Dynamic and Advanced Data Mining for Progressing Technological Development:
Innovations and Systemic Approaches

A B M Shawkat Ali
Central Queensland University, Australia

Yang Xiang
Central Queensland University, Australia

INFORMATION SCIENCE REFERENCE

Hershey · New York

Director of Editorial Content: Kristin Klinger
Senior Managing Editor: Jamie Snavely
Assistant Managing Editor: Michael Brehm
Publishing Assistant: Sean Woznicki
Typesetter: Kurt Smith, Sean Woznicki, Jamie Snavely
Cover Design: Lisa Tosheff
Printed at: Yurchak Printing Inc.

Published in the United States of America by
Information Science Reference (an imprint of IGI Global)
701 E. Chocolate Avenue
Hershey PA 17033
Tel: 717-533-8845
Fax: 717-533-8661
E-mail: cust@igi-global.com
Web site: http://www.igi-global.com/reference

Library of Congress Cataloging-in-Publication Data

Dynamic and advanced data mining for progressing technological development :
innovations and systemic approaches / A.B.M. Shawkat Ali and Yang Xiang,
editors.
    p. cm.
  Summary: "This book discusses advances in modern data mining research in
today's rapidly growing global and technological environment"--Provided by
publisher.
  Includes bibliographical references and index.
  ISBN 978-1-60566-908-3 (hardcover) -- ISBN 978-1-60566-909-0 (ebook) 1.
Data mining. 2. Technological innovations. I. Shawkat Ali, A. B. M. II.
Xiang, Yang, 1975-
  QA76.9.D343D956 2010
  303.48'3--dc22
                2009035155

British Cataloguing in Publication Data
A Cataloguing in Publication record for this book is available from the British Library.

Table of Contents

Detailed Table of Contents

Gulden Uchyigit, University of Brighton, UK

The increase in the information overload problem poses new challenges in the area of web personalization. Traditionally, data mining techniques have been extensively employed in the area of personalization, in particular data processing, user modeling and the classification phases. More recently the popularity of the semantic web has posed new challenges in the area of web personalization necessitating the need for more richer semantic based information to be utilized in all phases of the personalization process. The use of the semantic information allows for better understanding of the information in the domain which leads to more precise definition of the user's interests, preferences and needs, hence improving the personalization process. Data mining algorithms are employed to extract richer semantic information from the data to be utilized in all phases of the personalization process. This chapter presents a state-of-the-art survey of the techniques which can be used to semantically enhance the data processing, user modeling and the classification phases of the web personalization process.

Savo Kordic, Edith Cowan University, Australia
Chiou Peng Lam, Edith Cowan University, Australia
Jitian Xiao, Edith Cowan University, Australia
Huaizhong Li, Wenzhou University, China

The productivity of chemical plants and petroleum refineries depends on the performance of alarm systems. Alarm history collected from distributed control systems (DCS) provides useful information about past plant alarm system performance. However, the discovery of patterns and relationships from such data can be very difficult and costly. Due to various factors such as a high volume of alarm data (especially during plant upsets), huge amounts of nuisance alarms, and very large numbers of individual alarm tags, manual identification and analysis of alarm logs is usually a labor-intensive and time-consuming task. This chapter describes a data mining approach for analyzing alarm logs in a chemical plant. The main idea of the approach is to investigate dependencies between alarms effectively by considering the temporal context and time intervals between different alarm types, and then employing a data mining technique capable of discovering patterns associated with these time intervals. A prototype has been implemented to allow an active exploration of the alarm grouping data space relevant to the tags of interest.

Chapter 3

Fu Xiao, Nanjing University, P.R. China
Xie Li, Nanjing University, P.R. China

Intrusion Detection Systems (IDSs) are widely deployed with increasing of unauthorized activities and attacks. However they often overload security managers by triggering thousands of alerts per day. And up to 99% of these alerts are false positives (i.e. alerts that are triggered incorrectly by benign events). This makes it extremely difficult for managers to correctly analyze security state and react to attacks. In this chapter the authors describe a novel system for reducing false positives in intrusion detection, which is called ODARM (an Outlier Detection-Based Alert Reduction Model). Their model based on a new data mining technique, outlier detection that needs no labeled training data, no domain knowledge and little human assistance. The main idea of their method is using frequent attribute values mined from historical alerts as the features of false positives, and then filtering false alerts by the score calculated based on these features. In order to filer alerts in real time, they also design a two-phrase framework that consists of the learning phrase and the online filtering phrase. Now they have finished the prototype implementation of our model. And through the experiments on DARPA 2000, they have proved that their model can effectively reduce false positives in IDS alerts. And on real-world dataset, their model has even higher reduction rate.

Chapter 4

Shady Shehata, University of Waterloo, Canada
Fakhri Karray, University of Waterloo, Canada
Mohamed Kamel, University of Waterloo, Canada

Most of text mining techniques are based on word and/or phrase analysis of the text. Statistical analysis of a term frequency captures the importance of the term within a document only. However, two terms can have the same frequency in their documents, but one term contributes more to the meaning of its sentences than the other term. Thus, the underlying model should indicate terms that capture the semantics of text. In this case, the model can capture terms that present the concepts of the sentence, which leads to discover the topic of the document. A new concept-based mining model that relies on the analysis of both the sentence and the document, rather than, the traditional analysis of the document dataset only is introduced. The concept-based model can effectively discriminate between non-important terms with respect to sentence semantics and terms which hold the concepts that represent the sentence meaning. The proposed model consists of concept-based statistical analyzer, conceptual ontological graph representation, and concept extractor. The term which contributes to the sentence semantics is assigned two different weights by the concept-based statistical analyzer and the conceptual ontological graph representation. These two weights are combined into a new weight. The concepts that have maximum combined weights are selected by the concept extractor. The concept-based model is used to enhance the quality of the text clustering, categorization and retrieval significantly.

Chapter 5

Mohammed M. Mazid, CQUniversity, Australia
A B M Shawkat Ali, CQUniversity, Australia
Kevin S. Tickle, CQUniversity, Australia

Intrusion detection has received enormous attention from the beginning of computer network technology. It is the task of detecting attacks against a network and its resources. To detect and counteract any unauthorized activity, it is desirable for network and system administrators to monitor the activities in their network. Over the last few years a number of intrusion detection systems have been developed and are in use for commercial and academic institutes. But still there have some challenges to be solved. This chapter will provide the review, demonstration and future direction on intrusion detection. The authors' emphasis on Intrusion Detection is various kinds of rule based techniques. The research aims are also to summarize the effectiveness and limitation of intrusion detection technologies in the medical diagnosis, control and model identification in engineering, decision making in marketing and finance, web and text mining, and some other research areas.

Chapter 6

Ming Xu, Hangzhou Dianzi University, P. R. China
Hong-Rong Yang, Hangzhou Dianzi University, P. R. China
Ning Zheng, Hangzhou Dianzi University, P. R. China

It is a pivotal task for a forensic investigator to search a hard disk to find interesting evidences. Currently, the most search tools in digital forensic field, which utilize text string match and index technology, produce high recall (100%) and low precision. Therefore, the investigators often waste vast time on huge irrelevant search hits. In this chapter, an improved method for ranking of search results was proposed to reduce human efforts on locating interesting hits. The K-UIH (the keyword and user interest hierarchies) was constructed by both investigator-defined keywords and user interest learnt from electronic evidence adaptive, and then the K-UIH was used to re-rank the search results. The experimental results indicated that the proposed method is feasible and valuable in digital forensic search process.

Chapter 7

J. L. van Velsen, Dutch Ministry of Justice, Research and Documentation
Centre (WODC), The Netherlands
R. Choenni, Dutch Ministry of Justice, Research and Documentation Centre (WODC),
The Netherlands

The authors describe a process of extracting a cointegrated model from a database. An important part of the process is a model generator that automatically searches for cointegrated models and orders them according to an information criterion. They build and test a non-heuristic model generator that mines for common factor models, a special kind of cointegrated models. An outlook on potential future developments is given.

Alexander Troussov, IBM, Ireland
Eugene Levner, Holon Institute of Technology and Bar-Ilan University, Israel
Cristian Bogdan, KTH – Royal Institute of Technology, Sweden
John Judge, IBM, Ireland
Dmitri Botvich, Waterford Institute of Technology, Ireland

Spreading activation (also known as spread of activation) is a method for searching associative networks, neural networks or semantic networks. The method is based on the idea of quickly spreading an associative relevancy measure over the network. Our goal is to give an expanded introduction to the method. The authors will demonstrate and describe in sufficient detail that this method can be applied to very diverse problems and applications. They present the method as a general framework. First they will present this method as a very general class of algorithms on large (or very large) so-called multidimensional networks which will serve a mathematical model. Then they will define so-called micro-applications of the method including local search, relationship/association search, polycentric queries, computing of dynamic local ranking, etc. Finally they will present different applications of the method including ontology-based text processing, unsupervised document clustering, collaborative tagging systems, etc.

Jesmin Nahar, Central Queensland University, Australia
Kevin S. Tickle, Central Queensland University, Australia
A B M Shawkat Ali, Central Queensland University, Australia

Extracting useful information from structured and unstructured biological data is crucial in the health industry. Some examples include medical practitioner's need:

- Identify breast cancer patient in the early stage.
- Estimate survival time of a heart disease patient.
- Recognize uncommon disease characteristics which suddenly appear.

Currently there is an explosion in biological data available in the data bases. But information extraction and true open access to data are require time to resolve issues such as ethical clearance. The emergence of novel IT technologies allows health practitioners to facilitate the comprehensive analyses of medical images, genomes, transcriptomes, and proteomes in health and disease. The information that is extracted from such technologies may soon exert a dramatic change in the pace of medical research and impact considerably on the care of patients. The current research will review the existing technologies being used in heart and cancer research. Finally this research will provide some possible solutions to overcome the limitations of existing technologies. In summary the primary objective of this research is investigate how existing modern machine learning techniques (with their strength and limitations) are being used in the indent of heartbeat related disease and the early detection of cancer in patients. After an extensive literature reviewed the following objectives are chosen; (1) develop a new approach to find the association between diseases such as high blood pressure, stroke and heartbeat; (2) propose an improved feature selection method to analyze huge images and microarray databases for machine learning algorithms in cancer research; (3) find an automatic distance function selection method for clustering tasks; (4) discover the most significant risk factors for specific cancers; (5) determine the preventive factors for specific cancers that are aligned with the most significant risk factors. Therefore we propose a research plan to attain these objectives within this chapter. The possible solutions of the above objectives are as follows; (1) new heartbeat identification techniques show promising association with the heartbeat patterns and diseases; (2) sensitivity based feature selection methods will be applied to early cancer patient classification; (3) meta learning approaches will be adopted in clustering algorithms to select an automatic distance function. (4) apriori algorithm will be applied to discover the significant risks and preventive factors for specific cancers. We expect this research will add significant contributions to the medical professional to enable more accurate diagnosis and better patient care. It will also contribute in other area such as biomedical modeling, medical image analysis and early diseases warning.

Chapter 10

This chapter provides the reader with an introduction to clustering algorithms and applications. A number of important well-known clustering methods are surveyed. We present a brief history of the development of the field of clustering, discuss various types of clustering, and mention some of the current research directions in the field of clustering. Algorithms are described for top-down and bottom-up hierarchical clustering, as are algorithms for K-Means clustering and for K-Medians clustering. The technique of representative points is also presented. Given the large data sets involved with clustering, the need to apply parallel computing to clustering arises, so we discuss issues related to parallel clustering as well. Throughout the chapter references are provided to works that contain a large number of experimental results. A comparison of the various clustering methods is given in tabular format. We conclude the chapter with a summary and an extensive list of references.

Chapter 11

As a data mining technique, independent component analysis (ICA) is used to separate mixed data signals into statistically independent sources. In this chapter, we apply ICA for modeling multivariate volatility of financial asset returns which is a useful tool in portfolio selection and risk management. In the finance literature, the generalized autoregressive conditional heteroscedasticity (GARCH) model and its variants such as EGARCH and GJR-GARCH models have become popular standard tools to model the volatility processes of financial time series. Although univariate GARCH models are successful in modeling volatilities of financial time series, the problem of modeling multivariate time series has always been challenging. Recently, Wu, Yu, & Li (2006) suggested using independent component analysis (ICA) to decompose multivariate time series into statistically independent time series components and then separately modeled the independent components by univariate GARCH models. In this chapter, we extend this class of ICA-GARCH models to allow more flexible univariate GARCH-type models. We also apply the proposed models to compute the value-at-risk (VaR) for risk management applications. Backtesting and out-of-sample tests suggest that the ICA-GARCH models have a clear cut advantage over some other approaches in value-at-risk estimation.

Chapter 12

Tich Phuoc Tran, University of Technology, Australia
Pohsiang Tsai, University of Technology, Australia
Tony Jan, University of Technology, Australia
Xiangjian He, University of Technology, Australia

Most of the currently available network security techniques are not able to cope with the dynamic and increasingly complex nature of cyber attacks on distributed computer systems. Therefore, an automated and adaptive defensive tool is imperative for computer networks. Alongside the existing prevention techniques such as encryption and firewalls, Intrusion Detection System (IDS) has established itself as an emerging technology that is able to detect unauthorized access and abuse of computer systems by both internal users and external offenders. Most of the novel approaches in this field have adopted Artificial Intelligence (AI) technologies such as Artificial Neural Networks (ANN) to improve performance as well as robustness of IDS. The true power and advantages of ANN lie in its ability to represent both linear and non-linear relationships and learn these relationships directly from the data being modeled. However, ANN is computationally expensive due to its demanding processing power and this leads to overfitting problem, i.e. the network is unable to extrapolate accurately once the input is outside of the training data range. These limitations challenge IDS with low detection rate, high false alarm rate and excessive computation cost. This chapter proposes a novel Machine Learning (ML) algorithm to alleviate those difficulties of existing AI techniques in the area of computer network security. The Intrusion Detection dataset provided by Knowledge Discovery and Data Mining (KDD-99) is used as a benchmark to compare our model with other existing techniques. Extensive empirical analysis suggests that the proposed method outperforms other state-of-the-art learning algorithms in terms of learning bias, generalization variance and computational cost. It is also reported to significantly improve the overall detection capability for difficult-to-detect novel attacks which are unseen or irregularly occur in the training phase.

Chapter 13

M. Ameer Ali, East West University, Bangladesh

Image segmentation especially fuzzy based image segmentation techniques are widely used due to effective segmentation performance. For this reason, a huge number of algorithms are proposed in the literature. This chapter presents a survey report of different types of classical and shape based fuzzy clustering algorithms which are available in the literature.

Chapter 14

Shyamala G. Nadathur, Monash University, Australia

These datasets have some unique characteristics and problems. Therefore there is a need for methods which allow modelling in spite of the uniqueness of the datasets, capable of dealing with missing data, allow integrating data from various sources, explicitly indicate statistical dependence and independence and allow modelling with uncertainties. These requirements have given rise to an influx of new methods, especially from the fields of machine learning and probabilistic graphical models. In particular, Bayesian Networks (BNs), which are a type of graphical network model with directed links that offer a general and versatile approach to capturing and reasoning with uncertainty. In this chapter some background mathematics/statistics, description and relevant aspects of building the networks are given to better understand s and appreciate BN's potential. There are also brief discussions of their applications, the unique value and the challenges of this modelling technique for the Domain. As will be seen in this chapter, with the additional advantages the BNs can offer, it is not surprising that it is becoming an increasingly popular modelling tool in Health Domain.

Chapter 15

Kwok Pan Pang, Monash University, Australia

Most research on time series analysis and forecasting is normally based on the assumption of no structural change, which implies that the mean and the variance of the parameter in the time series model are constant over time. However, when structural change occurs in the data, the time series analysis methods based on the assumption of no structural change will no longer be appropriate; and thus there emerges another approach to solving the problem of structural change. Almost all time series analysis or forecasting methods always assume that the structure is consistent and stable over time, and all available data will be used for the time series prediction and analysis. When any structural change occurs in the middle of time series data, any analysis result and forecasting drawn from full data set will be misleading. Structural change is quite common in the real world. In the study of a very large set of macroeconomic time series that represent the 'fundamentals' of the US economy, Stock and Watson (1996) has found evidence of structural instability in the majority of the series. Besides, ignoring structural change reduces the prediction accuracy. Persaran and Timmermann (2003), Hansen (2001) and Clement and Hendry (1998, 1999) showed that structural change is pervasive in time series data, ignoring structural breaks which often occur in time series significantly reduces the accuracy of the forecast, and results in misleading or wrong conclusions. This chapter mainly focuses on introducing the most common time series methods. We highlight the problems when applying to most real situations with structural changes, briefly introduce some existing structural change methods, and demonstrate how to apply structural change detection in time series decomposition.

Chapter 16

G. M. Shafiullah, Central Queensland University, Australia

Adam Thompson, Central Queensland University, Australia

Peter J. Wolfs, Curtin University of Technology, Australia

A B M Shawkat Ali, Central Queensland University, Australia

Emerging wireless sensor networking (WSN) and modern machine learning techniques have encouraged interest in the development of vehicle health monitoring (VHM) systems that ensure secure and reliable operation of the rail vehicle. The performance of rail vehicles running on railway tracks is governed by the dynamic behaviours of railway bogies especially in the cases of lateral instability and track irregularities. To ensure safety and reliability of railway in this chapter, a forecasting model has been developed to investigate vertical acceleration behaviour of railway wagons attached to a moving locomotive using modern machine learning techniques. Initially, an energy-efficient data acquisition model has been proposed for WSN applications using popular learning algorithms. Later, a prediction model has been developed to investigate both front and rear body vertical acceleration behaviour. Different types of model can be built using a uniform platform to evaluate their performances and estimate different attributes' correlation coefficient (CC), root mean square error (RMSE), mean absolute error (MAE), root relative squared error (RRSE), relative absolute error (RAE) and computation complexity for each of the algorithm. Finally, spectral analysis of front and rear body vertical condition is produced from the predicted data using Fast Fourier Transform (FFT) and used to generate precautionary signals and system status which can be used by the locomotive driver for deciding upon necessary actions.

Chapter 17

Matjaz Gams, Jozef Stefan Institute, Ljubljana, Slovenia

Matej Ozek, Jozef Stefan Institute, Ljubljana, Slovenia

The pharmaceutical industry was for a long time founded on rigid rules. With the new PAT initiative, control is becoming significantly more flexible. The Food and Drug Administration is even encouraging the industry to use methods like machine learning. We designed a new data mining method based on inducing ensemble decision trees from which rules are generated. The first improvement is specialization for process analysis with only few examples and many attributes. The second innovation is a graphical module interface enabling process operators to test the influence of parameters on the process itself. The first task is creating accurate knowledge on small datasets. We start by building many decision trees on the dataset. Next, we subtract only the best subparts of the constructed trees and create rules from those parts. A best tree subpart is in general a tree branch that covers most examples, is as short as possible and has no misclassified examples. Further on, the rules are weighed, regarding the number of examples and parameters included. The class value of the new case is calculated as a weighted average of all relevant rule predictions. With this procedure we retain clarity of the model and the ability to efficiently explain the classification result. In this way, overfiting of decision trees and overpruning of the basic rule learners are diminished to a great extend. From the rules, an expert system is designed that helps process operators. Regarding the second task of graphical interface, we modified the Orange [9] explanation module so that an operator at each step takes a look at several space planes, defined by two chosen attributes. The displayed attributes are the ones that appeared in the classification rules triggered by the new case. The operator can interactively change the current set of process parameters in order to check the improvement of the class value. The task of seeing the influence of combining all the attributes leading to a high quality end product (called design space) is now becoming human comprehensible, it does not demand a high-dimensional space vision any more. The method was successfully implemented on data provided by a pharmaceutical company. High classification accuracy was achieved in a readable form thus introducing new comprehensions.

Preface

World database is increasing very rapidly due to the uses of advanced computer technology. Data is available now everywhere, for instance, in businesses, science, medical, engineering and so on. Now a challenging question is how we can make these data be the useful elements. The solution is data mining. Data Mining is a comparatively new research area. But within short time, it has already established the discipline capability in many domains. This new technology is facing many challenges to solve users' real problems.

The objective of this book is to discuss advances in data mining research in today's dynamic and rapid growing global economical and technological environments. This book aims to provide readers the current state of knowledge, research results, and innovations in data mining, from different aspects such as techniques, algorithms, and applications. It introduces current development in this area by a systematic approach. The book will serve as an important reference tool for researchers and practitioners in data mining research, a handbook for upper level undergraduate students and postgraduate research students, and a repository for technologists. The value and main contribution of the book lies in the joint exploration of diverse issues towards design, implementation, analysis, evaluation of data mining solutions to the challenging problems in all areas of information technology and science.

Nowadays many data mining books focus on data mining technologies or narrow specific areas. The motivation for this book is to provide readers with the update that covers the current development of the methodology, techniques and applications. In this point, this book will be a special contribution to the data mining research area.

We believe the book to be a unique publication that systematically presents a cohesive view of all the important aspects of modern data mining. The scholarly value of this book and its contributions to the literature in the information technology discipline are that:

This book increases the understanding of modern data mining methodology and techniques. This book identifies the recent key challenges which are faced by data mining users. This book is helpful for first time data mining users, since methodology, techniques and application all are under in the a single cover. This book describes the most recent applications on data mining techniques.

The unique structures of our book include: literature review, focus the limitations of the existing techniques, possible solutions, and future trends of the data mining discipline. Data Mining new users and new researchers will be able to find help from this book easily.

The book is suitable to any one who needs an informative introduction to the current development, basic methodology and advanced techniques of data mining. It serves as a handbook for researchers, practitioners, and technologists. It can also be used as textbook for one-semester course for senior undergraduates and postgraduates. It facilitates discussion and idea sharing. It helps researchers exchange their views on experimental design and the future challenges on such discovery techniques. This book will also be helpful to those who are from outside of computer science discipline to understand data mining methodology.

This book is a web of interconnected and substantial materials about data mining methodology, techniques, and applications. The outline of the book is given below.

Chapter 1. Data Mining Techniques for Web Personalization: Algorithms and Applications.

Chapter 2. Patterns Relevant to the Temporal Data-Context of an Alarm of Interest.

Chapter 3. ODARM: An Outlier Detection-Based Alert Reduction Model.

Chapter 4. Concept-Based Mining Model.

Chapter 5. Intrusion Detection Using Machine Learning: Past and Present.

Chapter 6. A Re-Ranking Method of Search Results Based on Keyword and User Interest.

Chapter 7. On the Mining of Cointegrated Econometric Models.

Chapter 8. Spread of Activation Methods.

Chapter 9. Pattern Discovery from Biological Data.

Chapter 10. Introduction to Clustering: Algorithms and Applications.

Chapter 11. Financial Data Mining using Flexible ICA-GARCH Models.

Chapter 12. Machine Learning Techniques for Network Intrusion Detection.

Chapter 13. Fuzzy Clustering Based Image Segmentation Algorithms.

Chapter 14. Bayesian Networks in the Health Domain.

Chapter 15. Time Series Analysis.

Chapter 16. Application of Machine Learning techniques for Railway Health Monitoring.

Chapter 17. Use of Data Mining Techniques for Process Analysis on Small Databases.

Despite the fact that many researchers contributed to the text, this book is much more than an edited collection of chapters written by separate authors. It systematically presents a cohesive view of all the important aspects of modern data mining.

We are grateful to the researchers who contributed the chapters. We would like to acknowledge research grants we received, in particular, the Central Queensland University Research Advancement Award Scheme RAAS ECF 0804 and the Central Queensland University Research Development and Incentives Program RDI S 0805. We also would like to express our appreciations to the editors in IGI Global, especially Joel A. Gamon, for their excellent professional support.

Finally we are grateful to the family of each of us for their consistent and persistent supports. Shawkat would like to present the book to Jesmin, Nabila, Proma and Shadia. Yang would like to present the book to Abby, David and Julia.

A B M Shawkat Ali
Central Queensland University, Australia

Yang Xiang
Central Queensland University, Australia

Chapter 1
Data Mining Techniques for Web Personalization:
Algorithms and Applications

Gulden Uchyigit
University of Brighton, UK

ABSTRACT

The increase in the information overload problem poses new challenges in the area of web personalization. Traditionally, data mining techniques have been extensively employed in the area of personalization, in particular data processing, user modeling and the classification phases. More recently the popularity of the semantic web has posed new challenges in the area of web personalization necessitating the need for more richer semantic based information to be utilized in all phases of the personalization process. The use of the semantic information allows for better understanding of the information in the domain which leads to more precise definition of the user's interests, preferences and needs, hence improving the personalization process. data mining algorithms are employed to extract richer semantic information from the data to be utilized in all phases of the personalization process. This chapter presents a state-of-the-art survey of the techniques which can be used to semantically enhance the data processing, user modeling and the classification phases of the web personalization process.

INTRODUCTION

Personalization technologies have been popular in assisting users with the information overload problem. As the number of services and the volume of content continues to grow personalization technologies are more than ever in demand.

Mobasher (Mobasher et al., 2004) classifies web personalization into 3 groups. These are, manual decision rule systems, content-based recommender systems and collaborative based recommender

DOI: 10.4018/978-1-60566-908-3.ch001

systems. Manual decision rule systems allow the web site administrator to specify rules based on user demographics or on static profiles (collected through a registration process). Content-based recommender systems make personalized recommendations based on user profiles. Collaborative-based recommender systems make use of user ratings and make recommendations based on how other users in the group have rated similar items.

Data mining techniques have extensively been used in personalization systems, for instance text mining algorithms such as feature selection are employed in content-based recommender systems as way of representing user profiles. Other data mining algorithms such as clustering and rule learning algorithms are employed in collaborative recommender systems.

In recent years developments into extending the Web with semantic knowledge in an attempt to gain a deeper insight into the meaning of the data being created, stored and exchanged has taken the Web to a different level. This has lead to developments of semantically rich descriptions to achieve improvements in the area of personalization technologies (Pretschner and Gauch, 2004). Utilizing such semantic information provides a more precise understanding of the application domain, and provides a better means to define the user's needs, preferences and activities with regard to the system, hence improving the personalization process. Here data mining algorithms are employed to extract semantic meaning from data such as ontologies. Here, algorithms such as clustering, fuzzy sets, rule learning algorithms, natural language processing have been employed.

This chapter will present an overview of the state-of-the art techniques in the use of data mining techniques in personalization systems, and how they have been and will continue to shape personalization systems.

BACKGROUND

User Modeling

User modeling/profiling is an important component in computer systems which are able to adapt to the user's preferences, knowledge, capabilities and to the environmental factors. According to Kobsa (Kobsa, 2001) systems that take individual characteristics of the users into account and adapt their behaviour accordingly have been empirically shown to benefit users in many domains. Examples of adaptation include customized content (e.g. personalized finance pages or news collections), customized recommendations or advertisements based on past purchase behavior, customized (preferred) pricing, tailored email alerts, express transactions (Kobsa, 2001).

According to Kay (Kay 2000b), there are three main ways a user model can assist in *adaptation*. The first is the interaction between the user and the interface. This may be any action accomplished through the devices available including an active badge worn by the user, the user's speech via audio input to the system etc. The user model can be used to assist as the user interacts with the interface. For instance, if the user input is ambiguous the user model can be used to disambiguate the input. The second area where the user model can assist the adaptation process is during the information presentation phase. For instance, in some cases due to the disabilities of the user the information needs to be displayed differently to different users. More sophisticated systems may also be used to adapt the presented content.

Kay (Kay 200b), describes the first of the user modeling stages as the *elicitation* of the user model. This can be a very straight forward process for acquiring information about the user, by simply asking the user to fill in a questionnaire of their preferences, interests and knowledge, or it can be a more sophisticated process where elicitation tools such concept mapping interface (Kay 1999) can be used. Elicitation of the user model becomes a valuable process under circumstances where the adaptive interface is to be used by a diverse population.

As well as direct elicitation of the user profiling, the user profile can also be constructed by observing the user interacting with the system and automatically inferring the user's profile from his/her actions. The advantage of having the system automatically infer the user's model is that the user is not involved in the tedious task of defining their user model. In some circumstances the user is unable to correctly define their user model especially if the user is unfamiliar with the domain.

Stereotypes is another method for constructing the user profile. Groups of users or individuals are divided into stereotypes and generic stereotype user models are used to initialize their user model. The user models are then updated and refined as more information is gathered about the user's preferences, interest, knowledge and capabilities. A comprehensive overview of generic user modeling systems can be found in (Kobsa, 2001b).

Recommender Systems

Recommender systems are successful in assisting with the information overload problem. They are popular in application domains such as e-commerce, entertainment and news. Recommender systems fall into three main categories collaborative-based, content-based and hybrid systems.

Content-based recommender systems are employed on domains with large amounts of textual content. They have their roots in information filtering and text mining. Oard (Oard, 1997), describes a generic information filtering model as having four components: a method for representing the documents within the domain; a method for representing the user's information need; a method for making the comparison; and a method for utilizing the results of the comparison process. The goal of Oard's information filtering model is to automate the text filtering process, so that the results of the automated comparison process are equal to the user's judgment of the documents.

The content-based recommender systems were developed based on Oard's information filtering model. Content-based recommender systems automatically infer the user's profile from the contents of the documents the user has previously seen and rated. These profiles are then used as input to a classification algorithm, along with the new unseen documents from the domain. Those documents which are similar in content to the user's profile are assumed to be interesting and recommended to the user.

A popular and extensively used document and profile representation method employed by many information filtering methods including the content based method, is the so called *vector space representation* (Chen and Sycara, 1998), (Mladenic, 1996), (Lang, 1995), (Moukas, 1996), (Liberman, 1995), (Kamba and Koseki, 1997), (Armstrong et al., 1995). The vector space method (Baeza-Yates and Ribeiro-Neto, 1999) consider that each document (profile) is described as a set of keywords. The text document is viewed as a vector in n dimensional space, n being the number of different words in the document set. Such a representation is often referred to as *bag-of-words*, because of the loss of word ordering and text structure (see Figure 2). The tuple of weights associated with each word, reflecting the significance of that word for a given document, give the document's position in the vector space. The weights are related to the number of occurrences of each word within the document. The word weights in the vector space method are ultimately used to compute the *degree of similarity* between two feature vectors. This method can be used to decide whether a document represented as a weighted feature vector, and

Figure 1. Illustration of the bag-of-words document representation using word frequency

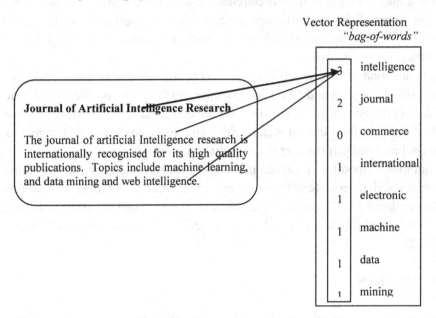

a profile are similar. If they are similar then an assumption is made that the document is relevant to the user. The vector space model evaluates the similarity of the document d_j with regard to a profile p as the correlation between the vectors d_j and p. This correlation can be quantified by the cosine of the angle between these two vectors. That is,

$$sim(d_j, p) = \frac{d_j \bullet p}{|d_j| \times |p|} = \frac{\sum_{i=1}^{t} w_{i,j} \times w_{i,p}}{\sqrt{\sum_{i=1}^{t} w_{i,p}^2 \times \sum_{i=1}^{t} w_{i,j}^2}}$$

(1)

Content-based systems suffer from shortcomings in the way they select items for recommendations. Items are recommended if the user has seen and liked similar items in the past.

Future recommendations will display limited diversity. Items relevant to a user, but bearing little resemblance to the snapshot of items the user has looked at in the past, will never be recommended in the future.

Collaborative-based recommender systems try to overcome these shortcomings presented by content-based systems. Collaborative-based systems (Terveen et al., 1997), (Breese et al., 1998), (Knostan et al., 1997), (Balabanovic and Shoham, 1997) are an alternative to the content-based methods. The basic idea is to move beyond the experience of an individual user profile and instead draw on the experiences of a community of users. Collaborative-based systems (Herlocker et al., 1999), (Konstan et al., 1997), (Terveen et al., 1997), (Kautz et al., 1997), (Resnick and Varian, 1997) are built on the assumption that a good way to find interesting content is to find other people who have similar tastes, and recommend the items that those users like. Typically, each target user is associated with a set of nearest neighbor users by comparing the profile information provided by the target user to the profiles of other users. These users then act as recommendation partners for the target user, and items that occur in their profiles can be recommended to the target user. In this way, items are recommended on the basis of *user* similarity rather than item similarity.

Collaborative-based method alone can prove ineffective for several reasons (Claypool et al., 1999). For instance, *the early rater problem*, arises when a prediction can not be provided for a given item because it's new and therefore it has not been rated and it can not be recommended, *the sparsity problem* which arises due to sparse nature of the ratings within the information matrices making the recommendations inaccurate, *the grey sheep problem* which arises when there are individuals who do not benefit from the collaborative recommendations because their opinions do not consistently agree or disagree with other people in the community.

To overcome, the problems posed by pure content and collaborative based recommender systems, hybrid recommender systems have been proposed. Hybrid systems combine two or more recommendation techniques to overcome the shortcomings of each individual technique (Balabanovic, 1998), (Balabanovic and Shoham, 1997), (Burke, 2002), (Claypool et al., 1999). These systems generally, use the content-based component to overcome the new item start up problem, if a new item is present then it can still be recommended regardless if it was seen and rated. The collaboration component overcomes the problem of over specialization as is the case with pure content based systems.

DATA PREPARATION: ONTOLOGY LEARNING, EXTRACTION AND PRE-PROCESSING

As previously described personalization techniques such as the content-based method employ the vector space representation. This data representation technique is popular because of it's simplicity and efficiency. However, it has the disadvantage that a lot of useful information is lost during the representation phase since the sentence structure is broken down to the individual words. In an attempt to minimize the loss of information during the representation phase it is important to retain the relationships between the words. One popular technique in doing this is to use conceptual hierarchies. In this section we present an overview of the existing techniques, algorithms and methodologies which have been employed for ontology learning.

The main component of ontology learning is the construction of the concept hierarchy. Concept hierarchies are useful because they are an intuitive way to describe information (Lawrie and Croft, 2000). Generally hierarchies are manually created by domain experts. This is a very cumbersome process and requires specialized knowledge from domain experts. This therefore necessitates tools for their automatic generation. Research into automatically constructing a hierarchy of concepts directly from data is extensive and includes work from a number of research groups including, machine learning, natural language processing and statistical analysis. One approach is to attempt to induce word categories directly from a corpus based on statistical co-occurrence (Evans et al., 1991), (Finch and Chater, 1994), (McMahon and Smith, 1996), (Nanas et al., 2003a). Another approach is to merge existing linguistic resources such as dictionaries and thesauri (Klavans et al., 1992), (Knight and Luk, 1994) or tuning a thesaurus (e.g WordNet) using a corpus (Miller et al., 1990a). Other methods include using natural language processing (NLP) methods to extract phrases and keywords from text (Sanderson and Croft, 1999), or to use an already constructed hierarchy such as yahoo and map the concepts onto this hierarchy.

Subsequent parts of this section include machine learning approaches and natural language processing approaches used for ontology learning.

Machine Learning Approaches

Learning ontologies from unstructured text is not an easy task. The system needs to automatically extract the concepts within the domain as well as extracting the relationships between the discovered concepts. Machine learning approaches in particular clustering techniques, rule based techniques, fuzzy logic and formal concept analysis techniques have been very popular for this purpose. This section presents an overview of the machine learning approaches which have been popular in discovering ontologies from unstructured text.

Clustering Algorithms

Clustering algorithms are very popular in ontology learning. They function by clustering the instances together based on their similarity. The clustering algorithms can be divided into *hierarchical* and *non-hierarchical* methods. Hierarchical methods construct a tree where each node represents a subset of the input items (documents), where the root of the tree represents all the items in the item set. Hierarchical methods can be divided into the *divisive* and *agglomerative* methods. Divisive methods begin with the entire set of items and partition the set until only an individual item remains. Agglomerative methods work in the opposite way, beginning with individual items, each item is represented as a cluster and merging these clusters until a single cluster remains. At the first step of *hierarchical agglomerative clustering* (HAC) algorithm, when each instance represents its own cluster, the similarities between each cluster are simply defined by the chosen similarity method rule to determine the similarity of these new clusters to each other. There are various rules which can be applied depending on the data, some of the measures are described below:

Single-Link: In this method the similarity of two clusters is determined by the similarity of the two closest (most similar) instances in the different clusters. So for each pair of clusters S_i and S_j,

$$sim(S_i, S_j) = \max\{\cos(d_i, d_j) \mid d_i \in S_i, d_j \in S_j\} \tag{2}$$

Complete-Link: In this method the similarity of two clusters is determined by the similarity of the two least similar instances of both clusters. This approach can be performed well in cases where the data forms the natural distinct categories, since it tends to produce tight (cohesive) spherical clusters. This is calculated as:

$$sim(S_i, S_j) = \min\{\cos(d_i, d_j)\} \tag{3}$$

Average-Link or *Group Average*: In this method, the similarity between two clusters is calculated as the average distance between all pairs of objects in both clusters, i.e. it's an intermediate solution between complete link and single-link. This is unweighted, or weighted by the size of the clusters. The weighted form is calculated as:

$$sim(S_i, S_j) = \frac{1}{n_i n_j} \sum \cos(d_i, d_j) \tag{4}$$

where n_i and n_j refer to the size of S_i and S_j respectively.

Hierarchical clustering methods are popular for ontology learning because they are able to naturally discover the concept hierarchy during the clustering process. Scatter/Gather (Lin and Pantel, 2001) is one of the earlier methods in which clustering is used to create document hierarchies. Recently new types of hierarchies have been introduced which rely on the terms used by a set of documents to expose some structure of the document collection. One such technique is lexical modification and another is subsumption.

Rule Learning Algorithms

These are algorithms that learn *association* rules or other attribute based rules. The algorithms are generally based on a *greedy search* of the attribute-value tests that can be added to the rule preserving its consistency with the training instances. Apriori algorithm is a simple algorithm which learns association rules between objects. Apriori is designed to operate on databases containing transactions (for example, the collections of items bought by customers). As is common in association rule mining, given a set of item sets (for instance, sets of retail transactions each listing individual item's purchased), the algorithm attempts to find subsets which are common to at least a minimum number S_c (the cutoff, or confidence threshold) of the item sets. Apriori uses a bottom up approach, where frequent subsets are extended one item at a time (a step known as candidate generation, and groups of candidates are tested against the data. The algorithm terminates when no further successful extensions are found. One example of an ontology learning tool is OntoEdit (Maedche and Staab, 2001), which is used to assist the ontology engineer during the ontology creation process. The algorithm semi automatically learns to construct an ontology from unstructured text. The algorithm uses a method for discovering *generalized* association rules. The input data for the learner is a set of transactions, each of which consists of set of items that appear together in the transaction. The algorithm extracts association rules represented by sets of items that occur together sufficiently often and presents the rules to the knowledge engineer. For example a shopping transaction may include the items purchased together. The generalized association rule may say that snacks are purchased together with drinks rather than crisps are purchased with beer.

Fuzzy Logic

Fuzzy logic provides the opportunity to model systems that are inherently imprecisely defined. Fuzzy logic is popular in modeling of textual data because of the uncertainty which is present in textual data. Fuzzy logic is built on theories of fuzzy sets. Fuzzy set theory deals with representation of classes whose boundaries are not well defined. The key idea is to associate a membership function with the elements of a class. The function takes values in the interval [0, 1] with 0 corresponding to no membership and 1 corresponding to full membership. Membership values between 0 and 1 indicate marginal elements in the class. In (Tho et al., 2006) fuzzy logic has also been used in generating of ontologies. Fuzzy logic is incorporated into ontologies to handle uncertainty in data.

Formal Concept Analysis

Formal Concept Analysis (FCA) is a method for deriving conceptual structures out of data. These structures can be graphically represented as conceptual hierarchies, allowing the analysis of complex structures and the discovery of dependencies within the data. FCA is increasingly applied in conceptual clustering, data analysis, information retrieval, knowledge discovery, and ontology engineering. Formal Concept Analysis is based on the philosophical understanding that a concept is constituted by two parts: its extension which consists of all objects belonging to the concept, and its intension which comprises all attributes shared by those objects. This understanding allows to derive all concepts from a given context (data table) and to introduce a subsumption hierarchy. The source data can be reconstructed at any given time, so that the interpretation of the data remains controllable. A data table is created with the objects as a left hand column and the attributes along the top. The relationships between each of the objects and their attributes are marked in the table. The set of objects which share the same attributes are determined. Each one of these pairs are then known as a formal concept. The sub-concept and super-concept are also determined form this which shows the hierarchy. A concept lattice is then determined using all the dependencies which is then determined as an ontology hierarchy. Use of FCA methods in ontology learning have been popular in recent years (Cimiano et al., 2005), (Quan et al., 2004).

Natural Language Processing (NLP)

NLP techniques have been used in (Lin and Pantel, 2001) to determine classes, where each concept is a cluster of words. Artequkt (Alani et al., 2003), which operates in the music domain, utalises NLP techniques in order to extract information about the artists. Artequkt uses WordNet and GATE (Bontcheva et al., 2004), an entity recognizing tool as the tools for identifying the information fragments. Relations between concepts are extracted by matching a *verb* with the entity pairs found in each sentence. The extracted information is then used to populate the ontology. The system in (Agirre et al., 2004) uses textual content from the web to enhance the concepts found in WordNet. The proposed method constructs a set of topically related words for each concept found in WordNet, where each word sense has an associated set of words. For example the word bank has the two sense: *river bank*: estuary, stream and as a *fiscal institute*: finance, money, credit, loan. The system queries the web for the documents related to each concept from WordNet and builds a set of words associated with each topic. The documents are retrieved by querying the web using a search engine and by asking for the documents that contain the words that are related to a particular sense and not contain words related to another sense. In (Sanchez and Moreno, 2005) the hierarchy construction algorithm is based on analyzing the neighborhood of an initial keyword that characterizes the desired search domain. In English the immediate anterior word for a keyword is the one frequently classifying it (expressing a semantic specialization of the meaning), whereas the immediate posterior one represents the domain where it is being applied. The previous word for a specific keyword is used for obtaining the taxonomical hierarchy of terms (e.g breast cancer will be subclass of cancer). The process is repeated recursively in order to create a deeper-level subclass (e.g metastatic breast cancer will be a subclass of breast cancer). On the other hand, the posterior word for the specific keyword is used to categorize the web resource considered as a tag that expresses the context in where the search domain is applied (e.g colon cancer research will be an application domain where colon cancer is applied). Following this is a polysemy detection algorithm is performed in order to disambiguate polysemic domains. Using this algorithm the agents construct a concept hierarchy of the domain.

The use of semantic techniques in personalization of the information search process has been very popular in recent years. It generally makes use of the user's context during the search process. Typical search engines retrieve information based on keywords given by users and return the information found as a list of search results. A problem with keyword-based search is that often they return a large list of search results with many of them irrelevant to the user. This problem can be avoided if users know exactly the right query terms to use. Such query terms are often hard to find by the user. Refining the query during the searching process can improve the search results. Ontology enhanced searching tools that map a user query onto an ontology (Parry, 2004) has been very popular. In (Widyantoro and Yen, 2002) a strategy for query refinement is presented. This approach is based on fuzzy ontology of term associations. The system uses its knowledge about term associations, which it determines using statistical co-occurrence of terms, to suggest a list of broader and narrower terms in addition to providing the results based on the original query term. The broader and narrower terms referring to whether the semantic meaning of one subsumes or covers the semantic meaning of the other. The narrower than terms are then used to narrow down the search results by focusing to the more specific context while still remaining in the context of the original query. The broader than is used to broaden the search results. The definition that term t_i is narrower-than term t_j is the ratio between the number of co-occurrences of both terms and the number of occurrences of term t_i. Therefore the more frequent term t_i and t_j co-occur and less frequent term t_i occurs in documents, t_i is narrower-than t_j. A membership value of 1.0 is obtained when a term always co-occurs with another term. In contrast, the membership value of narrower term relation between two terms that never co-occur will be 0. In (Gong et al., 2005) a search query expansion method which makes use of WordNet is proposed. It creates a collection-based term semantic network (TSN) using word co-occurrences in the collection. The query is expanded in three dimensions using WordNet to get the hypernym, hyponym and synonym of the relation (Miller et al., 1990b). To extract the TSN from the collection, Apriori association rule mining algorithm is used to mine out the association rules between the words. TSN is also used to filter out some of the noise words from WordNet. This is because WordNet can expand a query with too many words. This adds noise and detracts from the retrieval performance, thus leading to low precision. Each page is assigned with a combined weight depending on how the frequency of the original query, expanded hypernym, synonyms and hyponym. Each one of these weights is multiplied with a factor (α,β,γ) that are experimentally determined using the precision recall, the retrieval performance based on the expansion word. For instance hypernyms relation has less significant impart than hyponyms and synonym relation, hyponyms may bring more noise so its factor is less than the others.

USER MODELLING WITH SEMANTIC DATA

Integrating semantic information into the personalization process requires for this information to be integrated in all stages of the personalization stage including the user modeling process. Using conceptual hierarchies to represent the user's model has its advantages including determining the user's context. A hierarchical view of user interests enhances the semantics of the user's profile, as it is much closer to the human conception of a set of resources (Godoy and Amandi, 2006). Recent developments have integrated semantic knowledge with the user model to model context. Automatically constructing the user's model into a conceptual hierarchy allows the modeling of contextual information. In (Nanas et al., 2003b), a method of automatically constructing the user profile into a concept hierarchy is presented. The system starts by extracting the concepts from the domain and employing statistical feature selection methods. The concepts are then associated by defining the links between them. The extracted terms are linked using a sort of a "*sliding window*" The size of window defines the kind of associations that are taken into consideration. A small window of few words defines the *Local Context*, whereas, a larger window defines a *Topical Context*. The goal of topical context is to identify semantic relations between terms that are repeatedly used in discussing the topic. To identify topical correlations a window of 20 words are chosen, 10 words at either side of the term. Weights are assigned to the links between extracted terms. For instance to assign a weight w_{ij} to the link between the terms t_i and t_j the below formula is used:

$$w_{i,j} = \frac{fr_{ij}^2}{fr_i \cdot fr_j} \cdot \frac{1}{d} \qquad (5)$$

where, fr_{ij} is the number of times term t_i and t_j appear within the sliding window, fr_i and fr_j are respectively the number of occurrences of t_i and t_j in documents rated by the user, and d is the average distance between the two linked terms. Two extracted terms next to each other has a distance of 1, while if there are n words between two extracted terms then the distance is n+1. The hierarchy is identified by using topic subtopic relations between terms. The more documents that a term appears in the more general the term is assumed to be. Some of the profile terms will broadly define the underlying topic, while the others co-occur with a general term and provide its attributes, specialization and related concepts. Based on this hypothesis, the terms are ordered into a hierarchy according to frequency count in different documents.

Concept hierarchies can also be constructed by making use of a pre-constructed hierarchy such as yahoo (Sieg et al., 2005), (Pretschner and Gauch, 2004). In (Pretschner and Gauch, 2004) the user profile is created automatically while the user is browsing. The profile is essentially a reference ontology in which each concept has a weight indicating the user's perceived interests in that concept. Profiles are generated by analyzing the surfing behavior of the user, especially the content, length and the time spent on the page. For the reference ontologies existing hierarchies from yahoo.com are used. This process involves extracting the contents of documents which are linked from the hierarchy. Each concept in the yahoo hierarchy is represented as a feature vector. The contents of the links which are stored in the user's browsing cache are also represented as feature vectors. To determine user's profile these feature vectors and the concept feature vectors are compared using the cosine similarity, those concepts which are similar are inserted into the user profile. The concepts in the user profile is updated as the user continues to browse and search for information. A popular application of semantic information at present is in the area of education. Personalization techniques are the next new thing in e-learning systems (Gomes et al., 2006). Several approaches have been proposed to collect information about users such as preferences, following clicking behavior to collect likes and dislikes, and questionnaires asking for specific information to assess learner features (e.g tests, learner assessment dialogs, and preference forms). Ontologies can be used in defining course concepts (Gomes et al., 2006). In (Gomes et al., 2006) the system traces and learns which concepts the learner has understood, for instance number of correct or wrong answers associated with each concept. also associated with each concept is well learned or known etc. Representing learner profiles using ontologies is also a popular method (Dolog and Schafer, 2005). The advantages of this is that they can be exchanged which makes learner profiles interoperable. (Carmagnola et al., 2005) present a multidimensional matrix whose different planes contain the ontological representation of different types of knowledge. Each of these planes represent user actions, user model, domain, context adaptation goals and adaptation methods. The framework uses semantic rules for representation. The knowledge in each plane is represented in the form of a taxonomy, they are application independent and modular and can be used in different domains and application. Each domain is defined at different levels: at the first level there is the definition of general concepts. For example, for domain taxonomy, the first level includes macro domain such as: tourist information, financial domain, e-learning domain etc; for the adaptation goals-taxonomy, the first level specifies general goals such as: inducing/pushing; informing/explaining; suggesting/recommending, guiding/helping and so on for all the ontologies. At the following levels there are specialized concepts. For example for the tourist domain, the next level can include tourist categories (travel, food etc.) while the adaptation-goals taxonomy can include more specific goals such as explaining to support learning or clarify or to teach a new concept or correct mistakes. User modeling and adaptation rules can be applied at the points of intersection within the matrix. In (Mylonas et al., 2006) a fuzzy ontology framework for personalization of multimedia content is presented. The main idea here is to extract context and make use of the context within the personalization process. The user context is extracted from using fuzzy ontology. In the fuzzy ontology framework the concept link relationships are assigned a value [0, 1] which determines the degree to which each concept is related to each other. One concept can be related with some degree and the same concept can be related with another concept another degree. The user preference model is a representation of concepts. During the searching process the user's context stored in the preference model is combined with the document retrieved using the query alone. Developing user models which are generic which can be used in many different application areas can be very advantageous. In (Tchienehom, 2005) a generic profile model is presented which encapsulates the use of semantic information in the profile. The generic profile model is subdivided into four levels: the profile logical structure, the profile contents, the profile logical structure semantics and the content semantics.

ONTOLOGY-BASED RECOMMENDER SYSTEMS

In recent years, web trends expressing semantics about people and their relationships have gained a lot of interest. The friend of a friend (FOAF) project is a good example of one of the most popular ontologies. The FOAF project is an ontology which describes people and their friends (Middleton et al., 2002). Such ontologies are advantageous in that they are able provide an easy way of defining user groups based on their interests (Mori et al., 2005). Utilizing ontologies this way allows for groups of users with similar interests to be identified, hence, making the recommendation process more accurate. OntoCapi (Alani et al., 2002) is a system which helps to identify communities of people based on specific features which they have in common, for instance who attended same events, who co-authored same papers and who worked on same projects etc. OntoCapi uses a fixed ontology for identifying groups of users. OntoCapi is developed for the research domain, researchers are recommended papers depending on their research interests. Papers are recommended based on the similarity of the profiles of different researchers. An interesting aspect of the OntoCapis is that it is able to identify communities of interests using relations such as conference attendance, supervision, authorship, and research interest and project membership. In essence, OntoCapi uses all this information to develop the communities of interest. QuickStep (Middleton et al., 2002) is also a recommender system which heavily relies on a pre-defined ontology. The ontology used here is for the research domain and is computed by domain experts. The ontology contains usual information such as "*interface agents*" is-a "*agents*" paper. The concepts defined in the ontology hierarchy are represented by weighted feature vectors of example papers found in the domain. The system uses a kind of bootstrapping technique which uses each user's list of publications. It represents the user's papers as feature vectors and maps them to the concept hierarchy using the nearest neighbor algorithm.

It then uses those concepts to generate a profile for the user. Each concept is assigned with an interest value determined from the topics which the papers belong. The interest value is partly determined from the number of papers that belong to this topic and the user's interest in them. The recommendations are then formulated from the correlation between the user's current topics of interest and papers that are classified as belonging to those topics. The recommendation algorithm also makes use of the classification confidence, which is the classification measure of topic with the document. In (Mobasher et al., 2004), semantic attribute information and the user ratings given to the objects are used in providing the user with collaborative recommendations. Semantic information is extracted from the objects in the domain this semantic information is then aggregated. The aggregation reveals the semantic information which all the objects have in common. For instance, if the objects in the domain are descriptions of romantic movies and comedy movies, aggregating the extracted semantic information for these objects may reveal romantic comedies. As for making predictions whether the user will like certain items the combine the semantic similarity along with the ratings that the users have given to these individual items.

Context representation in mobile environments has also become popular in recent years. Representing context for these environments is usually multi-faceted, giving the user situation in terms of location, time, contacts, agenda, presence, device and application usage, personal profile and so on. The most important advantage of using an ontological description of these entities is that they can be augmented, enriched and synthesized using suitable reasoning mechanisms, with different goals. In (Buriano et al., 2006) a framework is presented which utalises ontologies to define dimensions such as "moving" or "alone/accompanied", "leisure/business" and so on. User's mood can also be represented in this way, all this can used in computing the recommendation. In (Cantador and Castells, 2006) a pre-defined ontology is used which is represented using semantic networks. User profiles are represented as concepts, where a weight represents the user's interest in a particular concept. Users are then clustered using Hierarchical agglomerative clustering, where concepts are clustered. The concepts and user clusters are then used to find emergent, focused semantic social networks. Several other recommender systems exist which utilize pre-defined ontologies to reason about the classes which exist in the ontology (Aroyo et al., 2006), (Blanco-Fernndez et al., 2004) and to base their recommendations on. In the recommendation process the system is very reliant on the data which is available for it to extract the user's interests. Recently free textual reviews have become popular for extracting opinion. In (Aciar et al., 2006) present an interesting framework for extracting semantic information from unstructured textual consumer reviews. To do this a pre-defined domain ontology is utilized where important concepts are identified from the textual review. These are the combined with a set of measures such as opinion quality, feature quality and overall assessment to select the relevant reviews and provide a recommendations to the user.

SUMMARY AND FUTURE WORK

Integrating of semantic information with the personalization process brings countless advantages to the personalization process. Most recently the use of ontologies have shown very promising results and have taken the personalization process to another level. Ontologies provide interoperability and enable reasoning about the knowledge in the domain as well as user's needs. Other advantages include in the way information is returned to the user. Using an ontology to represent the recommended output can be used for the explanation process (i.e giving reasons as to why certain recommendations were made). Explanations such as this are important for trust building between the user and the system. In this chapter we presented an overview of some of the techniques, algorithms, methodologies along with challenges of using semantic information in representation of domain knowledge, user needs and the recommendation algorithms.

Future trends in personalization systems will continue with the theme of improved user and domain representations. In particular systems will dynamically model the domain by extracting richer more precise knowledge from the domain and to be integrated in all stages of the personalization process. Software agents integrated with such personalization systems can be an interesting research direction, where the agents can autonomously and dynamically learn domain ontologies and share these ontologies with other agents.

Another interesting dimension of personalization technologies is their use with ubiquitous mobile applications. Improved personalization techniques which are able to model user's context can advance the personalized applications embedded on these devices.

Future research directions in application of personalization technologies will be increasingly popular as the basis of applications areas such as e-learning, e-business and e-health.

REFERENCES

Aciar, S., Zhang, D., Simoff, S., & Debenham, J. (2006). Recommender system based on consumer product reviews. In *Proceedings of the IEEE/WIC/ACM International Conference on Web Intelligence.*

Agirre, E., Alfonseca, E., & de Lacalle, O. L. (2004). *Approximating hierarchy-based similarity for wordnet nominal synsets using topic signatures.*

Alani, H., Kim, S., Weal, D. M. M., Hall, P. L. W., & Shadbolt, N. (2003). Automatic extraction of knowledge from web documents. In *Proceedings of 2nd International Semantic Web Conference - Workshop on Human Language Technology for the Semantic Web abd Web Service.*

Alani, H., O'Hara, K., & Shadbolt, N. (2002). *Ontocopi: Methods and tools for identifying communities of practice.*

Armstrong, R., Freitag, D., Joachims, T., & Mitchel, T. (1995). Webwatcher: A learning apprentice for the world wide web. In *AAAI Spring Synopsium on Information Gathering from Heterogenous, Distributed Environments.*

Aroyo, L., Bellekens, P., Bjorkman, M., Broekstra, J., & Houben, G. (2006). Ontology-based personalisation in user adaptive systems. In *2nd International Workshop on Web Personalisation Recommender Systems and Intelligent User Interfaces in Conjunction with 7th International Conference in Adaptive Hypermedia.*

Baeza-Yates, R., & Ribeiro-Neto, B. (1999). *Modern Information Retrieval.* Reading MA: Addison Wesley.

Balabanovic, M. (1998). *Learning to Surf: Multi-agent Systems for Adaptive Web Page Recommendation.* PhD thesis, Department of Computer Science, Stanford University.

Balabanovic, M., & Shoham, Y. (1997). Fab: Content-based, collaborative recommendation. *Communications of the ACM, 40*(3), 66–72. doi:10.1145/245108.245124

Blanco-Fernndez, Y., & Gil-Solla, J. J. P.-A. A. Ramos- Cabrer, M., Barragns-Martnez, B., Garca-Duque, M. L.-N. J., FernndezVilas1, A., & Daz-Redondo, R. P. (2004). Avatar: An advanced multi-agent recommender system of personalized TV contents by semantic reasoning. In *Web Information Systems WISE 2004*. Berlin: Springer-Verlag.

Bontcheva, K., Tablan, V., Maynard, D., & Cunningham, H. (2004). Evolving gate to meet new challenges in language engineering. *Natural Language Engineering*, 10.

Breese, J., Heckerman, D., & Kadie, C. (1998). Empirical analysis of predictive algorithms for collaborative filtering. In *Proceedings of the Fourteenth Conference on Uncertainty in Artificial Intelligence*. San Francisco: Morgan Kaufmann Publisher.

Buriano, L., Marchetti, M., Carmagnola, F., Cena, F., Gena, C., & Torre, I. (2006). The role of ontologies in context-aware recommender systems. In *7th International Conference on Mobile Data Management*

Burke, R. (2002). Hybrid recommender systems: Survey and experiments. *User Modeling and User-Adapted Interaction, 12*(4). doi:10.1023/A:1021240730564

Cantador, I., & Castells, P. (2006). A multilayered ontology-based user profiles and semantic social networks for recommender systems. In *2nd International Workshop on Web Personalisation Recommender Systems and Intelligent User Interfaces in Conjunction with 7th International Conference in Adaptive Hypermedia.*

Carmagnola, F., Cena, F., Gena, C., & Torre, I. (2005). A multidimensional approach for the semantic representation of taxonomies and rules in adaptive hypermedia systems. In *PerSWeb05 Workshop on Personalization on the Semantic Web in conjunction with UM05.*

Chen, L., & Sycara, K. (1998). Webmate: A personal agent for browsing and searching. In *2nd International Conference on Autonomous Agents,* Minneapolis, MN.

Cimiano, P., Hotho, A., & Staab, S. (2005). Learning concept hierarchies from text corpa using formal concept hierarchies. *Journal of Artificial Intelligence Research,* (24): 305339.

Claypool, M., Gokhale, A., Miranda, T., Murnikov, P., Netes, D., & Sartin, M. (1999). Combining content-based and collaborative filters in an online newspaper. In *SIGIR '99 Workshop on Recommender Systems: Algorithms and Evaluation,* Berkeley, CA., P. & Schafer, M. (2005). Learner modeling on the semantic web. In *PerSWeb05 Workshop on Personalization on the Semantic Web in conjunction with UM05.*

Evans, D., Hersh, W., Monarch, I., Lefferts, R., & Henderson, S. (1991). Automatic indexing of abstracts via natural-language processing using a simple thesaurus. *Medical Decision Making, 11*(3), 108–115.

Finch, S., & Chater, N. (1994). Learning syntactic categories: A statistical approach. In M. Oaksford, & G. Brown, (Eds.), *Neurodynamics and Psychology.* New York: Academic Press.

Godoy, D., & Amandi, A. (2006). Modeling user interests by conceptual clustering. *Information Systems, 31*(4), 247–265. doi:10.1016/j.is.2005.02.008

Gomes, P., & Antunes, B. L. R., Santos, A., Barbeira, J., & Carvalho, R. (2006). Using ontologies for elearning personalization. In *eLearning Conference.*

Gong, Z., Cheang, C. W., & U, L. H. (2005). Web query expansion by wordnet. In *Database and Expert Systems Applications*, (pp. 166-175). Berlin: Springer Verlag.

Herlocker, J., Konstan, J., Borchers, A., & Reidl, J. (1999). An algorithmic framework for performing collaborative filtering. In *Proceedings of the Conference on Research and Development in Information Retrieval.*

Kamba, T., H. S. & Koseki, Y. (1997). Antagonomy: A personalised newspaper on the world wide web. *International Journal of Human-Computer Studies, 46*(6), 789–803. doi:10.1006/ijhc.1996.0113

Kautz, H., Selman, B., & Shah, M. (1997). Referral web: Combining social networks and collaborative filtering. *Communications of the ACM, 40*(3), 63–65. doi:10.1145/245108.245123

Klavans, J., Chodrow, M., & Wacholder, N. (1992). *Building a knowledge base from parsed definitions.* In K. Jansen, G. Heidorn, & S. Richardson, (Eds.), *Natural Language Processing: The PLNLP Approach.* Amsterdam: Kluwer Academic Publishers.

Knight, K., & Luk, S. (1994). Building a large scale knowledge base for machine translation. In *Proceedings of the Thirteenth National Conference on Artificial Intelligence,* (pp. 773-778). Menlo Park, CA: AAAI Press.

Knostan, J., Miller, B., Maltz, D., Herlocker, J., Gordon, L., & Riedl, J. (1997). Grouplens: Applying collaborative filtering to Usenet news. *Communications of the ACM, 40*(3), 77–87. doi:10.1145/245108.245126

Lang, K. (1995). Newsweeder: Learning to filter Netnews. In *12th International Conference on Machine Learning.*

Lawrie, D., & Croft, W. (2000). Discovering and comparing topic hierarchies. In *Proceedings of RIAO.*

Liberman, H. (1995). Letzia: An agent that assists in web browsing. In *Proceedings of the 1995 International Joint Conference on Artificial Intelligence*, Montreal, Canada.

Lin, D., & Pantel, P. (2001*).* Induction of semantic classes from natural language text. In *Knowledge Discovery and Data Mining*, (pp. 317-322).

Maedche, A., & Staab, S. (2001). Ontology learning for the semantic web. *IEEE Intelligent Systems, 18*(2), 72–79. doi:10.1109/5254.920602

McMahon, J., & Smith, F. (1996). Improving statistical language model with performance with automatically generated word hierarchies. *Computational Linguistics, 2*(22), 217–247.

Middleton, S., Alani, H., Shadbolt, N., & Roure, D. D. (2002). *Exploiting synergy between ontologies and recommender systems.* In Semantic Web Workshop.

Miller, G., Beckwith, R., Fellbaum, C., Gross, D., & Miller, K. (1990a). Introduction to wordnet: An online lexical database. *Journal of Lexicography, 3*(4), 235–244. doi:10.1093/ijl/3.4.235

Miller, G. A., Beckwith, R., Fellbaum, C., Gross, D., & Miller, K. J. (1990b). Introduction to wordnet: An on-line lexical database. *International Journal of Lexicography, 3*(4), 235–244. doi:10.1093/ijl/3.4.235

Mladenic, D. (1996). *Personal WebWatcher: design and implementation.* Technical report, Department for Intelligent Systems, J. Stefan Institute [Ljubljana, Slovenia.]. *Jamova, 39,* 11000.

Mobasher, B., Jin, X., & Zhou, Y. (2004). Semantically enhanced collaborative filtering on the web. In *Web Mining: FromWeb to SemanticWeb: First EuropeanWeb Mining Forum,* (pp. 57-76).

Mori, J., Matsuo, Y., & Ishizuka, M. (2005). Finding user semantics on the web using word co-occurrence information. In *PerSWeb05 Workshop on Personalization on the Semantic Web in conjunction with UM05.*

Moukas, A. (1996). Amalthaea: Information discovery and filtering using a multi-agent evolving ecosystem. In *Proc. 1st Intl. Conf. on the Practical Application of Intelligent Agents and Multi Agent Technology,* London.

Mylonas, P., Vallet, D., Fernndez, M., Castells, P., & Avrithis, Y. (2006). Ontology-based personalization for multimedia content. In *3rd European Semantic Web Conference - Semantic Web Personalization Workshop.*

Nanas, N., Uren, V., & Roeck, A. D. (2003a). Building and applying a concept hierarchy representation of a user profile. In *Proceedings of the 26th annual international ACM SIGIR conference on Research and development in information retrieval,* (pp. 198-204). New York: ACM Press.

Nanas, N., Uren, V., & Roeck, A. D. (2003b). Building and applying a concept hierarchy representation of a user profile. In *Annual ACM Conference on Research and Development in Information Retrieval archive Proceedings of the 26th annual international ACM SIGIR conference on Research and development in information retrieval.*

Oard, D. (1997). The state of the art in text filtering. *User Modeling and User-Adapted Interaction,* 7.

Parry, D. (2004). A fuzzy ontology for medical document retrieval. In *ACSW Frontiers '04: Proceedings of the second workshop on Australasian information security, Data Mining and Web Intelligence, and Software Internationalisation,* (pp. 121-126). Darlinghurst, Australia: Australian Computer Society, Inc.

Pazzani, M., & Billsus, D. (1997). Learning and revising user profiles: The identification of interesting web sites. *Machine Learning, 27,* 313–331. doi:10.1023/A:1007369909943

Pretschner, A., & Gauch, S. (2004). Ontology based personalized search and browsing. *Web Intelligence and Agent Systems, 1*(4), 219–234.

Quan, T. T., Hui, S. C., & Cao, T. H. (2004). Foga: A fuzzy ontology generation framework for scholarly semantic web. In *Workshop on Knowledge Discovery and Ontologies In conjunction with ECML/PKDD.*

Resnick, P., & Varian, H. (1997). Recommender systems. *Communications of the ACM, 40*(3), 56–58. doi:10.1145/245108.245121

Sanchez, D., & Moreno, A. (2005). A multi-agent system for distributed ontology learning. In *EUMAS*, (pp. 504-505).

Sanderson, M., & Croft, W. B. (1999). Deriving concept hierarchies from text. In *Research and Development in Information Retrieval*, (pp. 206-213).

Sieg, A., Mobasher, B., Burke, R., Prabu, G., & Lytinen, S. (2005). Representing user information context with ontologies. In *Proceedings of the 3rd International Conference on Universal Access in Human-Computer Interaction*.

Tchienehom, P. L. (2005). Profiles semantics for personalized information access. In *PerSWeb05 Workshop on Personalization on the Semantic Web in conjunction with UM05*.

Terveen, L., Hill, W., Amento, B., McDonald, D., & Creter, J. (1997). Phoaks: A system for sharing recommendations. *Communications of the ACM, 40*(3), 59–62. doi:10.1145/245108.245122

Tho, Q. T., Hui, S. C., Fong, A., & Cao, T. H. (2006). Automatic fuzzy ontology generation for semantic web. *IEEE Transactions on Knowledge and Data Engineering, 18*(6), 842–856. doi:10.1109/TKDE.2006.87

Widyantoro, D. H., & Yen, J. (2002). Using fuzzy ontology for query refinement in a personalized abstract search engine. In *10th IEEE International Conference on Fuzzy Systems*, (pp. 705-708).

Chapter 2
Patterns Relevant to the Temporal Data–Context of an Alarm of Interest

Savo Kordic
Edith Cowan University, Australia

Chiou Peng Lam
Edith Cowan University, Australia

Jitian Xiao
Edith Cowan University, Australia

Huaizhong Li
Wenzhou University, China

ABSTRACT

The productivity of chemical plants and petroleum refineries depends on the performance of alarm systems. Alarm history collected from distributed control systems (DCS) provides useful information about past plant alarm system performance. However, the discovery of patterns and relationships from such data can be very difficult and costly. Due to various factors such as a high volume of alarm data (especially during plant upsets), huge amounts of nuisance alarms, and very large numbers of individual alarm tags, manual identification and analysis of alarm logs is usually a labor-intensive and time-consuming task. This chapter describes a data mining approach for analyzing alarm logs in a chemical plant. The main idea of the approach is to investigate dependencies between alarms effectively by considering the temporal context and time intervals between different alarm types, and then employing a data mining technique capable of discovering patterns associated with these time intervals. A prototype has been implemented to allow an active exploration of the alarm grouping data space relevant to the tags of interest.

DOI: 10.4018/978-1-60566-908-3.ch002

INTRODUCTION

Complex industrial processes such as chemical plants and petroleum refineries produce large amounts of alarm information on a daily basis, due to the many different types of alarm that can occur in a relatively short period of time. Additionally, in the last two decades, "software alarms" were introduced in *distributed control systems*. These can be implemented simply by changing computer settings, which is an inexpensive process compared to installing "real alarms". Thus many process engineers choose to add extra alarm points to the existing DCS to monitor anything about which they may be concerned. Consequently, in many emergency situations excessive numbers of inappropriate alarms are generated, making the alarm system difficult to use when it is most urgently needed. A recent example is the 2005 explosion at the BP Texas City Refinery (OSHA, 2005) which left 15 people dead. BP North America was found to be responsible for the tragedy by (BP, 2007), and was fined a record $50 million and spent more than $1 billion for the inspection and refurbishment of all main process units in the refinery.

According to Shook (2004) the typical alarm management strategy for monitoring an alarm system includes collecting all alarms from all consoles, performing analysis to identify "nuisance alarm" occurrences, assessing the original performance, and then spending a few days over the period of a month to detect and reconfigure the worst nuisance alarms. The final task is to calculate statistics based on monthly alarm occurrences in order to show the frequency of alarms. While it is possible to manually extract the information required for incident reviews or alarm rationalization, the extensive quantity and complexity of data (typically collected from more than one database) have made the analysis and decomposition a very laborious task.

It is possible to identify frequent patterns on the basis of event changes over time by using *temporal windows*. However, a typical chemical alarm database is characterized by a large search space with skewed frequency distribution. Furthermore, since there can be several levels of alarms in an industrial plant, the discovered patterns or associations between **high frequency** alarms may indicate some trivial preventive actions and not necessarily provide unexpected or useful information about the state of the chemical process, while at the same time high-priority safety alarms which have a low frequency may be discarded. In contrast, setting a **low frequency** threshold level uniformly for all alarm tags might not only be computationally very expensive (with thousands of generated rules) but also there could be many spurious relationships between different support level alarms.

Therefore, despite a wealth of plant information, the data mining task of finding meaningful patterns and interesting relationships in chemical databases is difficult. This chapter presents a novel approach to developing techniques and tools that support alarm rationalization in legacy systems by extracting relationships of alarm points from alarm data in a cost-effective way.

RELATED WORK

Temporal data mining (Roddick & Spiliopoulou, 2002) is concerned with the analysis of sequences of events or itemsets in large sequential databases, where records are either chronologically ordered lists of events or indexed by transaction-time, respectively. The task of temporal data mining is different from the non-temporal discovery of relationships among itemsets such as association rules (Agrawal, Imielinski, & Swami, 1993), since of particular interest in temporal data mining is the discovery of causal relationships and temporal patterns and rules. Thus techniques for finding temporal patterns take *time* into account by observing differences in the temporal data.

In temporal data mining, the discovery process usually includes sliding time windows or time constraints. Srikant & Agrawal (1996) developed the GSP algorithm which generalizes the sequential pattern framework by including the *maximum* and *minimum time periods* between adjacent elements of the sequential patterns and allows items to be selected within a user-specified transaction-time window. The idea of Zaki (2000) was to incorporate into the mining process additional constraints such as the maximum length of a pattern, and constraints on an item's inclusion in a sequence.

Over the last decade other researchers extended the sequential pattern mining framework in various ways such as considering multidimensionality and periodicity. Lu, Han, & Feng (1998) proposed the use of *multidimensional inter-transaction* association rules where essentially dimensional attributes such as time and location were divided into equal length intervals. In the case of *cyclic association rules* (Özden, Ramaswamy, & Silberschatz, 1998) the sequences were segmented into a range of equally spaced time-periods and then these were used for discovering regular cyclic variations over time. Instead of looking for full periodic patterns, Han, Dong, & Yin (1999) considered only a set of desired time periods called *partial periodic patterns*. Ma & Hellerstein (2001) generalized the concept of partial periodicity by taking into account time tolerances, and Cao, Cheung, & Mamoulis (2004) proposed a method for automatic discovery of frequent partial periodic patterns by using a structure called the *abbreviated list table*.

More relevant to our research, based on a real plant mining problem is discovery of temporal rules in telecommunications networks where data is given as a sequence of events ordered with respect to the time of alarm occurrence. One of the main difficulties when analyzing event sequences in WINEPI (Mannila, Toivonen, & Verkamo, 1995) was to specify the window size within which an *episode* (i.e. a partially ordered set of events) must occur. If the window is too small information will be lost or if the window is too big then unrelated alarms could be included, making the process of detecting *frequent episodes* increasingly difficult. Basically there are three types of episodes: a *serial episode* which occurs in a fixed order (i.e. time-ordered events), a *parallel episode* which is an unordered collection of events (i.e. trivial partial order), and a *composite episode* which is built from a serial and a parallel episode. While the WINEPI algorithm calculates the frequency of an episode as the fraction of windows in which the episode occurs, the subsequent algorithm MINEPI (Mannila & Toivonen, 1996) directly calculates the frequency of an episode β in a given event sequence *s* as the number of *minimal occurrences* (*mo*) of β in the sequence *s*, within a given time bound. Therefore, the frequency of an episode will depend on the user-given time bound between events. Bettini, Wang, & Jajodia (1998) generalized the framework of mining temporal relationships by introducing time-interval constraints on events, and representing event structures as a rooted directed acyclic graph.

More recently, Casas-Garriga (2003) described the concept of *unbounded episodes* where the proposed algorithm automatically extends the window width during the mining process based on the size of the episodes being counted. Laxman, Sastry, & Unnikrishnan (2007a) introduced the non-overlapping occurrences counting method which has the advantage in comparison to overlapping methods in terms of actual space and efficiency during the discovery of episodes. Some recent work in temporal data mining also focuses on the significance of discovered episodes. For instance, Gwadera, Atallah, & Szpankowski (2005) showed that the lower and upper thresholds of statistically significant episodes can be determined by comparing the actual observed frequency with the estimated frequency generated by a Bernoulli distribution model. It is also desirable to consider the duration of important events. An application of this general idea to data from the manufacturing plants of General Motors is presented by Laxman, Sastry, &

Unnikrishnan (2007b). In this chapter we focus on the analysis of alarm sequences in a chemical plant, in which not only the duration of events but also the time between events is considered. Critical to our study are the duration of activation and return alarm intervals, and the differences in the distribution of events within time-intervals. Such information is essential for the elimination of irrelevant data points in a chemical process sense.

THEORETICAL FRAMEWORK

In this section a framework that facilitates understanding of the phenomena under investigation is discussed.

Alarm Events

Alarms are used as a mechanism for alerting operators to take actions that would alleviate or prevent an abnormal situation. Alarm data is a discrete type of data that will be generated only if a signal exceeds its limits.

Alarm Database and Event Intervals

Alarm databases in a chemical plant consist of records of time-stamped alarm events which include activation (ALM), return (RTN) and acknowledge (ACK) event types. We assume that a possible alarm sequence could be "ALM" → "RTN", or "ALM" → "ACK" → "RTN", but not "ALM" → "ACK" → "ALM". Note that the *acknowledge* type only indicates an operator action to stop the alarm going off, but no remedial action is taken, thus it is not considered in our research.

An *alarm sequence* can be seen as a series of event types occurring at specific times. The role of time is crucial, so a successful conceptual framework cannot rely purely on simple time points representing the instantaneous events (i.e. points at which alarm tags activate). A design that would be adequate should allow the representation of alarm events with *duration*. Since any two event types are separated in time, each interval between events can be seen as a temporal window. For simplicity and without loss of generality, let us consider only three alarms, namely, *TAG 1*, *TAG 2* and *TAG 3* in a chemical process. Alarms which are activated after the event when *TAG 1* is activated and before *TAG 1* is returned, form an *activation-return* (A-R) temporal window. The recognition that *TAG 2* and *3* for example, also occur within the (A-R) interval of *TAG 1*, implies change in both *TAG 2* and *3* over the duration of *TAG 1*. Although there may not exist both a causal and a temporal order, the main principle underlying our design is that *TAG 1* must precede *TAG 2* and *3*.

Temporal Orders and Intervals

The study design assumes that the temporal order between alarm events is preserved, and changes in alarms are manifested as disturbances until the system is returned to a normal state. Obviously, we want to investigate two questions when an alarm activation event (for example, *TAG 1* activation) occurs:

1. What are the next likely set of alarms or alarm groups which will be activated after the activation of *TAG 1*?
2. Are the alarms or alarm groups identified in Question 1 associated with the activation of *TAG 1*?

The answer to the first question provides the statistical prediction for the occurrence of alarm events. For example, if it is known that *TAG 2* is likely to be activated after the activation of *TAG 1*, and *TAG 2* is a critical alarm, then necessary precautions can be taken after the event of *TAG 1's* activation to avoid a disastrous consequence.

In order to answer the second question, we consider the nature of the alarm events in a chemical process. In a simplistic sense, if the activation of *TAG 1* causes the activation of *TAG 2*, then when *TAG 1* returns, the cause for *TAG 2* is eliminated. Therefore, it can be expected that *TAG 2* will return shortly after *TAG 1* returns. For this reason, an appropriate conceptual framework should also support representation of return events. The return event (RTN) of *TAG 1* marks the beginning of a verifying window where the window *time-width* is the process lag length. All alarm return events in the verifying window form the members in the verifying *return-time-width interval* (R-W) window which is associated with the activation time window. There must be a finite amount of time for all tags associated with the problem to return. If *TAG 1* is activated again before the process lag is reached, the activation of *TAG 1* marks the end of the verifying *return-activation* (R-A) window. Activation events in the activation-return (A-R) window are pruned if their return events do not appear in the associated verifying window.

Event Interval Filtering

Two strategies, incorporating chemical process related heuristics, are designed to remove spurious data points. These are:

Return-Point Strategy (R-p)

The rationale used here is that a *dependent* variable should return after the *independent* variable (i.e. a cause alarm) has returned. If the cause of the problem is resolved then all subsequent alarm tags related to the problem should return some time after the initial alarm tag associated with the cause has returned.

It is expected that after a transportation lag, return of the cause alarm will propagate to all associated alarms and thus cause the associated alarms to return. Thus, the relationship can be described in terms of the intersection between activation events in the activation-return (A-R) window and return events in the return-activation (R-A) or return-time-width interval (R-W) window. Formally we could write this criterion as

R-p = Activations (A-R) ∩ *Returns (R-A, or R-W)*

Activation-Point Strategy (A-p)

The heuristic used here relates to activations of alarm tags after the cause of the problem has been resolved. The rationale is that dependant variables (*consequence alarms*) once returned, should not re-activate after the *independent* variable is returned (i.e. the cause alarm is eliminated). Thus, the relationship can

Figure 1. Two filtering strategies

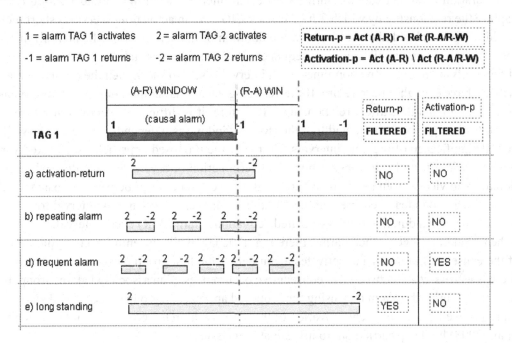

be described in terms of the difference between activation events in activation-return (A-R) windows and activation events in return-activation (R-A) or return-time-width interval (R-W) windows. Formally we could write this criterion as:

A-p = Activations (A-R) ∩ Activations (R-A, or R-W)

Two heuristic-based preprocessing strategies that incorporate domain specific concepts, and their filtering effects related to four types of alarms are shown in Figure 1. In this example, we assume that *TAG 1* is a causal alarm and *TAG 2* is a consequential alarm.

Specifically, we need to be concerned with the temporal order of events and represent durations that reflect possible causal dependencies. With an efficient alarm system, there should be no more than one alarm indicating an abnormal situation, as shown in case (a) of Figure 1. However, a perfect association between the variables under investigation may not exist. Operator related problems and inadequately configured alarm systems with improper *setpoints* (i.e. a minimum/maximum operating range) or poorly defined alarm limits or *deadbands* (i.e. a signal band where no action occurs) can cause repeating alarms, frequent alarms and long standing alarms.

Filtering Limitations

Return-point and *Activation-point* filtering strategies require some specific amount of time that is sufficient for consequential alarms to follow the cause alarm in time, in both activation-return and return-activation/time temporal ordering. The following is the list of possible filtering limitations.

- The duration of an activation-return (A-R) event-interval (window) should be *long enough* to capture the relationship by which *TAG 1* causes *TAG 2*. If an activation interval is short then there could be some related alarms, however, the duration of the activation (A-R interval) may not be long enough to capture all causal consequences if a causal process takes time.

- If the verifying return-activation/time-width interval is set *too short*, then the consequential alarm will not have enough time to return. If the verifying interval is set **too long**, then many events may come and go and thus affect relationships. Therefore, it is difficult to decide *how close is close enough* when giving the time width of the (R-W) window, as it depends on the size as well as the causal significance of the time intervals. Currently the proposed approach uses a fixed verifying window width for all alarm tags. Thus the determination of a verifying window width requires domain knowledge from the domain experts about the 'process lag' between propagating alarms. It may be a good idea to ensure that the duration of the verifying window interval for each alarm reflects the actual duration of its associated activation-return (A-R) event interval.

- When an alarm triggers other alarms, there is a 'time lag' while the entire event sequence finishes. If the cause alarm returns and activates again before the first group of associated alarms returns, there is a *cross-effect* between two consecutive occurrences of an associated alarm group. In order to correctly mine the alarm data using the proposed approach, a group of associated alarms should all return well before any new activation of the alarms within the group. Further research (Kordic et al., 2008) has been carried out to investigate this issue.

FORMAL BACKGROUND AND NOTATIONS

In this section we define formal concepts and notations that we will use to describe our mining methods. We follow the basic definitions introduced by Mannila, Toivonen & Verkamo (1997) in defining alarm sequences.

Definition 1. (Time Point)

A *time point* is an integer that represents the occurrence time of an alarm event. Let t_a and t_b be time points and there is a partial order between time points $t_a \leq t_b$.

Definition 2. (Time Interval)

A *time interval* is a contiguous sequence with a range of time points such that

$$[t_a, t_b] \equiv \{t: t_a \leq t \leq t_b\}$$

The duration of the interval $w = |t_b - t_a|$ is the *width* of the time interval.

Definition 3. (Alarm Sequence)

Given a class of event types T, an *alarm* is a pair of terms *(a, t)* where $a \in T$ and t is the *occurrence time* represented as an integer. An **alarm sequence** S is an ordered collection of alarms defined as $S =$

$\{(a_1,t_1),(a_2,t_2),...,(a_n,t_n)$, such that $a_i \in T$ for all $i=1,2,...,n$, and $t_i \leq t_{i+1}$ for all $i=1,...,n-1$.

Example 1

In our research we consider alarm *activation* and alarm *return* knowledge. While activations are represented as positive integers, returns are represented as negative integers. An example of an alarm sequence is

S = {(1, 5), (2, 12), (-1, 19), (-2, 23), (1, 30), (2, 32), (-1, 35)}

Notice that a pair of terms (alarm tag and occurrence time), have been recorded for each event that occurred in the time interval [5, 35]. For instance, the first member of the sequence (1, 5) indicates that *alarm TAG 1* is activated at the occurrence time = 5, and the third element of the sequence (-1, 19), indicates that *alarm TAG 1* is returned at occurrence time = 19.

Definition 4. (Activation-Return Interval Window)

An *activation-return* (A-R) window W_{A-R} is a subsequence of an entire event sequence S with respect to an event interval $W_{A-R}=(S, t_{act}, t_{ret})$. It consists of the alarm pairs *(a, t)* from sequence S, where $a \in T$ and $t_{ret}>t\geq t_{act}$. Intuitively, *activation-return* windows are constructed by using the activation instances of a target tag, where the activation event marks the beginning of an interval window and the return event of the target alarm indicates the end of a window.

Definition 5. (Return-Activation/Width Interval Window)

A *return-activation/width* (R-A/W) window $W_{R-A/R-w}$ is a subsequence of an entire event sequence S with respect to an event interval $W_{R-A}=(S, t_{ret}, t_{act})$ or $W_{R-w}=(s, t_{ret}, t_w)$. It consists of the alarm pairs *(a, t)* from sequence S, where $a \in T$ and $t_{act}>t\geq t_{ret}$ or $t_w>t\geq t_{ret}$. Intuitively, verifying *return-activation/width* windows will be formed either if an alarm tag is re-activated or the user given maximal width w of the window is reached.

Definition 6. (Interval Event-Set)

An *interval event-set* Φ is a partially ordered set of alarm types $a_1 \leq a_2 \leq,...,\leq a_n$ containing activation events pruned with either the Return-point (R-p) or the Activation-point (A-p) filtering strategy. Interval event-sets do not contain duplicate event types.

Definition 7. (Parallel Episode Frequency)

Let C be a collection of *interval event-sets* with respect to all event intervals of a specific tag of interest a_k. Let E be a set of the distinct alarm tags $a_1 a_2,...,a_n$ such that $E \subseteq T$. An *interval event-set* Φ is said to contain E if and only if $E \subseteq \Phi$, and $\Phi \in C$. We define the *frequency (E)* of an unordered (parallel) episode as the number of *interval event-sets* which contain all the members in E. Given a threshold *minimum support* for the minimal frequency, the set E is frequent if *frequency (E) $\geq$ minimum support*.

THE PROPOSED MINING PROCESS

The overall algorithm involving three phases is shown below. Essentially, it relies on a context-based segmentation strategy, and incorporates some frequent itemset mining techniques.

Algorithm

The pseudo-code for the main algorithm is shown below.

```
Input: sequence of historical alarm event logs
Output: frequent episode
(Phase 1): Data Generation and Preparation
Extract the relevant information associated with alarm tags from
simulation event log-file or alarm database and put into an appro-
priate format
(Phase 2): Data Segmentation and Filtering
FOR ALL target alarm tags in the event log file
     Extract the W_{A-R(i)} and the  W_{R-A/W(i)}  sets of transactions
     FOR EACH alarm tag
          Do filtering based on Return-point (R-p) strategy or Acti-
vation-point (A-p) strategy
     END FOR
END FOR
(Phase 3): Discovery of Interesting Patterns
DO "frequent itemset mining" to obtain a set of co-occurring alarm
tags associated with each tag of interest
```

Phase 1: Data Generation and Preparation

The strategy in our experiments was to use a systematic and data-driven approach achieved by increasing model/data complexity in order to evaluate and refine the developed techniques. The proposed approach was evaluated initially using simulated data produced from a Matlab (MathWorks, 2009) model of the Vinyl Acetate chemical process, and then using real chemical plant data with more than 100 distinct alarm tags.

Generation of Simulated Alarms Using the Vinyl Acetate Matlab Model

The Vinyl Acetate model can be used to accurately simulate a Vinyl Acetate process. However, unlike a real Vinyl Acetate plant, the Matlab model does not have alarm monitors built in and hence it cannot produce alarms which would be caused by setpoint changes or disturbances in the process. Figure 2 shows the simulated alarm monitors (AM), the associated alarm tags, and the monitored measurement variables.

Figure 2. Alarm tags and monitored measurement variables

AM	TAG	Monitored Variable
AM01	1	%O2 in the Reactor Inlet
AM02	2	Gas Recycle Stream Pressure
AM03	3	HAc Tank Level
AM04	4	Vaporizer Level
AM05	5	Vaporizer Pressure
AM06	6	Heater Exit Temperature
AM07	7	Reactor Exit Temperature
AM08	8	Separator Level
AM09	9	Separator Temperature
AM10	10	Separator Vapor Flowrate
AM11	11	Compressor Exit Temperature
AM12	12	Absorber Level
AM13	13	Absorber Scrub Flowrate
AM14	14	Circulation Stream Temperature
AM15	15	Absorber Circulation Flowrate
AM16	16	Scrub Stream Temperature
AM17	17	%CO2 in the Gas Recycle
AM18	18	%C2H6 in the Gas Recycle
AM19	19	FEHE Hot Exit Temperature
AM20	20	%H2O in the Column Bottom
AM21	21	5th Tray Temperature
AM22	22	Decanter Temperature
AM23	23	Decanter Organic Level
AM24	24	Decanter Aqueous Level
AM25	25	Column Bottom Level
AM26	26	Liquid Recycle Flowrate
AM27		Column Bottom VAc Composition

In order to simulate alarms using the Matlab model, it was necessary to perform simulations twice. The first simulation was performed to obtain the normal measurement outputs of the Vinyl Acetate model under normal operating conditions. Then the second simulation was performed to obtain the disturbed measurement outputs of the model under disturbance. The difference between normal measurement outputs and the disturbed measurement outputs was used to generate discrete alarm data associated with the injection of disturbances. For simplicity, it was assumed that a simulated alarm is activated if the following condition is satisfied:

$$Abs\left(\frac{\left(D_m - N_m\right)}{N_m}\right) \geq S_{am}$$

where D_m is the disturbed output magnitude, N_m is the normal output magnitude and S_{am} is the sensitivity of the simulated alarm monitor. Note that the simulated alarm will return to normal if the above condition is not satisfied. The signal detection sensitivity for all alarm monitors was set to be equal to 0.0005.

Simulated Data Pre-Processing

The Vinyl data consists of records of alarm logs which characterize the actual state of the plant at particular points in time, representing the status of 27 alarm monitors. Using a simple algorithm, the event log file is processed to produce formatted alarm data as shown in Figure 3. Note that the symbol (A) stands for *activated* and (R) for *returned*. Also note that Figure 3 shows a simple record representing only the first 8 alarm monitors.

The approach captures the first time instance an alarm tag goes into activation and the time instance the alarm tag is returned. For example, in the column associated with TAG 1 in Figure 3, it shows that TAG 1 was activated at 1:32 and returned at 1:35, thus the duration of this tag being in an activation state was 3 minutes. TAG 1 is re-activated at 1:37. Similarly, TAG 6 was activated at 1:33 and it returned at 1:36. The collection of alarm activations/returns and time-stamps associated with a defined set of alarm tag identifiers as shown in Figure 3 forms an alarm sequence. The starting point of the activation-return (A-R) window is defined as the time the tag of interest went into activation and the ending point is where it went into the corresponding return state. For example, if the tag of interest is TAG 1 in Figure 3, the event interval windows are defined as $W_{A-R(1)}$, from 1:32 to 1:35 and $W_{A-R(2)}$ from 1:37 to 1:39. A second type of window (denoted as $W_{R-A/R-w}$) used here is defined by a fixed user-defined duration after a tag of interest moves back into a return state (after being activated). This user-defined duration may be shortened if the tag of interest is reactivated. Again, using a user-defined window width of 3 minutes and TAG 1 as an example, its $W_{R-A/R-w(1)}$ should start from 1:35 and end 3 minutes later at 1:38, but as TAG 1 is re-activated again at 1:37 this window will terminate at the point TAG 1 is re-activated (i.e. a duration of 2 minutes instead of 3 minutes).

Figure 3. An example of an alarm sequence

Time	TAG							
Interval (every 1 minute)	1	2	3	4	5	6	7	8
R1 1:32	(A) 1							
R2 1:33						(A) 6		
R3 1:34		(A) 2						
R4 1:35	(R) -1				(A) 5			(A) 8
R5 1:36		(R) -2				(R) -6	(A) 7	
R6 1:37	(A) 1						(R) -7	
R7 1:38					(R) - 5			
R8 1:39	(R) -1		(A) 3					

Real Plant Data Pre-Processing

Since different vendors of modern control systems generate their own format for messages, the format of plant alarm data is both software and hardware dependent. As a minimum requirement, the alarm event log consists of records with fields that store information such as a *unique identifier* for each alarm tag, *time/date, alarm priorities, alarm settings* and the possible *states* of an alarm tag [ALM, RTN]. When an alarm tag is in an activation [ALM] state, it implies that the value of the associated process variable is outside its normal operational setting, and when this value returns to the normal operational setting, the alarm tag is then in a return [RTN] state. It is important to check an event log file carefully because real plant data tends to be inconsistent, with errors, missing values, outliners, and duplicate values. The data pre-processing steps are summarized as follows:

- *Removal of irrelevant records* - records in the alarm databases (or alarm log files) are irrelevant to the pattern discovery aim if the data fields have no [ALM] or [RTN] values. For example, all the records in the database containing [ACK] values.
- *Removal of irrelevant attributes (database fields)* – each extracted event has only three important attributes – alarm tag identifier, its state, and the time of the event occurrence.
- *Removal of redundant data* - the same events may be recorded two or more times. Examples of such values are multiple [ALMs] with identical alarm stamps but with only one [RTN].
- *Removal of outliners* that fall outside the activation-return and return-activation boundaries. Examples of such values are [RTN] with no [ALM] at the beginning of the file, and [ALM] with no [RTN] at the end of the file, due to inaccurate sampling.
- *Data substitution* – finally, an alarm sequence is created where each event has an associated time of occurrence given as an integer number, and also activation and return event types are represented as positive and negative integers, respectively.

Phase 2: Data Segmentation and Filtering

This phase extracts a sequence of alarm events from the alarm event log database (file) of a chemical plant. Since we consider both activation and return events, it is possible to segment the entire alarm sequence by using the activation instances of a target tag, where the activation event marks the beginning of a sliding widow and the return event of the target alarm indicates the end of a window. Thus if the total number of activations of a specified alarm tag is n, then the whole alarm sequence can be segmented into n windows of W_{A-R}. Similarly the whole alarm sequence can also be segmented into n windows of type $W_{R-A/R-w}$ if there are n returns associated with the tag of interest. Obviously, this segmentation is an event-based extraction within a clear contextual meaning. At each point in time, the window is shifted along to the next activation instance of the tag of interest. Each of the n windows of W_{A-R} captures data that indicates which other alarm tags also went into activation while the alarm tag of interest was in activation. On the other hand, each of the n windows of $W_{R-A/R-w}$ captures data that show which other alarm tags also returned within a user-defined window after the tag of interest returned.

The Segmentation and Filtering Algorithm

Problem: suppose we are given a sequence $s = (s, T_S, T_E)$ where T_S is the starting time and T_E is the ending time, an integer a_k represents a specified target alarm tag, and a window width w. Find all *interval event-sets* with respect to the target alarm tag.

The pseudo-code for the segmentation and R-p filtering is shown below.

```
Input: a sequence s, a window width w, and a specific tag of inter-
est a Output: the collection C of interval event-sets with respect
  k
to tag of interest
 /* initialisation*/
A:= {∅}, R:= {∅}, C:= {∅ };
k:= 0;
    FOR each a  in s
             k
            A ← subset of activation segment (W   [k]);
                                              A-R
            R ← subset of return segment (W       [k], w);
                                           R-A/R-w
            C[k] ← intersection (A ∩ R);
k:= k + 1;
      END FOR
Output C
```

The main idea of the algorithm is the following: during each shift of the window $W_{A\text{-}R\,(k)} + W_{R\text{-}A/R\text{-}w\,(k)}$, we recognize all unique activations and return events and place them into sets (A and R). Next, we store the intersection of two sets A∩R into a collection of event-sets *C*. In the recognition phase the total time spent going through the loop will be linear since there are $O(n)$ shifts of the window. The body of the for-loop consists of four assignment statements, and thus the time taken to execute the body once is $O(1)$. Therefore, the time spent by the algorithm is $O(n) + O(1)$. As the lower-order term can be neglected, the time complexity is $O(n)$ unless there is only one occurrence of a_k. In this case $k = 1$, and consequently the time complexity is $O(1)$.

Phase 3: Discovery of Interesting Patterns

At the end of the first two phases the unstructured data has been partitioned into a cluster of information on the basis of its relation to the activation and return of an alarm tag of interest.

Figure 4. An example of processing interval event-sets associated with TAG 3 using the Return-point strategy and a window width of 30 minutes

$W_{A\text{-}R(k)}$ of TAG 3 (activations)	$W_{R\text{-}A/R\text{-}w(k)}$ of TAG 3 w=30 min (returns)	Found in $W_{A\text{-}R(k)}$ and $W_{R\text{-}A/R\text{-}w(k)}$ of TAG 3
3 16 9 4 18 6 11 8 23 27 14 12 20 17 2 25 5 7 19	-3 -16	3 16
3 16 9 4 18 11 6 8 23 27 14 20 12 17 5 25 2 1 7 19 24	-3 -16	3 16
3 16 9 4 18 6 11 8 23 27 14 20 12 17 5 25 2 1 7 19 24	-3 -4 -16	3 16 4
3 16 9 4 18 6 11 8 23 27 14 20 12	-3 -16	3 16

Example 2

Figure 4 shows an example of processing event-sets associated with TAG 3 using the R-p filtering strategy and a window width of 30 minutes.

The collection of resulting event-sets in column 3 of Figure 4 is used in the next step to find a data driven frequency threshold value that can be used subsequently for finding patterns of interest.

CASE STUDY

To evaluate the proposed method two simulated data sets were generated with varying complexity and fault durations.

Case 1: Simulated Fault Data Set 1

The duration of the first simulation was 10080 minutes which represents one week's operation of the Vinyl Acetate process. The measurement outputs were monitored and sampled at a frequency of 1 sample in one minute. The sampled measurement outputs were then streamed into a data file. After the completion of the simulation, the data file contained 27 columns and 10080 rows, each column representing a measurement output, and each row representing one minute intervals in the simulation. The second simulation is performed to simulate the response of the Vinyl Acetate process under disturbances. Frequent disturbances of one type, namely the *loss of %O2 in the Reactor Inlet* (associated with alarm TAG 1), were injected into the Vinyl Acetate process to induce a response in measurement outputs. Each fault was injected 10 times and lasted for different durations. Similar to the normal simulation, the duration of the second simulation was also 10080 minutes. Again, the measurement outputs were monitored and sampled at a frequency of 1 sample in one minute. The sampled measurement outputs were then streamed into the second data file. Using the normal process output stored in the first data file and the disturbed process output stored in the second data file, it is straightforward to obtain the changes in the process measurements which were caused by the injected disturbances using the formula given in the section "Generation of Simulated Alarms using the Vinyl Acetate Matlab Model".

An implementation of the FP-growth (Han et al., 2000) algorithm was used to output all frequent patterns associated with each alarm tag of interest. Firstly, we wanted to demonstrate the effectiveness of the filtering, and thus we set the minimum frequency very low at 1 occurrence. Figure 5 illustrates the effect of the A-point and R-point filtering on *simulated dataset 1* with respect to faults associated with alarm TAG 1. In this experiment we compared the quantities of patterns discovered without filtering (activations), with the quantities of patterns discovered using a verifying group and filtering.

Figure 5 shows that overall the numbers of frequent patterns dropped dramatically in the case of R-point filtering. The number of frequent patterns ranged from 799795 for the activations with no filtering, down to 255 for the activations with R-point filtering.

Next, we examined the validity of the discovered patterns. For the simulated dataset 1, we set the minimum frequency a bit higher - equal to 8 occurrences - to find more statistically significant (frequent) rules relating to 10 injected faults. In our research we are only interested in finding **primary and consequential** alarms, and therefore in rules that have a specific target tag appearing in the antecedent. The idea of mining *maximal frequent itemsets* (Bayardo, 1998; Burdick, Calimlim, & Gehrke, 2005;

Figure 5. The effect of the A-point and R-point filtering on simulated dataset 1

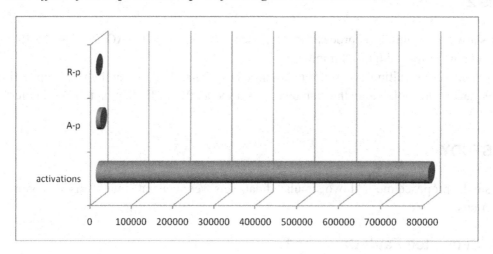

Gouda & Zaki, 2001) is to use a very concise set of frequent itemsets called maximal frequent itemsets. For a given maximal frequent event set $E = a_1, a_2... a_m, m \geq 2$, the consequent Y will be the event set $E - a_1$. Thus the confidence of composite episode *confidence* $a_1 => (Y)$ is calculated as *frequency* $(a_1 \cup Y)$ / *frequency* (a_1). Calculating the confidences of episodes is not difficult since the alarm sequence is segmented into sets of windows associated with each primary alarm tag.

Figure 6 shows rules with respect to the first ten alarm tags. In terms of checking whether the group of associated alarms is correct, the results sets associated with fault TAG 1 (loss of %O2) can be checked against the Vinyl Acetate process flowsheet chart illustrated in Kordic et al. (2008). Based on the Vinyl Acetate flowsheet analysis and the alarm status display, the loss of Oxygen feed (TAG 1) in the reactor could significantly affect temperature change in the Reactor (TAG 7), Heat Exchanger (TAG 6), Separator (TAG 9), and Vaporizer Level (TAG 4).

Case 2: Simulated Fault Data Set 2

Frequent disturbances were injected into the Vinyl Acetate process to induce a response in measurement outputs. Only one type of disturbance was introduced in this simulation, namely the *loss of the fresh HAc feed stream* (associated with alarm TAG 3), with each fault lasting over different durations. The fault was injected 10 times. The measurement outputs were monitored and sampled at a frequency of 1 sample in *five* seconds. After the completion of the simulation, the data file contained 27 columns and 60481 rows, each column representing a measurement output, and each row representing a five second interval in the simulation.

Similarly to the effect of the A-point and R-point filtering on simulated dataset 1, the numbers of frequent patterns dropped dramatically in the case of both A-point and R-point filtering. This time the number of frequent patterns ranged from 2069255 for the activations with no filtering, down to only 11 for the activations with R-point filtering. We have also developed a prototype data mining tool that reduces the effort needed for pre-processing, data segmentation and analysis of alarm log files. As shown in Figure 7, a graphical user interface was created to allow user interaction.

Figure 6. An example of processing selected comparative results for simulated dataset 1 with respect to minimum frequency = 8 occurrences, minimum confidence = 40%, R-point filtering and verifying window width w = 900 seconds

TAG	Frequent Episodes	*frequency*	*confidence*
1 %O2 (fault) [AM01]	1 => (6 7 9 4)	10	10/10 = 100%
2 Press [AM02]	2 => ( ) *below minimum frequency*	-	-
3 HAc-L [AM03]	3 => ( ) *below minimum frequency*	-	-
4 Vap-L [AM04]	4 => ( ) *below minimum frequency*	-	-
5 Vap-P [AM05]	5 => ( ) *below minimum frequency*	-	-
6 Pre-T [AM06]	6 => ( ) *below minimum frequency*	-	-
7 RCT-T [AM07]	7 => (12)	12	12/29 = 41%
8 Sep-L [AM08]	8 => () *below minimum frequency*	-	-
9 Sep-T [AM09]	9 => () *below minimum frequency*	-	-
10 Sep-V [AM10]	FIXED		
...	...	...	...

Case 3: Chemical Plant Data Set

To evaluate the efficiency of mined results we also used real petrochemical plant data with more than 100 distinct alarm tags. Due to the confidentiality agreement involved, we will only present some of the advantages of our approach with respect to this dataset. The chemical plant data sample was given as a 'dump file' containing records of alarm logs taken from an Oracle database. These alarm records represented the actual state of the plant over a period of 12 days. An example of the plant data after irrelevant data fields were removed is given below:

23/03/2005 ALM 08:55:49 TAGB1924

23/03/2005 RTN 08:55:54 TAGB1925

...

Please note that in the above example, and wherever else 'real plant data' is shown, tag labels have been changed to protect the **confidentiality** of the data provided by the industrial partner.

Choosing the right support threshold is critical in terms of finding interesting patterns. There were 116 alarm tags, and only 7 alarm tags had a frequency greater than 100 occurrences. 87.1% of the events (i.e. the first 101 alarm tags) have a frequency that is less than 50 occurrences (2.7%). A common misconception is that the higher the value associated with support then the greater will be the degree of interestingness (McGarry, 2005) to the user. For example a pattern with a support value of 90% may be considered better than one with a support value of 30%. Thus a user may arbitrarily determine a high support value for finding patterns of interest from a data set, and then if no patterns are found, it may lead to the misconception that there are no interesting patterns in the data set. The concept here is that "the story is in the data". For example, if the occurrence of a group of co-related tags in the data set has a frequency of 10% then that is the value to use, rather than selecting an arbitrary value. For this reason, our approach is to set a sufficient threshold for each alarm tag independently, prior to the data mining phase.

We have also developed a prototype data mining tool to aid in the analysis of an alarm tag of interest. As shown in Figure 8, a graphical user interface was created to speed up the process and to provide an intuitive means of interpreting the results - especially for databases with a large number of alarm tags. The example shown in Figure 8 describes the temporal relationships between alarms with respect to target alarm 5 representing *TAG T08UA976*.

A-R Durations

1186,1379,1518,1644,1439,1653,2058,11822,719,290,1333,886,3104,424, 760,914,813,960,844,892, 960,1043,735,632,781,789,888,837,942,885,910, 1656,1256,1017,1342,423,694,708,1371,1182,943,

Figure 7. A graphical user interface was created to allow user interaction

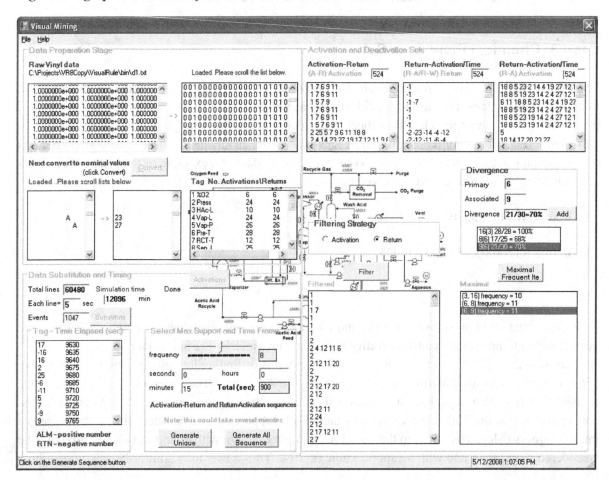

Figure 8. A graphical user interface was created for exploration of tags

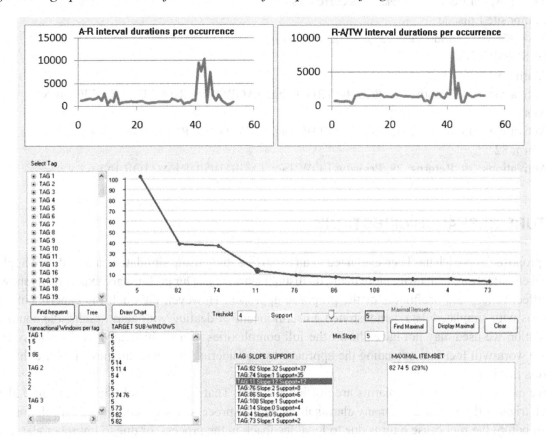

87594,10337,759,7482, 2269,1109,2536,1127,761,339,492,945

R-A/TW Durations

743,757,704,702,732,642,373,1503,1612,1688,1686,1545,1516,1581,1574,1541,1747,1355,1408,135
9,1381,1787,1639,1507,1401,1407,1422,1335,1378,1339,1570,720,813,488,1886,1653,1802,1418,11
03,1908,1745,8538,1125,3420,593,611,1973,1500,1323,1576,1649,1524,1532

The aim of this procedure is to extract relevant information from vast amounts of data in order to indicate a threshold that characterizes the context of tag-dependent data. The level of skewness could be calculated with respect to minor interval changes in the curve's slope. The number of times the consequential alarm occurred within the windows of the primary tag and the rate of change in slope interval are factors taken into account to provide the user with guidance in selecting the confidence threshold value. Note that we expected that an extreme skewness to the right may indicate a chattering alarm.

Threshold relevant to data context of Alarm 5

Minimum support = 12 occurrences

Serial episodes

5 = > (82) confidence = 37%, 20 occurrences

5 = > (74) confidence = 35%, 19 occurrences
Composite Episode
5 => (82, 74) confidence = 29%, 16 occurrences
DESCRIPTION
Alarm: 5
Activations: 53, Returns: 53, Priority: HIGH Tag: TAGRO976, REACTOR 5 OFFNORM
Alarm 74
Activations: 35, Returns: 35, Priority: LOW Tag: TAGRI1049, REACTOR INLET
Alarm 82
Activations: 29, Returns: 29, Priority: LOW Tag: TAGRI1050, REACTOR INLET

FUTURE RESEARCH DIRECTIONS

The proposed approach has been evaluated in an extensive study using simulated data, and then applied to real chemical plant data with more than 100 distinct alarm tags. Our preliminary experiments showed the effectiveness and usefulness of the proposed approach. However, although the experiments and analysis with simulated data demonstrated a useful means of dealing with alarm faults, the computer simulation we used may not have shown the full complexities of a sophisticated, real alarm system. Future work will focus on extending the approach by considering an interestingness measure that can address this issue.

We can assume that some alarms are not independent. That is, there could be a root cause alarm which triggers the activation of many alarms in a chemical process. These "consequential" alarms may return before the root cause returns due to local feedback in the process, or due to improper alarm settings. However, by definition an interval *event set Φ* does not contain duplicate events (only the first incidence of an event is recorded) although in an activation-return window there may be multiple occurrences of any consequential alarm tag. If this alarm tag does not occur frequently elsewhere in the alarm sequence, it is probably a good indication that the alarm is a consequence of the primary cause. Based on the objective statistical strength of discovered patterns we can find which alarms occur most often in the data context of the particular tag of interest. For instance, given an event sequence s and the set of all windows Δ (s, win_a) with respect to target TAG A, if we know that the subsequent TAG B occurs 20 times in Δ (s, win_a) and only 25 times in the entire sequence s, this may indicate that the connection between tag A and B is significant, since 20/25 = 0.8. On the other hand, if the value is low, say 0.1, this value may indicate events that are not very dependent. In other words, by comparing the *total number of occurrences* of a particular alarm tag (in the data context of the primary tag) against its frequency in the entire sequence, we can find the degree of dependency for this particular tag. However, more rigorous testing is required to determine the applicability of this measure.

CONCLUSION

To summarize, in this chapter we have presented an approach for analyzing large alarm databases. A crucial element in this investigation is to determine intervals related to co-occurrences of the particular alarm tag of interest. The approach combines a context-based segmentation strategy with a data mining technique to address the problem of discovery of interesting patterns from historical alarm event logs. The discovered groups of co-occurring alarms can be used to support alarm rationalization by identifying redundant alarms and system bad actors. We showed the efficiency of our filtering strategies and the relevance of discovered patterns. We illustrated how instead of selecting an arbitrary value for all alarms in an alarm sequence, we could set a sufficient threshold for each alarm tag independently. The approach is more cost effective for identifying primary and consequential alarms than any manual alarm analysis of event logs, which is very costly in terms of time and labour.

REFERENCES

Agrawal, R., Imielinski, T., & Swami, A. (1993). Mining association rules between sets of items in large databases. In *Proceedings of the 1993 ACM SIGMOD International Conference on Management of Data (SIGMOD'93)* (pp. 207-216). New York: ACM.

Bayardo, R. J. (1998). Efficiently mining long patterns from databases. In *Proceedings of the 1998 ACM SIGMOD International Conference on Management of Data (SIGMOD'98)* (pp. 85-93). New York: ACM.

Bettini, C., Wang, X. S., & Jajodia, S. (1998). Mining Temporal Relationships with Multiple Granularities in Time Sequences. *Data Eng. Bull., 21*(1), 32–38.

BP. (2007). *BP America announces resolution of Texas City, Alaska, propane trading, law enforcement investigations.* Retrieved April 2008, from http://www.bp.com

Burdick, D., Calimlim, M., & Gehrke, J. (2005). MAFIA: A Maximal Frequent Itemset Algorithm. *IEEE Transactions on Knowledge and Data Engineering, 17*(11), 1490–1504. doi:10.1109/TKDE.2005.183

Cao, H., Cheung, D. W., & Mamoulis, N. (2004). Discovering Partial Periodic Patterns in Discrete Data Sequences In *Advances in Knowledge Discovery and Data Mining* (Vol. 3056, pp. 653-658). Berlin: Springer.

Casas-Garriga, G. (2003). *Discovering unbounded episodes in sequential data.* Paper presented at the Principles and Practice of Knowledge Discovery in Databases (PKDD'03), Dubrovnik Croatia.

Gouda, K., & Zaki, M. J. (2001). Efficiently Mining Maximal Frequent Itemsets. In *Proceedings of the 2001 IEEE International Conference on Data Mining* (pp. 163-170). Washington, DC: IEEE Computer Society.

Gwadera, R., Atallah, M. J., & Szpankowski, W. (2005). Reliable detection of episodes in event sequences. *Knowledge and Information Systems, 7*(4), 415–437. doi:10.1007/s10115-004-0174-5

Han, J., Dong, G., & Yin, Y. (1999). Efficient Mining of Partial Periodic Patterns in Time Series Database. In *Proceedings of the 15th International Conference on Data Engineering* (pp. 106-115). Washington, DC: IEE Computer Society.

Han, J., Pei, J., Yin, Y., & Mao, R. (2000). *Mining Frequent Patterns without Candidate Generation (SIGMOD'00).* Paper presented at the 2000 ACM SIGMOD Intl. Conference on Management of Data, Dallas, TX.

Kordic, S., Lam, P., Xiao, J., & Li, H. (2008). Analysis of Alarm Sequences in a Chemical Plant. In *Proceedings of the 4th international conference on Advanced Data Mining and Applications* (Vol. 5139, pp. 135-146). Berlin: Springer-Verlag.

Laxman, S., Sastry, P., & Umnikrishnan, K. (2007b). Discovering Frequent Generalized Episodes When Events Persist for Different Durations. *IEEE Transactions on Knowledge and Data Engineering, 19*(9), 1188–1201. doi:10.1109/TKDE.2007.1055

Laxman, S., Sastry, P. S., & Unnikrishnan, K. P. (2007a). A fast algorithm for finding frequent episodes in event streams. In *Proceedings of the 13th ACM SIGKDD International Conference on Knowledge Discovery and Data Mining* (pp. 410-419). New York: ACM.

Lu, H., Han, J., & Feng, L. (1998). *Stock Movement Prediction and N-dimensional Inter-Transaction Association Rules.* Paper presented at the SIGMOD Workshop Research Issues on Data Mining and Knowledge Discovery (DMKD '98), Seattle, Washington.

Ma, H., & Hellerstein, J. L. (2001). Mining Partially Periodic Event Patterns with Unknown Periods. In *Proceedings of the 17th International Conference on Data Engineering* (pp. 205-214). Washington, DC: IEEE Computer Society.

Mannila, H., & Toivonen, H. (1996). Discovering generalized episodes using minimal occurrences. In *The Second International Conference on Knowledge Discovery and Data Mining (KDD-96)* (pp. 146-151). Menlo Park, CA: AAAI Press.

Mannila, H., Toivonen, H., & Verkamo, A. I. (1995). *Discovering frequent episodes in sequences.* Paper presented at the First International Conference on Knowledge Discovery and Data Mining (KDD '95), Montreal, Canada.

Mannila, H., Toivonen, H., & Verkamo, A. I. (1997). Discovery of Frequent Episodes in Event Sequences. *Data Mining and Knowledge Discovery, 1*(3), 259–289. doi:10.1023/A:1009748302351

MathWorks. T. (2009). *MATLAB - The Language of Technical Computing.* Retrieved 20 January, 2009, from http://www.mathworks.com/products/matlab/

McGarry, K. (2005). A survey of interestingness measures for knowledge discovery. *20*(1), 39 - 61.

OSHA. (2005). *OSHA Fines BP Products North America More Than $21 Million Following Texas City Explosion.* Retrieved May, 2008, from http://www.osha.gov/pls/oshaweb

Özden, B., Ramaswamy, S., & Silberschatz, A. (1998). *Cyclic Association Rules.* Paper presented at the Fourteenth International Conference on Data Engineering (ICDE '98), Orlando, Florida.

Roddick, J. F., & Spiliopoulou, M. (2002). A Survey of Temporal Knowledge Discovery Paradigms and Methods. *IEEE Transactions on Knowledge and Data Engineering, 14*(4), 750–767. doi:10.1109/TKDE.2002.1019212

Shook, D. (2004). *Alarm management* [white paper]. Retrieved July 7, 2004, from http://www.matrikon.com/download/products/lit/Matrikon_Alarm_Management_Whitepaper.pdf

Srikant, R., & Agrawal, R. (1996). *Mining Sequential Patterns: Generalizations and Performance Improvements.* Paper presented at the 5th Int. Conf. Extending Database Technology (EDBT), Avignon, France.

Zaki, M. J. (2000). Sequence Mining in Categorical Domains: Incorporating Constraints. In *Proceedings of the Ninth International Conference on Information and Knowledge Management* (pp. 422-429). New York: ACM.

KEY TERMS AND DEFINITIONS

Data Mining: is usually defined as the process of extracting and analyzing previously unknown, hidden patterns and relationships from data that has been collected.

Data Preprocessing: is the process that includes various procedures such as data cleaning, data reduction, and data filtering to transform the raw data into a suitable form for data mining.

Case Study: is an intensive study that is carried out in order to investigate various strategies and prove the efficiency of the proposed tools and techniques.

Frequent Episodes: is a data mining framework for discovery of temporal rules in telecommunications networks. Basically there are three types of episodes: a serial episode which occurs in a fixed order, a parallel episode which is an unordered collection of events, and a composite episode which is built from a serial and a parallel episode.

Domain Knowledge: is the knowledge which is specific to a domain such as knowledge obtained from experts in the field.

Simulated Data: A large volume of alarm data was generated using a computer model of the plant that simulates the behavior of a chemical process.

Simulation Model: A simulation model such as the Matlab model of the Vinyl Acetate plant was designed to closely represent the behavior of the chemical plant.

Chapter 3
ODARM:
An Outlier Detection–Based Alert Reduction Model

Fu Xiao
Nanjing University, P. R. China

Xie Li
Nanjing University, P. R. China

ABSTRACT

Intrusion Detection Systems (IDSs) are widely deployed with increasing of unauthorized activities and attacks. However they often overload security managers by triggering thousands of alerts per day. And up to 99% of these alerts are false positives (i.e. alerts that are triggered incorrectly by benign events). This makes it extremely difficult for managers to correctly analyze security state and react to attacks. In this chapter the authors describe a novel system for reducing false positives in intrusion detection, which is called ODARM (an Outlier Detection-Based Alert Reduction Model). Their model based on a new data mining technique, outlier detection that needs no labeled training data, no domain knowledge and little human assistance. The main idea of their method is using frequent attribute values mined from historical alerts as the features of false positives, and then filtering false alerts by the score calculated based on these features. In order to filter alerts in real time, they also design a two-phrase framework that consists of the learning phrase and the online filtering phrase. Now they have finished the prototype implementation of our model. And through the experiments on DARPA 2000, they have proved that their model can effectively reduce false positives in IDS alerts. And on real-world dataset, their model has even higher reduction rate.

INTRODUCTION

With increasing of unauthorized activities and attacks, intrusion detection systems (IDS) have been widely deployed during the last decade, and their value as security components has been demonstrated. But this technique still has some problems. For example, practitioners and researchers have observed

DOI: 10.4018/978-1-60566-908-3.ch003

that IDS can easily trigger thousands of alerts per day, up to 99% of which are false positives (i.e. alerts that are triggered incorrectly by benign events) (Julisch & Dacier, 2002). This flood of mostly false alerts has made it very difficult for managers to analyze security state. Moreover the reactions to dangerous attacks are often delayed, because the alerts for them are hidden in huge amounts of trivial ones and are often neglected. So how to reduce false positives is an important problem needing researchers pay more attentions to.

Now one popular solution to this problem is using certain algorithms (e.g. machine learning or statistical algorithms) to identify true alerts and filter false ones from raw data. Some related methods have been proposed, such as classification-based method, root cause analysis-based method and so on, but most of these methods have three limitations. Firstly, they usually need a lot of labeled training data or domain knowledge to build their alert reduction model. However these data are often difficult to obtain. Secondly, most of them are off-line model which will delay the reaction to attacks. Thirdly, most of them can not adapt to new situations. In this chapter we proposed a novel method, which hasn't above limitations. It is based on a new data mining technique, outlier detection. This technique has been successfully applied in many fields (e.g. fraud detection, weather prediction), but has not been used to reduce false positives.

In order to filter IDS alerts better, we have designed a special outlier detection algorithm for this field, i.e. an improved frequent pattern-based outlier detection algorithm. It assigns each alert an outlier score, which indicates how abnormal the alert is. The score is calculated based on how many frequent attribute values the alert contains. Usually the more frequent patterns an alert has, the higher its score is, and the more likely it is a false positive. In order to filer alerts in real time, we also design a two-phrase framework. In the learning phrase, we build the feature set of false positives and calculate the threshold of true alerts based on this set. Then in the online filtering phrase, we compare the outlier score of each newcome alerts with this threshold so as to determine whether it is false positive or not. And the feature set is automatically updated so as to keep its accuracy. Based on above algorithm and framework, we have built a new alert reduction system named ODARM (an Outlier Detection-Based Alert Reduction Model). And we have validated ODARM by experiments on both DARPA 2000 dataset and real-world data. The results on DARPA 2000 show that when 86% of alerts have been filtered by our model, 100% of true alerts still remain. And on real-world dataset ORARM has even higher reduction rate.

The rest of this chapter is organized as follows. The next section discusses related work. The section "Outlier Detection-Based Alert Reduction" introduces the design of our outlier detection-based alert reduction system. The next section presents our experiments and gives detailed analysis of the final result. The last section concludes the chapter and introduces the future work.

RELATED WORK

Related work towards alert reduction technique, which aims at identifying and reducing IDS alerts, is described in the first section. And then the next section reviews current outlier detection algorithms.

Alert Reduction

There is still not so much work on identifying and reducing IDS alerts. Current methods can be divided into three categories, which are described as follows:

Method based on Classification. The main idea of this method is building an alert classifier that tells true from false positives. Tadeusz Pietraszek has presented one such system (Pietraszek, 2004). It firstly generates training examples based on the analyst's feedback. Then these data are used by machine learning techniques to initially build and subsequently update the classifier. Finally the classifier is used to process new alerts. This method can classify alerts automatically. But its main shortcoming is producing labeled training data is labor intensive and error prone.

Method based on Root Cause Analysis. This method firstly discovers and understands the root causes of IDS alerts. Then according to these causes, the alerts triggered by attacks can be distinguished from those triggered by benign evens. Klaus Julisch has proposed such a model based on conceptual clustering (Julisch & Dacier, 2002; Julisch, 2001; Julisch, 2003). It generalizes alerts according to the Generalization Hierarchies built on each alert attribute. And the final generalized alerts will be presented to users to help root causes analysis. The main disadvantage of this method is Generalization Hierarchies are not easy to build. It depends on the experience of domain experts and collecting enough background knowledge. Moreover this kind of methods only supports offline process.

Methods based on the Assumption that "Frequent Alert Sequences Are Likely Resulted from Normal Behaviors". Now many alert reduction methods belong to this category. For example, Clifton & Gengo (2000) applied frequent episode mining on IDS alerts. When the frequent sequences of alerts that have the same destination were found, they would be presented to users in order to determine whether they were false positives or not. Alharby & Imai (2005) and Manganaris et al. (2000) have designed similar methods, but Alharby & Imai (2005) used continuous and discontinuous patterns to model false positives, and Manganaris et al. (2000) used frequent itemsets and association rules to model them. Viinikka et al. (2006) filtered IDS alerts by monitoring alert flow. They modeled regularities in alert flows with classical time series methods. After removing the periodic components, slowly changed trend and random noise from time series, the remaining was regarded as true alerts. All methods mentioned above are based on modeling false positives by frequent or periodic alert sequences. It is effective in the environment where normal behaviors seldom change. However it often mistakes the new normal behaviors or infrequent ones for true alerts.

Our work differs from the above in that we use an unsupervised data mining technique, outlier detection, which needs no labeled training data and domain knowledge. In addition, it needs little human assistance. So our model can overcome the shortages that classification or root cause analysis based methods have. Although our method is also based on frequent patterns, it is quite different from the third category of methods, because they are build on different assumptions. Our method assumes that alerts containing many frequent attribute values are likely resulted from normal behaviors. However the third category uses frequent alert sequences to identify these alerts. In other words, in our model, the frequent pattern is made up of alert attributes. But in the third category of methods, frequent pattern is constituted by alerts. Moreover current alert reduction methods such as Viinikka et al. (2006) and Julisch (2003) can obtain true alerts only after removing all false positives or clustering all alerts. But our method can directly identify the outliers (true alerts) in larger amounts of data, so the cost wasted for processing false positives will be reduced and the reaction to attacks will be more rapid. In addition, our model can constantly update the feature set so that it is adaptive to new normal behaviors. It is the third category of methods can't do.

Alert correlation (Ning et al., 2004), which is a little similar to above work, is another kind of technique for analyzing intrusion alerts. However it mainly focuses on the reconstruction of attack scenarios, while our focus is identifying and reducing false positives.

Outlier Detection

Outlier detection is a new data mining technique which has absorbed many attentions recently. It is quite different from traditional data mining techniques (e.g., clustering), because data focused by this technique are those deviating from the common data model. However, these data are often more valuable in fact. For example, in fraud detection, they are likely to be illegal use of credit cards. This technique has already been applied in several fields. And in the field of network security, people have successfully used outlier detection to implement IDS (Ertoz et al., 2003; Dokas et a., 2002). However this technique has not been applied in alert reduction till now.

Researchers have already proposed many algorithms for outlier detection, which mainly include following categories: **Statistical Distribution-Based Outlier Detection** (Barnett & Lewis, 1994) identifies outliers with respect to the distribution or probability model (e.g., a normal distribution) for the given data set. But it can not work well without the data distribution. **Distance-Based Outlier Detection** (Knorr & Ng, 1997) regard those objects that do not have "enough" neighbors as outliers, where neighbors are defined based on distance from the given object. The above two algorithms both depend on the overall or "global" distribution of the given set of data points. However, data are usually not uniformly distributed. So **Density-Based Local Outlier Detection** (Breunig, 2000) is proposed, which addresses this problem by local outliers. However this kind of algorithms usually has high computing cost. **Frequent Pattern-Based Outlier Detection** (He et al., 2005) is another algorithm that can address this problem. It defines the outlier degree of an object by how many frequent pattern it contains. Those objects that contain fewest frequent patterns are regarded as outliers. Besides the algorithms above, there are also some other ones, such as **Deviation-Based Outlier Detection** (Arning et al., 1996). For the length of this chapter is limited, we will not introduce them here.

OUTLIER DETECTION-BASED ALERT REDUCTION

Definitions and Notations

Before introducing our model, we firstly define some concepts that are central to this chapter, including false alert, true alert, feature set of false alert, threshold of true alert, frequent attack, and global frequent itemset.

False Alert and **True Alert**. In this chapter, we refer to false positives as false alerts, i.e. alerts mistakenly triggered by benign events. And we refer to true positives as true alerts, i.e. alerts related to real attacks.

Feature Set of False Positives. It is a dataset composed of false positives' features. These features describe the characters of false alerts and can be used to identify them. In this chapter, we use the frequent itemsets (also called frequent patterns) as features. These frequent patterns are the combinations of attribute values. And they are discovered from IDS alerts by the mining algorithm.

Threshold of True Alerts. It is the threshold for distinguishing true alerts from false ones. Alerts whose outlier scores bigger than this threshold are treated as false positives, otherwise true. In this chapter, we use the largest outlier score of all candidate true alerts to set this threshold.

Frequent Attack. Some attacks will trigger many similar alerts, especially probing and DoS attacks. For example, the DoS attack exploring Solaris' sadmind vulnerability often triggers many "Sadmind_ Amslverif_Overflow" alerts in IDS. We call this kind of attacks frequent attack.

Global Frequent Itemset. Some itemset is only frequent in a long run, i.e. the two occurrences of it usually after a long time interval. In this chapter, this kind of itemset is called global frequent itemset.

Choosing an Appropriate Outlier Detection Algorithm

As mentioned in "Outlier Detection," a lot of outlier detection algorithms have been proposed now. In order to choosing an appropriate algorithm for alert reduction, we should firstly understand the characters of IDS alerts and make clear their requirements for outlier detection technique. IDS alerts are the time-series data and their distribution are usually not uniform, i.e. they are often the mixture of several alert clusters, and the densities of these clusters are not equal. Furthermore, Alharby et al. have proposed that any prospective technique for alert reduction should have high scalability, low cost and independent reduction process which can support any type of IDSs. In addition, this technique should be able to deal with noisy data and any type of attributes contained in the alerts (Alharby & Imai, 2005).

Considering these, we carefully studied current outlier detection algorithms. Then we selected the frequent pattern-based method (FP-Outlier) (He et al., 2005) to filter false positives. The reason is that it can meet all the requirements mentioned above. Moreover it is one of the two algorithms that can process uneven data (distance-based method is the other one, but it has high computing cost). We have proved by experiment that this method is very effective in alert reduction.

Improved FP-Outlier Algorithm

Frequent pattern-based outlier detection (i.e. FP-Outlier) is presented by Zengyou He et al. This method is built on the following truth: given a set of supermarket transactions, where each transaction is a set of literals (called items). Frequent itemsets are those combinations of items that have transaction support above predefined minimum support (support means percentage of transactions containing these itemset). If a transaction contains many frequent itemsets, it means that this transaction is unlikely to be an outlier because it possesses the "common features". There are mainly three steps in this algorithm: Firstly, all frequent itemsets are found in the dataset by certain mining algorithm. Secondly the outlier score of each transaction is calculated based on these frequent patterns (i.e. frequent itemsets). Finally, transactions are sorted ascendingly according to their outlier scores, and the top p% of which are selected as candidate outliers. In the second step, the outlier score is defined by Frequent Pattern Outlier Factor (FPOF). Given a transaction t, its FPOF is calculated as follows:

$$FPOF(\text{t}) = \frac{\sum\limits_{X \subseteq t, X \in FPS(D, minisupport\ t)} support(X)}{\left\| FPS(D, minisupport\ t) \right\|} \tag{1}$$

In formula 1, $D = \{t_1, t_2 \ldots t_n\}$ is a set of n transactions. Same as the definition in association rule mining (Agrawal et al., 1993), *Support(X)* denotes the ratio between the number of transactions that contain itemset X and the number of transactions in D. *minisupport* is a user defined threshold. It defines the minimal support of frequent itemset (Agrawal et al., 1993). And *FPS(D, minisupport)* is a set of frequent patterns mined from D with *minisupport*.

The key idea of FP-Outlier is using frequent itemsets as features to identify "normal" data. So the more frequent and repeated the normal behaviors are, the better this algorithm can work. After analyzing IDS alerts, we found that they just had above characters. For example, a Snort deployed in the network of our laboratory can produce more than 30,000 alerts a week, and 95% of them are 4 types, viz., "SNMP public access udp", "SNMP request udp", "(http_inspect) BARE BYTE UNICODE ENCODING" and "NETBIOS SMB IPC$ unicode share access". Through carefully analyzing, we believe that they are all triggered by configuration problems. It means all of them are false positives. Thus it is obvious that if we mine frequent itemsets from IDS alerts, the frequent patterns we get will mostly come from false positives. So these patterns can be regarded as features of false positives and used to filter them.

In order to make the FP-Outlier algorithm more fit for IDS alerts, we have improved it in two aspects.

Our first improvement is assigning each alert attribute a weight. That is because we have observed that when determine whether or not an alert is false positive, the attributes of this alert usually have different impact to the final decision. For example, there are two alerts. The first one contains frequent pattern "AlertType = SNMP public access udp". And the second one contains frequent pattern "port = 80". In general the first one is more likely to be a false positive than the second, because port 80 is common to both attacks and normal events. In order to show this difference, we should assign a higher weight to the "AlertType" attribute than to the "Destination/Source Port" attribute.

Frequent pattern is composed by alert attributes, so it will have a weight too. Its weight is defined as follows:

Definition 1 (Weight of a Frequent Pattern) Let $A=\{A_1, A_2 ... A_n\}$ be a set of alert attributes name, each with an associated domain of value. The weight of A_i has been given as w_i ($1 \leq i \leq n$). A frequent pattern X which contains A is a tuple over A. Then the weight of X is defined as:

$$Weight(X) = \max\{w_i | w_i \text{ is the weight of } A_i, A_i \in A \text{ and } A \text{ is contained by } X, 1 \leq i \leq n\}.$$

In other words, the weight of a frequent pattern is equal to the largest weight of all alert attributes contained by it.

The weight value can be automatically designed by the techniques frequently used in information retrieval, such as the formula proposed by A. Leuski (2001). But in our experiments, they are empirically set by us for simplify the process. We will introduce how to set the weight value in "Results Obtained from DARPA 2000 Data Set." And we have also proved by experiment that assigning alert attributes different weights can really improve performance. Detail of the experiment is also shown in "Results Obtained from DARPA 2000 Data Set."

Our second improvement to FP-Outlier is using dynamic feature set to describe normal behaviors (i.e. false positives). With the arriving of new alerts, new type of normal behavior also emerges. So in order to keep the feature set up to date, the frequent pattern describing new behaviors should be constantly added to features set. This improvement will cause the value of $\|FPS(D, minisupport)\|$ in formula 1 also change constantly. Then the outlier score of alerts in different period will become incomparable. For example, with the growth of alert set, the number of frequent patterns will also increase. Then even for the same alert, the outlier score calculated in the early time will be bigger than the one calculated later. It is obviously inappropriate. In order to solve this problem, we removed $\|FPS(D, minisupport)\|$ from our calculating of outlier score. This change will not violate FP-Outlier's basic idea (i.e. determine the outlier degree of an object by how many frequent pattern it contains).So it is the needless cost for us in deed.

According to above improvements, given an alert t, the FPOF that defines its outlier score will be changed to follows:

$$Weight(X) = \max\{w_i \,|\, w_i \text{ is the weight of } A_i, A_i \in A \text{ and } A \text{ is contained by } X, 1 \le i \le n\} \qquad (2)$$

Base on this formula, we present an algorithm *CalculateOutlierScore* to calculate each alert's outlier score. Following is the pseudo code of this algorithm.

Real-Time Framework for Alert Reduction

This section gives a detailed introduction on how to use the improved algorithm to filter false positives. The original FP-Outlier algorithms are only designed for off-line process. The main shortcoming of off-line process is that attack-related alerts can't be presented to users immediately and the reactions to them are often delayed. So we design a real-time alert reduction framework to solve this problem. This framework consists of the learning phrase and the online filtering phrase (shown in figure 2).

Learning Phrase

The main work in this phrase is building the feature set of false positives and calculating the threshold of true alerts. The definitions of feature set and threshold have been already been given in the previous section.

There are two difficulties in this phrase: Firstly, new type of false positives continually emerges, so it is difficult to determine how many data are enough for building the feature set. Secondly, not all frequent patterns mined from IDS alerts can be used as features. That's because frequent attack (Re. section Definitions and Notations) can also trigger many similar IDS alerts. Frequent patterns mined from these alerts are obviously not features of false positives.

In order to address the first problem, we design a block-by-block mining method. At first, the alerts sequence is divided into several blocks. Each block contains n alerts which have neighboring timestamps. Then we mine frequent patterns in every block, and the patterns found are put into feature set. If the

Figure 1. Algorithm to calculate each alerts outlier score

```
Algorithm CalculateOutlierScore
Input: FPset    // the dataset of frequent pattern
         alert     // the alert to be processed
Output: OutlierScore  //the Outlier score of the input alert
01 begin
02     for each frequent itemset X in FPset do begin
03        if alert contains X then
04           OutlierScore = OutlierScore + weight(X)*support(X)
05        end if
06     end
```

Figure 2. Real-time framework for alert reduction

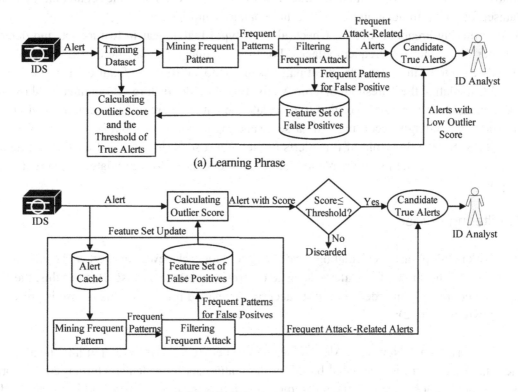

(a) Learning Phrase

(b) Online Filtering Phrase

next two or three blocks all can not contribute new features, the feature set will be regarded as stable and we can stop collecting new alerts. Because global frequent itemsets (Re. section Definitions and Notations) are only frequent in a long run, we have to combine all blocks and mine them to find this kind of pattern in the end. It should be noticed that the supporting instances of frequent patterns are all more than one predefined minimal value.

As to the second problem, we designed an algorithm to automatically filter this kind of pattern. We have observed that alerts triggered by frequent attack usually occur many times in a short period, and they often have the same destination or source address. But false positives usually don't have these characters. So this is helpful to identify them. In our filtering algorithm, we designed two statistics: the first one is the number of certain type of alerts from the same source IP in the last T seconds, and the second one is the number of certain type of alerts to the same destination IP in the last T seconds. We calculate the two statistics for each alert type in the frequent itemsets. If any statistic is large than predefined threshold (e.g. in DARPA 2000, we define this threshold is 15 alerts per minute), this type of alerts will be regarded as triggered by frequent attack.

Detailed process in learning phrase is presented as follows (shown in figure 2):

- Step1 Constructing Feature Set. Collect n alerts in the order of arrival as one block and mine them for frequent patterns (we use Apriori algorithm to mine frequent itemset). Add new patterns into the feature set, and then collect next n alerts. Repeat above process until the next k blocks (we choose k =3) all contributes no new patterns. Combine all blocks into one set and mine the whole dataset for global frequent itemsets. Put these patterns into feature set.

- Step2 Filtering Frequent Attacks. Check all alert types that appear in feature set, and determine whether or not they are frequent attacks. For those frequent attacks, the outlier score of related alerts are set to 0, and related frequent patterns are removed from the feature set.
- Step3 Calculating the Threshold of True Alerts. Based on the feature set obtained in above steps, use CalculateOutlierScore algorithm to calculate the outlier score of each remaining alert. Alerts are sorted ascendingly according to their score and top p% of them is put into the set of candidate true alerts. Set the threshold of true alerts to the largest score in the set of candidate true alerts. And after all alerts in this set are recommended to users, the set of candidate true alerts is reset to empty.

Online Filtering Phrase

The main work in this phrase is calculating the outlier score for each newcome alert, and then comparing this score with the threshold of true alerts, so as to determine it is true or false. Besides this, the feature set is updated continually in order to keep its accuracy. Detailed process in this phrase is presented as follows (shown in figure 2):

- Step1 Filtering Each Newcome Alert. When a new alert come, it is firstly put into the alert cache, then its outlier score is calculated based on the feature set by CalculateOutlierScore algorithm. If the score is not bigger than the threshold, this alert is regarded as true and is recommended to users, otherwise it is discarded.
- Step2 Updating the Feature Set. As soon as the account of alerts in cache is equal to n, a frequent itemset mining is executed on these alerts. If the result contain some frequent patterns that the feature set hasn't, filter frequent attacks from these new patterns (similar to step2 in the learning phrase) and the remaining are added into the feature set. As to the patterns that the feature set already has, we only need to update the support, i.e., their supports in feature set are set to the mean of new support and the old one. All frequent attack-related alerts are put into the set of candidate true alerts and then recommended to users. Finally, store all alerts in cache into alert database, and then clear up the cache.

We should mention that with the coming of new alerts, the threshold calculated based on the early feature set will become inaccurate gradually. Moreover, although the feature set is updated continually, some global patterns are still possibly missed. So it is necessary to mine the whole alert databases so as to adjust the threshold and the support of frequent patterns. This process can be done at comparatively long intervals. And in order to avoid affecting the real-time filtering, it had better be executed in background offline.

EXPERIMENTS

We have built a prototype implementation of our alert reduction model using the Weka framework (Witten & Frank, 2000). The prototype has been validated on DARPA 2000 dataset. And in order to assess the performance of our method in a real setting, we also applied it to real network data from our laboratory. We summarize the results obtained in this section. Before presenting the results, we will introduce the measures used in our experiments firstly. They are *reduction rate*, *completeness* and *soundness*. Their definitions are given as follows:

Definition 2 (Reduction Rate) Let N be the total number of alerts and N_f be the number of alerts filtered by the systems. The reduction rate Rr, which assesses how many alerts can be filtered by the system, is defined as the ratio between N_f and N, i.e.,

$$FPOF(t) = \sum_{X \subseteq t, X \in FPS(D, \min i \sup port\ t)} support(X) \times weight(X)$$

(3)

Definition 3 (Completeness) Let td be the number of true alerts correctly detected by the system, and tm be the number of true alerts missed by the system. The completeness Rc, which evaluates how well the system can detect true alerts, is defined as the ratio between td and the total number of true alerts, i.e.,

$$Rr = \frac{N_f}{N}$$

(4)

Definition 4 (Soundness) Let td be the number of true alerts correctly detected by the system, N be the total number of alerts and N_f be the number of alerts filtered by the systems. Then $N-N_f$ means the number of candidate true alerts. The soundness Rs, which measures how correctly the alerts are recommended, is defined as the ratio between td and the total number of candidate true alerts recommended by the system, i.e.,

$$Rc = \frac{td}{td + tm}$$

(5)

Results Obtained from DARPA 2000 Data Set

DARPA 2000 is a famous synthetic data set for intrusion detection-related tests. It includes two scenarios: LLDOS 1.0 and LLDOS 2.0.2. Because the purpose of our experiment on DARPA 2000 is just verifying the feasibility and studying how to set the parameters, we did not use too many data so as to simplify our implementation. The dataset we used is phrase 2 to phrase 4 from DMZ in LLDOS 1.0. On this dataset, the IDS (we use RealSecure) can produce 886 alerts, which include 51 true alerts and 835 false positives. There are 45 attributes in each alert. And in our alert reduction method, we mainly use 5 of them for analysis. They are "alert type", "source IP", "source port", "destination IP" and "destination port".

Our experiment on DARPA 2000 is composed by two parts: Firstly we studied the effect of main parameters (including p, minisupport and weights of alert attributes) used in our model so as to choose appropriate values for them. And then we test how well our real-time framework work.

Experiments on Alert Attribute's Weight

In our experiment, the value of alert attribute's weight was empirically set. After carefully studying many IDS alerts, we have found some general rules for setting the weight. For example, according to our observation, the alert type of false positive seldom appears in true alerts. So the weight of "alert type" can be set comparatively high. And because some hosts (e.g. web server and proxy) are hot destinations of both attacks and normal services, the weight of "destination IP" is usually smaller than "alert type". The weight of "source IP" is usually similar to "destination IP", because we found that many false positives and true alerts were triggered by few special hosts, such as web proxy. In addition, the weight of port is usually small, because many ports (such as 80, 23, 21 and so on) are common targets of both attacks and normal services. And many ports (such as 21) are used by both hackers and legal users as source port.

However above guideline can not produce exact weight values. So in order to get appropriate value, we calculated the weight of alert attributes by following steps: Firstly, we sampled n alerts randomly from all IDS alerts (in our experiment, n = 30), and manually classified them into true alerts and false positives. Secondly, for each alert attributes i, all frequent values were found, and the total number (recorded as S_i) of frequent values that appeared in both false positives and true ones was calculated. After that, the weight of attribute i (i.e. $weight_i$) was calculated according to formula 6:

$$Rs = \frac{td}{N - N_f} \tag{6}$$

Finally, above steps were repeated 2 times, and the weight of each attribute was set to the mean of the results. For example, figure 3 shows the distribution of attribute "destination port". According to this figure, we can see that 4 attribute values appear frequently. And among them, one is contained by both false positives and true alerts. So the weight of "destination port" is set to 1-1/4≈0.8. The reason why we set the weight in this way is that in our model, frequent attribute values are regarded as the features of false positives. So if they also appear in true alerts, their ability as special features of false positives will be weakened. And accordingly their weights should also be small. In another word, the more frequent values appear in both true alerts and false ones, the smaller this attribute's weight is.

Figure 3. Distribution of "destination port"

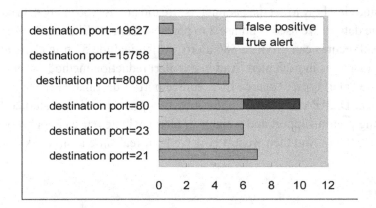

Figure 4. Performance with different attribute weights

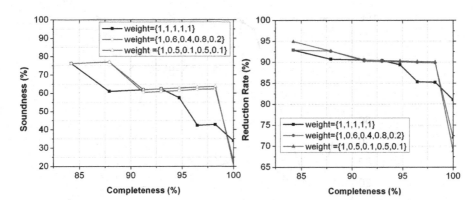

After above processing, the final weights of "alert type", "source IP", "destination IP", "source port", and "destination port" we got were respectively 1, 0.8, 0.6, 0.4, and 0.2 (they are all approximate value). This result is also consistent with our general observation of IDS alerts. In order to verify our conclusion on the weight of alert attribute, we assigned three groups of weights for alerts and observed the corresponding results. In the first group, all alert attributes had the same weight values (i.e.1). In the second group, the weights of "alert type", "source IP", "destination IP", "source port", and "destination port" were respectively 1, 0.8, 0.6, 0.4, and 0.2. And in the third group, the weight of "alert type" was 1, the weight of "destination IP" and "source IP" were both 0.5, and the weight of "source port" and "destination port" were both 0.1. Then we set minisupport to 3%.

The result of this experiment (shown in figure 4) exactly proved our assumption. From it, we can see that after setting different weights for alert attributes according to their importance, both soundness and reduction rate of our model are improved to some extent. And we are also surprised to find when the weights are respectively set to {1, 0.6, 0.4, 0.8, 0.2} and {1, 0.5, 0.1, 0.5, 0.1}, the results obtained are very similar. We think that is caused by the characters of data in DARPA 2000. It also means our model is not very sensitive to parameters. And slight inaccuracy of the parameter's value does not influence the result too much. This will make our model more practical.

Experiments on Other Parameters

Effect of p. Parameter p denotes the proportion of candidate true alerts in the whole dataset (re. Section Choosing an Appropriate Outlier Detection Algorithm). It is mainly used in the learning phrase and determines the threshold of true alerts. In order to study how p influences the performance of our method, we change the value of p and obtain two groups of data. In this experiment, the weights of alert attributes are set to {1, 0.6, 0.4, 0.8, 0.2} (they are respectively the weights of "alert type", "source IP", "destination IP", "source port",, and "destination port"), and the minisupport is set to 5%. Figure 5 shows the result:

From above figure, we can see that it is difficult to achieve both high completeness and good soundness. Increasing of p leads to higher completeness, but the soundness often decreases too. In alert reduction systems, missing true alerts is usually more serious than incorrectly recommending false positives to users, so completeness is more important. In other words, the value of p should firstly ensure high

Figure 5. Performance with different value of p

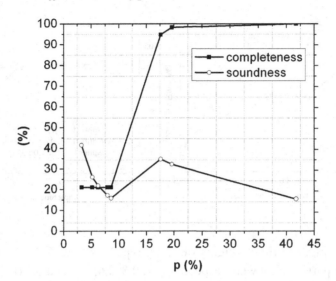

completeness. Then on the base of it, the soundness and reduction rate should also be comparatively high. So according to figure 5, we think that the value between 15% and 20% is appropriate for p.

Effect of minisupport. Parameter minisupport defines the minimal value of support for frequent patterns mining. Small minisupport will bring more frequent patterns, but the possibility that the patterns are mined from frequent attacks also grows. In order to study what value of minisupport is appropriate, we set it respectively to 5% and 3%. When minisupport was equal to 5%, the frequent patterns mined from the dataset did not contain any frequent attacks, while equal to 3%, they contained a frequent attack 'Sadmind Amslverify Overflow'.

The final result of this experiment is shown in figure 6 (In this experiment, the weight is still {1, 0.6, 0.4, 0.8, 0.2}). From it, we can see that when minisupport is 3%, our method has better completeness and soundness. We believe that is because the feature set of false positives in this situation is more precise than that when minisupport is 5% (It should be noticed that this precision is based on removing all unsuitable features, i.e., patterns from frequent attacks).

Efficiency of Our Real-time Framework. Based on above result, we also test the efficiency of our real-time framework on DARPA 2000. In the learning phrase, we firstly regarded every 100 alerts as one block in the order of arrival. Then we mined each block for frequent patterns. After mining 4 blocks, the feature set of false positives was stable, so we stop collecting training data. 12 frequent patterns can be found after mining these 400 alerts. Because there is no frequent attack in them, all patterns were regarded as features. Then we set weights to {1, 0.6, 0.4, 0.8, 0.2}, and calculated the outlier score for these alerts. After sorting alerts ascendingly by their outlier scores, we found that the maximal score in the top 15% alerts is 0.054. So the threshold of true alerts is set to 0.054.

In the online filtering phrase, the remaining 485 alerts were input to our prototype one by one. We mined every 100 alerts so that the new feature of false positives can be found and added into the feature set in time. In our experiment, new patterns can be found only when mining the first 100 alerts. Among these patterns (i.e., "Alert Type = Admind", "Alert Type = Sadmind_Amslverify_Overflow" and "Source IP = 202.077.162.213"), only the alerts that type of "Sadmind_Amslverify_Overflow" denoted a frequent

Figure 6. Performance with different value of minisupport

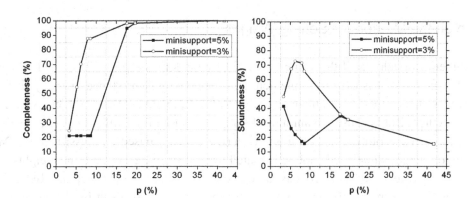

attack, so the corresponding patterns (i.e., "Alert Type = Sadmind_Amslverify_Overflow") can not be added into the feature set.

After 485 alerts had been processed, 70 alerts were recommended to users as true alerts. The reduction rate is 86%. Because 50 alerts among them were really true, and there are totally 51 true alerts in the dataset, the completeness of our prototype is 98%, and the soundness is 71%. However, after analyzing all recommended alerts, we found that the only true alert missed by our prototype was a duplicated one. In fact, when RealSecure detects an intruder breaks into a host by telnet, it will generate 3 types of alerts for this single attack step, i.e., "TelnetEnvAll", "TelnetXdisplay" and "TelnetTerminaltype". And we only missed the alert that type of "TelnetTerminaltype". Users can still identify this attack step by the other two alerts. So the completeness of our prototype can be regarded as 100% considering this.

Results Obtained from Real Data

Due to various limitations of synthetic dataset (McHugh, 2000), we have repeated our experiments on real-world IDS alerts. This dataset is collected over the period of 2 weeks in the network of our laboratory. The network includes 10 hosts, which connect to the Internet through one proxy server. A network-based IDS (snort) recorded information exchanged between the Internet and the intranet. There are totally 65528 alerts in this dataset, 95% of which are 4 types of alerts, i.e., "SNMP public access udp", "SNMP request udp", "(http_inspect) BARE BYTE UNICODE ENCODING" and "NETBIOS SMB IPC$ unicode share access".

In this experiment, we regarded 1000 alerts as one block, and used the same set of parameters as for DARPA 2000. By executing similar steps as in the previous paragraph, we obtained 5258 candidate true alerts finally, and the reduction rate is 92%. After thoroughly analyzing, we found that all alerts filtered by our prototype were false positives, so the completeness is 100%. Among the true alerts recommended by our prototype, the account of alerts triggered by real attacks was 2620, so the soundness is 50%. By comparing with the result obtained from DARPA 2000, we found that our model has higher reduction rate but lower soundness on real dataset. The likely explanation of this fact is that real dataset contains fewer intrusions and more redundancy than DARPA 2000. We believe that if we fit the parameters to the real data, the performance of our prototype can be even high.

Analysis

Discussion on the Method for Setting Weights

In our experiment, we calculated the value of weight by random sampling. This method has several advantages, for example, it is easy to implement and the weights it produced are very fit for current dataset. However, this method needs manual analysis of sample alerts. This conflicts with the idea of unsupervised method. But because the amount of samples is little, it is still better than the alert reduction methods that need a lot of labeled training data (e.g. method based on classification). Moreover, the calculation of weight value needs not be repeated for every dataset. In fact, the weights calculated by this method can be regarded as reference values. And we have proved in section "Results Obtained from Real Data," that even on different dataset, we can also get well result by the same parameters. The weight value can also be automatically designed by the techniques frequently used in information retrieval (Re. section Definitions and Notations). But as we known, the cost of these techniques is high. So in order to reduce cost and simply the implement, we choose the manual method temporarily. Now we are looking for low-cost automatic method.

Discussion on the Adaptability of our Model

In practice, the behaviors of attackers and normal users are both frequently changed. So the alert reduction system must be adaptive to this change, i.e. it should be able to identify the false positives triggered by new normal behaviors, and avoid to mistakenly filter out true alerts caused by new attacks. Our model also did some efforts in this aspect.

In order to identify new false positives, we designed a dynamic feature set (re. section Improved FP-Outlier Algorithm), i.e. with the arriving of new alerts, the new frequent patterns which represent new false positives are continually mined and put into the feature set, so that the accuracy of feature set can be kept. The experiment shown before has proved the effectiveness of this method. However it still has some limitations. For example, only when the amount of false positives triggered by new normal behaviors is larger than a predefined threshold, can their feature patterns be discovered. In order to identify these false positives more rapidly, we can choose low threshold. But this will possibly bring unrelated frequent patterns to feature set. So a trade-off has to be found between them.

As far as the change of attackers' behaviors, we believe that it has little effect on our model. Because our model is based on profiling false positives by frequent attribute values. And any alert (no matter it has new type or not) which does not possess the features of false positives will be regarded as true alert. This is similar to the idea of anomaly detection in the field of IDS. In other words, new or unknown attacks can be identified by our model unless they have the same features with false positives. However even in the later situation, our model can also identify most of them by the algorithms for filtering frequent attacks (re. section Real-Time Framework for Alert Reduction).

CONCLUSION

In this chapter, we present a novel alert reduction method based on a new data mining technique, i.e., outlier detection. And we also build a real-time framework to filter false IDS alerts using this method.

Now we have finished the prototype implementation of our model. And through the experiments on DARPA 2000, we have proved that when 86% of alerts have been filtered by our model, 100% of true alerts still remain. And on real-world dataset, our model has even higher reduction rate. However, our method also has some shortages, for example, now its soundness is still not perfect. In the future, we will study how to improve the soundness of our model. We have observed that the more accurate the feature set is, the higher soundness we can obtain. In addition, accurate outlier score can also bring high soundness. So our future work in this aspect will mainly focus on the two factors. In addition, we will look for low-cost automatic method for setting weights and do more experiments on real-world IDS alerts so as to know how our model works with alerts generated by multiple IDSs.

REFERENCES

Agrawal, R., Imielinski, T., & Swami, A. (1993). Database Mining: A Performance Perspective. *IEEE Transactions on Knowledge and Data Engineering, 5*(6), 914–925. doi:10.1109/69.250074

Alharby, A., & Imai, H. (2005). IDS False Alarm Reduction Using Continuous and Discontinuous Patterns. In *Proceeding of ACNS 2005* (pp. 192-205). Heidelberg: Springer.

Arning, A., Agrawal, R., & Raghavan, P. (1996). A Linear Method for Deviation Detection in Large Databases. In *Proceeding of 2nd International Conference on Data Mining and Knowledge Discovery* (pp. 164-169). New York: ACM Press.

Barnett, V., & Lewis, T. (1994). *Outliers in Statistical Data*. New York: John Wiley & Sons.

Breunig, M., Kriegel, H., Ng, R., & Sander, J. (2000). LOF: Identifying Density-Based Local Outliers. In *Proceeding of 2000 ACM-SIGMOD International Conference on Management of Data,* (pp. 93-104). New York: ACM Press.

Clifton, C., & Gengo, G. (2000). Developing Custom Intrusion Detection Filters Using Data Mining. In *Proceeding of 21st Century Military Communications Conference* (pp. 440-443). New York: IEEE Press.

Dokas, P., Ertoz, L., Kumar, V., Lazarevic, A., Srivastava, J., & Tan, P. (2002). Data Mining for Network Intrusion Detection. In *Proceeding of NSF Workshop on Next Generation Data Mining* (pp. 21-30). Cambridge, MA: AAAI/MIT Press.

Ertoz, L., Eilertson, E., Lazarevic, A., Tan, P., Dokas, P., Kumar, V., et al. (2003). Detection of Novel Network Attacks Using Data Mining. *Proceeding of ICDM Workshop on Data Mining for Computer Security* (pp. 1-10). New York: IEEE Press.

He, Z., Xu, X., Huang, J. Z., & Deng, S. (2005). FP-Outlier: Frequent Pattern Based Outlier Detection. *Computer Science and Information System, 2*(1), 103–118. doi:10.2298/CSIS0501103H

Julisch, K. (2001). Mining Alarm Clusters to Improve Alarm Handling Efficiency. In *Proceeding of the 17th Annual Computer Security Applications Conference* (pp. 12-21). New York: IEEE Press.

Julisch, K. (2003). Clustering Intrusion Detection Alarms to Support Root Cause Analysis. *ACM Transactions on Information and System Security, 6*(4), 443–471. doi:10.1145/950191.950192

Julisch, K., & Dacier, M. (2002). Mining Intrusion Detection Alarms for Actionable Knowledge. In *Proceeding of the 8th ACM International Conference on Knowledge Discovery and Data Mining*, (pp. 366-375). New York: ACM Press.

Knorr, E., & Ng, R. (1997). A unified notion of outliers: Properties and computation. In *Proceeding of 3rd Int. Conf. Knowledge Discovery and Data Mining* (pp. 219-222). New York: ACM Press.

Leuski, A. (2001). Evaluation Document Clustering of Interactive Information Retrieval. In *Proceeding of ACM CIKM'01*, (pp. 33-40). New York: ACM Press.

Manganaris, S., Christensen, M., & Zerkle, D. (2000). A Data Mining Analysis of RTID Alarms. *Computer Networks*, *34*(4), 571–577. doi:10.1016/S1389-1286(00)00138-9

McHugh, J. (2000). The 1998 Lincoln Laboratory IDS Evaluation (A Critique). In *Proceeding of RAID 2000* (pp. 145-161). Heidelberg: Springer.

Ning, P., Cui, Y., Reeves, D., & Xu, D. (2004). Tools and Techniques for Analyzing Intrusion Alerts. *ACM Transactions on Information and System Security*, *7*(2), 273–318. doi:10.1145/996943.996947

Pietraszek, T. (2004). Using Adaptive Alert Classification to Reduce False Positives in Intrusion Detection. In *Proceeding of RAID 2004* (pp. 102-124). Heidelberg: Springer.

Viinikka, J., Debar, H., Mé, L., & Séguier, R. (2006). Time Series Modeling for IDS Alert Management. In *Proceeding of 2006 ACM Symposium on Information, computer and communications security*, (pp. 102-113). New York: ACM Press.

Witten, I. H., & Frank, E. (2000). *Data Mining: Practical Machine Learning Tools with Java Implementations*. San Francisco: Morgan Kaufmann.

Chapter 4
Concept–Based Mining Model

Shady Shehata
University of Waterloo, Canada

Fakhri Karray
University of Waterloo, Canada

Mohamed Kamel
University of Waterloo, Canada

ABSTRACT

Most of text mining techniques are based on word and/or phrase analysis of the text. Statistical analysis of a term frequency captures the importance of the term within a document only. However, two terms can have the same frequency in their documents, but one term contributes more to the meaning of its sentences than the other term. Thus, the underlying model should indicate terms that capture the semantics of text. In this case, the model can capture terms that present the concepts of the sentence, which leads to discover the topic of the document. A new concept-based mining model that relies on the analysis of both the sentence and the document, rather than, the traditional analysis of the document dataset only is introduced. The concept-based model can effectively discriminate between non-important terms with respect to sentence semantics and terms which hold the concepts that represent the sentence meaning. The proposed model consists of concept-based statistical analyzer, conceptual ontological graph representation, and concept extractor. The term which contributes to the sentence semantics is assigned two different weights by the concept-based statistical analyzer and the conceptual ontological graph representation. These two weights are combined into a new weight. The concepts that have maximum combined weights are selected by the concept extractor. The concept-based model is used to enhance the quality of the text clustering, categorization and retrieval significantly.

INTRODUCTION

Due to the daily rapid growth of the information, there are considerable needs in extracting and discovering valuable knowledge from the vast amount of information found in different data sources today such

DOI: 10.4018/978-1-60566-908-3.ch004

as World Wide Web. Data mining in general is the field of extracting useful information, and sometimes high-level knowledge, from large sets of raw data. It has been the attention of many researchers to find efficient ways to extract useful information automatically from such information sources.

Text Mining is the process of deriving high quality information from text by discovering patterns and trends through different written resources. Text mining is generally considered more difficult than traditional data mining. This is attributed to the fact that traditional databases have fixed and known structure, while text documents are unstructured, or, as in the case of web documents, semi-structured. Thus, text mining involves a series of steps for data pre-processing and modeling in order to condition the data for structured data mining. Text mining can help in many tasks that otherwise would require large manual effort. Common problems solved by text mining include, but not limited to, searching through documents, organizing documents, comparing documents, extracting key information, and summarizing documents. Methods in information retrieval, machine learning, information theory, and probability are employed to solve those problems.

Natural Language Processing (NLP) is both a modern computational technology and a method of investigating and evaluating claims about human language itself. NLP is a term that links back into the history of Artificial Intelligence (AI), the general study of cognitive function by computational processes, with an emphasis on the role of knowledge representations. The need for representations of human knowledge of the world is required in order to understand human language with computers. Text mining attempts to discover new, previously unknown information by applying techniques from natural language processing and data mining.

The problem introduced by text mining is that natural language was developed for humans to communicate with one another and to record information. Computers are a long way from understanding natural language. Humans have the ability to understand the meaning of text and humans can easily overcome obstacles that computers cannot easily handle such as spelling variations and contextual meaning. However, although human mind can understand the meaning of unstructured data, human lacks the computer's ability to process text in large volumes or at high speeds. Herein lays the key to create a new technology called concept-based mining that combines the human way of understanding with the speed and accuracy of a computer.

MAIN FOCUS

Most of text mining techniques are based on word and/or phrase analysis of the text. Statistical analysis of a term frequency captures the importance of the term within a document only. However, two terms can have the same frequency in their documents, but one term contributes more to the meaning of its sentences than the other term. Thus, a mining model should indicate terms that capture the semantics of text. In this case, the model can capture terms that present the concepts of the sentence, which leads to discover the topic of the document. Research suggests that there are important concepts either words or phrases in each sentence that can truly present the meaning of a sentence.

BACKGROUND

Typical text mining tasks include but not limited to text clustering, text categorization and document retrieval. Clustering is unsupervised learning paradigm where clustering methods try to identify inherent groupings of the text documents so that a set of clusters are produced in which clusters exhibit high intra-cluster similarity and low inter-cluster similarity. Generally, text document clustering methods attempt to segregate the documents into groups where each group represents some topic that is different than those topics represented by the other groups (Aas & Eikvil 1999; Salton, Wong, & Yang 1975; Salton & McGill 1983).

Categorization, one of the traditional text mining techniques, is supervised learning paradigm where categorization methods try to assign a document to one or more categories, based on the document content. Classifiers are trained from examples to conduct the category assignment automatically. To facilitate effective and efficient learning, each category is treated as a binary classification problem. The issue here is whether or not a document should be assigned to a particular category or not.

There has been considerable research in the area of document retrieval for over 30 years (Belkin and Croft 1987), dominated by the use of statistical methods to automatically match natural language user queries against data records. There has been interest in using natural language processing to enhance single term matching by adding phrases (Fagan 1989), yet to date natural language processing techniques have not significantly improved performance of document retrieval (Cole 1998), although much effort has been expended in various attempts. The motivation and drive for using natural language processing (NLP) in document retrieval is mostly intuitive; users decide on the relevance of documents by reading and analyzing them. Thus, if a system can automate document analysis, this should help in the process of deciding on document relevance.

NLP-based semantic analysis is the process of relating syntactic structures, from the levels of phrases, clauses, sentences and paragraphs to the level of the writing as a whole, to their language-independent meanings. Generally, the semantic structure of a sentence can be characterized by a form of verb argument structure. This underlying structure allows the creation of a composite meaning representation from the meanings of the individual concepts in a sentence. The verb argument structure permits a link between the arguments in the surface structures of the input text and their associated semantic roles. The study of the roles associated with verbs is referred to a thematic role or case role analysis (Jurafsky & Martin 2000). Thematic roles, first proposed by Gruber and Fillmore (Fillmore 1968), are sets of categories that provide a shallow semantic language to characterize the verb arguments.

Recently, there have been many attempts to label thematic roles in a sentence automatically. Gildea and Jurafsky (Gildea & Jurafsky 2002) were the first to apply a statistical learning technique to the FrameNet database. They presented a discriminative model for determining the most probable role for a constituent, given the frame, predicator, and other features. These probabilities, trained on the FrameNet database, depend on the verb, the head words of the constituents, the voice of the verb (active, passive), the syntactic category (Sentence [S], Noun Phrase [NP], Verb Phrase [VP], Proposition Phrase [PP], and so on) and the grammatical function (subject and object) of the constituent to be labeled. The authors tested their model on a pre-release version of the FrameNet I corpus with approximately 50,000 sentences and 67 frame types. Gildea and Jurafsky's model was trained by first using Collins' parser (Collins 1999), and then deriving its features from the parsing, the original sentence, and the correct FrameNet annotation of that sentence.

Figure 1. Concept-based mining model

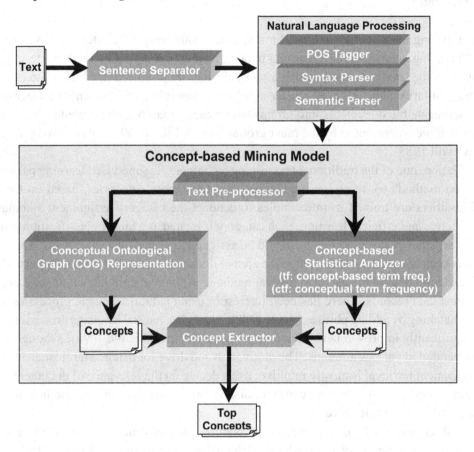

A machine learning algorithm for shallow semantic parsing was proposed in (Pradhan et al. 2005). It is an extension of the work in (Gildea & Jurafsky 2002). The algorithm of (Pradhan et al. 2005) is based on using Support Vector Machines (SVM) which results in improved performance over that of earlier classifiers by (Gildea & Jurafsky 2002). Shallow semantic parsing is formulated as a multi-class categorization problem. SVMs are used to identify the arguments of a given verb in a sentence and classify them by the semantic roles that they play such as AGENT, THEME, GOAL.

Concept-Based Mining Model

In this chapter, a novel concept-based model is presented. In the presented model, each sentence is labeled by a semantic role labeler that determines the terms which contribute to the sentence semantics associated with their semantic roles in a sentence. Each term that has a semantic role in the sentence, is called concept. Concepts can be either a word or phrase and it is totally dependent on the semantic structure of the sentence. The concept-based model analyzes each term within a sentence and a document using the following three components as shown in Figure 1.

The first component is the concept-based statistical analyzer that analyzes each term on the sentence and the document levels. After each sentence is labeled by a semantic role labeler, each term is statistically weighted based on its contribution to the meaning of the sentence. This weight discriminates between non-important and important terms with respect to the sentence semantics. The second component is the Conceptual Ontological Graph (COG) representation which is based on the conceptual graph theory and utilizes graph properties. The COG representation captures the semantic structure of each term within a sentence and a document, rather than the term frequency within a document only. After each sentence is labeled by a semantic role labeler, all the labeled terms are placed in the COG representation according to their contribution to the meaning of the sentence. Some terms could provide shallow concepts about the meaning of a sentence, but, other terms could provide key concepts that hold the actual meaning of a sentence. Each concept in the COG representation is weighted based on its position in the representation. Thus, the COG representation is used to provide a definite separation among concepts that contribute to the meaning of a sentence. Therefore, the COG representation presents concepts into a hierarchical manner. The key concepts are captured and weighted based on their positions in the COG representation. Consider the following sentence "We have noted how some electronic techniques, developed for the defense effort, have eventually been used in commerce and industry". In this sentence, the semantic role labeler identifies three target words (verbs), marked by bold, which are the verbs that represent the semantic structure of the meaning of the sentence. These verbs are **noted**, **developed**, and **used**. The topic of this sentence is about X **noted** Y. More detailed information about Y is induced from the structure of the verb **developed** and the verb **used**. In this example, the conceptual graph of the verb **noted** is the most general graph that is placed in the highest level of the COG representation. The conceptual graphs of **developed** and **used** verbs present more detailed information about the sentence as illustrated in Figure 2.

At this point, concepts are assigned two different weights using two different techniques which are the concept-based statistical analyzer and the COG representation. It is important to note that both of them achieve the same functionality, in different ways. The output of the two techniques is the important weighted concepts with respect to the sentence semantics that each technique captures. However, the weighted concepts that are computed by each technique could not be exactly the same. The important concepts to the concept-based statistical analyzer could be non-important to the COG representation and vice versa. Therefore, the third component, which is the concept extractor, combines the two different weights computed by the concept-based statistical analyzer and the COG representation to denote the important concepts with respect to the two techniques. The extracted top concepts are used to build standard normalized feature vectors using the standard vector space model (VSM) for the purpose of text mining.

The statistical analyzer weighting is calculated by:

$$\text{weight}_{\text{stat}_i} = tf\text{weight}_i + ctf\text{weight}_i \qquad (1)$$

The COG weighting is calculated by:

$$\text{weight}_{\text{COG}_i} = tf\text{weight}_i * L_{\text{COG}_i} \qquad (2)$$

The combined concept-based weighting of the top concepts is calculated by:

$$\text{weight}_{\text{comb}_i} = \text{weight}_{\text{stat}_i} * \text{weight}_{\text{COG}_i} \qquad (3)$$

Figure 2. Conceptual ontological graph

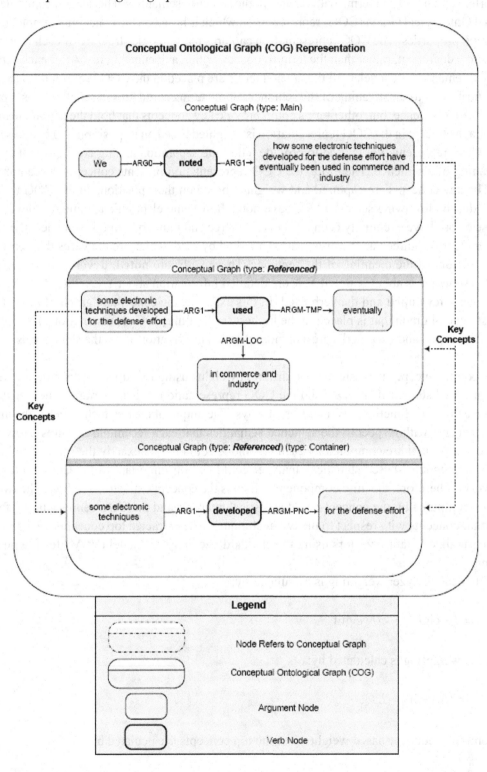

where

- The *tf*weight$_i$ value presents the weight of concept i at the document-level.
- The *ctf*weight$_i$ value presents the weight of the concept i at the sentence-level based on the contribution of concept i to the semantics of the sentences.
- The L_{COG_i} value measures the importance of each level in the COG representation. The values of this measure, which are 1,2,3,4, and 5, are assigned to One, Unreferenced, Main, Container, and Referenced levels in the COG representation respectively.

Consider the Following Sentence

"We have noted how some electronic techniques, developed for the defense effort, have eventually been used in commerce and industry".

In this sentence, the semantic role labeler identifies three target words (verbs), marked by bold, which are the verbs that represent the semantic structure of the meaning of the sentence. These verbs are noted, developed, and used. Each one of these verbs has its own arguments as follows:

- [ARG0 We] [TARGET noted] [ARG1 how some electronic techniques developed for the defense effort have eventually been used in commerce and industry]
- We have noted how [ARG1 some electronic techniques] [TARGET developed] [ARGM-PNC for the defense effort] have eventually been used in commerce and industry
- We have noted how [ARG1 some electronic techniques developed for the defense effort] have [ARGM-TMP eventually] been [TARGET used] [ARGM-LOC in commerce and industry]

Arguments labels are numbered Arg0, Arg1, Arg2, and so on depending on the valency of the verb in sentence. The meaning of each argument label is defined relative to each verb in a lexicon of Frames Files. Because the meaning of each argument number is defined on a per-verb basis, there is no straightforward mapping of meaning between arguments with the same number. Generality, Arg0 is very consistently assigned an Agent-type meaning, while Arg1 has a Patient or Theme meaning almost. Thus, this sentence consists of the following three verb argument structures:

- First verb argument structure: [ARG0 We], [TARGET noted], and [ARG1 how some electronic techniques developed for the defense effort have eventually been used in commerce and industry]
- Second verb argument structure: [ARG1 some electronic techniques], [TARGET developed], and [ARGM-PNC for the defense effort]
- Third verb argument structure: [ARG1 some electronic techniques developed for the defense effort], [ARGM-TMP eventually], [TARGET used], and [ARGM-LOC in commerce and industry]

Table 1. Concept-based term analysis

Row Number	Sentence Concepts	CTF
(1)	Note	1
(2)	electron techniqu develop defens	
	effort evenut commerc industri	1
(3)	electron technique	3
(4)	Develop	3
(5)	defens effort	3
(6)	electron techniqu develop defens effort	2
(7)	Eventu	2
(8)	commerc industri	2
	Individual Concepts	**CTF**
(9)	Electron	3
(10)	Technique	3
(11)	Defens	3
(12)	Effort	3
(13)	Evenut	2
(14)	Commerc	2
(15)	Industri	2

A cleaning step is performed to remove stop-words that have no significance, and to stem the words using the popular Porter Stemmer algorithm. The terms generated after this step are called concepts as follows:

- Concepts in the first verb argument structure: "note", "electron techniqu develop defens effort evenut commerc industri"
- Concepts in the second verb argument structure: "electron techniqu", "develop", and "defens effort"
- Concepts in the third verb argument structure: "electron techniqu develop defens effort", "eventu", and "commerc industri".

It is imperative to note that these concepts are extracted from the same sentence. Thus, the concepts mentioned in this example sentence are: "note", "electron techniqu develop defens effort evenut commerc industri", "electron techniqu", "develop", "defens effort", "electron techniqu develop defens effort", "eventu", and "commerc industri".

The traditional analysis methods assign same weight for the words that appear in the same sentence. However, the concept-based term analysis discriminates among terms that represents the sentence concepts. This analysis is entirely based on the semantic analysis of the sentence. In this example, some concepts have higher conceptual term frequency *ctf* than others as shown in Table 1. In such cases, these concepts (with high *ctf*) contribute to the meaning of the sentence more than other concepts (with low *ctf*).

As shown in Table 1, the concept-based term analysis computes the *ctf* measure for: the concepts extracted from the verb argument structures of the sentence, which are in Table 1 from row (1) to row

(8), the concepts overlapped with other concepts that are in Table 1 from row (3) to row (8), and the individual concepts in the sentence, which are in Table 1 from row (9) to row (15).

In this example, the topic of the sentence is about the electronic techniques. These concepts have the highest *ctf* value with 3. In addition, the concept note which has the lowest *ctf*, has no significant effect on the topic of the sentence. Thus, the concepts with high *ctf* such as electronic, techniques, developed, defense, and effort present indeed the topic of the sentence.

Applications of the Concept-Based Mining Model

Most of the current text mining methods are based on the Vector Space Model (Salton, Wong, & Yang 1975; Salton & McGill 1983) which is a widely used data representation for text clustering, classification, and retrieval. The VSM represents each document as a feature vector of the terms (words or phrases) in the document. Each feature vector contains term-weights (usually term-frequencies) of the terms in the document. The similarity between the documents is measured by one of several similarity measures that are based on such a feature vector. Examples include the cosine measure and the Jaccard measure.

To test the effectiveness of using the concepts extracted by the proposed concept-based model as an accurate measure to present terms in the document, the introduced concept-based model is applied to text clustering, categorization and text retrieval.

The similarities which are calculated by the concept-based model are used to compute a similarity matrix among documents. Three standard document clustering techniques are used for testing the effect of the concept-based similarity on clustering: (1) Hierarchical Agglomerative Clustering (HAC), (2) Single Pass Clustering, and (3) k-Nearest Neighbor (kNN) as discussed in (Shehata, Karray & Kamel 2006). The concept-based similarity between two documents d_1 and d_2 is calculated by:

$$sim_c(d_1, d_2) = \sum_{i=1}^{m} \max(\frac{l_{i}}{S_{i_1}}, \frac{l_{i}}{S_{i_2}}) * weight_{i_1} * weight_{i_2},$$

(4)

where

$$weight_{i_1} = tfweight_{i_1} + ctfweight_{i_1}$$
$$weight_{i_2} = tfweight_{i_2} + ctfweight_{i_2}$$

The concept-based weight of concept i_1 in document d_1 is presented by $weight_{i_1}$. In calculating $weight_{i_1}$, the $tfweight_{i_1}$ value presents the weight of concept i in the first document d_1 at the document-level and the $ctfweight_{i_1}$ value presents the weight of the concept i in the first document d_1 at the sentence-level based on the contribution of concept i to the semantics of the sentences in d_1. The sum between the two values of $tfweight_{i_1}$ and $ctfweight_{i_1}$ presents an accurate measure of the contribution of each concept to the meaning of the sentences and to the topics mentioned in a document. The term $weight_{i_2}$ is applied to the second document d_2.

Equation (4) assigns a higher score, as the matching concept length approaches the length of its verb argument structure, because this concept tends to hold more conceptual information related to the meaning of its sentence.

In equation 1, the tf_{ij_1} value is normalized by the length of the document vector of the term frequency tf_{ij} in the first document d_1, where $j = 1, 2,...,cn_1$

$$tfweight_{i_1} = \frac{tf_{ij_1}}{\sqrt{\sum_{j=1}^{cn_1} (tf_{ij_1})^2}} \qquad (5)$$

cn_1 is the total number of the concepts which has a term frequency value in the document d_1. In equation 2, the ctf_{ij_1} value is normalized by the length of the document vector of the conceptual term frequency ctf_{ij} in the first document d_1 where $j = 1, 2,...,cn_1$

$$ctfweight_{i_1} = \frac{ctf_{ij_1}}{\sqrt{\sum_{j=1}^{cn_1} (ctf_{ij_1})^2}} \qquad (6)$$

cn_1 is the total number of concepts which has a conceptual term frequency value in the document d_1. The same normalization equations are applied to the weights of the concepts in the second document d_2 as shown in equations 3 and 4

$$tfweight_{i_2} = \frac{tf_{ik_2}}{\sqrt{\sum_{k=1}^{cn_2} (tf_{ik_2})^2}} \qquad (7)$$

$$tfweight_{i_1} = \frac{tf_{ij_1}}{\sqrt{\sum_{j=1}^{cn_1} (tf_{ij_1})^2}} \qquad (8)$$

For the single-term similarity measure, the cosine correlation similarity measure is adopted with the popular TF-IDF (Term Frequency/Inverse Document Frequency) term weighting. Recall that the cosine measure calculates the cosine of the angle between the two document vectors d_1 and d_2. Accordingly, the single-term similarity measure (sim_s) is $sim_s(d_1, d_2) = \cos(x, y) = \frac{d_1 \cdot d_2}{\|d_1\| \|d_2\|}$.

The concept-based weighting as shown in Equation (3) that is calculated by the concept-based model is used to compute a document-concept matrix between documents and concepts. Three standard document categorization techniques are used for testing the effect of the concepts on categorization quality: (1) Support Vector Machine (SVM), (2) Rocchio, and (3) Naïve Bayesian (NB) as discussed in (Shehata, Karray & Kamel 2007).

The process of the text retrieval is explained as follows. First, the COG representations are constructed from the input text documents. Secondly, the concepts, which have the referenced type, are extracted from the COG levels and ranked. Thirdly, the highest ranked concepts are indexed as fields associated to their documents for the text retrieval purpose. Lastly, Lucene search engine (Apache lucene) is used for testing the effect of associating concepts as indexed fields with their documents on text retrieval as discussed in (Shehata, Karray & Kamel 2006; Shehata, Karray & Kamel 2007).

It is observed that the results produced by the concept-based model in text clustering, categorization, and retrieval have higher quality than those produced by traditional techniques. This is due to the fact that weighting based on the matching of concepts in each document, is showed to have a more significant effect on the quality of the text mining due to the similarity's insensitivity to noisy terms that can lead to an incorrect similarity measure. The concepts are less sensitive to noise when it comes to calculating normalized feature vectors. This is due to the fact that these concepts are originally extracted by the semantic role labeler and analyzed using two different techniques with respect to the sentence and document levels. Thus, the matching among these concepts is less likely to be found in non-relevant documents to a concept.

FUTURE TRENDS

There are a number of suggestions to extend this work. One direction is to link the presented work to web document categorization, clustering and retrieval. Another future direction is to investigate the usage of such models on other corpora and its effect on document mining results, compared to that of traditional methods.

CONCLUSION

This work bridges the gap between natural language processing and text categorization disciplines. A new concept-based model composed of three components, is proposed to improve the text categorization quality. By exploiting the semantic structure of the sentences in documents, a better text categorization result is achieved. These components are the concept-based statistical analyzer, the conceptual ontological graph (COG) and the concept extractor.

The concept-based model allows choosing concepts based on their weights which represent the contribution of each concept to the meaning of the sentence. This leads to perform concept matching and weighting calculations in each document in a very robust and accurate way. The quality of the categorization, clustering and retrieval results achieved by the presented model surpasses that of traditional weighting approaches significantly. There are a number of suggestions to extend this work. One direction is to link the presented work to web document clustering, categorization, and retrieval. Another direction is to investigate the usage of such model on other corpora and its effect on clustering, categorization and retrieval compared to that of traditional methods.

REFERENCES

Aas, K., & Eikvil, L. (1999, June). *Text categorisation: A survey* (Tech. Rep. 941). Oslo, Norway: Norwegian Computing Center.

Apache jakarta lucene search engine, version 1.3. (n.d.). Retrieved from http://lucene.apache.org/

Belkin, N., & Croft, W. (1987). Retrieval techniques. *Annual Review of Information Science & Technology, 22*, 109–145.

Cole, R. (1998). *Survey of the State of the Art in Human Language Technology (Studies in Natural Language Processing)*. Cambridge, UK: Cambridge University Press.

Fagan, J. (1989). The effectiveness of a nonsyntactic approach to automatic phrase indexing for document retrieval. *Journal of the American Society for Information Science American Society for Information Science, 40*(2), 115–132. doi:10.1002/(SICI)1097-4571(198903)40:2<115::AID-ASI6>3.0.CO;2-B

Fillmore, C. (1968). *The case for case. Chapter in: Universals in Linguistic Theory*. New York: Holt, Rinehart and Winston, Inc.

Gildea, D., & Daniel, J. (2002). Automatic labeling of semantic roles. *Computational Linguistics Journal, 28*(3), 245–288. doi:10.1162/089120102760275983

Jurafsky, D., & Martin, J. (2000). *Speech and Language Processing*. Upper Saddle River, NJ: Prentice Hall Inc.

Pradhan, S., Hacioglu, K., Krugler, V., Ward, W., Martin, J., & Jurafsky, D. (2005). Support vector learning for semantic argument classification. *Machine Learning Journal, 60*(1-3), 11–39. doi:10.1007/s10994-005-0912-2

Salton, G., & McGill, M. (1983). *Introduction to Modern Information Retrieval*. New York: McGraw-Hill.

Salton, G., Wong, A., & Yang, C. (1975). A vector space model for automatic indexing. *Communications of the ACM, 18*(11), 112–117. doi:10.1145/361219.361220

Shehata, S., Karray, F., & Kamel, M. (2006). Enhancing text retrieval performance using conceptual ontological graph, In *Workshops Proceedings of the IEEE International Conference on Data Mining (ICDM)*, (pp. 39–44).

Shehata, S., Karray, F., & Kamel, M. (2006). Enhancing text clustering using concept-based mining model, In *Proceedings of the IEEE International Conference on Data Mining (ICDM)*, (pp. 1043-1048).

Shehata, S., Karray, F., & Kamel, M. (2007). A concept-based model for enhancing text categorization, In *Proceedings of the 13th ACM SIGKDD International Conference on Knowledge Discovery and Data Mining (KDD)*, (pp. 629-637).

Shehata, S., Karray, F., & Kamel, M. (2007). Enhancing search engine quality using concept-based text retrieval, In *Proceedings of the 13th IEEE/WIC/ACM International Conference on Web Intelligence (WI)*, USA.

KEY TERMS AND DEFINITIONS

Concept: In the new presented model, concept is a labeled term.

Data Mining (sometimes called data or knowledge discovery): The process of analyzing data from different perspectives and summarizing it into useful information.

Document Clustering: The act of collecting similar documents into bins, where similarity is some function on a document.

Document Retrieval: Defined as the matching of some stated user query against useful parts of free-text records.

Label: A thematic role is assigned to a verb argument. e.g.: "John" has subject (or Agent) label. "the ball" has object (or theme) label.

Term: Either an argument or a verb. Term is also either a word or a phrase (which is a sequence of words).

Document Categorization (also known as document classification): The task of automatically assigning a set of documents into categories from a predefined set.

Text Mining (sometimes alternately referred to as text data mining): Refers generally to the process of deriving high quality information from text.

Thematic Role: A way of classifying the arguments of natural language predicates into a closed set of participant types which were thought to have a special status in grammar.

Knowledge Representation (KR): The study of how knowledge about the world can be represented and what kinds of reasoning can be done with that knowledge.

Verb-Argument Structure: A verb associated with terms that are semantically related with respect to a sentence meaning (e.g. John hits the ball) "hits" is the verb, "John" and "the ball" are the arguments of the verb "hits".

Chapter 5
Intrusion Detection Using Machine Learning:
Past and Present

Mohammed M. Mazid
CQUniversity, Australia

A B M Shawkat Ali
CQUniversity, Australia

Kevin S. Tickle
CQUniversity, Australia

ABSTRACT

Intrusion detection has received enormous attention from the beginning of computer network technology. It is the task of detecting attacks against a network and its resources. To detect and counteract any unauthorized activity, it is desirable for network and system administrators to monitor the activities in their network. Over the last few years a number of intrusion detection systems have been developed and are in use for commercial and academic institutes. But still there have some challenges to be solved. This chapter will provide the review, demonstration and future direction on intrusion detection. The authors' emphasis on Intrusion Detection is various kinds of rule based techniques. The research aims are also to summarize the effectiveness and limitation of intrusion detection technologies in the medical diagnosis, control and model identification in engineering, decision making in marketing and finance, web and text mining, and some other research areas.

INTRODUCTION

Intrusion is a frequently used word in various sectors. As this is relating to unwanted events, users from every field have their great concern on this topic. Researchers are trying their best to define this term more elaborately and preciously. In terms of general security, intrusion is an attack that attempt from outsiders of a periphery. Intrusion in medical expression is defined as 'a tooth is forced upward into the

DOI: 10.4018/978-1-60566-908-3.ch005

bone tissue by a force outside the mouth' (Park et al., 2005). In geology, an intrusion is a body of igneous rock that formed by molten magma. It cools beneath the Earth's crust.

In terms of computer security, intrusion is a system compromise or breach of security incident regarding computer. This involves gaining control of a computer system from the owner or an authorized administrator. This can be done by an "insider" who has permission to use the computer with normal user privileges. It can be by an "outsider" from another network or perhaps even in another country. They exploit vulnerabilities in an unprotected network service on the computer to gain unauthorized entry and control.

There are various kinds of intrusions. Some of the examples are as follows:

* Virus, worm, or "Trojan horse" – these are sort of programming code created for harmful purpose. Generally these spread out through internet by downloading files, copy files form one computer to another computer, using pirated software, email, etc.
* Stealing password: Password stealing is one of the notorious types of intrusions at the present time. Hackers steal password of bank account, email account, confidential database, etc. over the internet. Different types of tools and ways are used to steal password such as – sniffer or "shoulder surfing" (watching over someone's shoulder while they type their password), brute-force guessing, password cracking software, trial and error method, etc.
* Gaining illegal access: Hacker gains illegal access of terminal or steals information while users transferring file using less secured data transferring method such as old-style telnet, ftp, IMAP or POP email, etc.
* An exploitable vulnerability in a network services like FTP, Apache or Microsoft IIS, SSH, a name server, etc.
* Physically accessing a computer and rebooting it to an unsecured administrative mode or taking advantage of other weaknesses that come from a vendor who assumes that anyone using the keyboard and mouse directly is "trusted"

Another example of intrusion is "root kits". "Root kits" gain elevated privileges on a computer. It is often installed by different types of "Trojan horse" programs. It hides the intruder's presence on the system. A Trojan horse is a program that acts like a real program a user may wish to run, but also performs unauthorized actions. These Trojan horse programs will make it look like nothing at all is wrong with systems, even though it may have gigabytes of pirated software installed on it, may be flooding the network and disrupting service for everyone on local area network.

Another common post-intrusion action is to install a sniffer or password logger, perhaps by replacing the operating system's own SSH (Secure SHell) or FTP (File Transfer Protocol) server. This exploits trust relationships that often exist with other local or university computers (e.g., the Homer or Dante clusters), other institutions and government agencies that may have a research relationship with, or even to/from people's home computers on cable modem or DSL (Digital Subscriber Line) lines. Any one may not think about the act of logging in from one computer to another as a trust relationship, but these are indeed relationships between computers that involve a level of trust (namely secret passwords, which are the first line of defence). Intruders prey on these trust relationships to extend their reach into computer networks.

Determining whether or not an intrusion has taken place is sometimes a very difficult task. Root kits and Trojan horses make the job even more difficult and work so well because they take advantage of a discrepancy between the knowledge level of the intruder and the system administrator and users. Often the only way to know for sure if an intrusion has occurred is to examine the network traffic external to the suspect computer system, or to examine the computer and system using trusted tools (perhaps by rebooting it from a special forensic CD-ROM or by taking the disk drive to another computer that you know is secure).

Intrusion Detection System

An intrusion detection system (IDS) is a software tool to use for computer security. The goal of IDS is simply to protect the system or network from any kind of intrusions such as network packet listening, stealing information, authority abuse, unauthorized network connections, falsification of identity, etc. However the task of detecting intrusion is not simple for many reasons which we have discussed in the following section of this chapter. Most of the time, it works as a dynamic monitoring entity of firewalls. Generally it monitors the traffic of a network like a network sniffer or observe system log file of computers. Then it collects the data and searches for any abnormal behaviour. There are different types of approaches of Intrusion Detection. According to Verwoerd and Hunt (Verwoerd & Hunt, 2002), category and their subcategory of different type of IDS approaches are given below.

- Conceptual outline
- Anomaly Modelling Techniques
  - Statistical models
  - Immune system approach
  - Protocol verification
  - File checking
  - Taint checking
  - Neural nets
  - WhiteListing
- Misuse detection modelling technique
  - Expression matching
  - State transition analysis
  - Dedicated languages
  - Generic algorithms
  - Burglar alarms
- Probe techniques
  - Host log monitoring
  - Promiscuous network monitoring
  - Host network monitoring
  - Target based IDS

Agent Based IDS

Using of agent in IDS has a great significant role in improving its performance especially decision making and intrusion detecting. A basic task of an agent is to carry out some predefined job without manual interference and supervision. It is programmed in such a way that it change itself in order to suit different conditions, can make decisions intelligently and able to work with other agents and units of IDS. It works independently and observes the environment where it is deployed to act back on the environment (Weiss, 1999). IDS can be comprised of many agents with similar or dissimilar type of tasks. If one agent is affected or attacked then other agents back up affected agent to carry out the entire process without any interruption. In some agent based IDS, there is provision to manipulate agents manually in case of a typical situation such as maintenance.

An agent runs independently for IDS to monitor any violation of usual work and reports unusual or abnormal behaviours to the appropriate transceiver. Various kinds of tasks monitored by agents are password cracking and access violation, spreading of Trojan horses, interceptions, Spoofing, scanning ports and services, remote OS Fingerprinting, network packet listening, stealing information, authority abuse, unauthorized network connections, falsification of identity, information altering and deletion, unauthorized transmission and creation of data (sets), unauthorized configuration changes to systems and network services (servers), Ping flood (Smurf), Send mail flood, SYN flood, Distributed Denial of Service (DdoS), Buffer Overflow, Remote System Shutdown, Web Application attacks, etc.(Kazienko & Dorosz, 2004) After gathering information regarding the above kind of abnormal activities, agent reports to the transceiver. In case of multiple agents based IDS, the transceiver could get a same type of notification from different agent. Based on information provided by different agents, the transceiver or monitor generates an alarm or notifies for further action.

How Agents Work in IDS

According to agents working approach, agents can be categorized two types. In first type of approach, agents use a communication infrastructure by which agents communicate with each other. This is called Agent Communication Language (ACL) (Gowadiam et al., 2005). JADE (Bellifemine et al, 2005) is a FIPA (FIPA, 2005) specified software framework by which agents can communicate with each other. JADE offers various services such as a Directory Facilitator (DF), library of interaction protocols, and distributed agent platform to develop proper agent communication facilities. Agent platform monitors agents' activities such as start, suspend, terminate, etc. Interaction protocols arrange interaction among agents such as request, query, subscribe, etc. and provide a series of acceptable messages and semantics for those messages. The second type of approach, agents do not communicate with each other rather they notify their findings on regular basis to a component called a transceiver. Spafford & Zamboni (2000) and Balasubramaniyan et al. (1998) have proposed such framework known as AAFID (Autonomous Agents for Intrusion Detection). In this type of framework, the transceiver resides in each host machine, collects data from agents and proceeds data for further action.

Advantages of Agents

There are different types of IDSs proposed. Of these systems, the agent based IDSs are very popular and promising for the following reasons(Slagell, 2001):

Reduction of data movement: Agents gather data on the spot and process immediately. So it reduces traffic over the network for data handling and saves time.

Flexibility: Each agent runs as an individual so it does not need help from others to perform its' own task. If any agent is removed from the system for modification or any improvement, the IDS will continue its operation.

Load-balance: Agents can balance the workload of IDS by spreading tasks over a number of machines.

Detection of distributed attacks: The use of mobile agents makes it easier to correlate and detect distributed attacks.

Fault-tolerance: As an agent can work on its own, that means if any agent of the IDS is affected or attacked and stops working, IDS will not stop. This makes IDS fault tolerant.

LITERATURE REVIEW

As detection intrusion is a great concern in computer world, there are several detection systems developed since early 80's. According to Patcha et al.(2007) there are three broad categories for the analysis and detection of intrusions. Those are Signature or Misuse Detection System, Anomaly Detection System and Hybrid or Compound Detection System. Some literature reviews on IDS are discussed as follows.

Intrusion Detection Expert System (IDES) (Denning & Neumann, 1985; Lunt et al. 1992) is one of the earliest IDS developed by Stanford Research Institute (SRI) in the early 1980's. Later on, an enhanced version of IDES called Next-generation Intrusion Detection Expert System (NIDES) (Anderson et al. 1994; Anderson et al. 1995) has come with additional features. However, it produces a high false signal in the case of irregular distributed data.

Haystack, proposed by Smaha (1998), is another primitive IDS which uses descriptive statistics to generate a user behaviour model for few particular user groups. Limitations of Haystack are it was designed to work in an offline environment with manual attribute selection for good indicators of intrusive activity.

Statistical Packet Anomaly Detection Engine (SPADE) (Staniford et al. 2002) is an anomaly detection system which works with a popular intrusion detection and prevention software SNORT (Roesch, 1999). Because of classification of random unseen packets, it produces a high false alarm rate. Ye et al.(2002) proposed a host based anomaly IDS which is also based on statistical analysis. Hotellings T^2 test has been use to analyse the trail of intruders activities.

Using system call modelling and sequence analysis, Eskin et al. (2001) has developed sliding window based IDS. However this IDS has some disadvantages. For a monitoring system, computational overhead is very high. Another problem is for irregular nature of systems calls, this IDS produces a significant number of false positive alarms.

Valdes et al. (2000) has used Naïve Bayesian networks for IDS which is able to detect distributed attacks. Some weakness of this IDS are

- Identical to a threshold based system
- Child node based interactions could produce inappropriate decision

Principal Component Analysis (PCA) based anomaly detection system developed by Shyu et al. (2003) has reduced the dimensionality of the audit data. In this IDS, PCA has been used as an outlier detection scheme. Using the KDD CUP99 data this IDS has shown better detection rate.

Yeung et al. (2003) presents IDS using hidden Markov model with profiling system call sequences and shell command sequences. This IDS uses minimum likelihood among all training sequences to eliminate anomalous behaviours. A disadvantage of this IDS is overlooking of unique identification of general user.

Packet Header Anomaly Detector (PHAD) (Mahoney & Chan, 2001), Learning Rules for Anomaly Detection (LERAD) (Mahoney & Chan, 2002) and Application Layer Anomaly Detector (ALAD) (Mahoney & Chan, 2002) are time-based IDS. In time based models, occurrence of an event is calculated using probability of previous events. To detect intrusions, PHAD, ALAD, and LERAD monitor predefined attributes. In these IDS, multivariate problems are segmented into univariate problems which affect the efficiency of detecting attacks. Another problem of these IDS is computationally expense for large data sets.

Asaka et al. (1999) have developed an Intrusion Detection System which was named IDA (stands for the Intrusion Detection Agent system). This IDA has two eccentric characteristics which are tracing the origin of intrusion by use of agents and the other is to find out or trace specific events that may relate to intrusions instead of continuously monitoring user activities. As the authors of this paper state 'Our goal is not to detect all intrusions precisely but to detect many intrusions efficiently' (Asaka et al., 1999). Many types of attack detection are not implemented in this paper such as remote attacks, attacker inside organization, etc. The performance of IDS is not tested with traditional intrusion data.

Helmer et al. (2002) have developed an agent based IDS which travel between monitored systems in a network of distributed systems, collect data from data cleaning agents, sort associated data and notify the findings to a user interface and database. Agent systems with lightweight agent support allow runtime addition of new capabilities to agents. Helmer et al. (2002) describe the design of Multi-agent IDS and show how lightweight agent capabilities allow the addition of communication and collaboration capabilities to the mobile agents in their IDS. While this has many facilities, experiments were only performed with 'sendmail' data and not tested on other intrusion detection related databases.

Balasubramaniyan et al. (1998) have developed an architecture for a distributed Intrusion Detection System based on multiple independent entities. These entities, called autonomous agents, work collectively. This approach solves some of the problems such as configurability, scalability or efficiency. In this paper, the authors many IDS's desirable characteristics such as fault tolerance, resistance to subversion, minimal overhead of the system, minimal human supervision, graceful degradation, dynamic reconfiguration, etc. But their proposed architecture is not implemented practically. So the performance of IDS is uncertain.

Barrus and Rowe (1998) propose a distributed architecture with autonomous agents to monitor security-related activity within a network. Each agent operates cooperatively yet independently of the others, providing for efficiency, real-time response and distribution of resources. This architecture provides significant advantages in scalability, flexibility, extensibility, fault tolerance, and resistance to compromise. They also propose a scheme of escalating levels of alertness, and a way to notify other agents on other computers in a network of attacks so they can take primitive or reactive measures. They design a neural network to measure and determine alert threshold values. A communication protocol is proposed to relay these alerts throughout the network. Manual intervention and inability to handle huge data are major two deficiencies of this IDS.

Crosbie and Spafford (1998) have developed prototype architecture of a defence mechanism for computer systems. Many intrusion detection problems, their key aspects and a few solutions have been explained in this paper. Instead of earlier footsteps of single monolithic module of intrusion detection systems, this IDS has implemented small and independent agents to monitor the system and distinguish the abnormal behaviour. The authors claimed that this IDS has more flexibility, scalability and resilience of the agent. But this IDS needs human interaction and system wait for human decision in complex situations. Detecting intrusion inside the organization is one of the major aspects of IDS which is not discussed in this paper. Performance of the IDS has also not been tested.

Carver et al. (2000) have emphasized Intrusion Response (IR) because delayed response to attack extends an opportunity to attackers. If IR is delayed by ten hours, a skilled attacker will be 80% successful and for thirty hours, the attacker is almost 100% successful. Research by (Cohen, 2008) indicates that the success of an attack is dependent on the time gap between detection and response. So Carver et al. (2000) presented a window of vulnerability based on the time when intrusion is detected and action is taken. Assorted number of software agents work collectively to deal with this window by providing automated response to any abnormal actions. While the approach of this IDS is effective, it is not tested with any intrusion related data, and hence there are questions about its performance. Tracing of the source of intrusion is an important feature of IDS but it is not discussed in this paper.

Bernardes and Santos(2000) offers the use of mobile agent mechanisms. A number of mobile agents move constantly within an organization internal information ways. The basic tasks of these independent small agents are to monitor the communication paths of the organization. Unfortunately, an efficiency test was not done for the IDS and continuous communication among agents could overhead the system. Sometimes many agents with a dissimilar assessment of a same issue could be time consuming for a final decision.

Immunity-based agents are deployed Dasgupta and Gonzalez (2002) in their IDS approach. These agents travel from machine to machine and observe different types of intrusion related or any other abnormal activities in the network. Agents follow a hierarchy for communicating with each other and for executing actions which threaten security. These agents can learn and adapt to their environment dynamically and can detect both known and unknown intrusions. However, there is no discussion on how to reduce network overhead caused by agents roaming around in network and the IDS does not have an intruder tracing system.

Autonomous software agents, especially when equipped with mobility, promise an interesting design approach for intrusion detection. Krugel and Toth(2001) evaluate the implications of applying mobile agent technology and present taxonomy to classify different architectures. Sparta, an actual implementation of a mobile agent based system is described well.

Brian and Dasgupta (2001) has implemented a distributed agent architecture for intrusion detection and response in networked computers. Unlike conventional IDS, this security system attempts to emulate mechanisms of the natural immune system using Java-based mobile software agents. These security agents monitor multiple levels (packet, process, system, and user) of networked computers to determine correlation among the observed anomalous patterns, reporting such abnormal behaviours to the network administrator and/or possibly taking some action to counter a suspected security violation.

Jansen et al. (1999) have highlighted relatively unexplored terrain of using mobile agents for intrusion detection and response. They have discussed a number of issues such as ways to apply agent mobility, shortcomings of current IDS designs, various approaches of their implementations, automated response to an intrusion as soon as detected, tracing the path of an attacker, etc. But handling huge data sets and comparison with other IDS is not discussed in this paper.

Jazayeri and Lugmayr(2000) has developed an IDS named as Gypsy. It is a component-based mobile agent. Some excellent features of Gypsy's are dynamically extensible agents according to environment, use of lightweight agents, remote administration tools for servers and agents, etc. Gypsy agents fol-

Table 1. Shows rules generation techniques used in different types of detection policy by different authors

Authors	Year	Intrusion Detection type	Rule Generations Techniques
Javitz and Valdes Javitz and Valdes Porras and Valdes	1991 1993 1998	Anomaly detection	Intensity audit record distribution, categorical and counting measures
Frank Bloedorn et al.	1994 2001	Classification	Decision Trees
Crosbie and Spafford	1995	Anomaly detection	Parse trees
Ryan et al.	1998	Anomaly detection	Pure feed forward neural network
Sinclair et al.	1999	Classification	Decision Trees
Warrender et al.	1999	Anomaly detection	Hidden Markov model(HMM)
Warrender et al.	1999	Anomaly detection	Associative rules
Ghosh et al	1999	Classification	Elman-network with leaky bucket
Marchette	1999	Anomaly detection	Mixture model
Hofmeyr and Forrest	1999	Anomaly detection	Collection of non-self bit vectors
Ghosh et al.	1999	Classification	Pure feed forward neural network with leaky bucket
Lee Lee and Stolfo Lee and Stolfo Lee et al. Lee et al. Lee et al. Lee et al.	1999 1998 2000 1999a 1999b 2000 2001	Classification	Associative rule and Frequent episode generation
Neri	2000	Classification	Associative rules represented in a Horn clause language
Fan et al.	2000	Classification	Ordered associative rules and Frequent episodes
Dickerson and Dickerson Dickerson et al.	2000 2001	Classification	Fuzzy logic rules
Chittur	2001	Classification	Decision trees
Fan Lee et. al.	2001 2001	Classification	Associative rule and Frequent episode generation
Bloedorn et al.	2001	Anomaly detection	Outliers from clusters
Singh and Kandula	2001	Classification	Associative rule and Frequent episode generation
Barbar´a et. al.	2001	Anomaly detection	Contingency table for Naive Bayes classifier
Dasgupta and Gonz´alez	2001	Classification	Classifier on statistics of attributes
Li et al.	2002	Classification	Association rules
Mahoney and Chan	2002	Anomaly detection	Conditional probabilities
Mahoney and Chan Mahoney and Chan Chan et. al.	2003a 2003b 2003	Anomaly detection	Rules with probabilities of consequence given antecedent
Didaci et al. Giacinto and Roli	2002 2002	Classification	Pure feed forward neural network
Dasgupta and Gonz´alez	2002	Anomaly detection	Collection of rules specifying non-self area

Table 1. continued

Authors	Year	Intrusion Detection type	Rule Generations Techniques
Eskin et al. Portnoy et al.	2002 2001	Anomaly detection	Outliers from clusters
Eskin et al.	2002	Anomaly detection	Outliers from clusters
Chan et al.	2003	Anomaly detection	Outlying clusters with high or low density
Marin et al.	2001	Classification	Learning vector quantization(LVQ)
Staniford et al.	2002	Port scan detection	Bayes network and connections between detected anomalous events
Sequeira and Zaki	2002	Anomaly detection	Minimum before preventative samples
Yeung and Chow	2002	Anomaly detection	Parzen-window
Lane	2000	Anomaly detection	Set of instances representing normal activity
Eskin et al. Honig et al.	2002 2002	Anomaly detection	Support vector machine(SVM)
Mukkamala et. al. Mukkamala and Sung	2002 2003	Classification	Support vector machine(SVM) for each class
Lane	2000	Anomaly detection	Hidden Markov model(HMM)
Eskin Eskin Eskin et al.	2000 2000 2000	Anomaly detection	Probabilistic model7
Kumar	1995	Misuse detection	Colored Petrinets
Staniford-Chen et al.	1996	Misuse detection	Graphs defined by ruleset
Tolle and Niggermann	2000	Classification	Mapping function from graphs to classification
Helmer et al.	1999	Classification	Associative rule and Frequent episode generation
Sinclair et al.	1999	Classification	Rules with wild cards

low a chain of command. Under a supervisor agent that travels through the network according to their itinerary, there could be many worker agents. Many IDS related problem has been considered including trace back of intrusion. However, the authors did not discuss how to fetch huge amounts of data from log files and reduce network overhead using many agents.

Protecting computer and network systems from intruder is one of the burning issues with a huge amount of work on Intrusion Detection. The main objective is to discover robust and efficient ways of detection intrusion. In Table 1 we have shown some of the work done on Intrusion Detection by various researchers.

ALGORITHM DESCRIPTION

Association Rule Mining (ARM) is one of the most important and substantial techniques in machine learning. It is particularly important for extracting knowledge from large databases by discovering frequent itemsets and associating item relationships between or among items of a data file. ARM is a powerful exploratory technique with a wide range of applications such as marketing policies, medical diagnosis, financial forecast, credit fraud detection, public administration and actuarial studies, text mining, various kinds of scientific research, telecommunication services and many other research areas. Emerging importance of ARM encourage machine learning researchers to develop magnificent number of algorithm such as Apriori (Agrawal et al., 1993), Predictive Apriori (Scheffer, 2001), Tertius (Flach & Lachiche, 2001), CLOSET (Pei, 2000), MAFIA (Burdick, 2001), ELACT (Zaki, 2000), CHARM (Zaki et al.1999) and many others. Still researchers are showing their great interest for further improvement of ARM. As a result significant number of algorithms has been introduced in last few years.

Credit for development of Association Rule Mining is mostly attributed to Agrawal (Agrawal et al.,1993). Association rule is an expression of X⇒Y (read as 'if X then Y'), where X and Y are itemsets in a database D. The expression can be illustrated as 'if a customer buys item X then likely to buy item Y' or 'if a patient is infected by disease X then likely to be infected by disease Y', and so on. The itemset of the left hand side of the arrow is called antecedent and itemset of the right hand side of the arrow is called consequent. Each expression is called a rule. A rule can contain from two to an unrestricted number of items with or without the conjunction AND or OR operands. An item of a rule is selected from the frequent itemset of the data file. Frequent itemsets are the items that occur more frequently. Basically, ARM follows two major steps to produce rules from a data file: first, find all the frequent itemsets; second, generate strong association rules from the frequent itemsets. The best rules are picked on the basis of different types of interestingness measures. Precision of a rule mostly depends on interestingness of that rule. Some measures of interestingness of rules are described in the following section.

Measure of Interestingness

Measures of interestingness are the matrices to measure rules weight. There are numbers of matrices. However there is no common metric to measure ARM rule's interestingness. Here are some Measures of Interestingness.

Support

Support for ARM is introduced by Agrawal et al.(1993). It measures the frequency of association, i.e. how many times the specific item has been occurred in a dataset. An itemset with greater support is called frequent or large itemset. In terms of probability theory we can express support as:

$$\text{Support} = P(A \cap B) = \frac{\text{Number of transactions containing both A and B}}{\text{Total number of transactions}}$$

where A and B are itemsets in a database D.

Confidence

Confidence measures the strength of the association (Bastide, 2000). It determines how frequently item B occurs in the transaction that contains A. Confidence expresses the conditional probability of an item. The definition of confidence is

Figure 1. Producing frequent itemsets

A small data file D

Transaction ID	Items
1	Desktop, Flash Memory
2	Laptop, Printer, Webcam, Mouse
3	Desktop, Printer, Webcam, Flash Memory
4	Laptop, Printer, Flash Memory, Webcam, Mouse
5	Laptop, Printer, Webcam

First of Scan D →

C_1(Itemsets)

Itemset	Sup.
Desktop	2
Flash Memory	3
Laptop	3
Printer	4
Webcam	4
Mouse	2

L_1(After pruning from C_1)

Itemset	Sup.
Flash Memory	3
Laptop	3
Printer	4
Webcam	4

C_2(itemsets from L_1)

Itemset
Flash Memory, Laptop
Flash Memory, Printer
Flash Memory, Webcam
Laptop, Printer
Laptop, Webcam
Printer, Webcam

Second Scan D →

C_2(counting support of itemsets)

Itemset	Sup.
Flash Memory, Laptop	1
Flash Memory, Printer	2
Flash Memory, Webcam	2
Laptop, Printer	3
Laptop, Webcam	3
Printer, Webcam	4

L_2(after pruning from C_2)

Itemset	Sup.
Laptop, Printer	3
Laptop, Webcam	3
Printer, Webcam	4

C_3(itemsets from L_2)

Itemset
Laptop, Printer
Laptop, Webcam
Printer, Webcam

Third Scan D →

C_3(counting support of itemsets)

Itemset	Qty
Laptop, Printer, Webcam	3

L_3(rule/s with predefined support)

Itemset	Qty
Laptop, Printer, Webcam	3

$$\text{Confidence} = P(A \mid B) = \frac{P(A \cap B)}{P(A)} = \frac{\text{Number of transactions containing both A and B}}{\text{Number of transactions containing A}}$$

where A and B are itemsets in a database D.

Predictive Accuracy

Predictive accuracy is another way to measure interestingness of a generated rule. Basically this accuracy is used for the Predictive Apriori rule measurement. According to Scheffer (2001), the definition of predictive accuracy is:

Let **D** be a data file with r number of records. If *[x → y]* is an Association Rule which is generated by a static process P then the predictive accuracy of *[x → y]* is

$c([x \rightarrow y])=Pr[r$ satisfies $y|r$ satisfies $x]$

where distribution of r is govern by the static process P and the Predictive Accuracy is the conditional probability of $x \rightarrow r$ and $y \rightarrow r$.

The process of generating candidate is most important part for rule generation. The procedure is described briefly in the following section.

General Procedure for Rule Generation in ARM

In Figure 1, initially every item is considered as a candidate C_1 itemset. After counting their supports, the candidate itemsets {Desktop} and {Mouse} are discarded because they appear in fewer than three transactions. In the next iteration, candidate C2 itemsets are generated using only the frequent C_1 itemsets because the Apriori principle ensures that all supersets of the infrequent C_1 itemsets must be infrequent. After pruning the C_1 candidate itemset, Apriori uses mathematical formula of combination and create the C_3 candidate itemset. Thus this iteration processes go on until the frequent candidate itemsets is null. In Figure1, the process of candidate generation in Association Rule Mining is explained briefly.

Figure 2. Algorithm for frequent itemset generation of the Apriori algorithm

```
1:   n=1
2:   FREQₙ={i|i Є I Λ σ ({i}) ≥ N x minsup}          {Find all frequent 1-
itemset}
3:   repeat
4:       n=n+1
5:       CANDTₙ=Apriori-gen(FREQₙ -1)                {Generate candidate
itemsets}
6:       for each transaction t Є T do
7:           CANDTₜ = subset(Cₙ, t).                 {Identify all candidates that
belong to t }
8:           for each candidate itemset candt Є CANDTₜ do
9:               σ(candt) = σ(candt) + 1.            {Increment of support
count}
10:          end for
11:      end for
12:  FREQₙ={ candt | candt Є CANDTₙ Λ σ(candt) ≥ N x minsup}{Extract the frequent n-
itemset}
13:  until FREQₙ=Ø
14:  result = ∪FREQₙ
```

Figure 3. Algorithm for rule generation with Apriori

```
1:   for each frequent k-itemset fₖ, k≥2 do
2:   CONSQₘ ={i|i Є freqₖ}          {Find all frequent 1-itemset}
3:   call ap-genrules(freqₖ, CONSQₘ)
4:   end for
```

Each algorithm has its own way to generate rules. Here are some popular ARM algorithms with rule generating pseudocode. These algorithms belong to the category of unsupervised learning methods.

Apriori

The Apriori algorithm was first proposed by Agrawal et al.(1993). It uses prior knowledge of frequent items for association rule mining. The basic idea of the Apriori algorithm is to generate frequent item-sets of a given dataset and then scan the dataset to check if their counts are really large. The process is

Figure 4. Algorithm of the procedure of ap-genrules(freq$_k$, CONSQ$_m$)

```
1:   n=|freq_n|                                    {size of frequent itemset}
2:   m=|CONSQ_m|                                   {size of rule consequent}
3:   if n>m+1 then
4:       CONSQ_m+1=appriori-gen(CONSQ_m)
5:       for each consq_m+1 ∈ CONSQ_m+1 do
6:           conf= σ(freq_n)/ σ(freq_n - consq_m+1)
7:           if conf≥ minconf then
8:               output the rule (freq_n - consq_m+1) → consq_m+1
9:           else
10:              delete consq_m+1 form consq_m+1
11:          end if
12:      end for
13:      call ap-genrules(freq_k, consq_m+1)
14:  end if
```

Figure 5. Algorithm Predictive Apriori for ap-genrules(f$_k$, H$_m$)procedure

```
1.   Input: • intended number of association rules n to display,
                • database D with items z_1, . . . , z_n
2.   Set the support threshold of the rule body supp_body_min = 1
3.   For i = 1, . . . , n DO:
     Construct a number of association rules of length i at random
     and measure their confidence conf provided supp(X) > 0.
     Let π_i(conf) be the distribution of confidences.
4.   For all conf, compute π(conf)
5.   Let FREQ_0 = {∅} be the set of frequent item sets of length 0.
6.   For i = 1, . . . , n - 1 Do:
     While (i = 1||FREQ_i-1 ≠∅)
         (a) Determine all frequent item sets X of length i with supp(X) > supp_body-min
         (b) For all X ∈ FREQ_i call RuleGen(X)
         (c) If best[n] has changed in RuleGen Then
             Increase supp_body-min so that,
             E(conf|1, supp_body-min) > E(conf(best[n])|conf(best[n]), supp(best[n])).
         (d) If supp_body-min > size of database D Then Exit.
         (e) If supp_body-min has been increased in step 6(d) Then
             Delete all item sets X from FREQ_i with supp(X) < supp_body-min
7.   Output: best[n]
```

iterative and candidates of any pass are generated by joining frequent itemsets of the proceeding pass. Apriori is a confidence-based Association Rule Mining algorithm. The confidence is simply accuracy to evaluate rules, produced by this algorithm. The rules are ranked according to the confidence value. If two or more rules share the same confidence then they are initially ordered using their support and secondly the time of discovery.

Simple Steps of Apriori

- Produce frequent itemsets of length 1
- Repeat until count of new frequent itemsets are zero (0)
  - From length n frequent itemsets, produce n+1 candidate itemsets
  - Prune infrequent candidate of length n
  - Count the support of each candidate by scanning the DB
  - Retaining the frequent candidate, eliminate the infrequent one
- Produce Apriori rules based on support and confidence

The algorithm for frequent itemset generation of the Apriori algorithm (Tan et al., 2005) is shown Figure 2. Here $CANDT_n$ denote the set of candidate n-itemsets and $FREQ_n$ denote the set of frequent n-itemsets.

Figure 3 and Figure 4 show the pseudocode for the rule generation steps (Tan et al., 2005).

Figure 6. Algorithm of the procedure of RuleGen(X)

RuleGen(X) finds the best rules with rule body X

1. Set $supp_{rule-min}$ so that
   $E(conf \mid supp_{rule-min} /supp(X), supp(X)) > E(conf(best[r])\mid conf(best[r]), supp(best[r]))$

2. For $j = 1, \ldots, n - |X|$ (number of items not in X) **Do**
   (a) **If** j = 1 **Then**
       Set $Y_1 = \{\{z\} \mid z \in \{z_1, \ldots, z_k\}, z \notin X\}$
   Else generate Y_j analogous to the generation of candidate item sets.
   (b) **For** all $y \in Y_j$ **Do**
       i. **Calculate** $supp(X \cap y)$.
       ii. **If** $supp(X \cap y) \leq supp_{rule-min}$ **Then**
       delete y from Y_j and continue with the next y at 2b.
       iii. **Calculate** the predictive accuracy of $X \Rightarrow y$

       iv. **If** the predictive accuracy of $X \Rightarrow y$ is among the best r AND
       (there is no other rule in best[r] which is at least equally accurate AND
       which subsumes $X \Rightarrow y$) **Then**
       update best[r],
       remove rules which are subsumed by other at least equally accurate rules.
       Set $supp_{rule-min}$, so that
           $E(c \mid supp_{rule-min} / supp_{body-min}, supp_{body-min})$
           $\geq E(conf(best[r])\mid conf(best[r]), supp(best[r]))$.

3. **If** any rule has been removed out of best[r] in step 2(b)iv **Then** recur from step 1.

Predictive Apriori

In the case of Apriori, every so often we can find rules with higher confidence but low support on respective items of generated rules. Sometimes, rules are produced with large support but low confidence. Scheffer (2001) introduced this algorithm with the concept of 'larger support has to trade against a higher confidence'. Predictive Apriori is also a confidence-based ARM algorithm. But rules ranked by this algorithm are sorted according to 'expected predicted accuracy'. The interestingness measure of Predictive Apriori suits the requirements of a classification task (Mutter et al., 2004). It tries to maximize expected accuracy of an association rule rather than confidence in Apriori. Figure 5 and Figure 6 show the pseudocode of Predictive Apriori (Tan et al., 2005).

Tertius

The Tertius system implements a top-down rule discovery system employing the confirmation measure (Flach & Lachiche 2001). Tertius uses a first-order logic representation that deals with structured, multi-relational knowledge. It allows users to choose the most convenient option among several possible options. Generated rules from Tertius are descriptive rather than predictive. Descriptive approaches include clustering, association rule learning, learning of attribute dependencies, subgroup discovery, and multiple predicate learning (Flach & Lachiche 2001). Tertius is able to deal with extensional knowledge, either with explicit negation or under the Closed-World Assumption. In case of explicit negation, truth-values of all ground facts are specified in advance. If an unknown value is appeared, it is compared with the predefined truth-values. The value is assigned to explicit negative if it does not match with truth-values. When there is no predefined truth-value, no assumption is made. Under Closed-World Assumption, values that currently not known as true are assumed as false. This approach is conservative regarding value ranking. The ranking of value is performed on true ground facts only. Tertius algorithm also considers induction of integrity constraints in databases, learning mixed theories of predicate definitions and integrity constraints. Figure 7 shows the algorithm for sorting rules in Tertius (Deltour, 2001).

Figure 7. Algorithm for sorting rules in Tertius

```
t-stack← {empty rule}
while t-stack is not empty
        rule ←first rule of the t-stack
        if ruleEval(rule)
                refine rule
                for each child
                        if calculateOptimistic(child)
                                calculate optimistic estimate
                                if ruleExplore(child)
                                        if storeInNodes(child)
                                                add child to t-stack
                                        if calculateConfirmation(child)
                                                calculate confirmation
                                        if storeInResults(child)
                                                add child to results
                sort t-stack according to optimistic estimate
        else break
```

Apriori, Predictive Apriori and Tertius are widely known algorithms for data mining. These algorithms are being used in WEKA (Witten & Frank 2000) data mining software. In the following section we will evaluate performance of those algorithms using Meta Learning technique.

EXPERIMENT OUTCOME

We compare three popular algorithms of ARM, namely, Apriori, Predictive Apriori and Tertius on some prominent data files IDS. We organized this experiment into three main steps: first we compare the algorithms across a number of different measures of accuracy providing a comprehensive empirical evaluation of the performance of three association algorithms on 15 UCI Repository data sets (Blake & Merz, 2007). Initially we apply ARM algorithms on these 15 well known data sets to compare the outcomes. The details of the data sets statistical characteristics are provided in Table 2. We then characterize the datasets using the central tendency measures and some other basic statistical measures. Finally, the empirical results are combined with the dataset characteristic measures to generate rules describing which algorithm is best suited to which type of problems.

Data Preparation

After selecting data files without any missing values, we have applied three algorithms of Association Rule Mining, Apriori, Predictive Apriori and Tertius using WEKA (Witten & Frank 2000). For Association Rule Mining, WEKA uses 'unsupervised discretized' value of attributes. We have used 3-bin discretization and the other parameter settings of Discretize option of the software have been kept as default. As

Table 2. Basic properties of 15 data repository files

Data file Name	No. of Instance	No. of Attribute			No. of Class
		Total	Nominal	Numeric	
page-blocks	5473	11	1	10	1
vehicle	846	19	1	18	1
Market Basket	1000	12	3	10	2
liver disorders	345	7	1	6	1
ionosphere	351	35	1	34	1
Zoo	101	18	17	1	1
ecoli	336	8	1	7	1
cmc	1473	10	2	8	X^1
breast cancer	286	10	10	0	1
prostoperative patient data	90	9	9	0	1
bridges version1	107	13	10	3	1
Iris	150	5	1	4	1
tae	151	6	3	3	1
haberman	306	4	2	2	1
car	1728	7	7	0	1

well, parameter settings for each algorithm were the default and we always chose the first 10 best rules. Table 2 shows the basic properties of 15 UCI Repository data sets (Blake & Merz, 2007).

Meta Learning Process

In our experiment we converted nominal data to numeric using Java programming and analysing those data using MATLAB (2008). A popular data mining tool, See5 (RuleQuest, 2008), has been used to get final rules.

Experimental Design

In the first step of our experiment, we have compared average confidence of the 10 best rules of 15 data files. On the basis of confidence, Apriori always showed supremacy compared to the other two algorithms (Predictive Apriori and Tertius). The details of the comparative study are provided in Figure 4-6. Rules generated from Tertius are worst in terms of confidence comparison. Then we compared between Apriori and Predictive Apriori in terms of average confidence and predictive accuracy of the initially selected 15 data files (The details of the data sets description are provided in Table 2). We have converted Nominal data to numeric values to perform the statistical analysis. We have considered simple, statistical and information theoretic measures to identify the dataset characteristics. The details of statistical characteristics comparisons are provided in Table 7. Some of the statistical formulation is available in MATLAB Statistics Toolbox (MATLAB, 2008). By using See5 (RuleQuest, 2008) data mining tools with the most co-related attributes, we generated rules to identified which algorithm was suitable for which type of problem. Finally, we examined the rules by the statistical measures. The details of the rule descriptions are provided in Figure 2.

Performance Analysis

In the experiment, we have compared Apriori, Predictive Apriori and Tertius with 'confidence' in the first step. Apriori always shows the best performance in this experiment. The details of the 'confidence' based performance of 3 algorithms are shown in Figure 8, Figure 9 and Figure 10.

As in the first step of this experiment, Apriori and Predictive Apriori showed better performance. Tertius had the worst among those in terms of 'confidence' based comparisons. So we compared Apriori and Predictive Apriori with 'confidence' and 'predictive accuracy' respectively. Then we found out which algorithm is better between them. The details of the data sets comparisons are provided in Table 3.

Rule Generation

As a part of the meta-learning process, we have used data from Table 7 and generated rules using See5 data mining tools. See 5 basically classified the data characteristics on the basis of Mode and Geometric Mean. The details of the characteristics rules are provided in Figure 11.

Figure 8. Performance of Apriori based on average confidence

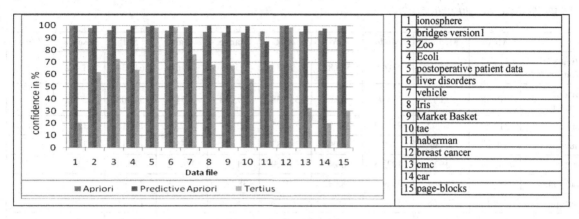

Figure 9. Performance of Predictive Apriori based on average confidence

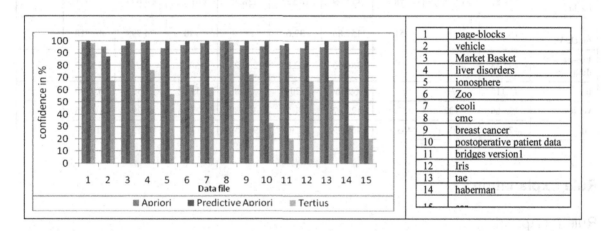

Figure 10. Performance of Tertius based on average confidence

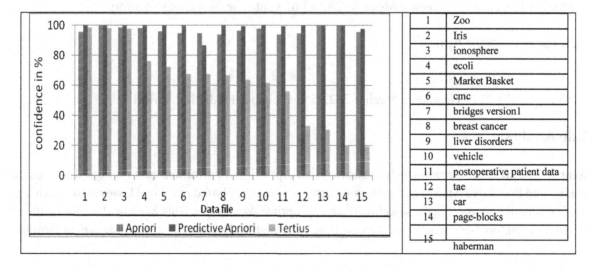

Table 3. Using statistical formulation and comparison between confidence and 'predictive accuracy' we have generated the following table

	Mean	Median	Mode	GM	IQR	Range	Var	Std	Zscore	Class
Breast Cancer	584.19	607.2	607.2	576.85	96.3	252.7	8416.6	64.934	23.462	2
Bridge version	212.48	233.75	225.92	198.64	55.938	193.58	6034.9	54.408	6.7602	1
car	312.88	250.92	222.67	282.95	207.25	268	16230	116.15	3.91	1
cmc	5.4593	5.444	4.7778	4.7094	2.5833	7.1111	8.559	1.7011	17.247	2
ecoli	187.87	192	192.43	186.47	3.6429	149	326.72	17.149	3.263	2
haberman	39.779	38.667	36.667	38.032	9	38.667	59.655	7.0808	11.44	2
ionosphere	269.18	337.68	51.176	209.21	200.76	344.26	18575	132.11	4.4927	2
iris	149.19	149	148	149.16	4.25	11	7.8595	2.7971	40.272	1
Liver disorders	112.88	112	111.17	112.36	4.2083	71	114.82	9.8548	18.25	2
Market basket	175.81	177.67	178.5	173.69	18.125	138.75	661.93	24.643	15.954	2
Page blocksW	160.81	158.9	151.8	157.86	32.6	142.8	750	24.799	16.018	1
Pos-patient data	497.88	435.31	421.13	486.96	142.88	230.25	15001	92	5.8092	2
tae	71.115	71	71.4	69.56	20	34.8	233.42	11.303	3.2965	2
vehicle	123.06	122	121.72	122.37	11.5	32.889	123.46	8.2291	10.275	2
zoo	472.73	480.71	463.35	469.99	57.368	96.059	3139.7	40.134	10.75	2

Rule Explanation

Rule for Apriori

If

Mode > 121.72 and Geometric Mean <= 282.95 of a data file then choose Apriori.

Rule for Predictive Apriori

If

Mode <= 121.72 or Geometric Mean > 282.95 then choose Predictive Apriori

Rule Analysis

Comparative study of three algorithms showed that Apriori had performed best on confidence based ranking and Predictive Apriori had performed better on accuracy based ranking. However the main aim of this research is to assist in the selection of an appropriate Association Rule Mining algorithm without the need for trial-and-error testing of the vast array of available algorithms. Based on statistical formula-

Figure 11. Characteristics rules generated by See5

```
See5 [Release 2.03]
Options:
       Rule-based classifiers
       Pruning confidence level 99%
Read 15 cases (9 attributes)
Rules:
Rule 1: (6/2, lift 2.3)
       Mode > 121.72 & Geomean <= 282.95 ⇒ class 1  [0.625]
Rule 2: (6, lift 1.2)
       Mode <= 121.72  ⇒ class 2  [0.875]
Rule 3: (3, lift 1.1)
       Geomean > 282.95 ⇒  class 2  [0.800]
Default class: 2
Evaluation on training data (15 cases):
            Rules
       ----------------
       No    Errors
        3    2(13.3%)  <<
       (a)  (b)   <-classified as
       ---- ----
        4         (a): class 1
        2    9    (b): class 2
Time: 0.0 secs
```

tion measurement and meta-learning process, we can recommend an algorithm by analysing Mode and GM of a data file. Although we have used nine statistical measurements, the rules emphasize only two of them. We aim to continue this research by considering more association problems, extracting better rules using other participating statistical measurements.

LIMITATION OF THE EXISTING ALGORITHM

Although ARM plays a big role among different machine learning algorithms, there are some fundamental challenges still needs to overcome. Some of those challenges are (Ali & Wasimi 2007):

- Multiple scans of transaction database
- Handling huge number of candidates
- Tedious workload on CPU when counting support for each candidate
- Wrong judgment because of the straight-forward interpretation of the rules
- Sometimes the number of strong rules found can be very small.
- Sometimes the number of strong rules can be very large.
- Produced set of strong rules which are expected and do not lead to new insight.
- Meaningless rules which do not help for any decision.

    Data files for mining are huge with millions of transactions and hundreds of attributes which could lead an enormous number itemset. 'A frequent pattern of length l implies the presence of $2l - 2$ additional frequent patterns as well, each of which is explicitly examined by such algorithms'(Zaki & Hsiao 2005).

For a simple example, a data file with 4 items could produce 14 itemsets. Details of possible itemsets are shown in Figure 12.

Moreover, addition of new dimension makes the task more complex. Thus carefully designed algorithms are an expectation in data mining studies. Usage of ARM is increasing rapidly in various research and commercial area. As a result, the models for ARM should be comprehensible depend of the application domain. These illustrate that data mining must pay concern to computational efficiency and simple models. Furthermore, even though the data sets can be very large, the limitations of the information in the data have to be carefully studied and the effect of skewed or long-tail distributions has to be assessed.

Researchers have proposed two ways to solve these problems. The first one is to mine only maximal frequent itemsets (Agrawal et al.,2000; Bayardo,1998; Gouda & Zaki,2001; Lin & Kedem,1998), which are typically fewer in order of magnitude than all frequent patterns. The second is to mine only the frequent closed sets (Pasquier et al.,1999; Wang et al.,2003; Zaki, 2000; Bastide et al.,2000): 'Closed sets are lossless in the sense that they can be used to uniquely determine the set of all frequent itemsets and their exact frequency' (Zaki & Hsiao 2005).

PROPOSED NEW IDS

Computational approaches to science are known as Computer Science. Dodig-Crnkovic (2002) states Computer Science draws upon three areas of science; mathematics, logic and natural science. Typically any type of computer science based research and development is an iterative process. The researchers begin with a basic idea for an algorithm then proceeds to implement this, dealing with any issues that arise. Buchanan (1988) describes three steps of performing computer science research, being directly applicable to this study.

Theoretical Steps

This research will involve the development of a number of algorithmic solutions to the problems that have identified. Following are the techniques/methods can be used in this research:

Figure 12. Possible itemsets of four items

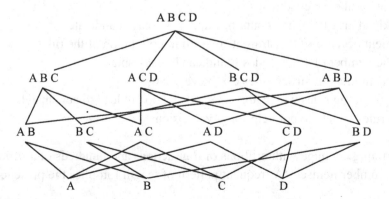

Developing an Agent Based IDS

First of all, developing an IDS which will use an agent. At this point, we prefer a single agent considering system workload and network overhead. It will be an intelligent category of agent and will reside at network server. It will work with firewall to provide network environment more secure. Basic task of our agent is to collect system log file and analyzes data using meta-learning technique. Analyzing training data, this agent will produce detection model at a predefined time interval. So it will help the IDS to detect every type of intrusion such as misuse intrusions, anomaly intrusions, etc. Fault tolerance is one of the basic and very important features of any software or support tool. Taking this into consideration, a backup agent will always support the main agent.

Meta Learning Process

Meta learning is one of the important branches of Machine Learning. In this technique automatic learning algorithms are applied on pre processed data to conduct machine learning experiments. One important feature of it is to solve problems using Machine Learning (ML) and Data Mining (DM) tools. The successful applications should have continuous adaptation to new needs. Learning from previous experience is more desirable than beginning fresh on new tasks for a model. Meta-learning techniques can help this by searching for patterns across tasks. Another advantage of meta-learning is if a base-learner fails to execute tasks efficiently, the meta-agent can support the base-learner promptly. There are different types of meta learning techniques (Vilalta et al.,2004) such as

Dataset Characterization
Dataset characterization types of technique are Statistical and Information-Theoretic Characterization, Model-Based Characterization and Landmarking.

Mapping Datasets to Predictive Models
This technique is subdivided by Hand-Crafting Meta Rules, Learning at the Meta-Level and Ranking Models.

Combining Base-Learners
Subcategories of this technique are Stacked Generalization, Boosting, Meta-Decision Trees, Composition of Inductive Applications, Meta-learning for Pre-processing.

Dataset characterization technique with Combining Base-Learners has been used in this research. Preliminary flowchart of the model that we will follow is shown in Figure 13.

One Pass Algorithm to Generate Association Rules

Another fundamental issue is to choose the right type of mining algorithms. As we will use ARM algorithms, we will concentrate more on this topic. Association rules can be found in two steps: 1) finding large itemsets (support is greater than user specified support) for a given threshold support and 2) generate desired association rules for a given confidence. In the following subsections, we will discuss the issues that need to be considered to generate and maintain frequent itemsets and association rules in data streams. Since data streams of a system log file are rapid, time-varying streams of data elements, itemsets which are frequent are changing as well. Often these changes make the model built on old data inconsistent with the new data, and frequent updating of the model is necessary. This problem is known as concept drifting (Dasgupta & Gonzalez 2002). From the aspect of association rule mining, when data is changing over time, some frequent itemsets may become non-frequent and some non-frequent itemsets may become frequent. If we store only the counts of frequent itemsets in the data structure, when we need the counts for potential non-frequent itemsets which would become frequent itemsets later, we cannot get this information. Therefore, the technique to handle concept drifting needs to be considered. Krugel & Toth (2001) proposed a method to reflect the concept drifts by boundary movements in the Closed Enumeration Tree (CET).

Compact Data Structure

An efficient and compact data structure is needed to store, update and retrieve the collected information. This is due huge amounts of data handling and limited memory. Failure in developing such a data structure will largely decrease the efficiency of the mining algorithm because, even if we store the information in disks, the additional I/O operations will increase the processing time. The data structure needs to be incrementally maintained since it is not possible to rescan the entire input each time. Manku & Motwani (2002) have used a lattice data structure to store itemsets. Li et al. (2004) employ a prefix tree data structure. Giannella et al.(2003) used FP-tree construct to store itemsets. As those three are most popular and efficient among data structures, we will use a hybrid data structure considering those three structures.

Efficient Memory Management

The next fundamental issue should be considered is how to optimize the memory space consumed when running the mining algorithm. This includes how to store the information we collect from system log file,

Figure 13. A Meta learning frame work

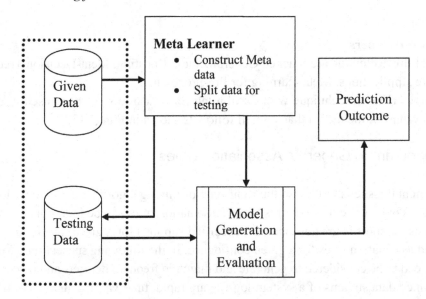

updated and retrieved those efficiently. Fully addressing these issues in the mining algorithm can greatly improve its performance. Use of Java programming language to develop this system is more preferable. The real-time specification for Java extends the Java platform to support real-time processing. It also introduces a region-based memory model, called scoped memory (Eskin, 2000a), which side-steps the Java garbage collector. Scoped memory is a proven technique to manage memory efficiently.

Generating Long Itemsets

Handling long itemsets efficiently consuming minimal time is another major issue for ARM based rule mining. If researchers use an efficient compact hybrid data structure using Java programming, he/she will be able to handle and generate long itemsets, enabling rule accuracy. This will lead to better performance of the intrusion detection system.

Engineering Steps

The adopted algorithm/s must then be engineered into steps that are efficient for the computer to process. Basically, the process to the techniques can be demonstrated through the results of the program.

The proposed system architecture is shown in Figure 14.

Analytical Steps

The validation stage involves taking a final look at the system to determine if the developed methods have satisfied the research goals. The collection of DARPA (Lincoln Laboratary, 2008) data from Lincoln Laboratory is used to analyse the results. Using these results, we can define the strong points of the algorithm that proposed by me and its weak points. At the preliminarily stage of research DARPA KDD99 dataset have been used.

Data Description

We have used DARPA intrusion detection evaluation datasets from MIT Lincoln Lab (Lincoln Laboratory, 2008). This datasets provide researchers to evaluate performance of different IDS methodologies. DARPA KDD99 (Lincoln Laboratory, 2008) dataset represents data as rows of TCP/IP dump. Each row consists of 41 attributes which describe about features of computer connection. These attributes can be grouped into 4 categories. Those are:

- **Basic attributes:** these attributes are about packet header of a connection.
- **Content attributes:** these are about domain knowledge and some other information such as failed login attempts.
- **Time based traffic attributes:** these attributes are relating to time window such as attempts to connect with same host within 2 second interval.
- **Host based traffic attributes:** these attributes are about individual host history within a timeframe.

Figure 14. Proposed architecture of Intrusion Detection System

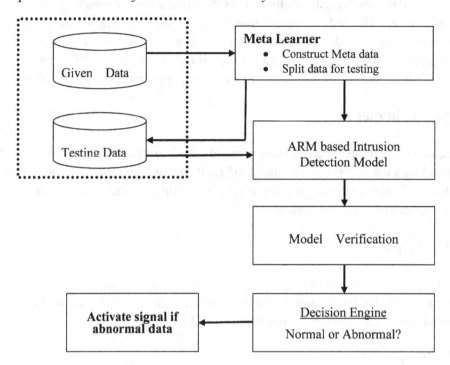

DARPA KDD99 dataset contains 494019 data of training connections. Based upon discriminate analysis(Lane, 2000) we have used first 8 and last attributes. Those attributes are Protocol Type, Service, Land, Wrong fragment, Num_failed_logins(Number of failed logins), Logged_in(indication for successful logged in user), Root_shell(whether the root shell is obtained by the user) and Is_guest_login(whether the logged in person is guest). The last attribute "attack_type" has 38 types of attacks which can be categorized into four types (Jemili et al.,2007). Those are Denial of service (DoS), Remote to local (r2l), User to root (u2r) and Probe.

Analytical Experiment

We consider some most common measures of rule interestingness such as support, confidence, lift, leverage, coverage and correlation for classifiers evaluation in our analytical experiment. First, we measure the algorithm performance individually by calculating support, confidence, lift, leverage, coverage and correlation using WEKA(Witten & Frank 2000) data mining software. We choose the first 10 best rules for each algorithm. Secondly, we measure the performance by calculating average of each measure.

In Table 8 we have presented the average of each measure of interestingness. Although each algorithm is showing the highest confidence level which is 1, there is a wide variation of average-support. Apriori algorithm has picked up rules with highest support (more than 85%) which is pretty impressive for this database. With respect to all other measures such as Lift, Leverage, Coverage and Correlation; Apriori showed better performance as well.

Finally we have calculated the ranking performance (Ali & Smith, 2006) for the above algorithms based on support, confidence, lift, leverage, coverage and correlation. The best performing algorithm

Table 5. Average of 10 best rules of DARPA KDD99 dataset for Apriori

Apriori	Support	Confidence	Lift	Leverage	Coverage	Correlation
Rule 1	0.851753266	1	1.0015002	0.001275851	0.853031031	0.092839545
Rule 2	0.851745169	1	1.0015002	0.001275839	0.853022922	0.092836568
Rule 3	0.851708733	1	1.0015002	0.001275785	0.852986432	0.092823177
Rule 4	0.851700636	1	1.0015002	0.001275773	0.852978323	0.092820202
Rule 5	0.851753266	1	1.0013885	0.001181025	0.85293593	0.089317841
Rule 6	0.851753266	1	1.0013885	0.001181025	0.85293593	0.089317841
Rule 7	0.851745169	1	1.0013885	0.001181013	0.852927822	0.089314978
Rule 8	0.851745169	1	1.0013885	0.001181013	0.852927822	0.089314978
Rule 9	0.851708733	1	1.0013885	0.001180963	0.852891336	0.089302094
Rule 10	0.851708733	1	1.0013885	0.001180963	0.852891336	0.089302094
Average	**0.851732214**	**1**	**1.0014332**	**0.001218925**	**0.852952888**	**0.090718932**

on each of these measures is assigned the rank of 1 and the worst is 0. Thus, the rank of the jth algorithm on the ith dataset is calculated as:

$$R_{ij} = 1 - \frac{e_{ij} - \max(e_i)}{\min(e_i) - \max(e_i)}$$

Table 6. Average of 10 best rules of DARPA KDD99 dataset for Predictive Apriori

Predictive Apriori	support	Confidence	Lift	Leverage	Coverage	Correlation
Rule 1	0.00053439	1	1.7419517	0.00022761	0.000930882	0.019917424
Rule 2	0.00053439	1	1.7419517	0.00022761	0.000930882	0.019917424
Rule 3	0.00053439	1	1.1741103	0.00007925	0.000627433	0.00964845
Rule 4	0.00053439	1	1.0020121	0.00000107	0.000535465	0.001037206
Rule 5	0.000524269	1	1.74195171	0.00022330	0.000913252	0.01972781
Rule 6	0.000467591	1	1.0020121	0.00000094	0.000468532	0.000970185
Rule 7	0.000467591	1	1.0000567	0.00000003	0.000467618	0.000162837
Rule 8	0.000445325	1	2.59952227	0.00027401	0.001157633	0.026695035
Rule 9	0.000445325	1	2.59922137	0.00027399	0.001157499	0.026692524
Rule 10	0.00040889	1	2.59952227	0.00025160	0.001062917	0.025579198
Average	**0.000489655**	**1**	**1.72023127**	**0.00015594**	**0.000825211**	**0.015034809**

Table 7. Average of 10 best rules of DARPA KDD99 dataset for Tertius

Tertius						
	Support	**Confi dence**	**Lift**	**Leverage**	**Coverage**	**Correlation**
Rule 1	0.0000020242	1	494021	0.0000020242	1	1
Rule 2	0.0000020242	1	494021	0.0000020242	1	1
Rule 3	0.0000020242	1	494021	0.0000020242	1	1
Rule 4	0.0000020242	1	494021	0.0000020242	1	1
Rule 5	0.0000020242	1	494021	0.0000020242	1	1
Rule 6	0.0000020242	1	494021	0.0000020242	1	1
Rule 7	0.0000020242	1	494021	0.0000020242	1	1
Rule 8	0.0000020242	1	494021	0.0000020242	1	1
Rule 9	0.0000020242	1	494021	0.0000020242	1	1
Rule 10	0.0000020242	1	494021	0.0000020242	1	1
Average	**0.0000020242**	**1**	**494021**	**0.0000020242**	**1**	**1**

where e_{ij} is the percentage of correct classification for the jth algorithm on dataset *i*, and e_i is a vector accuracy for dataset i. A detailed comparison of algorithm performance can be evaluated from this equation.

We have again evaluated the performance of all the algorithms using the total number of best and worst performances. The total number of the best and worst ranking for support, confidence, lift, leverage, coverage, correlation and computational complexity for all the algorithms are evaluated by using the following equation:

$$C_i = \frac{1}{r}\left(\frac{s_i - f_i}{n}\right) + \frac{1}{r}$$

where $\rho = 2$ is the weight shifting parameter, s_i is the total number of success or best cases for the ith algorithm, f_i is the total number of failure or worst cases for the same algorithm, and n is the total number of datasets.

Finally, we have measured the relative weighted performance for all the algorithms with two different weights for ranking average of support, confidence, lift, leverage, coverage, correlation and computational complexity using the following equation:

Table 8. Data analysis using interestingness measure of rules

	Support	**Confi dence**	**Lift**	**Leverage**	**Coverage**	**Correlation**
Apriori	0.851732214	1	1.001433	0.001219	0.852953	0.091
Predictive Apriori	0.000489655	1	1.720231	0.000156	0.000825	0.015
Tertius	0.000002024	1	494021	0.000002	1	1

$$Z = \mathrm{a}\,a_i + \mathrm{b}t_i$$

α and β are the weight parameters for ranking average performance against computational complexity. The average performance and computational complexity are denoted by a_i and t_i. By changing the values of β we have observed the effect of the relative importance of accuracy and computational complexity. From detailed analysis of the results we have a proposed best suitable learning technique that can handle intrusion detection significantly.

After carrying out the ranking performance, Apriori still attain the superiority among the three algorithms. However we have discussed the shortcoming of Apriori in Section 2.1. By overcoming those challenges, it is possible to produce a better Machine Learning algorithm with hybrid approach. This hybrid algorithm can be used to construct an efficient intrusion detection system.

DISCUSSION/ FUTURE DIRECTION

Detecting intrusion is one of the major concerns since the beginning of computer use. A great deal of research has been performed and many solutions have been suggested by researchers to prevent intrusions. Nowadays an extensive number of IDS are in the marketplace with attractive features such as rapid detection rate, flexibility, extensibility, fault tolerance, resistance to compromise, etc. Instead of using monolithic agent, currently multi agents are being deployed in multilevel of the network for intrusion detection purposes. This feature makes IDSs more flexible, scalable, and resilient. However, there are still huge numbers of issues unsolved. Some of those are incompatible with existing high speed network, automatic update with hackers' supplicated tools, etc. So improvement of contemporary IDS has become essential. In this research, we have widely investigated a number of Intrusion Detection Systems and related issues, particularly using Machine Learning techniques. In that regard, we have conducted a comparative study among some selective algorithms for data mining to find out the nature of the best algorithm. We have done another experiment for ranking performance with measures of rule interestingness. In both the experiments, Apriori attained the superiority among the algorithms. However, Apriori has many drawbacks such as multiple scans of the database, inefficient handling of large databases, time consuming, etc. It is very common to handle large databases to detect intrusion. For a robust and efficient IDS, development of algorithm is essential considering those shortcomings. We need to improve other deficiencies of IDS as well such as high false alarm, damage recoveries after attack, defending itself from attack, recognizing new attack and response immediately, etc. There is no common and efficient evaluation methodology to evaluate Intrusion Detection Systems. However, the Receiver Operating Characteristics (ROC) curve is widely used to evaluate IDS, even though those results are sometimes misleading and/or incomplete. It is very difficult to implement all the characteristics in IDS, in terms of complicacy and efficiency. But those features are imperative for a robust and efficient Intrusion Detection System in order to secure computer systems and networks.

REFERENCES

Agrawal, R., Aggarwal, C., & Prasad, V. V. V. (2000). Depth First Generation of Long Patterns. In *Proc. Seventh Int'l Conference Knowledge Discovery and Data Mining*.

Agrawal, R., Imielinski, T. T., & Swami, A. (1993). Mining associations between sets of items in large databases. In *Proc. of the ACM SIGMOD Int'l Conference on Management of Data*, Washington, DC, (pp. 207-216).

Ali, A. B. M. S., & Smith, K. A. (2006). On learning algorithm selection for classification. *Journal on Applied Soft Computing, 6*, 119–138. doi:10.1016/j.asoc.2004.12.002

Ali, A. B. M. S., & Wasimi, S. A. (2007). *Data Mining: Methods and Techniques*. Victoria Australia: Thomson Publishers.

Anderson, D., Frivold, T., Tamaru, A., & Valdes, A. (1994). Next Generation Intrusion Detection Expert System (NIDES). *Software Users Manual, Beta-Update release, Computer Science Laboratory*, (Tech. Rep. SRI-CSL-95-0). Menlo Park, CA: SRI International.

Anderson, D., Lunt, T. F., Javitz, H., Tamaru, A., & Valdes, A. (1995). *Detecting Unusual Program Behavior Using the Statistical Component of the Next-generation Intrusion Detection Expert System (NIDES)* (SRI-CSL-95-06). Menlo Park, CA: SRI International.

Asaka, M., Taguchi, A., & Goto, S. (1999). The implementation of IDA: an intrusion detection agent system. In *Proceedings of the 11th FIRST Conference*.

Balasubramaniyan, J., Fernandez, J. O., Isacoff, D., Spafford, E., & Zamboni, D. (1998). *An architecture for intrusion detection using autonomous agents, COAST.* (Tech. Rep. 98/5). West Lafayette, IN: Purdue University.

Barbar'a, D., Wu, N., & Jajodia, S. (2001). Detecting novel network intrusions using bayes estimators. In *Proc. of the First SIAM Int. Conf. on Data Mining (SDM 2001)*. Chicago: Society for Industrial and Applied Mathematics (SIAM).

Barrus, J., & Rowe, N. C. (1998). A distributed autonomous-agent network intrusion detection and response system. In *Proceedings of the command and control research and technology symposium*, Monterey, CA.

Bastide, Y., Taouil, R. N., Pasquier, Y., Stumme, G., & Lakhal, L. (2000). Mining Frequent Patterns with Counting Inference. *SIGKDD Explorations*, (Vol. 2).

Bayardo, R. J. (1998). Efficiently Mining Long Patterns from Databases. In *Proc. ACM SIGMOD Conference Management of Data*.

Bellifemine, F., Poggi, A., & Rimassa, G. (1999). JADE - a FIPA compliant agent framework. In *Proceedings of the fourth international conference and exhibition on the practical application of intelligent agents and multi-agents*, London.

Bernardes, M. C., & Moreira, E. S. (2000). Implementation of an intrusion detection system based on mobile agents. In *International symposium on software engineering for parallel and distributed systems*, (pp. 158-164).

Blake, C., & Merz, C. J. (2007). *UCI Repository of machine learning databases*. University of California. Retrived on February 15, 2009 from http://archive.ics.uci.edu/ml/

Bloedorn, E., Christiansen, A. D., Hill, W., Skorupka, C., Talbot, L. M., & Tivel, J. (2001). *Data mining for network intrusion detection: How to get started*. Retrieved from http://citeseer.nj.nec.com/523955. html

Brian, H., & Dasgupta, D. (2001). Mobile security agents for network traffic analysis. In *Proceedings of the second DARPA Information Survivability Conference and Exposition II (DISCEX-II)*, Anaheim, CA.

Buchanan, B. G. (1988). What do expert systems offer the science of Artificial Intelligence. *Proceedings of the fourth Australian conference on applications of expert systems*. (pp. 1-30). Sydney: University of Technology.

Burdick, D., Calimlim, M., & Gehrke, J. (2001). MAFIA: a macimal frequent itemset algorithm for transactional databases. In *International conference on Data Engineering*.

Carver, C. A., Hill, J. M. D., Surdu, J. R., & Pooch, U. W. (2000). A methodology for using intelligent agents to provide automated intrusion response. In *IEEE Systems, Man, and Cybernetics Information Assurance and Security Workshop*, West Point, NY.

Chan, P. K., Mahoney, M. V., & Arshad, M. H. (2003). Managing Cyber Threats: Issues, Approaches and Challenges. In *Learning Rules and Clusters for Anomaly Detection in Network Traffic*. Amsterdam: Kluwer Academic Publishers.

Chittur, A. (2001). *Model generation for an intrusion detection system using genetic algorithms*. High School Honors Thesis, Ossining High School, in cooperation with Columbia Univ.

Cohen, F. B. (1999). Simulating Cyber Attacks, Defenses, and Consequences. In *Strategic Security Intelligence*. Retrieved April 7, 2009 from http://all.net/journal/ntb/simulate/simulate.html

Crosbie, M., & Spafford, E. (1995). Defending a computer system using autonomous agents. In *Proceedings of the 18th national information systems security conference*.

Crosbie, M., & Spafford, E. H. (1995). *Active defense of a computer system using autonomous agents*, (Technical Report CSD-TR- 95-008). West Lafayette, IN: Purdue Univ.

Dasgupta, D., & Gonzalez, F. (2002). An immunity-based technique to characterize intrusions in computer networks. *IEEE Transactions on Evolutionary Computation, 6*(3).

Dasgupta, D., & Gonz'alez, F. A. (2001). An intelligent decision support system for intrusion detection and response. In *Proc. of International Workshop on Mathematical Methods, Models and Architectures for Computer Networks Security (MMM-ACNS)*, St.Petersburg. Berlin: Springer-Verlag.

Deltour, A. (2001). *Tertius extension to Weka*. Department of Computer Science, University of Bristol. Retrieved April 01, 2009, from http://www.cs.bris.ac.uk/Publications/pub_master.jsp?pubyear=2001

Denning, D. E., & Neumann, P. G. (1985). *Requirements and Model for IDES—A Real-time Intrusion Detection System*, (Tech. Rep. # 83F83-01-00). Menlo Park, CA: SRI International.

Dickerson, J. E., & Dickerson, J. A. (2000). Fuzzy network profiling for intrusion detection. In *Proc. of NAFIPS 19th International Conference of the North American Fuzzy Information Processing Society, Atlanta*, (pp. 301–306). North American Fuzzy Information Processing Society (NAFIPS).

Dickerson, J. E., Juslin, J., Koukousoula, O., & Dickerson, J. A. (2001). Fuzzy intrusion detection. *In IFSA World Congress and 20th North American Fuzzy Information Processing Society (NAFIPS) International Conf.*, Vancouver, Canada, North American Fuzzy Information Processing Society (NAFIPS). *3*, 1506–1510

Didaci, L., Giacinto, G., & Roli, F. (2002). Ensemble learning for intrusion detection in computer networks. *ACM Journal.*

Dodig-Crnkovic, G. (2002). Scientific Methods in Computer Science. *Proceedings Conference for the Promotion of Research in IT at New Universities and at University Colleges in Sweden.*

Eskin, E. (2000). Detecting errors within a corpus using anomaly detection. In *Proc. of 2000 North American Chapter of the Association of Computational Linguistics (NAACL-2000)*, Seattle. North American Chapter of the Association of Computational Linguistics(NAACL).

Eskin, E. (2000a). Anomaly detection over noisy data using learned probability distributions. In *Proc. 17th International Conf. on Machine Learning*, (pp. 255–262). San Francisco: Morgan Kaufmann.

Eskin, E., Arnold, A., Preraua, M., Portnoy, L., & Stolfo, S. J. (2002, May). A geometric framework for unsupervised anomaly detection: Detecting intrusions in unlabeled data. In D. Barbar & S. Jajodia (Eds.), *Data Mining for Security Applications*. Boston: Kluwer Academic Publishers.

Eskin, E., Miller, M., Zhong, Z.-D., Yi, G., Lee, W.-A., & Stolfo, S. J. (2000). Adaptive model generation for intrusion detection systems. In *Workshop on Intrusion Detection and Prevention, 7th ACM Conference on Computer Security, Athens*. New York: ACM.

Eskin, E., Stolfo, S. J., & Lee, W. (2001). Modeling system calls for intrusion detection with dynamic window sizes. In *Proceedings of the DARPA Information Survivability Conference& Exposition II*, Anaheim, CA, (pp. 165–175).

Fan, W. (2001). *Cost-Sensitive, Scalable and Adaptive Learning Using Ensemble-based Methods*. Ph. D. thesis, Columbia Univ.

Fan, W., Lee, W., Stolfo, S. J., & Miller, M. (2000). A multiple model cost-sensitive approach for intrusion detection. In R. L. de M'antaras & E. Plaza (Eds.), *Proc. of Machine Learning: ECML 2000, 11th European Conference on Machine Learning*, Barcelona, Spain, (LNCS Vol. 1810, pp. 142–153).

FIPA. (2005). *FIPA Specification Lifecycle, IEEE Foundation for Intelligent Physical Agents*. Retrieved December 10, 2008 from http://www.fipa.org/specifications/lifecycle.html

Flach, P. A., & Lachiche, N. (2001). *Confirmation-guided discovery of first-order rules with Tertius*, (pp. 61-95). Amsterdam: Kluwer Academic Publishers.

Frank, J. (1994). Artificial intelligence and intrusion detection: Current and future directions. In *Proc. of the 17th National Computer Security Conference*. Baltimore: National Institute of Standards and Technology (NIST).

Gaffney, J. E., & Ulvila, J. W. (2001). Evaluation of intrusion detectors: a decision theory approach. In *Proceedings of the 2001 IEEE Symposium on Security and Privacy*, Oakland, CA, (pp. 50–61).

Ghosh, A. K., Schwartzbard, A., & Schatz, M. (1999). Learning program behavior profiles for intrusion detection. In *Proc. 1st USENIX Workshop on Intrusion Detection and Network Monitoring, Santa Clara, CA*, (pp. 51–62). USENIX.

Giacinto, G., & Roli, F. (2002). Intrusion detection in computer networks by multiple classifier systems. In *Proc. of the 16th International Conference on Pattern Recognition (ICPR)*, Quebec City, Canada, (Vol. 2, pp. 390–393). Washington, DC: IEEE press.

Giannella, C., Han, J., Pei, J., Yan, X., &. Yu P., S. (2003). Mining Frequent Patterns in Data Streams at Multiple Time Granularities. In *Data Mining: Next Generation Challenges and Future Directions*. Cambridge, MA: AAAI/MIT.

Gouda, K., & Zaki, M. J. (2001). Efficiently Mining Maximal Frequent Itemsets. In *Proc. First IEEE Int'l Conference Data Mining*.

Gowadiam, V., Farkas, C., & Valtora, M. (2005). PAID: A probabilistic agent-based intrusion detection system. *Computers & Security, 24*(7), 529–545. doi:10.1016/j.cose.2005.06.008

Helmer, G., Wong, J., Honavar, V., & Miller, L. (1999). *Automated discovery of concise predictive rules for intrusion detection*, (Technical Report 99-01). Ames, IA: Iowa State University.

Helmer, G.G., Wong, J.S.K., Honavar, V. & Miller, L. (2002). Lightweight agents for intrusion detection. *Journal of Systems and Software*.

Hofmeyr, S. A., & Forrest, S. (1999). Immunizing computer networks: Getting all the machines in your network to fight the hacker disease. In *Proc. of the 1999 IEEE Symp. on Security and Privacy*, Oakland, CA. Washington, DC: IEEE Computer Society Press.

Honig, A., Howard, A., Eskin, E., & Stolfo, S. J. (2002). Adaptive model generation: An architecture for the deployment of data miningbased intrusion detection systems. In D. Barbar & S. Jajodia (Eds.), *Data Mining for Security Applications*. Boston: Kluwer Academic Publishers.

Jansen, W., Mell, P., Karygiannis, T. & Marks, D. (1999). *Applying mobile agents to intrusion detection and response*. National Institute of Standards and Technology Computer Security Division, NIST Interim Report (IR) e 6416.

Javitz, H. S., & Valdes, A. (1991). The SRI IDES StatisticalAnomaly Detector. In *Proc. 1991 IEEE Computer Society Symposium on Research in Security and Privacy*, Oakland, CA. Washington, DC: IEEE Computer Society.

Javitz, H. S., & Valdes, A. (1993). *The NIDES statistical component: Description and justification*. Technical report. Menlo Park, CA: SRI International.

Jazayeri, M., & Lugmayr, W. (2000). Gypsy: a component-based mobile agent system. In *Eighth euromicro workshop on parallel and distributed processing*, Greece.

Jemili, F., Zaghdoud, M. & Ahmed, M., Ben. (2007). A Framework for an Adaptive Intrusion Detection System using Bayesian Network. *IEEEXplore*, 66 – 70.

Kazienko, P., & Dorosz, P. (2004). *Intrusion Detection Systems (IDS) Part I, WindowSecurity.* Retrieved September 23, 2008 from http://www.windowsecurity.com/articles/intrusion_ detection_systems_ids_ part_i__network_intrusions_attack_symptoms_ids_tasks_and_ids_architecture.html

Krugel, C., & Toth, T. (2001). Sparta e a security policy reinforcement tool for large networks. *I-NetSec, 01*, 101–110.

Kumar, S. (1995). *Classification and Detection of Computer Intrusions.* Unpublished doctoral dissertation, Purdue University, West Lafayette, IN.

Lane, T. D. (2000), *Machine Learning Techniques for the computer security domain of anomaly detection.* Unpublished doctoral dissertation, Purdue Univ., West Lafayette, IN.

Lee, W. (1999). *A Data Mining Framework for Constructing Features and Models for Intrusion Detection Systems.* Doctoral dissertation, Columbia Univ., New York.

Lee, W., & Stolfo, S. J. (1998). Data mining approaches for intrusion detection. In *Proc. of the 7th USENIX Security Symp.* San Antonio, TX: USENIX.

Lee, W., & Stolfo, S. J. (2000). A framework for constructing features and models for intrusion detection systems. *Information and System Security, 3*(4), 227–261. doi:10.1145/382912.382914

Lee, W., Stolfo, S. J., Chan, P. K., Eskin, E., Fan, W., Miller, M., et al. (2001). Real time data mining-based intrusion detection. In *Proc. Second DARPA Information Survivability Conference and Exposition,* Anaheim, CA, (pp. 85–100). Washington, DC: IEEE Computer Society.

Lee, W., Stolfo, S. J., & Mok, K. W. (1999a). A data mining framework for building intrusion detection models. In *Proc. of the 1999 52 IEEE Symp. on Security and Privacy*, Oakland, CA, (pp. 120–132). Washington, DC: IEEE Computer Society Press.

Lee, W., Stolfo, S. J., & Mok, K. W. (1999b). Mining in a data-flow environment: Experience in network intrusion detection. In S. Chaudhuri & D. Madigan (Eds.), *Proc. of the Fifth International Conference on Knowledge Discovery and Data Mining (KDD-99),* San Diego, CA, (pp. 114–124). New York: ACM.

Lee, W., Stolfo, S. J., & Mok, K. W. (2000). Adaptive intrusion detection: A data mining approach. *Artificial Intelligence Review, 14*(6), 533–567. doi:10.1023/A:1006624031083

Lee, W., & Xiang, D. (2001). Information-theoretic measures for anomaly detection. *In Proc. of the 2001 IEEE Symp. on Security and Privacy*, Oakland, CA, (pp. 130–143). Washington, DC: IEEE Computer Society Press.

Li, H. F., Lee, S., Y. & Shan, M., K. (2004). An Efficient Algorithm for Mining Frequent Itemsets over the Entire History of Data Streams. In *Int'l Workshop on Knowledge Discovery in Data Streams*.

Li, Y., Wu, N., Jajodia, S. & Wang, X. S. (2002). Enhancing profiles for anomaly detection using time granularities. *Journal of Computer Security*.

Lin, D.-I., & Kedem, Z. M. (1998). Pincer-Search: A New Algorithm for Discovering the Maximum Frequent Set. In *Proc. Sixth Int'l Conference Extending Database Technology*.

Lincoln Labrotary. (2008). *1999 DARPA Intrusion Detection Evaluation Data Set*. Cambridge, MA: Massachusetts Institute of technology. Retrieved January 12, 2009 from http://www.ll.mit.edu/ mission/ communications/ist/ corpora/ideval/data/ 1999data.html

Lunt, T. F., Tamaru, A., Gilham, F., Jagannathm, R., Jalali, C., Neumann, P. G., et al. (1992). *A Real-time Intrusion Detection Expert System (IDES), Computer Science Laboratory*. Menlo Park, CA: SRI International.

Luo, J. (1999). *Integrating fuzzy logic with data mining methods for intrusion detection*. Master's thesis, Mississippi State Univ.

Mahoney, M. V., & Chan, P. K. (2001). *PHAD: Packet Header Anomaly Detection for Identifying Hostile Network Traffic Department of Computer Sciences*. Technical Report CS- 2001-4, Florida Institute of Technology, Melbourne, FL.

Mahoney, M. V., & Chan, P. K. (2002). Learning nonstationary models of normal network traffic for detecting novel attacks. In *Proc. of the 8th ACM SIGKDD International Conf. on Knowledge Discovery and Data mining,* Edmonton, Alberta, Canada, (pp. 376–385). New York: ACM Press.

Mahoney, M. V., & Chan, P. K. (2003a). Learning rules for anomaly detection of hostile network traffic. In *Proc. Third IEEE Intl. Conf. on Data Mining (ICDM),* Melbourne, FL, (pp. 601–604). Washington, DC: IEEE Computer Society Press.

Mahoney, M. V., & Chan, P. K. (2003b). An analysis of the 1999 darpa/lincoln laboratory evaluation data for network anomaly detection. In G. Vigna, E. Jonsson, and C. Kr¨ugel (Eds.), *Proc. 6th Intl. Symp. on Recent Advances in Intrusion Detection (RAID 2003)*, Pittsburgh, PA, (LNCS Vol. 53 2820, pp. 220–237). Berlin: Springer.

Manku, G.,S. & Motwani, R. (2002). Approximate Frequency Counts over Data Streams. *Int'l Conf. on Very Large Databases*.

Marchette, D. (1999). A statistical method for profiling network traffic. In *First USENIX Workshop on Intrusion Detection and Network Monitoring, Santa Clara, CA*, (pp. 119–128). USENIX.

Marin, J. A., Ragsdale, D., & Surdu, J. (2001). A hybrid approach to profile creation and intrusion detection. In *Proc. of DARPA Information Survivability Conference and Exposition*, IEEE Computer Society, Anaheim, CA.

Matlab. (2008). *Statistics Toolbox User's Guide, The MathWorksInc*, USA . Version 6.2

Mukkamala, S., & Sung, A. H. (2003). Identifying significant features for network forensic analysis using artificial intelligent techniques. *International Journal of Digital Evidence*, *1*(4), 1–17.

Mutter, S., Hall, M., & Frank, E. (2004). Using Classification to Evaluate the Output of Confidence based Association Rule Mining. In *Advances in Artificial Intelligence - AI 2004,* (LNAI Vol. 3339, pp. 538-549). Berlin: Springer.

Neri, F. (2000).Comparing local search with respect to genetic evolution to detect intrusion in computer networks. In *Proc. of the 2000 Congress on Evolutionary Computation CEC00, La Jolla, CA,* (pp. 238–243). Washington, DC: IEEE Press.

Park, H.-S., Kwon, O.-W., & Sung, J.-H. (2005). *Nonextraction treatment of an open bite with microscrew implant anchorage.* American Association of Orthodontists, U.S.A.

Pasquier, N., Bastide, Y., Taouil, R., & Lakhal, L. (1999). Discovering Frequent Closed Itemsets for Association Rules. In *Proc. Seventh Int'l Conference Database Theory.*

Patcha, A., & Park, J. M. (2007). An overview of anomaly detection techniques: Existing solutions and latest technological trends. In *Computer Networks,* (pp. 3448–3470).

Pei, J., Han, J., & Mao, R. (2000). Closet: An Efficient Algorithm for Mining Frequent Closed Itemsets. In *Proc. SIGMOD Int'l Workshop Data Mining and Knowledge Discovery.*

Pizlo, F. & Vitek, J. (2008). Memory Management for Real-time Java: State of the Art. *IEEE Xplore,* 248-254.

Porras, P. A., & Valdes, A. (1998). Live traffic analysis of TCP/IP gateways. In *Proc. of the 1998 ISOC Symp. on Network and Distributed Systems Security (NDSS'98),* Internet Society, San Diego.

Portnoy, L., Eskin, E., & Stolfo, S. J. (2001). Intrusion detection with unlabeled data using clustering. In *Proc. of ACM CSS Workshop on Data Mining Applied to Security (DMSA-2001),* Philadelphia. New York: ACM.

Roesch, M. (1999). Snort – lightweight intrusion detection for networks. In *Proceedings of the 13th USENIX Conference on System Administration Seattle,* Washington, (pp. 229–238).

RuleQuest. (2008). *RuleQuest Data mining tools, RuleQuest Research Pty Ltd.* Retrieved November 12, 2008 from http://www.rulequest.com/download.html

Ryan, J., Lin, M.-J., & Miikkulainen, R. (1998). Intrusion detection with neural networks. In M. I. Jordan, M. J. Kearns, & S. A. Solla (Eds.), *Advances in Neural Information Processing Systems,* (Vol. 10). Cambridge, MA: The MIT Press

Scheffer, T. (2001). Finding Association Rules that Trade Support Optimally Against Confidence. In *Proceedings of the 5th European Conference on Principles and Practice of Knowlege Discovery in Databases(PKDD'01),* Freiburg, Germany, (pp. 424-435). Berlin: Springer-Verlag.

Sequeira, K., & Zaki, M. (2002). Admit: Anomaly-based data mining for intrusions. In *Proc. of the 8th ACM SIGKDD International conf. on Knowledge Discovery and Data mining,* Edmonton, Alberta, Canada, (pp. 386–395). New York: ACM Press.

Shyu, M.-L., Chen, S.-C., Sarinnapakorn, K., & Chang, L. (2003). A novel anomaly detection scheme based on principal component classifier. In *Proceedings of the IEEE Foundations and New Directions of Data Mining Workshop,* Melbourne, FL (pp. 172–179).

Sinclair, C., Pierce, L., & Matzner, S. (1999). An application of machine learning to network intrusion detection. In *Proc. 15th Annual Computer Security Applications Conference (ACSAC '99),* Phoenix, (pp. 371–377). Washington, DC: IEEE Computer Society.

Singh, S., & Kandula, S. (2001). *Argus - a distributed network-intrusion detection system*. Undergraduate Thesis, Indian Institute of Technology.

Slagell, M. (2001). *The Design and Implementation of MAIDS (Mobile Agents for Intrusion Detection System)*. Master's thesis, Iowa State University, USA.

Smaha, S. E. (1988). Haystack: An intrusion detection system. In *Proceedings of the IEEE Fourth Aerospace Computer Security Applications Conference*, Orlando, FL, (pp. 37–44).

Spafford, E. H., & Zamboni, D. (2000). Intrusion detection using autonomous agents. *Computer Networks*, *34*(4), 547–570. doi:10.1016/S1389-1286(00)00136-5

Staniford, S., Hoagland, J. A., & McAlerney, J. M. (2002). Practical automated detection of stealthy portscans. *Journal of Computer Security, 10*(1-2), 105–136.

Staniford-Chen, S., Cheung, S., Crawford, R., Dilger, M., Frank, J., Hoagland, J., et al. (1996). GrIDS – A graphbased intrusion detection system for large networks. In *Proc. of the 19th National Information Systems Security Conference*, Baltimore, MD. National Institute of Standards and Technology (NIST).

Tan, P.-N., Steinbach, M., & Kumar, V. (2005). Association Analysis: Basic Concepts and Algorithms. In *Introduction to Data Mining*, (pp. 327-414). Reading, MA: Addison-Wesley

T¨olle, J., & Niggermann, O. (2000). Supporting intrusion detection by graph clustering and graph drawing. In *Proc. of Third International Workshop on Recent Advances in Intrusion Detection (RAID 2000)*, Toulouse, France, (LNCS Vol. 1907). Berlin: Springer.

Valdes, A., & Skinner, K. (2000). Adaptive model-based monitoring for cyber attack detection. In *Recent Advances in Intrusion Detection Toulouse*, France, (pp. 80–92).

Verwoerd, T., & Hunt, R. (2002). Intrusion detection techniques and approaches. *Computer Communications*, 1356–1365. doi:10.1016/S0140-3664(02)00037-3

Vilalta, R., Carrier, G., C., Brazdil. P. & Soares, C. (2004). Using Meta-Learning to Support Data Mining. *International Journal of Computer Science & Applications, I*, 1, 31 – 45.

Wang, J., Han, J., & Pei, J. (2003). Closet+: Searching for the Best Strategies for Mining Frequent Closed Itemsets. In *Proc. ACM SIGKDD Int'l Conference Knowledge Discovery and Data Mining*.

Warrender, C., Forrest, S., & Pearlmutter, B. A. (1999). Detecting intrusions using system calls: Alternative data models. In *Proc. of the 1999 IEEE Symp. on Security and Privacy,* Oakland, CA,(pp. 133–145). Washington, DC: IEEE Computer Society Press.

Weiss, G. (1999). *Multi-Agent System: A modern approach to distributed artificial intelligence*. Cambridge, MA: The MIT Press.

Witten, I. H., & Frank, E. (2000). *Data Mining: Practical Machine Learning Tool and Technique with Java Implementation*. San Francisco: Morgan Kaufmann.

Ye, N., Emran, S. M., Chen, Q., & Vilbert, S. (2002). Multivariate statistical analysis of audit trails for host-based intrusion detection. *IEEE Transactions on Computers*, 810–820. doi:10.1109/TC.2002.1017701

Yeung, D.-Y., & Chow, C. (2002). Parzen-window network intrusion detectors. In *Proc. of the Sixteenth International Conference on Pattern Recognition*, (Vol. 4, pp. 385–388), Quebec City, Canada. Washington, DC: IEEE Computer Society.

Yeung, D.-Y., & Ding, Y. (2003). Host-based intrusion detection using dynamic and static behavioral models. In *Pattern Recognition*, (pp. 229–243).

Zaki M., J. & Hsiao, C-J. (2005). Efficient Algorithms for Mining Closed Itemsets and Their Lattice Structure. *IEEE Computer Society, 17.*

Zaki, M. J. (2000). Scalable algorithms for association mining. *IEEE Transactions on Knowledge and Data Engineering*, 12.

Zaki, M. J. (2000). Generating Non-Redundant Association Rules. In *Proc. Sixth ACM SIGKDD Int'l Conference Knowledge Discovery and Data Mining*.

Zaki, M. J., & Hsiao, C. J. (1999). *CHARM: An efficient algorithm for closed association rule mining*. New York: Rensselaer Polytechnic Institute.

KEY TERMS AND DEFINITIONS

Intrusion: A system compromise or breach of security incident regarding computer. This involves gaining control of a computer system from the owner or an authorized administrator.

Association Rule Mining: Association Rule Mining (ARM) is one of the most important and substantial techniques for data mining. It discovers frequent items and associates between or among those items. ARM is a technique with a wide range of applications such as marketing policies, medical diagnosis, financial forecast, scientific research, telecommunication services and many other research areas.

Machine Learning: Machine Learning is a technique that makes a machine to learn or to perform a specific task. This learning is based on data analysis, previous experiences, etc. With the help of Machine Learning a machine can behave more intelligently and can do tasks more intelligently.

Meta Learning: Meta learning is one of the important branches of Machine Learning. The basic idea of Meta Learning is learning from past experience. In this technique automatic learning algorithms are applied on pre processed data to conduct machine learning experiments.

Apriori: Apriori is one of the most popular algorithms of Association Rule Mining. It uses prior knowledge of frequent items for rule generation. Confidence is the metric for ranking generated rule by Apriori.

Measure of interestingness: Measures of interestingness are the matrices to measure rules weight. Most of them are derived from statistical calculation. There are numbers of matrices such as support, confidence, predictive accuracy, conviction, lift, leverage, coverage, etc.

Agent Based IDS: This type of Intrusion Detection System (IDS) uses one or more agents to detect intrusive activities in system. Agents are assigned to perform specific task to make the IDS robust. There are different types of agents such as mobile agent, autonomous agent, multi-sensor based agent, intelligent agent, network agent, distributed agent, etc.

ENDNOTE

[1]   X denotes none

Chapter 6
A Re-Ranking Method of Search Results Based on Keyword and User Interest

Ming Xu
Hangzhou Dianzi University, P. R. China

Hong-Rong Yang
Hangzhou Dianzi University, P. R. China

Ning Zheng
Hangzhou Dianzi University, P. R. China

ABSTRACT

*It is a pivotal task for a forensic investigator to search a hard disk to find interesting evidences. Currently, most search tools in **digital forensic** field, which utilize text string match and index technology, produce high recall (100%) and low precision. Therefore, the investigators often waste vast time on huge irrelevant search hits. In this chapter, an improved method for ranking of search results was proposed to reduce human efforts on locating interesting hits. The **K-UIH** (the keyword and user interest hierarchies) was constructed by both investigator-defined keywords and user interest learnt from electronic evidence adaptive, and then the **K-UIH** was used to re-rank the search results. The experimental results indicated that the proposed method is feasible and valuable in **digital forensic** search process.*

INTRODUCTION

The most common activity task for a forensic investigator is to search a hard disk for interesting evidences. The investigator needs to focus on specific evidence and important indicators of suspicious activity (e.g., specific key word searches). Unfortunately, the large size of modern hard disk makes it extremely difficult and wastes investigator's vast time on huge irrelevant search hits. Many commercial or open sources tools have been developed to assist investigators to find relevant hits among large amounts of data, e.g., Forensic Tool Kit (AccessData, 2009), Encase (Guidance Software, 2009), etc. Nevertheless,

DOI: 10.4018/978-1-60566-908-3.ch006

huge number of search hits will be returned by search operations with high recall and low precision. What's more, these **digital forensic** text string search tools fail to group and/or order search hits in a manner that appreciably improves the investigator's ability to get to the relevant hits first.

In the works of Petrovic, and Franke (2007), they presented a new search procedure which makes use of the constrained edit distance in the pre-selection of the areas of the **digital forensic** search space that are interesting for the investigation. They divided the whole search space into several fragments and then computed constrained edit distance between each fragment and the query. However, our approach focuses on the entire hard disk instead of dividing it into small search spaces. Jee, Lee, and Hong (2007) also tried to improve search efficiency of **digital forensic**. Pattern matching board was used to build high speed bitwise search model for large-scale **digital forensic** investigations. This approach is different from ours, because we attempt to re-rank search results to reduce human efforts, and no additional hardware is used in the search process. It is not a new issue to personalize search results, which has been successfully applied in web information retrieval field. Kim and Chan (2008) learnt implicit interest from user to reorder search results. Various files on user's computer were used as the training set of user interest. Unfortunately, their user profile did not focus to represent from general to specific topics. The works of Kim and Chan (2008) sufficed this end. Their approach is to learn a user interest hierarchy (UIH) from the web pages visited by user. A divisive hierarchical clustering (DHC) algorithm was designed to group words into hierarchy where higher-level nodes are more general and lower-level ones are more specific. In their study (Kim, & Chan, 2006), a ranking algorithm was proposed to reorder the results with a learned user profile. In our search results re-ranking algorithm, large amounts of data from digital evidence can be used to learn user interest, but the primary goal of **digital forensic** search is to satisfy the investigator, which is different from web personalization.

However, during the digital investigation, developing a profile of the offender can help focus the search. Armed with a better understanding of the possible motivation, modus operandi (MO), and signatures, the investigator can be able to derive specific search criterion for forensic analysis (Rogers, 2003). After all, our approach attempts to automate extract user interest from digital artifact, no human effort act in this process. So we believe that identifying user interest is important in **digital forensic** search process, and the UIH method can be extending to **digital forensic** field after combined with investigator's focus.

Yang, Sun, and Sun (2006) also proposed an algorithm for learning hierarchical user interest models according to the Web pages which users had browsed. But they attempted to update user interest according to dynamic document set, while the dataset of the proposed method is based on static electronic evidence.

RELATED WORK

Dario Forto illustrated the importance of text searches in **digital forensic**s (Forte, 2004). He took GREP tool as example, and realized that its power depends on the technical expertise of investigator. Beebe, and Dietrich (2007) disclosed a general consensus that industry standard **digital forensic** tools are not scalable to large data sets. In their following work (Beebe, & Clark, 2007), a new and high-level text string search process model was presented. They proposed and empirically tested the feasibility and utility of post-retrieval thematically clustering of **digital forensic** search results. Our method also attempts to resort search results for quickly finding important hits. The difference is that we try to learn user interest from evidence and combine it with investigator-defined keyword to build adaptive user interest hierarchy, which is used to rank the search results.

In the works of Petrovic and Franke (2007), they presented a new search procedure which makes use of the constrained edit distance in the pre-selection of the areas of the **digital forensic** search space that are interesting for the investigation. They divided the whole search space into several fragments and then computed constrained edit distance between each fragment and the query. However, our approach focuses on the entire hard disk instead of dividing it into small search spaces. Jee, Lee, and Hong (2007) also tried to improve search efficiency of **digital forensic**. Pattern matching board was used to build high speed bitwise search model for large-scale **digital forensic** investigations. This approach is different from ours, because we attempt to re-rank search results to reduce human efforts, and no additional hardware is used in the search process. It is not a new issue to personalize search results, which has been successfully applied in web information retrieval field. Teevan, Dumais, and Horvitz (2005) learnt implicit interest from user to reorder search results. Various files on user's computer were used as the training set of user interest. Unfortunately, their user profile did not focus to represent general to specific topics. The work of Kim, and Chan (2008) sufficed this end. Their approach is to learn a user interest hierarchy (UIH) from web pages visited by user. A divisive hierarchical clustering (DHC) algorithm was designed to group words into hierarchy where higher-level nodes are more general and lower-level ones are more specific. In their study (Kim, & Chan, 2006), a ranking algorithm was proposed to reorder the results with a learned user profile. In our search results reranking algorithm, large amounts of data from digital evidence can be used to learn user interest, but the primary goal of **digital forensic** search is to satisfy the investigator, which is different from web personalization.

However, during the digital investigation, developing a profile of the offender can help focus the search. Armed with a better understanding of the possible motivation, modus operandi (MO), and signatures, the investigator can be able to derive specific search criterion for forensic analysis (Rogers, 2003). After all, our approach attempts to automate extract user interest from digital artifact, no human effort act in this process. So we believe that identifying user interest is important in **digital forensic** search process, and the UIH method can be extending to **digital forensic** field after combined with investigator's focus.

Yang, Sun, and Sun (2006) also proposed an algorithm for learning hierarchical user interest models according to the Web pages which users had browsed. But they attempted to update user interest according to dynamic document set, while the dataset of the proposed method is based on static electronic evidence.

THE K-UIH

K-UIH

In Kim's user interest hierarchy (Kim, &Chan, 2008), more general interest is represented by a larger set of words, which are extracted from web pages. Each web page can be assigned to a set of nodes for further processing. According to DHC algorithm, the similarity function and threshold-finding method greatly influence the clustering algorithm. The former measures how close the two words are related, and the latter determines what value of similarity is considered to be "strong" or "weak". Edges with weak weights are removed in **Similarity Matrix** (Denoted by SM). In this work, we fix the similarity function to AEMI-SP, and consider threshold-finding method based on MaxChildren.

Table 1. The sample data set

Page	words
1	computer academy journal Chinese science
2	computer academy conference deadline security submit
3	computer journal submit engineering
4	computer crime investigate network security forensic technology case
5	computer confident abuse identify material enterprise
6	paper submit review revise research study
7	paper submit review revise research

A UIH organizes a user's interests from general to specific. Towards the root of a UIH, more general or longer-term interests are represented by larger clusters of words, while towards the leaves, more specific or shorter-term interests are represented by smaller clusters of words. Before discussing our approach for building **K-UIH**, a picture of UIH is drawn to be taken as an example. To generate a UIH, seven web pages in bookmarks of web browser were collected as input. We firstly parsed the HTML documents and extracted text information from them without considering link or multimedia information. And then, the words were fragmented (Chinese pages) or stemmed (English pages) so that we can get all words in web page. At last, we filtered the words through a stop list (Frakes, & Baeza-Yates, 1992), which contains the most common words. The sample data set is shown in Table 1. It should be note that the samples throughout our study are in Chinese language. To illustrate our idea more intelligibly, we have translated them into English.

In Figure 1, the words in nodes come from the sample data set (Table 1). Each node represents a conceptual relationship if those terms occur together at the same web page. For example, in the left bottom of picture, 'journal' and 'Chinese' can be typed as journal submission, while in its brother node, 'conference' and 'deadline' are brought into conference program, but the exchange is not true. Additionally, these words are all related to some other words, such as 'research' and 'paper', which are contained in the parent node. While investigating the whole tree, it can be easily found that left side represents user interest about research and paper submission, and the right side is related to computer forensics.

In this study, we mainly focus on improving search efficiency of investigator. It seems natural to incorporate investigator's interest into UIH as a new tree, which we name it **K-UIH**. In **digital forensic** field, it is common that there is hundreds or thousands of files in digital evidence, so a huge UIH will be built by using original cluster algorithm. We attempt to utilize keywords inputted by investigator to localize original SM. Here, we should pay attention to a hypothesis: there exists an intersection between keywords set and SM words set, which means at least one word in keyword set also occurs in SM words set. It is believed that the investigator can easily seek important evidence if the input keyword is contained in the SM word set. The SM words set will limit and explain the actual meanings of the key words in the digital evidence contexts.

Note that we would like to see a small **K-UIH** contains one or more keywords, so a new threshold-finding method should be designed to suffice it. We observe a component of *SM*, called keyword similarity set (denoted by C), which contains similarities between keywords and other words. For example, in *SM*, if there are 10 edges connected between keywords and other words, the member number of C (denoted by n) is 10. We determine the threshold using the formula below:

Figure1. The sample user interest hierarchy

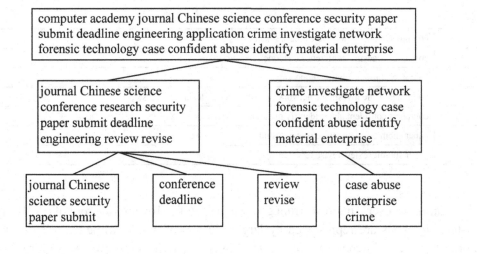

$$threshold = \{Max(s, C_i) \mid t = Min(n,t)\} \tag{1}$$

Before the threshold is computed, similarity values in *C* should be arranged in descend order (*i*=1, 2, ..., *n*). In equation 1, we define a constant *i* as the smaller one between *n* and *t*, which prevent too many similarity edges are under consideration. And then, the threshold is selected as the bigger one between c_i and *s*, which is also defined as a constant, i.e., 10. The role of *s* is similar to *t*. The value of *t* can be determined by MaxChildren method, which selects a threshold such that maximum of child clusters are generated and is guided to generate a shorter tree.

After localizing *SM* with the threshold discussed above, we will build **K-UIH** according to MaxChildren method and AEMI-SP similarity function as the same as original UIH algorithm. A simple example of **K-UIH** is shown in Figure 2.

In this mock case in figure 2, someone was suspected of making pirate sale of video, audio or games. The input keywords for searching were 'crack', 'manufacturer' and 'free'. As drawn in Figure 2, his interest was demonstrated well in the **K-UIH** we build. We are confident that search efficiency of digital investigation would be greatly improved by using **K-UIH**.

Figure 2. Sample adaptive user interest hierarchy

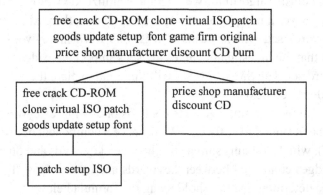

Figure 3. The proposed search procedure

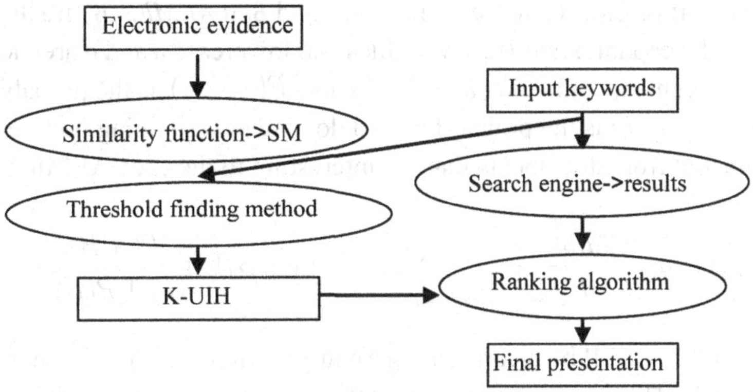

To illustrate the proposed approach clearly, the improved search process is summarized in Figure 3.

The first step inputs the electronic evidence, and parsed those documents and extracted text information from them without considering link or multimedia information, and then, the words were fragmented (Chinese pages) or stemmed (English pages) so that we can get all words in web page, at last, we filtered the words through a stop list.

The second step uses AEMI-SP as a similarity function, to calculate the "closeness" of two words; the third step builds a weighted undirected graph, called **Similarity Matrix**, with each vertex representing a word and each weight denoting the similarity between two words. Since related words are more likely to appear in the same document than unrelated terms, we measure co-occurrence of words in a document. At the same time, the investigator needs to input the keywords.

The third step uses SM, keywords inputted by investigator, and expression (1) to locate threshold.

The fourth step builts the **K-UIH** by MaxChildren and AEMI-SP. When we built the **K-UIH** between step 3 and 4, the common search evidence process based on inputted keywords should also be transacted to get search results.

The final step is using ranking algorithm and **K-UIH** to rank the search results. The ranking algorithm is presented in section 4.

Similarity Functions

The similarity function is used to calculate how strongly two words are related. We assume two words co-occurring within a window size are related, because related words are more likely to be close to each other than unrelated words. In this work, the window size is simply assumed to be the entire length of a document. That is, two words co-occur if they are in the same document.

The document frequency of a word calculates the number of documents that contain the word. Words that are commonly used in many documents are usually not informative in characterizing the content of the documents. Hence, the inverse document frequency (the reciprocal of document frequency) measures how informative a word is in characterizing the content. AEMI is an enhanced version of MI (Mutual Information) and EMI (Expected Mutual Information). Unlike MI which considers only one corner of the contingency matrix and EMI which sums the MI of all four corners of the contingency matrix,

AEMI sums supporting evidence and subtracts counter-evidence. AEMI could find more meaningful multiword phrases than MI or EMI. Consider variables A and B in $AEMI(A,B)$ are the events for the two terms (a and b), where the capital A and B are variables and lowercase a and b are the instances. $P(A=a)$ is the probability of a document containing a term of a and $P(A = \bar{a})$ is the probability of a document not having term a. $P(A=a, B=b)$ is the probability of a document containing both terms a and b. These probabilities are estimated from documents that are interesting to the user. AEMI(A,B) is defined as:

$$AEMI\ (A, B) = P(a,b)\log\frac{P(a,b)}{P(a)P(b)} - \sum_{(A=a,B=\bar{b})(A=\bar{a},B=b)} P(A,B)\log\frac{P(A,B)}{P(A)P(B)} \tag{2}$$

In this work, we enhance AEMI by incorporating a component for inverse document frequency (IDF) in the correlation function. The measures how informative a term is in characterizing the content. While involving the IDF, we adapt sigmoid function in order to emphasize more specific (informative) terms. The adjusted sigmoid function is called SP (specificity):

$$SP(m) = \frac{1}{1 + \exp(0.6 \times (m \times 10.5\text{ - }5))}, \text{where } SP(m) = \frac{1}{1 + \exp(0.6 \times (m \times 10.5\text{ - }5))}$$
$$m = MAX(P\ (a), P(b)), \text{where } m = MAX(P\ (a), P(b)) \tag{3}$$

We choose the larger probability so that SP is more conservative. The factor 0.6 smoothes the curve, and constants 10.5 and −5 shift the range of m from between 0 and 1 to between −5 and 5.5. The new range of −5 and 5.5 is slightly asymmetrical because we would like to give a small bias to more specific terms. For example, for a='ann' and b='perceptron', m is 0.2 and $SP(m)$ is 0.85, but for a = 'machin' and b = 'ann', m is 0.6 and $SP(m)$ is 0.31.

The correlation function:

$$AEMI - SP = AEMI \times \frac{SP}{2} \tag{4}$$

The usual range for $AEMI$ is 0.1–0.45 and SP is 0–1. To scale SP to a similar range as $AEMI$, we divide SP by 2.

The MaxChildren

The MaxChildren method is used to dynamically determine a reasonable threshold value to differentiate strong from weak correlation values between a pair of terms. The MaxChildren method selects a threshold such that maximum of child clusters are generated. This ensures that the resulting hierarchy tree does not degenerate too tall and thin. This preference stems from the fact that topics are in general more diverse than detailed and the library catalog taxonomy is typically short and wide. The MaxChildren calculates the number of child clusters for each boundary value between two quantized regions. The method ignores the first half of the boundary values to guarantee the selected threshold is not too low. The MaxChildren method recursively divides the selected best region until there are no changes on the number of child clusters.

SCORING OF THE FILE RETURNED BY TRADITIONAL SEARCH ENGINE

In this section, the ranking algorithm for reordering the search results returned by traditional search engine is discussed. The most important step is scoring each file in the search results. Therefore, a reasonable scoring method should be designed so that the more interesting file would be assigned a higher score. We are inspired by the H R .Kim's work which has made a good example of how to scoring search results depending on UIH (Kim, & Chan, 2006).

Given a file in search results, we firstly identify the terms both occur in the file and **K-UIH**. The number of distinct terms in **K-UIH** is denoted by m, and the number of distinct terms in the file is denoted by n. For each matching term t_i, we compute the score of it according to three sides: the deepest level of a node where a term of belongs to D_{t_i}, the length of a term such as how many words are in the term L_{t_i} and the frequency of a term F_{t_i}. The first one is related to **K-UIH** structure. The terms in more specific interests are harder to match, and the deepest level (depth) where the term matches indicates significance. If a term in a node also appears in several of its ancestors, we use the level (depth) closest to the leaves. The second one is related to the term itself. Longer terms (phrases) are more specific than shorter ones. If a file contains a long search term typed in by investigator, the file is more likely what the investigator is looking for. And the last one is about the importance of the term in file. More frequent terms are more significant than less frequent terms. A document that contains a search term many times will be more related to a investigator's interest than a document that has the term only once. The emphasis of term (such as specially-formatted term) (Kim, & Chan, 2006) is ignored in this work because many of evidences have no visual character. The significance of a term can be measured by estimating the probability. $P(D_{t_i})$ represents the probability of marching term t_i at depth D_{t_i} in **K-UIH**, $P(L_{t_i})$ is defined in the similar way of length L_{t_i}, and $P(F_{t_i})$ represents the one of F_{t_i} in the file. Lower probability indicates the matching term is more significant. Assuming independence among these three characteristics, we estimate the score of term S_{t_i} below:

$$
\begin{cases}
P(D_{t_i}) = \dfrac{\text{number of distinct terms at depth } D_{t_i} \text{ in AUIH}}{m} \\[2ex]
P(L_{t_i}) = \dfrac{\text{number of distinct terms of length } L_{t_i} \text{ in AUIH}}{m} \\[2ex]
P(F_{t_i}) = \dfrac{\text{number of distinct terms with frequency } F_{t_i} \text{ in file}}{n} \\[2ex]
S_{t_i} = -w_1 \log_2 P(D_{t_i}) - w_2 \log_2 P(L_{t_i}) - w_3 \log_2 P(F_{t_i})
\end{cases}
\tag{5}
$$

In this research, the weight is assigned simply $w_1 = w_2 = w_1 = 1/3$.

The score of file is computed by summing the score of each matching term, i.e.

$$
S_{f_i} = \sum_{i=1}^{l} S_{t_i}
\tag{6}
$$

Table 2. The test cases

Case	Description	Evidence size(hard disk)
A	Abusing resource inside the enterprise	40G
B	Drug trafficking via Email	40G
C	Spreading sex information via Internet	40G

where l is the total number of matching terms in a file. The final presentation of search results is arranged in a descend order of file score.

PRELIMINARY EVALUATION

Evaluation Data Set

At the beginning of the evaluation experiments, the test data set of the digital evidences is necessary to be collected. Three mock cases were constructed for the purpose of evaluating the feasibility of the proposed methodology in cyber crime cases. Table 2 lists the detail of cases. The three cases listed in table 2 are all popular in modern society. Another important factor in the evaluation is the set of searching keywords, which will be determined by an experienced volunteer as an investigator. This volunteer should be well familiar with these cases, and has access to the electronic evidence. Hence, we are confident that the keyword set would be realistic and valuable for an investigation.

Performance Evaluating

There are a great many **digital forensic** software integrated with search tool, such as FTK (AccessData) and Encase (Guidance Software). However, many of these tools are insensitive to sorting search results other than group them to simple categories, i.e., hits counts.

We evaluate the performance of the proposed approach by comparing it with the dtSearch tool (DtSearch, 2009). The dtSearch is a common-used desk search tool, which reorders the search results by comprehensively computing file score according their relevancies to the keywords.

The search efficiency of the **digital forensic** can be measured on whether the search hit is relevant to case or interesting to investigator. Thereby, the investigative relevancy of every hit in search results set produced by our method and dtSearch will be determined by the volunteer. To make a quantitative measurement, we categorize relevancy as 'relevant' and 'irrelevant'. A hit is marked as 'relevant' when this hit is important for investigation, and the 'irrelevant' hits are those that have no relation to the case. Given a fix number of search results, more 'relevant' hits represent better performance. Two specific measures precision p and recall r are given as follows:

$$p = \frac{\text{the number of relevant hits}}{\text{the number of total hits}} \tag{7}$$

Table 3. Building the SM with IE Favourites and IE browsing history

Percentage of search hits	10%	20%	50%	100%
Case A	80.5%	82.1%	84.6%	90%
Case B	82.7%	85.5%	87.8%	91.4%
Case C	**89.5%**	**92.0%**	**92.3%**	**95.1%**

$$r = \frac{\text{the number of relevant hits}}{\text{the number of total relevant hits in data set}} \qquad (8)$$

Note that the mainly aim is to reduce time spent on analysing search results, so we mainly focus on the precision of search hits in the experiments.

Experiments

To test the availability of the proposed approach, a test tool is implemented in C under a Linux operation system. There are several factors that affect the performance of the tool. Other than similarity function and threshold finding method discussed in UIH algorithm (Kim, & Chan, 2008), four parameters are important in the proposed approach. Those are the value of s and t in equation 1, the size of keyword set, the percentage of reviewed hits and the scope of training set. We will focus on these factors in the following sections.

The Values of s and t

The first parameter we study is *s* and *t* shown in equation 1 (section 3). The *s* and *t* play important roles in threshold finding stage of the proposed method. Simply, s is selected in set {1.5, 2, 2.5, 3, 3.5}, and t is selected in set {5, 10, 15, 20, 25}. The best precision and recall is achieved when s and t pair is (2.5, 10), which is used in the following experiments.

The Size of Keyword Set

The second parameter is the size of keyword set, i.e. the number of keywords in keyword set. In a sense, single keyword is not enough, and the performance will be better when more keywords occur in SM. On the other side, the investigator would be experienced and not necessary to input too many keywords. Hence, more than 2 keywords are considered in our experiments.

Table 4. Building SM with IE Favourites, IE browsing history and Email archive

Percentage of search hits	10%	20%	50%	100%
Case A	84.5%	86.7%	87.9%	89.0%
Case B	**92.5%**	**93.0%**	**94.4%**	**94.7%**
Case C	85.1%	86.8%	86.5%	88.2%

Table 5. Building SM with all text files in hard disk

Percentage of search hits	10%	20%	50%	100%
Case A	**88.1%**	**89.2%**	**90.7%**	**92.6%**
Case B	84.4%	85.9%	87.7%	90.6%
Case C	87.5%	88.5%	90.2%	92.3%

The Percentage of the Reviewed Hits and the Scope of the Training Set

The proposed approach is based on learning user interest from the electronic evidence. Therefore, the scope of the training set is important for building SM and **K-UIH**. The common text evidences in computer include the IE Favourites, the IE browsing history, the E-mail archive, the desktop files, the 'My Document' files and other text files in hard disk.

Dissimilar user interest hierarchies would be built using different scopes of training set and produced the dissimilar results. Another factor in experiments is the percentage of search hits reviewed by investigator. Because huge amount of hits could be returned by each search process, the investigator would like to find important evidence by reviewing parts of search results. We assumed that the search results are reviewed from end to end. The results using different training sets and different percentages of reviewed hits are illustrated in Table 3, 4, and 5 respectively. The table 3 describes the precisions with different training sets and percentages of reviewed hits when using IE Favourites and IE browsing history build the SM; the table 4 describes the results when using IE Favourites, IE browsing history and Email archive build the SM; and the table 5 describes the results when using all text files in hard disk build the SM. As shown in Table 3, 4, and 5, the best performances (bold) are obtained with different training set for different cases. For example, the suspect of case B, which is about drug trafficking via Email, would left important evidence in Email archive (in table 4). So the precision is higher than others when Email archive occupies moderate part of the training set. In the similar way, we achieve best performance in case C when IE archive is considered well (in table 3). In case A, employee might store key evidence in anyplace of hard disk, hence, so the highest precision is obtained when the whole data are considered (in table 5).

Figure 4. The precision of the proposed approach and dtSearch in case A

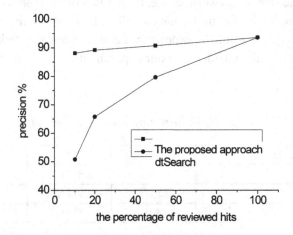

Figure 5. The precision of the proposed approach and dtSearch in case B

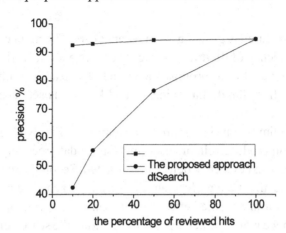

Comparing with dtSearch Tool

In this section, we compare the proposed approach with dtSearch. Different cases are considered singly in this evaluation. The results of the precision of the proposed approach and dtSearch in case A, B, and C are shown in Figure 4, 5, and 6 respectively. where the x-axis represents the the percentage of reviewed hits, and the y-axis represents the precision.

From these figures, we can easily found that higher precision is obtained by the proposed approach, especially when the percentage of reviewed hits is low. It shows that using our proposed approach can locate relevant hits more quickly than using the dtsearch tool.

At last, we should be aware that the proposed method, in some circumstances, there will be some restrictions. For example, in some cases, the investigator is interested in credit card account numbers, so the input keywords can be a digital string, instead of the meaningful terms. However, the search process would be toilless in these cases because a long digital string (i.e., credit card account numbers) may occur in fewer files than a meaningful terms. The proposed method is mainly focused to improve the efficiency of an investigator when he is facing many results returned by the search engine.

Figure 6. The precision of the proposed approach and dtSearch in case C

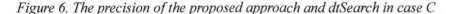

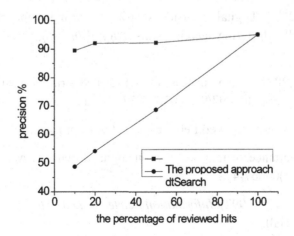

CONCLUSION

The field of **digital forensic** search is growing up in recent years. The main contribution of this chapter is to enhance the search efficiency of **digital forensic**. There are a lot of works about using user interest to improve the search efficiency. In our proposed approach, the search results are reordered based on the **K-UIH**, which is learnt from the digital evidence and keywords set. The experimental results are promising.

However, there are some limitations in our proposed approach. Firstly, there should be more enough text evidence in case that can produce reliable user interest. So data recovery is necessary because the criminal may delete important text evidence before investigated. Secondly, the investigator's experience is another important factor to affect the performance of this approach. The more appropriate keywords proposed by investigator occur in SM, the better presentation of investigator's interest can be given by **K-UIH** and better performance would be achieved. Furthermore, the search efficiency can be improved when the scope of training set is limited according to the specific case. Finally, in our proposed approach, a new **K-UIH** should be built for each new search process, so additional computing is required. However, the primary goal of this work is to reduce human effort on investigation and human time spent on analysing the search results. We endeavour to find some ways to reduce the complexity of the proposed approach, which is part of our future work. We also plan using other elements (e.g., hit counts of web page, access time of file and so on) to build a richer **K-UIH**.

ACKNOWLEDGMENT

This work is based upon work funded by Zhejiang Povincial Natural Science Foundation of China under Grant No. Y1090114, and Zhejiang Povincial Science and Technology Program of China under Grant No. 2008C21075.

REFERENCES

AccessData. Corp. (2009). *Forensic Toolkit.* Retrieved February 1, 2009, from http://accessdata.com/forensictoolkit.html.

Beebe, N., & Clark, J. G. (2007). Digital forensic text string searching–improving information retrieval effectiveness by thematically clustering search results. *Digital Investigation, 4,* 49–54. doi:10.1016/j.diin.2007.06.005

Beebe, N., & Dietrich, G. (2007). A new process model for text string searching. *Advances in Digital Forensics, 3*(242), 179–191. doi:10.1007/978-0-387-73742-3_12

DtSearch, Inc. (2009). *dtSearch.* Retrieved February 5, 2009, from http://www.dtsearch.com/

Forte, D. (2004). The importance of text searches in digital forensics. *Network Security, 4,* 13–15. doi:10.1016/S1353-4858(04)00067-4

Frakes, W. B., & Baeza-Yates, R. (1992). *Information Retrieval: Data Structures and Algorithms.* Upper Saddle River, NJ: Prentice-Hall.

Guidance Software, Inc. (2009). *EnCase Forensic.* Retrieved February 5, 2009, from http://www.guidancesoftware.com/products/ef_index.asp

Jee, H., Lee, J., & Hong, D. (2007). High speed bitwise search for digital forensic system. In *Proceedings of world academy of science, engineering and technology, 26*, 104-107.

Kim, H., & Chan, P. K. (2006). Personalized search results with user interest hierarchies learnt from bookmarks. In *Advances in Web Mining and Web Usage Analysis*, (pp. 158-176). Berlin: Springer.

Kim, H., & Chan, P. K. (2008). Learning implicit user interest hierarchy for context in personalization. *Applied Intelligence, 28*(2), 153–166. doi:10.1007/s10489-007-0056-0

Petrovic, S., & Franke, K. (2007). Improving the efficiency of digital forensic search by means of the constrained edit distance. In *Proceedings of the Third International Symposium on Information Assurance and Security,* IEEE Computer Society, (pp. 405-410).

Rogers, M. (2003). The role of criminal profiling in the computer forensics process. *Computers & Security, 22*(4), 292–298. doi:10.1016/S0167-4048(03)00405-X

Teevan, J., Dumais, S. T., & Horvitz, E. (2005). Personalizing search via automated analysis of interests and activities. In *Proceedings of the 28th annual international ACM SIGIR conference on Research and development in information retrieval*, (pp. 449-456). New York: ACM.

Yang, F. Q., Sun, T. L., & Sun, J. G. (2006). Learning hierarchical user interest models from web pages. *Wuhan University Journal of Natural Sciences, 11*(1), 6–10. doi:10.1007/BF02831694

KEY TERMS AND DEFINITIONS

Digital Forensic: A branch of forensic science pertaining to legal evidence found in computers and digital storage mediums. Digital forensics is also known as computer forensics.

K-UIH(keyword and User Interest Hierarchies): Constructed by both investigator-defined keywords and investigated user interest at different abstraction levels. The investigated user interest can be learned implicitly from the contents (words/phrases) in a set of electronic evidence.

Similarity Matrix: A weight matrix between two words.

Chapter 7
On the Mining of Cointegrated Econometric Models

J. L. van Velsen
Dutch Ministry of Justice, Research and Documentation Centre (WODC), The Netherlands

R. Choenni
Dutch Ministry of Justice, Research and Documentation Centre (WODC), The Netherlands

ABSTRACT

The authors describe a process of extracting a cointegrated model from a database. An important part of the process is a model generator that automatically searches for cointegrated models and orders them according to an information criterion. They build and test a non-heuristic model generator that mines for common factor models, a special kind of cointegrated models. An outlook on potential future developments is given.

INTRODUCTION AND MOTIVATION

Research and development in data mining started with the extraction of association rules from vast amount of data. Today, data mining has evolved in a wide variety of directions, ranging from complexity control of algorithms to the development of applications for many domains, such as counter terrorism, medical diagnosing, marketing and so on (Antonie, Zaïane & Coman, 2001; Bach, 2003; Banek, Min Tjoa & Stolba, 2006; Bhattacharyya, 1999; Choenni, 2000; Wang & Han, 2000). The extraction of econometric models, however, has received relatively little attention in the field of data mining.

An econometric model is a model that specifies the statistical relationship that is believed to hold between its variables. These models play a central role in many fields of research and become increasingly important in forecasting tools. For example, in finance, stock prices may be expressed in terms of other stock prices and macro-economic variables, such as industrial production and interest rates (Cheung & Ng, 1998; Nasseh & Strauss, 2000; Pesaran & Timmermann, 2000). Another example, within government forecasting, is the modelling of recorded crime, which may be expressed in terms of demographic and

DOI: 10.4018/978-1-60566-908-3.ch007

macro-economic variables, such as the number of young males and unemployment (Deadman, 2003; Greenberg, 2001; Hale & Sabbagh, 1991). Two common econometric models are the linear regression model and the cointegrated model.

The parameters of an econometric model are estimated from historical data of the variables. This requires assumptions on how the variables evolve in time. In a linear regression model, all variables are assumed stationary. Loosely speaking, a variable is stationary if its statistical properties, such as its mean, do not depend on time. (We will come to a more precise definition of stationarity in the text.) If one or more variables are non-stationary, the regression is spurious. A well-known example is the regression of two independent integrated variables: Based on statistical significance testing, there seems to be a strong relation between the variables, while, in fact, they are independent (Granger & Newbold, 1974). (An integrated variable is a special kind of non-stationary variable, its definition will be given in the text.)

Today, model generators exist that search for the best linear regression model out of a large group of candidate models. For example, given historical data of a stationary response variable and of a collection of N stationary candidate predictor variables, the program PcGets (Krolzig & Hendry, 2001) heuristically searches for the best model through the set of 2^N-1 candidate models. This generator employs a form of backwards regression: Starting with a large subset of the set of N candidate predictor variables and based on significance testing and information criteria, candidate variables are dropped during iteration steps.

Our objective is the mining of cointegrated models. In this case, the variables evolve in time in such a way that they are all integrated, but linear combinations of the variables exist that are stationary. Cointegrated models are very common in econometric modelling. For a detailed example with two data sets, see (Johansen, 1995). Because cointegrated models cannot be found with a generator that operates under the assumptions of a linear regression model (stationary variables), the mining of cointegrated models is an interesting new development in the mining of econometric models.

The outline of this chapter is as follows. First, we discuss the basics of integration and cointegration and specify the structure of the cointegrated model. Second, we give the exact formulation of the problem. Third, we discuss the process of extracting a cointegrated model from a data set and give the ingredients of a non-heuristic model generator. These ingredients are statistical tests and methods to compare models, such as information criteria. Fourth, we give an example of extracting a cointegrated model from a data set. Fifth, we study the performance of a non-heuristic model generator with a Monte Carlo simulation. Finally, we conclude and give an outlook on further developments.

INTEGRATION, COINTEGRATION AND THE COINTEGRATED MODEL

In this section, we present the structure of the cointegrated model that we want to mine. First, we consider single variables and give the definition of an integrated variable. Second, we discuss the joint dynamics of multiple variables and give an introduction to cointegration. Finally, we come to the cointegrated model.

A Single Variable: Integration

We consider an econometric variable z that is defined at discrete times $at+t_0$. Here, t is a non-negative integer, a is some unit of time, such as a year or a day, and t_0 is the origin of time. The random number z_t denotes the value of the variable at time $at+t_0$. For example, if z is a daily stock price and t_0 is the closing time at a certain initial day, then z_t is the closing price t days later. We now come to the definition of an integrated variable. In order to do so, we first discuss the statistical properties of a stationary variable. For a more formal discussion of stationarity, we refer to text books on time series such as (Hamilton, 1994).

A basic example of a stationary variable z is the so-called autoregressive z satisfying

$$z_t = c + \phi z_{t-1} + \sigma \varepsilon_t \quad with \quad |\phi| < 1 \tag{1}$$

Here, ε_t and $\varepsilon_{t'}$, with $t \neq t'$, are statistically independent Gaussian numbers with vanishing mean and unit variance and c, φ and σ are parameters. The mean μ_t and autocovariance $\gamma_{tt'}$ of z are given by (Hamilton, 1994)

$$\mu_t = <z_t> = \frac{c}{1-\phi} \quad and \quad \gamma_{tt'} = <(z_t - \mu_t)(z_{t'} - \mu_{t'})> = \frac{\sigma^2 \phi^{|t-t'|}}{1-\phi^2}, \tag{2}$$

where "$<>$" denotes a statistical average. The essential thing of Eq. (2) is that μ_t does not depend on t and that $\gamma_{tt'}$ depends only on on the absolute time-difference $|t-t'|$. In other words, μ_t and $\gamma_{tt'}$ do not change if we shift time or interchange t and t'. Because of these properties, z is a stationary variable. The result for the mean of z can be understood by writing Eq. (1) in error correction (EC) form:

$$\Delta z_t = c + (\varphi - 1)z_{t-1} + \sigma \varepsilon_t. \tag{3}$$

Here, Δ is the difference operator defined as $\Delta z_t = z_t - z_{t-1}$. If $c + (\varphi - 1)z_{t-1} > 0$ (or equivalently $z_{t-1} < c/(1-\varphi)$), then $<\Delta z_t> > 0$ and if $c + (\varphi - 1)z_{t-1} < 0$ (or equivalently $z_{t-1} > c/(1-\varphi)$), then $<\Delta z_t> < 0$. That is, the term $c + (\varphi - 1)z_{t-1}$ in Eq. (3) drives z towards $c/(1-\varphi)$, which is the mean of z cf. Eq. (2). For this reason, $c + (\varphi - 1)z_{t-1}$ is called the EC term of Eq. (3).

A variable is integrated of order p (or I(p) for short) if $\Delta^h z$ is stationary for $h=p$ while it is non-stationary for $0 \leq h < p$. Here, p is a positive integer and h is a non-negative integer. (By definition, the operator Δ^0 equals multiplication with unity.) An example of an I(1) variable is the random walk z satisfying

$$z_t = c + z_{t-1} + \sigma \varepsilon_t. \tag{4}$$

The mean and autocovariance of the random walk are given by

$$\mu_t = z_0 + ct \quad and \quad \gamma_{tt'} = \sigma^2 \min(t, t'). \tag{5}$$

Because μ_t depends on t and $\gamma_{tt'}$ does not depend on $|t-t'|$, the random walk is non-stationary. By writing Eq. (4) as

$$\Delta z_t = c + \sigma \varepsilon_t, \tag{6}$$

we see that Δz is stationary. From this it follows that the random walk is an I(1) variable. Note that, unlike the EC form (3) of the autoregressive z, the right-hand-side of Eq. (6) has no term that corrects Δz_t.

Many econometric variables are integrated rather than stationary. For example, the return of a stock price z is generally assumed stationary. The return at time $at+t_0$ is defined as $(z_t - z_{t-1})/z_{t-1}$ and approximately equals $\Delta \ln(z_t)$. Here, "ln" denotes the natural logaritm. This means that $\Delta \ln(z)$ is stationary and $\ln(z)$ is an I(1) variable.

Multiple Variables: Cointegration

In the previous section, we discussed individual variables. Now, we consider the joint dynamics of $M \geq 2$ variables collected in an M-dimensional columnvector Z. The vector Z satisfies

$$Z_t = C + (1_M + \alpha\beta^T)Z_{t-1} + \Sigma^{1/2}E_t,$$
(7)

or, equivalently, as a vector error correction model (VECM),

$$\Delta Z_t = C + \alpha\beta^T Z_{t-1} + \Sigma^{1/2}E_t.$$
(8)

Here, 1_M is the $M \times M$ identity matrix, α and β are $M \times r$ matrices of rank $r \leq M$, C is an M-dimensional columnvector of constants, Σ is an $M \times M$ covariance matrix and E is an M-dimensional Gaussian columnvector. The symbol "T" denotes the transpose of a matrix or vector. The matrices α and β are such that $(1_M + \alpha\beta^T)$ has r eigenvalues within the complex unit circle.

The joint model of Eq. (7) is a multivariate generalization of Eqs. (1) and (4). If $r=0$ (this means that α and β are absent), then it is a generalization of Eq. (4) and if $r=M$, then it is a generalization of Eq. (1). (Similarly, Eq. (8) is a multivariate generalization of Eq. (6) if $r=0$ and of Eq. (3) if $r=M$.) Remarkably, because $M \geq 2$, there exists an intermediate regime with $0 < r < M$ in which all variables of Z are I(1) but there exist linear combinations of the variables that are stationary. In this regime, we say that Z is cointegrated. The interpretation of cointegration is as follows: The non-stationary parts of all M variables of Z can be written as linear combinations of a *smaller* number of $(M-r)$ distinct random walks. Because there are less random walks than variables, there exist linear combinations of the variables in which the random walks drop out. The M prefactors of such linear combinations are said to constitute M-dimensional cointegration vectors. A superposition of two cointegration vectors is again a cointegration vector. That is, cointegration vectors are not unique. However, the r-dimensional space spanned by the cointegration vectors is unique and equals col(β), where "col" denotes the columnspace of a matrix.

To give a definite example of cointegration, we have simulated Eq. (7) with M=4, r=2, C=0 and

$$\alpha = \frac{1}{2}\begin{pmatrix} -1 & 0 \\ -1 & 1 \\ 0 & 0 \\ 0 & 0 \end{pmatrix}, \quad \beta = \begin{pmatrix} 1 & 1 \\ 0 & -1 \\ 0 & -1 \\ -1/2 & 1/2 \end{pmatrix}, \quad \Sigma = \begin{pmatrix} 1 & 0 & 0 & 1/2 \\ 0 & 1 & 0 & 0 \\ 0 & 0 & 1 & 0 \\ 1/2 & 0 & 0 & 1 \end{pmatrix}$$
(9)

Figure 1. The non-stationary variables Z_1, Z_2, Z_3 and Z_4 as a function of t (a) and the stationary linear combination corresponding to the first column of β (b) and the second column of β (c)

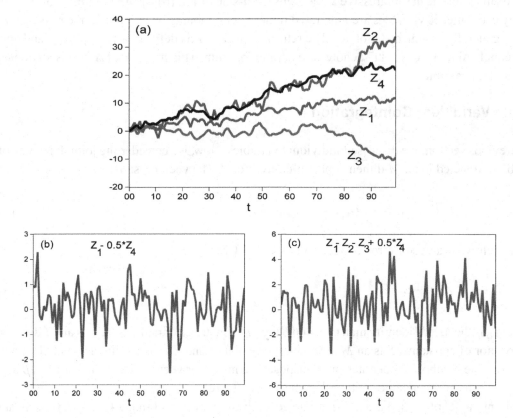

The results of the simulation are presented in Fig. 1. In panel (a), we have plotted all four variables of Z as a function of t with $t \in \{0,..,99\}$. In panels (b) and (c), we have plotted the stationary variables corresponding to, respectively, the first and second column of β. In the simulation, we have chosen a specific stochastic initial condition for Z. To understand why this is necessary, consider simulating the autoregressive z of Eq. (1). This would require a Gaussian with mean $c/(1-\varphi)$ and variance $\sigma^2/(1-\varphi^2)$ for the initial condition. Note that in Fig. 1, Z_1, Z_2, Z_3 and Z_4 denote the four elements of Z, *not* the vector Z at t=1 to 4. From now on, Z with a single index either refers to Z at a certain time or to a certain element of Z (a variable). Which of the two applies will be clear from the context.

The Cointegrated Model

In the previous subsection, we discussed the joint dynamics of the M variables of Z. Now, we wish to relate one of these variables, say Z_1, to the other variables Z_i with $i \in \{2,..,M\}$. The relevance of this relation will be explained in the next section ("Formulation of the problem"). The relation takes the form

$$\Delta Z_{1,t} = c + \sum_{i=2}^{M} \xi_i \Delta Z_{i,t} + \lambda \left(Z_{1,t-1} - \sum_{i=2}^{M} \vartheta_i Z_{i,t-1} \right) + \sigma \varepsilon_t. \tag{10}$$

The model of Eq. (10) is called a partial or conditional error correction model (ECM): Given its parameters c, ξ_i, θ_i, λ and σ, we may generate data for Z_1 provided that we are given data for Z_i with $i \in \{2,..,M\}$. The parameters of Eq. (10) are a function of C, α, β and Σ (Johansen, 1995). Without giving the detailed connection here, we note that $\lambda=0$ corresponds to $r=0$ (Z is not cointegrated) and that $\lambda<0$ corresponds to $0<r<M$ (Z is cointegrated). In the first case ($\lambda=0$), the partial model is a linear regression model and in the second case ($\lambda<0$), it is a cointegrated model. The model (10) is the central result of this section: with $\lambda<0$, it is the cointegrated model that we want to mine from a database. Note that, in this case, because the ΔZ_i with $i \in \{1,..,M\}$ are stationary, the term with the brackets in Eq. (10) (the EC term) is stationary as well. That is, the M-dimensional columnvector $(1,-\theta)^T$ is a cointegration vector. (By definition, the i-th element of the (M-1)-dimensional rowvector θ equals θ_{i+1}.) If $\lambda=0$, the EC term is switched off and no linear combination of the elements of Z exists that is stationary.

To conclude this section, we give three definite examples of the relation between the joint model (8) and the partial model (10). In all three examples, Z is cointegrated and we set $C=0$. First, with the matrices of Eq. (9), we have $c=0$, $\lambda=-1$, $\theta=\xi=(0,0,1/2)$ (the vector ξ is defined in the same way as θ) and $\sigma=(1/2)\sqrt{3}$:

$$Z_{1,t} = \frac{1}{2}Z_{4,t} + \frac{\sqrt{3}}{2}\varepsilon_t. \qquad (11)$$

Note that the cointegrated model (11) corresponds to the linear combination in panel (b) of Fig. 1. Second, if we scale the matrices α and β of Eq. (9) such that $\alpha\beta^T \rightarrow \alpha\beta^T/2$, then we have $c=0$, $\lambda=-1/2$, $\theta=\xi=(0,0,1/2)$ and $\sigma=(1/2)\sqrt{3}$:

$$\Delta Z_{1,t} = \frac{1}{2}\Delta Z_{4,t} - \frac{1}{2}\left(Z_{1,t-1} - \frac{1}{2}Z_{4,t-1}\right) + \frac{\sqrt{3}}{2}\varepsilon_t, \qquad (12)$$

or, equivalently,

$$Z_{1,t} = \frac{1}{2}Z_{4,t} + \eta_t, \quad \eta_t = \frac{1}{2}\eta_{t-1} + \frac{\sqrt{3}}{2}\varepsilon_t. \qquad (13)$$

Finally, if we take the matrices α and β of Eq. (9) and $\Sigma=1_4$, then we have $c=0$, $\lambda=-1$, $\xi=(0,0,0)$, $\theta=(0,0,1/2)$ and $\sigma=1$:

$$\Delta Z_{1,t} = -\left(Z_{1,t-1} - \frac{1}{2}Z_{4,t-1}\right) + \varepsilon_t,$$

or, equivalently,

$$Z_{1,t} = \frac{1}{2}Z_{4,t-1} + \varepsilon_t. \qquad (14)$$

The relation between Z_1 and Z_4 is instantaneous in Eqs. (11) and (12) and retarded in Eq. (14). The difference between Eqs. (11) and (12) is that in the first, the autocovariance $\gamma_{tt'}$ of $Z_1-(1/2)Z_4$ is given by Eq. (2) with $\varphi=0$ while in the latter, it is given by Eq. (2) with $\varphi=1/2$. The models of Eqs. (11) and (12) are called common factor models because $\theta=\xi$. The instantaneous relation between Z_1 and Z_4 is a result of $\theta=\xi$.

FORMULATION OF THE PROBLEM

We are given a database holding a set $\{Z_{1,t}{}^*;t=\{0,..,T-1\}\}$ of T realizations of Z_1 (the variable we want to model) and a set $\{Z_{i,t}{}^*;i=\{2,..,M\},t=\{0,..,T-1\}\}$ of T realizations of $(M-1)$ variables Z_i with $i\in\{2,..,M\}$ (the variables on which Z_1 may depend). In the regime of tall data ($T \gg M$), one can reliably estimate the full model (8), but the corresponding partial model (10) is not immediately clear. In the regime of wide data ($M \gg T$), one cannot estimate the full model. In the same regime, however, partial models of the form of (10) with less parameters than T can be estimated. From these considerations, it follows that partial models are the natural choice when mining a database. There is, however, one major drawback to partial models: If Z_i with $i\in\{2,..,M\}$ are not weakly exogenous (Engle, Hendry & Richard, 1983) for the parameters of the partial model, then estimates of its parameters are inefficient. (This is generally not known beforehand and has to be checked empirically.)

Our objective is to find the cointegrated model of the form (10) from a set Q of candidate models. (Note that we generally do not know beforehand that the cointegrated model exists. This is a thing that has to be checked empirically.) In the regime of tall data, the set of $2^{M-1}(2^{M-1}-1)$ candidate models Q is defined as

$$Q = \{\Delta Z_{1,t}^* = c^* + \sum_{i\in H}\xi_i^*\Delta Z_{i,t} + \lambda^*(Z_{1,t-1} - \sum_{i\in S}\vartheta_i^*Z_{i,t-1}^*) + \sigma^*\varepsilon_t^*; H \in P(\{2,..,M\}), S \in P(\{2,..,M\}) \setminus \{\}\}$$

(15)

Here, the starred parameters denote maximum likelihood (ML) estimates based on the T realizations of Z, ε_t^* with $t=\{1,..,T-1\}$ are the residuals, $P(\{2,..,M\})$ is the power set of $\{2,..,M\}$ and $\{\}$ denotes the empty set. In the regime of wide data, Q is defined in the same way, but models with more than $T-1$ parameters are excluded. This means that Q holds

$$\sum_{m=0}^{T-5}\binom{M-1}{m} \sum_{l=1}^{T-4-m}\binom{M-1}{l}$$

models.

Because the number of elements of Q grows exponentially with M for tall data and exponentially with T for wide data, the search through Q can generally not be done manually and requires some sort of automated approach. Also, the number of elements of Q is often too large to allow for a full search through Q. That is, one has to come up with an algorithm to heuristically search through Q. Another way to control the complexity is to consider restricted sets Q' such as the common factor sets with $c^*=0$, $H=S$ and $\xi^*=\theta^*$ and with $c^*=0$, $\lambda^*=-1$, $H=S$ and $\xi^*=\theta^*$. (By definition, the i-th element of the

(M-1)-dimensional rowvector ξ^* equals ξ^*_{i+1} if $i+1 \in H$ and vanishes otherwise; The same holds for the elements of θ^*.) The disadvantage of restricted sets is that the cointegrated model may not be in Q'. (This objective can be overcome by checking the elements Q'.)

As an example of a tall data set, consider the realizations plotted in Fig. 1. This corresponds to M=4 and T=100. The set Q holds 56 models and the restricted set Q' with c^*=0, λ^*=-1, H=S and ξ^*=θ^* holds 7 models. Given these data, we wish to establish that Eq. (11) is the cointegrated model of Z_1. In other words, our objective (data $\rightarrow$ cointegrated model) is nearly the exact opposite of what we have done in the simulation example (joint model $\rightarrow$ data).

THE PROCESS OF SELECTING A MODEL WITH A NON-HEURISTIC MODEL GENERATOR

The process of selecting an element of Q (or Q') is indicated in Fig. 2 and consists of three blocks: A preliminary data analysis (I), building, checking and comparing all elements of Q (or Q') (II) and validating the final model (III). The second block is automated with a non-heuristic model generator. The first block can be done manually or be incorporated in the generator. The third block, however, deals with the interpretation and plausibility of models and has to be done manually. We now describe the contents of the three blocks (the gray boxes in Fig. 2) in the following subsections.

Preliminary Data Analysis

In both data regimes, we verify that all M variables of Z are I(1) (a necessary condition for cointegration) by doing ADF tests (Said & Dickey, 1984). In addition, for tall data, we perform a Johansen trace test (Johansen, 1995) on the joint model. The null hypothesis of this test is that r={0,..,M-1} and the alternative hypothesis is that all variables are stationary (r=M). Starting with r=0, we continue by raising r with unity until the null hypothesis is not rejected (say at the 0.05 level). If we find that 0<r<M, then Z is cointegrated. (By putting restrictions on β, we can also do an additional check (on top the ADF tests) that all M variables of Z are I(1).)

For tall data, we check if the residuals E^* of the joint model (8) have no serial correlation. (This can, of course, not be done for wide data.) To test for this, we use an LM test (Johansen, 1995). In case of serial correlation, we extend the right-hand-side of (8) with lagged ΔZ_t. This means that (10) should also be extended with lagged first-differenced variables and that Q is to be redefined accordingly.

Building, Checking and Comparing Models

After building all elements of Q, the generator first needs to create the set q $\subset$ Q of well-specified models. Second, it needs to compare the elements of q and select the best model.

Checking Models and Creating q

A model becomes an element of q if it passes three kinds of tests:

Figure 2. Schematic representation of the process of extracting a model from the data

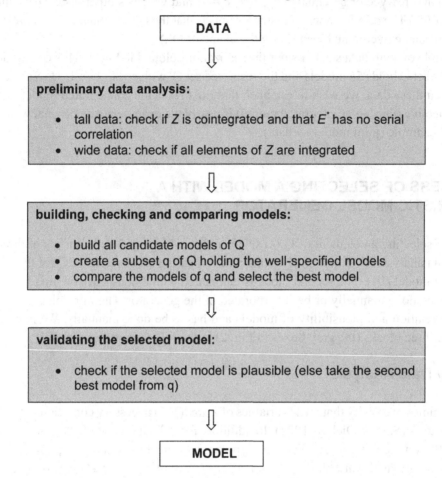

1. A cointegration test
2. A test if the residuals ε_t^* have no serial correlation
3. A test if the estimated cointegration vector $(1, -\theta^*)$ suffers from strong exogeneity

Cointegration Tests

There are two tests for cointegration in partial models: ECM tests and the Engle-Granger (EG) test. In the ECM test of Banerjee, Dolado, Hendry and Smith (1986) one tests for $\lambda=0$ (no cointegration) versus $\lambda<0$ (cointegration) while treating the $\lambda\theta_i$'s as free parameters. The EG test (Engle & Granger, 1987) consists of estimating the EC term (the term in brackets on the right-hand-side of Eq. (10)) and the null hypothesis is that the EC term has a unit root (no cointegration) and the alternative is that the EC term is stationary (cointegration). Both tests have their advantages and disadvantages (Ericsson & MacKinnon, 2002). Generally, ECM tests perform much better than the EG test. However, for a common factor model, both tests have the same performance, but the EG test does not require weak exogeneity.

Serial Correlation

The residuals ε_t^* may not have any serial correlation, else the regression is spurious. To test for this, we use the BG LM test (Breusch, 1978; Godfrey, 1978). The null hypothesis of this test is that the residuals have no serial correlation and the alternatives are that the residuals have an autoregressive moving average parametrization up to a certain order d, typically $d=1$ or $d=2$.

Strong Exogeneity

To check whether the estimated cointegration vector $(1,-\theta^*)$ has suffered from strong exogeneity, the generator imposes the restriction that $(1,-\theta^*)$ is in $col(\beta')$. Here, β' is the matrix corresponding to the joint model holding all variables in the cointegrated model (for wide data) and $\beta'=\beta$ (for tall data). The matrix β' is estimated with the restriction that $(1,-\theta^*)$ is in its columnspace and rejection of the null hypothesis indicates that $(1,-\theta^*)$ has suffered from strong exogeneity (Johansen, 1995).

Selecting the Best Model

The elements of q are compared with BIC (Schwarz, 1978), which trades off the quality of the fit (sum of squared residuals) and the number of parameters to achieve that fit. A perfect fit with a large number of parameters and a very loose fit with only one parameter, are generally not preferred by BIC. These extreme cases correspond to, respectively, extracting too much and too little information from the data set. Extracting too much information is bad because the data set is just some specific collection of re-alizations that could easily have been different and extracting too little information is bad for obvious reasons. (The criterion BIC requires ML estimation, which motivates the ML estimation in Eq. (15).)

Validating the Selected Model

Before accepting a model, we must inspect its parameters to make sure it makes sense. Particularly for wide data, there will be models that meet all statistical tests, but cannot be argued to be plausible.

EXTRACTING A MODEL FROM THE DATA OF THE SIMULATION EXAMPLE

In this section, we manually investigate the data set of Fig. 1. ADF tests indicate that none of the four variables of Z rejects the null hypothesis of a unit root with a constant (the smallest of the four prob-abilities equals 0.69). Because $T>>M$, the data are tall and we can estimate the joint model (8). The Johansen trace test indicates $r=2$ (probabilities of the null with $r=0$ and $r=1$ equal 0.00, while the prob-ability of the null with $r=2$ equals 0.14). As an additional check that the variables are non-stationary, we restrict one of the two columns of β by setting three out of its four elements to zero (the estimated non-vanishing element picks up one of the four variables). The probabilities of the nulls corresponding to the four restricted β's all vanish. To conclude the preliminary analysis, we perform an LM test on E^*. The probabilities of no serial correlation at lags one and two, equal, respectively, 0.41 and 0.90, such that (8) is well-specified.

We now define the restricted set Q' of 7 models with $c^*=0$, $\lambda^*=-1$, $S=H$ and $\theta^*=\varphi^*$ and build, check and compare the elements of Q'. Because Q' is a set of common factor models, we use the EG proce-dure to check for cointegration. The results are listed in Tab. 1. To graphically illustrate the meaning of the EG test, we have plotted the residuals of models 1 and 2 in Fig. 3. Note that the EG test unjustfully indicates that model 3 is cointegrated. In conclusion, for this particular data set, we have found the cor-rect cointegrated model (11).

A MONTE CARLO SIMULATION

In the previous section, we have found the correct cointegrated model (11) for a particular data set. In this section, we generate 10000 data sets (realizations of Z) and build a non-heuristic model generator that automatically performs the same tasks as the ones of the previous section (building all elements of Q' with $c^*=0$, $\lambda^*=-1$, $S=H$ and $\theta^*=\varphi^*$, calculating the EG and BG LM statistics, calculating BIC and selecting the best model out of the well-specified ones). We consider two cases: case I where the parameters of Eq. (8) are that of the simulation example (the correct cointegrated model is given by Eq. (11)) and case II where we scale the matrices α and β such that $\alpha\beta^{\mathrm{T}} \to \alpha\beta^{\mathrm{T}}/2$ (the correct cointegrated model is now given by Eq. (12) and is not an element of Q'.)

Like in the previous section, we consider a model cointegrated if the EG probability is less than 0.05. For the BG LM statistic (with $d=2$), however, we consider three possibilities: rejection of a model if the probability of its residuals having no serial correlation is lower 0.10, 0.05 or 0.00 (the last corresponds to switching off the BG LM test). Taking a higher critical BG LM probability means that in case I, the generator will more often reject the correct cointegrated model than for a lower critical BG LM probability. That is, the generator more often makes a type I error (rejection of the true model). On the other hand, in case II, a higher critical BG LM probability more often signifies that the correct cointegrated model is not in Q' than a lower critical BG LM probability. That is, the generator is more often prevented from making a type II error (accepting a false model).

The results of the Monte Carlo simulation are given in Fig. 4. As expected, a low critical BG LM probability is advantageous in case I ($\lambda=-1$) and a high critical BG LM probability is advantageous in case II ($\lambda=-1/2$).

Figure 4. Results of the Monte Carlo simulation for case I ($\lambda=-1$) and case II ($\lambda=-1/2$). The numbers 1 to 7 on the horizontal axis of each graph indicate the models of Q' cf. the numbering of Tab. 1. The

Figure 3. Residuals of model 1 (left panel, lower solid line) and model 2 (right panel, lower solid line). The residuals of model 1 are clearly stationary (vanishing EG probability) while that of 2 are non-stationary (EG probability equals 0.58). The scales on the left of the two panels correspond to the residuals, the scales on the right correspond to Z_1 (upper solid lines) and the fitted Z_1 (dashed lines).

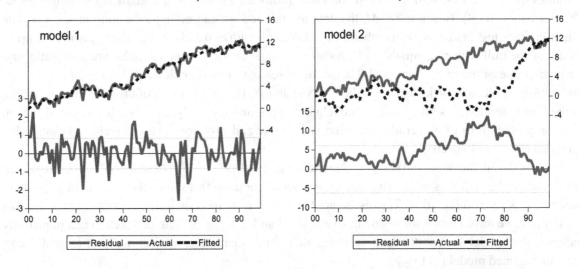

Table 1. Results of checking and comparing the 7 models of Q'. The column 'EG' holds the probabilities that the residuals have a unit root (according to the critical values of MacKinnon (1996)). The column 'BG LM' holds the probabilities that the residuals have no serial correlation (for the alternatives, we used d=2). The column 'BIC' holds the numerical values of BIC. A cross denotes rejection of a model (based on the EG and BG LM test). Models 1,4,5,6 and 7 are well-specified and model 1 is selected the best model because it has the lowest BIC (indicated with an arterisk).

model	S	EG	BG LM	BIC
1 *	{4}	0.00	1.00	2.51
2 X	{3}	0.58 X	0.00 X	6.51
3 X	{2}	0.00	0.00 X	3.96
4	{3,4}	0.00	1.00	2.55
5	{2,4}	0.00	0.99	2.55
6	{2,3}	0.00	1.00	3.26
7	{2,3,4}	0.00	1.00	2.59

number 8 means that the generator rejects all models in Q'. The vertical axis indicates the frequency of the selected model.

CONCLUSION AND FUTURE RESEARCH

In conclusion, we have described a process of extracting a cointegrated model from a database holding T realizations of a response variable and T realizations of $(M\text{-}1)$ potential predictor variables. This process consists of a preliminary data analysis (step I), building, checking and comparing models (step II) and a posterior analysis (step III). The essential ingredients of step II are a cointegration check (EG or ECM test), checking if the residuals have no serial correlation (BG LM test) and comparing the well-specified models with BIC. We have built a non-heuristic model generator that mines for common factor models and simulated its behavior with several critical BG LM probabilities to investigate the trade-off between type I and type II errors.

In future work, one can go beyond the simulated generator in two ways: letting go of the restriction of common factor models and making the search heuristic to control the complexity. For common factor models, a heuristic search can be done as follows. Starting with a large subset of potential predictor variables, we remove a predictor variable and see if the corresponding model is well-specified. This is done for all predictor variables separately and out of the resulting well-specified models, we take the one with the smallest BIC - provided that its BIC is smaller than that of the larger model - and repeat the procedure from there. By choosing several initial conditions (the large subsets of potential predictor variables), we can reduce the probability of getting stuck in a model that is only optimal locally. The initial conditions should be such that each potential predictor variable is considered in several combinations with other potential predictor variables. Without the restriction of common factor models, a heuristic search is more complicated because one has to distinguish between predictor variables inside and outside the EC term. In this case, there are several possibilities: We can, for example, remove predictor variables outside and inside the EC term sequentially; Another strategy is to remove predictor variables outside the EC term while, at each step, perform a heuristic search through all possibilities inside the EC term.

REFERENCES

Antonie, M.-L., Zaïane, O. R., & Coman, A. (2001). Application of data mining techniques for medical image classification. In O. R. Zaïane & S. J. Simoff (Eds.), *Proc. 2nd Int. Workshop on Multimedia Data Mining (MDM/KDD2001)* (pp. 94-101).

Bach, M. P. (2003). Data mining applications in public organizations. In L. Budin, V. Lužar-Stiffler, Z. Bekić & V. H. Dobrić (Eds.), *Proc. of the 25th Int. Conf. on Information Technology Interfaces* (pp. 211-216). Zagreb, Croatia: SRCE University Computing Centre.

Banek, M., Min Tjoa, A., & Stolba, N. (2006). In A. Min Tjoa & J. Trujillo (Eds.), *Lecture Notes in Computer Science 4081* (pp. 185-194). Berlin: Springer.

Banerjee, A., Dolado, J. J., Hendry, D. F., & Smith, G. W. (1986). Exploring equilibrium relationships in econometrics through static models: Some Monte Carlo evidence. *Oxford Bulletin of Economics and Statistics, 48*(3), 253–277.

Bhattacharyya, S. (1999). Direct marketing performance modeling using genetic algorithms. *INFORMS Journal on Computing, 11*(3), 248–257. doi:10.1287/ijoc.11.3.248

Breusch, T. S. (1978). Testing for autocorrelation in dynamic linear models. *Australian Economic Papers, 17*(31), 334–355. doi:10.1111/j.1467-8454.1978.tb00635.x

Cheung, Y.-W., & Ng, L. K. (1998). International evidence on the stock market and aggregate economic activity. *Journal of Empirical Finance, 5*(3), 281–296. doi:10.1016/S0927-5398(97)00025-X

Choenni, R. (2000). Design and implementation of a genetic-based algorithm for data mining. In A. El Abbadi, M. L. Brodie, S. Chakravarthy, U. Dayal, N. Kamel, G. Schlageter & K.-Y. Whang (Eds.), *Proc. of the 26th Int. Conf. on Very Large Data Bases (VLDB)* (pp. 33-42). San Francisco: Morgan Kaufmann Publishers Inc.

Deadman, D. (2003). Forecasting residential burglary. *International Journal of Forecasting, 19*(4), 567–578. doi:10.1016/S0169-2070(03)00091-8

Engle, R. F., & Granger, C. W. J. (1987). Co-integration and error-correction: Representation, estimation and testing. *Econometrica, 55*, 251–276. doi:10.2307/1913236

Engle, R. F., Hendry, D. F., & Richard, J.-F. (1983). Exogeneity. *Econometrica, 51*(2), 277–304. doi:10.2307/1911990

Ericsson, N. R., & MacKinnon, J. G. (2002). Distributions of error correction tests for cointegration. *The Econometrics Journal, 5*(2), 285. doi:10.1111/1368-423X.00085

Godfrey, L. G. (1978). Testing against general autoregressive and moving average error models when the regressors include lagged dependent variables. *Econometrica, 46*(6), 1293–1301. doi:10.2307/1913829

Granger, C. W. J., & Newbold, P. (1974). Spurious regression in econometrics. *Journal of Econometrics, 2*, 111–120. doi:10.1016/0304-4076(74)90034-7

Greenberg, D. F. (2001). Time series analysis of crime rates. *Journal of Quantitative Criminology, 17*(4), 291–327. doi:10.1023/A:1012507119569

Hale, C., & Sabbagh, D. (1991). Testing the relationship between unemployment and crime: A methodological comment and empirical analysis using time series data from England and Wales. *Journal of Research in Crime and Delinquency, 28*(4), 400. doi:10.1177/0022427891028004002

Hamilton, J. D. (1994). *Time Series Analysis.* Princeton, NJ: Princeton University Press.

Johansen, S. (1995). *Likelihood-Based Inference in Cointegrated Vector Autoregressive Models.* Oxford, UK: Oxford University Press.

Krolzig, H.-M., & Hendry, D. F. (2001). Computer automation of general-to-specific model selection procedures. *Journal of Economic Dynamics & Control, 25*(6-7), 831–866. doi:10.1016/S0165-1889(00)00058-0

MacKinnon, J. G. (1996). Numerical distribution functions for unit root and cointegration tests. *Journal of Applied Econometrics, 11*(6), 601–618. doi:10.1002/(SICI)1099-1255(199611)11:6<601::AID-JAE417>3.0.CO;2-T

Nasseh, A., & Strauss, J. (2000). Stock prices and domestic and international macroeconomic activity: A cointegration approach. *The Quarterly Review of Economics and Finance, 40*(2), 229–245. doi:10.1016/S1062-9769(99)00054-X

Pesaran, M. H., & Timmermann, A. (2000). A recursive approach to predicting UK stock returns. *The Economic Journal, 110*(460), 159–191. doi:10.1111/1468-0297.00495

Said, S. E., & Dickey, D. A. (1984). Testing for unit roots in autoregressive-moving average models of unknown order. *Biometrika, 71*(3), 599–607. doi:10.1093/biomet/71.3.599

Schwarz, G. (1978). Estimating the dimension of a model. *Annals of Statistics, 6*(2), 461–464. doi:10.1214/aos/1176344136

Wang, K., He, Y., & Han, J. (2000). Mining frequent itemsets using support constraints. In A. El Abbadi, M. L. Brodie, S. Chakravarthy, U. Dayal, N. Kamel, G. Schlageter & K.-Y. Whang (Eds.), *Proc. of the 26th Int. Conf. on Very Large Data Bases (VLDB)* (pp. 43-52). San Francisco CA: Morgan Kaufmann Publishers Inc.

Chapter 8
Spreading Activation Methods

Alexander Troussov
IBM, Ireland

Eugene Levner
Holon Institute of Technology and Bar-Ilan University, Israel

Cristian Bogdan
KTH – Royal Institute of Technology, Sweden

John Judge
IBM, Ireland

Dmitri Botvich
Waterford Institute of Technology, Ireland

ABSTRACT

Spreading activation (also known as spread of activation) is a method for searching associative networks, neural networks or semantic networks. The method is based on the idea of quickly spreading an associative relevancy measure over the network. The goal is to give an expanded introduction to the method. The authors will demonstrate and describe in sufficient detail that this method can be applied to very diverse problems and applications. They present the method as a general framework. First they will present this method as a very general class of algorithms on large (or very large) so-called multidimensional networks which will serve a mathematical model. Then they will define so-called micro-applications of the method including local search, relationship/association search, polycentric queries, computing of dynamic local ranking, etc. Finally they will present different applications of the method including ontology-based text processing, unsupervised document clustering, collaborative tagging systems, etc.

INTRODUCTION

The proliferation of Web 2.0 and Enterprise 2.0 technologies has lead to the emergence of massive networks connecting people and various digital artifacts. The efficiency of human navigation in such networks depends on the availability of a powerful and intelligent backend which provides guidance

DOI: 10.4018/978-1-60566-908-3.ch008

and recommendations. Spreading activation, as a versatile graphmining tool, which has near linear performance, might soon play a significant role in the engineering of software for Web 2.0 applications. There is an increased need for a new generic and formal understanding of spreading activation as a class of algorithms rather than a particular algorithm with many parameters.

In this chapter we will provide both high level formal general description of the method as well as provide different applications of the framework.

We present spreading activation in a generic form, as a set of methods suitable for mining multidimensional networks with oriented weighted links. These graphmining methods might produce results similar to those which might be achieved by soft clustering and fuzzy inferencing. The input object is a function on nodes of the network, and the spread of activation is a technique which provides "spreading" of this function through the network links. The result of the spreading activation is a new function on the nodes. The properties of that function strongly depend on the original function and the parameters of the spreading activation. For instance, when the underlying network is a network of ontological concepts, parameters governing spread might be chosen in such a way that allows "smoothing" of the original function and interpreting the resulting function as "conceptual" summaries of the initial non-zero valued nodes.

Methods of spreading activation are inherently methods of so called "soft computing" and in the applications section we will demonstrate that spreading activation is able to model very complex phenomena taking into account the inherently imprecise dimensions of nuanced empirical reality, like natural language processing and social network analysis.

Web 2.0 and Enterprise 2.0 trends encourage the use of data before providing a fully developed structure and, consequently, this leads to the creation of massive multidimensional networks. Web 2.0 relies on social networking, and some level of ambiguity is innate in social interaction. Even those networks which supposed to support annotation and categorization of content, like folksonomies, don't posses "the truth, the whole truth, nothing but the truth". Spreading activation, as a method tolerant to incompleteness, errors and inconsistencies in data, scalable and fast, is a graphmining technique which can be used for Web 2.0 applications.

This chapter provides a survey of the literature, and is illustrated by use cases from the EU Project Nepomuk (which built a social semantic desktop). New experimental materials are based on exploitation of the IBM spreading activation based library "IBM LanguageWare Multidimensional Network Miner for Socio-Semantic Applications" (which is freely available for download from IBM site for emergent technologies alphaWorks).

SPREADING ACTIVATION METHODS FRAMEWORK (SAM FRAMEWORK)

In this section we'll introduce spreading activation (a phenomenon observed in the nervous systems of living organisms) as a cognitive psychology phenomenon, provide a description of graph algorithms imitating this phenomenon, and we will trace the roots of activation spread method back to numerical simulations in physics.

Origin of Spreading Activation Methods

In neurophysiology interactions between neurons is modeled by way of activation which propagates from one neuron to another via connections called synapses to transmit information using chemical signals. The first spreading activation models were used in cognitive psychology to model this processes of memory retrieval (Collins, A.M. & Loftus, E.F., 1975; Anderson, J.,1983).

This framework was later exploited in Artificial Intelligence (AI) as a processing framework for semantic networks and ontologies, and applied to Information Retrieval (Crestani, F., 1997; Aleman-Meza, Halaschek, Arpinar, & Sheth, 2003; Rocha, C, Schwabe, D. & Poggi de Aragao, M., 2004; Schumacher, K., Sintek, M. & Sauermann, L., 2008) as the result of direct transfer of information retrieval ideas from cognitive sciences to AI. There are also various papers where the same methods were proposed without mentioning activation spread – in computer supported cooperative work (Sandor, O., Bogdan, C. & Bowers, J., 1997), in graph-clustering (Stein, B. & Nigemman, O., 1999).

Although the idea expressed in the name of the model (Anderson, J.,1983) "A spreading activation theory of memory" allows us to understand many features of graph-methods exposed in this chapter and see potential domains of application; this model can't be directly translated into a graphmining algorithm, since the traversal of a graph with loops is not defined. As we'll show later, the application domain of the algorithms inspired by cognitive sciences might be much broader.

Outline of the Basic Algorithm

Input to the algorithm is a function on nodes of an oriented graph with typed, weighted arcs. Frequently, the function is quite sparse, and so can be easily stored as a list of nodes with non-zero activation values. The algorithm works in one or more iterations (the number of iterations is regulated by several parameters and conditions). On each iteration

- the list of nodes is expanded to include neighboring nodes (including both neighbors following incoming links, and neighbors which have links to the nodes in the list)
- the activation value at each node in the list is recomputed based on the values of the function on nodes which linked to the given node and the types of connections which exist between them
- The list is purged by excluding the nodes with the values less than a given threshold.

The output of the algorithm is then the list of nodes (value of the function after spread of activation) ranked according their activation values.

Spreading Activation Methods (SAM) Framework

A formal description of the Spreading Activation Methods (SAM) Framework requires the introduction of some notation.

A multidimensional network can be modeled as a directed graph, which is a pair

$$G = (V,E)$$

where

V – is the set of vertices v_i

E – is the set of edges e_j (although in oriented graphs edges are referred to as arcs)

init: $E \to V$ – is the mapping which provides initial nodes for arcs

term: $E \to V$ – is the mapping which provides terminal nodes for arcs

imp – is importance value of arcs and nodes.

For instance, *imp(v)* where the node v is a geographical location, might be the population. *Imp(e)* number of phone calls from person *init(e)* to person *term(e)*.

w – "weights", for instance, the sigmoidal function of *imp*.

$w(e_j)$=0 means that effectively arc e_j is ignored $w(e_j)$=1 means that activation of *init(e_j)* strongly affects the activation of *term(e_j)*. For instance, when the nodes represent "words", synonym links might be assigned the value 1.

$F(E)$ – is the "activation" function, usually a real valued function on nodes of the network.

Spreading activation method (SAM) algorithms employ iterative steps where activation is propagated between neighboring nodes. Many applications use SAM for local search on massive networks with a small number of initially activated nodes; in this case traversal optimization is usually done by a breadth-first search graph algorithm and the importance of various constraints to improve performance of activation spread becomes of greater value.

Generic description of SAM algorithms needs to include iterative re-computation of activation (also sometimes called pulses of activation).

Generic description of spreading activation methods (SAM) framework

1. Initialisation: Sets the parameters of the algorithm, network, and initial $F(E)$ as a list of non-zero valued nodes V_n
2. Iterations: (each iteration is one pulse of SAM)
    a. List Expansion: the list is expanded to include neighbors (including both neighbors following outgoing links, and neighbors which have links to the nodes in the list). Newly added nodes receive a zero valued level of activation
    b. Recomputation: the value at each node in the list is recomputed based on the values of the function on nodes which have links to the given node and types of connections
    c. List Purging: The list is purged - we exclude the nodes with the values less than a threshold.
    d. Conditions Check To Break Iterations: like maximum number of iterations to be performed.

3.   Output: The list of nodes (value of the function after spread of activation) ranked according F values.

Generic Description of Recomputation Phase

We have the list of nodes V_n.

1. Input/Output Through Links Computation.
For each node v we compute the input signal to each arc e, such that init(e)=v. This computation can be based on the value F(v), the outdegree of a node etc. For instance, if the node v has n outgoing arcs of the same type, each arc e might get input signal:

I (e) = F(init(e)) · (1 / outdegree(v)**beta)

where beta might be equal to 1. It could be also less than one, in which case the node v will propagate more activation to its neighbors than it has.
    When the signal ("activation") passes through a link e, the activation usually experiences decay by a factor w(e):

O (e) = I(e) · $w(e)$

2. Input/Output of Node Activation
Before the pulse, the node v has the activation level F(v).
    Through incoming links v get more activation:

Input(v) = Σ O(e)

for all links e such that init(e) $\in V_n$, term(e) = v.
    By dissipating the activation through outgoing links, the node v might lose activation:

Output(v) = Σ I(e)

for all links e such that init(e) = v, term(e) $\in V_n$

3. Computation of the New Level of Activation
A new value $F_{new}(v)$ is computed based on values of F(v), Input (v), and Output(v), for example

$F_{new}(v)$ = F(v) + Input (v)

SAM and Methods of Numerical Simulation in Physics

Spreading activation algorithms were introduced in 1990s; however the same iterative methods were used long before in numerical simulation in physics, mechanics, chemistry and engineering sciences

(Morton, K.W. & Mayers, D.F., 2005; Rübenkönig, O., 2006). The major distinctions of these algorithms from what is called now as spreading activation are:

a)   in physics – such algorithms usually work on a regular mesh (so that the local topology of the graph is encoded into formulas of the recomputation stage)
b)   in physics – initial conditions, or initial activation – are usually assigned to all nodes on the mesh; and the use of algorithms for efficient graph traversal is not needed. For instance, steps 2a (List expansion) and 2b (List Purging) in the generic description of SAM framework might be skipped.

For instance, one dimensional heat transfer equations might be numerically simulated on a one-dimensional mesh, by iterative methods. On each iteration recomputation stage is based on the formula below:

$$F_{new}(v) = (F(RightNeighbor(v)) + F(LeftNeighbor(v))) / 2$$

Using a different formula, one can simulate the behavior of an oscillating string (although this will require storing tree values at each node - position, mass and velocity of the material point corresponding to the node).

Using the same iterative algorithm, with one set of parameters one can emulate heat transfer; with another set of parameters the same algorithm will show us the behavior of oscillating strings. But the phenomena of heat propagation and string oscillation are quite different (for instance, heat propagation might lead to "thermal death" - the state of equilibrium where the level of activation is the same for all nodes, while oscillation might continue forever). Our illustration concern only basics, while real modeling might be much more complicated, for instance, hear transfer might lead to combustion, where after reaching some level of activation a node generates more "heat" than it gets from neighboring nodes.

This recall to physics gives us useful insight into the high potential of SAM framework and directions for future work:

*   There are numerous possible modifications of SAM algorithms
*   Changing parameters of spreading activation significantly affects the results
*   Selection of "correct" parameters for new applications of SAM might be potentially a hard task, and must be based on the creation of a "correct" model for the phenomena in question
*   Understanding the nature ("the physics") of what and how is propagated on the network, requires domain specific knowledge.
*   Discovering how to do this efficiently is computer science.

Applications described in this chapter use formulae similar to "heat transfer", which ensures fast convergence after limited number of iterations.

Theorizing about potential areas of applications for SAM algorithms which are more similar to "oscillation", we can suggest that such algorithms might be potentially used to rank web-sites based not only on their current status, but also on the trend (like the site becomes popular).

Figure 1. This is a two-dimensional numerical simulation done by the Galaxy library (Troussov, A., Judge, J., & Sogrin, M., 2007). Parameters of the algorithm were tuned to work with networks like WordNet to detect focus concepts of documents. For example, if four concepts (depicted at the corners of the mesh) are mentioned in the text, SAM computes that the center of the mesh got the highest value. Note, that if parameters of the algorithm were chosen to emulate heat transfer, the highest level activation will stay with initial four nodes.

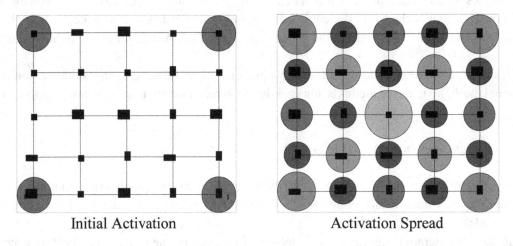

Initial Activation   Activation Spread

Classification of SAM Algorithms Based on the Distribution of Initial Activation

An important dimension of classification of SAM algorithms is the intended mode of the use with respect to the distribution of nodes with non-zero level of initial activation:

- egocentric applications – where SAM algorithms are used mainly to process egocentric queries (i.e. only one node on a network has non-zero level of activation on the initialization stage)
- polycentric applications – where several nodes on a network have non-zero level of activation on the initialization stage;
- omnicentric applications – where most of the nodes on a network have non-zero level of activation on the initialization stage.

Examples of egocentric applications are described in (Kinsella et al., 2008) and (Nepomuk PSEW Recommendation). Polycentric applications are described in (Troussov, Sogrin, Judge, & Botvich, 2008a; Troussov et al., 2008b). In omnicentric spreading activation, we probably should talk about redistribution of activation, rather than about spreading of activation. And indeed, the authors of such algorithms (Levner, Pinto, Rosso, Alcaide, & Sharma, 2007b) don't call their algorithm as the algorithms of spreading activation. Nevertheless we believe that these algorithms must be presented together with "classical" spreading activation algorithms as described in section 2.2. Having the single umbrella of the SAM framework allows to focus on the core part of these algorithms – i.e. recomputation step in iterations; and simplify knowledge transfer across the application domains of SAM algorithms.

Spreading Activation as a Graphmining Technique

As we have already seen, the technique of SAM is quite polymorphic. In this section we interpret the results of spreading activation in terms of graph mining.

First of all, one can think that after running SAM the most activated nodes will be those nodes, which get the activation from multiple sources, or, in other words, those nodes which minimize the "distance" to the nodes which were initially activated. Therefore these nodes might be considered as potential centroids of strong clusters induced by the initial activation. Since partitioning of the nodes according to these clusters is not immediately available (and is not needed in many applications), SAM algorithms might be considered as methods of soft clustering.

On the other hand, the most activated nodes are those nodes, which are connected to the initial conditions by particular types of directed links (arcs with large weights). Therefore we might consider SAM as an efficient scheme for computing fuzzy inferencing. For such applications replacing a single valued function F by a vector function might be useful.

We conclude by noting that SAM algorithms might be used for soft clustering and fuzzy inferencing on networks.

COMPOSITION OF MULTIDIMENSIONAL NETWORKS AND PERTAINING NAVIGATION METHODS

Successful application of graph-based mining methods strongly depends on the understanding of the phenomena encountered in the modelled networks. In this section we outline socio-semantic aspects of modern networks and discuss the problem of related item recommendation.

Composition of Multidimensional Networks

The proliferation of Web 2.0 technologies has lead to the emergence of massive networks connecting people and various digital artifacts. Collaborative tagging systems like Del.icio.us give us examples of such networks. Most of the data in such systems might be represented as a network with four types of nodes: people, resources, tags and instances of tagging (Mika, 2005). In Del.icio.us there are no direct links between people or links between resources, instances of tagging usually have three links: link to the user, link to the resource, and link to the tag used.

Social networks are traditionally modeled by graphs. "Advances in digital technologies invite consideration of organizing within communities as a process that is accomplished by global, flexible, adaptive, and ad hoc networks that can be created, maintained, dissolved, and reconstituted with remarkable alacrity. Increasingly these networks are multidimensional including individuals as well as digital artifacts and concepts." – (Contractor, 2007). Since most of such networks are now based on computer mediation (Facebook, LinkedIn, IBM internal social network Beehive), more types of links between people are known, and more digital artifacts might be accounted for, thus providing "the opportunity to capture, tag, and manifest high-resolution high-fidelity relational "metadata" (which node is connected to which other node) from these multidimensional networks" (Contractor, 2008).

Enterprise 2.0 usually adds new dimensions and new connections (for example, since identity management on the intranet is simple, it is easy to add additional links from, for example, a corporate remake of Facebook to a corporate remake of Delicious).

Communication networks are of particular interest to business and security applications.

Lexico-semantic resources (such as WordNet or medical ontologies) are important resources for knowledge-based methods in language engineering; the semantic web and the Nepomuk Social Semantic Desktop (Sauermann, 2005; Groza et al., 2007; Sauermann, Kiesel, Schumacher, & Bernardi, 2009) rely on the use of ontologies. The data for ontologies and their relatives (catalogs, thesauri, taxonomies, topic maps, semantic networks etc) are graphs with vertices corresponding to concepts (and their instances) and labeled (weighted) arcs denoting relationship.

Navigating Networked Data using Polycentric Fuzzy Queries

The content of the network brought to life by Web 2 is influenced by premises which encourage utilising data before providing structure, the result being that often the content of these networks is usually of mixed quality. The composition of the networks which are based on Semantic Web technologies frequently includes nodes and links which are more related to the technologies underpinning the functioning of these networks, than to the potential interpretation of these networks by humans.

The efficiency of human navigation in modern networks depends on the availability of suitable user interfaces powered by an "intelligent" back end which provides guidance and recommendations based on soft computing methods. Later in this chapter we describe how the "pile" based GUI (Graphical User Interface) called Nepomuk-Simple and the IBM library Galaxy (Troussov, A., Judge, J. & Sogrin, M., 2007) can be used for such guided navigation through the network of Personal Information Management Ontology concepts in the scenario of the social semantic desktop as pertaining to the EU 6th framework project Nepomuk.

In navigation on networks, one of the most important guiding tools is related item recommendation - that is given a set of nodes on a network, to recommend potentially relevant nodes. The role of related item recommendation is to reduce cognitive load, provide guidance in navigation and browsing, contextualize, simplify, and make sense of otherwise complex interlinked data.

Related item recommendation is different from search, since the goal of recommendation is not to find nodes with particular properties (the user herself frequently would not be able to specify what exactly she would like to have as a recommendation), but the search of nodes with strong cumulative direct and indirect connections to the initial set of nodes. Therefore we consider the problem of related item recommendation on networked data as a problem of *"how to find something without having searched for it"*, or, in technical terms, as a problem of processing fuzzy (underspecified) polycentric queries on multidimensional networks. As argued in (Troussov et al., 2008b), processing of such queries might, for instance, require the use of fuzzy logic, soft clustering and fuzzy inferencing, and spreading activation is one of the technique particularly suitable for the task.

Spreading Activation for Processing Polycentric Queries

The application of an SAM algorithm to processing polycentric queries might be straightforward: take the nodes from the query and propagate activation to other nodes; however, better results might be achieved if the query processor is constructed as a hybrid system and is used as a component of a bigger system for processing fuzzy polycentric queries. Troussov et al., (2008b) describes components of the software architecture to process fuzzy polycentric queries. This includes

- Query generator
- Processor of fuzzy polycentric queries
- Post processing
- Explanatory module

The use case of tag recommendation for enterprise collaborative tagging systems illustrates all aspects of such architecture. As we mentioned above, people, resources and tags are "wired" together by instances of tagging; to achieve tag recommendation one can put an activation in the nodes representing the user and the resource. After propagation, the list of most activated people, resources, tag and instances of tagging might be post processed, to show only tags.

The explanatory module might take the list of most activated instances, and convert it into explanations like "the list of all people who have the same geographical location or are connected through the reporting chain to you, who use this tag this resource".

Results of recommendation will depend on which tags are mostly frequently used by the user, by the tags used by the people who have significant overlap in tagged resources with the user, etc. In general, this will be a community based tag recommendation (Sigurbjörnsson, B., & van Zwol, R., 2008). However, spreading activation is a method of soft computing; this means that if the external community grows, the results of recommendation will tend to be skewed towards the most popular tags in the whole community. To make the results of tag recommendations more "community based", the query processor might have two parts: firstly, spreading activation from the user and the resource is used to detect the subcommunity most connected to the user and the resource; secondly, activation starts from the members of this community.

The same architecture based on SAM framework, might be used to provide other services for collaborative tagging systems. For example, expertise location in the scenario like "who can explain these documents to me from the point of view of semantic web technologies?" might be construed as a polycentric query which include several resources, tags and people. Processing of polycentric queries based on a generic graphmining technique, like SAM, might take into account multiple relations like relations between people, hyperlinks between resources, relation that the tag JSP might be semantically close to the tag Java. It also can take into account timestamps (when a particular instances of tagging occurred) and use this information about temporal aspects of collaborative tagging systems (thus addressing the problem of tag expiration).

Collaborative tagging systems are socio-technical systems, and therefore we cannot assume that everyone will use the system in the same way and with the same purposes in mind as others. For instance, in addition to tagging topicality of the content of the resources, people might use evocative tags or tags needed to manage their workflow instead of (or in addition to) building folksonomies (user generated taxonomies).

Composition and Navigation Summary for Multidimensional Networks

Many modern multidimensional networks are created by the proliferation of socio-technical systems, which requires careful considerations regarding what humans bring into such networks, such as semantics, social aspects and task management. Related item recommendations for networked data facilitate guided navigation; such recommendations (done in a predictive search mode), introduce fuzzification and serendipity aspects in browsing. The use case of collaborative tagging systems demonstrates the advantages of navigating networked data using polycentric fuzzy queries, and the advantages of using SAM algorithms for processing such queries. Spreading activation methods might be used as a primary method for related item recommendation.

Ontology Based Text Processing

SAM algorithms might be used for ontology based text processing to allow us to detect the relevancy of ontological concepts to a text by propagating the relevancy measure from concepts mentioned in the text to other concepts not mentioned in the text. Iterative redistribution of relevance might also improve the ranking of concepts according to their relevancy to the text in a similar way as PageRank provides ranking of web sites. The rationale of applying SAM algorithms might be explained as follows:

1. Text understanding is inferencing, although a computational approach by clustering ontological concepts mentioned in the text might be somewhat useful
2. Soft clustering, fuzzy inferencing and other methods of soft computing are suitable for knowledge-based analytics on term mentions when our knowledge is incomplete and inconsistent, and when the parsing methods used to process text are "shallow"
3. Spreading activation is a method which combines elements of soft clustering and fuzzy inferencing.
4. and therefore spreading activation on ontological networks taking concepts mentioned in a text as the initial input, and propagating this "input" to other concepts might work (although the exact parameters of such propagation are not known in advance)

This section is based mainly on the results of the EU 6th Framework project Nepomuk (2006-2008). This project created a social semantic desktop (SSD), based on the Semantic Web technologies (Decker, & Frank, 2004; Sauermann, Bernardi, & Dengel, 2005), and is available for download from (Nepomuk Installation). Semantic web technologies are used to annotate resources and relate them to the Personal Information Management (PIMO) ontology (Sauermann, & Dengel, 2007). IBM/Nepomuk components are available as one Java library "Galaxy" (Troussov, Judge, & Sogrin, 2007), and address the problems of the consumability of SSD, especially in the corporate environment by providing automatic metadata generation for free texts and scalable back-end for social software. Galaxy is library of components centered around a core spreading activation component – the primary graph-mining technique used in all stages of processing.

The nature of PIMO ontology excludes the use of methods tailored to the particular domain and use of particular lexico-semantic resources, and therefore spreading activation methods, which work based on the local topology, are especially suitable. In this section we'll describe ontology-based methods used in Galaxy in text processing applications, while section 4.3 describes applications of the Galaxy to related item recommendation (based on both text processing and link analysis).

Major steps in Nepomuk use of PIMO ontology for text processing are:

1. Converting of PIMO ontology to a lexico-semantic resource
2. Mapping from free texts into PIMO ontology
3. Analytics on term mention which allow to reason which concepts sits well together resulting in term disambiguation and creation of metadata

The task of converting a Nepomuk PIMO ontology into a lexico-semantic resource is addressed in (Davis, B., Handschuh, S., Troussov, A., Judge, J., & Sogrin, M., 2008; Troussov et al., 2008c).

Mapping from free texts to a PIMO ontology is done in Galaxy by exploiting IBM LanguageWare lexical analyzer which was influenced by the approach developed in above mentioned papers. This mapping allows us to build semantic models of documents. We define semantic models of free texts as a function on nodes of a semantic network which shows the relevance of corresponding ontological concepts to the text. This semantic model might be built by an ontology aware lexical analyzer or a parser. We call this model - Semantic Function Space Model (SFSM). This model covers traditional Vector Space Model (VSM), and it is somewhat similar to it. However, VSM is an algebraic model, while Function Space Model can be studied by the methods of function analysis (find local extremes, make function "more smooth"), etc involving graphmining.

Galaxy library uses SAM to "improve" the SFSM, assuming that the model represents a cohesive coherent text (not random list of words). This empirical approach to language understanding is based on the use of fuzzy inferencing methods (like mentioning of *car* in a sentence increases out awareness that the term *Jaguar* mentioned in the same text refers to a *car*, not an animal) and soft clustering (*Dublin* in Ireland might be the geographical focus of a text which mentions *Clonsilla, Drumcondra*, and *Malahide*). To this end, Galaxy uses spreading activation methods which essentially provide soft clustering and fuzzy inference, i.e. activation from the concepts mentioned in text is propagated to other concepts in PIMO, new concepts even those not mentioned in the text, might be discovered as relevant to the text, the concepts mentioned in the text mutually corroborate each other in similar way as Google's PageRank algorithm discovers the relative importance of web pages (Langville & Meyer, 2006).

One can say that SAM adds dimension of soft computing methods to the methods traditionally used in ontology-based text processing; and this makes Galaxy tolerant to incompleteness and inconsistencies in data.

Galaxy's text processing also utilizes the empiric known as one sense per discourse. The whole procedure follows following steps:

1. Run spreading activation on SFSM
2. Find the most activated concept which is considered as the major focus of the text
3. Disambiguate mentioning of ambiguous concepts based on their proximity to the focus
4. repeat stages 1-3 till all mentions are disambiguated

Galaxy's spreading activation algorithm, closely follows the SAM framework and exhibits features important for the optimization of performance and for the development of data driven solutions. For example, links are typed, and don't have individual weights w(e) responsible for the decay of the signal when passing through links. Galaxy works with oriented arcs, however, since spreading activation for text processing applications requires operations of list expansion (so there is a need for fast retrieval of neighbors which have links to the nodes in the list), links are actually stored as bidirectional, although direction is another dimension of links.

Figure 2. This figure is based on the diagram "Ontologies and their relatives" from Paul Buitelaar's "Lexical Semantics and Ontologies" Tutorial at ACL/HCSnet, July 2006, Melbourne, Australia. We show that SAM algorithms are a method of soft computing suitable for ontology-based text processing.

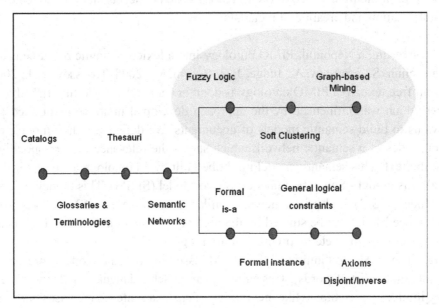

Fuzzification of Graph Clustering Algorithms

Among various document clustering algorithms that have been proposed so far, the most useful are those that automatically reveal the number of clusters and assign each target document to exactly one cluster. However, in many real situations, there not exists an exact boundary between different clusters. In this sub section, we introduce a fuzzy version of the MajorClust algorithm (Stein, B. & Nigemman, O., 1999). The proposed fuzzy clustering method assigns documents to more than one category by taking into account a membership function for both, edges and nodes of the corresponding underlying graph. Thus, the clustering problem is formulated in terms of weighted fuzzy graphs. The fuzzy approach permits to decrease some negative effects which appear in clustering of large-sized corpora with noisy data.

Clustering of documents is a well-known problem that has been approached in some cases by using a priori known characteristics of the target corpus such as the exact number of clusters to be obtained, although other approaches permit to derive this characteristic automatically. MajorClust is one of the most promising and successful algorithms for unsupervised document clustering. This graph theory based algorithm assigns each document to that cluster the majority of its neighbours belong to. The node neighbourhood is calculated by using some specific similarity measure which is assumed to be the weight of each edge (similarity) between the nodes (documents) of the graph (corpus). MajorClust automatically reveals the number of clusters and assigns each target document to exactly one cluster (often named a class, or a category). However, in many real situations, there not exists an exact boundary between different categories.

Therefore, a different approach is needed in order to determine how to assign some document to more than one category. We suggest to take advantage of the observed MajorClust qualities and the fuzzy logic in order to obtain a Fuzzy-MClust algorithm. The presence of multiple attributes (features) of the documents (key words, abstracts, different types of tokens, etc.) is modelled with the help of multiple edges between any pairs of nodes that are supplied with fuzzy weights which may be either fuzzy numbers or linguistic variables.

The main feature of the new algorithm, FuzzyMClust differing it from MajorClust and other clustering algorithms is that all the items (for example, the documents to be grouped) are allowed to belong to two and more clusters (categories).

The Taxonomy of Clustering Algorithms

Clustering analysis refers to the partitioning of a data set into clusters, so that the data in each subset (ideally) share some common trait, often proximity, according to some defined distance measure (Mirkin, 1996; MacKay, 2003; Alexandrov, Gelbukh, & Rosso, 2005). Clustering methods are usually classified with respect to their underlying algorithmic approaches; iterative (or partitional) and density based are some instances belonging to this classification. Hierarchical algorithms find successive clusters using previously established ones, whereas partitional algorithms determine all clusters at once. Hierarchical algorithms can be agglomerative ("bottom-up") or divisive ("top-down"); agglomerative algorithms begin with each element as a separate cluster and merge them into successively larger clusters. Divisive algorithms begin with the whole set and proceed to divide it into successively smaller clusters.

Iterative algorithms start with some initial clusters (their number either being unknown in advance or given a priori) and intend to successively improve the existing cluster set by changing their "representatives" ("centers of gravity", "centroids"), like in K-Means (MacKay, 2003) or by iterative node-exchanging (like in Kernighan, & Lin, 1970).

Clustering approaches are usually classified, with respect to their underlying algorithmic approaches, to hierarchical and iterative (or partitional). Hierarchical algorithms find successive clusters using previously established clusters, whereas partitional algorithms determine all clusters at once.

Hierarchical algorithms can be agglomerative ("bottom-up") or divisive ("top-down"); agglomerative algorithms begin with each element as a separate cluster and merge them into successively larger clusters. Divisive algorithms begin with the whole set and proceed to divide it into successively smaller clusters. Iterative algorithms start with some initial clusters (their number either being unknown in advance or given a priori) and intend to successively improve an existing cluster set by changing their "representatives" ("centers of gravity", "centroids"), like in K-Means (Mirkin, 1996) or by iterative node-exchanging. An interesting and perspective version of iterative algorithms is MajorClust (Stein, B. & Nigemman, O., 1999) which automatically reveals the number of clusters, unknown in advance, and successively increases the total "strength" or "connectivity" of the cluster set by iterative moving nodes between the clusters.

Depending on whether the algorithms work with crisp (hard) data or uncertain (noisy, fuzzy) data, they can have hard or fuzzy versions. For example, the basic MajorClust belongs to the family of hard-data algorithms while this paper deals with its fuzzy version, called FuzzyMClust.

Basic MajorClust

MajorClust operationalizes iterative propagation of nodes into clusters according to the principle "maximum attraction wins" (Stein, B. & Nigemman, O., 1999).

The algorithm starts by assigning each point in the initial set its own cluster. Within the following re-labelling steps, a point adopts the same cluster label as the majority of its weighted neighbours. If several such clusters exist, one of them is chosen randomly. The algorithm terminates if no point changes its cluster membership.

Algorithm MajorClust

```
Input: object set D, similarity measure φ : D × D →  [0; 1], simi-
larity threshold τ. Output: function δ : D → N, which assigns a
cluster label to each point.
Initialisation
 (01) i := 0, ready := false
 (02) for all p from D do i := i + 1, δ (p) := i end do
Iterations
(03) while ready = false do
      (04) ready := true
      (05) for all q from D do
            Recomputation
            (06)  δ* := i if  Σ{φ(p, q)| φ(p; q) ≥ τ and δ(p) = i} is
maximum.
            Output
            (07) if δ(q) ≠ δ* then δ(q) := δ*, ready := false
      (08)  end do
(09) end do
```

Remark. The similarity threshold τ is not a problem-specific parameter but a constant that serves for noise filtering purposes. Its typical value is 0.3.

MajorClust algorithm is used for omnicentric applications and therefore steps List Expansion and List Purging are absent. MajorClust algorithm might be rewritten in the notations of section 2.3 as follows.

Activation function $F(E)$ in MajorClust algorithm is a vector function of dimensionality N. After each iterations all components of vector $F(v) = \{a_1, a_2, ..., a_N\}$ are zero valued, except of one: $a_i = 1$ means that the node v has cluster label i. On each iterations the node v gets input from its neighbors (excepts of those neighbors with connectivity less than the threshold τ), computed by the same method as described in 2.3

$$\text{Input}(v) = \Sigma\, O(e)$$

Computation of the new level of activation at the Recomputation stage is given by the following formula:

$$F_{new}(v) = \{a_1, a_2, ..., a_N\},$$

where $a_i = 1$ if $\text{Input}_i(v) \geq \text{Input}_j(v)$ for all j, $1 \leq j \leq N$, otherwise $a_i = 0$.

Rendering MajorClust algorithm as SAM framework algorithm, gives us directions for possibly useful modifications. For example, requirement of MajorClust algorithm that all components of vector $F(v)$ are zero valued, except of one, might be too restrictive. Rejection of this requirements leads to fuzzification of MajorClust algorithm, including those described in 4.2.3.

Fuzzy Modifications of the Basic MajorClust

Fuzzy Weights of Edges and Nodes in FuzzyMClust

For simplicity, we start with describing the case of a single attribute, when M=1.

The measure of membership of any edge i in a cluster k is presented by a membership function μ_{ik}, where $0 \leq \mu_{ik} \leq 1$, and $\Sigma_k \mu_{ik} = 1$ for any i.

We will need the following definitions. A node j is called *inner* if all its neighbours belong to the same cluster as the node j. If an edge i connects nodes x and y, we will say that x and y are the *end nodes* of the edge i. A node j is called *boundary* if some of its neighbours belong to a cluster (or several clusters) other than the cluster containing the node j itself.

The main ideas behind the above concept of the fuzzy membership function μ_{ik} is that the edges connecting the inner nodes in a cluster may have a larger "degree of belonging" to a cluster than the "peripheral" edges (which, in a sense, reflects a greater "strength of connectivity" between a pair of nodes). For instance, the edges (indexed i) connecting the "inner nodes" in a cluster (indexed k) are assigned $\mu_{ik} = 1$ whereas the edges linking the "boundary nodes" in a cluster have $\mu_{ik} < 1$. The latter dependence reflects the fact that in the forthcoming algorithm the boundary nodes have more chances to leave a current cluster than the inner ones, so the "strength of connectivity" of a corresponding edge in the current cluster is smaller. As a simple instance case, we define $\mu_{ik} = a_{ik}/b_i$, where a_{ik} is the number of those neighbours of the end nodes of i that belong to the same cluster k as the end nodes of i, and b_i is the number of all neighbours to the end nodes of i. In a more advanced case, we define $\mu_{ik} = A_{ik}/B_i$, where A_{ik} is the sum of the weights of edges linking the end nodes of i with those neighbours of the end nodes of i that belong to the same cluster k as the end nodes of i, and B_i is the total sum of the weights of the edges adjacent to the edge i. Fuzzy approach can lead to better practical results (Klawonn & Höppner, 2003).

Furthermore, we introduce the measure of membership of any item (node) j in any cluster k, which is presented by the membership function γ_{jk}, where $0 \leq \gamma_{jk} \leq 1$, and $\Sigma_k \gamma_{jk} = 1$ for any j. Notice that these weights are assigned to nodes, rather than to the edges, this specific feature being absent in all previous algorithms of MajorClust type. The value of the membership function γ_{jk} reflects the semantic correspondence of node j to cluster k, and is defined according to the ´fitness´ of node j to cluster k as defined in (Levner et al., 2007b). The idea behind this concept is to increase the role of the nodes having a larger fitness to their clusters. In formula (1) and the text below, γ_{jk} is a function of a cluster C_k containing node j: $\gamma_{jk} = \gamma_{jk}(C_k)$ which may dynamically change in the algorithm suggested below as soon as C_k changes. The objective function in the clustering problem becomes more general than that in (Stein, B. & Nigemman, O., 1999) so that the weights of nodes are being taken into account, as follows:

Maximize $\Lambda(C) = \Sigma_{k=1,\ldots,K} |C_k| \lambda_k, + \Sigma_{j=1,\ldots,n} \gamma_{jk}(C_k),$ (1)

where

C denotes the decomposition of the given graph G into clusters,

$C_1, C_2, ..., C_K$ are clusters in the decomposition C,

$\Lambda(C)$ denotes the total weighted connectivity of G(C),

λ_k designates the edge connectivity of cluster $G(C_k)$, this is, according to Stein and Busch (2005), the cardinality of the set of edges of minimum total weight $\Sigma_i \mu_{ik}$ that must be removed in order to make graph $G(C_k)$, disconnected, the weight μ_{ik} of any edge i in cluster k being defined as above, for example, $\mu_{ki} = a_{ik}/b_i$, and

$\gamma_{jk}(C_k)$ is the fitness of node j to cluster k.

Linguistic Weights of Edges and Nodes in FuzzyMClust and Grading

The fuzzy weights of edges and nodes (that is, in informal terms, the fuzzy semantic correlations between the documents and the fuzzy fitness of documents to categories) can be presented not only in the form of fuzzy numbers defined between 0 and 1 reflecting a flexible (fuzzy) measure of fitness which sometimes called "a responsibility" (Levner, Alcaide, & Sicilia, 2007a). Moreover they even may be linguistic variables (*small, medium, large,* etc). In the latter case, they are assigned the so-called ´grades´ introduced in Levner and Alcaide (2006). The presence of fuzzy weights on edges and nodes permit us to avoid several well-known drawbacks and flaws of the standard MajorClust. The most important among them are the following:

1) When MajorClust runs, it may include nodes with weak links, i.e. with a small number of neighbours which inevitably leads to the decrease of the objective function already achieved.
2) MajorClust assigns each node to that cluster the majority of its neighbours belong to, and when doing this, the algorithm does not specify the case when there are several "equivalent" clusters equally matching the node. The recommendation by (Stein, B. & Nigemman, O., 1999) to make this assignment in an arbitrary manner, may lead to the loss of a neighbouring good solution.
3) MajorClust scans nodes of the original graph in an arbitrary order, which may lead to the loss of good neighbouring solutions.
4) MajorClust does not take into account different multiple attributes characterizing multi-dimensional links between the items (nodes) as well as the different contribution (weights) of different attributes.
5) MajorClust takes into account only one local minimum among many others (which may lead to the loss of much better solutions than the one selected).

These flaws will be avoided in the fuzzy algorithm suggested, by the price of greater computational efforts (the running time) and a larger required memory.

Fuzzy Multi-Attribute Membership Functions and Their Borda Ranking

We consider a multi-attribute case which implies that the edges, in fact, of M different types (colors) corresponding to M different attributes (in paper (Levner, Alcaide, & Sicilia, 2007a) there are five attributes), each colored edge having its own membership function μ_{ki}^m, where $m= 1,...,M$.

Connections between pairs of nodes being of a multi-attribute nature, represented by multiple arcs between each pair of nodes, lead to a generalization of Stein and Nigemman's graph model (1999) to the clustering model defined on a colored multigraph (the arcs now are non-homogenous, they are colored in M different colors corresponding to M different attributes).

Suppose that there are *N* documents and *K attributes* (called also criteria or experts), and that the *k*th attribute has an associated weight w_k. First we assume that $w_k = 1$, however, later we consider that each w_k is a positive, *not necessarily integer*, number. A preference order (sometimes called a permutation or total order) supplied by each attribute ranks the documents in each category from the most preferred to the least preferred without ties. An alternative view is to consider separately each document and to rank the categories with respect to the fitness (correspondence) of this document to different categories. A preference order in which x_1 is ranked first, x_2 is ranked second, and so forth, is written here as x_1, x_2, . . ., x_N. We shall discuss an algorithm for aggregating information provided by different attributes and obtaining a consensus preference order integrating the information from all the attributes.

Borda's voting method works as follows. Given *N* documents, if points (grades) $N - 1$, $N - 2$, . . ., and 0 are assigned to the first-ranked, second-ranked, . . ., and last-ranked document in each attribute's ("expert's") preference order, then the winning document is the one with the greatest total number of points. In other words, if r_{ik} is the rank of alternative *i* by attribute *k*, the *Borda count* for document *i* is $b_i = \sum_k (N - r_{ik})$. The alternatives are then ordered according to these counts. The ties are handled by evaluating the rank for a tied alternative as the average of the associated rankings.

Using a fuzzy Borda (see Levner and Alcaide, 2006), we can find a consensus fitness of nodes to clusters coordinated for different attributes, and, in long run, a better total fitness of nodes to the obtained clusters than the standard MajorClust.

The objective function in the clustering problem in the multi-attribute case becomes more general than (1) but retains the same structure, with the weights of attributes being taken into account and the additional index corresponding to the multiple attributes being added, as follows:

Maximize $\Lambda_{multi}(C') =$

$$\Sigma_{m=1,\ldots,M} \Sigma_{k=1,\ldots,K} v_m |C'_k| \lambda_k^m + \Sigma_{m=1,\ldots,M} \Sigma_{j=1,\ldots,n} w_m \gamma_{jk}^m (C'_k),$$

where

C' denotes the multi-attribute decomposition of the given graph G into clusters,

$C'_1, C'_2, \ldots, C'_K$ are clusters in the decomposition C',

$\Lambda_{multi}(C')$ denotes the total weighted connectivity of G(C'),

λ_k^m designates the edge connectivity of cluster G(C'_k), with respect to attribute *m*,

$\gamma_{jk}^m (C'_k)$ is the fitness of node j to cluster k, with respect to attribute *m*.

Finding the Fitness by a Borda Voting Method

The goal of text categorization is the classification of documents into a fixed number of predefined categories. Each document can be either in exactly one category, or in several categories, or in no category at all. Using a computer-aided procedure, the objective is to do the category assignments automatically. Our text classifier consists of five steps: First, identify (a) *the set of attributes* characterizing the documents; (b) *the set of predefined categories,* and (c) *the set of classifying words and expressions* within each category. These three sets can be either fixed, or flexible being extended or decreased during the interactive classification process. Second, compute the *fitness* measure f_{ij}^k of document i to category j with respect to attribute k. The fitness f_{ij}^k is a function of three arguments: (1) the number of words in the attribute k of document i that coincide with predefined classifying words and expressions in category j; (2) the size (the number of words) of attribute k of document i, and (3) the number of the classifying words in category j. At the third step, using the set of decision rules of the *if-then* type and the Borda voting method, described below, the algorithm defines *weights* (relative importance) of categories v_j and *weights* w_k of attributes $\{k\}$ which maybe either linguistic values (like, *very strong, strong, medium, weak, very weak*) or crisp magnitudes ranked in intervals [1, 100] or [0, 1]. The fourth step defines the complete fitness f_{ij} of document i to category j, by using an additive approach: $f_{ij} = \sum_k w_k f_{ij}^k$, where the latter value can be either fuzzy or crisp. Finally, the fifth step distributes the documents among the categories using standard methods of cluster-analysis aimed either to maximize the total validity of classification as in (Levner, Alcaide, & Sicilia, 2007a), or to maximize the total "fitness" of available documents to their assigned categories $F(C) = (1/N)\sum_{i,j} v_j f_{ij} x_{ij} \times 100$, where $x_{ij} = 1$ if document i is assigned to category j and 0 otherwise, and N is the number of documents, under predetermined constraints on the cardinality of category sets and running time of the classifying procedure.

An approach pursued at the third step of the algorithm is the Borda ranking method.

Clustering Algorithm on a Multigraph – A Generalization of MajorClust

Initially, our algorithm assigns each node of the multigraph to its own elementary cluster.

Then the membership functions are independently computed for all attributes and integrated by using a combination of the fuzzy Borda method and grading (see Levner and Alcaide 2006). As a result the consensus fusion of all attributes is done, multi-color membership functions are reduced to the integrated membership function presented by formula (2), and the clustering problem on the multigraph is reduced to a clustering problem on a conventional graph with a generalized connectivity function (2).

Next, the iterative step is done, but in contrast to the basic MajorClust, we extend the procedure in two dimensions:

- "*in width*", that is, instead of considering a single node at each iterative step, we consider in parallel Q *best variants supplying them with their corresponding membership functions,*
- and "in depth", that is, each of Q variants is examined at each iterative step in a "look-ahead mode", and then Q new best results in the considered series of two sequential steps, - which provide Q best values of the generalized objective function (2) are chosen.

In more detail, at each iterative step the algorithm works as follows:

- For each node j, select at most Q "best" clusters, providing the maximum increase (increment) for the value of the objective function (2), or close to the maximum;
- Define the membership function for any of Q variants, defined at each iterative step as

$$\alpha_{jk} = \Lambda_{multi} (C'_{jk}) / \Lambda^*_{multi} (C'_{j}), \tag{2}$$

where

Q is a integer threshold value determined by the decision maker;

$\Lambda_{multi} (C'_{jk})$ is the current increase (increment) for the value of the objective function (2) provided by the inclusion of node j into a cluster k; and

$\Lambda^*_{multi} (C'_{j})$ is the maximum increase (increment) for the value of the objective function (2) provided by the inclusion of node j into clusters, among all Q variants: $\Lambda^*_{multi} (C'_{j}) = \max_{k} \Lambda_{multi} (C'_{jk})$;

- For all of Q variants examine next step in a "look-ahead mode", and then choose Q new best results in the considered series of two sequential steps.

The order of node scan is defined by the following decision rules R1-R3.

Rule R1. If there are several nodes having majority (or the maximum value of the corresponding objective function) in certain clusters, then choose first the node having the maximal number of neighbours.

Rule R2. If there are several nodes having both the majority and the maximum number of neighbours in certain clusters then choose first the node whose inclusion leads to the maximum increase of the objective function.

Rule R3. If, at some iterative step, the inclusion of some node would lead to the decrease of the objective function, this node should be skipped (that is, it will not be allocated into any new cluster at that step).

The algorithm stops when the next iterative step do not change the clustering (this is *Rule* 4) or any further node move leads to deteriorating of the achieved quality (defined by formula (2) (this is *Rule* 5) or according to other stopping rules R6-R7 below:

Rule 6. If the number of steps exceeds the given threshold then stop.

Rule 7. If the increase in the objective function at H current steps is less than ε (H and ε are given by the experts and decision makers in advance) then stop.

Text Classification Fitness Finding Method

The method works in five steps: First, it identified (a) the set of five attributes characterizing the documents, namely, title, key words, abstract, bibliography, and authors' bio (b) the set of 72 categories predefined by experts and (c) the set of classifying words and expressions in each category.

Second, the algorithm automatically computed the *fitness* value f_{ij}^k of document i with respect to category j with respect to attribute k; here the simple relation has been used:

$$f_{ij}^k = \min\{1,\, g_{ij}^k / \alpha_j^k\},$$

where g_{ij}^k is the number of words in attribute k of document i coinciding with classifying words in category j; α_j^k is the minimal number of classifying words in category j with respect to attribute k whose presence in k is sufficient to provide the maximum fitness $f_{ij}^k = 1$ (this value is predefined by experts). For example, consider attribute $k = abstract$ of a document $i = i^*$, and assume that α_j^k is defined to be 5, then if four words in k are found among classifying words of category j it implies that fitness $f_{ij}^k = 0.8$. Another example: if the attribute $k = title$ and $\alpha_j^k = 1$ then any document with at least one classifying word of category j in its title attains $f_{ij}^k = 1$.

At the third step, using the set of decision rules of *if-then* type and the Borda voting method, described above, the algorithm broke ties by defining *weights* (relative importance) of categories v_j and *weights* w_k of attributes which were either linguistic variables or magnitudes ranked in interval $[0, 1]$. The fourth step defined the complete fitness f_{ij} of each document i to category j, by using an additive approach: $f_{ij} = \sum_k w_k f_{ij}^k$. The fifth step finally distributed the documents among the categories using the cluster-analysis algorithm aimed to maximize the total classification quality, which, in our case, the total fitness of available documents to their assigned categories $F(C) = (1/N)\sum_{i,j} v_j f_{ij} x_{ij} \times 100$, under predetermined constraints on the cardinality of category sets. Two diagrams representing the quality of classification (in %), are presented in Fig.3, first, as a function of the different strategies (characterized by $\alpha_j^k = \alpha$ for all j, k with the values of α equal to 3, 5, 7, 10 and 12, respectively) with respect to a fixed value (50) of the size s of the classifying sets and, second, as a function of the different sizes of the classifying sets (from 40 to 80) with respect to a fixed $\alpha = 7$. The white column in each column series corresponds to the automatic classification based on all five attributes, the black one takes into account only two attributes *title* and *key words*, and the grey one corresponds to manual experts' evaluations based on attribute *title* only.

Figure 3. Fitness of classification

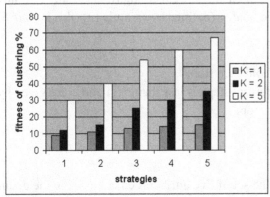 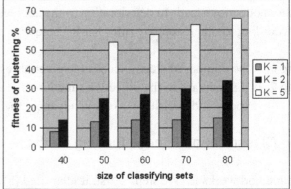

The Butterfly Effect

In Figure 4 below we can observe the so-called "butterfly effect", which appears when some documents (nodes) of the dataset (graph) may belong to more than one cluster, in this case the fuzzy algorithm works better than the crisp one.

Figure 4 (a) depicts an example when the classical MajorClust algorithm has found two clusters and, then, according to formula (1) this clustering of eight nodes obtains a score of 21 (C=7x3 + 1x0 = 21). On the other hand, Figure 4 (b) demonstrates how the fuzzy algorithm works when some nodes can belong simultaneously to several different clusters. We assume that the algorithm uses formula (2) where, for the simplicity, we take $\gamma jk(Ck) = 0$; even in this simplified case the fuzzy algorithm wins. Two variants are presented: in Figure 4(b) we consider the case when the membership values are shared equally between two cluster with the membership value 0.5; then the obtained score is 21 (C=2x((3+0.5)x3) + 1x0 = 21). Note that the value of the objective function is here the same as in the case 1(a). However, if the documents (nodes) are highly relevant to the both databases with the membership function values 1 then the fuzzy algorithm yields a better score which is presented in Figure 4 (b): C=2x((3+1)x3) + 1x0=24. It worth noticing that this effect becomes even stronger if $\gamma jk(Ck) > 0$.

Discussions and Future Research

Consensus between contradicting attributes is achieved with the help of a fuzzy version of the Borda voting method. Special attention in the definition and operation of the so called fuzzifier will be needed, since it controls the amount of overlapping among the obtained clusters and, it is well known that for those corpora with varying data density, noisy data and big number of target clusters, some negative effects may appear. These effects are formalized with the help of the fuzzy if-then rules and the standard Mamdani-type inference scheme/.

Our efforts are devoted to employ fuzzy clustering on text corpora since we have observed a good performance of the MajorClust in this context. However, we consider that there exist different areas of application for this new clustering algorithm which includes not only data analysis but also pattern recognition, spatial databases, production management, etc. in the case when any object can be assigned to more than a unique category.

Figure 4. Butterfly effect in fuzzy clustering (a) use classical MajorClust, whereas (b) use the F-MajorClust approach

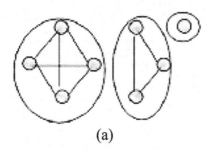   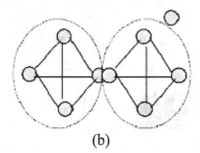

(a)   (b)

Related Item Recommendation for Networked Data

Nepomuk-Simple is an early, general-purpose application of the SAM framework. It was designed and developed within the EU 6th framework project Nepomuk to allow knowledge workers to organize and explore their data, and it is organized around the Pile user interface metaphor. Nepomuk related item recommendations described in this chapter are based on IBM Galaxy library (Troussov, A., Judge, J. & Sogrin, M., 2007) and are described in (Groza et al., 2007; Sauermann, Kiesel, Schumacher, & Bernardi, 2009).

The Pile metaphor is based on early observations by T.W. Malone (1983) that physical desktops differ quite a lot from virtual ones, which are based on folders. As different from the hierarchical folder structure on virtual desktops, real-world desktop surfaces are used by people to group items that are related to each other or to a task. Such groupings are called piles, and it would be expected that a user works with a handful of piles at a given moment, a much smaller scale than the thousands of folders on computer desktops today. Another point of difference from folders is that piles can contain non-file elements such as ontology concepts. Along these lines of including semantic content in piles, items visualized as files by desktop systems, are represented with their most important metadata in piles (e.g. the subject and author of an e-mail rather than an .eml file). Within the Pile-based interface of Nepomuk-Simple, "spreading activation" helps the user manage their piles in two major ways: (1) given a pile with its items, it recommends possible candidate items to add to the pile and (2) given an item, recommend possible candidate piles to add it to. We are considering a number of other ways in which activation spread can help pile-based user interfaces, which are detailed in (Troussov et al., 2008b).

The Nepomuk-Simple user interface is laid out around three main sections (Fig. 5): the pile items (left), the pile item properties (statements, top right), and pile-based views (low-right) such as timeline

Figure 5. The recommendations view "what else to add to the pile" of the Nepomuk-Simple pile-based user interface. Based on the item text and the content of the pile, additional items are recommended and thus show a relevance score with + signs (lower-middle)

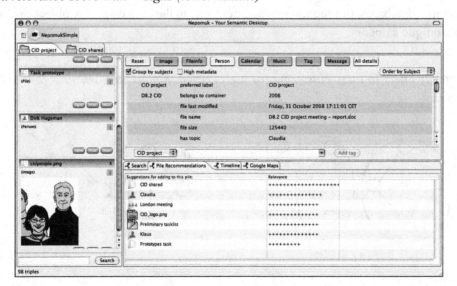

view, map view, or recommendation view, which is the main focus of the present description. Multiple piles can be open at the same time. To add items to the pile, the user can easily drag and drop them from various sources (traditional file folder explorers, semantic explorers, other piles, statements about pile items), or transfer them from applications such as the Mozilla Firefox web browser and the Mozilla Thunderbird e-mail client.

While the timeline view and the map view are based on time-related and respectively location-related statements about pile items, the recommendation view shows other items in the user's Nepomuk-based local semantic data store that are potential candidates for the present pile, with a relevance level computed by the SAM. First several topics are computed for pile items based on their text content, and these topics constitute the initial foci of the activation spread. Then the spread takes place through the statements (RDF relations) of the local semantic data store. In effect, this is a fuzzy polycentric query allowing us to make full use of the SAM power, beyond the egocentric queries used by the PIMO recommender.

The second major way of using SAM in the pile context is to recommend a pile for a given item. We have implemented such recommendations as plugins for applications in the Mozilla suite. With the Nepomuk-Simple plugin, the Firefox web browser shows on its status bar the name of the highest-relevance pile for the content viewed, if any (Fig. 6). This recommendation is based on the text content which is then matched against the profile of each Pile using SAM mechanisms.

In a similar manner, the user can get a pile recommendation when reading their e-mail with the Mozilla Thunderbird mail client.

The Nepomuk-Simple recommendation component uses the graph mining functionality of Galaxy and data in the Nepomuk RDF repository to perform two operations:

Figure 6. Pile recommendation for a webpage. Based on the item text and the content of the existing piles, some piles may be recommended and thus show a relevance score with + signs (lower right)

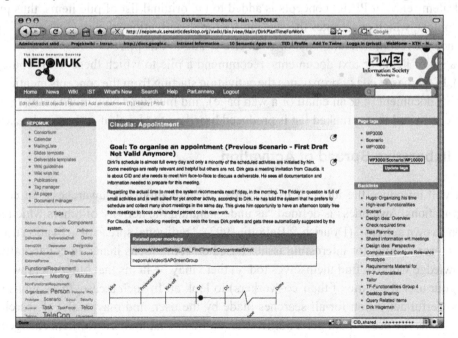

1. Process a text document, disambiguate lexical expressions used within it and determine its focus or topic. This process is described in more detail in Section 4.1. Here we want to explain the results to provide better view on how to use results of such processing in interactive applications like Nepomuk-Simple. Disambiguated lexical expressions or document's focus as PIMO concepts can be used to enhance document's metadata or to provide additional hyperlinks when presenting a document to users. This is not simple parsing of texts to find mentions of concepts, but advanced semantic analysis of text (which includes some fuzzy inferencing which concepts sits well together in a cohesive coherent text) which allows to detect relevance of the concepts to the text, even if they are not mentioned, and provide relevancy measure which might be better than those obtained by frequency-based term-weighting schemes.

2. Generate recommendations of items related to one or more "starting" nodes. By related item we mean PIMO items which are most strongly linked to the starting items through multiple indirect linkages. Items which already directly linked to the starting nodes are not returned in the list of related items. Several related item recommender functions are implemented

    a. Given an item, return a list of related items.

    b. Given a text document, return a list of items related to it. This function uses and extends semantic text analysis to provide more recommendations to the user.

In order to perform these functions, the Nepomuk-simple item recommendation functionality is implemented according to the following principles:

*   Given a collection such as a Nepomuk-Simple pile, return a list of related items, which are recommended to add to it (Fig. 5). First Galaxy checks whether some of the pile items are texts which can be analysed. Then for each such text found in the pile Galaxy performs ontology-based text processing and creates the list of most relevant PIMO concepts for the respective item. The list of all such item-relevant PIMO concepts is added to the original list of pile items, thus providing a richer context, which constitutes the starting set for an activation spread which then is processed to produce the recommendation list of what else to add to this pile.

*   Given a set of items or text documents, recommend a pile to which these items could be added (Fig. 6). In this case Galaxy propagates the activation starting from the concepts mentioned in each respective document (e.g. an email or a web page), and measures how much activation comes to each pile item and then a ranked list is produced based on the level of activation in each pile.

Mutual Collaborative Spread of Activation

This section will introduce the ideas of using spread of activation for "awareness" in collaborative software applications. Awareness is defined "as understanding the activity of others which provides a context for one's own activity" (Dourish & Bellotti, 1992). Traditional spread of activation use scenarios assume a lone user looking for interesting issues based on some focus items. In collaborative settings (as most knowledge workers find themselves today) there may be items that other users would like (to some extent) our user (or some of their co-workers) to look at. In such a case, these items should get even more powerful activation for all searches made by the user, and maybe also if searches are not made explicitly, i.e. the user would get a notification on items that their co-workers changed and were searched for in the past, or are simply related to some objects they work with. Therefore the user will become more aware of the relevant work of co-workers.

The theoretical framework for such spread of activation, which we could call Mutual collaborative Spread of Activation (SoA), is described in (Sandor, Bogdan, & Bowers, 1997). The set of items that are in the user interest (hence set the starting point for a polycentric query) are in the user focus. The focus is thus covered by the current activation spread scenarios. The set of items that others (co-workers) would like the user to look at are said to have a nimbus towards the user. The nimbus is not considered by the current SoA scenarios, however, it is easy to notice that the nimbus can spread through the network exactly as the focus does, using the same Spread of Activation methods. The addition of nimbus to this framework leads us to the "mutual collaborative" characterization of this approach.

Focus is a bit different from a simple polycentric search in that it has a persistence dimension. The focus models the "interests" of a user, which can be extracted from the explicit searches the user made, but also from other sources, such as the Piles created, the objects looked at, etc. Nimbus also has similar long-term properties. Also important is the time evolution of focus and nimbus: for example the nimbus of a "meeting" calendar item will depreciate a lot after the meeting time. In spreading activation terms, this will lead to much lower (or zero) initial activation.

Further Considerations

Mining of Web 2.0

In the section 3.5 we already outlined potential applications of the SAM Framework to mining networks created by Web 2.0 using collaborative tagging system as an example. SAM can be used for community detection, community based-tag recommendation, expertise location and other functionalities of collaborative tagging systems. The use of spread of activation techniques has an apparent advantage over other methods since as a generic graphmining technique it is capable of taking into account multiple relations.

Applications to Social Network Analysis

In Section 3.1. we mentioned that modern computer mediated social network become multidimensional including people as well as digital artifacts and concepts. Kinsella et al. (2008) provides examples of usage SAM algorithms for mining digital social networks.

Modeling of Temporal Aspects of Massive Dynamic Networks

Temporal aspects such as the passage of time or even the time at which a given interaction happens can affect the needs of socio-semantic applications: ad-hoc communities of interest are formed and dissolved, events are tied to the particular points in time when they occur, metadata (like tags in Del.icio.us) might "expire", and not fit to the cognitive needs of a user at a given point in time. Numerous collections of longitudinal data, or data with timestamps (e.g. phone calls registered by telephone companies, emails) needs mining which will allow us to identify trends, to predict future activities, to find recurring patterns of events, etc. The results of such mining are needed to set competitive tariffs for traffic, to create better tools for workflow management, to provide time-sensitive search and navigation, etc. Levner, Troussov, and Judge (2009) provides outlook on potential use of SAM framework for modelling temporal aspects of massive dynamic networks, including considerations on data representation, graphmining, goals of mining and the potential range of application domains.

Krieger (2008) and (Levner, Troussov, & Judge, 2009) identify two approaches to model the temporal aspect of this type of data: synchronic (study the network at particular time slices) and diachronic (the network and its linkage is dynamic).

The idea of using SAM algorithms for synchronic analysis is based on the experiments which demonstrate that omni-centric spreading activation is capable of detecting network structures not only on micro-level, but also on mezo- and mega-levels. One can analyse a network at different time-slices using the same persistent methods, and therefore detect trends.

The possibility of using SAM algorithms for diachronic applications is based on a data representation where timestamps are themselves nodes of a multidimensional network. Each timestamp node represents the moment when an event occurred and they are linked together forming a "timeline." Events are then linked to time stamps indicating the point in the timeline at which a given event occurred. By activating specific nodes an egocentric SAM can be employed to detect recurring combinations of events in a short period of time. This can then in turn be used to anticipate future actions or needs and so can be used to suggest recommended actions for example a workflow application.

The Fig. 7 below illustrates this principle. A series of 3 events in succession is detected. At some later point 2 of the same 3 events occur together. By activating the nodes corresponding to these 2 events and using SAM the nodes corresponding to the previous time points receive activation, and so too does the node corresponding to the third event. Using this a system can then determine that it is likely that the third event will also occur and suggest opening the appropriate application to the user.

Figure 7. Activation spreaded from the time stamp T_y after several iterations reaches the node labelled as "Travel Reservation". The cumulative level of activation at this node allows us to detect that the node "Travel Reservation" might be relevant to current user activities.

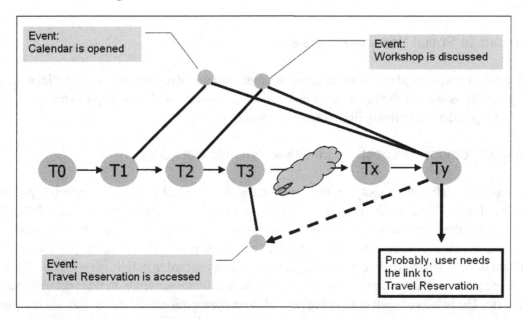

OPTIMIZING SAM RESULTS

Tuning of parameters governing SAM algorithms might be a difficult task. While in some cases a domain expert can easily decide on approximate values of the parameters, in other domains it might be a much harder task. For instance, in ontology-based text processing, it is easy to decide that synonymy relations are of major importance, and to translate this decision into assigning parameter values for weights of synonymy links, so that the decay of the activation passed through the link of the type "synonym" would be minimal; however, decisions for other semantic relations (like "antonymy") might be not so obvious.

Analysis of stability and convergence properties of SAM algorithms might be an important direction for future work. Such analysis might be useful to find stability regions using parameter and data perturbation.

Since SAM algorithms are usually very fast, supervised machine learning might be useful in situations where training material (gold standard) is available. For example, SAM library Galaxy (Troussov, A., Judge, J. & Sogrin, M., 2007) has subsecond performance in all applications in the EU Nepomuk social semantic desktop (Groza et al., 2007; Sauermann, Kiesel, Schumacher, & Bernardi, 2009), and most of the parameters governing behavior of the algorithm are stored in a configuration file. External application can run numerous tests of Galaxy changing parameters of algorithms, and compare results with the gold standard. Thus the manual search of good parameters for an SAM algorithm might be done by computers as a (randomised) search in the parameter space.

Cascading of spreading activation results is an intuitive way to create algorithms with desired properties. For instance, in the section 3.4 we suggested that to create a robust community-based tag recommendation solution, one can: at the first round to apply SAM algorithm to detect the community, and, at the second round to use the detected community for spreading activation to get robust tag recommendations.

CONCLUSION

Spreading activation algorithms are well established in information retrieval, recent publications discussed in this chapter show that these type of algorithms also gained prominence in the natural language processing (including ontology-based text processing and text clustering).

The spreading activation based library Galaxy (Troussov, A., Judge, J. & Sogrin, M., 1997) was used in the social semantic desktop built by the EU 6th framework project Nepomuk (2006-2008) for related item recommendation on multidimensional networked data found in the Personal Information Management Ontology (PIMO) which Nepomuk uses. Multidimensional networks of this type include people and the things they create (documents, emails, calendar entries etc.) and do (tasks, workflow items etc.). Preliminary results of this exploitation tentatively suggest that spreading activation based methods can be very useful for navigation in web 2.0 and semantic web applications. In this chapter we have outlined potential applications of spreading activation to collaborative tagging systems, computer mediated social networks and for modeling temporal aspects of massive dynamic multidimensional networks. As a soft computing method, spreading activation methods are useful to provide "fuzzification" of graph mining, which is needed to model complex phenomena by taking into account the inherently imprecise dimensions of nuanced empirical reality. By shifting focus from breadth-first search optimisation to the recomputation stage, where the activation function in a node of the network is recomputed based on the values of the function in neighbour nodes, we have extended the traditional definition of spreading activation algorithms. We presented the method as a Spreading Activation Methods (SAM) framework, which covers a very general class of algorithms on large multidimensional networks used for iterative local search, relationship/association search, and the computation of dynamic local ranking scores. This allows knowledge transfer, whereby the methods used in particular SAM algorithms and applications, might be easily reused in other domains.

Proliferation of Web 2.0 and Web 3.0 creates massive computer mediated networks. It is expected that by the year 2010, the majority of Web information will be created automatically as log files of Web services (such as Facebook) and by "The Internet of Things". Graphs serve as suitable models for such multidimensional networks. Real time mining of such networks requires the use of scalable algorithms with real time, linear or near-linear performance, such as those which can be implemented using the SAM framework.

ACKNOWLEDGMENT

This research was partially supported by the European Commission under contract IST-2006-027705 NEPOMUK. The authors would especially like to thank all IBM and KTH contributors to the Nepomuk project. Dr. Alexander Troussov's work was done in collaboration with the Centre for Next Generation Localisation (CNGL), which is funded under Science Foundation Ireland's CSET programme: Grant# 07/CE2/I1142. We would like to thank Dr. A.Nevidomsky and M.Sogrin for some helpful discussions.

REFERENCES

Aleman-Meza, B., Halaschek, C., Arpinar, I., & Sheth, A. (2003). Context-Aware Semantic Association Ranking. In *Proceedings of SWDB'03, Berlin, Germany*, 33-50.

Alexandrov, M., Gelbukh, A., & Rosso, P. (2005). An approach to clustering abstracts. In *Proc. of NLDB 2005 Conference*, (LNCS Vol. 3513, pp. 275–285). Berlin: Springer Verlag.

Anderson, J. (1983). A Spreading Activation Theory of Memory. *Journal of Verbal Learning and Verbal Behavior*, (22): 261–295. doi:10.1016/S0022-5371(83)90201-3

Collins, A. M., & Loftus, E. F. (1975). A spreading-activation theory of semantic processing. *Psychological Review*, *82*(6), 407–428. doi:10.1037/0033-295X.82.6.407

Contractor, N. (2007). *From Disasters to WoW: Using a Multi-theoretical, Multilevel Network Framework to Understand and Enable Communities*. Retrieved March 8, 2009, from http://www.friemel.com/asna/keynotes.php

Contractor, N. (2008). *The Emergence of Multidimensional Networks*. Retrieved November 30, 2008, from http://www.hctd.net/newsletters/fall2007/Noshir Contractor.pdf

Crestani, F. (1997). Application of Spreading Activation Techniques in Information Retrieval. *Artificial Intelligence Review*, *11*(6), 453–482. doi:10.1023/A:1006569829653

Davis, B., Handschuh, S., Troussov, A., Judge, J., & Sogrin, M. (2008). Linguistically Light Lexical Extensions for Ontologies. In *Proceedings of the 6th edition of the Language Resources and Evaluation Conference (LREC) in Marrakech, Morocco 26th May - 1st June 2008.*

Decker, S., & Frank, M. (2004). *The Social Semantic Desktop.* Technical Report DERI-TR-2004-05-02, Digital Enterprise Research Institute (DERI). Retrieved March 8, 2009, from http://www.deri.ie/fileadmin/documents/DERI-TR-2004-05-02.pdf

Dourish, P., & Bellotti, V. (1992). Awareness and coordination in shared workspaces. In *Proceedings of the 1992 ACM conference on Computer-supported cooperative work*, Toronto, Ontario, Canada, (pp. 107 – 114).

Groza, T., Handschuh, S., Moeller, K., Grimnes, G., Sauermann, L., Minack, E., et al. (2007). The NEPOMUK Project - On the way to the Social Semantic Desktop. In *Proceedings of International Conferences on new Media technology (I-MEDIA-2007) and Semantic Systems (I-SEMANTICS-07), Graz, Austria, September 5-7*, (pp. 201-210).

Kernighan, B., & Lin, S. (1970). An efficient heuristic procedure for partitioning graphs. *The Bell System Technical Journal, 49*(2), 291–308.

Kinsella, S., Harth, A., Troussov, A., Sogrin, M., Judge, J., Hayes, C., & Breslin, J. G. (2008). Navigating and Annotating Semantically-Enabled Networks of People and Associated Objects. In T. Friemel, (ed.), *Why Context Matters: Applications of Social Network Analysis*, (pp. 79-96). Wiesbaden, Germany: VS Verlag

Klawonn, F., & Höppner, F. (2003). What is fuzzy about fuzzy clustering-understanding and improving the concept of the fuzzifier. In *Advances in Intelligent Data Analysis,* (pp. 254–264).

Krieger, H.-U. (2008). Where Temporal Description Logics Fail: Representing Temporally-Changing Relationships. In *Proceedings of the 31st annual German conference on Advances in Artificial Intelligence Kaiserslautern, Germany*, (LNAI Vol. 5243, pp. 249 – 257).

Langville, A. N., & Meyer, C. (2006). *Google's PageRank and Beyond: The Science of Search Engine Rankings.* Princeton, NJ: Princeton University Press.

Levner, E., & Alcaide, D. (2006). Environmental risk ranking: Theory and applications for emergency planning. *Scientific Israel - Technological Advantages, 8*(1-2), 11–21.

Levner, E., Alcaide, D., & Sicilia, J. (2007a). Text Classification Using the Fuzzy Borda Method and Semantic Grades. In *Proc. of WILF-2007 (CLIP-2007).* (LNCS Vol. 4578, pp. 422–429). Berlin: Springer.

Levner, E., Pinto, D., Rosso, P., Alcaide, D., & Sharma, R. R. K. (2007b). Fuzzifying Clustering Algorithms: The Case Study of MajorClust. In A. Gelbukh & A.F. Kuri Morales (Eds.), *Lecture Notes on Artificial Intelligence 4827*, (pp. 821–830). Berlin: Springer.

Levner, E., Troussov, A., & Judge, J. (2009). Graph-based Mining of Digital Content. *CNGL tutorial, Dublin, Ireland, January 19-21.*

MacKay, D. J. (2003). *Information Theory, Inference and Learning Algorithms*. Cambridge, MA: Cambridge University Press.

Malone, T. W. (1983). How do people organize their desks? Implications for designing office information systems. *ACM Transactions on Office Information Systems, 1*, 99–112. doi:10.1145/357423.357430

Mika, P. (2005). Ontologies are us: A unified model of social networks and semantics. *Lecture Notes in Computer Science, 3729, Galway, Ireland*, (pp. 122-136). Berlin: Springer-Verlag.

Mirkin, B. (1996). *Mathematical Classification and Clustering*. Dordrecht: Kluwer Academic Publishers.

Morton, K. W., & Mayers, D. F. (2005). *Numerical Solution of Partial Differential Equations, An Introduction*. Cambrdige, MA: Cambridge University Press.

Nepomuk Installation (n.d.). Retrieved March 8, 2009, from http://dev.nepomuk.semanticdesktop.org/wiki/UsingInstaller

Nepomuk PSEW Recommendation: Using the Recommendations View in PSEW. (n.d.). Retrieved March 7, 2009, from http://dev.nepomuk.semanticdesktop.org/wiki/UsingPsewRecommendations

Rocha, C., Schwabe, D., & Poggi de Aragao, M. (2004). A Hybrid Approach for Searching in the Semantic Web. In *Proceedings of the 13th international conference on World Wide Web, May 17-20, 2004, New York*, (pp. 374-383).

Rübenkönig, O. (2006). *The Finite Difference Method (FDM) - An introduction*. Albert Ludwigs University of Freiburg.

Sandor, O., Bogdan, C., & Bowers, J. (1997). Aether: An Awareness Engine for CSCW. In H. Hughes, W. Prinz, T. Rodden, & K. Schmidt (eds.), *ECSCW'97: Fifth European Conference on Computer Supported Cooperative Work, Lancaster, UK* (pp. 221-236). Amsterdam: Kluwer Academic Publishers.

Sauermann, L. (2005). The semantic desktop - a basis for personal knowledge management. In Maurer, H., Calude, C., Salomaa, A., and Tochtermann, K., (Eds.), *Proceedings of the I-KNOW 05. 5th International Conference on Knowledge Management*, (pp. 294–301).

Sauermann, L., Bernardi, A., & Dengel, A. (2005). Overview and outlook on the semantic desktop. In Decker, S., Park, J., Quan, D., & Sauermann, L., (Eds.), *Proceedings of the First Semantic Desktop Workshop at the ISWC Conference 2005*, (pp. 1–18).

Sauermann, L., Kiesel, M., Schumacher, K., & Bernardi, A. (2009). Semantic Desktop. *Social Semantic Web, 2009*, 337–362. doi:10.1007/978-3-540-72216-8_17

Sauermann, L., van Elst, L., & Dengel, A. (2007). Pimo – a framework for representing personal information models. In *Proc. of the I-SEMANTICS 2007*, (pp. 270–277).

Schumacher, K., Sintek, M., & Sauermann, L. (2008). Combining Fact and Document Retrieval with Spreading Activation for Semantic Desktop Search. In *The Semantic Web: Research and Applications, 5th European Semantic Web Conference, ESWC 2008, Tenerife, Canary Islands, Spain, June 1-5, 2008 Proceedings* (LNCS Vol. 5021, pp. 569-583). Berlin: Springer.

Sigurbjörnsson, B., & van Zwol, R. (2008). Flickr tag recommendation based on collective knowledge. In *Proceeding of the 17th international conference on World Wide Web, Beijing, China*, (pp. 327-336).

Stein, B., & Busch, M. (2005). Density-based cluster algorithms in low-dimensional and high-dimensional applications. In *Proc. of Second International Workshop on Text-Based Information Retrieval, TIR05*, (pp. 45–56).

Stein, B., & Nigemman, O. (1999). On the nature of structure and its identification. [Berlin: Springer.]. *Lecture Notes in Computer Science*, *1665*, 122–134. doi:10.1007/3-540-46784-X_13

Troussov, A., Judge, J., & Sogrin, M. (1997, December 13). *IBM LanguageWare Miner for Multidimensional Socio-Semantic Networks*. Retrieved March 8, 2009, from http://www.alphaworks.ibm.com/tech/galaxy

Troussov, A., Judge, J., Sogrin, M., Akrout, A., Davis, B., & Handschuh, S. (2008c). A Linguistic Light Approach to Multilingualism in Lexical Layers for Ontologies. In *Proceedings of the International Multiconference on Computer Science and Information Technology*, (pp. 375–379).

Troussov, A., Judge, J., Sogrin, M., Bogdan, C., Edlund, H., & Sundblad, Y. (2008b). Navigating Networked Data using Polycentric Fuzzy Queries and the Pile UI Metaphor Navigation. *Proceedings of the International SoNet Workshop*, (pp. 5-12).

Troussov, A., Sogrin, A., Judge, J., & Botvich, D. (2008a). Mining Socio-Semantic Networks Using Spreading Activation Technique. In *Proceedings of I-KNOW '08 and I-MEDIA '08, Graz, Austria, September 3-5, 2008*, (pp. 405-412).

Chapter 9
Pattern Discovery from Biological Data

Jesmin Nahar
Central Queensland University, Australia

Kevin S. Tickle
Central Queensland University, Australia

A B M Shawkat Ali
Central Queensland University, Australia

ABSTRACT

Extracting useful information from structured and unstructured biological data is crucial in the health industry. Some examples include medical practitioner's need to identify breast cancer patient in the early stage, estimate survival time of a heart disease patient, or recognize uncommon disease characteristics which suddenly appear. Currently there is an explosion in biological data available in the data bases. But information extraction and true open access to data are require time to resolve issues such as ethical clearance. The emergence of novel IT technologies allows health practitioners to facilitate the comprehensive analyses of medical images, genomes, transcriptomes, and proteomes in health and disease. The information that is extracted from such technologies may soon exert a dramatic change in the pace of medical research and impact considerably on the care of patients. The current research will review the existing technologies being used in heart and cancer research. Finally this research will provide some possible solutions to overcome the limitations of existing technologies. In summary the primary objective of this research is to investigate how existing modern machine learning techniques (with their strength and limitations) are being used in the indent of heartbeat related disease and the early detection of cancer in patients. After an extensive literature review these are the objectives chosen: to develop a new approach to find the association between diseases such as high blood pressure, stroke and heartbeat, to propose an improved feature selection method to analyze huge images and microarray databases for machine learning algorithms in cancer research, to find an automatic distance function selection method for clustering tasks, to discover the most significant risk factors for specific cancers,

DOI: 10.4018/978-1-60566-908-3.ch009

and to determine the preventive factors for specific cancers that are aligned with the most significant risk factors. Therefore we propose a research plan to attain these objectives within this chapter. The possible solutions of the above objectives are: new heartbeat identification techniques show promising association with the heartbeat patterns and diseases, sensitivity based feature selection methods will be applied to early cancer patient classification, meta learning approaches will be adopted in clustering algorithms to select an automatic distance function, and Apriori algorithm will be applied to discover the significant risks and preventive factors for specific cancers. We expect this research will add significant contributions to the medical professional to enable more accurate diagnosis and better patient care. It will also contribute in other area such as biomedical modeling, medical image analysis and early diseases warning.

INTRODUCTION

More frequently clinical decisions are often made based on medical practitioner knowledge and experience rather than on the knowledge hidden in the huge database. The limitations of this practice include unwanted biases, errors and excessive medical costs which affects the quality of service provided to patients (Palaniappan & Awang, 2008). Therefore, it is important to discover the hidden knowledge from a medical database to provide a better care of patient. Li et al., (2004) argue:

- 'Data mining techniques can be successfully applied to ovarian cancer detection with a reasonably high performance' (Li et al., 2004).
- 'The classification using features selected by the genetic algorithm consistently outperformed those selected by statistical testing in terms of accuracy and robustness' (Li et al., 2004).

Similarly many researchers in the machine learning community found that molecular level classification of human tissues has produced remarkable results, and indicated that the gene expression method could significantly aid in the development of efficient cancer diagnosis and classification platforms (Brown et al., 2000; Lu & Han, 2003; Statnikov et al., 2005; Yeh et al., 2007). Machine learning techniques are also widely explored in heart diseases (Ordonez et al., 2001), computer-based medical picture interpretation method contain a major application area provide significant support in medical diagnosis (Coppini et al., 1995; Zhu & Yan, 1997) and many more.

Magoulas & Prentza (2001) suggest, since the understanding of biological systems is not complete, so there are essential features and information hidden in the physiological signals which are not readily apparent. Moreover, the effects between the different subsystems are not distinguishable. Basically biological signals are characterized by substantial variability, caused either by spontaneous internal mechanisms or by external stimuli. Associations between the different parameters may be too complex to be solved with conventional techniques. Modern Machine Learning (ML) methods rely on these sets of data, which can be produced easier, and can help to model the nonlinear relationships that exist between these data, and extract parameters and features which can improve the current medical care (Magoulas, & Prentza, 2001).

As shown in Figure 1 that cancer and heart disease are the top two causes of death in the United Kingdom. Finding patterns in the data that can assist in the early detection of these diseases will have a significant impact on human health.

In summary, this chapter proposes some new solutions to overcome the existing limitations of cancer and heart disease by employing intelligent and statistical machine learning techniques to identify valid, novel, yet potentially useful and ultimately understandable patterns from the large biological data repositories.

This chapter provides a minimal background in human biology to better understand the remainder of the research. A more elaborate introduction can be found in (Marieb & Hoehn, 2006; Marieb & Mitchell, 2007).

BIOLOGICAL BACKGROUND

Human Biology

All over the world cancer is a serious threat for human health. Cancer is a group of diseases which have the common feature of uncontrolled growth of cells and have the ability to infiltrate and destroy normal body tissue. Normally, cancer cells may spread throughout the blood and lymph system to other parts of the body. Molecular actions are the cause of cancer which changes the properties of cells. Generally, in cancer cells the normal control systems to prevent cell overgrowth and the invasion of other tissues are disabled. The abnormal cells which are divided in an uncontrolled way form a tumour. This tumour can be malignant or benign which means life threatening and not dangerous. Malignant tumour might

Figure 1. Comparative death rates for different causes in UK (King & Bobins, 2006)

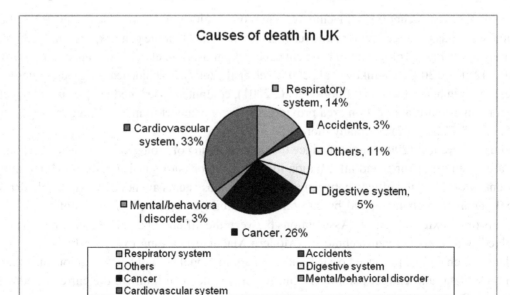

Figure 2. Affected cancer bladder shows by circle. (Source: http://www.ecureme.com/emyhealth/data/ Bladder_Cancer.asp)

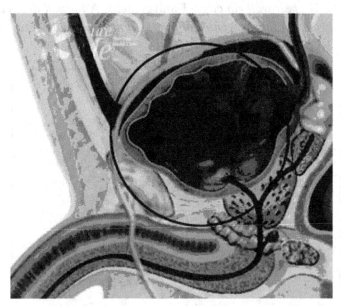

attack surrounding organs and tissues in a process called metastasis. The abnormalities in cancer cells cause for mutations in genes that control cell division. Day by day more genes become mutated. As a result, the number of mutations starts to increase, resulting in further abnormalities in that cell. Over time a number of mutated cells die, but abnormal cells multiply much more rapidly than normal cells.

There are 3 types of faulty genes. The first group, called proto-oncogenes enhance cell division and the mutated forms of these genes are called oncogenes. The second group are called tumor suppressors and they prevent cell division. The third group is DNA repair genes that prevent mutations that lead to cancer. There are different types of chromosomal aberrations that can occur in cancer cells-such as a part of chromosome can have more than the normal two copies. A portion of chromosome may also have only one copy or even no copies. The final type of aberration occurs when a part of a chromosome has moved to a different location, called event relocation. It should be mention that not all aberrations cause cancer (Jong, 2006).

There are more than 100 different types of cancer occurring in humans.

The causes of cancer may be inherited or acquired. The main categories of cancer comprise: Carcinoma – this type of cancer begins in the skin or in tissues that line or cover internal organs. Sarcoma –starts in bone, fat, muscle, blood vessels, cartilage or other connective or supportive tissue. Leukemia – this begins in the blood-forming tissue such as the bone marrow and produced large numbers of abnormal blood cell and enters the blood. Lymphoma and myeloma– this begins in the cells of the immune system. Central nervous system cancers are the type of cancer starting in the tissues of the brain and spinal cord (Cancer, org 2008).

Figure 3. Normal breast with lobular carcinoma in situ (LCIS) in an enlarged cross–section of the lobule. **Breast profile: A** *ducts,* **B** *lobules,* **C** *dilated section of duct to hold milk,* **D** *nipple,* **E** *fat,* **F** *pectoralis major muscle,* **G** *chest wall/rib cage.* **Enlargement: A** *normal duct cells,* **B** *ductal cancer cells,* **C** *basement membrane,* **D** *lumen (center of duct). (http://www.cancer.org/docroot/CRI/content/ CRI_2_2_1X_What_is_breast_cancer_5.asp?sitearea=)*

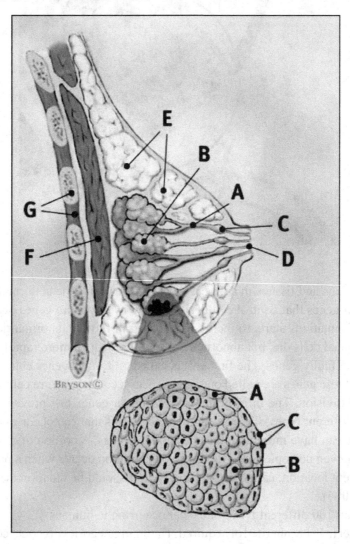

TYPES OF CANCERS

Among the vast range of cancers the following are the most common: Bladder Cancer, Breast Cancer, Cervical Cancer, Colon Cancer, Lung Cancer, Prostate Cancer, Leukemia, and Skin Cancer.

Figure 4. Cervical cancer (Source: http://www.righthealth.com/Health/Cervical_Cancer_Pictures/-od-definition _adam _2%25252F9163-s)

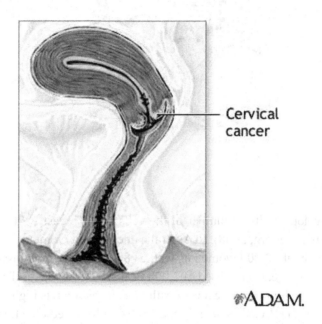

Bladder Cancer

Bladder cancer is a cancer where abnormal cells multiply without control in the bladder. In most of the cases, bladder cancer begins in cells lining the inside of the bladder and is called urothelial cell or transitional cell carcinoma (UCC or TCC). If the bladder cancer is only in the lining is called superficial bladder cancer, and if the cancer spreads into the muscle wall of the bladder, it is called invasive bladder cancer (Wikipedia, 2008). The American Cancer Society estimates that in the United States there will be about 68,810 new cases of bladder cancer diagnosed in 2008 (about 51,230 men and 17,580 women). The chance of a man developing this at any time during his life is about 1 in 27 and for a woman, 1 in 85. In 2008, there were about 14,100 deaths from bladder cancer in the United States (about 9,950 men and 4,150 women) (Cancer.org, 2008). The cancer affected bladder is presented in Figure 2.

Figure 5. Lung cancer (Source: http://search.live.com/images/)

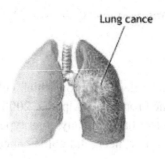

Figure 6. Prostate cancer (Source: http://health.allrefer.com/pictures-images/prostate-cancer.html)

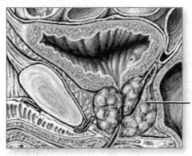

Prostate cancer

Breast Cancer

Breast cancer develops whilst a number of the cells in the breast start to grow out of spread to other parts of the body (Cancer.org, 2008). In Australia one in eight women will develop breast cancer before the age of 85 and about 12,000 women as well as 84 men were diagnosed with breast cancer in 2002. Statistics showed breast cancer caused 502,000 deaths (7% of cancer deaths; almost 1% of all deaths) worldwide in 2005. In USA breast cancer death rates for women is higher than those for any other cancer besides lung cancer.(Breast Cancer Statistics, 2008).It is predicted that by 2011, the number of new diagnoses will increase to about 14,800 women and 122 men (Wikipedia, 2008). The cancer affected breast is showed in Figure 3.

Cervical Cancer

Cervical cancer is a type of cancer that starts in the cervix (part of the female reproductive systems), the lower part of the uterus (womb) that opens at the top of the vagina (Figure 4). Generally, majority of the cases, early cervical cancer have no symptoms. Cervical cancer has two stages: early or pre invasive stage, and late or invasive stage. Cervical cancer is a major global health problem with prevalence and death rates. It is the number one killer of young women in under developed countries. In Korean women for example, cervical cancer is the third most common form of cancer, after stomach and breast cancer (Herzog, 2003). The American Cancer Society estimated that in 2008, about 11,070 cases of invasive cervical cancer were diagnosed in the United States. Research showed that non-invasive cervical cancer (carcinoma in situ) is about 4 times more common than invasive cervical cancer (Cervical cancer, 2008). In 2008, about 3,870 women died from cervical cancer in the United States. Hispanic women are affected over twice that in non-Hispanic white women, and African-American women develop this cancer about 50% more often than non-Hispanic white women (Cervical cancer, 2008).

Lung Cancer

There are various types of lung cancer, depending on which cells are affected. The majority of lung cancer begins in the cells that line the bronchi (Wikipedia, 2008). Statistics shows that both, men and women die from lung cancer more often than from any other type of cancer. Lung cancer accounted for more deaths than breast cancer, prostate cancer, and colon cancer in 2004. In that year, 108,355 men

Figure 7. Skin cancer (Source: http://www.taconichills.k12.ny.us/webquests/noncomdisease/skin%20 cancerpic.jpg)

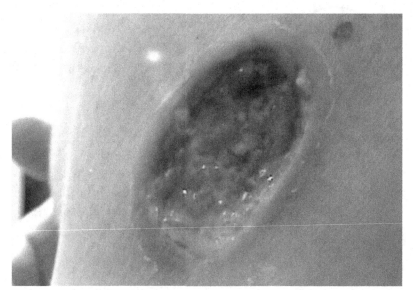

and 87,897 women were diagnosed with lung cancer, and 9,575 men and 68,431 women died from lung cancer. In 2008, there were about 215,020 new cases of lung cancer, which included 114,690 among men and 100,330 among women (Cancer.org, 2008). The cancer affected lung is shown in Figure 5.

Prostate Cancer

This type of cancer originates in the prostate with an uncontrolled (malignant) growth of cells in the prostate gland. It is a common malignancy in men older than 50 years of age and it may cause no symptoms in the early stage. Prostate cancer may remain in the prostate gland or may spread to nearby lymph nodes to other parts of the body. In USA prostate cancer is one of the most frequently diagnosed cancers. The statistics showed that in 2004 189,075 men were diagnosed with prostate cancer and 29,002 men died from prostate cancer. It is a second leading cause of death of males in the USA. In Australia one in nine males affects for prostate cancer at the age of 75 years and one on five by the age 85 years. The death rate of prostate cancer is lower, which is one in 84 men under the age of 75 years and one in 22 by the age of 85 (Pharmacy, 2008). The prostate cancer is shown in Figure 6.

Skin Cancer

Skin cancer is generally the common form of cancer which approximated that over 1 million new cases occur annually. Skin cancer occurs in the outer layers of your skin. Each year the annual rates of all forms of one's cancer are increasing, representing a growing public concern. Research estimated that nearly half of all Americans who live to age 65 will develop skin cancer at least once (Cpaaindia, 2008). The affected skin cancer is shown in Figure 7.

The data mining research has been using two methods to identify cancer in humans: image and micro array based methods. The following section provides the up-to-date development of cancer research involving data mining techniques.

Figure 8. Machine learning phase

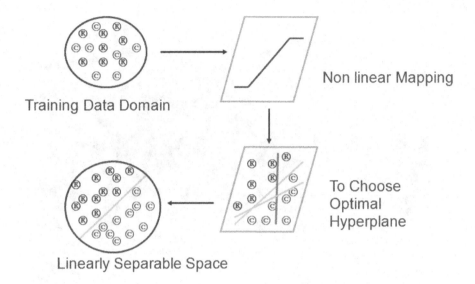

MACHINE LEARNING BACKGROUND

This section will reviews the existing solutions for cancer risk factor extraction, feature selection for a huge data base, gene clustering and finally cancer patient classification from biological data. A theoretical and technical discussion about the existing techniques will follow.

Machine Learning: An Overview

Before explaining machine learning, there is a need to clarify what is learning. Basically learning is a process of knowledge gathering. Similarly, a machine gathers knowledge from data, graph, image and some other sources through computer programming. Basically machine learning is a matter of finding statistical regularities or other patterns in the data. Mitchell (1997) gives the definition of machine learning as follows: 'A computer program is said to learn from experience E with respect to some class of tasks T and performance measure P, if its performance at tasks in T, as measured by P, improves with experience E.'

Now, given a set of attributes about potential cancer patients, and whether those patients actually had cancer, the computer could learn how to distinguish between likely cancer patients and possible false alarms. The symbol © means people already have cancer and ® means people are free from cancer (Figure 8). The first task in machine learning is data processing. A non-linear mapping is used to transform the data. After transformation, data become almost linearly separable. Then the machine tries to constructs some boundary such as line, circle, hyperplane etc to do the separation. Finally using optimisation techniques the machine fixes up the final separation boundary. Now, the process of learning is complete. This whole process in machine learning is called training as described in Figure 8.

At this moment the question is how efficient is the trained machine. To test this, there have a testing phase in the machine learning process. The symbol Ⓟ is a new unknown patient (Figure 9). The machine will identify whether the patient has cancer. Similarly the machine will transform the data first, and then

Figure 9. Machine evolution phase

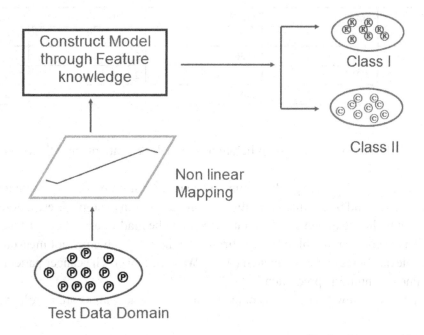

it will place the data in the model. Finally the model will predict whether the patient has cancer, and who has not. Therefore, using a variety of mathematical measures, the machine can test whether the prediction results are acceptable or not.

The whole process described in Figure 8 and 9 is called classification learning. Machine learning is not simply on classification. The following learning tasks are the main branches of machine learning (Mitchell, 1997):

Association learning: Learn relationships between the attributes. An association learning has the form LHS (Left Hand Side) --> RHS (Right Hand Side), where LHS and RHS are disjoint sets of items, the RHS set is likely to occur whenever the LHS set occurs. For instance, items in gene expression data can include genes that are highly expressed or repressed, as well as relevant facts describing the cellular environment of the genes (e.g. the diagnosis of a cancer sample from which a profile was obtained) (Creighton & Hanash, 2003). Association learning is one of the promising aspects of a knowledge discovery tool in the medical domain, and has been widely explored to date.

Classification: Classification is learning to put instances into pre-defined classes. The alternative name is supervised learning. Supervised learning is fairly common in classification problems because the goal is often to get the computer to learn a classification system that has been created. Cancer patient classification is a common example of classification learning. Generally, classification learning is suitable for any problem where deducing a classification is helpful and the classification is easy to determine (Breiman, et al., 1984).

Clustering: Clustering is discovering classes of instance that belong together. The alternative name is unsupervised learning. In this form of learning, the aim is not to maximize a utility function, but simply to locate similarities in the training data. The hypothesis is often that the clusters discovered will match reasonably well with an instinctive classification. For instance, clustering individuals based

Table 1. Microarray gene expressions

	Exp. 1	*Exp. 2*	*Exp. 3*	*Exp. 4*
Gene 1	-2.14	1.45	-6.32	0.25
Gene 2	1.74	-2.36	3.56	-1.25
Gene 3	-5.21		2.45	1.58
Gene 4	1.28	2.58	3.21	1.58

on patient gene information in one group belonging to diabetes patients and the other is diabetes free patients (Hand et al., 2001).

Numeric prediction: Learn to predict a numeric quantity instead of a class. Another popular name is estimation. The task could be continuous or discrete prediction. An example is estimation of the concentration of foreign bodies remaining in the human body can be made from other attributes such as White Blood Cell (WBC) count in the blood. Any attribute in the body which is not measured but related to other measurable attributes can be estimated (Ali & Wasimi, 2007). The cancer patient survivable time could be obtained by numeric prediction.

We did extensive review from various popular sources. The key areas are as follows:

- Cancer image classification
- Microarray cancer classification
- Heart beat aligned disease
- Risk factor identification
- Classification algorithms

Image Based Cancer Classification

Image is an optical picture about an object. Several cancer images are shown in the above section. Medical image data mining is used to collect effective models, relations, rules, changes, irregularities and common laws from mass amount of data and it became a separate important discipline called Medical Imaging. The image based machine learning technique can accelerate the processing speed and accuracy of the diagnosis decisions made by doctors. Recently the rapid development of digital medical devices, medical information databases have included not only the structured information of patients, but also non-structured medical image information (Wang et al., 2005). Antonie et al., (2001) argue that there are no methods to prevent breast cancer, which is why early detection represents a very important factor in cancer treatment and allows reaching a high survival rate. They suggest mammography as the most reliable method in early detection of breast cancer. Due to the high volume of mammograms to be read by physicians, the accuracy rate tends to decrease, and then the automatic reading of digital mammograms becomes highly desirable. Moreover, as they suggest, double reading of mammograms (consecutive reading by two physicians or radiologists) increased the accuracy, but the problem is high costing. Therefore, the computer aided diagnosis systems are necessary to assist the medical staff to achieve high efficiency and effectiveness. Wang et al., (2005) used decision tree algorithm for mammography classification and constructed a medical image classifier. They found that the system performed quite accurately and therefore revealed the potential of data mining in medical treatment assistance. The average precision of classification is above 98%. In their research, it was difficult to compute the continuous segments. Also, the noises were not considered in the decision tree model construction process so that the decision tree created fits the training example completely. Kusiak et al., (2001) used X-ray images of 50 patients and extracted the general information such as age and gender as well as eighteen feature information data for lung cancer. They used rough set theory as a data mining tool and improved the correctness rate of early diagnosis of lung cancer disease.

In cancer research, image based identification is gaining popularity. El-Baz et al., (2008) worked on CT images for early diagnosis of lung cancer. Rangaraj et al., (2007) developed the digital imaging and image analysis systems to detect mammographic features, classify them, and present visual prompts to the radiologist for breast cancer detection. Zhu et al., (2006) reviewed computer-assisted analysis of ultrasound and magnetic resonance images applied in the diagnosis and staging of prostatic cancer. Sheshadri & Kandaswamy (2007) proposed breast tissue classification based on texture based on related statistical measures. Also, Walker et al., (2001), Rodrigues et al., (2006), Twellmann et al., (2008), Nattkemper et al., (2005) worked on image data for early cancer detection.

Microarrays Based Cancer Classification

Microarray is an array of biological material, more specific deoxyribonucleic acid (DNA) molecules that can monitor expression level of thousands of genes concurrently. In case of microarray data, basically analyzed an expression matrix. Every column embodies all the gene expression levels from a single experiment, and each row represents the expression of a gene across all experiments. Every element in that data matrix is a log ratio. The log ratio is delineated as $\log_2 (T/R)$, where T is the gene expression level in the testing sample, R is the gene expression level in the reference sample.

The expression matrix can be presented as a matrix of colour rectangles. Each rectangle represents an element of the expression matrix as shown in Figure 10. The blank cell in the above table indicates the missing value.

In the above microarray expression black colour indicates that the log ratio is zero. Green expresses a negative log ratio and red indicates a positive log ratio. The meaning less color in this microarray expression is gray; it expresses the missing values in the matrix. Machine learning method has a various excellent statistical solutions to handle this missing value replacement.

Lu & Han et al., (2003) reviewed the cancer classification using gene expression and found it is a key challenging research area for cancer diagnosis and drug discovery. They also argue that DNA microarray technique has made simultaneous monitoring of thousands of gene expressions simultaneously, which opens the door for a researcher to explore the possibilities of cancer classification. Until today there are a number of methods proposed with promising performance. But there are still a lot of issues: managing high volume data, prediction evaluation, feature selections, modeling costs which need to be addressed and understood. They suggest that no single classifier is superior over all the others in the aspect of classification accuracy. Statistically based classifiers shown better accuracy but they are not sufficiently good classifiers in the case of cancer classification. Therefore more research is necessary to propose a superior classifier for cancer classification. Berrar et al., (2003) found that microarray data is characterized by a high-dimensional feature space often exceeding the sample space dimensionality by a factor of 100 or more. Moreover microarray data exhibit a high degree of noise. The current methods do not adequately address the problem of dimensionality and noise. In addition machine learning and data mining methods are based on statistics; most such techniques do not address the biologist's require-

Figure 10. A snapshot of microarray (Adapted from documentation of MeV, http://www.tigr.org/software/tm4/mev.html). T is the expression level in the testing sample; R is the gene expression level in the reference sample.

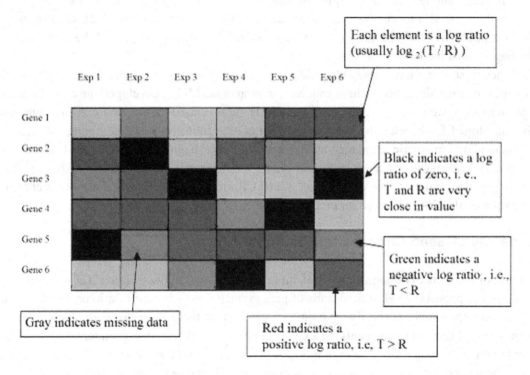

ment for sound mathematical confidence measures. Finally, the existing classification methods fail to incorporate misclassification costs. To overcome these limitations they proposed a probabilistic neural network (PNN) for muticlass cancer classification. The main disadvantage of PNNs is the fact that all training data must be stored in the input layer, requiring a large amount of memory. Sharma, & Paliwal (2008) face the small sample size (SSS) problem of gene expression data. This is a problem from the beginning of gene expression data handling. They utilized linear discriminant analysis (LDA), which is a well-known technique for feature extraction-based dimensionality reduction. Though, this technique cannot be functional for cancer classification because of the singularity of the within-class scatter matrix due to the SSS problem. Therefore, they suggest Gradient LDA technique which avoids the singularity problem associated with the within-class scatter matrix and shows its usefulness for cancer classification. The proposed method achieves lower misclassification error as compared to several other previous techniques. However improvements are needed to handle gene expression data. Recently several research studies have been done on microarray data for early cancer detection (Berns, 2000; Campbell et al., 2001; Veer et al., 2002; Pomeroy et al., 2002; Wong et al., 2008; Lee, 2008; Peterson & Coleman, 2008).

Heart Beat Related Diseases Study

Over the last decade machine learning people are involved to identify the patients in the early stage of heart diseases. Eberhart & Webber (1989) used an adaptive neural network to classify multichannel EEG patterns. Neural networks have been used to detect cardiac diseases from echocardiographic images

(Cios et al., 1997). In addition fuzzy discrimination analysis approaches for diagnosis of valvular heart disease have been applied and achieved a rate of true positive diagnosis of 81% while maintaining a rate of false positive diagnosis at the low level of 10% (Watanabe et al., 1996). Ordonez et al., (2001) used association rule mining algorithm in medical data to predict heart disease. They focus on two aspects in this work: mapping medical data to a transaction format suitable for mining association rules and identifying useful constraints. This research discovered several useful rules, for instance rule 1: if the patient has a perfusion defect and had a previous carotid surgery then he/she has a high probability of having heart disease. They suggest comparing the discovered association rules with classification rules obtained by a decision tree algorithm (Ordonez et al., 2001). Palaniappan & Awang (2008) developed a prototype Intelligent Heart Disease Prediction System (IHDPS) using data mining techniques, including Decision Trees, Naive Bayes and Neural Network. They stated that each technique has its unique strength in realizing the objectives of the defined mining goals. IHDPS can answer complex "what if" queries which traditional medical decision support systems cannot. They suggested using medical profiles such as age, sex, blood pressure and blood sugar to predict the likelihood of patients suffering from heart disease. While the proposed solution was based on 15 attributes, the list of attributes needs to expanded to provide a more comprehensive diagnostic system. Also, the model considers only categorical data and continuous data handling capability should be in the model. Additional data mining techniques can be incorporated to provide better diagnosis rather than three techniques only and the data set expanded. Finally they suggested it is most important to verify the system extensively with medical expert, especially cardiologists, before making the system available for public.

Risk Factors for Cancer

Bladder

Mihalakis et al., (2008) found that only 58.6% vs. 94.4%, 90.7%, and 92% of their sample reported that smoking was a risk factor for bladder cancer, respiratory problems, lung cancer and heart disease. D'Avanzo et al., (1995) declared that the attribute risk for cigarette smoking was significantly higher for bladder cancer among men (56%) than women (17%), whereas coffee consumption, low vegetable intake, and cystitis were more important (but not significantly so) among women. Michaud (2007) declared that in developed countries inflammation is liable to have an important role in bladder carcinogenesis. Johnson et al., (2008) suggested that pregnancy, parity, lactation, or a combination of these may play a protective role in bladder cancer by inhibiting tumor growth. It could be an important model system for studying the effects of pregnancy/lactation hormones on bladder cancer, which might lead to identification of additional risk factors of bladder cancer. Phillips et al., (2002) stated that around 50% of all (transitional cell carcinomas) TCCs are associated with cigarette smoking. Normally, there is an overall four-fold increase in risk, but this is related directly with length of smoking and number of cigarettes smoked. Nieder et al., (2006) estimated the alertness of smoking as a risk factor for bladder cancer. This study suggested the need for the American public to be better educated to help combat smoking related cancers.

Breast Cancer

Barak et al., (2008) argued that psychiatric morbidity may be confounding factor that affects cancer incidence and not particularly schizophrenia. They also stated that breast and ovarian cancer screening for all women who are on long term drugs that induce weight gain or hyperprolactinemia should not be neglected. Eltonsy et al., (2007) suggested that bilateral breast volume asymmetry estimated in screening mammograms should be studied as a risk factor for breast cancer. Maskery et al., (2006) found that invasive cancer incidence between Caffeine Index (CI) groups is much closer to significantly different in women who are pre-menopausal and Caucasian (p=0.091) contrasted to women who are postmenopausal and Caucasian (p=.573). The results of the logistic regression confirm menopausal status as the primary predictor of invasive breast cancer incidence in those populations. Future work will involve modifying lifestyle questions at multiple time points, and exploring other lifestyle variables (i.e. exercise frequency) in relation to breast cancer occurrence. In this way it may further explore how these lifestyle and life history factors impact breast cancer incidence. Matalliotakis et al., (2008) found that endometriosis was significantly associated with the risk of breast cancer in mothers (ORZ6.3 (95% CI, 2.2e17.8), P < 0.001) and in maternal aunts (ORZ5.9 (95% CI, 1.3e72.9), P < 0.001). In conclusion, the study demonstrated a 6.9-fold increased risk of family history of breast cancer in women with endometriosis. Sakr et al., (2008) investigated the familial risk of breast cancer in women with endometriosis. They found 8% carcinoma for patients with isolated papillary lesions and recommend surgical excision for papilloma. They also analyzed the risk factors for the association between malignancy and papillomas. Investigated results showed that age of more than 50 years and the presence of microcalcifications are independently related to the risk of malignancy. Pichard et al., (2008) stated the association of insulin resistance and obesity with breast cancer risk is biologically plausible and consistent. The main message of their reviewed literature is that weight gain and metabolic degradation throughout life are strong promoters of the risk for breast cancer.

Cervical Cancer

Almonte et al., (2008) stated that human papillomavirus (HPV) infection is a main cause for cervical cancer; other cofactors (high parity, long term use of oral contraceptives, smoking and co-infection with the human immunodeficiency virus might contribute significantly to the increased risk for developing cervical cancer among women persistently exposed to HPV. It is mentioned that lifetime number of male sexual partners and the sexual behavior of the male sexual partners are associated with an increased risk of HPV infection. The limitation of this work is this study was carried out in a relatively low-risk population. Smith et al., (2003) found that the relative risk of cervical cancer increases with increasing duration of oral contraceptive use. International Collaboration of Epidemiological Studies of Cervical Cancer, (2007) investigated that current oral contraceptives users increased the risk of invasive cervical cancer with increasing duration of use (relative risk for 5 or more years' use versus never use, 1·90 [95% CI 1·69–2·13]). They found that the risk declined after use ceased, and by 10 or more years had returned to that of never users. Haverkos et al., (2003) concluded that the data supported a role for cigarette smoking as a risk factor for cervical cancer. They proposed a multifactorial hypothesis involving a virus–tar interaction as the etiology of cervical cancer. Schiff man et al., (2007) found that almost all cases persistent infection with one of about 15 genotypes of carcinogenic human papillomavirus (HPV) causes. Steckley et al., (2002) established that smoking may play a major role in cervical cancer in developing countries, but less of a role in other countries.

Lung Cancer

Shen et al., (2008) suggested that food contamination by environmental polycyclic aromatic hydrocarbons may be an important risk factor for lung cancer in Xuanwei. Takahashi (2008) stated the difference in lung cancer risk between Japan and the West is probable to be the combination of five factors: lower alcohol intake in Japanese males; lower intake of total fat, SFAs and cholesterol in Japanese males; higher efficiency of filters in Japanese cigarettes; lower concentrations of carcinogens in Japanese cigarettes; and lung-cancerresistant hereditary factors among Japanese males. Stefani et al., (2008) stated that antioxidants pattern was inversely associated with lung cancer risk (OR 0.69, 0.51–0.96) whereas the high-meat pattern was associated with a strong increase in risk (OR 2.90, 95% CI 1.91–4.40.Cassidy et al., (2008) suggest that the LLP risk model could predict approximately two-thirds of lung cancer within 5-years, screening only 30% of the population. Zhu et al., (2004) concluded that IL-8 can act as an autocrine and/or paracrine growth factor for lung cancer cells and the mitogenic function of IL-8 in lung cancer is mediated mainly by CXCR1 receptor. Pacella-Norman (2002) found that tobacco smoking was a major risk factor for all of selected cancers with odds ratios ranging from 2.6 (95% CI 1.5 – 4.5) for oesophageal cancer in female ex-smokers to 50.9 (95% CI 12.6 – 204.6) for lung cancer in women, and 23.9 (95% CI 9.5 – 60.3) for lung cancer and 23.6 (95% CI 4.6 – 121.2) for laryngeal cancer in men who smoked 15 or more grams of tobacco a day.

Prostate Cancer

Stephen et al., (2008) mentioned that without adjustment for clinical characteristics, obesity was not significantly associated with prostate cancer risk in this equal-access, clinic-based population. However, after adjusting for the lower PSA (prostate-specific antigen) levels and the larger prostate size, obesity was associated with a 98% increased prostate cancer risk. Sobti et al., (2008) performed an attempt to gain insight into the polymorphic forms of hormonal genes and to correlate them to the susceptibility of prostate cancer in the north Indian population. In future the genegene interaction can be explored in to find out the exact cause of the disease and their contribution in the progression of prostate cancer. Giovannucci et al., (1999) evaluated prospectively the relationship between cigarette smoking and total, distant metastatic, and fatal prostate cancer in 47,781 male health professionals throughout the United States. Research indicates that tobacco use may have a substantial impact on mortality from prostate cancer. Within 10 years after quitting smoking, this excess risk is eliminated, so smoking cessation, even late in life, may reduce prostate cancer mortality. Sobti et al., (2008) performed to explore the role of various genotypes involved in steroid metabolism and synthesis in the causation of prostate cancer. In their study, the mutant genotype A2A2 had shown a significantly high risk for prostate cancer (OR53.04; P5 0.01).The geneegene interaction can be explored in the future to find out the exact cause of the disease and their contribution in the progression of prostate cancer. Reissigl et al., (2008) suggested that chronic inflammation may be a risk factor for prostate cancer development.

Skin Cancer

Yang et al., (2002) investigated the relationships between the concentrations of arsenic in drinking water around the world and the development of skin lesions in people have been documented for some years at various locations. Cercato et al., (2008) stated the risk factor of skin cancer which having a fair skin

(Odds ratio) OR: 2.05; 95% (Confident Intervals) CI: 1.38–3.04), light coloured eyes (OR: 1.38; 95% CI: 1.12–1.68), freckles OR: 1.32; 95% CI: 1.12–1.56), and older age (OR: 2.34; 95% CI: 1.96–2.80) is associated with occurrence of sunburns. Strengths of the study include the relatively large sample and response rate. Furthermore, our results are important in highlighting inappropriate sun-protective behaviour for children, contributing to knowledge of a population for which scanty evidence exists. Limitations include the selection of the most relevant and simple to detect items and the bias of mis-classification involved in the children/parents-assessment (i.e. skin colour). Oberyszyn, T. M (2008) reviewed the different risk factor of non-melanoma skin cancer which might be the responsible for gender, immunosuppressive status and more controversially vitamin D levels. Research showed that ultraviolet light B (UVB) is responsible for the majority of cutaneous damage and is supposed to be the single most important etiologic agent in the development of non-melanoma skin cancers (NMSC). Moehrle, M. (2008) studied that athletes practicing outdoor sports are at increased risk for melanoma and nonmelanoma skin cancer. Moreover the important sun exposure; exerciseinduced immunosuppression may increase the risk for nonmelanoma skin cancer and cutaneous melanoma (CM) in athletes. Further efforts to identify individuals with skin cancer should high-risk populations such as outdoor sportsmen. Bjarge et al., (2002) studied the relation between human papillomavirus infection and the subsequent risk of anal and perianal skin cancer. This study provides prospective epidemiological evidence of an association between infection with HPV 16 and 18 and anal and perianal skin cancer. Kennedy et al., (2003) investigated different environmental and genetic risk factors for skin cancer. Research showed that painful sunburns before the age of 20 was associated with an increased risk of all three types of nonmelanoma skin cancer as well as actinic keratoses.

Cancer Risk Factor Extraction

In the medical domain, a risk factor is anything that increases a person's chance of getting a disease. Some risk factors can be changed after a certain time, and others cannot. The list of risk factors for a cancer patient is long list, for instance, person's age, sex, and family medical history. Others are linked to cancer-causing factors in the environment. Still others are related to lifestyle choices such as tobacco and alcohol use, diet, and sun exposure. This is important to know what short of risk factor is the more significant for a specific cancer. Because having a risk factor for cancer means that a person is more likely to develop the disease at some point in their lives. However, having one or more risk factors does not necessarily mean that a person will get cancer (Cancer, org. 2008). Association learning is an appropriate technique to extract significant risk factor for a specific cancer.

ASSOCIATION LEARNING

In this section the standard definition of association learning is introduced (Agrawal et al., 1993; Ordonez, 2006; Ordonez & Omiecinski, 1999; Ordonez et al., 2000). An association rule is a simple rule, such as:

Smoking $\cap$ family_history_positve $\Rightarrow$ lung_cancer

Where 'Smoking ∩ family_history_positve' is called the body of the rule and lung_cancer is the head of the rule. It associates the rule body with its head.

In context of medical data, our example expresses the fact that people who are smoking and have past family history of lung cancer are likely to have risk of lung cancer.

Let D be a database consisting of one table over n attributes $\{a_1, a_2, ..., a_n\}$ and the table contain k instances. In the following an attribute-value-pair will be called an item. An item set is a set of distinct attribute-value-pairs. For instance, smoking, family_history_positve, lung_cancer and so on.

Let d be a database record and it satisfies an item set $X \subseteq \{a_1, a_2, ..., a_n\}$ if $X \subseteq d$. An association rule is an implication $X \rightarrow Y$ where $X, Y \subseteq \{a_1, a_2, ..., a_n\}$, $Y \neq \phi$; and $X \cap Y = \phi$.

The *support* (*s*) and *confidence* (*c*) are two measures of rule interestingness that reflect usefulness and certainty of a rule respectively. The association rules that satisfy user specified minimum support threshold (*minSup*) and minimum confidence threshold (*minCon*) are called strong association rules. The formulations of support and confidence measure are as follows:

Support $(X \rightarrow Y) = P(X \cap Y)$

Confidence $(X \rightarrow Y) = P(Y|X) = \dfrac{P(X \cap Y)}{P(X)}$

Where P is used for probability measure in support and conditional probability in confidence. A probabilistic interpretation of support and confidence is discussed in (Hastie et al., 2001). Another rule measure metric called lift (Bayardo & Agrawal, 1999), defined as

Lift $(X \rightarrow Y) = \dfrac{P(X \cap Y)}{P(X)P(Y)}$

Lift quantifies the relationship between X and Y. Basically, a lift value greater than 1 provides strong evidence that X and Y depend on each other. A lift value below 1 state X depends on the absence of Y or vice versa.

The task for association rule mining can be divided into two folds:

- find all combinations of the risk factors for a specific cancer whose supports are greater than a user-specified minimum support (threshold).
- use the risk factors from frequent risk factors to generate the desired rules. Generally the confidence of each rule is computed, and if it is above the confidence threshold, the retrieve the rule in the system.

Among the long list of association learning algorithms Apriori (Agrawal et al., 1993), Predictive Apriori (Scheffer, 2001), Tertius (Flach & Lachiche, 2001) are most popular algorithms in the machine learning community. The Apriori algorithm is a state of the art algorithm most of the association rule algorithms are somewhat variations of this algorithm (Agrawal et al., 1993). The working principle of Apriori is iterative. It first finds the set of large 1- risk factors, and then set of 2-risk factors, and so on. The number of scans over the transaction database is as many as the length of the maximal risk factors. Apriori is based on the following fact: The simple but powerful observation leads to the generation of a smaller candidate set using the set of large risk factors found in the previous iteration (Karabatak et al., 2006).

Several recent small-scale multigenic studies provide evidence of the promising potential of applying such a pathway-based multigenic approach in association studies (Han et al., 2004; Popanda et al., 2004; Gu et al., 2005). Cooke et al., (1999) were the first to use apriori algorithm on medical data records for heart perfusion measurements. The support and confidence of the generated rules were 80% and 81%. Ordonez & Omiecinski (1999) find apriori is useful for medical images segmentation. But the computation complexity was expensive in their study. Other research used several association and classification approaches to study breast cancer patterns. This study illustrates how these approaches can be used to predict and diagnose the occurrence of breast cancer (Pendharkar et al., 1999). They found apriori and ANN algorithm needed more time to perform the task. Vinnakota & Lam (2006) introduced the use of an association learning approach to uncover spatial associations between cancer mortality and socio-economic characteristics on the different community people in USA. They observed the critical aspect of association rule mining is its requirement of categorical data. Since the categorical combinations of the attributes depend on the discretising method and on the number of classes chosen to represent the data, it would be necessary for future studies to study the effects of these class interval selections on the results of association learning algorithm. Zhu et al., (2003) used the Apriori algorithm to generate the co-occurrences of medical concepts, which are then filtered through a set of predefined semantic templates to instantiate useful relations. They found the benefit from the use of association rule mining algorithms on that aspect. Their approach can performed efficiently in extracting medical knowledge from large databases. They suggest serial and parallel algorithms can make faster of apriori algorithm. Ho et al., (2004) presented an induction data mining approach in order to predict cervical cancer using a combination of demographic, environmental and genetic factors. They examined the risk factors for cervical cancer using logistic regression and a decision tree algorithm, and reported the relationship among demographic, environmental and genetic factors for cervical cancer using induction technique. In addition to the induction technique, they compared logistic regression and the decision tree algorithm, and presented the practical use of rule induction for the management of cervical cancer. Their emphasis was on a specific cancer with several limitations to their research. One being the limited access to data, relying on one single source subjecting themselves to bias in an otherwise potentially data rich subject group its. Sufficient validation for the generalisation of their findings to other geographic areas or groups was not performed. The other limitation was the lack of input variables for patient characteristics, such as exercise behavior, nutrition, stress, and depression. Further study limitations also included low sensitivity for the logistic regression and Chi-squared Automatic Interaction Detection (CHAID) algorithm. An association rule mining algorithm was applied to extract associations between the selected socioeconomic variables and the colorectal, lung, breast, and prostate cancers mortality from 1988 to 1992 cancer mortality rates in United States (Vinnakota & Lam, 2006). Geographic information system technology is used for data integration which is defined at different spatial resolutions, and to visualise and analyse the results from the association rule mining process. This study provided the emphasis on mortality rates. Nahar & Tickle (2008) employ apriori algorithm to extract risk factors for different cancer types. As far as it is known, this is the first risk factor extraction research using association rule mining algorithms. This research argues computational complexity is an important issue for apriori algorithm.

MACHINE LEARNING TECHNIQUES FOR CANCER PATIENT CLASSIFICATION

Classification is simply a task to classify predefined instances into classes. In machine learning, the algorithm constructs a procedure that maps instances into one of several predefined classes. After that, apply a rule, a boundary or a function to the sample's attributes, in order to identify the classes. Consider the data matrix (X_i, Y_i) $(i=1,\dots,n)$, where $X_i \in \Re^d$ denotes the d-dimensional predictor variable and the response for classification $Y_i \in \{0,1,\dots,m\}$, where m is the number of classes. In this case Y_i is either 1 or -1. All of the training patterns are said to be linearly separable if there exists weight vector ω and bias factor b such that the following inequalities satisfied:

$$\left(\omega \cdot \mathbf{x}_i\right) + b \geq 1; \qquad \text{if } y_i = 1$$

$$\left(\omega \cdot \mathbf{x}_i\right) + b \leq -1; \qquad \text{if } y_i = -1$$

Artificial Neural Network (ANN), Decision Tree (DT), Naive Bayes (NB) and Support Vector Machine (SVM) are the most popular classifier in the medical domain (Kaper et al., 2004; Qin et al., 2004, Schlogl et al., 2005, Lotte et al., 2007). The following section will focus on some important classification algorithms.

Artificial Neural Networks

Artificial Neural Network (ANN), originally derived from neurobiological models, are massively parallel, computer-intensive, and data-driven algorithmic systems composed of a multitude of highly interconnected nodes, known as neurons. According to Berry et al., (2000) neural networks are the most widely used and the least understood of the major data mining techniques.

Basically each elementary node of an ANN is able to receive an input signal from external sources or other nodes and the algorithmic procedure equipped in each node is sequentially activated to locally transforming the corresponding input signal into an output signal to other nodes or environment. Moreover, an ANN features a number of interconnected nodes serving as signal receivers and senders, the network architecture designed to describe connections between the nodes, and the training algorithm associated with finding values of network parameters (weights) for a particular network (Rumelhart et al., 1986). After the interactions of linked nodes, an output obtained from one node can serve as an input for others nodes and the conversion of inputs into outputs are activated by virtue of a certain transforming function that is typically monotone, but otherwise arbitrary. Meanwhile, the specified working function has to depend on parameters determined with a training set of inputs and outputs. The network architecture is the organization of nodes and the types of connections permitted. The nodes are arranged in a series of layers with connections between nodes in different layers, but not between nodes in the same layer. Generally, nodes in the neural network can be divided into three layers: the input layer, the output layer, and one or more hidden layers. The layer receiving the inputs is called the input layer. The final layer provides the target output signal is the output layer. Any layers between the input and output layers are hidden layers. A simple representation of a neural network with one hidden layer can be shown in Figure 11. (Rumelhart et al., 1986)

ANN can be classified into two different categories, feedforward and feedback networks. The feedback networks contain nodes that can be connected to them self, enabling a node to influence other nodes as well as it. Kohonen self-organizing network and the Hopfield network are examples of this type of network. The ADALINE and backpropagation neural networks (BPN) are the two typical examples of this kind of network. BPN is a network essentially using a gradient descent training algorithm and has been the most often utilized paradigm to date. For the gradient descent training algorithm, the step size, called the learning rate, must be specified first. The learning rate is crucial for BPN since smaller learning rates tend to slow down the learning process before convergence while larger ones may cause network oscillation and unable to converge (Rumelhart et al., 1986).

Khan et al., (2001) precisely classified the small round blue cell tumors (SRBCTs) of childhood with 96 genes by using an artificial neural network with an accuracy of 100%. They observed a disadvantage of ANNs is the fact that all training data must be stored in the pattern layer, requiring a large amount of memory. Chu & Wang (2006) report a novel radial basis function (RBF) neural network that successfully classified the lymphoma data set (Alizadeh et al., 2000) with 100% accuracy using only 9 genes. This approach also obtained 100% accuracy in the SRBCT data set (Khan et al., 2001) and the ovarian data (Schaner, et al., 2003) with only 8 genes and 4 genes, respectively (Chu & Wang, 2006).

However, Zhang argue while ANNs have shown much promise, many issues still remain unsolved or incompletely solved. As indicated earlier, more research should be devoted to developing more effective and efficient methods in neural model identification, feature variable selection, classifier combination, and uneven misclassification treatment (Zhang, 2000). Moreover, as a practical decision making tool, ANNs need to be systematically evaluated and compared with other new and traditional classifiers. Recently, several authors have pointed out the lack of the rigorous comparisons between neural network and other classifiers in the following literature (Duin, 1996; Flexer, 1996; Prechelt, 1996; Salzberg, 1997).

Decision Tree (DT)

In 1970s, Professor Ross (Quinlan, 1986, 1993) proposed for the first an algorithm named ID3 (Interactive Dichotomiser 3) to generate decision trees. Based on the theory of information gain, ID3 selects the

Figure 11. A three-layer backpropagation neural networks (Rumelhart et al., 1986)

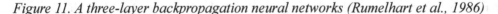

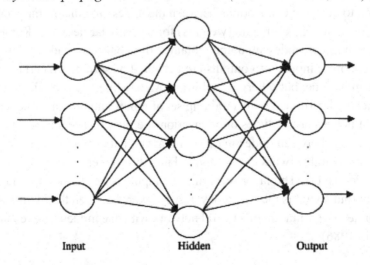

Input   Hidden   Output

Figure 12. A simple decision tree structure for weather data. The final decision is whether people should play Golf or not as indicated by 'yes' or 'no'.

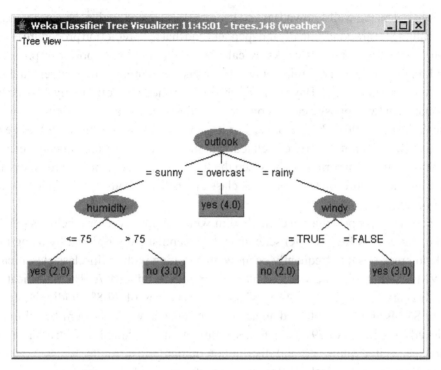

optimal information gain to as an attribute for branching of decision trees so that the trees thus built has a simple structure. Information gain is determined by the entropy of the sub-trees produced by a node of a decision tree using a certain attribute, as well as that of the whole data set. C4.5 is an extension and revision of ID3 algorithm. It uses information gain-ratio instead as a measurement method to segment attributes. Standardised information gain in this way can reduce the influence of ID3 drawback that segmentation nodes prefer too many sub-trees. C5.0 algorithm offers improvements for C4.5. Basically, a decision tree architecture looks like a flow-chart-like tree, with internal nodes representing an attribute. Initially a record flows through the tree along a path determined by a series of tests until a terminal node is reached and it is then given a class label. A simple decision tree is presented in Figure 12.

DT is useful for classification as they assign records to broad categories and output rules that can be easily translated. Different criteria are used to determine when splits in the tree occur (Han & Kamber, 2001). Porcel et al., (2008) use DT and shown 92.2% sensitivity, 98.3% specificity, and an area under the ROC curve of 0.976 for diagnosing tuberculosis.

A disadvantage of this approach is that there will always be information loss, because a decision tree selects one specific attribute for partitioning at each stage with a single starting point (Ross, 1993). Han & Kamber (2001) are pointed out that the efficiency and scalability become issues of concern when DT is used for large databases.

Naive Bayes (NB)

Naive Bayes is based on the well-known Bayes Theorem. It is termed 'naive' because it assumes that attributes of the training set are conditionally independent and that the prediction procedure is not influenced by any hidden or latent attributes. It works by calculating the maximum posterior probability of each class (John & Langley, 1995; Ali & Smith, 2006). In supervised learning environment and depending on the nature of its probability model, Bayes classifier can be trained very efficiently. Naive Bayes reaches its best performance in two opposite cases: completely independent features and functionally dependent features (Rish & Jayram, 2001). Naive Bayes has its worst performance between these extremes. The accuracy of naive Bayes is not directly correlated with the degree of feature dependencies measured as the class conditional mutual information between the features. Instead, a better predictor of naive bayes accuracy is the amount of information about the class that is lost because of the independence assumption (Friedman et al., 1997).

Hong & Cho (2008) proposed a novel method in which support vector machines (SVMs) are generated with the One Verses Rest (OVR) scheme and probabilistically ordered by using the NBs. This method is able to break ties that frequently occur when working with multi-class classification systems with OVR SVMs. SVMs with the winner-takes-all strategy produced 76.9% classification accuracy, while NBs with Pearson-correlated features yielded an accuracy of 74.8%, individually. The product based fusion of SVMs and NBs obtained an accuracy of 66.7%, while the sum-based fusion of SVMs and NBs achieved an accuracy of 79.6%. In terms of limitations (Mehmed, 2002): assumes attributes are statistically independent, assumes normal distribution on numeric attributes, classes must be mutually exclusive, redundant attributes mislead classification, attribute and class frequencies affect accuracy.

Support Vector Machine (SVM)

SVM is a comparative new machine learning algorithm. Basically it is a statistical based learning, which has been used for binary classification for the beginning. SVM model can usually be expressed in terms of a support vectors and can be applied to nonlinear problems using different kernel functions. Based on the support vectors information, SVM produces the final output function. The SVM algorithm creates a hyperplane- a subset of the points of the two classes, called a support vector. This separates the data among the classes with the maximum margin- meaning that the distance between the optimal hyperplane and the closest examples (the margin) is maximized (Cortes & Vapnik, 1995). SVMs basically perform the non-linear classification using a non-linear function called a kernel (Joachims, 1999). A non-linear kernel is a mathematical function that transforms the data from a non-linear feature space to nearly infinite linear feature space. Like ANNs, SVM is used in a wide range of pattern recognition and classification problems ranging from hand writing analysis, speech and text recognition, and protein function prediction to medical diagnosis problem (Baronti, 2005).

Recently, Lee and Lee (2003) also obtained 100% accuracy in lymphoma data set (Alizadeh et al., 2000) with a SVM classifier using at least 20 genes. Zhang et al., (2007) found SVM perform 94% accuracy with 95% sensitivity and 92% specificity respectively by using the detected peaks for ovarian cancer classification. They observed the disadvantages of SVM also, because it makes the final decision function sensitive to certain specific samples in the set. In addition the major limitations associated with SVM are (Platt, 1999): training is slow compared to Bayes classifier and decision trees, difficult to determine optimal parameters when training data is not linearly separable and difficult to understand structure of algorithm. One more significant issue for SVM is automatic kernel selection (Ali & Smith, 2006).

GENE CLUSTERING

Clustering is a type of categorization based on some rules on a group of object (in this case gene). A broad definition of clustering could be the process of categorising a finite number of gens into several groups where all members in the group are similar in some manner. As a result, a cluster is an aggregation of genes. All genes in the same cluster have common properties (e.g. distance) whose are different to the genes laying in other clusters. Generally there are two approaches to perform the clustering task: hierarchical and non-hierarchical. Hierarchical clustering repeatedly links pairs of clusters until every instance is included in the hierarchy. Non-hierarchical clustering performs data segmentation based on some metric of dissimilarity between segments and the degree of segmentation desired. Hierarchical clustering is comparatively more preferable. A hierarchical approach is presented in Figure 13 using 30 genes.

For the biologist who runs the clustering software, the quality of the clustering is of significant importance, as he or she interprets the clusters as associations of genes that behave similarly. Eisen et al., (1998) found hierarchical clustering using uncentered correlation distance and centroid linkage, K-means and self organizing map (SOM) are more popular clustering techniques.

K-Means

MacQueen (1967) developed K-means clustering algorithm for analysis of multivariate observations in 1967. Since then clustering techniques have been studied extensively in the areas of Statistics, Machine Learning, and Data Mining. K-means algorithm has been applied to many problem domains and has become one of the most used clustering algorithms. Matteucci even said that the K-means algorithm is one of the simplest unsupervised learning algorithms that solve the well known clustering problem (MacQueen, 1967). K-means clustering does not create a tree structure; it is assumed that the genes from the same cluster are biologically associated with all others by having physical or genetic interactions. For each cluster, only genes whose expression signals are similar to its centroid are selected. This can be accomplished by selecting the genes whose distances from their expression signals to their centroid are less than or equal to predefined threshold value. It should be noted that the size of biological association networks created by the k-means algorithm is decided based on the value set for the threshold, e.g., a larger threshold value results in a larger network created by k-means (Kim et al., 2008). Several studies demonstrate that K-means is a powerful tool for gene clustering task (Ciaramella et al., 2008; Liang, 2007; Peters, 2006).

The main drawback of the algorithm is that it requires predefined information regarding the number of clusters (i.e. k) to be found prior to start processing (Peters, 2006). If the data is not naturally clustered or the data size is quite large, one gets some strange result. The automatic distance function selection is another challenging issue for this clustering algorithm (Pun & Ali, 2007).

Figure 13. A hierarchical clustering approach. The X axis indicates the number of gene and Y axis indicates the distance.

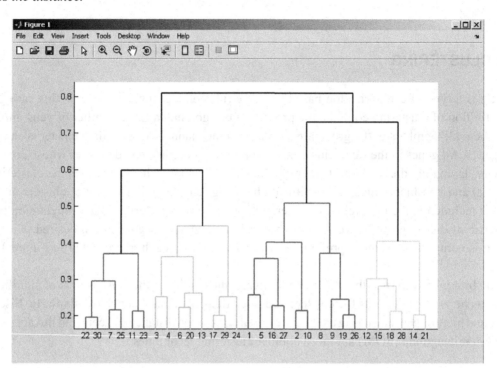

Self Organization Map (SOM)

The self-organizing map (SOM) is a popular visualising clustering technique invented by Professor Teuvo Kohonen which reduces the dimensions of data through the use of self-organizing neural networks. A SOM begins with a set of artificial neurons, each having its own physical location on the output map. Those neurons take part in a process where winner will take over (a competitive network). The node whose weights vector closest to the weights of inputs is considered the winner. When this node wins a competition, the neighbours' weights are also changed, albeit to a lesser extent. The further the neighbour is from the winner, the smaller its weight change. This process is then repeated for each input vector for a large number of cycles. Different inputs produce different winners. The net result is a SOM which is capable of associating output nodes with specific groups or patterns in the input data set (Kohonen, 2001). SOM has been already found an efficient gene clustering tools (Koop, et al., 2004; Chon & Park, 2008).

The basic limitation associated with SOM is of a value for each feature from training data in order to generate a map. Sometimes this simply is not possible and often it is very difficult to acquire all of this data, this problem is also referred to as missing data. Another problem is that every SOM is different and finds different similarities among the training vectors (Kohonen, 2001).

Figure 14. Lift performances measures with Apriori association rule mining algorithm for six cancer problems

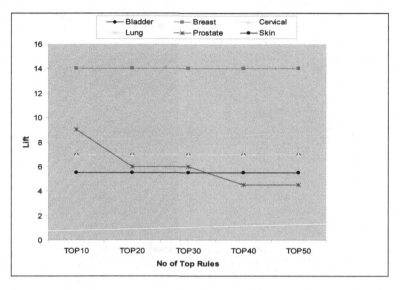

EXPERIMENTAL OUTCOME

Experiment One: Cancer Risk Factors Discovery

Three association rule mining algorithms have been considered: Apriori, Predictive Apriori and Tertius to discover significant risk factor for a specific cancer. We found among these three algorithms Apriori is the number one choice to extract significant risk factors from our cancer risk factors dataset (Nahar &

Figure 15. Leverage performances measures with Apriori association rule mining algorithm for six cancer problems

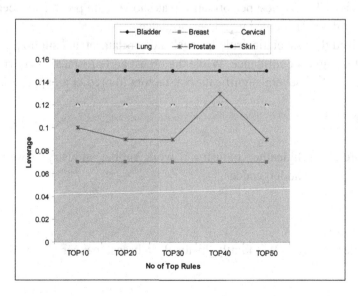

Figure 16. Conviction performances measures with Apriori association rule mining algorithm for six cancer problems

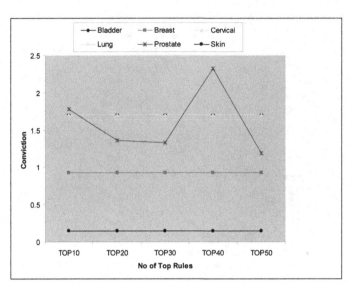

Tickle, 2008). The best rules were selected based on confidence and lift measures. All the reported rules obtained confidence 1. However, for the lift measure all the cancer datasets shows stable performance except prostate as shown in Figure 14. The breast data set shows highest lift values. On the other hand skin cancer problem showed the worst lift values.

Moreover verified Apriori performance with leverage measures as shown in Figure 15. As similar to lift measure we found except prostate cancer dataset, other cancers sets show steady performance. The highest performance was shown with skin cancer data set. On the other hand, breast cancer data set showed the worst performance in the leverage measure.

Finally we compare the apriori performance with conviction measure as shown in Figure 16. Conviction is a monotone in confidence and lift. We found similar steady performance for all the cancer data set except prostate cancer. The highest performance was shown with prostate cancer. On the other hand again the breast cancer data set showed worst performance.

Therefore we derived the association rule for each cancer dataset and summarized as below. All the generated rules had the highest confidence. While the breast and prostate cancer rules are very simple, the rest of the rules contained several significant risk factors to predict an appropriate cancer.

Relation: Bladder

Rule: (work_esposure ∩ work_leather_industry ∩ work_rubber_industry ∩ work_cable_industry ∩ work_printing_industry) ⇒ bladder_cancer

Relation: Breast

Rule: {gender (female) ∩ age(>40) ∩ family_history} ⇒ breast_cancer

Relation: Cervical

Rule: (poor_hygienic_practices ∩ low_socioeconomic_status ∩ low_vegetables ∩ sexually_transmitted_infections, smoking) ⇒ cervical_cancer

Relation: lung

Rule: (chemical_exposure ∩ smoking ∩ previous_lung_disease ∩ urban_residence ∩ family_history) ⇒ cervical_cancer

Relation: Prostrate

Rule: {family_history ∩ age (>50)} ⇒ prostrate_cancer

Relation: Skin

Rule: (weak_immune_system ∩ fragile_skin ∩ exposure_to_environmental_hazards ∩ previous_skin_cancer) ⇒ skin_cancer

All the generated rules have confidence 1. Therefore these rules are highly acceptable. Comparatively breast and prostrate cancer showed shorter rules comparing to other cancer. This research argues to consider more risk factors in the experimental data for breast and prostate cancer to extract most significant risk factors.

This study has demonstrated the use of association rule mining to identify some specific risk factors for a particular cancer problem. In this research we employed three types of association rule mining algorithms to extract significant risk factor for a specific cancer. Finally we suggested from our research to use Apriori algorithm for such type of tasks. All the generated rules had the highest level of confidence level. The main concern about Apriori is computational cost. But there is some solution to this question. This research will discuss one possible solution in the following chapter.

We have aim to extend this research by considering more risk factors in the raw data set for each cancer problem. Then association rule mining algorithm can extract more useful and significant risk factors for a particular cancer.

Experiment Two: Cancer Patient Classification

Proper cancer patient classification is an important task in the medical community. These sections will demonstrate the cancer patient classification by modern classification techniques using image and microarray data.

We considered several parameters to evaluate the machine learning algorithms. It is always better to justify any algorithm performance from different points of view. We considered two approaches to measure the performance. First, we observed the correctly classified performance for various algorithms and then we calculate the computational performance as well. Since the majority datasets hold less than 1000 instances, we preferred 10 fold cross validation procedure for our experiment. Moreover, we ran 10 times for each dataset. Therefore all the below results are started with (100). We used Percent_correct, i.e. accuracy, Mean_absolute_error, Root_mean_squared_error, Relative_absolute_error, Root_relative_ squared_error, True_negative_rate, False_negative_rate, F_measure, Kappa_statistic measures to evaluate the algorithms performances. These types of measures descriptions are available in any basic statistics books. Based on these measures we found SVM is the best suited algorithm to produce computer aided detection, CAD for breast cancer study.

Analysing: **Percent_correct**

Dataset NaiveBayes | SVM IBk AdaBoostM1 J48 PART

Dataset	NaiveBayes	SVM	IBk	AdaBoostM1	J48	PART
BcancerImage (100)	75.29	93.50	98.86	92.70	95.03	95.37
bcw_noise (100)	96.43	96.88	96.03	95.27	94.57	95.01
breast-cancer-wisconsin (100)	96.07	96.80	95.67	95.01	94.59	94.81
breastcancernsu (100)	49.88	71.55	61.45	59.71	54.76	53.79
breastmit (100)	51.26	90.90	86.04	65.04	73.49	73.67

Analysing: **Mean_absolute_error**

Dataset NaiveBayes | SVM IBk AdaBoostM1 J48 PART

Dataset	NaiveBayes	SVM	IBk	AdaBoostM1	J48	PART
BcancerImage (100)	0.24	0.07	0.01	0.13	0.06	0.05
bcw_noise (100)	0.04	0.03	0.04	0.06	0.06	0.05
breast-cancer-wisconsin (100)	0.04	0.03	0.04	0.07	0.06	0.06
breastcancernsu (100)	0.50	0.28	0.39	0.40	0.46	0.46
breastmit (100)	0.24	0.26	0.08	0.26	0.14	0.14

Analysing: **Root_mean_squared_error**

Dataset NaiveBayes | SVM IBk AdaBoostM1 J48 PART

```
-----------------------------------------------------------
```

BcancerImage (100) 0.48 | 0.24 0.06 0.24 0.20   0.18

bcw_noise (100) 0.18 | 0.16 0.19 0.19 0.22   0.21

breast-cancer-wisconsin (100) 0.18 | 0.160.19 0.22 0.20   0.20

breastcancernsu (100) 0.71 | 0.50 0.59 0.56 0.65   0.66

breastmit (100) 0.48 | 0.33 0.24 0.360.35   0.35

```
-----------------------------------------------------------
```

Analysing: **Relative_absolute_error**

Dataset NaiveBayes | SVM IBk AdaBoostM1 J48 PART

```
-----------------------------------------------------------
```

BcancerImage (100) 48.87 | 13.01 2.88 26.36 11.12   10.25

bcw_noise (100) 8.00 | 6.85 9.04 12.55 14.02   11.71

breast-cancer-wisconsin (100) 8.70 | 7.09 9.89 13.08 15.20   12.85

breastcancernsu (100) 100.12 | 56.83 77.74 79.93 91.30   92.47

breastmit (100) 70.03 | 75.45 22.58 74.37 40.69   39.38

```
-----------------------------------------------------------
```

Analysing: **Root_relative_squared_error**

Dataset NaiveBayes | SVM IBk AdaBoostM1 J48 PART

```
-----------------------------------------------------------
```

BcancerImage (100) 95.78 | 47.02 12.30 47.14 39.39   36.78

bcw_noise (100) 37.21 | 34.30 39.75 39.53 45.38   43.75

breast-cancer-wisconsin (100) 38.84 | 34.59 41.53 40.07 46.08   42.66

breastcancernsu (100) 140.80 | 99.15 117.25 112.47 130.79   131.80

breastmit (100) 115.81 | 79.17 57.91 85.49 83.99   83.93

Analysing: **True_negative_rate**

Dataset NaiveBayes | SVM IBk AdaBoostM1 J48 PART

BcancerImage (100) 0.70 | 0.98 0.99 0.930.96   0.96

bcw_noise (100) 0.98 | 0.96 0.910.92 0.93   0.93

breast-cancer-wisconsin (100) 0.95 | 0.97 0.97 0.97 0.95   0.96

breastcancernsu (100) 0.97 | 0.70 0.72 0.59 0.54   0.52

breastmit (100) 0.97 | 0.98 0.94 1.00 0.88   0.89

Analysing: **False_negative_rate**

Dataset NaiveBayes | SVM IBk AdaBoostM1 J48 PART

BcancerImage (100) 0.19 | 0.11 0.02 0.080.06   0.06

bcw_noise (100)| 0.02 0.01 0.03 0.04 0.04   0.04

breast-cancer-wisconsin (100) 0.03 | 0.04 0.070.07 0.08   0.08

breastcancernsu (100) 0.96 | 0.27 0.48 0.400.44   0.44

breastmit (100) 1.00 | 0.11 0.11 1.000.48   0.48

Analysing: **F_measure**

Dataset NaiveBayes | SVM IBk AdaBoostM1 J48 PART

```
----------------------------------------------------------------
```

BcancerImage (100) 0.76 | 0.93 0.99 0.920.95   0.95

bcw_noise (100) 0.97 | 0.98 0.970.96 0.96   0.96

breast-cancer-wisconsin (100) 0.95 | 0.95 0.94 0.930.92   0.92

breastcancernsu (100) 0.06 | 0.71 0.54 0.570.53   0.53

breastmit (100) 0.00 | 0.88 0.81 0.00 0.46   0.44

```
----------------------------------------------------------------
```

Analysing: **Kappa_statistic**

Dataset NaiveBayes | SVM IBk AdaBoostM1 J48 PART

```
----------------------------------------------------------------
```

BcancerImage (100) 0.51 | 0.87 0.98 0.85 0.90   0.91

bcw_noise (100) 0.92 | 0.93 0.91 0.90 0.88   0.89

breast-cancer-wisconsin (100) 0.91 | 0.93 0.90 0.890.88   0.88

breastcancernsu (100) 0.01 | 0.43 0.23 0.19 0.09   0.07

breastmit (100) 0.33 | 0.87 0.80 0.420.62   0.62

```
----------------------------------------------------------------
```

Analysing: **Time_training**

Dataset NaiveBayes | SVM IBk AdaBoostM1 J48 PART

```
----------------------------------------------------------------
```

BcancerImage (100) 0.01 | 0.15 0.00 0.12 0.04   0.05

bcw_noise (100) 0.01 | 0.15 0.00 0.09 0.02   0.03

breast-cancer-wisconsin (100) 0.00 | 0.13 0.00 0.04 0.01   0.02

breastcancernsu (100) 1.00 | 2.02 0.06 16.14 3.98   4.64

breastmit (100) 0.11 | 0.99 0.01 0.42 0.86   1.28

Analysing: **Time_testing**

Dataset NaiveBayes | SVM IBk AdaBoostM1 J48 PART

BcancerImage (100)| 0.00 0.06 0.00 0.00 0.00   0.00

bcw_noise (100)| 0.00 0.08 0.00 0.00 0.00   0.00

breast-cancer-wisconsin (100)| 0.00 0.04 0.00 0.00 0.00   0.00

breastcancernsu (100) 0.24 | 0.02 1.040.00 0.00   0.00

breastmit (100) 0.05 |0.23 0.00 0.00 0.00   0.00

The computational time was measured in seconds. We considered the computational performance in the two different phases: model buildup time called Time_training and model evolution time called Time_testing. Overall SVM is expensive in terms of computational cost compared toother algorithms. In the following section we propose sensitivity based feature selection for cancer patient classification. This approach will help SVM for faster cancer patient classification.

It would help to breast cancer computer aided detection (CAD) to choose an appropriate machine learning algorithm. For computer aided detection on the breast cancer dataset, we tested the algorithms performance from different angle by using useful statistical measures. These measures verified the algorithms classification performance. Moreover, we tested the computational performance for all the algorithms. We found SVM is the best suited machine learning algorithm for breast cancer study. It performed better in the scenarios, image and microarray breast data analysis. Comparatively it was best to handle image data. Since medical practitioners are struggling to recognize breast cancer problems in the early stages, microarray analysis could be a very useful technique for a breast cancer CAD system. We suggest both microarray and image based approach could be jointly adopted in the CAD system. This combined approach could verify more accurately any breast cancer present. We have planned to extend this research within the larger breast cancer domain. We will search the reasons why the image data is more meaningful for breast cancer study.

LIMITATION OF THE EXISTING TECHNIQUES

Several traditional methods are used to diagnose cancer and heart diseases, but at present the most popular diagnostic systems are:

- Blood test
- Ultrasound
- X-ray
- Biopsy
- MRI
- CT Scan
- Mammogram
- ECG

The current diagnostic system of breast cancer treatment has lot of limitations and in some cases the existing techniques carry out misleading information (Breast Ultrasound, 2008, Pusztai et al., 2006). That's why medical professionals suggest a combination of tests, such as Clinical breast examination, Mammogram, Ultrasound and Magnetic Resonance Imaging (MRI). However the combined diagnostics processes are expensive and involve long delays. Moreover there have some limitations, for instance early cancer detection, most appropriate risk factor identification; minor heart beat changing pattern recognition.

On the other hand computer aided detection (machine learning) is going popularity for cancer and heart disease identification. In that case we have to find out the best algorithms for cancer and heart beat related diseases identification in the early stages. The following section will provide some possible solution to overcome limitations of the existing machine learning techniques in the analysis of biological data.

FUTURE AIM

Heartbeat Identification

Heartbeat is the most important signal generator in human body which always carries the latest information about the body performance. Any uncommon signal gives the information about a certain change in the human body. This section will explain a new approach to find the association between the patterns of the heartbeat and some specific diseases.

The aim and objective of our research can be summarized as:

- Identify the association with the pattern of the heartbeat and some specified diseases using our proposed approach.
- Develop a new smoothing process to overcome the weakness of the Landmark smoothing process for heartbeat analysis.

Figure 17. Chart with Landmark smoothing process

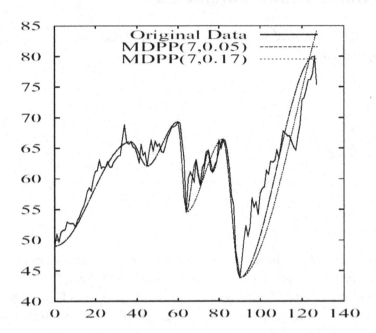

New Smoothing Process

We are proposing a smoothing process that can overcome the weakness of the Landmark Smoothing Process by Perng, et al., (2000). They proposed an idea of "Landmark Smoothing Process MDPP (D, P)". The process tries to minimize the fluctuation and noise in the data. The process used the Landmark (i.e. critical points) to re-construct the figure, and only the settled landmarks will be used to re-construct the figure. Figure 17 demonstrates an example of MDPP (D, P). It removes the fluctuations and smoothes the curves with 2 different parameters - P and D. The descriptions about the parameters P and D, and how the landmarks are removed will be provided in the next section. During the process, the useless landmarks will be removed. However, MDPP (D, P) focuses on two consecutive landmarks only, i.e. $(x_i, y_i), (x_{i+1}, y_{i+1})$; it fails to consider the next two landmarks, i.e. $(x_{i+3}, y_{i+3}), (x_{i+4}, y_{i+4})$.

MDPP (D, P) can be described as follows:

Given a sequence of landmark $((x_1, y_1), (x_2, y_2), \ldots (x_n, y_n))$, a minimal time interval D, and minimal vibration percentage P, the landmarks (x_1, y_1) and (x_{i+1}, y_{i+1}) will be removed if

$$X_{i+1} - x_i < D \text{ and } \frac{\left|(y_{i+1} - y_i)\right|}{\left(\left|y_i\right| + \left|y_{i+1}\right|\right)/2} < P$$

Our analysis indicates Landmark Smoothing Process may generate some misleading curves if it considers only two consecutive landmarks. Let figure 18 as an instance. Suppose we have five landmarks E, F, G, D, E, and F and G don't meet the criteria of MDPP(D,P) with the specified value of D and P, the final pattern will only appear as (i) according to the Landmark smoothing process. However,

Figure 18. Example to demonstrate the problem of Landmark smoothing process

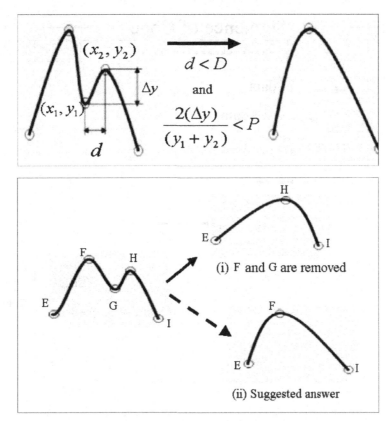

we should consider (ii) as the desirable pattern. It is more appropriate based on human intuition, as F is higher than H. Thus, MDPP (D,P) may generate some problems if it considers only two consecutive landmarks only.

In our research plan, we plan to propose an approach that will consider more landmarks so the above problem can be minimized.

Input Data Conversion

This process mainly converts the sequence of code to the data format that can be used in association discovery techniques.

We will apply the sliding window approach to generate all data for data mining. Let us use Figure 19 to demonstrate the idea. Suppose the sequence of the code is $(Z_1, Z_2,...Z_m)$, the first data will contain the first three codes, then, we slide one step ahead to obtain the second data, so on until the last data is obtained

For example, suppose the sequence of code is generated from one of heart beat diagram.

Let the sequence of code be "B1 C7 B2 C6 C7 B2"

It will generate the data set:

Figure 19. Converting the sequence of code to input format

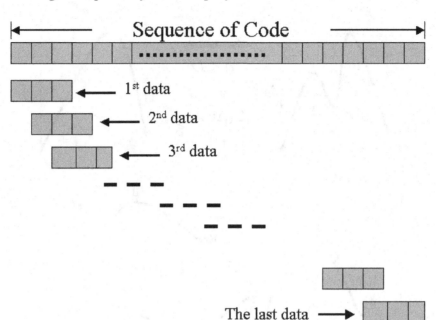

```
B1  C7  B2
C7  B2  C6
B2  C6  C7
C6  C7  B2
```

When the series is in a stable and constant situation, this series can be converted to a sequence of code that contains one element. In this situation, the length is less than three. Then, we are not able to slide window to generate a set of data. In order to distinguish the difference, we specify the data set generated from the stable series should contain one data, and the code of the data is "A1 0 0"

We generate one data set for each patient's heartbeat diagram. Then, we group all data sets to form a whole data set. As we described in Figure 17, there are four independent diagrams generated from the original heart beat diagram. Each independent diagram will generate one set of whole data. Thus we will obtain four sets of whole data. Each whole data set is represented as the data of one of attributes in data mining process.

Generating an Association Rule Using the Association Discovery Technique

In the final stage for finding the association rule association discovery is used to find items what imply the presence of other items in the same record. The discovery process produces association rule in the form: "If C input is used then R will likely happen."

The details about how Association Discovery works are described as following:

Let us assume we have an association rule indicated as LHS → RHS

|T| is the total number of records in the database.

|C| is the number of records covered by the LHS.

|R| is the number of records covered by RHS.

|C∩R| is the number of records covered by both the LHS and RHS, indicated by the overlapping area in Figure   20.

The five common measures can be expressed as follows.

$$Coverage = \frac{|C|}{|T|}, \quad Support.Factor = \frac{|C \cap R|}{|T|}, \quad Strength = \frac{|C \cap R|}{|C|},$$

$$Lift = strength \div \frac{|R|}{|T|} \quad Leverage = \frac{|C \cap R|}{|T|} - \frac{|C|}{|T|} \times \frac{|R|}{|T|}$$

In this research, the attributes *PM*, *PV*, *PPM* and *PPV* are specified in LHS; the attribute Disease code is specified in RHS.

Empirical experiments with real data will be used in our research project to validate and support our concept. However, in this proposal we will just use the following unreal case to exemplify how our approach and process work.

Suppose following five top rules are generated using Support.

R1: *PM*= (B1∩C1∩B2) and *PPV*= (C2∩A1∩B) ⇒ Acute Pulmonary Embolus (Support=0.95)

R2: *PM* = (C3∩B1∩B2) ⇒ Acute Pulmonary Embolus (Support=0.84)

R3: *PPV*= (B3∩C1∩B) and *PPM*= (A1∩B2∩C1) ⇒ Acute Pulmonary Embolus (Support=0.7)

Figure 20. Venn diagram

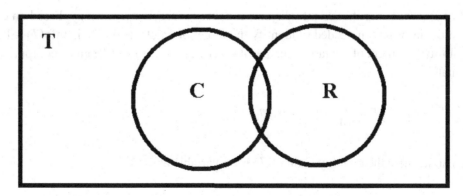

R4: PV= (B2∩B1∩C2) ⇒ Acute Pulmonary Embolus (Support=0.52)

R5: PPV= (B3∩C1∩B2) ⇒ Acute Pulmonary Embolus (Support=0.4)

It implies that the patient with Acute Pulmonary Embolus most likely has the pattern with the codes PM = (B1∩C1∩B2) and PPV= (C2∩A1∩B).

Sensitivity Based Feature Selection for Cancer Patient Classification

Lu and Han (2003) suggest any single classifier is not superior over all the others in the aspect of classification accuracy. After that we decided to involve several classifiers in a single system for proper feature selection to do cancer patient classification.
    The aim and objective of our research can be summarized as:

Evaluate several classification algorithms for a specific cancer problem and select the best performed classifier.

Reduce computational complexity by adopting attribute sensitivity analysis.

The sensitivity based feature selection approach is a several classifiers based approach. The following section will provide some mathmetical foundation about these methods.

Decision Tree C5.0

Decision Tree is a popular algorithm from the supervised learning group, which was first used by Quilan (Quilan, 1993) for data classification. Prof. Quilan first introduced ID3 decision tree algorithm then he updated the ID3 with new names such as C4.5 and C5.0. A decision tree is a simple rule based learning algorithm which is easy to understand. A simple decision tree is shown in Figure 12.
    Given the similar data matrix $[x_1, x_2, x_3, \cdots, x_n]$ and a probability distribution $P = (p_1, p_2, p_3, ..., p_n)$ the Entropy P is expressed as follows:

$$I(P) = -(p_1 \log(p_1) + p_2 \log(p_2) + p_3 \log(p_3) + \cdots + p_n \log(p_n))$$

If a set T of records is partitioned into disjoint exhaustive targets $y_1, y_2, y_3, ..., y_k$ based on categorical attribute, then the information needed to identify the target of an element of T is Info(T) = I(P), where P is the possibility allotment of the target i.e., partition $(y_1, y_2, y_3, ..., y_k)$ and P can be computed using the following equation:

$$P = (|y_1|/|T|, |y_2|/|T|, |y_3|/|T|, \cdots, |y_n|/|T|)$$

Now, we can identify the quantity Gain (X,T) for a variable as:

Figure 21. Working philosophy of PART algorithm (Witten and Frank, 2005)

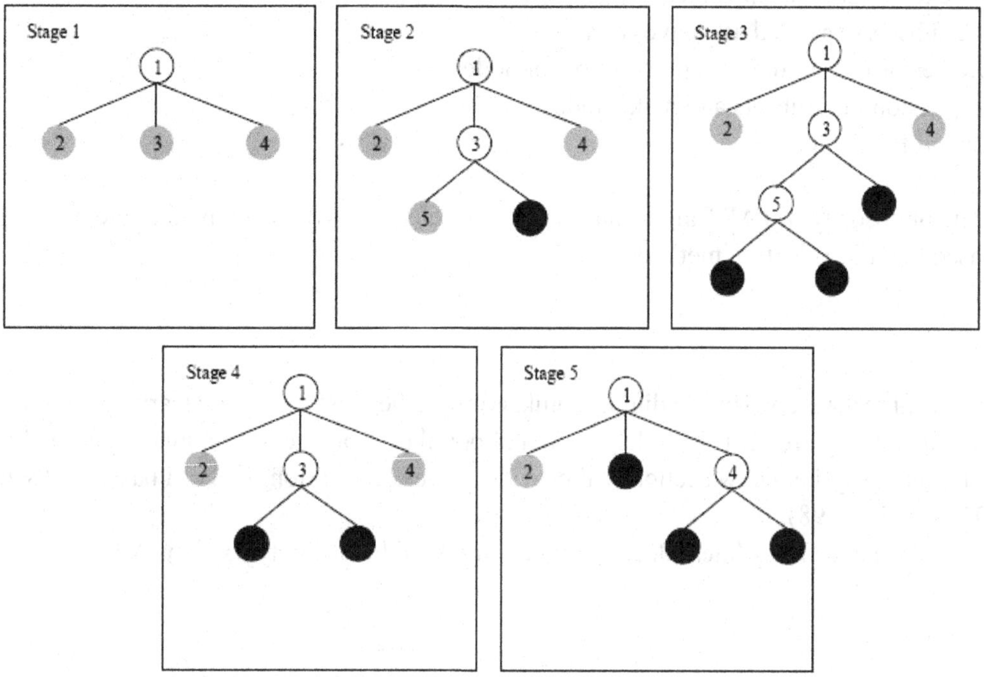

$$Gain(X,T) = Info(T) - Info(X,T)$$

Finally, the calculated gain to rank the features is used to build a decision tree.

PART

Part is comparative a recent scheme for producing sets of rules called "decision lists", which are ordered sets of rules in WEKA machine learning tools (Witten and Frank, 2005). They argue two popular rule based algorithms, C4.5 and RIPPER first generate an initial rule set and then they refine it using a complex optimization process to make them work better together. For this reason, unlike C4.5 and RIPPER, PART doesn't have to perform global optimization in order to generate rules (Frank and Witten, 1998). As a result Part is a faster algorithm compared with decision trees. The main philosophy of this algorithm is C4.5's heuristics algorithm and it works by forming pruned partial decision trees. Finally, it immediately converts them into a corresponding rule. A new data item is compared to each rule in the list in turn, and the item is assigned the category of the first matching rule (Cunningham and Holmes, 2000). The basic principle of PART algorithm is summarized in below with Figure 21.

PART Algorithm

'choose split of given set of examples into subsets
    while there are subsets that have not been expanded and

all the subsets expanded so far area leaves
choose next subset to be expanded and expand it
if all the subsets expanded are leaves and
estimated error for subtree ≥ estimate error for node
undo expansion into subsets and make node a leaf'
-Witten and Frank, 2005.

The basic philosophy of PART algorithm for feature selection will be adopted in the proposed Sensitivity Based Feature Selection method.

SVM

The SVM algorithm developed by Vladimir Vapnik, is one of the most successful learning algorithm from the supervised learning group. It is widely used and popular in businesses, engineering, medical, and science communities. The below section will provide a brief description on SVM based on (Scholkopf et al., 1997; Vapnik, 1998).

Suppose we want to find a linear decision function f with the property $f(x_i) = y_i$, $\forall i$.

$$y_i[(\mathbf{w} \cdot \mathbf{x}_i) + b] \geq 1, \quad \forall i \tag{1}$$

In practice, a separating hyperplane often does not exist. To allow for the possibility of examples violating (1), Vapnik introduce the slack variables ξ_i are:

$$\xi_i \geq 0, \quad \forall i \tag{2}$$

to get

$$y_i[(\mathbf{w} \cdot \mathbf{x}_i) + b] \geq 1 - \xi_i, \quad \forall i \tag{3}$$

The Support Vector (SV) approach to minimizing the guaranteed risk bound consists of the following. Minimize

$$\tau(\mathbf{w}, \xi) = \tfrac{1}{2}(\mathbf{w} \cdot \mathbf{w}) + \gamma \sum_{i=1}^{l} \xi_i \tag{4}$$

subject to the constraints (2) and (3).

Introducing Lagrange multipliers α_i and using the Kuhn_Tucker theorem of optimization theory, the solution is as follows:

$$\mathbf{w} = \sum_{i=1}^{l} y_i \alpha_i \mathbf{x}_i \tag{5}$$

with nonzero coefficients α_i only where the corresponding example (x_i, y_i) precisely meets the constraint (3). This x_i is called SVs. All residual example of the training set are immaterial. The constraint (3) is satisfied automatically (with $\xi_i = 0$), and they do not appear in the expansion (5). The coefficients α_i are found by solving the following quadratic optimization. Maximize

$$W(\alpha) = \sum_{i=1}^{l} \alpha_i - \frac{1}{2} \sum_{i,j=1}^{l} \alpha_i \alpha_j y_i y_j (\mathbf{x}_i \cdot \mathbf{x}_j)$$

(6)

subject to

$$0 \leq \alpha_i \leq \gamma, \quad i = 1, \cdots, l, \text{ and } 0 \leq \alpha_i \leq \gamma, \quad i = 1, \cdots, l, \sum_{i=1}^{l} \alpha_i y_i = 0 \text{ and } \sum_{i=1}^{l} \alpha_i y_i = 0$$

(7)

This is the time consuming process in SVM implementation. More general image or microarray data always holds too many features for a single problem. Due to this, proper feature selection is necessary before starting the quadratic optimization process to achieve a faster and useful decision. In that case, we like to introduce a sensitivity based feature selection approach for SVM.

After that, by linearity of the dot product, the decision function can be written as

$$f(\mathbf{x}) = \text{sgn} \left[\sum_{i=1}^{l} y_i \alpha_i \cdot (\mathbf{x} \cdot \mathbf{x}_i) + b \right].$$

(8)

To allow for much more general decision surfaces, one can first nonlinearly transform a set of input vectors $x_1, \ldots, x_l$ into a high-dimensional feature space. The decision function becomes

$$f(\mathbf{x}) = \text{sgn} \left[\sum_{i=1}^{l} y_i \alpha_i \cdot K(\mathbf{x}, \mathbf{x}_i) + b \right]$$

(9)

where RBF kernels is

$$K(\mathbf{x}, \mathbf{x}_i) = \exp(-\|\mathbf{x} - \mathbf{x}_i\|^2 / c)$$

(10)

As like RBF there have some other kernel, for instance Polynomial, Fisher, Sigmoid, etc are also available to extract SV for SVM

Finally the proposed sensitivity based feature selection approach is sketched in Figure 22.

Before start the sensitivity counting of a feature from a dataset, we will split the dataset into 10 folds. For each fold we will calculate the feature sensitivity by single iteration. Then in the sensitivity matrix we will place the feature ranking. At the identical time C5.0 and PART algorithm will work jointly. After completing the sensitivity matrix, based on the threshold value, the system will return the new feature matrix to SVM. Then the system will compare the SVM, C5.0, PART and reduced feature space performance of SVM. Finally the system will feed the best model for image and microarray based cancer classification. The whole approach will be implemented using Matlab Simulink package.

Automatic Clustering

The aim and objective of our research can be summarized as:

- Identify groups of co-regulated genes using clustering techniques.
- Discover spatial or temporal expression patterns using automated distance measure.

Alpaydin summarized the simple K-means clustering algorithm as follows (Alpaydin, 2004):

Initialize $\mathbf{m}_i$, $i = 1,\ldots,k$, for example, to k random $\mathbf{x}^t$

Repeat

For all $\mathbf{x}^t$ in X

$b_i^t \leftarrow 1$ if $\| \mathbf{x}^t - \mathbf{m}_i \| = \min_j \| \mathbf{x}^t - \mathbf{m}_j \|$

$b_i^t \leftarrow 0$ otherwise

For all $\mathbf{m}_i$, $i = 1,\ldots,k$

Figure 22. Proposed model for sensitivity based feature selection

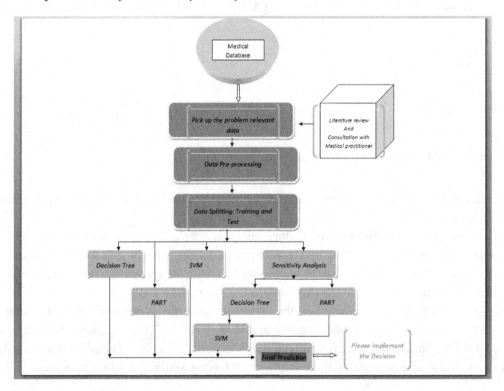

$$\mathbf{m}_i \leftarrow \text{sum over } t \ (b_i^t \mathbf{x}^t) \ / \ \text{sum over } t \ (b_i^t)$$

Until $\mathbf{m}_i$ converge

The vector $\mathbf{m}$ contains a reference to the sample mean of each cluster, $\mathbf{x}$ refers to each of our examples, and $\mathbf{b}$ contains the cluster level. One of the important factors is distance measure, $\min_j \| \mathbf{x}^t - \mathbf{m}_j \|$. *Euclidean, Manhattan* and *Minkowski* distance measure method are more frequently used metrics. There is no single distance measure method based on this that is best for clustering tasks.

However, we can introduce a meta learning approach to select unique distance measures method for clustering algorithm. We choose five values to construct the meta data characteristics. The five values are descriptive statistical measures are as follows:

- The minimum value of a gene sequence
- The lower quartile or first quartile of the same gene sequence
- The medium value of the same sequence
- The upper quartile or third quartile of the gene sequence
- The maximum value of the same gene sequence

Additional descriptive statistical measure could be added into the meta data characteristics matrix.

After constructing the new descriptive statistics based data matrix we will use Apriori/C5.0/PART algorithm to generate the rules corresponding with the distance measure method. Finally these rules will be adopted in the clustering algorithm for automatic gene expression data clustering.

DISCUSSIONS

The main problem of existing diagnostic systems is the inability for early detection. The majority of cases in the early stages of cancer and heart disease have no symptoms, so it is very hard to identify the stage and condition of the patients. For cancer, when symptoms are identified then the cancer cells have often already spread to other parts of the body. However, traditional diagnostic systems are expensive and take a long time to find out the disease status. As cancer and heart disease are the top 2 death rate for human, early detection of cancer and heart disease is an important issue.

From the vast range of literature reviewed it can be seen that existing machine learning techniques are being used in heart and cancer diagnoses. But there have some limitations of these machine learning techniques as well. This chapter provided a review on common cancer types. After that, we provided a brief summary on existing popular machine learning techniques. Finally we conducted two experiments to measure the machine learning algorithm performance. In the first experiment, three association rule mining algorithms have been considered, namely Apriori, Predictive Apriori and Tertius to discover significant risk factor for a specific cancer. From the experiment we observed Apriori is the number one choice to extract significant risk factor for our cancer risk factors dataset. In the second run we considered several parameters to evaluate the machine learning algorithms for early cancer patient classification. We considered two approaches to measure the performance. First, we observed the correctly classified performance for various algorithms and then we calculate the computational performance as well. Based on these measures we found SVM is the best suited algorithm to produce CAD for breast cancer study.

At the same time we summarized the limitations of all the existing tools. Towards the end, we focused on some possible future solutions. The significant mathematical background was built up in this chapter to find out the heartbeat related hidden diseases identification.

Fortunately, new treatments and technologies can increase the survival rate for the people with heart disease and cancer. Machine learning techniques provide a possible way forward in the early detection of these diseases.

REFERENCES

Agrawal, R., Imielinski, T., & Swami, A. (1993). Mining association rules between sets of items in large databases. In *ACM SIGMOD Conference*, (pp. 207–216).

Ali, S., & Smith, K. A. (2006). A meta-learning approach to automatic kernel selection for support vector machines. *Neurocomputing, 70*(1-3), 173–186. doi:10.1016/j.neucom.2006.03.004

Ali, S. & Smith, K. A. (2006). On Learning Algorithm Selection for Classification Applied Soft Computing, *Elsevier Science. 6*(2), 119-138.

Ali, S., & Wasimi, S. (2007). *Data Mining: Methods and Techniques*. Sydney: Thomson, Australia.

Alizadeh, A. A., Eisen, M. B., Davis, R. E., Ma, C., Lossos, I. S., & Rosenwald, A. (2000). Distinct types of diffuse large B-cell lymphoma identified by gene expression profiling. *Nature, 403*, 503–511. doi:10.1038/35000501

Almonte, M., Albero, G., Molano, M., Carcamo, C., García, P. J., & Pérez, G. (2008). Risk factors for Human Papillomavirus Exposure and Co-factors for Cervical Cancer in Latin America and the Caribbean. *Vaccine, 26*, L16–L36. doi:10.1016/j.vaccine.2008.06.008

Alpaydin, E. (2004). *Introduction To Machine Learning*. Cambridge, MA: MIT Press.

Antonie, M.-L., Zaiane, O. R., & Coman, A. (2001). Application of Data Mining Techniques for Medical Image Classification. In *Proceeding of the second International Workshop on Multimedia Data and Mining*, (pp. 94-101).

Barak, Y., Levy, T., Achiron, A., & Aizenberg, D. (2008). Breast cancer in women suffering from serious mental illness. *Schizophrenia Research, 102*, 249–253. doi:10.1016/j.schres.2008.03.017

Baronti, F. (2005). *Experimental Comparison of Machine Learning Approaches To Medical Domains: A Case Study Of Genotype Influence On Oral Cancer Development*. European conference on Emergent aspects in clinical data analaysis EACDA.

Bayardo, R. J., Jr., & Agrawal, R. (1999). International Conference on knowledge discovery and data mining. In *Proceedings of the Fifth ACMSIGKDD international conference on knowledge discovery and data mining*, San Diego, CA. (pp. 145 – 154).

Berns, A. (2000). Cancer: gene expression in diagnosis. *Nature, 403*, 491–492. doi:10.1038/35000684

Berrar, D. P., Downes, C. S., & Dubitzky, W. (2003). Multiclass Cancer Classification Using Gene Expression Profiling and Probabilistic Neural Networks. In *Proceeding of the Pacific Symposium on Biocomputing*, (pp. 5-16).

Berry, M. J. A., & Gordon, S. L. (2000). *Mastering Data Mining: The Art and Science of Customer Relationship Management*. New York: Wiley Computer Publishing.

Bjarge, T., Engeland, A., Luostarinen, T., Mork, J., Gislefoss, R. E., & Jellum, E. (2002). Human papillomavirus infection as a risk factor for anal and perianal skin cancer in a prospective study. *British Journal of Cancer*, *87*, 61–64. doi:10.1038/sj.bjc.6600350

Breast Cancer Statistics (2008). Retrieved February 12th, 2008, http://www.breastcancer.org/symptoms/understand_bc/statistics.jsp

Breast Ultrasound (2008). Retrieved from February 23, 2009, http://www.radiologyinfo.org/en/info.cfm?pg=breastus

Breiman, L., Friedman, J. H., Olshen, R. A., & Stone, C. J. (1984). Classification Based on Gene Expressions. In *International Joint Conference on Neural Networks*, Vancouver, Canada, (pp. 1930-1934).

Campbell, C., Li, Y., & Tipping, M. (2001). An efficient feature selection algorithm for classification of gene expression data. In *NIPS 2001 Workshop on Machine Learning Techniques for Bioinformatics*, Vancouver, Canada.

Cancer.org. (2008). Retrieved October 6th, 2008, http://www.cancer.org

Cassidy, A., Myles, J. P., Tongeren, M. V., Page, R. D., Liloglou, T., Duffy, S. W., & Field, J. K. (2008). The LLP risk model: an individual risk prediction model for lung cancer. *British Journal of Cancer*, *98*, 270–276. doi:10.1038/sj.bjc.6604158

Cercato, M. C., Nagore, E., Ramazzotti, V., Guillén, C., Terrenato, I., & Villena, J. (2008). Self and parent-assessed skin cancer risk factors in school-age children. *Preventive Medicine*, *47*, 133–135. doi:10.1016/j.ypmed.2008.03.004

Cervical cancer (2008). Retrieved February 12, 2009, from http://www.cancer.org/docroot/CRI/content/CRI_2_4_1X_What_are_the_key_statistics_for_cervical_cancer_8

Chon, T.-S., & Park, Y.-S. (2008). Self-Organizing Map. *Encyclopedia of Ecology*, (pp. 3203-3210).

Chu, F., & Wang, L. (2006). *Applying RBF Neural Networks to Cancer Classification and Regression Trees*. Wadsworth: Belmont, CA.

Ciaramella, A., Cocozza, S., Iorio, F., Miele, G., Napolitano, F., & Pinelli, M. (2008). Interactive data analysis and clustering of genomic data. *Neural Networks*, *21*(2-3), 368–378. doi:10.1016/j.neunet.2007.12.026

Cios, K. J., Chen, K., & Langenderfer, L. A. (1997). Use of Neural Networks in Detecting Cardiac Diseases from Echocardiographic Images. *IEEE Engineering in Medicine and Biology Magazine*, *16*(6).

Cooke, C. D., Ordonez, C., Garcia, E. V., Omiecinski, E., & Krawczynska, E. G. (1999). Data mining of large myocardial perfusion SPECT (MPS) databases to improve diagnostic decision making. *Journal of Nuclear Medicine, 40*(5).

Coppini, G., Poli, R., & Valli, G. (1995). Recovery of the 3-D shape of the left ventricle from echocardiographic images. *IEEE Transactions on Medical Imaging, 14*, 301–317. doi:10.1109/42.387712

Cortes, C., & Vapnik, V. (1995). Support-vector networks. *Machine Learning, 20*, 273–297.

Cpaaindia. (2008). www.cpaaindia.org, accessed 12th August, 2008.

Creighton, C., & Hanash, S. (2003). Mining gene expression databases for association rules. *Bioinformatics (Oxford, England), 19*(1), 79–86. doi:10.1093/bioinformatics/19.1.79

Cunningham, S. J., & Holmes, G. (2000). *Developing innovative applications in agriculture using data mining*. Tech. Report, Dept. of Computer Science, University of Waikato, New Zealand.

D'Avanzo, B., Vecchia, C. L., Negri, E., Decarli, A., & Benichou, J. (1995). Attributable risks for bladder cancer in Northern Italy. *Annals of Epidemiology, 5*, 427–431. doi:10.1016/1047-2797(95)00057-7

Dataset, (2008). Retrieved 17th August, 2008, from http://www.broad.mit.edu/cgi-bin/cancer/datasets. cgi

Duin, R. P. W. (1996). A note on comparing classifiers. *Pattern Recognition Letters, 17*, 529–536. doi:10.1016/0167-8655(95)00113-1

Eberhart, R. C., Dobbins, R. W., & Webber, W. R. S. (1989). CASENET: A Neural Network Tool for EEG waveform classification. In *Proc. IEEE Symposium on Computer Based Medical System*.

Eisen, M. B., Spellman, P. T., Brown, P. O., & Botstein, D. C. (1998). Analysis and display of genome-wide expression patterns. *Proceedings of the National Academy of Sciences of the United States of America, 95*, 14863–14868. doi:10.1073/pnas.95.25.14863

El-Baz, A., Gimelfarb, G., Falk, R., & Abo El-Ghar, M. A. (2008). Automatic analysis of 3D low dose CT images for early diagnosis of lung cancer. *Pattern Recognition*.

Eltonsy, N. H., Elmaghraby, A. S., & Tourassi, G. D. (2007). Bilateral Breast Volume Asymmetry in Screening Mammograms as a Potential Marker of Breast Cancer: Preliminary Experience. *Image Processing, IEEE International Conference on, 5*, 5-8.

Flach, P. A., & Lachiche, N. (2001). *Confirmation-guided discovery of first-order rules with Tertius*, (Vol. 42, pp. 61-95). Amsterdam: Kluwer Academic Publishers.

Flexer, A. (1996). Statistical evaluation of neural network experiments: Minimum requirements and current practice. In R. Trappl, (Ed.), *Proc. 13th Eur. Meeting Cybernetics Systems Research*, (pp. 1005–1008).

Frank, E., & Witten, I. H. (1998). Generating Accurate Rule Sets Without Global Optimization. In *The Proceedings of Fifteenth International Conference on Machine Learning*, (pp. 144-151).

Freedland, S. J., Wen, J., Wuerstle, M., Shah, A., Lai, D., Moalej, B., et al. (2008). Obesity Is a Significant Risk Factor for Prostate Cancer at the Time of Biopsy. *Urology.*

Friedman, N., Geiger, D., & Goldszmidt, M. (1997). Bayesian Network Classifiers. *Machine Learning*, *29*, 131–163. doi:10.1023/A:1007465528199

Giovannucci, E., Rimm, E. B., Ascherio, A., Colditz, G. A., Spiegelman, D., Stampfer, M. J., & Willett, W. C. (1999). Smoking and Risk of Total and Fatal Prostate Cancer in United States Health Professionals. *Cancer Epidemiology, Biomarkers & Prevention*, *8*, 277–282.

Gu, J., Zhao, H., Dinney, C. P., Zhu, Y., Leibovici, D., & Bermejo, C. E. (2005). Nucleotide excision repair gene polymorphisms and recurrence after treatment for superficial bladder cancer. *Clinical Cancer Research*, *11*, 1408–1415. doi:10.1158/1078-0432.CCR-04-1101

Han, J., Colditz, G. A., Samson, L. D., & Hunter, D. J. (2004). Polymorphisms in DNA double-strand break repair genes and skin cancer risk. *Cancer Research*, *64*, 3009–3013. doi:10.1158/0008-5472. CAN-04-0246

Han, J., & Kamber, M. (2001). *Data mining: concepts and techniques.* San Francisco: Morgan Kauffmann.

Hand, D., Mannila, H., & Smyth, P. (2001). *Principles of Data Mining.* Cambridge, MA: The MIT Press.

Hastie, T., Tibshirani, R., & Friedman, J. H. (2001). *The Elements of Statistical Learning* (1st ed.). New York: Springer.

Haverkos, H. W., Soon, G., Steckley, S. L., & Pickworth, W. (2003). Cigarette smoking and cervical cancer: Part I: a meta-analysis. *Biomedicine and Pharmacotherapy*, *57*, 67–77. doi:10.1016/S0753-3322(03)00196-3

Herzog, T. J. (2003). New approaches for the management of cervical cancer. *Gynecologic Oncology*, *90*, 22–27. doi:10.1016/S0090-8258(03)00466-9

Ho, S. H., Jee, S. H., Lee, J. E., & Park, J. S. (2004). Analysis on risk factors for cervical cancer using induction technique. *Expert Systems with Applications*, *27*(1), 97–105. doi:10.1016/j.eswa.2003.12.005

Hong, J.-H., & Cho, S.-B. (2008). A probabilistic multi-class strategy of one-vs.-rest support vector machines for cancer classification . *Neurocomputing*, *71*(16-18), 3275–3281. doi:10.1016/j.neucom.2008.04.033

Ibchelp, (2008). Retrieved August 17th, 2008 from http://www.ibchelp.org/pictures.html

Images, (2008). Retrieved 1st of October, 2008, from http://search.live.com/images/

International Collaboration of Epidemiological Studies of Cervical Cancer. (2007). Cervical cancer and hormonal contraceptives: collaborative reanalysis of individual data for 16 573 women with cervical cancer and 35 509 women without cervical cancer from 24 epidemiological studies. *Lancet*, *370*, 1609–1621. doi:10.1016/S0140-6736(07)61684-5

Joachims, T. (1999). Making large-scale SVM learning practical. In *Advances in Kernel Methods.*

John, G. H., & Langley, P. (1995). Estimating continuous distributions in Bayesian classifiers. In *Proceedings of the Eleventh Conference on Uncertainty in Artificial Intelligence*, San Mateo, CA, (pp. 338–345). San Francisco: Morgan Kaufmann.

Johnson, A. M., O'Connell, M. J., Messing, E. M., & Reeder, J. E. (2008). Decreased Bladder Cancer Growth in Parous Mice. *Urology, 72*, 470–473. doi:10.1016/j.urology.2008.04.028

Jong, K. (2006). *Machine learning for human cancer research*, PhD Thesis, Vrije Universiteit Amsterdam.

Kaper, M., Meinicke, P., Grossekathoefer, U., Lingner, T., & Ritter, H. (2004). BCI competition 2003–data set iib: support vector machines for the p300 speller paradigm. *IEEE Transactions on Bio-Medical Engineering, 51*, 1073–1076. doi:10.1109/TBME.2004.826698

Karabatak, M., Sengur, A., & Ince, M. C & Turkoglu, I. (2006). Texture Classification By Using Association Rules. In *Proceedings of The 5th International Symposium on Intelligent Manufacturing Systems*, (pp. 96-104).

Kennedy, C., Bajdik, C. D., & Willemze, R., Gruijl, Frank, R. de. & Bavinck, J. N. B. (2003). The Influence of Painful Sunburns and Lifetime Sun Exposure on the Risk of Actinic Keratoses, Seborrheic Warts, Melanocytic Nevi, Atypical Nevi, and Skin Cancer. *The Journal of Investigative Dermatology, 120*, 1087–1093. doi:10.1046/j.1523-1747.2003.12246.x

Khan, J. M., Wei, J. S., Ringner, M., Saal, L. H., Ladanyi, M., & Westermann, F. (2001). Classification and diagnostic prediction of cancers using gene expression profiling and artificial neural networks. *Nature Medicine, 7*, 673–679. doi:10.1038/89044

Kim, C. S., Riikonen, P., & Salakoski, T. (2008). Detecting biological associations between genes based on the theory of phase synchronization. *Bio Systems, 92*(2), 99–113. doi:10.1016/j.biosystems.2007.12.006

King, R. J. B., & Robins, M. W. (2006). *Cancer biology*, (3rd ed.). London: Pearson Education Limited, UK.

Kohonen, T. (2001). *Self-Organizing Maps,* (30, 3rd Ed.). Berlin: Springer.

Koop, K., Bakker, R. C., Eikmans, M., Baelde, H. J., de Heer, E., Paul, L. C., & Bruijn, J. A. (2004). Differentiation between chronic rejection and chronic cyclosporine toxicity by analysis of renal cortical mRNA. *Kidney International, 66*, 2038–2046. doi:10.1111/j.1523-1755.2004.00976.x

Kusiak, A., Kernstine, K. H., Kern, J. A., McLaughlin, K. A., Land, W. H., Jr., Timothy, M., et al. (2001). Application of Evolutionary Computation and Neural Network Hybrids for Breast Cancer Classification Using Mammogram and History Data. *Evolutionary Computation, Proceedings of the 2001 Congress on, 2*, 1147 – 1154.

Kusiak, A., Kernstine, K. H., Kern, J. A., McLaughlin, K. A., & Tseng, T. L. (2000). Data Mining: Medical and Engineering Case Studies. In *Proceedings of the Industrial Engineering Research, Conference*, Cleveland, Ohio, (pp. 1-7).

Lee, Y., & Lee, C. K. (2003). Classification of multiple cancer types by mulitcategory support vector machines using gene expression data. *Bioinformatics (Oxford, England)*, *19*, 1132–1139. doi:10.1093/bioinformatics/btg102

Lee, Z.-J. (2008). An integrated algorithm for gene selection and classification applied to microarray data of ovarian cancer. *Artificial Intelligence in Medicine*, *42*(1), 81–93. doi:10.1016/j.artmed.2007.09.004

Li, J., & Liu, H. (2006). *Kent Ridge Biomedical Data Set Repository, Singapore*. Retrieved 4th September, 2006 from http://sdmc.i2r.a-star.edu.sg/rp/

Li, L., Tang, H., Wu, Z., Gong, J., Gruidl, M., & Zou, J. (2004). Data mining techniques for cancer detection using serum proteomic profiling. *Artificial Intelligence in Medicine*, *32*(2), 71–83. doi:10.1016/j.artmed.2004.03.006

Liang, F. (2007). Use of SVD-based probit transformation in clustering gene expression profiles . *Computational Statistics & Data Analysis*, *51*(12), 6355–6366. doi:10.1016/j.csda.2007.01.022

Lotte, F., & Congedo, M., L'ecuyer, A., Lamarche, F. & Arnaldi, B. (2007). A review of classification algorithms for EEG-based brain–computer interfaces. *Journal of Neural Engineering*, *4*, 1–13. doi:10.1088/1741-2560/4/2/R01

Lu, Y., & Han, J. (2003). Cancer classification using gene expression data. *Information Systems*, *28*, 243–268. doi:10.1016/S0306-4379(02)00072-8

MacQueen, J. B. (1967). Some methods for classification and analysis of multivariate observations. In *Proceedings of 5th Berkeley Symposium on Mathematical Statistics and Probability*, Berkeley, University of California Press, (pp. 281-297).

Magoulas, G. D., & Prentza, A. (2001). *Machine learning in medical applications* (LNAI, pp. 300 – 307). Berlin: Springer.

Marieb, E. N., & Hoehn, K. N. (2006). *Human anatomy and physiology (7th edition)*. New York: Benjamin Cummings.

Marieb, E. N., & Mitchell, S. J. (2007). *Human anatomy and physiology lab manual, cat version* (9th edition). New York: Benjamin Cummings.

Maskery, S., Zhang, Y., Hu, H., Shriver, C., Hooke, J., & Liebman, M. (2006). Caffeine Intake, Race, and Risk of Invasive Breast Cancer Lessons Learned from Data Mining a Clinical Database. *Computer-Based Medical Systems*, (pp. 714 – 718).

Matalliotakis, I. A., Cakmak, H., Mahutte, N., Goumenou, A. G., Koumantakis, G., & Aydin, A. (2008). The familial risk of breast cancer in women with endometriosis from Yale series. *Surgical Oncology*, 1–5.

Mehmed, K. (2002). *Data Mining: Concepts, Models, Methods, and Algorithms*. Mahwah, NJ: Wiley-IEEE Press.

Michaud, D. S. (2007). Chronic inflammation and bladder cancer. *Urologic Oncology: Seminars and Original Investigations*, *25*, 260–268. doi:10.1016/j.urolonc.2006.10.002

Midgley, M. (2003). Biotechnology and the yuk factor. In *The Myths We Live By*. London: Routledge.

Mihalakis, A., Mygdalis, V., Anastasiou, I., Adamakis, I., Zervas, A., & Mitropoulos, D. (2008). Patient awareness of smoking as a risk factor for bladder cancer. *European Urology Supplements, 7*, 138. doi:10.1016/S1569-9056(08)60268-7

Mitchell, T. M. (1997). *Machine Learning*. New York: McGraw-Hill.

Moehrle, M. (2008). Outdoor sports and skin cancer. *Clinics in Dermatology, 26*(1), 12–15. doi:10.1016/j.clindermatol.2007.10.001

Nahar, J., & Tickle, K. S. (2008). Significant Risk Factor Extraction Using Rule Based Methods. In *IEEE International Workshop on Data Mining and Artificial Intelligence*, Khulna, Bangladesh.

Nattkemper, T. W., Arnrich, B., Lichte, O., Timm, W., Degenhard, A., & Pointon, L. (2005). Evaluation of radiological features for breast tumour classification in clinical screening with machine learning methods. *Artificial Intelligence in Medicine, 34*, 129–139. doi:10.1016/j.artmed.2004.09.001

Nieder, A. M., John, S., Messina, C. R., Granek, I. A., & Adler, H. L. (2006). Are Patients Aware of the Association Between Smoking and Bladder Cancer? *The Journal of Urology, 176*, 2405–2408. doi:10.1016/j.juro.2006.07.147

Oberyszyn, T. M. (2008). Non-melanoma skin cancer: Importance of gender, immunosuppressive status and vitamin D. *Cancer Letters, 261*(2), 127–136.

Ordonez, C. (2006). Association rule discovery with the train and test approach for heart disease prediction. *IEEE Transactions on Information Technology in Biomedicine, 10*(2), 334–343. doi:10.1109/TITB.2006.864475

Ordonez, C., & Omiecinski, E. (1999). Discovering association rules based on image content. In *IEEE Advances in Digital Libraries Conference (ADL'99)*, (pp. 38–49).

Ordonez, C., Omiecinski, E., Braal, L., Santana, C. A., Ezquerra, N., Taboada, J. A., et al. (2001). Mining Constrained Association Rules to Predict Heart Disease. In *Proceeding of the First IEEE International Conference on Data Mining (ICDM'01)*, (pp. 433-441).

Ordonez, C., Santana, C. A., & de Braal, L. (2000). Discovering interesting association rules in medical data. In *ACM DMKD Workshop*, (pp. 78–85).

Pacella-Norman, R., Urban, M. I., Sitas, F., Carrara, H., Sur, R., & Hale, M. (2002). Risk factors for oesophageal, lung, oral and laryngeal cancers in black South Africans. *British Journal of Cancer, 86*, 1751–1756. doi:10.1038/sj.bjc.6600338

Palaniappan, S., & Awang, R. (2008). Intelligent Heart Disease Prediction System Using Data Mining Techniques. *IJCSNS International Journal of Computer Science and Network Security, 8*(8), 343–350.

Pendharkar, P. C., Rodger, J. A., Yaverbaum, G. J., Herman, N., & Benner, M. (1999). Association, statistical, mathematical and neural approaches for mining breast cancer patterns. *Expert Systems with Applications, 17*, 223–232. doi:10.1016/S0957-4174(99)00036-6

Perng, C.-S., Wang, H., Zhang, S. R., & Parker, D. S. (2000). Landmarks: a new model for similarity based pattern querying in the time series databases. In *Proceedings of the 16ᵗʰ Int. Conference on Data Engineering,* San Diego, CA.

Peters, G. (2006). Some refinements of rough *k*-means clustering . *Pattern Recognition, 39,* 1481–149. doi:10.1016/j.patcog.2006.02.002

Peterson, L. E., & Coleman, M. A. (2008). Machine learning-based receiver operating characteristic (ROC) curves for crisp and fuzzy classification of DNA microarrays in cancer research. *International Journal of Approximate Reasoning, 47*(1), 17–36. doi:10.1016/j.ijar.2007.03.006

Pharmacy, (2008). Retrieved August 25, 2008 from http://www.pharmacy.gov.my/self_care_guide/Urogenital/Postate%20Cancer.pdf

Phillips, J., Kumar, V., & Bryden, G. (2002). Bladder Cancer. *Surgery (Oxford), 20,* 281–284. doi:10.1383/surg.20.12.281.14645

Pichard, C., & Plu-Bureau, G., Neves-e Castro, M. & Gompel, A. (2008). Insulin resistance, obesity and breast cancer risk. *Maturitas, 60*(1), 19–30. doi:10.1016/j.maturitas.2008.03.002

Platt, J. (1999). Probabilistic Outputs For Support Vector Machines And Comparison To Regularized Likelihood Methods. In A. Smola, P. Bartlett, B. Schoelkopf, D. Schuurmans, (eds.), *Advances in Large Margin Classifiers*, (pp. 61–74).

Pomeroy, S. L., Tamayo, P., Gaasenbeek, M., Sturla, L. M., & Angelo, M. (2002). Prediction of central nervous embryonal tumour outcome based on gene expression. *Nature, 415,* 436–442. doi:10.1038/415436a

Popanda, O., Schattenberg, T., Phong, C. T., Butkiewicz, D., Risch, A., & Edler, L. (2004). Specific combinations of DNA repair gene variants and increased risk for non-small cell lung cancer. *Carcinogenesis, 25,* 2433–2441. doi:10.1093/carcin/bgh264

Porcel, J. M., Alemán, C., Bielsa, S., Sarrapio, J., De Sevilla, T. F., & Esquerda, A. (2008). A decision tree for differentiating tuberculous from malignant pleural effusions. *Respiratory Medicine, 102*(8), 1159–1164. doi:10.1016/j.rmed.2008.03.001

Prechelt, L. (1996). A quantitative study of experimental evaluation of neural network algorithms: Current research practice. *Neural Networks, 9*(3), 457–462. doi:10.1016/0893-6080(95)00123-9

Pun, D., & Ali, S. (2007). Unique Distance Measure Approach for K-means (UDMA-Km) Clustering Algorithm. In *CD proceeding of The IEEE international conference,* (pp. 1-4).

Pusztai, L., Mazouni, C., Anderson, K., Wu, Y., & Symmans, W. F. (2006). Molecular Classification of Breast Cancer: Limitations and Potential. *The Oncologist, 11,* 868–877. doi:10.1634/theoncologist.11-8-868

Qin, L., Ding, L., & He, B. (2004). Motor imagery classification by means of source analysis for brain–computer interface applications. *Journal of Neural Engineering, 1,* 135–141. doi:10.1088/1741-2560/1/3/002

Quinlan, J. R. (1986). Induction of decision trees. *Machine Learning, 1,* 81–106.

Quinlan, R. (1993). *C4.5: Programs for Machine Learning*. San Francisco, CA: Morgan Kaufman Publishers.

Rangayyan, R. M., Ayres, F. J., & Desautels, J. E. L. (2007). A review of computer-aided diagnosis of breast cancer: Toward the detection of subtle signs. *Journal of the Franklin Institute, 344*(3-4), 312–348. doi:10.1016/j.jfranklin.2006.09.003

Reissigl, C. A., Wiunig, C. H., Neyer, M., Grunser, H., Remzi, M., & Pointner, J. (2008). Chronic inflammtion of the prostate as a risk factor for prostate cancer: a 4 year follow up study. *European Urology Supplements, 7*, 226. doi:10.1016/S1569-9056(08)60618-1

Rish, J. H., & Jayram, T. (2001). *An Analysis of Data Characteristics That Affect Naive Bayes Performance*. Technical Report RC21993, IBM T.J. Watson Research Center.

Rodrigues, P. S., Ruey-Feng, C., & Suri, J. S. (2006). Non-Extensive Entropy for CAD Systems of Breast Cancer Images. *Computer Graphics and Image Processing, SIBGRAPI '06, 19th Brazilian Symposium,* (pp. 121 – 128).

Ross, Q. J. (1993). *C4.5: Programs for machine learning*. San Francisco: Morgan Kaufmann Publishers.

Rumelhart, D. E., Hinton, G. E., & Williams, R. J. (1986). *Learning internal representations by error propagation in parallel distributed processing, 1*, 318–362. Cambridge, MA: MIT Press.

Sakr, R., Rouzier, R., Salem, C., Antoine, M., Chopier, J., Daraï, E., & Uzan, S. (2008). Risk of breast cancer associated with papilloma. [EJSO]. *European Journal of Surgical Oncology*, 1–5.

Salzberg, S. L. (1997). On comparing classifiers: Pitfalls to avoid and a recommended approach. *Data Mining and Knowledge Discovery, 1*, 317–328. doi:10.1023/A:1009752403260

Schaner, M. E., Ross, D. T., Ciaravino, G., Sorlie, T., Troyanskaya, O., & Diehn, M. (2003). Gene expression patterns in ovarian carcinomas. *Molecular Biology of the Cell, 14*, 4376–4386. doi:10.1091/mbc.E03-05-0279

Scheffer, T. (2001). Finding Association Rules that Trade Support Optimally Against Confidence. In *Proceedings of the 5th European Conference on Principles and Practice of Knowlege Discovery in Databases(PKDD'01)*, (pp. 424-435). Freiburg, Germany: Springer-Verlag.

Schiffman, M., Castle, P. E., Jeronimo, J., Rodriguez, A. C., & Wacholder, S. (2007). Human papillomavirus and cervical cancer. *Lancet, 370*, 890–907. doi:10.1016/S0140-6736(07)61416-0

Schlogl, A., Lee, F., Bischof, H., & Pfurtscheller, G. (2005). Characterization of four-class motor imagery EEG data for the BCI-competition. *Journal of Neural Engineering, 2*, L14–L22. doi:10.1088/1741-2560/2/4/L02

Scholkopf, B., Sung, K.-K., Burges, C. J. C., Girosi, F., Niyogi, P., Poggio, T., & Vapnik, V. (1997). Comparing support vector machines with Gaussian kernels to radial basis function classifiers. *IEEE Transactions on Signal Processing, 11*(45), 2758–2765. doi:10.1109/78.650102

Sharma, A., & Paliwal, K. K. (2008). Cancer classification by gradient LDA technique using microarray gene expression data. *Data & Knowledge Engineering, 66*(2), 338–347. doi:10.1016/j.datak.2008.04.004

Shen, M., Chapman, R. S., He, X., Liu, L. Z., Lai, H., Chen, W., & Lan, Q. (2008). Dietary factors, food contamination and lung cancer risk in Xuanwei, China. *Lung Cancer (Amsterdam, Netherlands), 61,* 275–282. doi:10.1016/j.lungcan.2007.12.024

Sheshadri, H. S., & Kandaswamy, A. (2007). Experimental investigation on breast tissue classification based on statistical feature extraction of mammograms. *Computerized Medical Imaging and Graphics, 31,* 46–48. doi:10.1016/j.compmedimag.2006.09.015

Smith, J. S., Green, J., Gonzalez, A. B. D., Appleby, P., Peto, J., & Plummer, M. (2003). Cervical cancer and use of hormonal contraceptives: a systematic review. *Lancet, 361,* 1159–1167. doi:10.1016/S0140-6736(03)12949-2

Sobti, R. C., Gupta, L., Singh, S. K., Seth, A., Kaur, P., & Thakur, H. (2008). Role of hormonal genes and risk of prostate cancer: gene-gene interactions in a North Indian population. *Cancer Genetics and Cytogenetics, 185,* 78–85. doi:10.1016/j.cancergencyto.2008.04.022

Statnikov, A., Aliferis, C. F., Tsamardinos, L., Hardin, D., & Levy, S. (2005). A comprehensive evaluation of multicategory classification methods for microarray gene expression cancer diagnosis. *Bioinformatics (Oxford, England), 21*(5), 631–643. doi:10.1093/bioinformatics/bti033

Steckley, S. L., Pickworth, W. B., & Haverkos, H. W. (2002). Cigarette smoking and cervical cancer: Part II: a geographic variability study. *Biomedicine and Pharmacotherapy, 57,* 78–83.

Stefani, E. D., Boffetta, P., Ronco, A. L., Deneo-Pellegrini, H., Acosta, G., Gutiérrez, L. P., & Mendilaharsu, M. (2008). Nutrient patterns and risk of lung cancer: A factor analysis in Uruguayan men. *Lung Cancer (Amsterdam, Netherlands), 61,* 283–291. doi:10.1016/j.lungcan.2008.01.004

Stephen, O., Freedland, J., Wen, J., Wuerstle, M., Shah, A., Lai, D., et al. (2008). Obesity Is a Significant Risk Factor for Prostate Cancer at the Time of Biopsy. *Urology.*

Takahashi, I., Matsuzaka, M., Umeda, T., Yamai, K., Nishimura, M., & Danjo, K. (2008). Differences in the influence of tobacco smoking on lung cancer between Japan and the USA: possible explanations for the 'smoking paradox' in Japan. *Public Health, 122,* 891–896. doi:10.1016/j.puhe.2007.10.004

Twellmann, T., Meyer-Baese, A., Lange, O., Foo, S., & Nattkemper, T. W. (2008). Model-free visualization of suspicious lesions in breast MRI based on supervised and unsupervised learning . *Engineering Applications of Artificial Intelligence, 21*(2), 129–140. doi:10.1016/j.engappai.2007.04.005

Vapnik, V. (1998). *Statistical Learning Theory.* Mahwah, NJ: John Wiley and Sons.

Veer, L. J. V., Dai, H., Vijver, M. J. V. D., He, Y. D., Hart, A. A. M., & Mao, M. (2002). Gene expression profiling predicts clinical outcome of breast cancer. *Nature, 415,* 530–536. doi:10.1038/415530a

Vinnakota, S., & Lam, N. S. N. (2006). Socioeconomic inequality of cancer mortality in the United States: a spatial data mining approach. *International Journal of Health Geographics,* 5–9.

Vinnakota, S., & Lam, N. S. N. (2006). Socioeconomic inequality of cancer mortality in the United States: a spatial data mining approach. *International Journal of Health Geographics*, 5–9.

Wang, S., Zhou, M., & Geng, G. (2005). Application of Fuzzy Cluster Analysis for Medical Image Data Mining. In *Proceedings of the IEEE International Conference on Mechatronics & Automation*, (pp. 631-636).

Watanabe, H., Yakowenko, W., Kim, Y., Anbe, J., & Tobi, T. (1996). Application of a Fuzzy Discrimination Analysis for Diagnosis of Valvular Heart Disease. *IEEE Trans. On Fuzzy Systems*.

Wikimedia, (2008). Retrieved October 2, 2008, from http://upload.wikimedia.org.

Wikipedia, (2008). Retrieved August 20, 2008 from http://en.wikipedia.org/wiki/Bladder_cancer

Witten, I. H., & Frank, E. (2005). *Data Mining: Practical machine learning tools and techniques*, (2nd Ed.). San Francisco: Morgan Kaufmann.

Wong, H.-S., & Wang, H.-Q. (2008). Constructing the gene regulation-level representation of microarray data for cancer classification. *Journal of Biomedical Informatics*, *41*(1), 95–100. doi:10.1016/j.jbi.2007.04.002

Yang, L., Peterson, P. J., Williams, W. P., Wang, W., Hou, S., & Tan, J. (2002). The Relationship Between Exposure to Arsenic Concentrations in Drinking Water and the Development of Skin Lesions in Farmers from Inner Mongolia, China. *Environmental Geochemistry and Health*, *24*(2).

Yeh, J.-Y., Wu, T.-S., Wu, M.-C., & Chang, D.-M. (2007). Applying Data Mining Techniques for Cancer Classification from Gene Expression Data. *International Conference on Convergence Information Technology*, (pp. 703-708).

Zalane, O. R. (2008). Principles of knowledge discovery in databases. *Bioinformatics (Oxford, England)*, *19*, 1132–1139.

Zhang, B., Pham, T. D., & Zhang, Y. (2007). *Bagging Support Vector Machine for Classification of SELDI-ToF Mass Spectra of Ovarian Cancer Serum Samples* (LNCS Vol. 4830). Berlin: Springer.

Zhang, G. P. (2000). Neural Networks for Classification: A Survey. *IEEE Transactions on Systems, Man and Cybernetics. Part C, Applications and Reviews*, *30*(4), 451–462. doi:10.1109/5326.897072

Zhu, A.-L., Li, J., & Leong, T.-Y. (2003). Automated Knowledge Extraction for Decision Model Construction: A Data Mining Approach. In *Proc. of AMIA Annu Symp.* (pp. 758–762).

Zhu, Y., Williams, S., & Zwiggelaar, R. (2004). A survey on histological image analysis-based assessment of three major biological factors influencing radiotherapy: proliferation, hypoxia and vasculature. *Computer Methods and Programs in Biomedicine*, *74*(3), 183–199. doi:10.1016/S0169-2607(03)00095-6

Zhu, Y., Williams, S., & Zwiggelaar, R. (2006). Computer technology in detection and staging of prostate carcinoma: A review. *Medical Image Analysis*, *10*(2), 178–199. doi:10.1016/j.media.2005.06.003

Zhu, Y., & Yan, H. (1997). Computerized tumor boundary detection using a Hopfield neural network. *IEEE Transactions on Medical Imaging*, *16*, 55–67. doi:10.1109/42.563666

Zhu, Y. M., Webster, S. J., Flower, D., & Woll, P. J. (2004). Interleukin-8/CXCL8 is a growth factor for human lung cancer cells. *British Journal of Cancer*, *91*, 1970–1976. doi:10.1038/sj.bjc.6602227

KEY TERMS AND DEFINITIONS

Machine Learning: Machine Learning is the learning of computer algorithms that progress mechanically through knowledge. The method of learning is based on different types of algorithms activities. The machine learning algorithms are basically subdivided into two folds: supervised and unsupervised learning.

Data Mining: The application area of machine learning is called data mining. It allows finding out the hidden information from a large database. Later that information could be useful to make a business, health, and engineering decision.

Algorithm: An algorithm is a stage by stage process for solving a problem. The word originates from the name of the mathematician, Mohammed ibn-Musa al-Khwarizmi. A computer program can be viewed as a detailed algorithm. In case of mathematics and computer science, an algorithm as a rule means a minute system that solves a regular problem.

Cancer: Cancer is a group of diseases with the common feature of uncontrolled growth of cells and has the ability to infiltrate and destroy normal body tissue. It is noticed that cancer cells be able to spread through the blood and lymph arrangements to other division of the body. Mainly, cancer affects on older people but sometimes kids get cancer which very often treated and cured.

Heart Disease: Heart disease is an assortment for different diseases affecting the heart. In 2007, it was the Primary cause of death in the United States, England, Canada and Wales. It is also noticed that heart disease killing one person in the United States alone. Heart disease includes a number of problems, for instance heart attack, angina affecting the heart and the blood vessels in the heart.

Biological Data: Biological data is basically collected from biological resources. Now-a-days this is stored as a digital form. The example of biological data is DNA base-pair sequences, cancer image data and microarray data, etc.

Clinical Decision: Clinical decision is generally decide from diagnosis and investigation through treatment and long-term care of the patient.

Chapter 10
Introduction to Clustering:
Algorithms and Applications

Raymond Greenlaw
Armstrong Atlantic State University, USA

Sanpawat Kantabutra
Chiang Mai University, Thailand

ABSTRACT

This chapter provides the reader with an introduction to clustering algorithms and applications. A number of important well-known clustering methods are surveyed. The authors present a brief history of the development of the field of clustering, discuss various types of clustering, and mention some of the current research directions in the field of clustering. Algorithms are described for top-down and bottom-up hierarchical clustering, as are algorithms for K-Means clustering and for K-Medians clustering. The technique of representative points is also presented. Given the large data sets involved with clustering, the need to apply parallel computing to clustering arises, so they discuss issues related to parallel clustering as well. Throughout the chapter references are provided to works that contain a large number of experimental results. A comparison of the various clustering methods is given in tabular format. They conclude the chapter with a summary and an extensive list of references.

BASICS OF CLUSTERING

Introduction

In today's world, information has become increasingly indispensable within our daily lives. This information includes financial, medical, and scientific data, and even something as mundane as grocery-shopping information with which we are intimately familiar. Many people have been discussing and exposing about the information era for years. The widespread use of the Internet and web-based applications has further fueled the use of information worldwide. Hand-in-hand with the ever-growing use of information (both

DOI: 10.4018/978-1-60566-908-3.ch010

in terms of the sheer volume of information, but as well in the increased total number of users) comes significantly greater complexity of data and information management. The vast sea of data appears to be limitless not only in quantity but also in dimension. Real-life applications can generate high-dimensional data. In genomics, for instance, a single gene expression profile could yield a vector of measurements whose dimension is in the range between 5,000 and 25,000 (Bühlmann, 2006). Many people have tried to manage data, and some have been able to manage data effectively. But, others have met with less success, and so new methods have emerged to cope with these more-complex situations.

Preferably we want to keep, extract, and maintain knowledge, as opposed to the data itself. Hopefully, the knowledge will be in some useful forms, where one can utilize the knowledge to make informed and strategic decisions. In addition, we would like to deal with smaller quantities of information to simplify decision making. One way to manage a data set is to group data that have certain similar characteristics; this method is called clustering (Hartigan, 1975), (Spath, 1980), (Jain & Dubes, 1988), (Kaufman Rousseeuw, 1990), (Dubes, 1993), (Everitt, 1993), (Mirkin, 1996), (Jain, Murty & Flynn, 1999), (Fasulo, 1999), (Kolatch, 2001), (Han, Kamber, & Tung, 2001), (Ghosh, 2002), (Berkin, 2002). Clustering allows us to work with a small, manageable set of groups rather than a complete data set that is typically unwieldy. In this chapter we will explore the topic of clustering. We provide an introduction to this subject, as well as describe various algorithms and applications of clustering. We begin with a definition of clustering.

Clustering Definition

Intuitively, *clustering* is a grouping of "similar" objects, where similarity is some predetermined function. More formally, given a set of *n* objects, the process of clustering partitions the set into different subsets of objects such that each subset shares specific common characteristics. The common characteristics are usually specified in terms of some mathematical relation. In geometric parlance, the objects can be viewed as points in some *d*-dimensional space. Clustering partitions these points into groups, where points in the same group are located near one another in space.

In Figure 1 we illustrate the partitioning of a set of points in two-dimensional space into four clusters. Each cluster is represented by a rectangle. Points in the same cluster are somewhat closer—more similar in terms of their Euclidean distance to one another than to points in other clusters. Notice in this case the number of points in each cluster is not perfectly balanced. The clusters have sizes from left-to-right, top-to-bottom of 33, 50, 23, and 16. However, rather than talking about the 122 points separately, we can talk about just four clusters. In base two this is almost a five-order magnitude decrease in the number of objects to consider. For large datasets the reduction in complexity of the number of items to discuss can be much greater still.

Examples of Clustering

Let us look at some of the far-reaching applications of clustering in this subsection by considering a few different domains in which clustering data are useful. In general, the field of clustering encompasses a number of different algorithms for grouping objects of similar kinds into respective categories. Clustering can also be viewed as an exploratory data-analysis tool to discover structural properties of data. Because typical objects can be translated into points in a *d*-dimensional space, examples of clustering abound in our daily lives. For example, a group of students majoring in computer science at a university may be

Figure 1. A set of points that is partitioned into four subsets

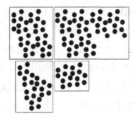

regarded as a cluster of people, and students majoring in other subjects can be grouped together as well. In this manner the majors (clusters in this case) partition the student body of a university.

In a marketing department of a dental-hygiene company, marketers may want to know the group of people who usually buy both toothpaste and dental floss because they can target their advertising campaign specifically to this cluster of people, perhaps offering a free small tube of toothpaste to those who buy two packages of floss. Biologists organize species of animals before a meaningful description of the differences among animals can be defined. In the field of medical sciences, clustering diseases, cures for diseases, or symptoms of diseases can lead to a useful taxonomy and thus increase our understanding of, relationships among, and potential treatments for diseases. In bioinformatics scientists often want to group genes from microarray data to describe the genes.

Of course, there are many other applications of clustering, and the list of such applications continues to grow.

Motivation

In the previous subsection we presented a number of examples of clustering. It is clear that as humans we are limited in our capacity to think about millions, billions, or trillions of data points, or to extract useful information from such a large volume of data. Thus if we could intelligently group similar items together, we could perhaps gain more perspective and insight into a large data set. In particular, we could extract real knowledge. But, how does one group similar items together? How does one do so efficiently? Furthermore, in the many problem domains where clustering has already been applied and for the new domains where applications of clustering are emerging, we want to have general techniques to construct clusters from the data. That is, we cannot always be applying ad hoc techniques to form clusters. The field of clustering has established methods that can be applied in a variety of settings. In this work we will cover a number of these methods, including those that span the greatest range of applications.

Overview of Chapter

This chapter is organized as follows. In section 2 we present a brief history of the development of the field of clustering. We include some background on clustering, talk about various types of clustering, and mention some of the current research directions in the field of clustering. In section 3 we discuss one of the classic methods of clustering called hierarchical clustering. We describe algorithms both from a top- down and bottom-up perspective. Next we cover algorithms for *K*-Means clustering in section 4, and algorithms for *K*-Medians clustering in section 5. The technique of representative points is described in section 6. Given the large data sets involved with clustering, the need to apply parallel computing to clustering arises. We discuss issues related to parallel clustering in section 7. Throughout the chapter references are provided, and many of these contain experimental results. Readers interested in specific applications of a particular technique are encouraged to pursue the references provided relating to that material. In section 8 we provide a comparison of the various clustering methods described. We conclude the chapter with a summary and an extensive list of references.

HISTORY

Introduction

When we talk about clustering in computer science, one must be careful not to confuse the type of clustering described in this article with another broad field called cluster computing. *Cluster computing* deals with using groups of computers together to solve complex problems. Our clustering involves partitioning of data. According to JSTOR, data clustering first appeared in the title of a 1954 article dealing with anthropological data. Some of the early references on clustering appeared in (Steinhaus, 1956), (Lloyd, 1957), (Hall & Ball, 1965), (MacQueen, 1967). These references were some of the initial ones to discuss methods for partitioning sets of data to simplify how the data might be considered and interpreted.

In general, clustering encompasses a number of different algorithms for grouping objects of similar kind into sets. All clustering algorithms, however, share the same purpose of learning some knowledge from a given data set. It is important to understand that clustering is an unsupervised classification. In clustering we are not provided with a set of predefined labeled patterns that in turn is used to predict a label of a newly emerged pattern. Clustering simply groups a given set of unlabeled patterns into meaningful clusters. Clustering is an important procedure in applications in all sciences and social sciences, ranging from biology, to physics, to anthropology, to political science, to psychology, to name a few. Techniques for clustering have developed very rapidly in the last decade, energized by both applications and the availability of inexpensive, powerful computers and the Internet. In what follows we examine some of the development in clustering.

The early papers focus on the *K*-Means clustering method. *K*-Means is the best-known, simplest, and most-popular clustering method. It was independently discovered by Steinhaus in 1956 (Steinhaus, 1956), Lloyd in 1957 (Lloyd, 1957), Ball and Hall in 1965 (Hall & Ball, 1965), and McQueen in 1967 (MacQueen, 1967). Since then, we have seen numerous developments in clustering techniques. We will not even attempt to cover them all here, but rather name a few of the classic methods in the literature. Hierarchical clustering methods were mentioned by Jain and Dubes (Jain & Dubes, 1988) and Kaufman and Rousseeuw (Kaufman Rousseeuw, 1990). Several versions of hierarchical clustering were discovered later on, such as with CURE (Guha, Rastogi & Shim, 1998) and CHAMELEON (Karypis, Han & Kumar, 1999). To merge or split subsets of points, as opposed to individual points, the distance between two points has to be generalized to the distance between subsets. This proximity measure is called a *linkage metric*. SLINK (Sibson, 1973), Voorhees' Method (Voorhees, 1986), and CLINK (Defays, 1977) are variations of hierarchical clustering that utilize a linkage metric. Jain and Dubes applied a minimum-spanning tree algorithm based on graph partitioning to hierarchical clustering (Jain & Dubes, 1988).

Statistics and probability theory have also been applied to clustering. Probabilistic models assume that the data comes from a mixture of several populations whose distributions we want to discover. BIRCH

(Zhang, Ramakrishnan & Livny, 1997) and STING (Wang, Yang, & Muntz, 1997) store "sufficient statistics" to achieve scalability and to facilitate queries, respectively. Wallace and Dowe invented SNOB which uses a mixture model in conjunction with the "minimum message length" principle (Wallace & Dowe, 1994). Cheeseman and Stutz utilized a mixture model to cover a broad variety of probability distributions (Cheeseman & Stutz, 1996). Fraley and Raftery designed a software tool that allows hierarchical, mixture-model clustering and discriminant analysis (Fraley & Raftery, 1999) .

To discover clusters of arbitrary shapes, density-based partitioning has been used in clustering. This idea of partitioning applies concepts of density, connectivity, and boundary to clustering. DBSCAN (Ester, Kriegel, Sander & Xu, 1996), GDBSCAN (Sander, Ester, Kriegel & Xu, 1998), OPTICS (Ankerst, Breunig, Kriegel & Sander, 1999), DBCLASD (Xu, Ester, Kreigel & Sander, 1998), and DENCLUE (Hinneburg & Keim, 1998) are examples of density-based clustering methods. As we mentioned earlier, real-life applications could have a very high number of dimensions or attributes. Clustering in such high-dimensional spaces presents enormous difficulty. This difficulty is usually known as *the curse of dimensionality*. Mathematically speaking, the distance to the nearest neighbor becomes indistinguishable from the distances to the majority of points in such a situation (Beyer, Goldstein, Ramakrishnan & Shaft, 1999). For more information, Aggarwal et al. presented interesting insights into the curse of dimensionality in (Aggarwal & Yu, 2000) .

Some clustering algorithms were designed to work well with high-dimensional data. These algorithms include CLIQUE (Aggarwal, Gehrke, Gunopulos, & Raghavan, 1998), ENCLUS (Cheng, Fu & Zhang, 1999), and MAFIA (Goil, Nagesh & Choufhary, 1999), (Nagesh, Goil & Choudhary, 2001). Artificial neural networks have also been applied in clustering such as self-organizing maps (Kohonen, 2001). When categorical data such as "male" and "female" are used in applications, numerical clustering techniques cannot directly be applied. ROCK (Guha, Rastogi & Shim, 1999), SNN (Ertoz, Steinbach & Kumar, 2003), CACTUS (Ganti, Gehrke & Raftery, 1999), and STIRR (Gibson, Kleinberg & Raghavan, 1998) were specifically designed to handle clustering with such data. In addition, there have been quite a few clustering techniques using evolutionary methods. Brown and Huntley applied simulated annealing in hierarchical clustering (Brown & Huntley, 1991) . Al-Sultan used a Tabu search approach to clustering (Al-Sultan, 1995). Hall et al. invented a genetic algorithm for fuzzy and hard *K-Means* clustering (Hall, Ozyurt & Bazdek, 1999). Genetic algorithms were also applied to clustering categorical data (Cristofor & Simovici, 2002).

The field of clustering is still very active. According to Google, as of November 2008, a search for "data clustering" produced 2,280,000 results. Despite its long history and numerous developments, clustering still poses a number of open research problems. We list several open problems in section 8. For more details and open problems, the extensive surveys on clustering by Jain et al. (Jain & Dubes, 1988), (Jain, Murty & Flynn, 1999) and Berkhin (Berkin, 2002) can be pursued.

Types of Clustering

As we noted early, clustering encompasses a number of different algorithms for grouping objects of similar kind into disjoint subsets of a set of objects. The following clustering methods are discussed in this chapter:

- *Hierarchical clustering*—This method allows us to partition data into a tree-like structure where moving deeper into the tree gives us a finer granularity (more clusters), while moving upward toward the root of the tree gives us a more coarse-grained view of the data. This technique is well established and efficient algorithms have been developed to compute hierarchical clusters. The technique and its variants have been applied to the following domains: molecular biology [19], astrophysics (White & Frenk, 1991), wireless-sensor networks (Bandyopadhay & Coyle, 2003), and search engines (Fich, 1993), among others.

- *K-Means*—Given a desired group number *K* and a set of data items or points, this algorithm partitions the data set into *K* groups in which similar items are placed into the same group. *K*-Means is among the oldest and simplest clustering method still in use, and the technique and its variants have been applied to the following domains: genomics (Gasch & Eisen, 2002), text mining (Steinbach, Karypis & Kumar, 2000), web mining (Lingras & West, 2004), and toxicology (Waring, Jolly, Ciurlionis, Lum, Praestgaard, Morfitt, et al, 2001), among others.

- *K-Medians*—This method is a discrete counterpart of *K-Means* clustering. *K-Medians* is an alternative to *K*-Means for non-continuous applications in which a mean is not well-defined. Some applications of *K*-Medians and its variants are involved with data streams (Babcock, Datar, Motwani, & O'Callaghan, 2003), photogrammetry and remote sensing (Doucette, Agouris, Stefanidis & Musavi, 2001), Internet content distribution (Laoutaris, Zissimopoulos & Stavrakakis, 2004), and phonetic classification (Gutkin & King, 2004), among others.

- *Representative points*—Clustering methods often produce a set of large clusters that is too fine for details and too large for storage. In this scenario we want some "representatives" of these clusters instead. In the case of spherically-shaped clusters, a single cluster only needs one representative point. In this chapter we extend the concept of representative points to clusters of any distributions. In such cases one cluster may need more than one representative point. In addition, we also extend the concept of representatives to use in cluster reconstruction. The ideas of representation have widely been applied to several areas such as face representation and classification (Graham & Allinson, 1998), image texture representation (Cula & Dana, 2001), and automatic music audio generation (Peeters, Burthe & Rodet, 2002), among others.

- *Parallel clustering*—Some clustering methods can be made to run significantly faster by utilizing two or more processors. Many clustering algorithms have been parallelized on various kinds of parallel machines. Examples are a parallel *K*-Means algorithm on a network of workstations (Kantabutra & Couch, 2000), a parallel hierarchical clustering on a parallel random access machine (Greenlaw & Kantabutra, 2008), and parallel *K*-Medians algorithms on parallel random access machines (Vittayakorn, Kantabutra & Tanprasert, 2008).

In the next section we mention some future research directions. Although we have covered many important clustering algorithms in this chapter, the reader can walk down other clustering avenues by exploring the extensive reference list given at the end of the chapter.

Research Directions

Clustering is still an active research area. In this section we mention three recent papers dealing with clustering. The first paper deals with multimedia mining. Kim et al. proposed a variation of hierarchical clustering called *SpaRClus* (**Spa**tial **R**elationship Pattern-Based Hierarchical **Clus**tering) to cluster image data (Kim, Jin & Han, 2008). The authors showed an algorithm called *SpIBag* (**Sp**atial **I**tem **Bag** Mining) that discovers frequent spatial patterns in images and then, based on *SpIBag*, the authors used

SpaRClus to cluster images. Experimentally, this method was shown to be effective and efficient. Most existing clustering algorithms produce a single clustering for a given data set even when the data can be clustered naturally in a number of ways.

Jain et al. addressed the difficult problem of uncovering disparate clusterings from the data in the second paper (Jain, Mekka & Dhillon, 2008). They also proposed methods to solve this problem. It was shown experimentally that their methods did well in uncovering multiple clusterings and were much improved over existing methods for a music-data set and a portrait-data set. The third paper shows that a particular problem related to hierarchical clustering is likely impossible to parallelize efficiently. More specifically, Greenlaw and Kantabutra addressed the parallel complexity of *bottom-up hierarchical clustering*. The authors defined a natural decision problem based on this algorithm and showed that this problem is one of the computationally most difficult problems in the COMPARATOR CIRCUIT VALUE PROBLEM class (Greenlaw & Kantabutra, 2008).

HIERARCHICAL CLUSTERING ALGORITHMS

Introduction

Clustering is a division of data into groups of "similar" objects, where each group is given a more-compact representation. In the clustering literature there are many methods to achieve this division of data. In this section we study one of the oldest methods called *hierarchical clustering*.

The hierarchical clustering problem is one of the most-popular ones in the clustering literature. Hierarchical clustering builds a *tree of clusters*. Sibling clusters in this tree partition the points associated with their parent, thereby producing a further refinement of the data. From the opposite viewpoint, parents remove structure from the representation of the data by grouping together the data corresponding to their children. This approach permits one to explore data using various levels of granularity. There are two widely studied methods for hierarchical clustering: *bottom-up* (Jain & Dubes, 1988) and *top-down* (Kaufman Rousseeuw, 1990). In subsection 3.2 we explore the top-down algorithm, and in subsection 3.3 we examine the bottom-up approach.

Top-Down Hierarchical Clustering Algorithm

As the name suggests, a top-down approach starts with one large cluster consisting of all of the data points and then recursively splits the most "appropriate" cluster. The process continues until a desired stopping condition is met. The stopping conditions can be one of several things such as a required number of clusters or a bound on the diameter of the "largest" cluster. Of course, the words "appropriate," "diameter," and "largest" have to be made precise for a given application and implementation. Our focus here is on the general principles behind the technique.

For a graph $G = (V, E)$ let $v(G)$ denote V, that is, the vertex set of G. The input to the top-down hierarchical clustering algorithm is a set S of n points x_i for $1 \leq i \leq n$, a distance function $d_S: S \times S \to R+$ that maps pairs of points to positive real numbers, and a bound K specifying the desired number of clusters. The output is a K-partition of S. We now present the *Top-Down Hierarchical Clustering Algorithm* in Table 1.

Table 1. The Top-Down Hierarchical Clustering Algorithm

Step	Top-Down Hierarchical Clustering Algorithm(S, d_s, K)
1.	$V \leftarrow \{1,\dots,n\}$;
2.	form the complete weighted graph $G = (V, E)$, where $i \in V$ corresponds to x_i, for $1 \le i \le n$, and edge $e = \{j, l\} \in E$ has weight $d_s(x_j, x_l)$ for all $1 \le j \ne l \le n$;
3.	partition-set $\leftarrow \{v(G)\}$;
4.	compute a minimum-cost spanning tree T of G;
5.	for $i \leftarrow 1$ to $K - 1$ do {
6.	delete the remaining highest-cost edge e from the remnants of T, and let T_2 and T_3 denote the two trees formed by this edge deletion from the tree T_1 of the remaining forest T;
7.	partition-set $\leftarrow$ partition-set $- \{v(T_1)\} \in \{v(T_2)\} \in \{v(T_3)\}$;
8.	}
9.	return partition-set;

Note that the algorithm subdivides the remaining clusters by splitting sets of points that are far apart. Since there are well-known algorithms for computing minimum-cost spanning trees efficiently, we see that this algorithm runs in polynomial time. We next turn our attention to the Bottom-Up Hierarchical Clustering Algorithm.

Bottom-Up Hierarchical Clustering Algorithm

The Top-Down Hierarchical Clustering Algorithm starts computing from the complete input set or the whole cluster, and progresses to produce smaller clusters until some desired-stopping criterion is met. That is, at each step of the algorithm a refinement of the partition is produced. The *Bottom-Up Hierarchical Clustering* Algorithm does just the opposite. A bottom-up approach starts with single-point clusters and then recursively merges two or more of the most "appropriate" clusters. The process continues in this fashion until a desired-stopping condition is met.

We use the notation $d_{min}(S_a, S_b)$ to denote the minimum *distance* between any pair of points, where one point comes from the set S_a and the other point comes from the set S_b. In the following algorithm we assume that n is even. The input conditions are as for the Top-Down Hierarchical Clustering Algorithm, and the output is a partition containing K clusters, as before. The *Bottom-Up Hierarchical Clustering* Algorithm can be described as follows (Table 2).

The algorithm operates in a bottom-up fashion. Without loss of generality, we have assumed that the number of input points is even. Depending on the distribution of the initial points, the algorithm may, for example, form $K - 1$ clusters having two points and one cluster containing the remaining points. If, for example, the points are distributed uniformly in the Cartesian plane and d_s is the *Euclidean distance*, then the clusters are expected to be roughly balanced in terms of their size. Note that there are no restrictions placed on the distance function d_s, as was the case for the Top-Down Hierarchical Clustering Algorithm. The algorithm clearly operates in polynomial time.

We should point out that for the same set of input points the Bottom-Up Hierarchical Clustering and Top-Down Hierarchical Clustering Algorithms may compute very different clusters.

Table 2. The Bottom-Up Hierarchical Clustering Algorithm

Step	Bottom-Up Hierarchical Clustering Algorithm(S, d_s, K)
1.	$S \leftarrow \{x_1, \ldots, x_n\}$
2.	for $i \leftarrow 1$ to $n/2$ do $C_i \leftarrow \in$;
3.	for $i \leftarrow 1$ to $n/2$ do {
4.	choose x and $y \in S$ such that $d_s(x,y)$ is a minimum;
5.	$C_i \leftarrow \{x, y\}$;
6.	$S \leftarrow S - C_i$;
7.	}
8.	partition-set $\leftarrow \{C_1, \ldots, C_{n/2}\}$;
9.	number-partitions $\leftarrow n/2$;
10.	while (number-partitions $> K$) do {
11.	choose C_a and C_b so that $d_{min}(C_a, C_b)$ is a minimum over partition-set;
12.	partition-set $\leftarrow$ partition-set $\in \{C_a \in C_b\} - \{C_a\} - \{C_b\}$;
13.	number-partitions—;
14.	}
15.	return partition-set;

Applications of Hierarchical Clustering

In this section we mention a couple of areas in which the hierarchical-clustering algorithms have been applied. Corpet applied a hierarchical-clustering algorithm to multiple-sequence alignment [19]. The sequences could be proteins or nucleic acids. This method is based on the dynamic-programming technique of pairwise alignment by initially using the hierarchical clustering to group the sequences to create sets of aligned sequences. In another more-complex application of hierarchical clustering, White and Frenk set up methods to calculate the characteristics of the galaxy population in a universe in which galaxy formation occurs gravitationally (White & Frenk, 1991). Their scheme applied to cosmogonies where structure grows through hierarchical clustering of a mixture of gas and dissipationless dark matter.

K-MEANS CLUSTERING

Introduction

K-Means is one of the most-common methods of clustering due to its simplicity. In this section we discuss *K-Means* in the Euclidean space. More precisely, the *similarity* of two points is defined to be the Euclidean distance between them, and the objective function of the *K-Means* problem is defined in terms of Euclidean distances.

We begin the discussion here with a couple of useful definitions. The first captures the notion of how far apart or how dissimilar two points are.

Definition 4.1 (Dissimilarity)

The *dissimilarity* of d-dimensional points x and y is defined to be the Euclidean distance between the two points. Let $d(x,y)$ denote the Euclidean distance of points x and y. That is,

$$\|x - y\| = d(x,y) = \sqrt{\sum_{i=1}^{d} (x_i - y_i)^2}$$

The next definition defines an error function.

Definition 4.2 (Squared-Error Function)

Let S be a set of d-dimensional points partitioned into K clusters, $\{C_i \mid i \in \{1, 2,\ldots, k\}\}$. The *squared-error function E* is

$$E = \sum_{i=1}^{K} \sum_{x \in C_i} d(\overline{C_i}, x),$$

where

$$\overline{C_i} = \frac{\sum_{x \in C_i} x}{|C_i|}$$

is the mean of cluster C_i. The sum in $\overline{C_i}$ is a component-wise sum of the points.

Next we present the definition of the *K-Means problem*.

Definition 4.3 (*K*-Means Problem)

Given a natural number K and a set S of n d-dimensional points, the *K-Means problem* is to find K clusters that partition S so that the squared-error function E is minimized.

The *K-Means* problem is known to be *NP*-complete (Wan, Wong, & Prusinkiewicz, 1988). Therefore, an efficient algorithm for finding a globally optimal solution to the problem does not exist, unless $P = NP$. Polynomial-time algorithms do exist, however, to approximate the solution to the *K-Means* problem. In the literature several methods to approximate *K-Means* solutions are as follows: *heuristics* (Lloyd, 1957), *distribution assumption* (Chinrungrueng & Sequin, 1995), (Wang & Zhang, 1995), *genetic* (Ratha, Jain, & Chung, 1995), *sampling* (Bradley & Fayyad, 1998), and *parallel computation approaches* (Ratha, Jain, & Chung, 1995), (Tsai, Horng, Tsai, Lee, Kao & Chen, 1997), (Kantabutra & Couch, 2000). These techniques target different aspects of the tradeoffs between the quality of the clustering and the execution time requirements. In the next subsection we will discuss a heuristic-based algorithm for the *K-Means* problem. The reader may explore other approaches by pursuing the references.

Heuristic *K*-Means Clustering Algorithm

To achieve a globally minimum-cost partitioning in the *K-Means* problem, an algorithm could use an exhaustive enumeration of all possible partitions for the given values of *n* and *K*. This process would be prohibitively expensive in computation time though because the number of partitions of a set of *n* objects into *K* nonempty clusters is given by the *Stirling numbers* of the second kind, and these are exponential in *n*. Thus, we settle for solutions based on heuristic algorithms.

Given a set *S* of *n* *d*-dimensional points, the *Heuristic K-Means Clustering* Algorithm forms *K* disjoint nonempty subsets $C_1, C_2, ..., C_K$ of points such that each point x_{ij} has the closest Euclidean distance to $\overline{C_i}$, $1 \leq i \leq K$, $1 \leq j \leq |C_i|$ (Kantabutra, 2001). That is, a point is in the cluster C_i if and only if it has closest Euclidean distance to $\overline{C_i}$. The algorithm achieves this result by trying to minimize the *squared-error function E* presented in Definition 4.2. The Heuristic *K*-Means Clustering Algorithm is measured by two criteria—*intra-cluster* cost and *inter-cluster* cost. The intra-cluster cost (the inner summation in Definition 4.2) represents the goodness of a given cluster. The inter-cluster cost (the outer summation in Definition 4.2) is the total intra-cluster cost of the *K* clusters; the inter-cluster cost represents the overall goodness of the clustering.

The heuristic principle of this algorithm is based on the hope that the overall cost is likely to be minimized upon completion of the algorithm, if the algorithm chooses the points that minimize the cost at each iteration. In a *K*-Means context, by minimizing each intra-cluster cost locally (that is, moving only points that reduce the squared-error function to a new appropriate cluster), we expect that the algorithm will globally yield a near-minimum inter-cluster solution. Note that for this algorithm we are using Euclidean distance, so no distance function is specified as input to the problem. The output of the algorithm is a set of *K* clusters. Using the heuristic principle as described, the algorithm can be specified as follows (Table 3).

The squared-error function *E* referred to in the algorithm is as given in Definition 4.2. The *K*-Means algorithm has time complexity of $O(nKr)$, where *n* is the number of points, *K* is the desired number of clusters, and *r* is the number of iterations of the while loop in the algorithm. This complexity seems simple until one realizes that *r* is unknown and can be very large. When the solution computed is sufficiently close to a local minimum, the algorithm converges at a linear rate (Du, Faber, & Gunzburger, 1999) . In addition to the potentially slow convergence, the outcome of the *Heuristic K-Means Clustering* Algorithm is, of course, dependent upon the choice of initial points. Various distributions of the initial points can yield undesirable outcomes for the clusters (Bradley & Fayyad, 1998). The *Heuristic K-Means Clustering* Algorithm only works well with spherical clusters, and splits clusters if they are not spherical (Kannan, Vempala & Vetta, 2000). Nevertheless, this algorithm does illustrate the basic approach taken in a number of *K*-Means heuristic algorithms.

Applications of Heuristic *K*-Means Clustering

In this section we mention a couple of areas in which the Heuristic *K*-Means Clustering Algorithm has been applied. Steinbach et al. applied *K-Means* and its variant to cluster documents (Steinbach, Karypis & Kumar, 2000). They compared hierarchical clustering and *K-Means* with a new variant of *K*-Means called *bisecting K-Means* in their study. Their results showed that the bisecting variant performed better than both regular *K*-Means and hierarchical clustering in document clustering. In the field of toxicology,

Table 3. The Heuristic K-Means Clustering Algorithm

Step	Heuristic K-Means Clustering Algorithm(S, K)
1.	randomly form K clusters of S that are approximately equal in size;
2.	compute the mean $\overline{C}_i$ for each of the K clusters;
3.	$E_I \leftarrow$ squared-error function of the K clusters;
4.	$E \leftarrow 0$;
5.	while ($E - E_I \neq 0$) {
6.	$E \leftarrow E_I$;
7.	compute distance $d(i,j) = \| \overline{C}_i - x_j \|$ for all $i \in$ 1, 2,..., K and $j \in$ 1, 2,..., n;
8.	compute memberships for the new K clusters using a point's closest distance to $\overline{C}_i$ to determine its membership;
9.	compute the new mean $\overline{C}_i$ for each of the K clusters;
10.	compute the new squared-error E_I for the K clusters;
11.	}
12.	return K clusters;

K-Means was used in the microarray analysis and gene-expression signature profiles (Waring, Jolly, et al, 2001). More specifically, K-Means was used to cluster gene-expression results, and these results were compared to the histopathology findings and clinical chemistry values to discover correlations among the histopathology, clinical chemistry, and gene-expression profiles induced by known hepatotoxins.

K-MEDIANS CLUSTERING

Introduction

In this section we survey a close cousin of K-Means clustering called *K-Medians* clustering. As with the K-Means problem, *K-Medians* clustering is a partitioning of a set of elements where the clustering is chosen to minimize some measure of dissimilarity. The difference is that a median of the *K-Medians* clustering must be a member of the cluster it determines, while a mean of the K-Means clustering does not have to satisfy this requirement.

We present several definitions related to *K-Medians* clustering in what follows. The definition of dissimilarity is the same as the one in the *K-Means* problem (see Definition 4.2). However, as we will see, there are some changes in the definition of the squared-error function E.

Definition 5.1 (Median)

Let S be a set of n d-dimensional points. A point $x \in S$ is a *median* of S if and only if $\sum_{i=1}^{|S|} d(x, y_i)$ is a minimum over all points in S.

Note that here again that the distance function d refers to Euclidean distance. This definition of the median coincides with the definition of the median for a set of real numbers when d is equal to one. The "central value" always minimizes $\sum_{i=1}^{|S|} d(x, y_i)$. We now provide the tweaked definition for the squared-error function (see Definition 4.2).

Definition 5.2 (Squared-Error Function)

Let S be a set of d-dimensional points and K a natural number. The *squared-error function E* is

$$E = \sum_{i=1}^{K} \sum_{x \in C_i} d(C_i^m, x),$$

where C_i^m is a median of cluster C_i.

Next we present the definition of the *K-Medians problem* using the new squared-error function.

Definition 5.3 (*K*-Medians Problem)

Given a natural number K and a set S of n d-dimensional points, the *K-Medians problem* is to find K clusters which partition S so that the squared-error function E is minimized.

As in the case of the K-Means problem, the *K-Medians* problem is known to be *NP*-complete (Young, 200). Hence, unless $P = NP$, to achieve a globally optimal partitioning in the *K-Medians* problem, the algorithm may have to use an enumeration of all possible partitions for a given value of K. As noted earlier for the K-Means problem, there are an exponential number of partitions to consider. Thus, here again, we turn our discussion to approximation algorithms. Several polynomial-time approximation algorithms for the *K*-Medians problem do exist (Young, 200), (Arora, Rahavan & Rao, 1998), (Charikar, Guha, Tardos & Shmoys, 1999). In the next section, however, we discuss a simple heuristic that can be applied to the problem. This algorithm illustrates the basic approach of the heuristic algorithms for the *K*-Medians problem.

Heuristic *K*-Medians Clustering Algorithm

Given a set S of n d-dimensional points, the *Heuristic K-Medians Clustering* Algorithm forms K disjoint nonempty clusters $C_1, C_2, ..., C_K$ of points. The algorithm tries to achieve a good approximation to the optimal solution by trying to minimize the squared-error function E. As in the case of the Heuristic K-Means Clustering Algorithm, the Heuristic K-Medians Clustering Algorithm is measured by two criteria—*intra-cluster* cost (the inner summation in Definition 5.2) and *inter-cluster* cost (the outer summation in Definition 5.2). In the *K-Medians* context, by minimizing each intra-cluster cost locally, we expect that the algorithm will globally yield a near-minimum inter-cluster solution.

Table 4. The Heuristic K-Medians Clustering Algorithm

Step	Heuristic K-Medians Clustering Algorithm (S, K)
1.	randomly form K clusters of S that are approximately equal in size;
2.	compute a median C_i^m for each of the K subsets;
3.	$E_l \leftarrow$ squared-error function of the K clusters;
4.	$E \leftarrow 0$;
5.	while $(E - E_l \neq 0)$ {
6.	$E \leftarrow E_l$;
7.	compute distance $d(i,j) = \| C_i^m - x_j \|$ for all $I \in 1, 2,..., K$ and $j \in 1, 2,..., n$;
8.	compute memberships for the new K clusters using a point's closest distance to C_i^m to determine its membership;
9.	compute the new mean C_i^m for each of the K clusters;
10.	compute the new squared-error E_l for the K clusters;
11.	}
12.	return K clusters;

Note that for this algorithm we are using Euclidean distance again, so no distance function is specified as input to the problem. The output of the algorithm is a set of K clusters. Using the heuristic principle as just described, the algorithm can be specified as follows (Table 4).

The squared-error E referred to in the algorithm is as given in Definition 5.2. The K-Medians algorithm has time complexity of $O(n^2Kr)$, where n is the number of points, K is the number of clusters, and r is the number of iterations of the while loop in the algorithm. Note that computing the medians takes $O(Kn^2)$. Similar remarks made pertaining to the running time of the Heuristic K-Means Clustering Algorithm apply here.

The Heuristic K-Means and K-Medians Clustering Algorithms are similar in many respects. They use the same concept of dissimilarity and similar squared-error functions. There are two distinct differences between the two algorithms though. First, the Heuristic K-Means Clustering Algorithm assumes that the solution lies in a continuous space, where the concept of a mean is well-defined; while the Heuristic K-Medians Clustering Algorithm allows for discrete spaces, in which there is no concept of means. Second, the running time of the *Heuristic K-Means Clustering* Algorithm is linear in n, while the running time of the *Heuristic K-Medians Clustering* Algorithm is quadratic in n due to the extra work of computing medians rather than means. In the K-Means problem, it takes linear time to compute a mean. The median is more difficult to compute than the mean. The median is required to be a member of the input set. The mean does not necessarily belong to the input set, although it belongs to the convex hull of possible input points. This inclusion in the point set increases the computational complexity of the Heuristic K-Medians Clustering Algorithm to $O(n^2)$ because, for a candidate point x to be a median, the algorithm must compute the distance $d(x,y)$ to all other $n - 1$ points y that are in the set.

Some applications necessitate the use of the *Heuristic K-Medians Clustering* Algorithm. For instance, suppose the problem is to cluster a group of web pages and we want to find the web page that is the representative of each cluster. Then we need to use the Heuristic *K*-Medians Clustering Algorithm because there is no well-defined notion of the mean of several web pages.

Applications of Heuristic *K*-Medians Clustering

In this section we mention a couple of areas in which the *Heuristic K-Medians Clustering* Algorithm has been applied. Laoutaris et al. studied a resource allocation problem in a graph concerning the joint optimization of capacity-allocation decisions and object-placement decisions given a single-capacity constraint (Laoutaris, Zissimopoulos & Stavrakakis, 2004). This study used a specific *K*-Medians algorithm as a building block, and the study has applications in Internet-content distribution and other domains. In phonetic classification a variant of *K*-Medians was used to divide a training class into *K* clusters (Gutkin & King, 2004) in the whole process of phoneme classification. The classification in this study was reportedly promising.

REPRESENTATIVE POINTS

Introduction

In the work described in the previous two sections, means and medians have been utilized to generate clusterings, but the means (respectively, medians) also in some sense *represent* the clusterings. Once the *K* means (*K* medians) for a *K*-Means (respectively, *K*-Medians) clustering of *n* points are known, one can regenerate the clustering from the means (respectively, medians) in $O(nK)$ time by placing each point into the cluster corresponding to the mean (respectively, median) nearest to that point (breaking ties in the same way). The problem with this scheme is that only clusters which are roughly spherical can be represented well by means (respectively, medians). One can begin to overcome this distribution dependence by representing each cluster with a set of well-separated points (Guha, Rastogi & Shim, 1998). The obvious question is whether one can also represent other non-spherical clusterings by the same technique.

In this section, we consider the inverse problem of representing an arbitrary cluster structure by subsets of *representative points* chosen to be nearer to cluster members than to non-members. Each subset of representative points is chosen to be nearer to members of one cluster rather than to points in any other subset. Once a set of subsets of representative points is in hand, one can determine cluster membership of a specific point in $O(|R|)$ time, where *R* is the set of representative points. This implies that one can determine the structure of all clusters in $O(n|R|)$ time. The concept of representative points can be used with any clustering scheme. For typical data distributions and clustering schemes, the number of representative points needed to represent clustering of the data is $O(K)$, where *K* is the number of clusters, so that storing these points instead of storing cluster-membership flags results in an $O(n)$ space savings in return for an $O(K)$ space usage. This observation means that the cluster structure of large data sets can be very efficiently stored by computing representative subsets, and that clusterings utilizing several different schemes may be computed and stored for future reuse in a size $O(K)$ which is usually much less than the number of points *n*.

To develop these ideas, we first define the concept of *cluster representation* and show how it relates to the traditional ideas of means and medians. We then develop a new and useful clustering algorithm chosen because it does not presume spherical distributions of data, and then consider how to represent the outcome of the clustering process for this model.

The size of the data set can often pose difficulty during the clustering process. It is thus a good idea to find a much smaller set of representative points that can capture the characteristics of the complete data set, and allow us to reconstruct the original clusters in a reasonable amount of time. We first present the definition of representative points for clusters.

Definition 6.1 (Representative Points)

Let S be a set of n d-dimensional points. Let C_1, C_2,..., C_K be a partition of S into K clusters. Let R_1, R_2,..., R_K be sets such that $R_i \subseteq C_i$ for all $i \in 1, 2,..., K$. The sets R_i are *representative points* for C_i for all $i \in 1, 2,..., K$ if and only if for all $x \in C_i$, there exists $r_i \in R_i$ such that for all $r_j \in R_j$ when $i \neq j$, we have $d(x,r_i) < d(x,r_j)$.

The next lemma shows that if we have a set of representative points, then we can efficiently reconstruct the corresponding clusters.

Lemma 6.1 (Time of Construction of Clusters)

Let S be a set of n d-dimensional points. Given representative points R_1, R_2,..., R_K of $\sum_{i=1}^{K} |R_i| = m$ points for K clusters of S, it takes $O(mn)$ time to reconstruct the clusters C_1, C_2,..., C_K, where $\bigcup_{i=1}^{K} C_i = S$.

Proof sketch: For each point $x \in S$ and each point $r_i \in R_i$, we compute all of the distances $d(x,r_i)$. This process takes $O(mn)$. For each point x, we find the smallest distance $d(x,r)$ to any representative point r. The index i such that r is an element of R_i indicates the cluster membership of the point x. This latter process also requires $O(mn)$ time. ∎

In reality, we want the number of representative points to be as small as possible. The required number of representative points seems to depend upon the number, density, and convexity of the clusters, as well as the distance among clusters. If the clusters are non-convex, more representative points are usually needed. The time complexity of computing the minimum set of representative points remains an open problem. There is a case in which the number of required representative points is $\Omega(n)$, and this is the worst case.

Figure 2 illustrates the case requiring $\Omega(n)$ representative points.

In the figure there are two comb-like clusters of points, and they overlap each other. The representative points for each cluster are denoted by **x** marks for the cluster on the left and circled **x** marks for the cluster on the right. This case shows that the number of representative points is $\Omega(n)$, where n is the total number of points in the set. As n grows in this same pattern, more representative points will be needed.

Heuristic Representative Algorithm

In this section a heuristic-based algorithm that finds a set of representative points for clusters is described. In order to design an effective algorithm, the clusters must be structured in some way. In other words, a cluster cannot just be a set of arbitrary points, but instead must satisfy some properties. In this section

Figure 2. A double comb-like set made up of two clusters that requires a large number of representative points

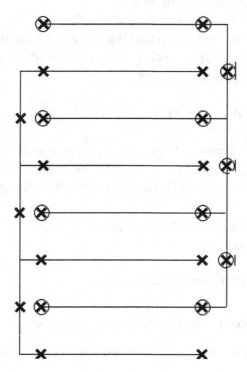

we assume that the clusters which we want to represent are Ψ*–clusters*. This special type of cluster is defined next.

Definition 6.2 (Ψ–Clustering Problem)

Let S be a set of d-dimensional points and Ψ a real number. The Ψ*-clustering problem* is to partition the set S into K clusters $C_1, C_2,..., C_K$ as follows:

1) For all $x, y \in C_i$, where $x \neq y$, there exists $z_1, z_2,..., z_t \in C_i$ such that
   - $d(x,z_1) < \Psi$,
   - $d(z_i,z_{i+1}) < \Psi$ for $1 \leq i \leq t$, and
   - $d(z_t,y) < \Psi$,

   where each C_i is a maximal cluster having this property.
2) The clusters $C_1, C_2,..., C_K$ are pairwise disjoint.

The clusters $C_1, C_2,..., C_K$ formed by this partitioning of S are called Ψ*–clusters*.

In graph-theoretic terms, given a graph $G = (V, E)$, where V is a set of vertices representing points and E is a set of edges with the property that an edge $\{v_i, v_j\} \in E$ if and only if $d(v_i, v_j) < \Psi$, the Ψ-clustering problem reduces to a problem of finding the connected components of a graph (Corpet, 1988). The following paragraphs introduce an algorithm that finds a set of representative points according to Definition 6.1. We first define single-cluster representation and then an algorithm for finding such a representation.

Table 5. The Heuristic Representative Algorithm

Step	Heuristic Representative Algorithm (Ψ-clusters $C_1, C_2,..., C_K, h$)
1.	$R_h \leftarrow C_h$;
2.	$P_{max} \leftarrow P_{max} \cup \{x\}$, where x is a random point;
3.	while ($P_{max} \neq \varnothing$) do {
4.	$P_{max} \leftarrow \varnothing$;
5.	$P \leftarrow \varnothing$;
6.	for all $r_i \in R_h$ do {
7.	for all $r_j \in R_h$ do {
8.	for all $x \in S - R_h$ do {
9.	if ($d(r_i,r_j) < d(x,r_j)$ and $i \neq j$) then
10.	$P \leftarrow P \cup \{r_j\}$;
11.	}
12.	if ($|P| > |P_{max}|$) then {
13.	$P_{max} \leftarrow P$;
14.	$r_{max} \leftarrow r_i$;
15.	}
16.	}
17.	}
18.	$tempset \leftarrow R_h$;
19.	for all $r_k \in R_h - (P_{max} \cup \{r_{max}\})$ do {
20.	for all $r_l \in R_h$ do {
21.	for all $x \in S - R_h$ do {
22.	if ($d(r_k,r_l) < d(x,r_l)$) then
23.	$tempset \leftarrow tempest - \{r_l\}$;
24.	}
25.	}
26.	if ($tempset \neq \varnothing$) then
27.	$R_h \leftarrow R_h - P_{max}$;
28.	else $R_h \leftarrow R_h - \{r_{max}\}$;
29.	}
30.	}
31.	return R_h;

Definition 6.3 (Single Cluster Representation Problem)

Let set $S = \bigcup_{i=1}^{K} C_i$ be a set of n points in d-dimensional space, where each C_i is a Ψ-cluster. Let h be a specific cluster number. The *single cluster representation problem* is to find a representative set $R_h \subseteq C_h$ such that for all $y \in C_h$ there exists $r_i \in R_h$ such that for all $x \in S - C_h$, we have $d(r_i,y) < d(x,y)$. The cluster R_h is called a *representative single cluster*.

We next describe an algorithm that takes as input a set $C_1, C_2, ..., C_K$ of Ψ-clusters and a designated cluster number h, and produces a representative single cluster R_h (Table 5).

The Heuristic Representative Algorithm just specified finds a set of representative points for a single cluster. To find a set of representative points for each of the K clusters, this algorithm must be invoked K times. In what follows we provide an algorithm for finding all K clusters. The algorithm that takes as input a set $C_1, C_2, ..., C_K$ of Ψ-clusters and returns as output a set of K representative single clusters (Table 6).

We should point out that the *K-Clusters Representative* Algorithm does *not* produce an optimal solution for the Ψ-clusters. However, in some cases the algorithm seems to provide a good approximation (Kantabutra, 2001). It is not hard to see that the time complexity for this algorithm is $O(n^3 K^2)$, where n is the number of points in the set S.

Applications of Clustering Using Representative Points

In this section we mention a couple of areas in which the clustering algorithms using representative points have been applied. As noted earlier, K-Means (Medians) in the K-Means (respectively, Medians) clustering can be viewed as K representatives of the K clusters. When fine details are not needed in the applications, these representatives could be used in a certain analysis to represent the data for each corresponding cluster. In a scenario where two exact replicas of databases are located in different geographic locations (say, one in Thailand and the other in the United States), representative points from one location could be sent to the other location for the clustering purpose, as opposed to sending the whole clusters. Once the representative points arrive at the other end, they could be used to reproduce the exact clusters in linear time.

CLUSTERING IN PARALLEL

Introduction

All clustering algorithms thus far presented in this chapter run in high-order polynomial time. In practice, however, clustering is usually applied to data sets of immense size. For instance, the size of the population in China is approximately 1.3 billion. If we want to do some clustering analysis using K-Means on this population, the running time would be asymptotically the quadratic order of 1.3 billion. For most applications, this time is simply too long to wait. Taking advantages of relatively inexpensive processors,

Table 6. The K-Clusters Representative Algorithm

Step	K-Clusters Representative Algorithm(Ψ-clusters $C_1, C_2, ..., C_K$)
1.	for $h = 1$ to K do {
2.	Heuristic Representative Algorithm($C_1, C_2, ..., C_K, h$);
3.	$T \leftarrow T \cup \{R_h\}$;
4.	}
5.	return T;

parallel computing could significantly reduce the computation time for large clustering problems. In the following sections we give two examples of clustering using parallel computation: one for a theoretical model and the other for a more-practical model.

In the theory of computation, an important subfield of theoretical computer science, computer scientists classify problems into *complexity classes* according to the resource requirements of the problem—for sequential computing typical resources studied are time and space, and for parallel computing time and the number of processors. Since proving lower bounds on the resource requirements to solve a problem is notoriously difficult, by grouping problems of similar difficulty into complexity classes, we can make relative statements about the computational complexity of problems. We have already seen that some problems in this paper have deterministic polynomial-time algorithms and so are in the complexity class *P*, whereas other problems discussed here are *NP*-complete.

In this section we focus on parallel-time complexity. We begin by introducing two models of parallel computation: first, an idealized model of parallel computation for which algorithm design is more intuitive and second, a more-practical-based parallel model. We then present a parallel algorithm for computing top-down hierarchical clusters. This algorithm is followed by a discussion of how to parallelize *K*-Means clustering on a group of workstations coordinating in parallel.

Parallel Models of Computation

In this subsection we describe two models of parallel computation: the *Parallel Random Access Machine* (*PRAM*) [32] and the *Cluster of Workstations* (*COWs*) (Wilkinson & Allen, 1998). We should note that these are just two of a wide variety of parallel models of computing which have been introduced. But, for an introduction to clustering in parallel, these models will suffice.

Parallel Random Access Machine

A *parallel random access machine,* or *PRAM* for short, is an idealized machine for designing parallel algorithms. In this model various important issues; such as processor synchronization, interprocessor communication, and processor startup; are abstracted away to allow algorithm designers to focus on exploiting the inherent parallelism of a problem. Here we provide a brief description of the model. A more-thorough description of the model can be found in (Greenlaw, Hoover & Ruzzo, 1995), for example.

A PRAM consists of a set of processors that run in lock step and which communicate via global shared memory. Processes run the same program and know their own index. Thus, they can skip certain parts of the program, if they wish. Each processor has a simple set of instructions such as addition, multiplication by two, branching, and indirect addressing. The input to the PRAM is placed in global shared memory, and the output is written there as well. Figure 3 provides an illustration of a PRAM. In this figure there are n processors labeled P1, P2,…, Pn; and m memory units. The values of n and m are not bounded although any computation that halts will, of course, just use a finite amount of resources.

In some variants of the PRAM a designated processor computes sequentially the number of processors that will be needed for a particular computation. The processor writes this value into global memory, and all processors whose index is less than this value will participate in the computation. Of course, there are issues that need to be clarified relating to global memory accesses, and we discuss those next.

Figure 3. A sample parallel random access machine that uses n processors and m memory cells in its computation

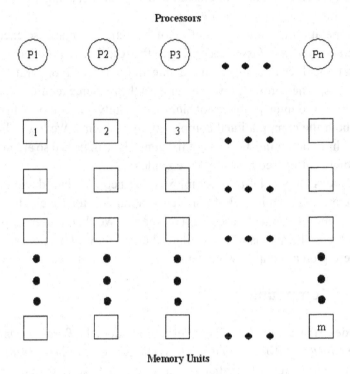

PRAM algorithms are expressed in pseudocode in the natural way. With respect to the ability (or the absence of it) to read or write, three main variants of the PRAM have been studied extensively. In increasing power, we have the variants as follows:

1. *Exclusive Read, Exclusive Write* (*EREW*), where each memory unit can be read or written to by only one processor at a given time.
2. *Concurrent Read, Exclusive Write* (*CREW*), where multiple processors can read a memory unit, but only one processor can write to a given memory cell at a particular time.
3. *Concurrent Read, Concurrent Write* (*CRCW*), where multiple processors can read a given memory cell at the same time, or where multiple processors can write to a given memory cell at the same time. Of course in the case of simultaneous writes, we need some arbitration scheme to determine which processor succeeds in writing. There are three primary models of concurrent writing that have been studied in the literature. The reader is referred to [32] for more details.

In some sense the EREW PRAM is the most-practical version of the PRAM, so an algorithm that runs in equivalent resource bounds on this model to one of the other variants is most desirable. Computationally speaking, as we noted earlier, the EREM PRAM is the weakest of the models followed by the CREW PRAM and then the CRCW PRAM.

Figure 4. Cluster of n workstations

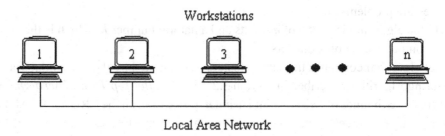

Cluster of Workstations

In this subsection we turn our attention to the other parallel model that we will discuss in this chapter. A cluster of workstations or personal computers is an (relatively) inexpensive alternative to a parallel computer. Such workstations are connected with an Ethernet network and use message-passing for communication among processors. In an Ethernet network, all communications consist of packets transmitted on a shared serial bus available to all processors (Wilkinson & Allen, 1998). Figure 4 shows a cluster of n workstations.

Workstations can be homogeneous or heterogeneous. *Message-Passing Interface (MPI)*, for example, can be used as a library routine in the C or FORTRAN programming language for communication among processes. For more details about this model the reader is referred to (Wilkinson & Allen, 1998).

PRAM Top-Down Hierarchical Clustering Algorithm

In order to provide the reader with a flavor for how clustering algorithms can be parallelized on the PRAM model, in this subsection we describe a *PRAM algorithm* for top-down hierarchical clustering (Table 7). We show that this algorithm runs very fast in parallel, more precisely, in a time that is only poly-logarithmic in the number of points to cluster. This algorithm requires the use of a polynomial number of processors. Problems having such time and processor bounds simultaneously are in the com-

Table 7. The Parallel Top-Down Hierarchical Clustering Algorithm

Step	Parallel Top-Down Hierarchical Clustering Algorithm (S, K)
1.	in parallel do {
2.	$V \leftarrow \{1,\ldots,n\}$;
3.	form the complete weighted graph $G = (V, E)$, where $i \in V$ corresponds to x_i, for $1 \leq i \leq n$, and edge $e = \{j, k\} \in E$ has weight $d_S(x_j, x_k)$ for all $1 \leq j \neq k \leq n$;
4.	}
5.	in parallel compute a minimum-cost spanning tree T of G;
6.	in parallel form the list L by sorting T's edges in descending order with respect to their weights;
7.	in parallel remove the first $K - 1$ edges from L and determine the K connected components which are formed by their removal;
8.	in parallel output these K connected components as the K clusters;

plexity class *NC* (see (Greenlaw, Hoover & Ruzzo, 1995) for more details). This class contains a wide variety of interesting problems.

The input to the algorithm is a set *S* of *n* points and a natural number *K,* which is the desired number of clusters. The output is a set of *K* clusters.

This parallel algorithm computes the same clusters as computed by the sequential Top-Down Hierarchical Clustering Algorithm described in section 3.2. The *Parallel Top-Down Hierarchical Clustering* Algorithm has resource bounds of $O(\log n)$ time using n^2 processors on the CREW PRAM. For a detailed analysis of the time and processor complexity of this algorithm, the reader is referred to (Greenlaw & Kantabutra, 2008). This algorithm shows that the top-down hierarchical clusters can be computed very quickly in parallel on the PRAM model; thus there is a great deal of parallelism inherent in this problem.

In the next subsection we describe a parallel algorithm for clustering on the COW model.

Parallel *K*-Means Algorithm on a Cluster of Workstations

Programming for a cluster of workstations is usually done using a *master-slave approach*. In a typical *cluster of workstations* setting, one process is designated as a *master process* and the other (usually identical) processes are designated as *slaves*. Both master and slave processes work together during the computation. The master process coordinates slave processes until the job is complete. Here we describe a parallel version of *K*-Means clustering for the COW. The algorithm will give the reader a feel for how clustering algorithms can be parallelized on the COW model.

Given a well-specified algorithm for the COW, the pseudocode can be implemented on an Ethernet network of homogenous workstations using the MPI for processor communication. The following is a description of the *Parallel K-Means Clustering* Algorithm (Table 8). We first describe code for the master process and then the code for a slave process. The input to the algorithm is a set *S* of *n* points and a natural number *K,* which is the desired number of clusters. The output is a set of *K* clusters.

Next we describe the slave process (Table 9). We assume that each slave process knows its own process identification number, and each calls its own identification number *myrank*. In the algorithm *P* is a subset of points initially sent to each slave process by the master process.

Let r_s be the number of iterations in the sequential Heuristic *K*-Means Clustering Algorithm, and let r_p be the number of iterations in its parallel counterpart. The time complexity of the serial Heuristic *K*-Means Clustering Algorithm is $O(r_s Kn)$, whereas the time complexity of the *Parallel K-Means Clustering* Algorithm is $O(r_p K|P|)$. Since r_s and r_p are inherently equivalent and $n >> |P|$, the complexity $O(r_p K|P|)$ is asymptotically better than $O(r_s Kn)$.

Table 8. The Parallel K-Means Clustering Algorithm

Step	Parallel *K*-Means Clustering Algorithm Master Process(*S*,*K*)
1.	randomly form *K* subsets of *S* of approximately equal size;
2.	send each subset to each of the *K* slaves;
3.	receive *K* resulting clusters from *K* slaves;
4.	return *K* clusters;

Table 9. The Parallel K-Means Clustering Algorithm slave process

Step	Parallel *K*-Means Clustering Algorithm Slave Process
1.	receive a subset P from the master process;
2.	while (squared-error E changes) do {
3.	compute a mean $\bar{x}_{myrank}$ of the subset P;
4.	broadcast the mean $\bar{x}_{myrank}$ to the other slaves;
5.	compute distance $d(i,j)$, $1 \leq i \leq K$, $1 \leq j \leq |P|$ of each point in P such that $d(i,j) = \| \bar{x}_i - x_j \|$;
6.	choose point members of the new K clusters according to their closest distances to $\bar{x}_i$, $1 \leq i \leq K$;
7.	broadcast K clusters computed in step 6 to the other slaves;
8.	form the new subset P by collecting points that belong to $\bar{x}_{myrank}$ that were sent from the other slaves in step 7;
9.	}
10.	send the subset P to master process;

Suppose n is sufficiently large, and the data are uniformly distributed. The cardinality of P would be close to n/K. We can measure the performance of the *Parallel K-Means Clustering* Algorithm against the performance of the serial algorithm by using speedup $T(K)$, where K is the number of processors (and clusters), as follows:

$$T(K) = \frac{serial\ time\ complexity}{parallel\ time\ complexity} = \frac{O(r_s K n)}{O(r_p K \,|\, P \,|)} = O(K)$$

Applications of Parallel Clustering

In this section we mention a couple of areas in which parallel clustering algorithms have been applied. In neurocomputing Feng et al. adopted data parallelism on PC cluster systems (Feng, Zhou, & Shen, 2007). In their paper they showed experimentally that a parallel hierarchical-clustering algorithm obtained a good quality of clustering and had a speedup over linear-clustering algorithms. Parallel clustering has also been applied in gene sequencing. Mudhireddy et al. invented a parallel hash-based EST-clustering algorithm for gene sequencing (Mudhireddy, Ercal & Frank, 2004). The clustering was done on 269,035 soybean EST sequences on a set of Linux machines. It was reported that their parallel algorithm obtained excellent speedup over its sequential counterpart.

COMPARISON OF CLUSTERING METHODS

In this chapter we have covered a wide range of clustering algorithms. Applying the various methods to problems of interest is rather like an art form. Here we compare and contrast some of the techniques to help the reader understand a bit better when one method might be preferred over another, and in which situations a particular method might be applied. There are no hard and fast rules of when to apply a given technique, and usually each application has its own nuances. Table 10 provides a comparison of bottom-up hierarchical clustering, heuristic K-Means clustering, heuristic K-Medians clustering, top-down hierarchical clustering, parallel K-Means clustering, and parallel top-down hierarchical clustering. Keep in mind that in many applications a hybrid form of these techniques will yield the best results.

SUMMARY AND OPEN PROBLEMS

This chapter has surveyed a number of well-known clustering techniques, including top-down hierarchical, bottom-up hierarchical, K-Means, K-Medians, representative points, and also looked at the parallelization of clustering. We have explored a number of application domains for these various methods. Research is ongoing on the subject of clustering. And, we would like to conclude this chapter by discussing a few open problems.

Table 10. A comparison of several clustering methods. (*) For a description of the parameters used in this column, see the text; for parallel algorithms t, p are time and processor bounds, respectively.

Clustering Method	Running Time*	Works Well on Data	Selected Applications Areas	Selected References
Bottom-Up Hierarchical Clustering	$O(n^2)$	Zoom features required	Molecular biology, astrophysics, wireless-sensor networks, and search engines	[7, 19, 31, 83]
Heuristic K-Means	$O(r_s Kn)$	Spherical, split clusters that are not spherical, continuous space	Genomics, text mining, web mining, and toxicology	[35, 62, 63, 73, 82]
Heuristic K-Medians	$O(n^2 Kr)$	Discrete space	Data streams, photogrammetry and remote sensing, Internet content distirubtion, and phonetic classification	[6, 23, 44, 61]
Top-Down Hierarchical Clustering	$O(n^2)$	Zoom features required	Multiple-sequence alignment and galaxy population calculations	[19. 83]
Parallel K-Means	$O(r_p K|P|)$	Spherical, split clusters that are not spherical, continuous space, very large data set	Genomics, text mining, web mining, and toxicology	[30, 66]
Parallel Top-Down Hierarchical Clustering	$O(\log n), n^2$	Very large data set	Multiple-sequence alignment and galaxy population calculations	[19. 41, 83]

- The first problem has to do with finding a "correct" value of K for both K-Means and K-Medians clusterings for arbitrary inputs. This problem seems very difficult. Up until now, nothing better than trial-and-error methods are known.
- Also in applications of K-Means and K-Medians clustering, can we predict or approximate the required number of iterations given some known characteristics of the inputs?
- The next problem involves a seven-year-old conjecture from (Kantabutra, 2001). The polynomial-time algorithm for finding a set of representative points presented in this chapter does *not* guarantee a minimum set of representative points. In fact, it is still not known whether such a polynomial-time algorithm exists. This problem is equivalent to determining whether finding a minimum set of representative points is *NP*-complete.
- Greenlaw and Kantabutra showed that a version of hierarchical-clustering problem, where no restriction is placed on the distance function, is *CC*-complete (Greenlaw & Kantabutra, 2008). It is open whether this problem remains *CC*-complete if the distance function is Euclidean.

In addition to these open problems, the references contained at the end of this chapter contain many additional items related to clustering. The interested reader is encouraged to pursue some of the references.

REFERENCES

Aggarwal, C. C., & Yu, P. S. (2000). Finding Generalized Projected Clusters in High Dimensional Spaces. *SIGMOD Record, 29*(2), 70–92. doi:10.1145/335191.335383

Agrawal, R., Gehrke, J., Gunopulos, D., & Raghavan, P. (1998). Automatic Subspace Clustering of High Dimensional Data for Data Mining Applications. In *Proceedings of the ACM SIGMOD Conference*, Seattle, Washington, (pp. 94-105).

Al-Sultan, K. (1995). A Tabu Search Approach to the Clustering Problem. *Pattern Recognition, 28*(9), 1443–1451. doi:10.1016/0031-3203(95)00022-R

Ankerst, M., Breunig, M., Kriegel, H.-P., & Sander, J. (1999). OPTICS: Ordering Points to Identify Clustering Structure. In *Proceedings of the ACM SIGMOD Conference*, Philadelphia, PA, (pp. 49-60).

Arora, S. Raghavan, P. and Rao S. (1998). Approximation Schemes for Euclidean *K-Medians* and Related Problems. In *Proceedings of the 30th Annual ACM Symposium on Theory of Computing*, Dallas, TX, (pp. 106-113).

Babcock, B., Datar, M., Motwani, R., & O'Callaghan, L. (2003). Maintaining Variance and K-Medians Over Data Stream Windows. In *Proceedings of the 22nd ACM SIGMOD-SIGACT-SIGART Symposium on Principles of Database Systems*, San Diego, CA, (pp. 234-243).

Bandyopadhyay, S., & Coyle, E. J. (2003). An Energy Efficient Hierarchical Clustering Algorithm for Wireless Sensor Networks. In *Proceedings of the 22nd Annual Joint Conference of the IEEE Computer and Communications Societies*, San Francisco, California.

Berkhin, P. (2002). *Survey of Clustering Data Mining Techniques*. Accrue Software, Inc.

Beyer, K., Goldstein, J., Ramakrishnan, R., & Shaft, U. (1999). When Is Nearest Neighbor Meaningful? In *Proceedings of the 7th ICDT Conference*, Jerusalem, Israel.

Bradley, P. S., & Fayyad, U. M. (1998). Refining Initial Points for *K-Means* Clustering. *Proceedings of the 15th International Conference on Machine Learning*, Madison, Wisconsin, (pp. 91-99).

Bradley, P. S., Fayyad, U. M., & Reina, C. (1998). Scaling Clustering Algorithms to Large Databases. In *American Association for Artificial Intelligence*.

Brown, D., & Huntley, C. (1991). *A Practical Application of Simulated Annealing to Clustering*. Technical Report IPC-TR-91-003, University of Virginia.

Bühlmann, P. (2006). Boosting and l^1-Penalty Methods for High-Dimensional Data with Some Applications in Genomics. In *From Data and Information Analysis to Knowledge Engineering*, (pp. 1-12). Berlin: Springer Science & Business.

Charikar, M., Guha, S., Tardos, É., & Shmoys, D. B. (1999, May). A Constant-Factor Approximation Algorithm for the *K-Medians* Problem. In *Proceedings of the 31st Annual ACM Symposium on Theory of Computing*, Atlanta, Georgia, (pp. 1-10).

Cheeseman, P., & Stutz, J. (1996). Bayesian Classification (AutoClass): Theory and Results. In *Advances in Knowledge Discovery and Data Mining*. Cambridge, MA: AAAI Press/MIT Press.

Cheng, C., Fu, A., & Zhang, Y. (1999). Entropy-Based Subspace Clustering for Mining Numerical Data. In *Proceedings of the 5th ACM SIGKDD Conference*, San Diego, California, (pp. 84-93).

Chinrungrueng, C., & Sequin, C. (1995, January). Optimal Adaptive *K-Means* Algorithm with Dynamic Adjustment of Learning Rate. *IEEE Transactions on Neural Networks, 6*, 157–169. doi:10.1109/72.363440

Cormen, T. H., Leiserson, C. E., & Rivest, R. L. (1990). *Introduction to Algorithms*. New York: McGraw-Hill.

Corpet, F. (1988). Multiple Sequence Alignment with Hierarchical Clustering. *Nucleic Acids Research, 16*(22), 10881–10890. doi:10.1093/nar/16.22.10881

Cristofor, D., & Simovici, D. A. (2002). An Information-Theoretical Approach to Clustering Categorical Databases Using Genetic Algorithms. In *Proceedings of the 2nd SIAM ICDM Conference*, Arlington, Virginia.

Cula, O. G., & Dana, K. J. (2001). Compact Representation of Bidirectional Texture Functions. In *Proceedings of the IEEE Computer Society Conference on Computer Vision and Pattern Recognition*, Hawaii, USA, December.

Defays, D. (1977). An Efficient Algorithm for a Complete Link Method. *The Computer Journal, 20*, 364–366. doi:10.1093/comjnl/20.4.364

Doucette, P., Agouris, P., Stefanidis, A., & Musavi, M. (2001, March). Self-Organized Clustering for Road Extraction in Classified Imagery. *Journal of Photogrammetry and Remote Sensing, 55*(5-6), 347–358. doi:10.1016/S0924-2716(01)00027-2

Du, Q., Faber, V., & Gunzburger, M. (1999). Centroidal Voronoi Tesselations: Applications and Algorithms. *SIAM Review*, *41*, 637–676. doi:10.1137/S0036144599352836

Dubes, R. C. (1993). Cluster Analysis and Related Issues. In *Handbook of Pattern Recognition and Computer Vision* (pp. 3-32). River Edge, NJ: World Scientific Publishing Co.

Ertoz, L. Steinbach, M. & Kumar, V. (2003, May). Finding Clusters of Different Sizes, Shapes, and Densities in Noisy, High Dimensional Data. In *Proceedings of the 3rd SIAM International Conference on Data Mining*, San Francisco.

Ester, M. Kriegel, H.-P., Sander, J. & Xu, X. (1996). A Density-Based Algorithm for Discovering Clusters in Large Spatial Databases with Noise. In *Proceedings of the 2nd ACM SIGKDD Conference*, Portland, Oregon, (pp. 226-231).

Everitt, B. (1993). *Cluster Analysis* (3rd edition). London: Edward Arnold.

Fasulo, D. (1999). *An Analysis of Recent Work on Clustering Algorithms*. Technical Report UW-CSE01-03-02, University of Washington.

Feng, Z., Zhou, B., & Shen, J. (2007). A Parallel Hierarchical Clustering Algorithm for PCs Cluster System. *Neurocomputing*, *70*(4-6), 809–818.

Ferragina, P., & Gulli, A. (2007). A Personalized Search Engine Based on Web-Snippet Hierarchical Clustering. *Software, Practice & Experience*, *38*(2), 189–225. doi:10.1002/spe.829

Fich, F. E. (1993). The Complexity of Computation on the Parallel Random Access Machine. In J. H. Reif, (Ed.) *Synthesis of Parallel Algorithms*, (pp. 843-899). San Francisco: Morgan Kaufmann.

Fraley, C., & Raftery, A. (1999). *MCLUST: Software for Model-Based Cluster and Discriminant Analysis*. Technical Report 342, Department of Statistics, University of Washington.

Ganti, V. Gehrke, J. & Ramakrishnan, R. (1999). CACTUS-Clustering Categorical Data Using Summaries. In *Proceedings of the 5th ACM SIGKDD Conference*, San Diego, CA, (pp.73-83).

Gasch, A. P., & Eisen, M. B. (2002). Exploring the Conditional Coregulation of Yeast Gene Expression Through Fuzzy *K*-Means Clustering. *Genome Biology*, *3*(11), 1–21. doi:10.1186/gb-2002-3-11-research0059

Ghosh, J. (2002). Scalable Clustering Methods for Data Mining. In *Handbook of Data Mining*. Mahwah, NJ: Lawrence Erlbaum.

Gibson, D., Kleinberg, J., & Raghavan, P. (1998). Clustering Categorical Data: An Approach Based on Dynamic Systems. In *Proceedings of the 24th International Conference on Very Large Databases*, New York, (pp. 311-323).

Goil, S., Nagesh, H., & Choudhary, A. (1999). *MAFIA: Efficient and Scalable Subspace Clustering for Very Large Data Sets*. Technical Report CPDC-TR-9906-010, Northwestern University.

Graham, D. B., & Allinson, N. M. (1998). Automatic Face Representation and Classification. In *Proceedings of British Machine Vision Conference*, Southampton, UK.

Greenlaw, R., Hoover, H. J., & Ruzzo, W. L. (1995). *Limits to Parallel: P-Completeness Theory*. Oxford, UK: Oxford University Press

Greenlaw, R., & Kantabutra, S. (2008). On the Parallel Complexity of Hierarchical Clustering and *CC-Complete* Problems. *Complexity, 14*(2), 18–28. doi:10.1002/cplx.20238

Guha, S., Rastogi, R., & Shim, K. (1998). CURE: An Efficient Clustering Algorithm for Large Databases. In *Proceedings of the ACM SIGMOD Conference*, Seattle, WA, (pp. 73-84).

Guha, S., Rastogi, R., & Shim, K. (1999). ROCK: A Robust Clustering Algorithm for Categorical Attributes. In *Proceedings of the 15th ICDE Conference*, Sydney, Australia, (pp. 512-521).

Gutkin, A., & King, S. (2004). Structural Representation of Speech for Phonetic Classification. In *Proceedings of the 17th International Conference on Pattern Recognition*, Cambridge, UK.

Hall, D. J., & Ball, G. B. (1965). *ISODATA: A Novel Method of Data Analysis and Pattern Classification*. Technical Report AD-699616, Stanford Research Institute, Menlo Park, California.

Hall, L. O., Ozyurt, B., & Bezdek, J. C. (1999). Clustering with a Genetically Optimized Approach. *IEEE Transactions on Evolutionary Computation, 3*(2), 103–112. doi:10.1109/4235.771164

Han, J., Kamber, M., & Tung, A. K. H. (2001). Spatial Clustering Methods in Data Mining: A Survey. In *Geographic Data Mining and Knowledge Discovery*. San Francisco: Taylor and Francis.

Hartigan, J. (1975). *Clustering Algorithms*. New York: John Wiley & Sons.

Hinneburg, A., & Keim, D. (1998). An Efficient Approach to Clustering Large Multimedia Databases with Noise. In *Proceedings of the 4th ACM SIGKDD Conference*, New York (pp. 58-65).

Jain, A., & Dubes, R. C. (1988). *Algorithms for Clustering Data*. Englewood Cliffs, NJ: Prentice-Hall.

Jain, A. K., Murty, M. N., & Flynn, P. J. (1999). Data Clustering: A Review. *ACM Computing Surveys, 31*(3), 264–323. doi:10.1145/331499.331504

Jain, P. Mekaa, R. & Dhillon, I. S. (2008). Simultaneous Unsupervised Learning of Disparate Clusterings. In *Proceedings of the SIAM International Conference on Data Mining, Atlanta*, Georgia.

Kannan, R., Vempala, S., & Vetta, A. (2000). On Clusterings: Good, Bad, and Spectral. In *Proceedings of the 41st Foundations of Computer Science*, Redondo Beach, CA.

Kantabutra, S. (2001). *Efficient Representation of Cluster Structure in Large Data Sets*. Ph.D. Dissertation, Tufts University, Medford, MA.

Kantabutra, S. & Couch, A. (2000). Parallel K-Means Clustering Algorithm on NOWs. *NECTEC Technical Journal, 1*(6).

Karypis, G., Han, E. H., & Kumar, V. (1999). CHAMELEON: A Hierarchical Clustering Algorithm Using Dynamic Modeling. *Computer, 32*, 68–75. doi:10.1109/2.781637

Kaufman, L. & Rousseeuw, P. (199). *Finding Groups in Data: An Introduction to Cluster Analysis*. New York: John Wiley & Sons.

Kim, S. Jin, X. & Han, J. (2008). SpaRClus: Spatial Relationship Pattern-Based Hierarchical Clustering. In *Proceedings of the SIAM International Conference on Data Mining, Atlanta*, Georgia.

Kohonen, T. (2001). Self-Organizing Maps. *Springer Series in Information Sciences, 30*. Berlin: Springer.

Kolatch, E. (2001). *Clustering Algorithms for Spatial Databases: A Survey*. PDF is available on the Web.

Laoutaris, N., Zissimopoulos, V., & Stavrakakis, I. (2004). Joint Object Placement and Node Dimensioning for Internet Content Distribution. *Information Processing Letters, 89*(6), 273–279. doi:10.1016/j.ipl.2003.12.002

Lingras, P., & West, C. (2004). Interval Set Clustering of Web Users with Rough *K*-Means. *Journal of Intelligent Information Systems, 23*(1), 5–16. doi:10.1023/B:JIIS.0000029668.88665.1a

Lloyd, S. (1957). *Least Square Quantization in PCM's*. Bell Telephone Laboratories Paper.

MacQueen, J. (1967). Some Methods for Classification and Analysis of Multivariate Observations. In *Proceedings of the Fifth Berkeley Symposium On Mathematical Statistics and Probability, 1*, 281-296.

Mirkin, B. (1996). *Mathematic Classification and Clustering*. Amsterdam: Kluwer Academic Publishers.

Mudhireddy, R., Ercal, F., & Frank, R. (2004). Parallel Hash-Based EST Clustering Algorithm for Gene Sequencing. *DNA and Cell Biology, 23*(10), 615–623. doi:10.1089/dna.2004.23.615

Nagesh, H., Goil, S., & Choudhary, A. (2001). Adaptive Grids for Clustering Massive Data Sets. In *Proceedings of the 1st SIAM ICDM Conference*, Chicago, IL.

Peeters, G., Burthe, A. L., & Rodet, X. (2002). Toward Automatic Music Audio Summary Generation from Signal Analysis. In *Proceedings of the International Conference on Music Information Retrieval*, Paris, France.

Ratha, N. K., Jain, A. K., & Chung, M. J. (1995). Clustering Using a Coarse-Grained Parallel Genetic Algorithm. In *Proceedings of the IEEE Computer Architectures for Machine Perception*, (pp. 331-338).

Sander, J., Ester, M., Kriegel, H.-P., & Xu, X. (1998). Density-Based Clustering in Spatial Databases: The Algorithm GDBSCAN and Its Applications. *Data Mining and Knowledge Discovery, 2*(2), 169–194. doi:10.1023/A:1009745219419

Sibson, R. (1973). SLINK: An Optimally Efficient Algorithm for the Single Link Cluster Method. *The Computer Journal, 16*, 30–34. doi:10.1093/comjnl/16.1.30

Spath, H. (1980). *Cluster Analysis Algorithms*. Chichester, UK: Ellis Horwood.

Steinbach, M., Karypis, G., & Kumar, V. (2000). A Comparison of Document Clustering Techniques. In *Proceedings of the 6th ACM SIGKDD International Conference on Knowledge Discovery and Data Mining*, Boston, MA.

Steinhaus, H. (1956). Sur La Division Des Corp Materiels En Parties. *Bull. Acad. Polon. Sci.*, C1. *III, IV*, 801–804.

Tsai, H., Horng, S., Tsai, S., Lee, S., Kao, T., & Chen, C. (1997). Parallel Clustering Algorithms on a Reconfigurable Array of Processors With Wider Bus Networks. In *Proceedings of the IEEE International Conference on Parallel and Distributed Systems.*

Vittayakorn, S., Kantabutra, S., & Tanprasert, C. (2008). The Parallel Complexities of the *K-Medians* Related Problems. In *Proceedings of the 5th International Conference on Electrical Engineering/Electronics, Computer, Telecommunications and Information Technology*, Krabi, Thailand, (pp. 9-12).

Voorhees, E. M. (1986). Implementing Agglomerative Hierarchical Clustering Algorithms for Use in Document Retrieval. *Information Processing & Management, 22*(6), 465–476. doi:10.1016/0306-4573(86)90097-X

Wallace, C., & Dowe, D. (1994). Intrinsic Classification by MML – The Snob Program. In *Proceedings of the 7th Australian Joint Conference on Artificial Intelligence*, Armidale, Australia, (pp. 37-44).

Wan, S. J., Wong, S. K. M., & Prusinkiewicz, P. (1998). An Algorithm for Multidimensional Data Clustering. *ACM Transactions on Mathematical Software, 14*, 153–162. doi:10.1145/45054.45056

Wang, F., & Zhang, Q. J. (1995). An Improved *K*-Means Clustering Algorithm and Application to Combined Multicodebook/MLP Neural Network Speech Recognition. In *. Proceedings of the IEEE Canadian Conference on Electrical and Computer Engineering, 2*, 999–1002.

Wang, W. Yang, J. & Muntz, R. (1997). STING: A Statistical Information Grid Approach to Spatial Data Mining. In *Proceedings of the 23rd Conference on VLDB*, Athens, Greece, (pp. 186-195).

Waring, J. F., Jolly, R. A., Ciurlionis, R., Lum, P. Y., Praestgaard, J. T., & Morfitt, D. C. (2001). Clustering of Hepatotoxins Based on Mechanism of Toxicity Using Gene Expression Profiles. *Toxicology and Applied Pharmacology, 175*(1), 28–42. doi:10.1006/taap.2001.9243

White, S. D. M., & Frenk, C. S. (1991). Galaxy Formation Through Hierarchical Clustering. *The Astrophysical Journal, 379*, 52–79. doi:10.1086/170483

Wilkinson, B., & Allen, M. (1998). *Parallel Programming, Techniques and Applications Using Networked Workstations and Parallel Computers.* Englewood Cliffs, NJ: Prentice Hall.

Xu, X., Ester, M., Kriegel, H.-P., & Sander, J. (1998). A Distribution-Based Clustering Algorithm for Mining in Large Spatial Databases. In *Proceedings of the 14th ICDE Conference*, Orlando, Florida, (pp. 324-331).

Young, N. E. (2000). Greedy Approximation Algorithm for *K-Medians* by Randomized Rounding. In *Proceedings of the ACM-SIAM Symposium on Discrete Algorithms*, San Francisco, CA.

Zhang, T., Ramakrishnan, R., & Livny, M. (1997). BIRCH: A New Data Clustering Algorithm and Its Applications. *Journal of Data Mining and Knowledge Discovery, 1*(2), 141–182. doi:10.1023/A:1009783824328

Chapter 11
Financial Data Mining Using Flexible ICA–GARCH Models

Philip L.H. Yu
The University of Hong Kong, Hong Kong

Edmond H.C. Wu
The Hong Kong Polytechnic University, Hong Kong

W.K. Li
The University of Hong Kong, Hong Kong

ABSTRACT

As a data mining technique, independent component analysis (ICA) is used to separate mixed data signals into statistically independent sources. In this chapter, we apply ICA for modeling multivariate volatility of financial asset returns which is a useful tool in portfolio selection and risk management. In the finance literature, the generalized autoregressive conditional heteroscedasticity (GARCH) model and its variants such as EGARCH and GJR-GARCH models have become popular standard tools to model the volatility processes of financial time series. Although univariate GARCH models are successful in modeling volatilities of financial time series, the problem of modeling multivariate time series has always been challenging. Recently, Wu, Yu, & Li (2006) suggested using independent component analysis (ICA) to decompose multivariate time series into statistically independent time series components and then separately modeled the independent components by univariate GARCH models. In this chapter, we extend this class of ICA-GARCH models to allow more flexible univariate GARCH-type models. We also apply the proposed models to compute the value-at-risk (VaR) for risk management applications. Backtesting and out-of-sample tests suggest that the ICA-GARCH models have a clear cut advantage over some other approaches in value-at-risk estimation.

DOI: 10.4018/978-1-60566-908-3.ch011

INTRODUCTION

In econometrics, volatility modeling of financial time series has received a lot of attention due to its wide applications in finance such as option pricing and risk management. Among the existing volatility models, one of the most important models is the autoregressive conditional heteroscedasticity (ARCH) model proposed by (Engle, 1982) which was further extended to generalized ARCH (GARCH) model by (Bollerslev, 1986). After the success of ARCH and GARCH models, researchers further proposed different types of GARCH models such as EGARCH (Nelson, 1991) and GJR-GARCH (Glosten, Jaganathan, & Runkle, 1993), etc. These univariate GARCH models are capable in capturing the dynamics of volatilities from the characteristics of financial time series.

Although GARCH models are successful in modeling volatilities of univariate financial time series, the problem of modeling multivariate time series still raises challenges in this research area. It is mainly because in existing multivariate GARCH models, the number of unknown parameters grows very fast with the number of time series in the model. For example, in (Engle, 2002), Engle et al. compared the complexity of several multivariate GARCH models and most of them have the complexity of $O(N^2)$ or even $O(N^3)$, where N is the number of time series.

However, in practice, we often need to extend the volatility modeling to high dimensional cases. For instance in portfolio optimization, a portfolio could contain several hundred of stocks. Therefore, new approaches are needed to deal with such situations.

Recently, (Wu, Yu & Li, 2006) suggested using independent component analysis (ICA) to decompose multivariate time series into statistically independent time series components and then separately modeled the independent components (ICs) by univariate GARCH models. Their experiment results showed that the ICA-GARCH models are more effective in capturing the time-varying features of volatilities and provide better value-at-risk estimate than existing methods including DCC (Engle, 2002), PCA-GARCH (Alexander, 2001) and RiskMetrics.

In this chapter, we extend this class of ICA-GARCH models to allow more flexible univariate GARCH-type models. In addition to the popular ICs extraction methods—FastICA algorithms, we also consider other ICA algorithms which can extract ICs from non-stationary data (Hyvärinen, 2001) as most financial time series are non-stationary.

The rest of this chapter is organized as follows: In Section 2, we introduce the univariate GARCH process and several of its extended models. Then, we propose flexible ICA-GARCH models for multivariate volatility modeling in Section 3. In Section 4, we consider the estimation of value at risk of a single asset or a portfolio based on the flexible ICA-GARCH models. Experimental results are given in Section 5. Finally, we conclude in Section 6.

VOLATILITY MODELS

In the following, we introduce several prevailing volatility models for financial time series.

GARCH *(p,q)* Model

In GARCH models, financial time series $\{y_t\}$ are assumed to be generated by a stochastic process with (conditional) time-varying volatility $\{\sigma_t\}$. The general GARCH (p,q) model ($p>0$ and $q\geq0$ are integers) is defined as

$$y_t = \mu + \varepsilon_t = \mu + \sigma_t z_t, \qquad\qquad z_t \sim D(0, 1) \tag{1}$$

$$\sigma_t^2 = \alpha_0 + \sum_{i=1}^{p} \beta_i \sigma_{t-i}^2 + \sum_{j=1}^{q} \alpha_j \varepsilon_{t-j}^2$$

where $\alpha_0 > 0$, $\alpha_i \geq 0$ for $i = 1, \cdots, q$ and $\beta_j \geq 0$ for $j = 1, \cdots, p$, and $D(0,1)$ represents a conditional distribution with zero mean and unit variance such as the standard Gaussian distribution $N(0,1)$ and the Student's t distribution (standardized to unit variance). Since GARCH(1,1) model was found to be adequate for many financial time series (Bollerslev, Chou, & Kroner, 1992), we focused on this model in our empirical analysis.

EGARCH *(p,q)* Model

Note that the volatility σ_t from the GARCH model is symmetric between positive and negative error shocks ε_t. However, higher volatilities are often seen for negative shocks than positive shocks. (Nelson 1991) proposed the exponential GARCH (EGARCH) model to allow volatility asymmetry:

$$\ln(\sigma_t^2) = \alpha_0 + \sum_{i=1}^{p} \beta_i \ln \sigma_{t-i}^2 + \sum_{j=1}^{q} \alpha_j \left[\frac{|\varepsilon_{t-j}|}{\sigma_{t-j}} - E\left\{ \frac{|\varepsilon_{t-j}|}{\sigma_{t-j}} \right\} \right] + \sum_{j=1}^{q} \gamma_i \frac{\varepsilon_{t-j}}{\sigma_{t-j}} \tag{2}$$

where $E\left\{ \frac{|\varepsilon_{t-j}|}{\sigma_{t-j}} \right\} = \sqrt{2/\pi}$ for standard Gaussian and $E\left\{ \frac{|\varepsilon_{t-j}|}{\sigma_{t-j}} \right\} = \sqrt{\frac{\nu-2}{\pi}} \frac{\Gamma\{\frac{\nu-1}{2}\}}{\Gamma\{\frac{\nu}{2}\}}$ for Student's t with degrees of freedom $\nu > 2$. Note that the γ_j governs the volatility asymmetry effect. For example, a negative γ_j implies that a negative shock increases future volatility while a positive shock reduces future volatility.

GJR-GARCH *(p,q)* Model

Another useful GARCH model that can describe the asymmetric conditional volatilities is the GJR-GARCH model (Glosten, Jaganathan, & Runkle 1993). The general GJR-GARCH (p,q) model assumes that the conditional variance at time t follows:

$$\sigma_t^2 = \alpha_0 + \sum_{i=1}^{p} \beta_i \sigma_{t-i}^2 + \sum_{j=1}^{q} \alpha_j \varepsilon_{t-j}^2 + \sum_{j=1}^{q} \gamma_j I_{t-j} \varepsilon_{t-j}^2 \tag{3}$$

where $I_{t-j} = 1$ if $\varepsilon_{t-j} < 0$; otherwise $I_{t-j} = 0$, and $\alpha_0 > 0$, $\beta_i \geq 0$, $\alpha_j \geq 0$, $\alpha_j + \gamma_j \geq 0$, $i = 1, \ldots, p$; $j = 1, \ldots, q$. So $\gamma_j > 0$ indicates that future volatility is always higher for a negative shock.

We note that GARCH and GJR-GARCH models allow for volatility clustering (i.e., persistence) by a combination of the β_i and α_j terms, whereas persistence in EGARCH models is entirely captured by the β_i terms.

THE FLEXIBLE ICA-GARCH MODELS

In this section, we first introduce the method of ICA and then describe the procedure of applying ICA in multivariate volatility modeling.

What is ICA?

Independent component analysis (ICA) (Comon, 1994) is a data mining technique which aims to express the observed data in terms of a linear combination of underlying latent variables. These latent variables are assumed to be non-Gaussian and mutually independent. A typical ICA model for an N-dimensional multivariate time series $\{x_t = (x_{it}, \ldots, x_{Nt})': t = 1, \ldots, T\}$ is:

$$x_t = As_t \tag{4}$$

where s_t is a vector of statistically independent latent variables called the independent components (ICs), and A is an unknown constant mixing matrix. In this paper, we only consider the case that A is a square matrix. The task of ICA is to identify both the ICs and the matrix A. That is to find W such that the unmixed data $y_t = Wx_t$ have components of y_t as independent as possible and hence y_t provides an estimate of s_t. In general, W differs from A^{-1} by a rotation and scale transformation.

Various algorithms for parameter estimation have been developed for ICA. Among them, a widely used one is the *FastICA algorithm* proposed by (Hyvärinen, 1999; Hyvärinen, & Oja, 1997), which is a fast fixed point algorithm (FastICA) for maximizing the non-Gaussianity of y_{it}. It was proven that the solutions to this optimization problem give the ICs (see (Hyvärinen, Karhunen, & Oja, 2001)). The FastICA algorithm aims to maximize a non-Gaussianity measure so-called negentropy which is approximated by the function $\{E[G(y)] - E[G(y_{gauss})]\}^2$ where G is a non-quadratic even function, y is an IC and y_{gauss} is Gaussian with the same variance to that of y. Some popular choices of $g = G'$ are the derivative of a standard Gaussian density (Guassian), the cubic power function (pow3) and the hyperbolic tangent (tanh).

Note that the FastICA algorithm assumes that all ICs are independently and identically distributed over time. However, a time-varying volatility is a common stylized fact in financial time series. It is thus more natural to assume that the ICs are non-stationary with variance changing over time.

An alternative approach to separate non-stationary multivariate time series was introduced in (Hyvärinen, 2001), where Hyvärinen proposed a *cumulant-based approach* to find the non-stationary components $\{y_{it}\}$. This approach aims to maximize the nonstationarity of y_{it} as measured by the fourth-order cross-cumulant of y_{it}:

$$\operatorname{cum}(y_{it}, y_{it}, y_{i,t-\tau}, y_{i,t-\tau}) = E\{y_{it}^2 y_{i,t-\tau}^2\} - E\{y_{it}^2\}E\{y_{i,t-\tau}^2\} - 2(E\{y_{it} y_{i,t-\tau}\})^2 \tag{5}$$

where τ is the time lag. If the series y_{it} is serially uncorrelated, and has zero mean and unit variance, this cumulant is simply the lag-τ autocorrelation of y_{it}^2, i.e., $\operatorname{corr}(y_{it}^2, y_{i,t-\tau}^2)$. The ICs are estimated by finding the linear combinations $w'x_t$, such that the absolute value of the cross-cumulant is maximized:

$$\max_{w} |\operatorname{cum}(w'x_t, w'x_t, w'x_{t-\tau}, w'x_{t-\tau})| \tag{6}$$

under the constraint: $\text{Var}(w'x_t) = 1$. In (Hyvärinen, 2001), Hyvärinen developed a fast fixed-point algorithm similar to the FastICA algorithm for separating ICs by nonstationarity, using cross-cumulants. Hyvärinen showed that the maximally nonstationary linear combinations give the ICs.

A second method of separation of nonstationary components is to use a *conditional-decorrelation approach* proposed by (Matsuoka, Ohya, & Kawamoto, 1995). They showed that if the latent components are conditionally uncorrelated and their local variances fluctuate independently of each other, the components and the mixing matrix can be determined uniquely. In this approach, the ICs are estimated by minimizing the conditional uncorrelatedness of y_t as measured by:

$$Q(W,t) = \sum_i \ln E_t\{y_{it}^2\} - \ln | E\{y_t y_t'\} |$$

(7)

where E_t represents the conditional expectation, which can be estimated based on the data around the time point t.

Building the Flexible ICA-GARCH Models

The flexible ICA-GARCH model works as follows: In the first step, we remove the autocorrelation of each return series x_{it} by an autoregressive AR(p_i) model:

$$x_{it} = \varphi_0 + \varphi_1 x_{i,t-1} + \cdots + \varphi_1 x_{i,t-p_i} + e_{it}$$

(8)

where e_{it} **is assumed to be a white noise series with mean zero and variance** σ_i^2. The AR order p_i is usually unknown and is determined by choosing the order with the smallest value in the Bayesian information criterion (BIC):

$$\text{BIC} = -2LLF + N_{para} \ln(N_{obs})$$

(9)

where LLF is the value of the maximized log-likelihood function of an AR model under consideration, N_{para} is the number of parameters in the model and N_{obs} is the sample size of the observed return series.

After choosing the appropriate AR model for each return series x_{it}, we use ICA to decompose the residual vector e_t (obtained from the fitted AR models) into independent components $\{s_{i,t}\}$, $i=1,\ldots,N$, i.e., $e_t = As_t$ with $s_t = (s_{1,t},\ldots,s_{N,t})'$. Then, we can model each IC $s_{i,t}$ by different univariate GARCH-type models mentioned in Section 2. More specifically, the following six GARCH-type models will be fitted for each IC:

- GARCH(1,1) with Gaussian error
- GARCH(1,1) with t error
- EGARCH(1,1) with Gaussian error
- EGARCH(1,1) with t error
- GJR-GARCH(1,1) with Gaussian error
- GJR-GARCH(1,1) with t error

By selecting the most suitable GARCH-type model automatically for each IC using the BIC criterion, we end up with a flexible class of ICA-GARCH models. We will describe this in details later.

Using the mixing matrix A, the (conditional) covariance matrix of the original return vector $x_t = (x_{1,t}, \ldots, x_{N,t})'$ at time t is given by:

$$H_t = AV_t A' \tag{10}$$

where V_t is a diagonal matrix with diagonal elements being the volatilities of independent components s_t.

Because the N components in s_t are independent, such an approach will not significantly increase the computational complexity while retaining a very high accuracy. The ICA-GARCH model allows the multivariate volatilities of N return series to be generated from N univariate GARCH-type models.

Selecting the Best ICA-GARCH Model

Notice that the likelihood function of the residual vectors $\{e_t\}$ is given by:

$$LF = \prod_{t=1}^{T} \{ p_i(w_i' e_t) \mid \det W \mid \} \tag{11}$$

where p_i is the density of the i-th IC fitted by a chosen GARCH-type model, and w_i' denotes the i-th row of W. As stated in Section 3.1, the ICs and the matrix W can be estimated using any one of the five methods: three FastICA algorithms, cumulant-based and conditional-decorrelation approaches. Also, for each of the five ICA models, the estimated ICs will be estimated by any one of the six GARCH-type models. Our task is to find the optimal ICA model and the most suitable univariate GARCH-type models for each IC. To do so, we propose to use an overall BIC to measure the fitness of an ICA-GARCH model.

First of all, for a certain ICA model $M_m (1 \leq m \leq 5)$, we can use the BIC to select the most suitable GARCH-type model for each IC. As all the ICs in the ICA model are mutually independent, we can determine the likelihood function of e using (11). Because the number of parameters of each GARCH-type model is also estimated, we can use these information to calculate an overall BIC of the ICA-GARCH model with ICs determined by the ICA model M_m:

$$\text{Overall} - \text{BIC}_m = \sum_{i=1}^{N} \text{BIC}_{im} \tag{12}$$

where BIC_{im} is the BIC value for the most suitable GARCH-type model for the i-th IC estimated using the ICA model M_m. Finally, we will choose the best ICA-GARCH model with minimal overall BIC value as the optimal model for the residuals $\{e_t\}$. Combining with the selected AR models, we obtain a flexible ICA-GARCH model for the original multivariate time series $\{x_t\}$.

ICA-GARCH FOR VOLATILITY ESTIMATION AND FORECASTING IN VAR APPLICATIONS

In this section, we introduce the estimation procedure of value at risk (VaR) by using the ICA-GARCH model for multivariate volatility modeling based on univariate GARCH models. There are a lot of researches in using GARCH models for VaR estimation. For example, (So & Yu, 2005) gave an empirical studies on VaR estimation using various GARCH models in different market indexes.

Value at Risk

We first briefly introduce the concept of value at risk. Value at risk (VaR) is a widely accepted measure of market risk in many risk management applications. VaR represents the maxial loss of an underlying asset that will occur during a target horizon with a specified probability. Mathematically, it is defined under a probabilistic framework:

$$p = \Pr(\Delta V_{t+1} \geq \text{VaR}) \tag{13}$$

where p is the prespecified probability of interest, such as $p = 5\%$ or $p = 1\%$.

For a single asset, the next day's profit (or loss if negative) is $\Delta V_{t+1} = Q_0(P_{t+1} - P_t)$, where Q_0 is the quantity of the underlying asset and P_t is the asset's market price at time t. Alternatively, we can use log returns to represent ΔV_{t+1}.

Our objective is to first estimate the volatilities of multivariate time series by using the proposed models, and then to compute the time-varying VaRs. In essence, the usefulness of VaR estimation relies on the accurate estimation of volatilities. Therefore, we are interested in assessing the performance of ICA-GARCH in VaR estimation.

The calculation of VaRs is as follows: we first need to fit one of the above models to the multivariate time series, and then use the estimated model parameters to forecast the next period volatility forecasts. Based on the forecasts of volatilities, we can compute the forecasts of VaRs using Monte Carlo simulation. More specifically, we use Monte Carlo simulation to generate a large number of hypothetical changes ΔV_{t+1}, e.g., 10,000. Then, we obtain the simulated distribution of ΔV_{t+1}. The 5% or 1% VaRs will be the 5% or 1% quantiles of the simulated ΔV_{t+1}.

Backtesting VaRs

Backtesting VaRs is a statistical framework that verifies whether the actual losses are consistent with the forecasting losses. It is a crucial model validation step to check whether or not a VaR model is adequate. We can also use backtesting to compare the performance of different volatility models in VaR estimation by using backtesting.

A common method to verify the accuracy of a model is to record the failure rate, which represents the proportion of times VaRs exceeded the actual loss in a given sample. Ideally, the failure rate should be an unbiased estimator of p, and the failure rate should converge to p as the sample size increases. That is, when we compare the actual losses with the estimated VaRs, the percentage of losses that exceed the VaRs should be close to the specified levels (e.g., 5% or 1%) if the volatilities forecast is accurate

Figure 1. Residual series

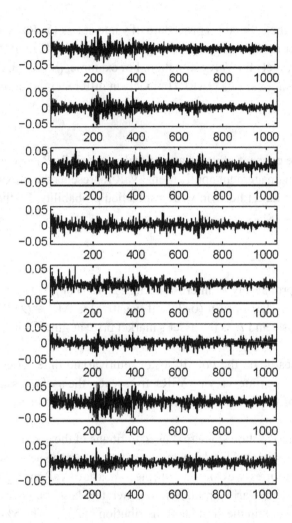

enough. For example, if we forecast the VaRs of the next 1,000 trading days, if the volatility model is good enough, the number of days that exceeds the VaRs should be close to 50 days if $p = 0.05$ or 10 days if $p = 0.01$.

EXPERIMENTS

There are two parts in this experimental section. In the first part, we test and validate the effectiveness of ICA-GARCH model in multivariate volatilities modeling. Then, we use backtesting to check the performance of the ICA-GARCH models for practical VaR applications.

Table 1. Selected models and parameter estimates of the flexible ICA-GARCH model

Series	IC1	IC2	IC3	IC4	IC5	IC6	IC7	IC8
Best model	GARCH-T	GARCH-T	EGARCH-T	GARCH-T	GJR-T	EGARCH	GJR	GJR-T
α_0	0.0135	0.0010	-0.0037	0.0083	0.0257	-0.0021	0.0054	0.0022
α_1	0.0712	0.0176	-0.0339	0.0914	0.0001	0.0722	0.0001	0.0164
β_1	0.9167	0.9816	0.9967	0.9021	0.9362	0.8575	0.9294	0.9721
γ_1	-	-	-0.1421	-	0.0697	-0.1008	0.1293	0.0189
d.f.*	11.156	9.798	4.735	8.453	10.032	-	-	7.077

* d.f. stands for the degrees of freedom of a t error

Data Description

We used the historical data of MSCI market price Index from eight developed financial markets, including (1) United States, (2) United Kingdom, (3) Japan, (4) Hong Kong, (5) Singapore, (6) Australia, (7) Germany and (8) Canada. All the indexes are US dollar based. The dataset is from the periods of July 9, 2001 to July 6, 2006, representing 1,302 daily observations.

For model comparison, we divide the dataset into two parts. The first part is the in-sample data consisting of the first 1,102 observations for model training while the remaining 200 observations are out-of-sample data for forecasting evaluation.

The daily returns x_{it} are calculated by $x_{it} = \ln(P_{it}) - \ln(P_{i,t-1})$, where P_{it} is the closing price of index i on the trading day t. Then, we employed the AR model to filter the autocorrelation of the return series. The in-sample residuals of the eight series are plotted in Figure 1.

Multivariate Volatility Modeling

Here, we choose five ICA algorithms: Cumulant-Based (CB), Conditional-Decorrelation (CD), and three versions of FastICA algorithms (FastICA(pow3), FastICA(tanh) and FastICA(Gaussian)). In the GARCH modeling of ICs, we provide six choices: GARCH, GARCH(T), EGARCH, EGARCH(T), GJR and GJR(T). The model selection is based on the BIC criterion we introduce in the previous section. The results are shown in Table 1.

According to the overall BIC measure, the flexible ICA-GARCH model selects the CD method as the best ICA algorithm to decompose the eight residual series. The GARCH models selected for each independent component are shown in the second row of Table 1. We note that five different GARCH-type models are chosen to model the eight residual series. The diversity of models selected implies the necessity of using flexible models to better reflect the complexity of multivariate volatility modeling such as heavy tailed distribution and volatility asymmetry.

To compare the performance of the flexible ICA-GARCH models with the standard ICA-GARCH models when all ICs are estimated by the same GARCH-type model, we also estimated their conditional volatilities which are shown in Figure 2, Figure 3, Figure 4, Figure 5 and Figure 6. Note that the ICA-GARCH, ICA-EGARCH, ICA-GARCH(T), ICA-GJR and ICA-GJR(T) models assume a common GARCH-type specification for all ICs.

Comparing with the residual series, we can see that the flexible ICA-GARCH is the best model in modeling the dynamic changes of volatilities. For example, the flexible ICA-GARCH indicates that

Figure 2. Conditional volatilities by flexible ICA-GARCH

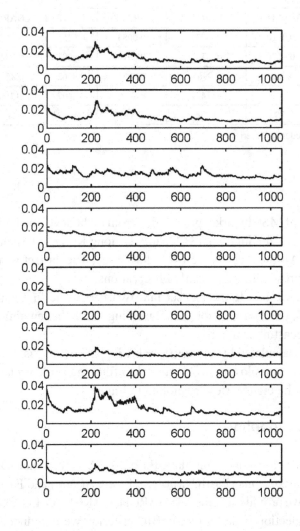

series No.1, No.2 and No.7 demonstrate greater volatilities around the 200-th observation whereas most of the other models are relatively flatten.

Experiments for Backtesting VaRs

In this section, we implemented the backtesting for the models considered. For risk management purposes, we consider 95 percent ($p = 0.05$) and 99 percent ($p = 0.01$) confidence levels of the VaRs. Since one can long (buy) or short (sell) a price index to make profit or loss, we therefore consider both positions for the VaR calculation. Actually, long position focuses on the left-hand tail of the return distribution while short position focuses on the right-hand tail. In this way, we can completely check the effectiveness of models on modeling the tail behavior.

Figure 3. Conditional volatilities by ICA-EGARCH

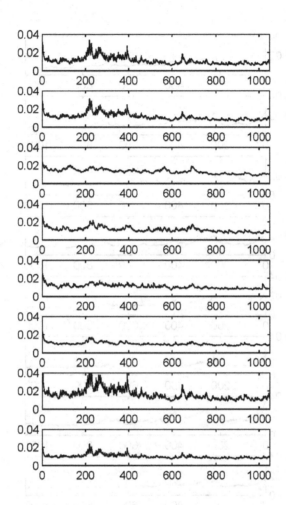

We also separately assess the performance of model estimation using in-sample data and evaluate the abilities of forecasting by using out-of-sample data described in the previous section. The corresponding results are listed in Table 2 and Table 3.

In backtesting, we suggest using the mean rank to measure and compare the overall performance of the seven models: flexible ICA-GARCH (Flex-ICA), ICA-GARCH, ICA-GARCH(T), ICA-EGARCH, ICA-EGARCH(T), ICA-GJR, and ICA-GJR(T). To calculate the mean rank, we first need to sort the values according to a standard from best to worst and assign ranks 1,2,...,7. The backtesting standard used here is the closeness to the specified level p. If more than one models have the same 'distance', these models share the ranks assigned to them. The overall mean ranks of the models are listed on the last row of each sub-table.

It is clear that the flexible ICA-GARCH model is the winner in most of the cases we considered, especially in prediction tests. From the VaR simulation, we can see that the flexible ICA-GARCH model

Figure 4. Conditional volatilities by ICA-GJR

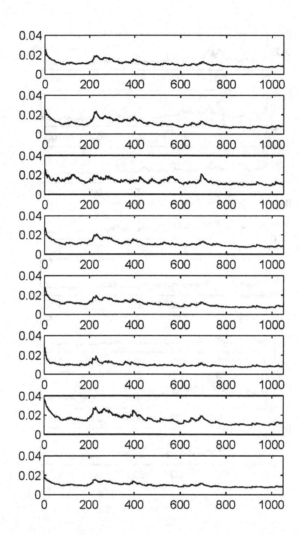

can improve the modeling quality significantly. The cost is that the computation times of a flexible model will be slightly greater.

We also construct an equally weighted portfolio (EWP) consisting with the eight indexes, that is, we give the same amount of investment to each index. Then, we would like to compute the portfolio VaR by using the models. To do so, we can forecast the portfolio's returns based on individual price index's forecasts. The formula is:

$$r_{p,t+1} = \ln\left(\frac{e^{r_{1,t+1}} + \cdots + e^{r_{N,t+1}}}{N}\right) \tag{14}$$

Figure 5. Conditional volatilities by ICA-EGARCH(T)

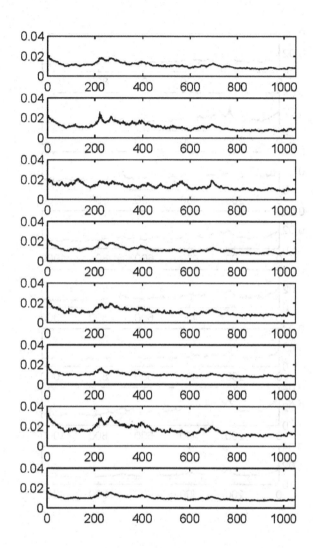

Where $r_{p,t+1}$ is the 1-day ahead log return forecast of the equally weighted portfolio with N indexes. The results of backtesting portfolio VaRs are shown in the second last row of each sub-table in Table 3. The results show that the flexible ICA-GARCH model again performs the best in estimating portfolio VaRs.

Figure 6. Conditional volatilities by ICA-GJR(T)

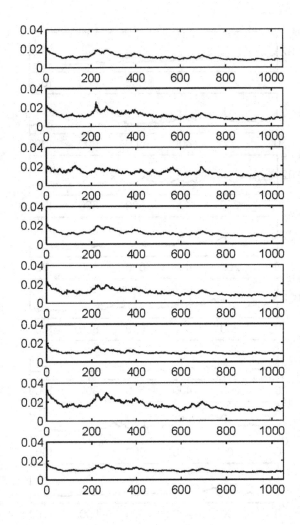

CONCLUSION

In this chapter, we have enriched the class of ICA-GARCH models by including more choices of ICA and GARCH models based on the BIC measure. The flexible ICA-GARCH model shows greater adaptability to mine hidden patterns from multivariate time series data. The experimental results validate the usefulness of the flexible ICA-GARCH models in multivariate volatility modeling and VaR estimation. It appears that the flexible ICA-GARCH models have some clear cut advantages over some existing models.

Two main advantages of the ICA technique are the suitability of ICA for non-Gaussian time series modeling and the independence property of the components. These two features greatly reduce the

Table 2. Backtesting VaR methods with in-sample data

Index	Flex-ICA	ICA	ICA-E	ICA-G	ICA-T	ICA-ET	ICA-GT
$p = 0.05$ Long Position							
US	.049	.050	.043	.058	.050	.057	.054
UK	.044	.039	.035	.041	.040	.038	.041
JP	.054	.050	.052	.058	.048	.057	.053
HK	.046	.038	.042	.045	.041	.044	.043
SG	.050	.042	.042	.044	.045	.051	.043
AU	.050	.045	.047	.048	.046	.047	.048
GE	.049	.043	.042	.055	.044	.052	.050
CA	.059	.048	.048	.053	.048	.054	.056
Rank	2.63	4.50	5.00	4.13	3.75	4.38	3.63
$p = 0.05$ Short Position							
US	.049	.051	.042	.052	.053	.047	.048
UK	.037	.041	.030	.045	.036	.034	.039
JP	.049	.045	.048	.045	.047	.057	.048
HK	.050	.053	.053	.057	.054	.051	.055
SG	.043	.044	.043	.051	.046	.051	.045
AU	.041	.039	.036	.043	.041	.032	.039
GE	.044	.047	.039	.043	.041	.046	.049
CA	.044	.042	.040	.048	.045	.045	.049
Rank	3.19	3.75	5.81	3.31	4.31	4.44	3.19
$p = 0.01$ Long Position							
US	.006	.010	.010	.009	.008	.004	.011
UK	.007	.015	.003	.006	.012	.004	.006
JP	.011	.008	.012	.012	.008	.011	.011
HK	.013	.010	.017	.012	.010	.014	.013
SG	.012	.010	.013	.019	.009	.015	.014
AU	.011	.016	.012	.015	.016	.012	.011
GE	.011	.010	.007	.005	.008	.005	.008
CA	.011	.011	.012	.012	.009	.009	.013
Rank	2.94	3.06	4.88	4.94	3.44	4.94	3.81
$p = 0.01$ Short Position							
US	.010	.009	.008	.011	.009	.009	.008
UK	.012	.005	.011	.012	.004	.008	.016
JP	.011	.010	.011	.012	.009	.007	.008
HK	.013	.010	.011	.010	.009	.011	.010
SG	.011	.011	.012	.015	.012	.012	.014
AU	.011	.012	.017	.019	.011	.017	.018
GE	.011	.005	.007	.006	.005	.008	.010
CA	.011	.010	.10	.010	.009	.009	.011
Rank	3.00	3.13	3.75	4.38	4.44	4.44	4.88

Table 3. Backtesting VaR methods with out-of-sample data

Index	Flex-ICA	ICA	ICA-E	ICA-G	ICA-T	ICA-ET	ICA-GT
p = 0.05 Long Position							
US	.010	.034	.035	.025	.046	.024	.026
UK	.045	.068	.082	.065	.072	.050	.068
JP	.063	.074	.077	.070	.074	.067	.070
HK	.054	.056	.059	.057	.056	.054	.055
SG	.040	.045	.062	.050	.047	.043	.055
AU	.053	.088	.111	.103	.092	.094	.099
GE	.033	.027	.047	.036	.031	.033	.030
CA	.055	.093	.126	.098	.095	.087	.106
EWP	.054	.065	.059	.048	.065	.055	.049
Rank	2.89	4.39	5.56	3.72	4.17	3.22	4.06
p = 0.05 Short Position							
US	.049	.040	.038	.033	.049	.028	.031
UK	.075	.054	.084	.067	.058	.053	.067
JP	.060	.070	.069	.069	.051	.063	.055
HK	.058	.037	.050	.034	.044	.031	.038
SG	.047	.046	.073	.053	.031	.028	.048
AU	.067	.061	.072	.070	.050	.059	.065
GE	.049	.035	.052	.029	.042	.031	.033
CA	.065	.053	.099	.079	.036	.054	.072
EWP	.051	.044	.047	.048	.057	.055	.045
Rank	3.00	3.89	4.83	4.94	2.94	4.39	4.00
p = 0.01 Long Position							
US	.001	.009	.008	.003	.007	.006	.000
UK	0	.014	.021	.016	.015	.013	.001
JP	.011	.030	.035	.026	.008	.028	.010
HK	.004	.015	.025	.018	.001	.010	.003
SG	.013	.023	.025	.020	.011	.021	.009
AU	.016	.031	.042	.034	.024	.034	.019
GE	.004	.012	.011	.009	.014	.008	.008
CA	.008	.039	.044	.049	.020	.044	.009
EWP	.012	.023	.013	.021	.031	.014	.033
Rank	3.44	3.78	5.11	4.44	3.83	3.78	3.61
p = 0.01 Short Position							
US	.009	.019	.011	.006	.021	.000	.006
UK	.014	.018	.021	.019	.020	.013	.019
JP	.010	.013	.018	.015	.011	.011	.011
HK	.006	.010	.011	.009	.008	.005	.003
SG	.011	.011	.019	.014	.010	.008	.014
AU	.019	.009	.026	.014	.007	.001	.021

Table 3. continued

GE	.006	.005	.013	.006	.006	.009	.010
CA	.019	.016	.020	.019	.016	.011	.019
EWP	.015	.018	.021	.024	.019	.008	.022
Rank	3.17	3.33	5.22	4.67	3.83	3.17	4.61

problems of model complexity and mis-specification. Moreover, since ICA also serves as a factor model, the independent components may carry financial implications. For example, we can check the proportion of variation explained by each IC and then we can identify some important factors that can interpret the results. Moreover, the relative loadings of each series on each common factor may reveal some interesting financial implications. For instance, we may be able to interpret one common IC as the global market volatility factor shared by all the market indexes series. Other independent factors may be classified as country-specific factors which have different impacts on different markets. Exploring such financial implications may help us to understand better the underlying relationships among the series in terms of their volatilities.

REFERENCES

Alexander, C. O. (2001). Orthogonal GARCH. In C.O. Alexander (Ed.), *Mastering Risk*, (Vol. 2). London: Financial Times-Prentice Hall.

Bollerslev, T. (1986). Generalized autoregressive conditional heteroscedasticity. *Journal of Econometrics*, *31*(3), 307–327. doi:10.1016/0304-4076(86)90063-1

Bollerslev, T., Chou, R. Y., & Kroner, K. F. (1992). ARCH modeling in finance; A review of the theory and empirical evidence. *Journal of Econometrics*, *52*, 5–59. doi:10.1016/0304-4076(92)90064-X

Comon, P. (1994). Independent component analysis: a new concept? *Signal Processing*, *36*, 287–314. doi:10.1016/0165-1684(94)90029-9

Engle, R. (1982). Autoregressive conditional heteroscedasticity with estimates of the variance of the U.K. inflation. *Econometrica*, *50*(4), 987–1008. doi:10.2307/1912773

Engle, R. (2002). Dynamic conditional correlation: A simple class of multivariate generalized autoregressive conditional heteroskedasticity models. *Journal of Business & Economic Statistics*, *20*(3), 339–350. doi:10.1198/073500102288618487

Glosten, L. R., Jaganathan, R., & Runkle, D. E. (1993). On the Relation between the Expected Value and the Volatility of the Nominal Excess Return on Stocks. *The Journal of Finance*, *48*(5), 1779–1801. doi:10.2307/2329067

Hyvärinen, A. (1999). Fast and robust fixed-point algorithms for independent component analysis. *IEEE Transactions on Neural Networks*, *10*(3), 626–634. doi:10.1109/72.761722

Hyvärinen, A. (2001). Blind source separation by nonstationarity of variance: A cumulant based approach. *IEEE Transactions on Neural Networks*, *12*(6), 1471–1474. doi:10.1109/72.963782

Hyvärinen, A., Karhunen, J., & Oja, E. (2001). *Independent Component Analysis*. New York: John Wiley & Sons.

Hyvärinen, A., & Oja, E. (1997). A fast fixed-point algorithm for independent component analysis. *Neural Computation*, *9*, 1483–1492. doi:10.1162/neco.1997.9.7.1483

Matsuoka, K., Ohya, M., & Kawamoto, M. (1995). A neural net for blind separation of nonstationary signals. *Neural Networks*, *8*, 411–419. doi:10.1016/0893-6080(94)00083-X

Nelson, D. B. (1991). Conditional heteroskedasticity in asset returns: A new approach. *Econometrica*, *59*, 347–370. doi:10.2307/2938260

So, M. K. P., & Yu, P. L. H. (2006). Empirical analysis of GARCH models in value at risk estimation. *Journal of International Financial Markets, Institutions and Money*, *16*(2), 180–197. doi:10.1016/j. intfin.2005.02.001

Wu, E. H. C., Yu, P. L. H., & Li, W. K. (2006). Value at Risk estimation using independent component analysis-generalized autoregressive conditional heteroscedasticity (ICA-GARCH) models. *International Journal of Neural Systems*, *16*(5), 371–382. doi:10.1142/S0129065706000779

Chapter 12
Machine Learning Techniques for Network Intrusion Detection

Tich Phuoc Tran
University of Technology, Australia

Pohsiang Tsai
University of Technology, Australia

Tony Jan
University of Technology, Australia

Xiangjian He
University of Technology, Australia

ABSTRACT

Most of the currently available network security techniques are not able to cope with the dynamic and increasingly complex nature of cyber attacks on distributed computer systems. Therefore, an automated and adaptive defensive tool is imperative for computer networks. Alongside the existing prevention techniques such as encryption and firewalls, Intrusion Detection System (IDS) has established itself as an emerging technology that is able to detect unauthorized access and abuse of computer systems by both internal users and external offenders. Most of the novel approaches in this field have adopted Artificial Intelligence (AI) technologies such as Artificial Neural Networks (ANN) to improve performance as well as robustness of IDS. The true power and advantages of ANN lie in its ability to represent both linear and non-linear relationships and learn these relationships directly from the data being modeled. However, ANN is computationally expensive due to its demanding processing power and this leads to overfitting problem, i.e. the network is unable to extrapolate accurately once the input is outside of the training data range. These limitations challenge IDS with low detection rate, high false alarm rate and excessive computation cost. This chapter proposes a novel Machine Learning (ML) algorithm to alleviate those difficulties of existing AI techniques in the area of computer network security. The Intrusion Detection dataset provided by Knowledge Discovery and Data Mining (KDD-99) is used as a benchmark to compare our model with other existing techniques. Extensive empirical analysis suggests that

DOI: 10.4018/978-1-60566-908-3.ch012

the proposed method outperforms other state-of-the-art learning algorithms in terms of learning bias, generalization variance and computational cost. It is also reported to significantly improve the overall detection capability for difficult-to-detect novel attacks which are unseen or irregularly occur in the training phase.

INTRODUCTION

Current security systems offer a reasonable level of protection; however, they cannot cope with the growing complexity of computer networks and hacking techniques. They have to face continuous environmental changes both with respect to what constitutes normal behavior and abnormal behavior. As the result, security systems suffer from *low detection rates* (missing out serious intrusion attacks) and *high false alarm rates* (falsely classifying a normal connection as an attack and therefore obstructing legitimate user access to the network resources). In order to overcome such challenging problems, there has been a great number of research conducted to apply *Machine Learning* (ML) algorithms to achieve a generalization capability from limited training data. In recent years, ML algorithms such as Artificial Neural Network (ANN), which is generally well regarded as the universal function approximator, have demonstrated successes in many network security applications. As a flexible "model-free" approach, ANN can fit the training data very well and thus provide a low learning bias. However, they are also susceptible to the overtting problem, which can cause instability in generalization. Some models of ANN also suffer from highly demanding computation power due to their large model complexity. For an ANN model to be useful, it should perform well on the training data and generalize reliably on the unseen data. Unfortunately, learning bias, generalization variance and model complexity are somewhat incompatible, i.e. reducing one element will inevitably increase the others. Therefore, a good tradeoff of these elements should be sought.

In this chapter, an innovative ML algorithm is proposed to alleviate the limitations of currently existing IDS, enhancing the performance of intrusion detection for rare and complicated attacks. By implementing *Adaptive Boosting* and *Semi-parametric* Radial-basis-function neural networks (RBFNN), the proposed model can minimize learning bias (how well the model fits the available sample data) and generalization variance (how stable the model is for unseen instances) at an affordable cost of computation.

This chapter starts with the related works of ML approaches for Network Security domain, followed by an extensive review of ANN models. Particularly, emphasis is put on the Generalized Regression Neural Network (GRNN) and vector-quantized GRNN. These models belong to the RBFNN family which has been reported for great successes in many applications. We also provide an overview of Ensemble Learning methods in which multiple classifiers are trained to solve the same problem and their decisions are then aggregated in some manner. It is theoretically and experimentally proved that such an ensemble model can achieve superior performance compared with individual classifiers. Next, the research proposal and its features are presented. The usefulness of this model will be illustrated through its application to the Network intrusion detection problem.

RELATED WORKS

An intrusion detection system (IDS) is defined as a protective system that monitors computers or networks for unauthorized activities based on network traffic or system usage behaviors, thereby detecting if a system is targeted by a network attack such as a denial of service attack. There are two types of IDS: (1) *misuse-based detection* in which events are compared against pre-defined patterns of known attacks and (2) *anomaly-based detection* which relies on detecting the activities deviating from system "normal" operations. Existing IDS face significant challenges in terms of detection speed, accuracy and system adaptability. Several techniques have been deployed to overcome these problems. A rule-based IDS uses *Expert Systems* (ES) in which the knowledge of a human expert is encoded into a set of rules. This allows a more effective knowledge management than that of a human expert in terms of reproducibility, consistency and completeness in identifying activities that match the defined characteristics of misuse and attacks (Ilgun, 1995). However, ES suffers from low flexibility and robustness. Unlike ES which can provide the user with a definitive answer, a Neural Network (NN) conducts an analysis of the information and generates a probability estimate of whether the data matches the characteristics that it has been trained to recognize. Cannady (1998) developed a network-based detection system in which 9 packet-level network data was retrieved from the RealSecure database and then classified by a feed-forward neural network (Cannady, 1998). Though this prototype is not a complete IDS, the results clearly demonstrate the potential of an ANN in detecting network attacks. Besides ANN, Support Vector Machines (SVMs) are also a good candidate for intrusion detection that plots the training vectors in high dimensional feature space, labeling each vector by its class. The data is then classified by determining a set of support vectors, which are members of the set of training inputs that outline a hyper plane in the feature space. SVMs are scalable as they are relatively insensitive to the number of data points (Ambwani, 2003). Several other ML paradigms including linear genetic programming, Bayesian networks, multivariate adaptive regression splines etc. have also been implemented for the design of IDS. In this chapter, we focus on emerging ANN and Boosting models.

Among intrusion detection models tested on KDD-99 dataset, most of them are reported to provide unacceptably low detection capability for U2R and R2L attacks. Some typical examples of such models include a rule-based predictive model (PNrule) (Agarwal, 2000) which is studied to effectively detect DoS and Probe attacks; the winning entry of KDD99 contest (Pfahringer, 2000) which is composed from 50×10 C5 decision trees fused by cost-sensitive bagged boosting. Similar techniques are also developed such as a decision tree forest constructed by Kernel Miner (KM) tool (Levin, 2000) and two layers of voting decision trees augmented with human security expertise (Miheev, 2000). Due to poor performance of these approaches on some sophisticated attacks, we are motivated to develop a new learning method to improve the overall detection performance on KDD 99 benchmark.

ARTIFICIAL NEURAL NETWORK

Artificial Neural Networks (ANN) is one of the most commonly used ML algorithms that have been successfully applied to different applications, including speech recognition, image analysis, adaptive control and many other disciplines. One of the most useful properties of an ANN is its ability to infer underlying functional dependencies between data samples. In this section, ANN is closely examined due to its complexity and importance in many classification and prediction applications. Firstly, Multilayer

Perceptron (MLP) is presented as the most popular ANN model. We then focus on a recently emerging ANN family, RBFNN, including GRNN and VQ-GRNN.

Multilayer Perceptron

Multilayer Perceptron (MLP) is the most popular network architecture in use today, initially proposed by Rumelhart and McClelland (Rumelhart & McClelland, 1986). This network uses a layered feed-forward topology in which the units each performs a biased weighted sum of their inputs and pass this activation level through a transfer function to produce their output. The network complexity can be configured by determining the number of layers, and the number of units in each layer (Bishop, 1995). After defining these values, the network can be trained from historical data.

During the training phase, weights and thresholds are adjusted automatically to minimize the prediction error made by the network. This error is defined as a function of the difference between actual outputs with the outputs generated by ANN. One of the most common error functions is the sum squared error, where the individual errors of output units on each case are squared and summed together. This concept of error can be further extended to an *error surface*. Each of the N weights and thresholds of the network is considered as a dimension in space and the network error is the $N+1$-th dimension. For any possible configuration of weights, an error surface can be produced by drawing the $N+1$-th error dimension (Bishop, 1995). Using this concept, the network training can be seen as an exploration of the error surface. The error associated with the current values of the model parameters is presented as a point in this surface. From this point, the training process needs to identify which direction it should progress to decrease the current error. This direction, in fact, is the one that reduces the steepness of the surface's gradient vector. It is also important to consider how large the steps (*learning rate*) should be to effectively reach the global minimum. Large steps may converge more quickly, but may also produce oscillations. On the other hand, very small steps may go in the correct direction, but they also require a large number of iterations. The rate in which the learning rate changes during training is called *learning momentum*. Employing appropriate values of the learning rate and momentum sometimes helps the training process escape the local minimum, and also to move rapidly over flat part of the error surface. The network training will be terminated when one of the stopping conditions is met such as when a given number of iterations (epochs) elapses, or when the error reaches an acceptable level, or when the error stops improving.

Generalized Regression Neural Network (GRNN)

A family of ANN models, RBFNN, has recently drawn great research attention due to its good generalization ability and a simple network structure that avoids unnecessary and lengthy calculations as compared to the Multilayer Feedforward Networks (MFN). Considering the node characteristics and the training algorithms, RBFNN are very different from MFN. The node characteristics for MFN are usually chosen as sigmoidal functions while for RBFNN, as indicated in the name, radial basis functions are employed. A popular algorithm in RFBNN family is the GRNN proposed by Specht (Spetch, 1991) which contains a hidden layer of radial units. Each radial unit models a Gaussian response surface which can be determined by its center point and a radius (Park & Sandberg, 1991). Because these functions are nonlinear, it is enough for a single hidden layer to describe any shape of function. The output of

Figure 1. Architecture of generalized regression neural network

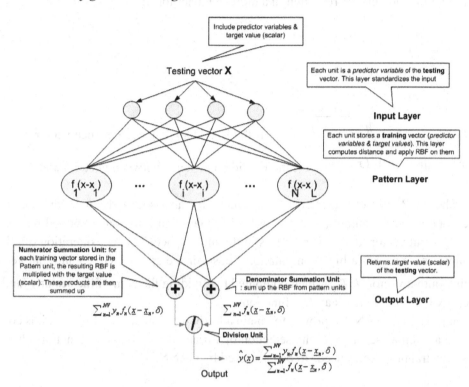

these Gaussians is then linearly weighted to produce the desired response. Figure 1 shows the generic architecture of the GRNN.

GRNN uses a single common radial bias function kernel bandwidth δ that is tuned during the learning phase. In particular, an optimal δ will produce the lowest learning Mean Squared Error (MSE). The following is the general form of GRNN which is similar to the equation proposed by Nadaraya (Nadaraya, 1964) and Watson (Watson, 1964):

$$\hat{y}\left(\underline{x}\right) = \frac{\sum_{n=1}^{NV} y_n f_n(\underline{x} - \underline{x}_n, \delta)}{\sum_{n=1}^{NV} f_n(\underline{x} - \underline{x}_n, \delta)} \tag{3-1}$$

With Gaussian function $f_n\left(\underline{x}\right) = \exp(\frac{-(\underline{x} - \underline{x}_i)^T(\underline{x} - \underline{x}_i)}{2\delta^2})$
Where

$\underline{x}$: Input vector (under line refers to vector)

$\underline{x}_n$: All other training vectors in the input space

δ: Single smoothing parameter chosen during network training

y_n: Scalar output related to $\underline{x}_n$

NV: Total number of training vectors

The Gaussian function can be rewritten in a more compact form:

$$f_i\left(d_i, \delta\right) = exp(\frac{-d^2}{2\delta^2})$$

(3-2)

Where

$d_i = \left\| x - \underline{x}_i \right\| = \sqrt{\left(x - \underline{x}_i\right)^T \left(x - \underline{x}_i\right)}$ is the Euclidian distance between vector x and

$d_i = \left\| x - \underline{x}_i \right\| = \sqrt{\left(x - \underline{x}_i\right)^T \left(x - \underline{x}_i\right)}$ $\underline{x}_n$ is the Euclidian distance between vector x and $\underline{x}_n$

From the above GRNN architecture, each input vector has an associated equal size Gaussian function and a corresponding scalar output (Spetch, 1991). The Gaussian function is applied on the Euclidian distances of an input vector to all other vectors in the input space. This consideration of all vectors in the whole input space causes a high computational cost for the system. Given an input vector $\underline{x}$, the corresponding output vector $\hat{y}\left(\underline{x}\right)$ is then computed by dividing the sum of the scalar y_n and Gaussian $f_n(.)$ products by the sum of Gaussian $f_n(.)$ functions.

In many applications, GRNN is proved to obtain a fairly high accuracy. However, it is computationally expensive as well as sensitive to the selection of variances for Gaussian functions due to the fact that every single training vector needs to be processed by GRNN.

Vector Quantized GRNN (VQ-GRNN)

When the number of data points in the training set is much larger than the number of degrees of freedom of the underlying process, we are constrained to have as many radial basis functions as the data points presented. Therefore, the classification problem is said to be over-determined. Consequently, the network may end up fitting misleading variations due to noise in the input data, thereby resulting a degraded generalization performance. GRNN normally suffers from this problem. In fact, GRNN is very computationally expensive because it incorporates each and every training example $\left(\underline{x}_i \rightarrow y_i\right)$ into its architecture. In order to overcome this problem, the Vector-quantized General Regression Neural Network (VQ-GRNN) was developed by Zaknich et al (Zaknich & Attikiouzel, 1988). It is a generalization of Specht's Probabilistic Neural Network (PNN) (Specht, 1990) and is related to Specht's General Regression Neural Network (GRNN) (Spetch, 1991) classifier. In particular, this method generalizes GRNN by quantizing the data space into clusters and assigning a specific weight to each of these clusters. Figure 2 shows the architecture of VQ-GRNN.

In this structure, the Euclidian distances from the input vector δ to the clusters within the input space $(c_1,...,c_M)$ are computed. The Gaussian function is then applied to these distances. After that, two summing units are computed. The first one is the summation of the Gaussian functions while the second one is derived by adding the products of cluster size Z_i, the associated scalar output and the Gaussian functions. Finally, these terms are fed into the division unit. The following is the summary of VQ-GRNN theory.

If there exists a corresponding scalar output y_n for each local region (cluster) which is represented by a center vector $\underline{c}_i$, then a GRNN can be approximated by a VQ-GRNN formulated as follow:

Figure 2. Architecture of Vector Quantized GRNN (VQ-GRNN)

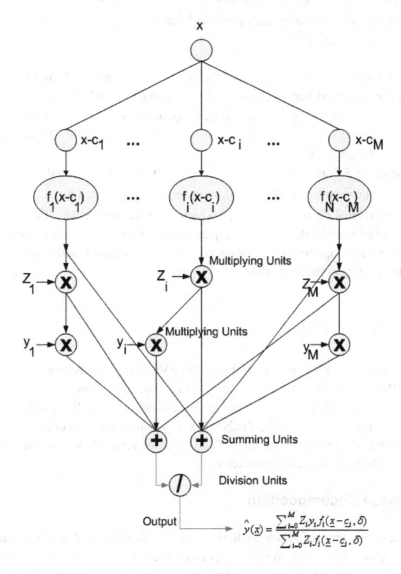

$$\hat{y}\left(\underline{x}\right) = \frac{\sum_{i=0}^{M} Z_i y_i f_i(\underline{x} - \underline{c}_i, \delta)}{\sum_{i=0}^{M} Z_i f_i(\underline{x} - \underline{c}_i, \delta)} \tag{3-3}$$

With Gaussian function $f_i\left(\underline{x}\right) = \dfrac{exp\left[-\left(\underline{x} - \underline{c}_i\right)^T \left(\underline{x} - \underline{c}_i\right)\right]}{2\delta^2}$

Where

$\underline{c}_i$ = center vector for cluster i in the input space

y_i = scalar output related to $\underline{c}_i$

Z_i = number of input vectors x_j within cluster $\underline{c}_i$

δ = single smoothing parameter chosen during network training

    M = number of unique centers $\underline{c}_i$

The Equation 3-3 can be seen as the general formulation for both GRNN and VQ-GRNN. In other words, GRNN can be computed from this equation by assuming that each cluster contains only one input vector ($Z_i = 1$), the y_i are real values (the output space is not quantized), the centre vectors $\underline{c}_i$ are replaced by with individual training vectors x_i and the number of clusters is equal to the number of individual input vectors ($M = NV$) (Jan, 2004).

Comparing Equation 3-3 and the Equation 3-1, the only difference is that VQ-GRNN applies its computation on a smaller number of clusters of input vectors represented by centers vectors $\underline{c}_i$ rather than dealing with individual input vectors $\underline{x}_n$ (Zaknich & Attikiouzel, 1988). This clustering relies on Gaussian characteristics in which the sum of multiple Gaussian functions within a cluster is approximated by a single Gaussian with magnitude of Z_j, provided that the individual functions are well concentrated (clustered) near the centers in the data space:

$$\sum_{i=0}^{Z_j} f_i\left(\underline{x} - \underline{x}_i, \delta\right) \approx Z_j f_j\left(\underline{x} - \underline{c}_j, \delta\right) \qquad (3\text{-}4)$$

By using the vector quantization technique, the resulting VQ-GRNN model is always a semi-parametric version of the GRNN which tends to smooth noisy data a little more than the GRNN. The VQ-GRNN retains the benefits of the GRNN with respect to generalization capabilities and ease of training by adjusting a single parameter δ, but the VQ-GRNN is always smaller in network size. In particular, with smaller size, VQ-GRNN is trained faster and the classification results have less variance, bias and less sensitive to the selection of smoothing parameters.

Bias and Variance Decomposition

One of the most desirable properties of a predictive model is its ability to *learn* from available data and *generalize* for new cases. The metric to evaluate performance of a model during learning process is the *learning bias* which is the difference between actual target values in the training set and the values learned by the model (Jan, 2004). It reflects how much a model misclassifies for a given dataset. Therefore, an accurate model should have low bias. Unlike learning bias which measures how well a model performs on an available training data, *generalization variance* can be used to measure performance stability of a model on new unseen data that never appears in the training set. In other words, it is the deviation of the performance of a model during the training phase compared with that of testing phase. A stable classifier should show similar accuracy on both old data and new data which is not seen by the model before, i.e. having low variance. It is impractical to achieve both low learning bias and low generalization variance due to their incompatibility. Attempts to reduce the bias component in the generalization error will inevitably cause an increase in variance and vice versa. This leads to *overfitting* and *underfitting* problems. When training a model, the training error and the generalization error (during parameter calibration process) gradually reduce. However, if the generalization error stops dropping, or begins rising, this indicates the overfitting problem. On the other hand, an underfitting model is not effective to model the underlying functions and hence, neither training nor generalization errors drops to a satisfactory level. From the variance-bias point of view, overfitting has low bias but high variance while underfitting suffers from high bias. Training a model for a long time tends to decrease bias but slowly increase variance; at some point, there will be an optimal tradeoff that minimizes the generalization error. Obtaining this tradeoff will produce a compromised solution for this problem of bias and variance. This theory is known as the *bias-variance dilemma* (Geman, Bienenstock, & Doursat, 1992).

The tradeoff of bias and variance often occurs when model complexity is adjusted to a certain level (Jan, 2004). In the case of overfitting, it is usually advisable to reduce the model complexity while further training is required for underfitting case. The Figure 3 demonstrates the relationship between model complexity and model risk which combines bias and variance. This suggests that between bias, variance and model complexity, there exists a certain relationship which can be useful in assessing model performance (Jan, 2004). A conceptual formulation of these three factors can be presented in a linear equation:

$$Cost = A* \text{Bias} + B*\text{Variance} + C*\text{Complexity}$$

Considering this cost, we can extend the bias-variance dilemma to a more complete picture of different issues relating to selecting the best model. Depending on nature of the problems, this cost function can vary from a simple function to a more complicated equation. Often in practice, model complexity can be seen as closely related to computational requirements of the model. From the Figure 3, this cost is highest at two extremes. Non-parametric models (right-end) with high complexity normally have low bias but high variance, and therefore suffer from the problem of overfitting. Simple models such as parametric models (left-end) with low variance but high bias on the other hands, can expect a risk of underfitting.

Figure 3. Risk function over model complexity

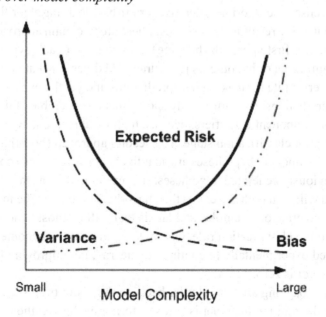

From previous sections, though the VQ-GRNN algorithm seems very robust to deal with unseen instances; its accuracy is sometimes not high enough for critical applications. This is because VQ-GRNN significantly reduces the model complexity of original GRNN to achieve low variance (system robustness) at the cost of higher bias (lowered accuracy). The next section discusses ensemble learning approaches which can be used to enhance accuracy of VQ-GRNN.

ENSEMBLE LEARNING

The goal of learning algorithms is to discover the underlying functional relationship of input variables. Ordinary ML methods work by searching through a space of possible functions, called *hypotheses*, to find the best approximation to the unknown function. The best hypothesis can be identified based on how well it fits the training data and how consistent it is with any available prior knowledge about the problem.

Ensemble learning algorithms take a different approach. Rather than finding one best learner to explain the data, they construct a set of learners, called a *committee* or *ensemble*, and then have those learners vote in some manner to predict the label of new data points. Even though the component learners within the ensemble are all attempting to solve the same problem, it is likely that each of them would have different strengths and weaknesses in different situations. Realizing and managing the situations in which the learner do not perform as well as expected is the key challenge for ensemble research (Costa, Filippi, & Pasero, 1995). A number of research (Kittler & Roli, 2000; Roli & Kittler, 2002; Windeatt & Roli, 2003) has supported a widespread view that for an ensemble to achieve best performance on a task, the component predictors should exhibit "diverse errors", meaning that they should have different error rates.

Bagging and Boosting

During training process, ensemble algorithms iteratively run a base learning algorithm (called *base learner*) and then forms a vote out of the resulting hypotheses. There are two main approaches to producing these component hypotheses. The first approach (bagging) is to construct each hypothesis independently in such a way that the resulting set of hypotheses is accurate and diverse – that is, each individual hypothesis has reasonably low error rate for making new predictions and yet the hypotheses disagree with each other in many of their predictions. It is empirically shown that an ensemble of those hypotheses is more accurate than any of its component classifiers, because their disagreements will "cancel out" when the ensemble comes to the joint classification stage. The second approach (boosting) is very similar to the first one except that the component hypotheses are adaptively constructed in a coupled fashion based on the performance of previously generated hypotheses. In particular, data instances that are misclassified by previous hypotheses will gain higher weights than the other examples. The intended effect is to force the weak learner to concentrate on examples and labels that will be most beneficial to the overall goal of finding a highly accurate classification rule. One of the remarkable phenomenon of this approach is that it has been observed experimentally to continue to "learn", i.e. improving the generalization error even after the training error is zero.

In short, boosting and bagging are very similar because they both train successive component classifiers with a subset of the training data that is "most informative" given the current set of component classifiers. In bagging, subsets of the raw training samples are independently and randomly selected, with replacement, according to a uniform probability distribution. In contrast, boosting creates each subset based on previous classification results, particularly; a probability distribution is introduced to prefer those samples on which previous classifiers are incorrect. The joint decision of boosting is the weighted combination of individual classifiers while bagging produces the final output as the majority vote of member classifiers.

Model Diversity

Although in general, classifier combinations can improve generalization performance, correlation between individual classifiers can be harmful to the ensemble (Alpaydin, 1993; Breiman, 1996; Krogh & Vedelsby, 1995; Lincoln & Skrzypek, 1989). The necessity for the *diversity* among the ensemble of classifiers in generalization and its benefits are discussed in several works in the literature (Krogh & Vedelsby, 1995; Rogova, 1994; Sharkey & Sharkey, 1997). It is proven that the better generalization performance of a combined classifier is not necessarily achieved by combining classifiers with better individual performance but by including independent classifiers in the ensemble. This classifier independence condition can be interpreted as *orthogonality*, *complementarity* or *disagreement* among individual classifiers. It is obvious that having identical classifiers combined will not produce any gain in the overall performance. One of the theoretical works proposed by Hansen and Salamon (Hansen & Salamon, 1990) claims that if the average error rate of a weak learner is less than 50% and the component classifiers in the ensemble are independent in the production of their errors, the expected error of that ensemble can be reduced to zero as the number of independent classifiers increases to infinity.

Several methods have been developed to enforce diversity on the classifiers within an ensemble. The four most commonly used methods include *using different combination schemes* (linearly and non-linearly), *using different base learning algorithms* (bagging and boosting), *using different training sets* and *using different feature subsets* (Kuncheva & Whitaker, 2003).

Margin Theory

Boosting is well-known for its empirical resistance to overfitting for various classification tasks. Their test error usually does not increase as their size becomes very large, and often is observed to decrease even after the training error reaches zero. Although the empirical success of a boosting algorithm depends on many factors (e.g. the type of data and how noisy it is, the capacity of the weak learning algorithm, the number of boosting iterations) the margin theory does provide a reasonable explanation of AdaBoost's success, both empirically and theoretically.

Let's consider a boosting method which can be formulated as a gradient optimization technique in function space (Schapire, Freund, Bartlett, & Lee, 1998) with the goal of minimizing the objective function

$$J\left(H\right) = \sum_i \exp(-y_i h_t(x_i))$$

Minimizing such objective function leads to maximizing the quantity $\rho_i = y_i h_t(x_i)$ which is the amount by which x_i is correctly classified. From this theory, it is important to introduce the concept of margin to explain how boosting methods work. Specifically, *margin* of a labeled example (x_n, y_n) is defined as

$$\rho_i = y_i h_t(x_i) \tag{4-5}$$

This margin can be thought of as a confidence measure of a classifier's predictive ability, or as a guarantee on the generalization performance. If the margin of a classifier is large, then it tends to perform well on test data. Conversely, if the margin is small, then the classifier tends not to perform so well.

An alternative way of viewing margin is to look at the convex linear combination of base hypotheses produced by boosting methods:

$$f(x_n) = \sum_{t=1}^{T} w_t h^{(t)}(x_n)$$

Where h^t is the hypothesis added at iteration t and w_t is its coefficient. This combination f can be viewed as a homogeneous *hyperplane* in a feature space, where each base hypothesis $h^{(t)}$ represents one feature or dimension. The margin of an example, as defined in Equation 4-1, is actually a signed distance from this example to the hyperplane. As soon as the training error is zero, the examples are on the right side and all have positive margin.

Applying the margin theory, some theoretical proofs have been derived for the upper bounds of training and generalization errors. These bounds suggest that if we can consistently find weak hypotheses that are slightly better than random guessing, then the training error drops exponentially fast. This guarantees that the boosting method converges within a small number of iterations.

BOOSTED MODIFIED PROBABILISTIC NEURAL NETWORK (BMPNN)

Currently available IDS have suffered from low detection accuracy and high false alarm rates, especially for rare and complicated attacks. For instance, the winning entries of KDD-99 competition do not provide satisfactory performance on U2R and R2L attack categories due to their low frequency and complicated nature. Several learning methods have been developed to increase the detection capability including ANN models. Such models, however, do not perform reliably for new unseen data. Alternative approaches tend to improve the generalization stability by reducing generalization variance at the cost of higher learning bias, i.e. allowing underfitting. This would degrade the overall performance to a certain level. In critical modeling applications, underfitting is not acceptable because a miss in detection may be very costly, i.e. causing the whole computer network compromised. Therefore, a detection system which can achieve both stable generalization and accurate data learning is very much desirable. Theoretically, both bias and variance may be reduced at the same time given infinite sized models. Nevertheless, this condition is generally infeasible since the model complexity must be limited in real life.

Motivated by the need of an accurate detection system for network security applications, this research proposes a learning algorithm which provides a good tradeoff for learning bias, generalization variance and computational requirement. We specifically focus on an emerging neural network family, the Radial

Basis Function Neural Networks (RBFNN). Particularly, GRNN (Spetch, 1991) and VQ-GRNN (Zaknich, 1998) draw most attention. In theory, the GRNN can achieve the optimal Bayesian estimate (with infinity network size) but with a cost of extremely demanding computation resource. The VQ-GRNN reduces the computationally extensive nonparametric GRNN to a semiparametric neural network by applying vector quantization techniques on the input space. This reduction significantly improves the robustness of the algorithm (low variance), but also affects its learning accuracy to some extent. To improve VQ-GRNN's performance in critical applications, an innovative learning method is proposed in this research, the Boosted Modified Probabilistic Neural Network (BMPNN). It integrates VQ-GRNN and a boosting method, the Stagewise Additive Modeling using Multiclass Exponential loss function - SAMME (Zhu, Rosset, Zhou, & Hastie, 2005). Compared with other multiclass boosting techniques, SAMME returns only one weighted classifier (rather than K) in each boosting iteration and the weak classifier only needs to be better than K-class random guessing (rather than 1/2). In our adaptation, SAMME is modified to adjust the reweighting of the base hypotheses in the joint classification using a diversity measure.

System Design

The proposed BMPNN algorithm has two major modules: (1) the *Adaptive Booster* iteratively produces base hypotheses on a weighted training dataset. The weights are updated adaptively based on the classification performance of component hypotheses. The generated hypotheses are then integrated via a weighted sum based on their diversity. (2) The *Modified Probabilistic Classifier* serves as the base learner which can be trained on weighted datasets. In each boosting iteration, a base hypothesis is created with associated accuracy and diversity measures. From this information, the data weights are updated for the next iteration and the final weighting of that hypothesis in the joint classification is computed (Figure 4).

Adaptive Booster (Master Algorithm)

In this research, we adapt SAMME (Zhu et al., 2005) which is a generalization of the Adaboost algorithm based on a generalization of the exponential loss, to handle multiclass problems and to work with base learners that output real valued class membership probability. We also modify SAMME to incorporate the diversity of generated base classifiers into the joint final hypothesis. In each boosting iteration, a generated base classifier is added into the ensemble and a Kohavi-Wolpert variance factor $\alpha \in [0,1]$ associated with the ensemble in that iteration is computed. A large value of α indicates the current ensemble is highly diverse and a low α refers to less diverse ensemble. Based on this diversity measure, the hypotheses weighting is adjusted such that a less diverse base hypotheses will have less impact (lower weight) in the final joint classification.

Let's consider a weighted dataset $S = \{(x_1, c_1), \ldots, (x_N, c_N)\}$ with $\mathbf{W}$ is the distribution (weights vector) and the output vector $c_i \in \{1, \ldots, K\}$

To deal with **multiclass classification problem**, the output vector c_i can be recoded with a K-dimensional vector y_i in which all entries equal to $-\dfrac{1}{K-1}$ except a value 1 in k-th position if the actual label of that vector is k, i.e.

$$y_i = (y_{i1}, y_{i2}, \ldots, y_{iK}), \quad i = 1 \ldots N$$

Figure 4. Overall BMPNN high-level design view

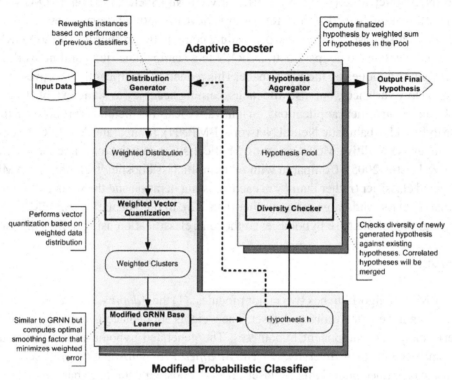

$$y_{ik} = \begin{cases} 1 & ,if\ c_i = k \\ -\dfrac{1}{K-1} & ,if\ c_i \neq k \end{cases}$$

The distribution W and the hypothess h are also recoded as a K-dimensional presentation:

$$W_i = (w_{i1}, w_{i2}, \ldots, w_{iK}),\ i = 1 \ldots N$$

$$h = (h_1, h_2, \ldots, h_K)$$

Unlike the standard Adaboost which uses the empirical loss, a population version of the loss is considered here. The weighted probability is then implemented to derive the update for the additive model (boosting) which outputs ***real-valued confidence-rated predictions*** (weighted class membership probabilities) rather than the classification labels. It is proved that, similar to the case of binary classification, optimizing the multiclass exponential loss approaches to the optimal Bayesian error. The solution given by optimizing the Lagrange is as follow:

$$C_k(x) = (K-1) \cdot \left[\log Prob_w \big(c = k \mid x \big) - \frac{1}{K} \sum_{k'=1}^{K} \log Prob_w \big(h(x) = k' \mid x \big) \right]$$

Where $Prob_w(h(x)=k|x)$ is the weighted class probability that the hypotheses $h(x)$ classify x as of class k given the input vector x, respectively.

The learning procedure of Adaptive Booster is listed below:

Input: $S = \{(x_1, y_1), \ldots, (x_N, y_N)\}$ and associated distribution **W**

Initialize $W_i^{(1)} = \dfrac{1}{N}$ for all $i = 1 \ldots N$, $\alpha^{(1)} = 1$

Do for $t = 1 \ldots T$

Generate base classifiers (*)

Train a classifier on the weighed sample $\{S, W^{(t)}\}$ using the Modified Probabilistic Classifier and obtain hypotheses $h^{(t)}: x \rightarrow [0,1]^K$

Compute Kohavi-Wolpert variance ($\alpha^{(t)}$) of current ensemble

$$\pm^{(t+1)} = \frac{1}{N.L^2} \sum_{j=1}^{N} l(x_j)(L - l(x_j))$$

Where L and $l(x_j)$ are the number of base classifiers generated so far in the ensemble and the number of classifiers that correctly classifies x_j. We have $L = t$.

Compute class probability estimates

$$C_k^{(t)}(x) = (K-1).\left[\log p_k^{(t)}(x) - \frac{1}{K}\sum_{k'=1}^{K}\log p_{k'}^{(t)}(x)\right], k = 1, .., K$$

Where $p_k^{(t)}(x) = Prob_w\left(h^{(t)}(x) = k|x\right)$ is the weighted class probability of class k.

Update weights

$$W_i^{(t+1)} = W_i^{(t)}.\exp\left[-\frac{K-1}{K}.\log p^{(t)}(x_i).h^{(t)}(x_i)\right], i = 1, .., n$$

Where $p(x_i) = Prob(x_i)$

Renormalize W

$$W_i = \frac{W_i}{\sum_{j=1}^{N} W_j}, i = 1 \ldots N$$

End for

Output

$$C_{final}(x) = \underset{k}{\mathrm{argmax}} \sum_{t=1}^{T} \pm^{(t)}.C_k^{(t)}(x)$$

5.1.2. Modified Probabilistic Classifier (Base Learner)

In this research, the base learner is implemented using VQ-GRNN which was initially introduced by Zaknich (Zaknich & Attikiouzel, 1988). This adaptation of VQ-GRNN is motivated by the necessity of a base learner suitable for ensemble learning. The base learner can produce confidence-rated outputs and it is modified such that it utilizes weights associated with training examples (to compute cluster center vectors and find a single smoothing factor) and incorporates these weights as penalties for mis-classifications (e.g. weighted MSE).

Our modified version of VQ-GRNN is similar to the original one in that a single kernel bandwidth is tuned to achieve satisfactory learning. They both cluster close training vectors according to a very simple procedure related to vector quantization. Note that the equation 3-3 can be extended to a multi-class classification problem by redefining the output vector as a *K*-dimensional vector where *K* is the number of classes.

$$y_i = \{y_{i1}, \ldots, y_{iK}\}^T$$

Where y_{ik} is the class membership probability of the *k*-th class of the vector x_i. If the vector x_i is of class *k*, then $y_{ik} = 1.0$ and $y_{ik} = 0$ for the remaining vector elements ($k \neq k'$). After training, an input vector *x* is classified as a class-*k* vector if the *k*-th element of the network output vector has the highest magnitude. The base learner has two major processes:

5.1.2.1. Vector Quantization Process

Vector quantization is used to partition the input space into localized regions or clusters which contain similar vectors. Each cluster is represented by its size Z_k and a center vector $\underline{c}_k$. The center is then associated with a desired output value. The number of radial basis function at each center equals the number of vectors that are represented by that center. In this way, the number of training vector pairs is reduced without changing the basic form of the network from that of GRNN. The main difference and also one of the key contributuons of our modified model over original VQ-GRNN is the implementation of a weighted averaging process to compute the center vector $\underline{c}_i$:

$$\underline{c}_k = \frac{\sum_{i=1}^{Z_k} W_i x_i}{Z_k}$$

where Z_k is the number of training vectors belonging to a cluster *k*.

Unlike the normal averaging approach of original VQ-GRNN, this process incorporates the weights of the input vectors (these weights are updated by the master boosting unit). This vector reduction approach improves computational efficiency, reduces significantly the model sensitivity to noise compared with the GRNN and makes the our modified learning method specially suited for boosting.

5.1.2.2. Training Process

VQ-GRNN's learning involves finding the optimal δ giving the minimum Mean Squared Error (MSE) for some fixed number of known sample vectors passing through the network. The choice of the bandwidth σ of the kernel is an important issue which used to challenge the kernel experts. Statisticians prefer to compute the value of σ based on some knowledge of the data statisics but it can also be determined experimentally. In most practical problems, the relationship between δ and the corresponding MSE is smooth, continuous and there is a single and unique value of σ which produces a minimum MSE. The optimum value of δ can be found very quickly by a convergent optimization algorithm based on recurrent parabolic curve fitting (Zaknich & Attikiouzel, 1993). It models the MSE versus σ curve as a parabola and iteratively finds the minimum point using Brent's method (Press, Flannery, Teukolsky, & Vetterling, 1986). When an initial estimate for δ is unknown, a very low starting value is chosen and it usually takes a few iterations through the testing data to converge to an adequate value. Our adaptation of VQ-GRNN uses the weights associated with data samples for computation of MSE. Particularly, our approach selects the single radial basis function bandwidth δ that produces the lowest *weighted mean squared error* (WMSE) for one iteration through the training data.

$$WMSE = \frac{\sum_{i=1}^{N}\left[W_i\left(\hat{y}_i\left(x_i\right)-y_i\right)\right]^2}{N}$$

where w_i and $\hat{y}_i$ are the associated weight and prediction of an example (x_i, y_i), $i = 1 \ldots N$

This modified VQ-GRNN can be seen as a kind of spherical function mixture model with data-directed center vector allocation. The relative widths of the spherical functions at each center are directly proportional to the relative number of training vectors assciated with each center. As the common bandwidth is varied during learning, the spherical functions always maintain their relative sizes with respect to each other.

In summary, the base learner extends the original GRNN by adapting the vector center reduction method of VQ-GRNN model and incoperating the weights associated with each training vector into the learning process. Particularly, these weights are utilized in the cluster center formation and MSE calculation for realzing the smoothing factor δ. These modifications improve performance of GRNN as well make it more applicable for boosting.

5.2. Remarks on BMPNN's Features

The radial basis function (RBF) used in the GRNN is actually a spherical kernel function used for nonparametric function estimation. As the number of training samples approaches infinity, the nonparametric estimation is not dependent on the parameters of the RBF. However, for finite training samples, there is always some dependence on the RBF parameters. This suggests that VQ-GRNN is a semiparametric approximation of the GRNN by reducing the input space. This semiparametric VQ-GRNN, when used as a base learner (referred as Modified Probabilistic Classifier) in the boosting framework, can still retain its superior performance. Subsequently, the overall BMPNN can achieve very high accuracy (low bias) as well as fast convergence. It also performs reliably for unseen data (low variance).

The high accuracy of BMPNN can be explained by the boosting effects of SAMME method implemented in the Adaptive Booster module. By sufficiently handling the multiclass problem and using confidence-rated predictions, SAMME is proved to be able to maximize the distribution margins of the training data. Also, our implementation of Kohavi-Wolpert variance (KW) in the reweighting of hypotheses in the joint classification can effectively enforce the ensemble diversity. Besides the merits of the Adaptive Booster module, the contributions of the Modified Probabilistic Classifier cannot be denied. That is, the base learner has very fast adaptation and it is modified to better integrate with the Adaptive Booster module. Particularly, after being modified, it can produce confidence rated outputs and fully utilize the weights given by the booster to each training example.

BMPNN is observed to be very robust to new data. This robustness is attributed to the margin maximization of boosting methods and the low generalization variance of VQ-GRNN base learner. Though

VQ-GRNN is a weak learner (high bias as the result of input space reduction), its performance is reported to be reliable, i.e. it is quite robust to overfitting.

Finally, the convergence of BMPNN is observed to be fast. This is because the base learner itself, as the reduced version of GRNN, has very short training time due to its computational efficiency. Moreover, the adaptive SAMME used in BMPNN has been theoretically and experimentally proved to converge to the optimal solution just after a relatively small number of iterations. Compared with VQ-GRNN, BMPNN can obtain much higher accuracy (competitive to the ideal GRNN) with a slightly increased computation. This additional computation added by the BMPNN is still lower than GRNN and other boosted algorithms.

6. APPLICATION TO NETWORK INTRUSION DETECTION

6.1. Intrusion Detection Data

To evaluate our proposed method, the KDD-99 dataset is used as a benchmark which was derived from the DARPA 98 dataset prepared by MIT Lincoln labs. The data contains 7 weeks of training traffic data and 2 weeks of testing data (McHugh, Christie, & Allen, 2000). Preprocessing was applied to abstract and summarize the raw *tcpdump* data to form network connections.

6.1.1. Attack Types and Categories

Each connection record in the KDD-99 dataset is labeled as either normal or one type of attack. There are totally 39 types of attacks which are grouped into 4 major categories(McHugh et al., 2000): Probe, Denial of Service (DoS), User to Root (U2R) and Remote to Local (R2L). In particular, Probe attacks refer to the incidents in which some malicious programs can automatically scan a network of computers to gather sensitive information or search for security vulnerabilities while an DoS attack prevents normal use of network resources for legitimate purposes by consuming the bandwidth or overloading the computational resources of the victim system. The R2L attacks occur when an intruder who has no valid account on a machine can exploit some system vulnerabilities to gain local access as a legitimate user by sending packets over a network. In contrast, U2R attacks assume that the attacker has already access to a system as a normal user account and he can exploit some security holes to gain user root privileges.

6.1.2. Features

41 features were used to summarize the connection information. These features are grouped as basic features and additional features respectively (McHugh et al., 2000).

6.1.2.1. Basic Features
Bro is used as the network analyzer to derive the 9 basic features from packet headers without inspecting the packet contents (Paxson, 1999). Some examples of basic features include duration of connection, protocol types and service types.

6.1.2.2. Additional Features

Content features: The payload of TCP packets is assessed by applying the domain knowledge. Examples of content-based features include the number of unsuccessful logins and whether the root access was gained or not.

Time based features: It is important to inspect the packets within some time interval to cope with the temporal nature of network attacks. These features are designed to capture properties within a 2 second temporal window. Number of connections to the same host is an example of time-based features.

Host based features: Utilize a historical window estimated over the number of connections (100 connections in KDD-99) instead of time. Host based features are therefore used to assess attacks which span over intervals longer than 2 seconds.

6.1.3. Component Datasets

The KDD-99 data consists of three components as detailed in Table 1. The entire KDD dataset is called "Whole KDD" which contains about 5 million records. A more concise version of "Whole KDD" is its "10% KDD" subset which contains 22 attack types and is normally used for training purpose. One side effect of this subset is that it contains more examples of attacks than normal connections and distributions of attack types are not represented equally. Also, DoS attacks account for the majority of this dataset due to its nature (McHugh et al., 2000).

It is believed that most novel attacks are variants of known attacks and the "signature" of known attacks can be sufficient to catch novel variants (Linger, Mead, & Lipson, 2004). Therefore, an IDS that can effectively learn and correlate known signatures to detect unknown attacks is desirable. In fact, IDS have to face with new situations that they never experienced before such as new cyber attacks with different technologies and imbalanced attack distributions. These changes in the network environments must be accommodated by adaptive IDS to maintain high accuracy and reliability. The KDD-99 contest took this issue into account by introducing "Corrected KDD" set that is not from the same probability distribution as the training data and it also contains 14 additional (unseen) attack types that are not included in the training data. This dataset is normally used for testing purpose (Table 1.)

6.2. Experiments on KDD-99 Data

To evaluate our proposed method, several experiments are conducted on the KDD 99 benchmark

6.2.1. Experiments Design

To conduct our experiments, a three-phase learning approach is deployed:

6.2.1.1. Preprocessing

The KDD-99 dataset contains attributes of different forms such as continuous, discrete and symbolic with varying resolutions and ranges. In order to build predictive models, preprocessing is required to transform this data into compatible format. Several techniques are deployed such as Data Reduction (remove duplicated data) Feature Selection (based on information gain) Data encoding and normalization.

Table 1. Component sets of KDD-99 dataset

Dataset	DoS	Probe	U2R	R2L	Total Attack	Total Normal
Whole KDD	3883370	41102	52	1126	3925650	972780
10% KDD	391458	4107	52	1126	396743	97277
Corrected KDD	229853	4166	70	16347	250436	60593

6.2.1.2. Classification

In this phase, our BMPNN algorithm and other conventional methods (Boosted J48, MLP and GRNN) will be trained on the "10% KDD" dataset to detect 5 class labels (Normal, Probe, DoS, U2R and R2L) using tenfold cross-validation. In each tenfold iteration, a sample of 50,000 records is randomly drawn from the "10% KDD" dataset and used as training set. Similarly, a sample of 10,000 records is obtained from "Corrected KDD" and used as validation set. The evaluation metrics computed from each iteration will then be averaged at the end of the cross-validation process.

6.2.1.3. Evaluation

The trained models will be tested on the "Test KDD" data. Specifically, the newly proposed BMPNN method is compared with different learning algorithms mentioned previously as well as the KDD-99 winner in terms of True Positive Rate (Detection Rate) and False Positive Rate (False Alarm). For each method, we also measure the required computation time which is the total time for a classifier to complete tenfold iterations, make predictions on test data and compute relevant metrics.

Because different attack categories have different severity levels, a misclassification cost must be considered. During the testing phase, the outputs of a classifier will be generated in form of a *Confusion Matrix* (*ConfM*) which summarizes the classification results. A *Cost Matrix* (*CostM*) is provided by the KDD-99 contest. The difference between *CostM* and *ConfM* is that an entry at row i and column j in the cost matrix, *CostM(i,j)*, represents the *cost* associated with a connection which actually belongs to class i and is classified as class j while the same position in the confusion matrix, *ConfM(i.j)*, displays the *number of connections* of type i and is classified (correctly or incorrectly) as class j. Given a test set, the average cost of a classifier is calculated as below (McHugh et al., 2000):

$$Cost = \frac{1}{N}\sum_{i=1}^{5}\sum_{j=1}^{5} ConfM\left(i,j\right) * CostM(i,j)$$

Where

N: total number of connections in the dataset
ConfM(i,j): the entry at row i, column j in the confusion matrix.
CostM(i,j): the entry at row i, column j in the cost matrix.

Taking into account all the above performance metrics, a "best" classifier is defined as the one that has high detection rate, low false positive and low overall penalty cost. However, at some times, such a best model is not possible to realize because some models will display their strengths under different performance metrics. Therefore, to compare between different classifiers, we need to consider both strengths and weaknesses of a classifier from different aspects (e.g. accuracy, robustness, algorithmic complexity, different use of machine resources and comprehensibility) and combine these factors to a compromised conclusion.

6.2.2. Experiment Results

Table 2 displays the detection performance of our model compared against KDD 99 winner (Pfahringer, 2000) and the PNrule approach (Agarwal, 2000).

Across the classes, MLP does not provide noticeable improvement in DR while its FAR is quite high in most cases (Probe, U2R, R2L and Normal). The GRNN is found not stable due to its high FAR and fluctuations in DR of different classes. The Boosted J48, on the other hands, provides stable detection rates for most of the classes but it does not really improve in FAR. Though no model can provide both highest DR and lowest FAR for all the classes, our BMPNN is suggested to be the most promising model which makes the best trade-off between detection capability (DR) and system robustness (FAR). That is, BMPNN can achieve both lowest FAR and highest DR for U2R and R2L attacks. For other classes, it remains very competitive compared with other methods. Moreover, due to the increase of correct classification on U2R and R2L which have high associated costs, our BMPNN is able to obtain a total cost of **0.1954** which is smaller than **0.2331** of the winner. It is also important to note that the test data used in our experiments follows a different distribution than in the training data and contains an additional 14 attack types not included in the training data. Therefore, achieving high detection rate on this test dataset suggests that our model is robust to data distribution changes and is able to detect unseen attacks.

To complete the whole cross-validation, testing and evaluation process, BMPNN takes 21.6 mins which faster than other highly accurate methods such as GRNN (44.2 mins) and other boosted algorithms (Boosted J48 – 35.4 mins). This effect of adaptive boosting mechanism implemented in BMPNN can significantly increase learning accuracy and lower generalization variance but may add some computation

Table 2. Overall detection rate (DR %) and false alarm rate (FAR %) evaluation

	Normal	Probe	DoS	U2R	R2L	DR/FAR (%)	Computation time (mins)
KDD 99 winner (Pfahringer, 2000)	99.5	83.3	97.1	13.2	8.4	DR	N/A
	27.0	35.2	0.1	28.6	1.2	FAR	
PNrule(Agarwal, 2000)	99.5	73.2	96.9	6.6	10.7	DR	N/A
	27.0	7.5	**0.05**	89.5	12.0	FAR	
MLP	98.4	86.0	97.0	14.3	11.9	DR	26.5
	30.0	40.1	0.8	51.5	20.0	FAR	
Boosted J48	99.5	**92.0**	96.9	11.8	17.1	DR	35.4
	13.3	6.7	0.09	20.1	8.7	FAR	
GRNN	91.1	85.3	**99.3**	4.4	12.8	DR	44.2
	35.2	21.4	0.56	33.3	15.7	FAR	
BMPNN	**99.8**	91.7	98.4	**22.7**	**18.2**	DR	**21.6**
	13.6	**3.3**	0.06	**19.8**	**1.1**	FAR	

overheads into BMPNN. However, as indicated in the experiments, BMPNN achieves superior detection rate and false alarm rate while other methods require much longer computation time. The traditional MLP does not perform very well in this problem with long computation time and high FAR.

The Figure 5 and Figure 6 compare Detection rates (highest values are in bold) and False alarms (lowest values are in bold) of the classifiers on KDD-99 dataset.

In summary, our proposed BMPNN can significantly reduce the total misclassification cost compared with KDD-99 winner. Its detection rates are the highest for Normal, U2R and R2L categories and very close to that of the best performing classifiers for Probe and DoS categories. Moreover, false alarm rates obtained by BMPNN are often the lowest compared to other methods. Finally, the low training time suggests that our BMPNN is very computationally efficient in comparison with other approaches.

7. CONCLUSION AND FUTURE RESEARCH

7.1. Conclusion

This chapter shows how boosting can be utilized to improve performance of a semi-parametric classifier. In particular, a novel learning technique, referred as Boosted Modified Probabilistic Neural Network (BMPNN) is proposed in which an RBF neural network (base learner) is trained iteratively with weighted data by a boosting method (adaptive booster). For each iteration, the data is weighted based on the performance of previous base classifiers. These base classifiers are then combined to form a joint classification. To obtain classification capability, the base learner uses a hybrid scheme which consists of both learning approaches: unsupervised learning (vector quantization) quantizes the input space into a smaller number of clusters while supervised learning (GRNN) computes final output as the weighted combination of the cluster centers' classification values. The base learner, therefore, is similar to the VQ-GRNN which can obtain more compact network size than original GRNN at the cost of lower or similar predictive accuracy. The difference between the adapted base learner and VQ-GRNN is that we incorporate weights of data instances into learning process, i.e. to compute cluster centers and find the optimal value of radial basis function's bandwidth. The adaptive booster is implemented by adapting the SAMME boosting algorithm. It is modified to more effectively enforce diversity using the Kohavi-Wolpert variance. The BMPNN model is then applied to the Network Intrusion Detection problem. It is found that our proposed technique outperforms other existing algorithms not only on minority and distributed U2R and R2L attacks but also majority classes.

In conclusion, the empirical analysis from this research suggests that BMPNN achieves superior performance compared with other state-of-the-art techniques in terms of accuracy, system robustness and misclassification costs while requires "affordable" computation. However, no system is absolutely secure given the best possible detection algorithms. That is true as long as the system is connected to other networks. The absolute security can only be achieved by disconnecting the system from the outside world which is against the principal benefits of internetworking – accessibility of information. This means that protecting our resources from cyber attacks is an ongoing task and computer security is always an active and challenging research area.

Figure 5. Detection rate comparision

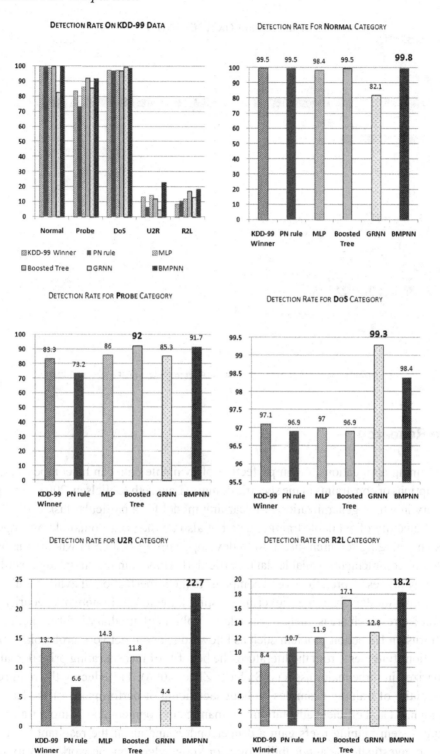

Figure 6. False alarm comparision

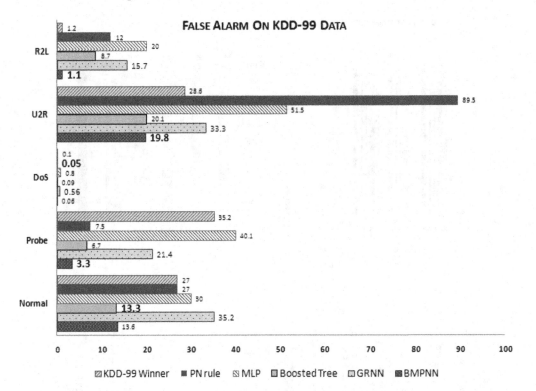

7.2. Future Research

In some data mining applications, the imperfection of available data can be compensated by utilizing relevant assumptions or constraints of the specific domain (Langseth & Nielsen, 2003). This phenomenon leads to a theory in which generalization of a learning model for a particular task depends not only on the quality and quantity of available training data but also on the prior domain knowledge existing for the task. It is an emerging research direction to develop learning system in which domain knowledge is incorporated to complement available data. Particularly, this domain knowledge can be utilized to guide the learning process more effectively, compensate the imperfection of available training data and prevent the learning models from rediscovering existing knowledge. In network security which is one of the most studied research areas, there exists a large volume of auxiliary information that we can use to solve the Intrusion Detection problem such as knowledge about network protocols, intrusive activities and protection strategies. From the literature, the benefits of incorporating prior domain knowledge can be summarized in three major aspects (Sinha & Zhao, 2008): 1) Reducing the requirements to the quality and quantity of training examples without sacrificing of performance of the learning systems. 2) Quick deployment and efficient adaptation to dynamic environment and 3) more transparent outputs of the learning system helping users gain a deeper understanding of the resultant model. Under this light, we plan to investigate the applicability of prior knowledge from network security domain in the Intrusion Detection problem.

REFERENCES

Agarwal, R., & Joshi, M. V. (2000). *PNrule: A New Framework for Learning Classifier Models in Data Mining*. Paper presented at the Technical Report.

Alpaydin, E. (1993). *Multiple networks for function learning*. Paper presented at the Proceedings of the IEEE International Conference on Neural Networks.

Ambwani, T. (2003). *Multi class support vector machine implementation to intrusion detection*. Paper presented at the Proceedings of the International Joint Conference of Neural Networks.

Bishop, C. M. (1995). *Neural Networks for Pattern Recognition*. Oxford, UK: Oxford University Press.

Breiman, L. (1996). Bagging predictors. *Machine Learning, 24*, 123–140.

Cannady, J. (1998). *Artificial neural networks for misuse detection*. Paper presented at the Proceedings of the National Information Systems Security Conference.

Costa, M., Filippi, E., & Pasero, E. (Eds.). (1995). *Artificial neural network ensembles: a bayesian standpoint*. Singapore: World Scientic.

Geman, S., Bienenstock, E., & Doursat, R. (1992). Neural networks and the bias/variance dilemma. *Neural Computation, 4*, 1–58. doi:10.1162/neco.1992.4.1.1

Hansen, L., & Salamon, P. (1990). Neural network ensembles. *IEEE Transactions on Pattern Analysis and Machine Intelligence, 12*, 993–1001. doi:10.1109/34.58871

Ilgun, K., Kemmerer, R., & Porras, P. (1995). State transition analysis: a rule-based intrusion detection approach. *IEEE Transactions on Software Engineering*, 181–199. doi:10.1109/32.372146

Jan, T. (2004). *Neural Network Based Threat Assessment for Automated Visual Surveillance*. Paper presented at the Proc. of International Joint Conference on Neural Networks IJCNN Budapest, Hungary.

Kittler, J., & Roli, F. (Eds.). (2000). *First International Workshop on Multiple Classier Systems,* Cagliari, Italy, (LNCS Vol. 1857).

Krogh, A., & Vedelsby, J. (1995). Neural network ensembles, cross validation, and active learning. *Advances in Neural Information Processing Systems, 7*, 231–238.

Kuncheva, L. I., & Whitaker, C. J. (2003). Measures of diversity in classifier ensembles and their relationship with the ensemble accuracy. *Machine Learning, 51*, 181–207. doi:10.1023/A:1022859003006

Langseth, H., & Nielsen, T. D. (2003). Fusion of domain knowledge with data for structural learning in object oriented domains. *Journal of Machine Learning Research, 4*, 339–368. doi:10.1162/jmlr.2003.4.3.339

Levin, I. (2000). *KDD-99 Classifier Learning Contest: LLSoft's Results Overview*. Paper presented at the SIGKDD Explorations.

Lincoln, W., & Skrzypek, J. (1989). Synergy of clustering multiple back propagation networks. *Advances in Neural Information Processing Systems, 2*, 650–659.

Linger, R. C., Mead, N. R., & Lipson, H. F. (2004). *Requirements Definition for Survivable Network Systems*. Pittsburgh, PA: Software Engineering Institute, Carnegie Mellon University.

McHugh, J., Christie, A., & Allen, J. (2000). Defending Yourself: The Role of Intrusion Detection Systems. *Software IEEE*, *17*(5), 42–51. doi:10.1109/52.877859

Miheev, V., & Vopilov, A. Shabalin, I. (2000). *The MP13 Approach to the KDD'99 Classifier Learning Contest.* Paper presented at the SIGKDD Explorations.

Nadaraya, E. A. (1964). On estimating regression. *Theory of Probability and Its Applications*, *9*, 141–142. doi:10.1137/1109020

Park, J., & Sandberg, I. W. (1991). Universal approximation using radial basis function networks. *Neural Computation*, *2*(3), 246. doi:10.1162/neco.1991.3.2.246

Paxson, V. (1999). *Bro: a system for detecting network intruders in real-time*. Paper presented at the Computer Networks.

Pfahringer, B. (2000). *Winning the KDD99 Classification Cup: Bagged Boosting*. Paper presented at the SIGKDD Explorations.

Press, W. H., Flannery, B. P., Teukolsky, S. A., & Vetterling, W. T. (1986). *Numerical Recipies. The art of Scientific Computing*. Cambridge, UK: Cambridge University Press.

Rogova, G. (1994). Combining the results of several neural network classifiers. *Neural Networks*, *7*, 777–781. doi:10.1016/0893-6080(94)90099-X

Roli, F., & Kittler, J. (Eds.). (2002). *Third International Workshop on Multiple Classier Systems* Cagliari, Italy, (LNCS Vol. 2364).

Rumelhart, D. E., & McClelland, J. L. (1986). *Parallel Distributed Processing: Explorations in the Microstructure of Cognition* (Vol. 2). Cambrdige, MA: The MIT Press.

Schapire, R. E., Freund, Y., Bartlett, P., & Lee, W. S. (1998). Boosting the margin: A new explanation for the effectiveness of voting methods. *Annals of Statistics*, *26*(5), 1651–1686. doi:10.1214/aos/1024691352

Sharkey, A. J. C., & Sharkey, N. E. (1997). Combining diverse neural nets. *The Knowledge Engineering Review*, *12*(3), 231–247. doi:10.1017/S0269888997003123

Sinha, A. P., & Zhao, H. (2008). *Incorporating domain knowledge into data mining classifiers: An application in indirect lending*. Paper presented at the Decision Support Systems.

Specht, D. F. (1990). Probabilistic neural networks. *Neural Networks*, *3*, 109–118. doi:10.1016/0893-6080(90)90049-Q

Spetch, D. F. (1991). A general regression neural network. *IEEE Transactions on Neural Networks*, *2*(6), 568–576. doi:10.1109/72.97934

Watson, G. S. (1964). Smooth regression analysis. *Sankhya Series*, *26*, 359–372.

Windeatt, T., & Roli, F. (Eds.). (2003). *Multiple Classier Systems, 4th International Workshop, MCS 2003*. Guilford, UK: Springer.

Zaknich, A. (1998). Introduction to the modified probabilistic neural network for general signal processing applications. *IEEE Transactions on Signal Processing, 46*(7), 1980–1990. doi:10.1109/78.700969

Zaknich, A., & Attikiouzel, Y. (1988). *An unsupervised clustering algorithm for the modified probabilistic neural network.* Paper presented at the IEEE International Workshop on Intelligent Signal Processing and Communications Systems, Melbourne, Australia.

Zaknich, A., & Attikiouzel, Y. (1993). *Automatic optimization of the modified probabilistic neural network for pattern recognition and time series analysis.* Paper presented at the Proc. First Australia and New Zealand Conference Intelligence Information System, Perth, Australia.

Zhu, J., Rosset, S., Zhou, H., & Hastie, T. (2005). Multiclass adaboost. *Technical Report #430.*

Chapter 13
Fuzzy Clustering Based Image Segmentation Algorithms

M. Ameer Ali
East West University, Bangladesh

ABSTRACT

Image segmentation especially fuzzy based image segmentation techniques are widely used due to effective segmentation performance. For this reason, a huge number of algorithms are proposed in the literature. This chapter presents a survey report of different types of classical and shape based fuzzy clustering algorithms which are available in the literature.

1. INTRODUCTION

The application of digital images is rapidly expanding due to the ever-increasing demand of computer, Internet and multimedia technologies in all aspect of human lives, which makes digital image processing a most important research area. Digital image processing encompasses a wide and varied field of applications from medical science to document processing and generally refers to the manipulation and analysis of pictorial information. Image processing is mainly divided into six distinct classes: i) Representation and modelling, ii) Enhancement, iii) Restoration, iv) Analysis, v) Reconstruction, and vi) Compression. Image analysis embraces feature extraction, segmentation and object classification (Baxes, 1994; Duda & Hart, 1973; Gonzalez & Woods, 2002; Jahne, 1997; Jain, 1989), with segmentation for instance, being applied to separate desired objects in an image so that measurements can subsequently be made upon them.

Segmentation is particularly important as it is often the pre-processing step in many image processing algorithms. In general, image segmentation refers to the practice of separating mutually exclusive homogeneous regions (objects) of interest in an image. The objects are partitioned into a number of

DOI: 10.4018/978-1-60566-908-3.ch013

non-intersecting regions in such a way that each region is homogeneous and the union of two adjacent regions is always non-homogeneous. Most natural objects are non-homogeneous however, and the definition of what exactly constitutes an object depends very much on the application and the user, which contradicts the above generic image segmentation definition (Gonzalez & Woods, 2002; Karmakar, Dooley, & Rahman, 2001; Spirkovska, 1993; Haralick & Shapiro, 1985; Fu & Mui, 1981).

Segmentation has been used in a wide range of applications, with some of the most popular being, though not limited to: automatic car assembling in robotic vision, airport identification from aerial photographs, security systems, object-based image identification and retrieval, object recognition, second generation image coding, criminal investigation, computer graphic, pattern recognition, and diverse applications in medical science such as cancerous cell detection, segmentation of brain images, skin treatment, intrathoracic airway trees, and abnormality detection of heart ventricles (Karmakar, Dooley, & Rahman, 2001; Pham & Prince, 1999; Liu, et al, 1997; Pal & Pal, 1993).

Different applications require different types of digital image. The most commonly used images are *light intensity* (LI), *range* (depth) image (RI), *computerized tomography* (CT), thermal and *magnetic resonance images* (MRI). The research published to date on image segmentation is highly dependent on the image type, its dimensions and application domain and so for this reason, there is no single generalized technique that is suitable for all images (Pal & Pal, 1993; Karmakar, 2002).

There are numerous image segmentation techniques in the literature, which can be broadly classified into two categories (Pal & Pal, 1993) namely: i) *classical* and ii) *fuzzy mathematical*. The former (Canny, 1986; Basu, 1987) comprises the five main classes (Pal & Pal, 1993) shown in Figure 1: i) Gray level thresholding (Otsu, 1980; Taxt, Flynn, & Jain, 1989; Yanowitz & Bruckstein, 1988), ii) Iterative pixel classification (e.g. relaxation, *Markov random fields* and neural network based techniques) (Andrey & Tarroux, 1998; Gosh, Pal, & Pal, 1993; Geman & Geman, 1984), iii) Surface-based segmentation (Besl & Jain, 1988), iv) Colour segmentation (Overheim & Wagner, 1982), and v) Edge detection (Canny, 1986; Haddon, 1988) . Fuzzy mathematical techniques are widely used in multifarious computer vision applications as they are far better able to handle and segment images, particularly noisy images, by using fuzzy membership values. The various fuzzy mathematical techniques identified in Figure 1 will be examined in greater detail in Section 2. There are also other image segmentation techniques which are not classified in either category, including those based upon *Markov random models*, Bayesian principles and the Gibbs distribution, with further details being given in (Geman & Geman, 1984; Derin & Elliot, 1987; Derin et al, 1984; Hansen & Elliot, 1982; Jain, 1981).

Segmentation is certainly one of the most challenging tasks in image processing and computer vision for many reasons, some of which are (Karmakar, Dooley, & Rahman, 2001; Spirkovska. 1993; Haralick & Shapiro, 1985; Pal & Pal, 1993):

- Image types such as MRI, CT or *Single Photon Emission Computed Tomography* (SPECT) contain inherent constraints that make the resulting image noisy and may include or introduce some visual artefacts.
- Image data can be ambiguous and susceptible to noise and high frequency distortion as in SPECT imaging for instance, where object edges become fuzzy and ill-defined.
- The shape of the same object can differ from image to image due to having different domain and capturing techniques as well as various orientations. An object's structure may not be well defined in many natural images and can also be very hard to accurately locate the contour of an object.

Figure 1. General classification of image segmentation techniques

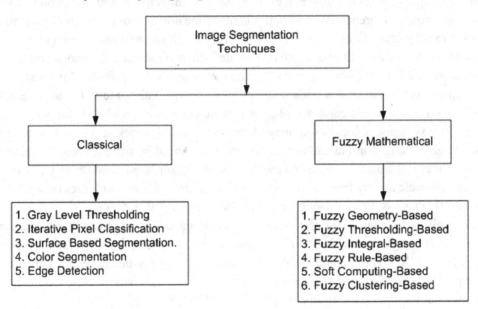

- The distributions of gray scale pixel values of the same object are not the same for all images and even in the same image, pixels belonging to the same class may have different intensities and distributions.

- Objects to be segmented are highly domain and application dependent-for example, in order to automatically estimate the myocardial wall thickness from a captured X-ray image of the human heart region, the inner and outer contours of the heart's left ventricle may be the two objects required to be segmented, while for another application, the entire heart may need to be segmented.

- The properties of an object can differ in their representation depending upon the type of image and its domain, so there needs to be a trade-off between the desired properties that are to be employed for segmentation. For example, some gray scale images have a Poisson distribution, though this would not be true for either an RI or MRI image, so the segmentation strategy requires both semantic and *a priori* information concerning the image type and with other relevant object information such as the number of objects in the image.

Thus, it can be concluded that most images contain some form of ambiguity. Pal and Pal (1993) showed that gray tones (LI) images possess ambiguities because of possible multi-valued brightness levels. This ambiguity may be defined in terms of grayness and/or spatiality. The gray ambiguity represents *indefiniteness* in deciding whether a pixel is either black or white, while spatial ambiguity means *indefiniteness* in the shape and geometry of a region contained in the image. Classical techniques produce a crisp (hard) decision, though such decisions are unsuitable for ambiguous and ill-defined data. For this reason, it is crucially important to have a segmentation strategy for image processing systems that is able to handle all types of uncertainty at any processing stage. Prewitt first suggested that image segmentation yielded fuzzy regions (Karmakar, 2002; Prewitt, 1970), which was the catalyst for the development of various fuzzy-based techniques, which have since proven to be very effective in efficiently handling such ill-defined image data, by assigning a membership value to every pixel (datum), which denotes the possibility of belongingness of that pixel to a region (cluster). This is main discriminating feature between fuzzy and hard decision-making and is one of the main motivations for using fuzzy-based image segmentation techniques.

In a fuzzy system, every image contains a number of regions $R_1, R_2, ..., R_c$ where c is the number of regions (objects) (Medasani, Krishnapuram, & Keller, 1999; Kruse, Gebhardt, & Klawonn, 1995; Bloch, 1994; Yang, 1993), with a number of pixels forming a region and each pixel in a region assigned a membership value which measures the probability of that pixel belonging to that particular region. Each datum $X(x,y)$ of image I having coordinates (x,y) is assigned a membership value μ by mapping the gray levels into the close interval ranging from 0 to 1, so the membership function μ for I can be defined as- $\mu(X): \Omega \rightarrow [0,1]$ where Ω denotes a universal reference set of all values for all the data in image I.

In using a fuzzy technique, the particular characteristics of an image including brightness, contrast, edges, regions, connectivity and complexity can be represented by *linguistic variables* such as VERY COMPLEX, COMPLEX and SIMPLE (Chacon, Aguilar, & Delgado, 2002). Medasani *et al* (1999) used both fuzzy and crisp methods to measure geometric properties such as area, perimeter, height, extrinsic and intrinsic diameter and elongatedness, together with non-geometric properties like average pixel intensity, entropy, and homogeneity for both real and synthetic images. They showed that fuzzy techniques consistently provided better results than crisp techniques for all images due to using fuzzy membership functions and also tested both approaches upon noisy data, with experimental results confirming their superiority for both geometric and non-geometric properties. It was also proven that if fuzzy techniques are applied in noisy conditions, it is not necessary to apply noise removal techniques to the image, even in textured regions where noise removal is often very difficult.

Any segmented image therefore will inherently produce fuzzy regions (objects) (Karmakar, 2002), so fuzzy-based image segmentation techniques do afford an attractive and effective approach for handling imprecise image information by employing fuzzy membership functions for each datum. This was the overriding reason for making literature on fuzzy image segmentation.

The organization of the chapter: Section 2 describes the different types of fuzzy image segmentation techniques while existing fuzzy clustering algorithms are detailed in Section 3. Different types of existing classical fuzzy clustering techniques and shape based fuzzy clustering techniques are presented in Section 4 and Section 5 respectively. Some concluding remarks are provided in Section 6.

2. FUZZY IMAGE SEGMENTATION TECHNIQUES

Fuzzy image segmentation techniques have become very popular (Karmakar, Dooley, & Rahman, 2001) due to the rapid development of fuzzy set theory based on mathematical models, genetic algorithms and neural networks, and are widely used in diverse applications including image processing, pattern recognition, robotic vision, engineering tools, security and computer vision systems. Fuzzy image segmentation techniques as shown in Figure 1, are broadly classified into six categories (Tizhoosh, 1997):- i) Fuzzy geometric, ii) Fuzzy thresholding, iii) Fuzzy integral-based, iv) Fuzzy rule-based, v) Soft computing-based, and vi) Fuzzy clustering. A detailed description of existing fuzzy clustering techniques is now provided.

Figure 2. Example showing four clusters

3. EXISTING FUZZY CLUSTERING ALGORITHMS

Clustering is the process of separating or grouping a given set of unlabeled patterns into a number of clusters such that the patterns drawn from the same cluster are *similar* to each other in some sense, while those are assigned to different clusters are *dissimilar* (Hoppner, 1999; Bezdek, 1984; Bezdek, 1981; Hung & Yang, 2001; Chintalapudi & Kam, 1998). Most of the time, objects are defined by a set of features and so those with similar features are classified into one cluster (Chintalapudi & Kam, 1998). For a physical interpretation of the clustering process, the example shown in Figure 2 contains four separate clusters.

As highlighted in Section 1, there are mainly two types of clustering, namely *hard* (crisp) (HC) and *fuzzy*-based (Karmakar, Dooley, & Rahman, 2001). In a HC algorithm (Ruspini, 1969; Dubes & Jain, 1998), the decision boundary is fully defined and one pattern is classified into one and only one cluster, i.e. the clusters are mutually exclusive (Hung & Yang, 2001; Chintalapudi & Kam, 1998). However in the real world, the boundaries between clusters are not clearly defined. Some patterns may belong to more than one cluster and so in this case, fuzzy-based clustering techniques (Bezdek, 1984; Bezdek, 1981; Krishnapuram & Keller, 1993; Fan, Zhen, & Xie, 2003) provide a better and more efficient approach to classifying these patterns by assigning a membership value to each individual pattern. As mentioned in Section 1, among fuzzy-based techniques, fuzzy clustering is considered for the literature review due to their effective segmentation performance. Fuzzy clustering algorithms are broadly classified into two groups: i) Classical and ii) Shape-based (Hoppner, 1999). There exist many classical fuzzy clustering algorithms in the literature, among the most popular and widely used being: i) *Fuzzy c-means* (FCM) (Bezdek, 1981), ii) *Suppressed fuzzy c-means* (SFCM) (Fan, Zhen, & Xie, 2003), iii) *Possibilistic c-means* (PCM) (Krishnapuram & Keller, 1993), and (iv) *Gustafson-Kessel* (GK) (Gustafson & Kessel, 1979), while from a shape-based fuzzy clustering viewpoint, well-established and popular algorithms include: i) Circular shape-based (Man & Gath, 1994), ii) Elliptical shape-based (Gath & Hoory, 1995), and (iii) *Generic shape-based* techniques (Ameer Ali, Dooley, & Karmakar, 2006). A detailed review of the above mentioned classical fuzzy clustering algorithms is now provided.

4. CLASSICAL FUZZY CLUSTERING ALGORITHMS

Clustering algorithms that use general feature sets such as PL, PI or CIL are generally treated as classical fuzzy clustering techniques. These are dependent on both the features used and the type of objects in an image. A review of the three main classical fuzzy clustering techniques mentioned above is now detailed.

4.1 Fuzzy c-Means Algorithm

The FCM algorithm (Bezdek, 1981) was developed by Bezdek in 1981 and is still the most popular classical fuzzy clustering technique, widely used directly or indirectly in image processing. It performs classification based on the iterative minimization of the following objective function and constraints (Bezdek, 1984; Bezdek, 1981; Chen & Wang, 1999; Antonio, Candenas, & Martin, 1999: Shen, Shi, & Zhang, 2001; Gustafson & Kessel, 1979; Wei & Mendel, 1994; Hathaway & Bezdek, 1986; Dave, 1992a):

$$J_q\left(\mu, V, X\right) = \sum_{i=1}^{c} \sum_{j=1}^{n} \left(\mu_{ij}\right)^q D_{ij}^2 \tag{1}$$

subject to

$$0 \leq \mu_{ij} \leq 1 \; ; $$

$$i \in \left\{1,...,c\right\} \text{ and } i \in \left\{1,...,c\right\} \; j \in \left\{1,...,c\right\} \text{ and } j \in \left\{1,...,c\right\} \tag{2}$$

$$\sum_{i=1}^{c} \mu_{ij} = 1 \; ; \; j \in \left\{1,...,c\right\} \tag{3}$$

$$0 < \sum_{j=1}^{n} \mu_{ij} < n \; ; \; i \in \left\{1,...,c\right\} \tag{4}$$

Where n and c are the number of data and clusters respectively. μ is the fuzzy partition matrix containing membership values $[\mu_{ij}]$, q is the fuzzifier where $1 < q \leq \infty$, V is cluster centre vector $[v_i]$, X is a data vector $[x_j]$ and $D_{ij} = d(x_j, v_i)$ is the distance between datum x_j and v_i. Using a Lagrangian multiplier, the following can be derived by optimizing the objective function in (1) with respect to μ and V.

$$\mu_{ij} = \cfrac{1}{\sum_{k=1}^{c} \left(\cfrac{D_{ij}}{D_{kj}}\right)^{2/(q-1)}} \tag{5}$$

$$v_i = \frac{\sum\limits_{j=1}^{n} \left(\mu_{ij}\right)^q x_j}{\sum\limits_{j=1}^{n} \left(\mu_{ij}\right)^q} \tag{6}$$

The membership values are initialized randomly and both these and the cluster centres are iteratively updated until the maximum change in μ_{ij} becomes less than or equal to a specified threshold ζ. q is normally set to 2 as this is the best value for the fuzzifier (Step 1) while the membership μ_{ij} is randomly initialized in Step 2. The cluster centre v_i and membership values μ_{ij} are then iteratively updated using (6) and (5) respectively (Steps 3.1-3.2) until either the maximum number of iterations (max_Iteration) or threshold ζ is reached (Step 3.3). The complete FCM algorithm is given in Algorithm 1, which for n data points incurs O(n) computational time complexity (Karmakar, 2002; Yang & Wu, 2004).

Algorithm 1. *Fuzzy c-Means* (FCM) Algorithm

Pre condition: Objects to be segmented, number of clusters c, threshold ζ and the maximum number of iterations max_Iteration.
Post condition: Final segmented regions $\Re$.
1. Fix q=2.
2. Initialize μ_{ij}.
1. FOR l=1,2,3,…,max_Iteration
        3.1 Update cluster centres v_i using (6).
        3.2 Update membership values $\mu_{ij}^{(l)}$ using (5)
        3.3 IF $\left\| \mu_{ij}^{(l)} - \mu_{ij}^{(l-1)} \right\| \le \xi$ THEN STOP.

The number of clusters c, fuzzifier q and threshold ζ all need to be set manually. The selection of q is especially important because if $q=1$ then FCM produces crisp (HC) instead of fuzzy regions. Also (5) and (6) are not sufficient to achieve the local minimum of (1) (Wei & Mendel, 1994; Tolias & Panas, 1998), since if any of the distance value $D_{ij}=0$, (5) will be undefined. FCM strongly supports probability, but not the degree of *typicality* because it has the constraints in (2)-(4) which preclude the trivial solution $\mu_{ij}=0$. The relative membership values in (5) are calculated using these constraints which can be interpreted as the degree of sharing, but not the degree of *typicality* as required in many fuzzy set theory applications (Krishnapuram, 1994). Antonio *at el* (Antonio, Candenas, & Martin, 1999) tried to solve this problem by considering the Euclidean distance, the Mahalnobis distance and the covariance matrix in (Gustafson & Kessel, 1979), and proposed the following two new objective functions:

$$J_{Ec}\left(\mu, V, X\right) = \sum_{i=1}^{c} \sum_{j=1}^{n} \mu_{ij} D_{ij}^2 \tag{7}$$

$$J_{Mh}\left(\mu, V, X\right) = \sum_{i=1}^{c} \sum_{j=1}^{n} \mu_{ij}^{3/2} D_{ij}^2 \sqrt{\left|G_i^{-1}\right|} \tag{8}$$

Figure 3. (a) Original cow image, (b) Manually segmented reference of (a). (c)-(e) Segmented results of (a)

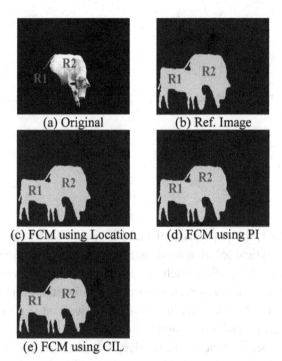

(a) Original   (b) Ref. Image

(c) FCM using Location   (d) FCM using PI

(e) FCM using CIL

where the $J_{Ec}(\mu, V, X)$ and $J_{Mh}(\mu, V, X)$ functions use the Euclidean and Mahalnobis distances respectively and G_i^{-1} is the covariance matrix for all data in the ith cluster. According to (Antonio, Candenas, & Martin, 1999), if the *membership function density* is defined as $\mu_{ij}\sqrt{\mu_{ij}}\sqrt{\left|G_i^{-1}\right|}$, then the membership values are respectively updated for the Euclidean and Mahalnobis distances by:

$$\mu_{ij}\left(Ec\right) = \frac{\left(\mu_{ij}\sqrt{\left|G_i^{-1}\right|}\sum_{k=1}^{n}\mu_{ik}\right)^{1/(q-1)}}{\sum_{i=1}^{c}\left(\mu_{ij}\sqrt{\left|G_i^{-1}\right|}\sum_{k=1}^{n}\mu_{ik}\right)^{1/(q-1)}}$$

(9)

$$\mu_{ij}\left(Mh\right) = \frac{\left(\mu_{ij}^{3/2}\sqrt{\left|G_i^{-1}\right|}\right)^{1/(q-1)}}{\sum_{i=1}^{c}\left(\mu_{ij}^{3/2}\sqrt{\left|G_i^{-1}\right|}\right)^{1/(q-1)}}$$

(10)

And the cluster centres are correspondingly updated by:

$$v_i = \frac{\sum_{j=1}^{n} \left(\mu_{ij} \right)^2 x_j}{\sum_{j=1}^{n} \left(\mu_{ij} \right)^2}$$

(11)

where the fuzzy covariance matrix for the kth cluster denoted by G_k is defined as:

$$G_k = \frac{\sum_{j=1}^{n} \mu_{kj}^2 \left(x_j - v_k \right) \left(x_j - v_k \right)^T}{\sum_{j=1}^{n} \mu_{kj}^2}$$

(12)

As mentioned in Section 1, the popularity of FCM is firmly based upon its flexible mathematical foundations and being an analytical solution for constraint optimized functions. This means it is possible to incorporate image feature information, such as *pixel location* (PL), *pixel intensity* (PI), and shape within its theoretical framework for segmentation purposes, and furthermore it is able to both effectively handle noisy and large datasets. FCM does arbitrarily divide objects into a given number regions (objects) whenever PL, PI, and *combination of pixel intensity and location* (CIL) are used as the selected features in the image segmentation process (Ameer Ali, Dooley, & Karmakar, 2005a). The experimental results of FCM separately using PL, PI, and CIL are given below in Figure 3.

4.2 Suppressed Fuzzy c-Means Algorithm

By using a fuzzifier q and membership value μ_{ij}, the performance of FCM is better than any HC technique (Ruspini, 1969), though the convergence speed is much lower. Moreover, if the fuzzifier is large ($q > 2$), it increases the gap between the membership values which may lead to a decrease the overall segmentation performance of FCM (Hoppner, 1999). To address these issues, the *rival checked fuzzy c-means* (RCFCM) algorithm (Wei & Xie, 2000) was introduced on the basis of competitive learning, by magnifying the largest membership value and suppressing the second largest membership value. The main step in the RCFCM algorithm is to modify μ_{ij} in the FCM algorithm as follows.

Assume the largest membership value of datum x_j for the pth cluster is μ_{pj} and its second largest membership value in the sth cluster is μ_{sj}. After modification, the membership value of x_j belonging to each cluster is then:

$$\mu_{pj} = \mu_{pj} + (1 - \alpha)\mu_{sj}$$

(13)

$$\mu_{sj} = \alpha\mu_{sj}$$

(14)

where $0 \leq \alpha \leq 1$. The main problem with RCFCM is that it only pays attention to the largest and second largest membership values, so if the choice of α is unsuitable, it can lead to the second largest membership value to be modified being actually less than some others, which causes a disturbance in the original order (Fan, Zhen, & Xie, 2003). For this reason, the convergence of RCFCM is not assured and so to solve this, the *suppressed fuzzy c-means* (SFCM) algorithm was introduced to magnify only the largest membership value and to suppress the rest (Fan, Zhen, & Xie, 2003). If μ_{pj} is the largest membership value for datum x_j, the modified values are:

$$\mu_{pj} = 1 - \alpha \sum_{i \neq p}^{c} \mu_{ij} = 1 - \alpha + \alpha \mu_{pj} \tag{15}$$

$$\mu_{ij} = \alpha \mu_{ij}; \ \mu_{ij} = \alpha \mu_{ij} \ i \neq p; \ i \neq p \tag{16}$$

where the various parameters are as defined above. Since SFCM prizes the largest and suppresses all other membership values, it does not disturb the original order and so eliminates the drawback of RCFCM. When $\alpha=0$, SFCM produces the same results as HC, while for $\alpha=1$ it becomes the FCM algorithm, so this establishes a more natural and realistic relationship between the HC and FCM algorithms, so that for a suitable α value, SFCM can compromise the advantages of faster convergence speed of HC techniques, with the better clustering performance of FCM without impacting on the time complexity which remains the same as FCM, i.e., $O(n)$.

Since SFCM reduces the sensitivity of the fuzzifier q it actually improves the segmentation performance of FCM. A sample experimental result of SFCM is shown in Figure 4.

4.3 Possibilistic c-Means Algorithm

FCM uses a probabilistic constraint (3) so that the sum of the membership values of a datum across all clusters is 1. The membership values generated by FCM using constraint (3) represent the degree of sharing, but not the degree of *typicality* or compatibility with an elastic constraint. *Typicality* here means the actual degree of belongingness of a datum to a cluster rather than an arbitrary division of data (Krishnapuram & Keller, 1993; Krishnapuram, 1994; Zadeh, 1978). Krishnapuram *et al* addressed these issues by proposing the *possibilistic c-means* (PCM) algorithm whose membership values represent the degree of *typicality* rather than the degree of sharing and as consequence constraint (3) is eliminated (Krishnapuram & Keller, 1993; Krishnapuram & Keller, 1996). Every cluster is independent of the other clusters in PCM and the FCM objective function is modified as follows:

$$J_q\left(\mu, V, X\right) = \sum_{i=1}^{c} \sum_{j=1}^{n} \left(\mu_{ij}\right)^q D_{ij}^2 + \sum_{i=1}^{c} \eta_i \sum_{j=1}^{n} \left(1 - \mu_{ij}\right)^q \tag{17}$$

subject to:

$$0 \leq \mu_{ij} \leq 1; \ i \in \{1,...,c\} \ \text{and} \ 0 \leq \mu_{ij} \leq 1 \ i \in \{1,...,c\} \ j \in \{1,...,c\}; \ i \in \{1,...,c\} \ \text{and} \ j \in \{1,...,c\} \tag{18}$$

Figure 4. (a) Original babacoot image, (b) Manually segmented reference of (a). (c)-(e) Segmented results of (a)

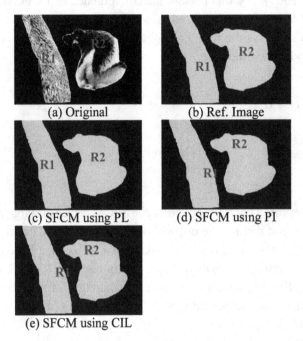

(a) Original   (b) Ref. Image

(c) SFCM using PL   (d) SFCM using PI

(e) SFCM using CIL

$$0 < \sum_{j=1}^{n} \mu_{ij} < n \;;\; 0 < \sum_{j=1}^{n} \mu_{ij} < n \; i \in \left\{1,...,c\right\} ; i \in \left\{1,...,c\right\} \tag{19}$$

$$\max \mu_{ij} > 0 \;;\; \max \mu_{ij} > 0 \; j \in \left\{1,...,c\right\} ; j \in \left\{1,...,c\right\} \tag{20}$$

where η_i is the *scale* (resolution) parameter that determines the zone of influence of a particular cluster. The PCM algorithm is applied twice, using the scale η_I the first time by setting:

$$\eta_i = \frac{\sum_{j=1}^{n} \left(\mu_{ij}\right)^q D_{ij}^2}{\sum_{j=1}^{n} \left(\mu_{ij}\right)^q} \tag{21}$$

and the second time:

$$\eta_i = \frac{\sum_{x_j \in \left(\pi_i\right)_\alpha} D_{ij}^2}{\left|\left(\pi_i\right)_\alpha\right|} \tag{22}$$

where $(\pi_i)_\alpha$ is an appropriate α-cut of π_i. By minimizing the objective function $J_q(\mu, V, X)$ in (17), the membership value μ_{ij} and cluster centre v_i can be calculated using the following two equations that are iteratively updated:

$$\mu_{ij} = \frac{1}{1 + \left(\dfrac{D_{ij}}{\eta_i}\right)^{2/(q-1)}}$$

(23)

$$v_i = \frac{\sum_{j=1}^{n} \left(\mu_{ij}\right)^q x_j}{\sum_{j=1}^{n} \left(\mu_{ij}\right)^q}$$

(24)

Algorithm 2. *Possibilistic c-Means Algorithm* (PCM)

Precondition: Objects to be segmented, number of clusters c, max_ Iteration.

Post condition: The final segmented regions $\Re$.

1. Fix c, and q=2.
2. Initialize μ_{ij}^0.
3. Estimate η_i using **(21)**.
4. FOR l=1,2,3,…, max_Iteration
    5. Update prototypes v_i using (24)
    6. Compute $\mu_{ij}^{(l+1)}$ using (23)
    7. IF $\left(\left\|\mu_{ij}^{(l+1)} - \mu_{ij}^l\right\| < \xi\right)$ THEN STOP.
  ENDFOR
8. Estimate η_i applying (22).
9. FOR l=1,2,3,…, max_Iteration
    10. Update cluster centre v_i using (24).
    11. Update $\mu_{ij}^{(l+1)}$ using (23).
    12. IF $\left(\left\|\mu_{ij}^{(l+1)} - \mu_{ij}^l\right\| < \xi\right)$ THEN STOP.
  ENDFOR
13. Return $\Re$.

If the fuzzifier $q=1$, PCM produces crisp (HC) regions. PCM provides good-segmented results for noisy data, but it is highly dependent on the initialization and the estimation of scale parameter η_i, for which FCM can be effectively used for both purposes. The computational time required for PCM is $O(n)$ (Karmakar, 2002; Yang & Wu, 2004). It should be noted that PCM can generate trivial solutions since the solution spaces are not constant over all clusters, moreover it only achieves a local minimum

Figure 5. (a) Original scene image, (b) Manually segmented reference of (a). (c)-(e) Segmented results of (a)

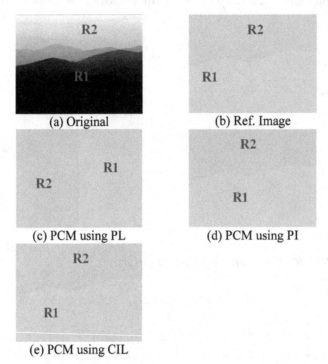

(a) Original

(b) Ref. Image

(c) PCM using PL

(d) PCM using PI

(e) PCM using CIL

and so is unable to minimize the objective function (17) in a global sense (Yang & Wu, 2004; Krishnapuram & Keller, 1996; Ahang & Leung, 2004; Barni, Cappellini, & Mecocci, 1996). The performance of PCM for noisy data can be improved using the modifications proposed in (Li, Huang, & Li, 2003; Schneider, 2000), though again only a local not global minimum can be reached. The improvement in (Li, Huang, & Li, 2003) may increase the possible number of local minima which produce a number of *bad* minimizers that are likely to trap PCM iterations into poor classification. The detail algorithm is presented in Algorithm 2.

In summary, PCM gives more emphasis to *typicality*, that means it is able to separate visually distinctive objects well, but conversely produces poorer segmentation performance when objects are not visually different. Figure 5 highlights the experimental results of PCM separately using PL, PI, and CIL.

4.4 Gustafson-Kessel Algorithm

The *Gustafson-Kessel* (GK) algorithm (Gustafson & Kessel, 1979) is a powerful clustering technique that has been used in various image processing, classification and system identification applications (Bezdek, 1981; Dave, 1992a). It is characterised by adapting automatically the local data distance metric to the shape of the cluster using a covariance matrix and adapting the distance inducing matrix correspondingly (Gustafson & Kessel, 1979; Huang, Li, & Ban, 2003; Babuska, Van der Veen, & Kaymak, 2002; Krishnapuram & Kim, 1999). The GK algorithm is based on the iterative optimization of the following FCM-type objective function (Bezdek, 1984; Bezdek, 1981):

$$J_q\left(\mu, V, X\right) = \sum_{j=1}^{n}\sum_{i=1}^{c}\left(\mu_{ij}\right)^{q} D_{ij}^{'2} \tag{25}$$

$$0 \leq \mu_{ij} \leq 1 \ ; \ i \in \left\{1,...,c\right\} \ \text{and} \ 0 \leq \mu_{ij} \leq 1 \ j \in \left\{1,...,n\right\} \ ; \ i \in \left\{1,...,c\right\} \ \text{and} \ j \in \left\{1,...,n\right\} \tag{26}$$

$$\sum_{i=1}^{c}\mu_{ij} = 1 \ ; \ j \in \left\{1,...,n\right\} \tag{27}$$

where $D_{ij}^{'}$ is the data distance norm calculated for clusters of different shapes in one dataset that is given by:

$$D_{ij}^{'2} = \left(x_j - v_i\right)^{T} A_i \left(x_j - v_i\right) \tag{28}$$

where A_i is the *norm inducing* matrix, which allows the distance to adapt to the local topological structure of the data (Huang, Li, & Ban, 2003; Babuska, Van der Veen, & Kaymak, 2002). Using the Lagrangian multiplier in (25), the membership value μ_{ij} can be calculated as follows:

IF $\left(D_{ij}^{'} = 0\right)$

THEN $\mu_{ij} = 1$ maintaining $\sum_{i=1}^{c}\mu_{ij} = 1$ \hfill (29)

ELSE $\mu_{ij} = \dfrac{1}{\sum_{k=1}^{c}\left(\dfrac{D_{ij}^{'}}{D_{kj}^{'}}\right)^{\frac{2}{q-1}}}$ \hfill (30)

The cluster centre v_i is updated as:

$$v_i = \frac{\sum_{j=1}^{n}\left(\mu_{ij}\right)^{q} x_j}{\sum_{j=1}^{n}\left(\mu_{ij}\right)^{q}} \tag{31}$$

To adapt to the structure of the cluster shape, the distance norm inducing matrix A_i is used which increases the distance of the furthest data points while decreasing those data points close to the cluster centre. A_i is defined as:

$$S_{fi} = \frac{\sum_{j=1}^{n} \left(\mu_{ij}\right)^{q} \left(x_{j} - v_{i}\right)^{T} \left(x_{j} - v_{i}\right)}{\sum_{j=1}^{n} \left(\mu_{ij}\right)^{q}} \tag{32}$$

$$A_{i} = \left| \rho_{i} \det \left(S_{fi}\right)^{1/P'} \left(S_{fi}\right)^{-1} \right| \tag{33}$$

where S_{fi} is the *fuzzy covariance* matrix, P' is the dimension of hyper-spherical cluster, and ρ_i is the cluster volume, which is usually set to 1. In the GK algorithm, the parameters values are set to $q=2$ and $\rho_i=1$ (Step 1) followed by the initialization of membership values μ_{ij} (Step 2). The cluster centre v_i is updated using (31) in Step 3.1, while the data distance norm is calculated (Steps 3.2 and 3.3) to iteratively update the membership value μ_{ij} using (29) and (30) (Step 3.4) until either fulfilling the specified threshold ζ or the maximum number of iterations is exceeded (Step 3.5). The detailed steps of the GK algorithm are given in Algorithm 3.

The performance of the GK algorithm is not very good for either small datasets or when data within a cluster are (approximately) linearly correlated, because in such cases the covariance matrix becomes singular. Babuska *et al.* (2002) overcame these drawbacks by considering the ratio of the maximum and minimum eigenvalues (Babuska, Van der Veen, & Kaymak, 2002) in calculating the *fuzzy covariance matrix*.

Algorithm 3: *Gustafson-Kessel* (GK) Algorithm

Precondition: Objects to be segmented, number of clusters c, threshold ζ and max_Iteration.
Post condition: The final segmented regions $\Re$.
1. Fix $q=2$ and set $\rho_i=1$.
2. Initialize μ_{ij}.
3. FOR $1=1,2,3,…,$ max_Iteration
    3.1 Update cluster centre v_i using (31).
    3.2 Compute cluster covariance matrix using (32) and (33).
    3.3 Calculate data distance norm by (28).
    3.4 Update $\mu_{ij}^{(l)}$ using (29) and (30).
    3.5 IF $\left(\left| \mu_{ij}^{(l)} - \mu_{ij}^{(l-1)} \right| \leq \xi \right)$ THEN STOP.

In summarising, the GK algorithm adapts the local structure of the cluster shape using a *distance norm inducing matrix A_i*, with the *modified GK* algorithm (Babuska, Van der Veen, & Kaymak, 2002) able to effectively handle both large and small datasets. These characteristics are exploited by using the GK algorithm as key part of the shape-based algorithm (Ameer Ali, Dooley, & Karmakar, 2006) for integrating generic shape information into the clustering framework. To clarify the performance of GK, a sample experimental result is provided in Figure 6.

4.5 MISR Algorithm

Based on the analysis, the fuzzy clustering algorithms including FCM, SFCM and PCM are highly dependent on the features used. For example, FCM using PI is suitable feature for one type image for segmenting objects while using PL produces better results for other. In some cases, FCM using CIL shows good segmentation performance (Ameer Ali, Dooley, & Karmakar, 2005a; Ameer Ali, Dooley, & Karmakar, 2005b; Ameer Ali, Karmakar, & Dooley, 2004a; Ameer Ali, Dooley, & Karmakar, 2004; Ameer Ali, Karmakar, & Dooley, 2004b; Ameer Ali, Dooley, & Karmakar, 2003). This raises an open question which feature set produces best segmentation results for which type of image (Ameer Ali, Dooley, & Karmakar, 2005a). Addressing this issue, Ameer *et al* proposed a new algorithm namely *merging initially segmented regions* (MISR) (Ameer Ali, Dooley, & Karmakar, 2005a) which merges initially segmented similar regions produced by clustering algorithm separately using a pair of feature set from PI, PL, and CIL. The detailed description of the MISR algorithm is given in Algorithm 4 with the full details in below.

It is shown in (Ameer Ali, Dooley, & Karmakar, 2005a), FCM using either CIL or PI is unable to properly segment the objects having *similar surface variations* (SSV) which requires to apply PL feature for segmentation process. For this reason, the foreground (objects) of an image (*f*) is segmented by FCM using CIL (Step 1) to separate the objects having SSV from those having *dissimilar surface variations* (DSV) (Step 2). To complete the segmentation process, objects with SSV are segmented by SFCM using PL (Step 3) as SFCM outperforms FCM mentioned in Section 4.2. For the case of objects having DSV, if there is more than one such object then it requires several processes to complete the segmentation process. In this regard, the feature sets for initial segmentation are selected based on the overlapping regions. To select the best feature set, two cases are considered, namely $\theta_1' > \frac{\pi}{4}$ and $\theta_1' \leq \frac{\pi}{4}$.

Figure 6. (a) Original crocodile image, (b) Ref. Image of (a), (c) Segmented results using GK

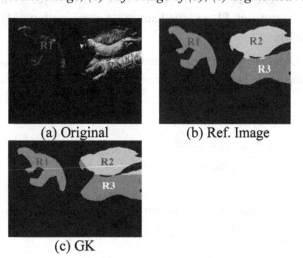

(a) Original   (b) Ref. Image

(c) GK

Algorithm 4: Fuzzy Image Segmentation Considering Surface Characteristics and Feature Set Selection (FISFS) Algorithm

Precondition: Objects (f) to be segmented, number of clusters c, *connectivity_Flag*, θ_1', θ_2' and θ_3'.

Post condition: The final segmented regions $\Re$.

1. Segment f by FCM using CIL into regions represented by R^C.
2. Find R_k^M and R^D for R^C.
3. IF ($k \geq 1$) THEN FOR $i = 1, \ldots, k$
        Segment R_i^M into M regions by SFCM using PL.
    END IF
4. IF ($D \geq 2$) THEN
            Connectivity_Flag=TRUE
            IF $D = 2$ THEN
                IF $\left(\theta_1' > \pi/4\right)$ THEN
                    Connectivity_Flag=FALSE
                    Segment R^D into D regions for R^I and R^C.
                ELSE
                    Select feature sets considering overlapping.
                    Segment R^D into D regions.
                END IF
            ELSE
                Segment R^D using R^I and R^C.
            END IF
    END IF

(i)   When $\theta_1' > \pi/4$, CIL dominates PL in the segmentation process and there is a high pixel misclassification risk when merging, because of the existence of two objects with vastly differing brightness values so PI will outweigh PL and the feature set combination of CIL and PI will generate a lower degree of overlap.

(ii) When $\theta_1' \leq \pi/4$, in order to decrease misclassification, the feature sets are selected based on the minimum value of the angle between the corresponding decision boundaries as follows:

$$feature\ sets = \begin{cases} CIL, PL & if\ \theta_1'\ is\ \min imum \\ PL, PI & if\ \theta_2'\ is\ \min imum \\ CIL, PI & if\ \theta_3'\ is\ \min imum \end{cases} \tag{34}$$

where θ_1' = angle between the decision boundaries for FCM using only CIL and PL; θ_2' = angle for FCM using only PL and PI; θ_3' = angle for FCM using only CIL and PI.

To apply the merging technique, two cases need to be considered namely if: i) there are more than two objects having DSV ($D>2$) and ii) two objects have DSV ($D=2$).

For the former, PI and CIL are used together with the *Connectivity_Flag* being set because using the connectivity property will correctly classify those pixels that are misclassified by PI. For the case of $D=2$, in applying the *Connectivity_Flag* is set to **FALSE** for $\theta_1' > \pi/4$ (Step 4), otherwise it is set **TRUE**. The reason for this is that if $\theta_1' > \pi/4$ it can be intuitively argued that connectivity should not be applied because while each region consists of having objects of distinct pixel intensities, either one or more pixels of a region may possess a similar intensity to another region that is actually connected to it. In such circumstances to reduce the possibility of pixel misclassification, connectivity is not applied. The complete processing steps for the MISR algorithm are given in Algorithm 4.

The experimental result of the MISR algorithm is given below in **Figure 7** (b) and **Figure 8** (b).

In analysing the overall segmentation performance of existing fuzzy clustering algorithms however, is highly dependent on the domain, image type and features used. For example, in using a particular clustering algorithm such as FCM, *pixel location* (PL) may be a better feature for one type of image, while *pixel intensity* (PI) is more appropriate for another, while in other cases, fuzzy clustering using a *combination of PI and PL* (CIL) may lead to superior segmented results. This raises the obvious question, as to which feature set produces the best results for which type of images, which clearly limits the generalization capability of any particular clustering algorithm (Ameer Ali, Karmakar, & Dooley, 2004b; Ameer Ali, Dooley, & Karmakar, 2003). This is why it is not possible to segment all objects in all images within a general framework i.e. existing clustering algorithms are unable to correctly segment all object types which limits their use in practical applications. This motivated generalise the existing clustering

Figure 7. (a) Original horse image, (b) segmented results using MISR

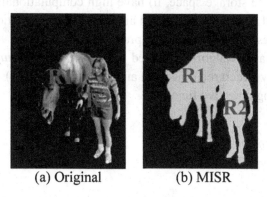

(a) Original   (b) MISR

Figure 8. (a) Original scene image, (b) Segmented results using MISR

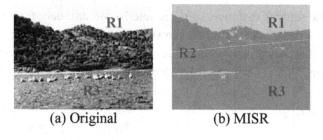

(a) Original   (b) MISR

algorithms thereby increasing their relevance to real world applications and hence developed MISR algorithm. The performance of the MISR algorithm is highly dependent on the initially segmented results, and while effective for certain image types, in other cases it is unable to correctly segment all objects because for instance, if the selected features contain PI for the initial segmentation of a particular image, it generates ambiguous results and the merging technique leads to poorer segmentation performance. This meant consideration had to be given to other features to be integrated into the clustering framework. As shape is perceptually very important in object recognition, this provided a strong incentive to examine the feasibility of incorporating shape information into the fuzzy clustering segmentation framework. The shape based fuzzy clustering algorithms are detailed in the following section.

5. SHAPE-BASED FUZZY CLUSTERING ALGORITHMS

The motivation to incorporate shape information into the fuzzy clustering framework is detailed in Section 4. The shape based algorithms are presented as follows.

5.1 Circular Shape-Based Clustering Algorithms

For many applications as for example contour detection of the heart's inner and outer left ventricle, segmentation is followed by recognition of curved or circular shaped objects. For this reason, a number of methods have been proposed using the Hough Transform with the aim of being able to segment circular, curved or arced shaped objects as detailed in (Chen & Chung, 2001; Athertom & Kerbyson, 1999; Olson, 1999; Chatzis & Pitas, 1997; Wu & Li, 1996-Bulot et al, 1996). These algorithms are restricted in their performance to segmenting only these regular geometric shapes and furthermore have some inherent problems: i) they require large storage space, ii) have high computational complexity, iii) are unable to detect substructure shaped objects, and iv) local and global peak detection in multi-dimensional accumulator array, which serves to limit their use in practical applications.

To address these issues, a new algorithm called *fuzzy c-shell clustering* (FCS) was introduced to detect and separate circularly structured objects in an image (Dave, 1990). This works by the iterative minimization of the following objective function:

$$J_s\left(\mu, V, R\right) = \sum_{i=1}^{c} \sum_{j=1}^{n} \left(\mu_{ij}\right)^q d_{ij}^2 \tag{35}$$

d_{ij} is the *shell distance* which measures the distance of a datum x_j from the ith cluster shell so $d_{ij}^2 = \left(D_{ij} - r_i\right)^2$, where r_i is the circular radius of the ith cluster prototype shell. This objective function is based on measuring the squared distance, so d_{ij}^2 is determined uniquely for a given datum x_j and prototype (v_i, r_i). Consider the two cluster example shown in Figure 9 for datum x_j, where v_1 and v_2 are the cluster centers, and r_1 and r_2 the corresponding cluster radii, with d_{1j} and d_{2j} as the data distances.

For the FCS algorithm, $\forall j$ and $c < n$, the following sets are defined as:

$$I_j = \left\{ i \Big| 1 \leq i \leq c \wedge d_{ij} = 0 \right\}, \tag{36}$$

Figure 9. Geometrical interpretation of shell distances d_{1j} and d_{2j}

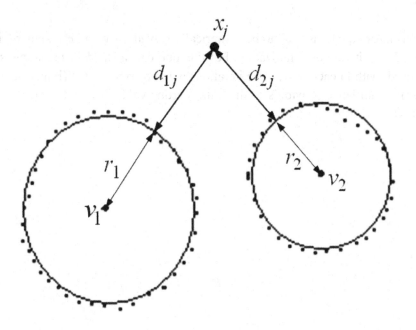

and

$$\bar{I}_j = \left\{1, 2, \ldots, c\right\} - I_j \tag{37}$$

The objective function J_s is then a globally minimal only if:

$$I_j = \varphi \Rightarrow \mu_{ij} = \frac{1}{\sum_{k=1}^{c}\left(\dfrac{d_{ij}}{d_{kj}}\right)^{2/(q-1)}} \tag{38}$$

or

$$I_j \neq \varphi \Rightarrow \mu_{ij} = 0, \ \forall i \in \bar{I}_j \ \text{ and } \ I_j \neq \varphi \Rightarrow \mu_{ij} = 0 \ \forall i \in \bar{I}_j \ \sum_{i=1}^{c}\mu_{ij} = 1, \ \forall i \in \bar{I}_j \ \text{ and } \ \sum_{i=1}^{c}\mu_{ij} = 1 \tag{39}$$

and the following equations are satisfied for cluster centre v_i and radius r_i:

$$\sum_{j=1}^{n}\left(\mu_{ij}\right)^{q}\frac{d_{ij}}{D_{ij}}\left(x_j - v_i\right) = 0 \tag{40}$$

$$\sum_{j=1}^{n} \left(\mu_{ij} \right)^{q} d_{ij} = 0 \qquad (41)$$

These two non-linear equations need to be numerically solved for v_i and r_i together with the objective function in (35) for iterative minimization. For this purpose, a standard technique such as Newton's method is used, with in each case, three iterations being recommended (Babuska, Van der Veen, & Kaymak, 2002). To initialize Newton's method, the starting value of v_i and r_i have to be calculated from the following:

$$v_i = \frac{\sum_{j=1}^{n} \left(\mu_{ij} \right)^{q} x_j}{\sum_{j=1}^{n} \left(\mu_{ij} \right)^{q}} \qquad (42)$$

$$r_i = \frac{\sum_{j=1}^{n} \left(\mu_{ij} \right)^{q} D_{ij}}{\sum_{j=1}^{n} \left(\mu_{ij} \right)^{q}} \qquad (43)$$

The main difference between the FCS algorithm and FCM is that FCS uses the ratio $\dfrac{d_{ij}}{D_{ij}}$ which is the ratio between the data distance from the cluster shell to that from the cluster centre, which can be construed as normalising d_{ij} by D_{ij}, which represents a true measure of scatter with respect to the cluster prototype (Dave, 1992b; Krishnapuram, 1995a; Krishnapuram, 1995b). Incidentally, FCM can be viewed as a special case of FCS where the shell radius is made zero. While FCS provides better results for detecting and representing circular substructures in two-dimensional datasets, since it involves the numerical solution of non-linear equations, it has limited practical value and so is unsuitable for generic object-based segmentation, except if the objects are either circular or ring shaped. Man *et al.* (Man & Gath, 1994) introduced *fuzzy clustering of ring shaped clusters* (FKR) to detect and separate objects having ring and compact spherical shapes by including the circular shape information into the bedrock of the FCM algorithm. The FKR algorithm works based upon the following objective function:

$$J_q \left(\mu, R, V \right) = \sum_{j=1}^{n} \sum_{i=1}^{c} \left(\mu_{ij} \right)^{q} d_{ij}^{2} \qquad (44)$$

subject to the constraints and parameters given in Sections 4.1 and above in this section. A graphical interpretation of d_{ij} in the FKR algorithm is illustrated in Figure 10.

The objective function in (44) is iteratively minimized for μ_{ij}, r_i, and v_i respectively by:

$$\mu_{ij} = \frac{1}{\sum_{k=1}^{c} \left(\dfrac{d_{ij}}{d_{kj}} \right)^{\frac{2}{q-1}}} \qquad (45)$$

Figure 10. Calculation of data distance (d_{ij}) and representation of other circular parameters

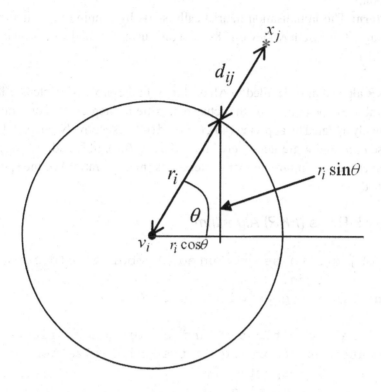

$$r_i = \frac{\sum\limits_{j=1}^{n}\left(\mu_{ij}\right)^q D_{ij}}{\sum\limits_{j=1}^{n}\left(\mu_{ij}\right)^q} \qquad (46)$$

$$v_i = \frac{\sum\limits_{j=1}^{n}\left(\mu_{ij}\right)^q \begin{pmatrix} x_{j1} - r_i \cos\theta \\ x_{j2} - r_i \sin\theta \end{pmatrix}}{\sum\limits_{j=1}^{n}\left(\mu_{ij}\right)^q} \qquad (47)$$

In terms of segmentation performance, FKR is very sensitive to the choice of initial conditions. If initial cluster centres and radii are randomly selected, the algorithm can become trapped in spurious local optima and so for this reason data are classified into two groupings: i) concentric patterns (ring shaped clusters and compact spherical), and ii) excentric (intersected) patterns, with examples of both being given in Figure 11 (a) and (b) respectively.

FKR is initialized depending on the type of data pattern as follows:

(i) **Concentric pattern:** The initial cluster centre v_i is chosen uniformly distributed around the centre of gravity (mean) of all data points. The initial cluster radius r_i is uniformly distributed between the minimum and maximum distance values between the centre of gravity of the whole dataset and the data point.

(ii) **Excentric pattern:** The initialisation heuristically starts by running three iterations of *fuzzy k-means* (FKM) algorithm (Gath & Geva, 1989) and then using its final values on μ_{ij} and v_i as initial conditions for FKR.

The complete FKR algorithm is detailed in Algorithm 5. In the processing steps, FKR is initialized using either (i) or (ii) above depending upon the actual data pattern (Step 2). For concentric data patterns, $\mu_{ij}, r_i,$ and v_i are iteratively updated by applying (45), (46) and (47) respectively (Steps 3.1.1–3.1.3), while for the excentric case r_i, μ_{ij} and v_i are iteratively updated using (46), (45) and (47) respectively (Steps 3.2.1–3.2.3) until either the maximum number of iterations (max_Iteration) or the specified threshold ζ in Step 3.3 is fulfilled.

Algorithm 5: Fuzzy k-Rings *(FKR) Algorithm*

Precondition: Objects to be segmented, number of clusters c, threshold ζ, and max_Iteration.
Post condition: Final segmented regions $\Re$.
1. Fix $q=2$.
2. Choose initial conditions v_i and r_i for concentric or μ_{ij} and v_i for excentric patterns according to the initialization process detailed in (i) or (ii) respectively.
3. FOR $1=1,2,\ldots,$ max_Iteration
    3.1 IF *concentric data patterns* THEN
        3.1.1 Update $\mu_{ij}^{(l)}$ using (45).
        3.1.2 Calculate r_i by (46).
        3.1.3 Update v_i using (47).
    3.2 ELSE
        3.2.1 Calculate r_i by (46).
        3.2.2 Update $\mu_{ij}^{(l)}$ using (45).
        3.2.3 Update v_i using (47).
    3.3 IF $\left(\left\| \mu_{ij}^{(l)} - \mu_{ij}^{(l-1)} \right\| \leq \xi \right)$ THEN STOP.

FKR works well for objects having ring, compact spherical shapes or a combination of these as shown by the example in Figure 12, where four circular objects have been correctly classified. It is not so effective in segmenting region-based circular objects as illustrated in the example in Figure 13, because the objects are not ring-shaped and improper scaling during iteration increases the misclassification error. FKR is also unable to segment arbitrary-shaped objects in an image as the example in Figure 14 (a) highlights, where both objects are arbitrarily shaped and though they are well separated FKR fails to segment them (Figure 14 (b)) because its mathematical model only considers circular information.

Figure 11. Typical examples of (a) Concentric data patterns, (b) Excentric data patterns

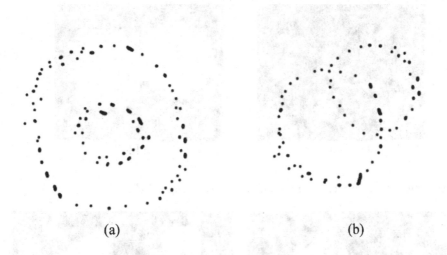

(a)　　　　　　　　　　　　　　(b)

FKR is also highly dependent on the type of datasets (concentric and excentric) and the initialization process.

As both FCS and FKR are designed for specific geometrically shaped objects such as rings and circles, they are only able to effectively segment these object types and are generally ineffectual in segmenting arbitrary-shaped objects. For this reason, both these well-established algorithms are only considered for comparative purposes in evaluating the various image segmentation results of the proposed algorithms in the shape-based framework.

5.2 Elliptical Shape-Based Algorithms

Since the ellipse is a generalized form of circle, to detect circular and elliptically shaped objects, the circular shape-based clustering theory presented in the previous section is now generalized. A number of algorithms to detect elliptical shaped objects have been introduced based on the Hough Transform

Figure 12. (a) Original example image, (b) Segmented results using FKR

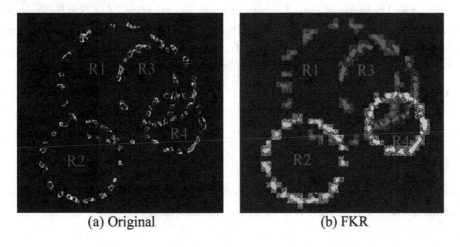

(a) Original　　　　　　　　　　(b) FKR

Figure 13. (a) Original sun image, (b) Segmented results using FKR

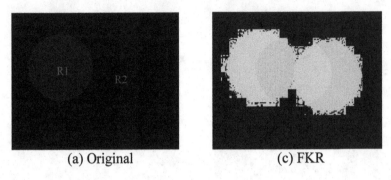

(a) Original   (c) FKR

Figure 14. (a) Original man image, (b) Segmented results using FKR

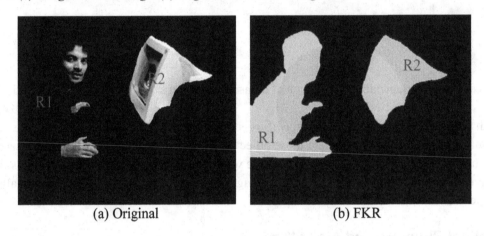

(a) Original   (b) FKR

(Zhang & Liu, 2005; Yang, Jiang, & Ren, 2004; Manso, Prestes, & Petraglia, 2003; Bennett, Burridge, & Saito, 1999; McLaughlin, 1998; Guil & Zapata, 1997), though these have the same drawbacks as those mentioned in Section 5.1 for the circular Hough Transform, together with the additional issue of bin splitting and bias (Dave, 1992b). These were the main factors behind the development of the *fuzzy c-ellipsoidal shell clustering* (FCES) algorithm (Dave, 1992b; Dave & Patel, 1990; Frigui & Krishnapuram, 1996; Dave & Bhaswan, 1992), which incorporates elliptic shape information into the shell clustering framework to detect and separate elliptical substructure as an extension of FCS. The various processing steps of FCS can be directly used, with the only difference being that for FCES, the norm is used in the distance measurement. The distance of a datum x_j from the shell is calculated as:

$$d_{ij}^2 = \left(D_{ij}' - r_i \right)^2 \tag{48}$$

$$D_{ij}'^2 = \left(x_j - v_i \right) A_i \left(x_j - v_i \right)^T \tag{49}$$

where A_i is the symmetric, positive definite matrix of the ith cluster that takes account of the orientation and scaling of the shell. The following two cases are considered for A_i.

Case 1: All A_i are the same i.e. $A_i = A$, for $\forall i$ such that A is a constant.

Case 2: $A_i \neq A_j$ for $i \neq j$, with all A_i being constants.

For both cases A_i must be known *a priori*, otherwise they must be determined, with an adaptive norm being introduced to find A_i in (Dave, 1992b; Dave & Bhaswan, 1992) as follows:

$$A_i^* = \left[\rho_i \det\left(S_{fi}'\right) \right]^{1/P'} \left(S_{fi}'\right)^{-1}, \ A_i^* = \left[\rho_i \det\left(S_{fi}'\right) \right]^{1/P'} \left(S_{fi}'\right)^{-1} \ 1 \leq i \leq c , \ 1 \leq i \leq c \tag{50}$$

$$S_{fi}' = \sum_{j=1}^{n} \left(\mu_{ij}\right)^q \frac{d_{ij}}{D_{ij}'} \left(x_j - v_i\right)\left(x_j - v_i\right)^T \tag{51}$$

where S_{fi}' is the covariance matrix, $det(A_i) = \rho_i = $ constant for each i and $\rho_i = 1$; A_i^* is the local minimum of the function and P' is the dimension of hyper-spherical shell.

While the FCES algorithm is effectively able to segment elliptically shaped objects, it involves either the solution of coupled non-linear equations or uses a non-linear algebraic distance, which can deteriorate the performance of the algorithm for scattered data and so is not suitable for practical applications. To address these issues, Gath *et al.* (1995) proposed a *fuzzy k-ellipses* (FKE) algorithm incorporating elliptical shape information into the framework of FCM, with the aim of being able to segment ring and elliptically shaped objects (Gath & Hoory, 1995) and their combination. FKE is based on the following FCM-type objective function:

$$J_q\left(\mu, V^{(1)}, V^{(2)}, R\right) = \sum_{i=1}^{c} \sum_{j=1}^{n} \left(\mu_{ij}\right)^q d_{ij}^2 \tag{52}$$

subject to all the constraints defined in Section 4.1.where

$$d_{ij} = \left\| x_j - v_i^{(1)} \right\| + \left\| x_j - v_i^{(2)} \right\| - r_i = D_{ij}^{(1)} + D_{ij}^{(2)} - r_i \tag{53}$$

and $v_i^{(1)}$, $v_i^{(2)}$ are the two foci, while r_i is the radius of the ith cluster. $D_{ij}^{(1)}$ and $D_{ij}^{(2)}$ are the Euclidean distances of a datum x_j from the two foci respectively. As illustrated in Figure 15, v_i, a_i and b_i are the ellipse centre, major and minor axes respectively, f_i is the half focal distance, θ_i is the tilt angle and $r_i = 2a_i$. FKE iteratively minimizes the objective function in (52) based on the following equations for cluster radius r_i, membership value μ_{ij} and the two foci $v_i^{(1)}$ and $v_i^{(2)}$.

Applying Lagrange optimization techniques to (52) with its constraints, the cluster radius r_i is:

Figure 15. Ellipse representation and its main parameters

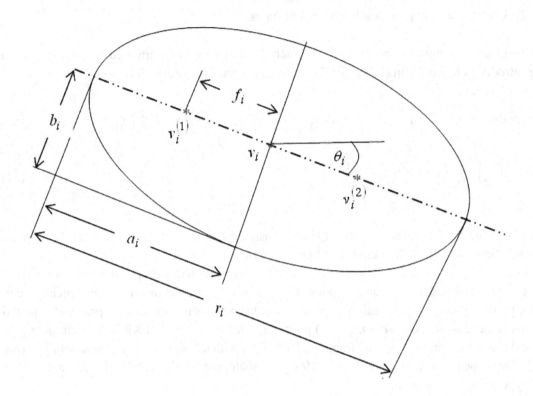

$$r_i = \frac{\sum_{j=1}^{n} \left(\mu_{ij}\right)^q \left(D_{ij}^{(1)} + D_{ij}^{(2)}\right)}{\sum_{j=1}^{n} \left(\mu_{ij}\right)^q}$$

(54)

The foci $v_i^{(1)}$ and $v_i^{(1)}$ $v_i^{(2)}$ and $v_i^{(2)}$ of the elliptical shape object are updated using:

$$v_i^{(1)} = \frac{\sum_{j=1}^{n} \left(\mu_{ij}\right)^q \begin{bmatrix} x_{j1} - \left(r_i - D_{ij}^{(2)}\right)\cos\theta_{ij}^{(1)} \\ x_{j2} - \left(r_i - D_{ij}^{(2)}\right)\sin\theta_{ij}^{(1)} \end{bmatrix}}{\sum_{j=1}^{n} \left(\mu_{ij}\right)^q}$$

(55)

$$v_i^{(2)} = \frac{\sum_{j=1}^{n} \left(\mu_{ij}\right)^q \begin{bmatrix} x_{j1} - \left(r_i - D_{ij}^{(1)}\right)\cos\theta_{ij}^{(2)} \\ x_{j2} - \left(r_i - D_{ij}^{(1)}\right)\sin\theta_{ij}^{(2)} \end{bmatrix}}{\sum_{j=1}^{n} \left(\mu_{ij}\right)^q}$$

(56)

and the membership value μ_{ij} is defined as:

$$\mu_{ij} = \frac{1}{\sum\limits_{k=1}^{c} \left(\dfrac{d_{ij}}{d_{kj}}\right)^{2/(q-1)}} \qquad (57)$$

FKE is initialized in the following way:

(i)   Initialize like FKR (see Section 5.1) based upon the data patterns.
(ii) Run 10 iterations of the FKR algorithm.
(iii) Updated cluster centre v_i is split into two foci using the fuzzy variance matrix of the ith cluster, S_{fi}:

$$S_{fi} = \frac{\sum\limits_{j=1}^{n} \left(\mu_{ij}\right)^q \left(x_j - v_i\right)\left(x_j - v_i\right)^T}{\sum\limits_{j=1}^{n} \left(\mu_{ij}\right)^q} = E_i^{-1} A_i^{''} E_i \qquad (58)$$

where E_i is the eigenvector and $A_i^{''}$ the eigenvalue matrix, which are respectively defined as:

$$E_i = \begin{pmatrix} \cos\theta_i & \sin\theta_i \\ -\sin\theta_i & \cos\theta_i \end{pmatrix} \qquad (59)$$

Figure 16. (a) Original image, (b) Segmented results using FKE

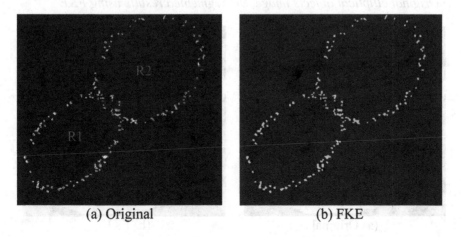

(a) Original   (b) FKE

$$A_i'' = \begin{pmatrix} \dfrac{1}{2}a_i^2 & 0 \\ 0 & \dfrac{1}{2}b_i^2 \end{pmatrix}$$

(60)

where θ_i is the tilt angle of the ellipse shown in Figure 15.

For FKE processing, the membership value μ_{ij} and the two foci $v_i^{(1)}$ and $v_i^{(2)}$ are initialized (Steps 2.1-2.3), while r_j, $v_i^{(1)}$, $v_i^{(2)}$, and μ_{ij} are updated using (54), (55), (56), and (57) respectively during each iteration (Steps 3.1-3.3) until fulfilling either the specified threshold ζ or maximum number of iterations (max_Iteration) in Step 3.4. The complete steps of the FKE algorithm are outlined in Algorithm 6.

FKE can segment effectively ring, elliptic or combination of both object types in an image. An example is shown in Figure 16, where FKE clearly separates the two objects, as one is circular and the other elliptical in shape. If however the objects are either circular or elliptic region-based in shape, FKE, like FKR in Section 5.1, cannot segment them due to improper scaling and its mathematical model only supporting shapes not regions as is clearly shown in Figure 17.

Not surprisingly, since FKE is a generalisation of the FKR algorithm, it also fails to segment arbitrary-shaped objects because it only considers elliptical shape information as confirmed by the example in Figure 18, where both objects despite being well separated, are neither circular nor elliptically shaped. Another drawback of FKE is that it is also highly dependent on the initialization and data type just like FKR.

Algorithm 6. Fuzzy k-Ellipse *(FKE) Algorithm*

Precondition: Objects to be segmented, number of clusters c, max_Iteration, threshold ζ.
Post condition: Final segmented regions $\Re$.
1. Fix $q=2$.
2. Fix the initial conditions for μ_{ij} and foci matrices $v_i^{(1)}$ and $v_i^{(2)}$:

Figure 17. (a) Original elliptical objects image, (b) Segmented results using FKE

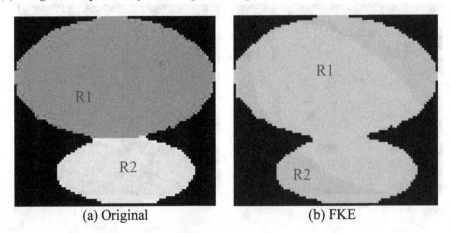

(a) Original   (b) FKE

Figure 18. (a) Original babacoot image, (b) Segmented results using FKE

 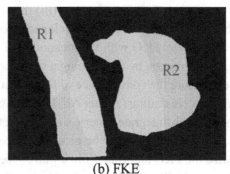

(a) Original   (b) FKE

```
     2.1 For the excentric case, start from any partition and run 10
iterations with the FKM algorithm. For the concentric case fix the
cluster centres uniformly distributed in the vicinity of the centre
of all data.
     2.2 Run 10 iterations of the FKR algorithm.
     2.3 Calculate fuzzy variance matrix S_{fi} applying (58) and then
find eigenvector and eigenvalue matrices.
     2.4 Split each cluster centre into two foci using (59) and
(60).
3.    FOR l=1,2,…,max_Iteration
     3.1 Update r_i using (54).
     3.2 Update v_i^{(1)} and v_i^{(2)} using (55) and (56) respectively.
     3.3 Update μ_{ij}^{(l)} by (57).
     3.4 IF (||μ_{ij}^{(l)} − μ_{ij}^{(l−1)}|| ≤ ξ) THEN STOP.
```

5.3 Generic Shape-Based Clustering Techniques

As the circular and elliptical shape based algorithms are unable to segment arbitrary-shaped objects, to address this limitation, a new shape-based clustering algorithm called *image segmentation using fuzzy clustering and integrating generic shape information* (FCGS) has been introduces, which incorporates generic shape information into the fuzzy clustering framework by exploiting a B-splines (Francis, 1994; Hearn & Baker, 1994) representation of an initial object's shape (Ameer Ali, Karmakar, & Dooley, 2008; Ameer Ali, Karmakar, & Dooley, 2005a). In the FCGS algorithm, the generic shape information is integrated considering the same technique used in the GK algorithm. The shape is initialized using B-splines while the intersection point is calculated using the polar coordinate system detailed in (Ameer Ali, Karmakar, & Dooley, 2005a). The shape of the cluster is iteratively updated using the concepts of circular shape clustering algorithm used in (Man & Gath, 1994). Even though the FCGS algorithm is able to segment arbitrary shaped objects in an image well, it suffers from the disadvantages including:

(i) it does not follow the optimization criteria clustering algorithm, (ii) the FCGS algorithm is unable to find out the proper intersection point, and (iii) the scaling of clusters during iterations is not proper. Addressing these issues, Ameer *at el* has developed a new *detection and separation of generic shaped object using fuzzy clustering* (FKG with the meaning of fuzzy k-generic shaped) algorithm that incorporates generic shape information by introducing a shape constraint to make certain the optimization criteria is upheld to both ensure the convergence of the objective function and preservation of the original object shape during iterative scaling (Ameer Ali, Dooley, & Karmakar, 2006; Ameer Ali, Karmakar, & Dooley, 2005b). To seamlessly integrate generic shape information into the segmentation process, an object shape descriptor i.e., a contour, needs to be provided as part of the initialization process.

To initialize the FKG algorithm, the initial shape contour points can be either provided manually or generated automatically which is adopted in FCGS (Ameer Ali, Karmakar, & Dooley, 2008). In order however, to automatically initialize the contour of the corresponding object in the FKG algorithm the following two steps are required: (i) the GK algorithm is used for initial segmentation and (ii) the boundary points of each region are scanned with all outliers discarded and these are then treated as the corresponding contour points. These contour points are used to measure the data distance from the boundary point in a similar strategy to that employed in the FCS, FKR, FCES, FKE, and FCGS algorithms.

It is the paramount the importance in any clustering-based segmentation strategy of calculating the data distance d_{ij} of a datum for subsequent use in an objective function. Using an analogous strategy to that used for the FCGS algorithm, d_{ij} is calculated from the respective contour shape points in the FKG algorithm. For the *butterfly* image and its corresponding B-spline shape representation in Figure 19 (a) and (b), the intersection point x'_{ij} on the contour of datum x_j can be calculated using either a Polar or Cartesian coordinate system.

In the FKG algorithm, the actual intersection point is calculated as shown in Figure 20 (c) and com-

Figure 19. (a) Original butterfly object; (b) Example of the intersection point between datum x_j and the B-splines shape contour of (a) along line l_1

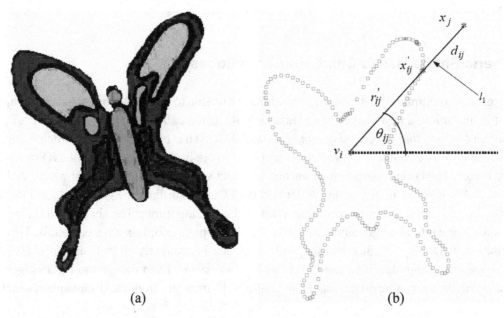

(a)   (b)

Figure 20. (a) Original branch image, Intersection point calculation of datum x_j on the B-splines representation shape using the Polar (b) and Cartesian (c) coordinate system

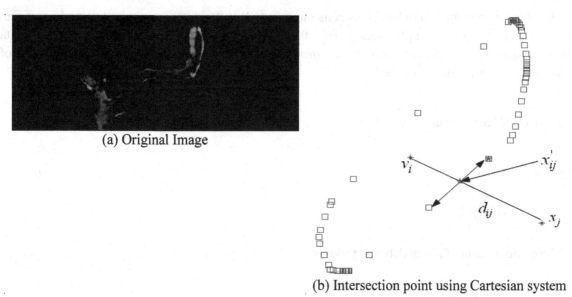

(a) Original Image

(b) Intersection point using Cartesian system

prises the following key processing steps: (i) find two points on the contour of the curve those are closest to and lie on opposite sides of the line l_1 and (ii) as the shape descriptor usually generates a straight line between these two consecutive contour points, the meeting point between the line passing through these two points and l_1 is the *intersection point* x_{ij}' of the corresponding datum x_j.

A unique feature of the FKG algorithm is that for the first time a dedicated shape constraint is incorporated into the fuzzy clustering framework to ensure convergence by preserving the initial shape of an object during the subsequent iterative shape scaling process. The shape constraint used for segmenting arbitrary-shaped objects is formally defined as:

$$\frac{r_{ij}'}{\sum_{t=1}^{n} r_{ij}'} = k_{ij} \tag{61}$$

where r_{ij}' is the distance between the intersection point x_{ij}' and the ith cluster centre v_i and k_{ij} is a constant of the jth datum in the ith cluster. The objective function for the FKG algorithm can now be formally defined based upon FCM (Bezdek, 1984) as follows:

$$J_q\left(\mu, V\right) = \sum_{j=1}^{n} \sum_{i=1}^{c} \left(\mu_{ij}\right)^q d_{ij}^2 \tag{62}$$

subject to $\sum_{i=1}^{c} \mu_{ij} = 1$ and $r_{ij}' \Big/ \sum_{t=1}^{n} r_{it}' = k_{ij}$ \hfill (63) where $d_{ij} = D_{ij} - r'_{ij}$

The objective function in (62) with its constraints in (63) is iteratively minimised using Lagrangian optimisation techniques. For optimisation, if $d_{ij} = 0$ then a HC (crisp) decision is necessary and the jth data will be classified into i^{th} cluster, otherwise the membership value will be updated based on the value of d_{ij}. The membership value is defined as:

IF $d_{ij} = 0$ THEN $\mu_{ij} = 1$ maintaining $\sum_{i=1}^{c} \mu_{ij} = 1$ (64)

ELSE $\mu_{ij} = \dfrac{1}{\sum_{k=1}^{c} \left(\dfrac{d_{ij}}{d_{kj}} \right)^{\frac{2}{q-1}}}$ (65)

The contour radius r'_{ij} is updated as follows:

$$r'_{ij} = D_{ij} - \frac{k_{ij} \sum_{t=1}^{n} D_{ij} - D_{ij}}{k_{ij} \sum_{t=1}^{n} \dfrac{1-k_{it}}{\mu_{it}} - \dfrac{1-k_{ij}}{\mu_{ij}}} \left(\frac{1-k_{ij}}{\mu_{ij}} \right)$$ (66)

When the second term in (66) becomes small i.e., tends to zero, the initial shape may become over-scaled when it is updated and so to reduce the impact of this effect, the r'_{ij} update is controlled as follows:

$$r'_{ij}(new) = \lambda r'_{ij} + (1-\lambda) r'^{(0)}_{ij}$$ (67)

where r'_{ij} and $r'^{(0)}_{ij}$ are the current and initial values of r'_{ij} respectively, and λ is an empirically selected data constant which is a trade-off between the current and initial object shapes.

Using the same optimisation technique as in (62) and (63), the ith cluster centre v_i can be calculated from:

$$f_x = x_{j1} - D_{ij} \frac{x'_{ij1} - v_{i1}}{r'_{ij}} + x'_{ij1} - r'_{ij} \frac{x_{j1} - v_{i1}}{D_{ij}}$$ (68)

$$f_y = S_{j2} - D_{ij} \frac{x'_{ij2} - v_{i2}}{r'_{ij}} + x'_{ij2} - r'_{ij} \frac{x_{j2} - v_{i2}}{D_{ij}}$$ (69)

$$v_i = \frac{\sum_{j=1}^{n}\left(\mu_{ij}\right)^q \begin{pmatrix} f_x \\ f_y \end{pmatrix}}{2\sum_{j=1}^{n}\left(\mu_{ij}\right)^q} \qquad (70)$$

where for an image, the 2-D data and cluster centre are given by $x_j = \begin{bmatrix} x_{j1} \\ x_{j2} \end{bmatrix}$ and $v_i = \begin{bmatrix} v_{i1} \\ v_{i2} \end{bmatrix}$ respectively. The complete steps for the FKG algorithm are provided in Algorithm 7.

So the total computational complexity of the FKG algorithm is $O(n\,m')$ i.e. it is dependent on the number of average cluster contour points m'. For most real world images, the number of contour points will be at least $O\left(\sqrt{\frac{n}{c}}\right)$ i.e. $O(m') = O(\sqrt{n})$ (Karmakar, 2002) so in the best case, the overall computational time complexity will be $O\left(n^{3/2}\right)$. However in the worst case, especially for the objects that comprise only the contour, then $n \cong c\,m'$ and the overall computational complexity of FKG will be $O(n^2)$.

In analysing the segmentation performance of the FKG algorithm, the segmented results were both qualitatively and numerically compared with seven other shape-based clustering algorithms, namely FKR, FKE, GK, FCS, FCES, FISFS and FCGS. Representative samples of the manually segmented reference regions together with the original images are shown in Figure 21 (a)-(b) to Figure 22 (a)-(b).

Algorithm 7. Detection and Separation of Generic Shaped Object using Fuzzy Clustering *(FKG)* Algorithm

Precondition: Objects to be segmented, the number of clusters c, max_Iteration and threshold ζ.
Post condition: Final segmented regions $\Re$.
1.   Initialize the shape.
2.   Find intersection point and calculate initial r'_{ij}.
3.   Calculate k_{ij} using (63).
4.   FOR $l = 1, 2, 3, …,$ max_Iteration

Figure 21. (a) Original camel image, (b) Segmented results of (a) using FKG

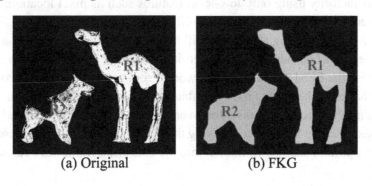

(a) Original   (b) FKG

Figure 22. (a) Original cow image, (b) Segmented results of (a) using FKG

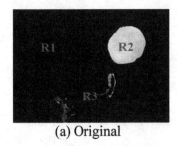 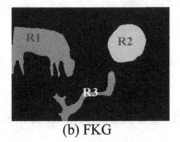

(a) Original   (b) FKG

4.1 Update $\mu_{ij}^{(l)}$ using (64) and (65).

4.2 Update r_{ij}' using (66) and (67).

4.3 Update v_i using (70).

4.4 IF $\left\| \mu_{ij}^{(l)} - \mu_{ij}^{(l-1)} \right\| \leq \xi$ THEN STOP.

In analysing the overall performance of the shape based fuzzy clustering algorithm, the circular shape based algorithm is suitable to segment only circular shaped objects. To generalise the performance of the circular shaped algorithms and to enhance the application area of the image segmentation techniques, the elliptical shape based algorithm is developed considering the elliptical shape information and these are fit for only elliptical and circular object segmentation. Since the circular and elliptical shape base algorithms are limited only to segment circular and elliptical objects respectively, the generic shape based fuzzy clustering algorithm is developed incorporating generic shape information into the fuzzy clustering framework which being able to segment arbitrary-shaped objects and hence broader the application area of segmentation.

6. SUMMARY

This chapter has reviewed various classical fuzzy clustering algorithms, with FCM being chosen as the design platform for the new clustering framework as it is able to incorporate object specific information like pixel location, intensity and shape within its generic structure.

For object-based image segmentation, classical fuzzy clustering algorithms like FCM are unable to segment objects satisfactorily using only low-level features such as pixel location, intensity and their combination. Different objects can be segmented well using different features in FCM, though no single algorithm is suitable for segmenting all objects within a general framework using a particular feature. To address this, Ameer *at el* introduced a new algorithm *merging initially segmented regions* (MISR) that aims to generalise the FCM clustering framework. From the critical analysis of the experimental results for MISR, it has been shown that its segmentation performance for objects having DSV is highly dependent on the initially segmented results. Moreover, in some cases MISR produced poor segmentation performance for objects having SSV due to applying the PL feature, so to address these matters a strategy is mandated that incorporates shape information into the clustering framework for segmentation.

The circular shape information is integrated into the clustering framework namely *fuzzy c-shell* (FCS) and *fuzzy k-rings* (FKR) to segment circular shaped objects. These algorithms are able to segment only circular shaped objects properly due to considering only circular information in segmentation process. As there are limited circular objects in real world, it demands to generalise the circular shaped algorithm. Since ellipse is a generalised form of circle, to improve the segmentation performance, the elliptical shape information is integrated into clustering framework namely *fuzzy c-elliptical shell* (FCES) and *fuzzy k-ellipses* (FKE) to segment elliptical, circular and combination of these two objects effectively. Both of these algorithms are unable to segment arbitrary shaped objects, as there are limited only in circular and elliptical in shape. For this, with the aim of segmenting generic shape based objects, *detection and separation of generic shaped objects using fuzzy clustering* (FKG) is developed and this is able to arbitrary shaped objects properly. This increases the application area of image segmentation and will be helpful to apply in real world object segmentation in MPEG-4 which is already applied for synthetic images.

REFERENCE

Ameer Ali, M., Dooley, L. S., & Karmakar, G. C. (2003). Fuzzy image segmentation using location and intensity information. In *Proceedings of the IASTED International Conference on Visualization, Imaging and Image Processing* (pp. 399-404).

Ameer Ali, M., Dooley, L. S., & Karmakar, G. C. (2004). Fuzzy image segmentation considering object surface similarity. In *Proceedings of the International Symposium on Communication Systems, Networks, and Digital Signal Processing* (pp. 516-519).

Ameer Ali, M., Dooley, L. S., & Karmakar, G. C. (2005a). Automatic feature set selection for merging image segmentation results using fuzzy clustering. In *Proceedings of the International Conference on Computer and Information Technology* (pp. 337-342).

Ameer Ali, M., Dooley, L. S., & Karmakar, G. C. (2005b). Fuzzy image segmentation combining ring and elliptic shaped clustering algorithms. In *Proceedings of the International Conference on Information Technology: Coding and Computing* (pp. 118-122).

Ameer Ali, M., Dooley, L. S., & Karmakar, G. C. (2006). Object based segmentation using fuzzy clustering. In *Proceedings of the IEEE International Conference on Acoustics, Speech, and Signal Processing*.

Ameer Ali, M., Karmakar, C. G., & Dooley, L. S. (2008). Image segmentation using fuzzy clustering and integrating generic shape information. *Malaysian Journal of Computer Science.*

Ameer Ali, M., Karmakar, G. C., & Dooley, L. S. (2004a). Fuzzy image segmentation using suppressed fuzzy c-means clustering. In *Proceedings of the International Conference on Computer and Information Technology* (pp. 363-368).

Ameer Ali, M., Karmakar, G. C., & Dooley, L. S. (2004b). Image segmentation using fuzzy clustering incorporating spatial information. In *Proceedings of the IASTED International Conference on Artificial Intelligence and Applications* (pp. 878-881).

Ameer Ali, M., Karmakar, G. C., & Dooley, L. S. (2005a). Fuzzy image segmentation using shape information. In *Proceedings of the IEEE International Conference on Multimedia and Expo (ICME'05)*.

Ameer Ali, M., Karmakar, G. C., & Dooley, L. S. (2005b). Fuzzy image segmentation of generic shaped clusters. In Proceedings of the IEEE International Conference on Image Processing (ICIP'05) (pp. 1202-1205).

Andrey, P., & Tarroux, P. (1998). Unsupervised segmentation of Markov random field modelled textured images using selectionist relaxation. *IEEE Transactions on Pattern Analysis and Machine Intelligence, 20*, 252–262. doi:10.1109/34.667883

Antonio, F. S., Candenas, J. M., & Martin, F. (1999). Membership functions in the fuzzy c-means algorithm. *International Journal on Fuzzy Sets and Systems, 101*, 49–58. doi:10.1016/S0165-0114(97)00062-6

Athertom, T. J., & Kerbyson, D. J. (1999). Size invariant circle detection. *Image and Vision Computing, 17*, 795–803. doi:10.1016/S0262-8856(98)00160-7

Babuska, R., Van der Veen, P. J., & Kaymak, U. (2002). Improved covariance estimation for Gustafson-Kessel clustering. In *Proceedings of the IEEE International Conference on Fuzzy Systems* (pp. 1081-1085).

Barni, M., Cappellini, V., & Mecocci, A. (1996). Comments on 'A possibilistic approach to clustering. *IEEE transactions on Fuzzy Systems, 4*(3), 385–396. doi:10.1109/91.531780

Basu, S. (1987). Image segmentation by semantic method. *Pattern Recognition, 20*, 497–511. doi:10.1016/0031-3203(87)90077-X

Baxes, G. A. (1994). *Digital image processing: Principles and applications*. Hoboken, NJ: John Wiley & Sons, Inc.

Bennett, N., Burridge, R., & Saito, N. (1999). A method to detect and characterize ellipses using the hough transform. *IEEE Transactions on Pattern Analysis and Machine Intelligence, 21*(7), 652–657. doi:10.1109/34.777377

Besl, P. C., & Jain, R. C. (1988). Segmentation using variable surface fitting. *IEEE Transactions on Pattern Analysis and Machine Intelligence, 10*, 167–192. doi:10.1109/34.3881

Bezdek, J. C. (1981). *Pattern Recognition with Fuzzy Objective Function Algorithm*. New York: Plenum Press.

Bezdek, J. C. (1984). FCM: The fuzzy c-means clustering algorithm. *Computers & Geosciences, 10*, 191–203. doi:10.1016/0098-3004(84)90020-7

Bloch, I. (1994). Fuzzy sets in image processing. In *Proceedings of the ACM Symposium on Applied Computing* (pp. 175-179).

Bulot, R., et al. (1996). Contour segmentation using hough transform. In *Proceedings of the International Conference on Image Processing* (pp. 583-586).

Canny, J. F. (1986). A computational approach to edge detection. *IEEE Transactions on Pattern Analysis and Machine Intelligence, 8,* 679–698. doi:10.1109/TPAMI.1986.4767851

Chacon, M. I., Aguilar, L., & Delgado, A. (2002). Definition and applications of a fuzzy image processing scheme. In *Proceedings of the IEEE Digital Signal Processing Workshop* (pp. 102-107).

Chatzis, V., & Pitas, I. (1997). Fuzzy cell Hough transform for curve detection. *Pattern Recognition, 30*(12), 2031–2042. doi:10.1016/S0031-3203(97)00025-3

Chen, M. S., & Wang, S. W. (1999). Fuzzy clustering analysis for optimizing fuzzy membership functions. *International Journal on Fuzzy Sets and Systems, 103,* 239–254. doi:10.1016/S0165-0114(98)00224-3

Chen, T. C., & Chung, K. L. (2001). An efficient randomized algorithm for detecting circles. *Computer Vision and Image Understanding, 83,* 172–191. doi:10.1006/cviu.2001.0923

Chintalapudi, K. K., & Kam, M. (1998). The credibilistic fuzzy c-means clustering algorithm. In *Proceedings of the IEEE International Conference on Systems, Man, and Cybernetics* (pp. 2034-2039).

Dave, R. N. (1990). Fuzzy shell-clustering and applications to circle detection in digital images. *International Journal of General Systems, 16,* 343–355. doi:10.1080/03081079008935087

Dave, R. N. (1992a). Boundary detection through fuzzy clustering. In *Proceedings of the IEEE International Conference on Fuzzy Systems* (pp. 127-134).

Dave, R. N. (1992b). Generalized fuzzy c-shells clustering and detection of circular and elliptical boundaries. *Pattern Recognition, 25*(7), 713–721. doi:10.1016/0031-3203(92)90134-5

Dave, R. N., & Bhaswan, K. (1992). Adaptive fuzzy c-shells clustering and detection of ellipses. *IEEE Transactions on Neural Networks, 3*(5), 643–662. doi:10.1109/72.159055

Dave, R. N., & Patel, K. J. (1990). Fuzzy ellipsoidal-shell clustering algorithm and detection of elliptical shapes. In . *Proceedings of the SPIE Intelligent Robots Computer Vision IX, 1381,* 320–333.

Derin, H. (1984). Byes smoothing algorithms for segmentation of binary images modelled by Markov random fields. *IEEE Transactions on Pattern Analysis and Machine Intelligence, 6,* 707–720. doi:10.1109/TPAMI.1984.4767595

Derin, H., & Elliot, H. (1987). Modelling and segmentation of noisy and textured images using Gibbs random fields. *IEEE Transactions on Pattern Analysis and Machine Intelligence, 9*(1), 39–55. doi:10.1109/TPAMI.1987.4767871

Dubes, R., & Jain, A. K. (1998). *Algorithms for clustering data.* Englewood Cliffs, NJ: Prentice-Hall.

Duda, R. O., & Hart, P. E. (1973). *Pattern Classification and Scene Analysis.* Hoboken, NJ: John Wiley & Sons, Inc.

Fan, J. L., Zhen, W. Z., & Xie, W. X. (2003). Suppressed fuzzy c-means clustering algorithm. *Pattern Recognition Letters, 24,* 1607–1612. doi:10.1016/S0167-8655(02)00401-4

Francis, S. H. (1994). *Computer Graphics.* Upper Saddle River, NJ: Prentice Hall.

Frigui, H., & Krishnapuram, R. (1996). Letters: A comparison of fuzzy shell-clustering methods for the detection of ellipses. *IEEE transactions on Fuzzy Systems, 4*(2). doi:10.1109/91.493912

Fu, K. S., & Mui, J. K. (1981). A survey on image segmentation. *Pattern Recognition, 13*(1), 3–16. doi:10.1016/0031-3203(81)90028-5

Gath, I., & Geva, A. B. (1989). Unsupervised optimal fuzzy clustering. *IEEE Transactions on Pattern Analysis and Machine Intelligence, 14*(7), 773–781. doi:10.1109/34.192473

Gath, I., & Hoory, D. (1995). Fuzzy clustering of elliptic ring-shaped clusters. *Pattern Recognition Letters, 16*(7), 727–741. doi:10.1016/0167-8655(95)00030-K

Geman, S., & Geman, D. (1984). Stochastic relaxation, Gibbs distribution, and the Bayesian restoration of images. *IEEE Transactions on Pattern Analysis and Machine Intelligence, 6*, 721–741. doi:10.1109/TPAMI.1984.4767596

Gonzalez, R. C., & Woods, R. E. (2002). *Digital Image Processing*. Upper Saddle River, NJ: Prentice Hall, Inc.

Gosh, A., Pal, N. R., & Pal, S. K. (1993). Self-organization for object extraction using multilayer neural networks and fuzziness measure. *IEEE transactions on Fuzzy Systems, 1*(1), 54–68. doi:10.1109/TFUZZ.1993.390285

Groll, L., & Jakel, J. (2005). A new convergence proof of fuzzy c-means. *IEEE transactions on Fuzzy Systems, 13*(5), 717–720. doi:10.1109/TFUZZ.2005.856560

Guil, N., & Zapata, E. L. (1997). Lower order circle and ellipse hough transform. *Pattern Recognition, 30*(10), 1729–1744. doi:10.1016/S0031-3203(96)00191-4

Gustafson, D. E., & Kessel, W. C. (1979). Fuzzy clustering with a fuzzy covariance matrix. In *Proceedings of IEEE Conference on Decision Control* (pp. 761-766).

Haddon, J. F. (1988). Generalized threshold selection for edge detection. *Pattern Recognition, 21*(3), 195–203. doi:10.1016/0031-3203(88)90054-4

Hansen, F. R., & Elliot, H. (1982). Image segmentation using simple Markov random field models. *Computer Graphics and Image Processing, 20*, 101–132. doi:10.1016/0146-664X(82)90040-5

Haralick, R. M., & Shapiro, L. G. (1985). Survey, image segmentation techniques. *Computer Vision Graphics and Image Processing, 29*, 100–132. doi:10.1016/S0734-189X(85)90153-7

Hathaway, R. J., & Bezdek, J. C. (1986). Local convergence of the fuzzy c-means algorithm. *Pattern Recognition, 19*(6), 477–480. doi:10.1016/0031-3203(86)90047-6

Hearn, D., & Baker, M. P. (1994). *Computer Graphics*. Upper Saddle River, NJ: Prentice Hall.

Hoppner, F., et al. (1999). *Fuzzy Cluster Analysis: methods for classification, data analysis, and image recognition*. New York: John Wiley & Sons, Ltd.

Huang, J. J., Li, S. Y., & Ban, X. J. (2003). A fast approach to building rough data model through G-K fuzzy clustering. In *Proceedings of the Second International Conference on Machine Learning and Cybernetics* (pp. 1559-1564).

Hung, M. C., & Yang, D. L. (2001). An efficient fuzzy c-means clustering algorithm. In *Proceedings of the IEEE International Conference on Data Mining* (pp. 225-232).

Jahne, B. (1997). *Digital Image Processing*. New York: Springer-Verlag.

Jain, A. K. (1981). Advances in mathematical models for image processing. In *IEEE Proceedings* (pp. 502-528).

Jain, A. K. (1989). *Fundamentals of Digital Image Processing*. Upper Saddle River, NJ: Prentice Hall, Inc.

Karmakar, G. C. (2002). *An Integrated Fuzzy Rule-Based Image Segmentation Framework*. Unpublished doctoral dissertation. Monash University: Australia.

Karmakar, G. C., Dooley, S. L., & Rahman, S. M. (2001). Review on fuzzy image segmentation techniques. In *Design and Management of Multimedia Information Systems: Opportunities and Challenges* (pp. 282-313). Hershey, PA: Idea Group Publishing.

Kohler, R. (1981). A segmentation system based on thresholding. *Computer Graphics and Image Processing, 15*, 319–338. doi:10.1016/S0146-664X(81)80015-9

Krishnapuram, R. (1994). Generation of membership functions via possibilistic clustering. In *Proceedings of the IEEE World Congress on Computational Intelligence,* USA (pp. 902-908).

Krishnapuram, R. (1995a). Fuzzy and possibilistic shell clustering algorithms and their application to boundary detection and surface approximation-Part II. *IEEE transactions on Fuzzy Systems, 3*(1), 44–60. doi:10.1109/91.366570

Krishnapuram, R. (1995b). Fuzzy and possibilistic shell clustering algorithms and their application to boundary detection and surface approximation-Part I. *IEEE transactions on Fuzzy Systems, 3*(1), 29–43. doi:10.1109/91.366564

Krishnapuram, R., & Keller, J. M. (1993). A possibilistic approach to clustering. *International Journal of Fuzzy Systems, 2*(2), 98–110. doi:10.1109/91.227387

Krishnapuram, R., & Keller, J. M. (1996). The possibilistic c-means algorithm: Insights and recommendation. *IEEE transactions on Fuzzy Systems, 4*(3), 385–396. doi:10.1109/91.531779

Krishnapuram, R., & Kim, J. (1999). A note on the Gustafson-Kessel and adaptive fuzzy clustering algorithms. *IEEE transactions on Fuzzy Systems, 7*(4), 453–461. doi:10.1109/91.784208

Kruse, R., Gebhardt, J., & Klawonn, F. (1995). *Foundations of Fuzzy Syztems*. New York: John Wiley & Sons, Inc.

Li, K., Huang, H. K., & Li, K. L. (2003). A modified PCM clustering algorithm. In *Proceedings of the IEEE International Conference on Machine Learning and Cybernetics (*pp. 1174-1179).

Liu, J., et al. (1997). A comparative study of texture measures for human skin treatment. In *Proceedings of the International Conference on Information, Communications, and Signal Processing*, Singapore (pp. 170-174).

Man, Y., & Gath, I. (1994). Detection and separation of ring shaped clusters using fuzzy clustering. *IEEE Transactions on Pattern Analysis and Machine Intelligence, 16*(8), 855–861. doi:10.1109/34.308484

Manso, P. M. B., Prestes, R. F., & Petraglia, M. R. (2003). Detection of ellipses using modified hough transform. In *Proceedings of the IEEE International Symposium on Industrial Electronics* (pp. 1151-1154).

McLaughlin, R. A. (1998). Randomized Hough transform: Improved ellipse detection with comparison. *Pattern Recognition Letters, 19*(3-4), 299–305. doi:10.1016/S0167-8655(98)00010-5

Medasani, S., Krishnapuram, R., & Keller, J. (1999). Are fuzzy definitions of basic attributes of image objects really useful? *IEEE Transactions on Systems, Man, and Cybernetics, 29*(4), 378–386. doi:10.1109/3468.769756

Olson, C. F. (1999). Constrained hough transforms for curve detection. *Computer Vision and Image Understanding, 73*(3), 329–345. doi:10.1006/cviu.1998.0728

Otsu, N. (1980). A threshold selection method from gray-level histogram. *IEEE Transactions on Systems, Man, and Cybernetics, 9*, 62–66.

Overheim, R. D., & Wagner, D. L. (1982). *Light and Color*. New York: Wiley.

Pal, N. R., & Pal, S. K. (1993). A review on image segmentation techniques. *Pattern Recognition, 26*(9), 1277–1294. doi:10.1016/0031-3203(93)90135-J

Pham, D. L., & Prince, J. L. (1999). An adaptive fuzzy c-means algorithm for image segmentation in the presence of intensity inhomogeneities. *Pattern Recognition Letters, 20*(1), 57–68. doi:10.1016/S0167-8655(98)00121-4

Prewitt, J. M. (1970). *Object Enhancement and Extraction*. New York: Academics Press, Ltd.

Rosenfeld, A., & Smith, R. C. (1981). Thresholding using relaxation. *IEEE Transactions on Pattern Analysis and Machine Intelligence, 3*, 598–606. doi:10.1109/TPAMI.1981.4767152

Ruspini, E. H. (1969). A new approach to clustering. In *Proceedings of the IEEE Conference on Information and Control* (pp. 22-32).

Schneider, A. (2000). Weighted possibilistic c-means clustering algorithm. In *Proceedings of the IEEE International Conference on Fuzzy Systems* (pp. 176-180).

Shen, Y., Shi, H., & Zhang, J. Q. (2001). Improvement and optimization of a fuzzy c-means clustering algorithm. In *Proceedings of the IEEE Instrumentation and Measurement Technology Conference* (pp. 1430-1433).

Spirkovska, L. (1993). *A summary of image segmentation techniques* (NASA Technical Memorandum).

Taxt, T., Flynn, P. J., & Jain, A. K. (1989). Segmentation of document images. *IEEE Transactions on Pattern Analysis and Machine Intelligence, 11*(12), 1322–1329. doi:10.1109/34.41371

Tizhoosh, H. R. (1997). *Fuzzy image processing*. Berlin, Germany: Springer. Retrieved from http://watfast.uwaterloo.ca/tizhoosh/fip.htm

Tolias, Y. A., & Panas, S. M. (1998). Image segmentation by a fuzzy clustering algorithm using adaptive spatially constrained membership functions. *IEEE Transactions on Systems, Man, and Cybernetics, 28*(3), 359–369. doi:10.1109/3468.668967

Wei, L. M., & Xie, W. X. (2000). Rival checked fuzzy c-means algorithm. In *Proceedings of the Acta Electronica Sinica* [Chinese] (pp. 63-66).

Wei, W., & Mendel, J. M. (1994). Optimality test for the fuzzy c-means algorithm. *Pattern Recognition, 27*(11), 1567–1573. doi:10.1016/0031-3203(94)90134-1

Wu, P. S., & Li, M. (1996). A novel hough transform for curve detection. *IEEE Transactions on Systems, Man, and Cybernetics, 4*, 2722–2727.

Yang, M. S. (1993). A survey of fuzzy clustering. *Mathematical and Computer Modelling, 18*(11), 1–16. doi:10.1016/0895-7177(93)90202-A

Yang, M. S., & Wu, K. L. (2004). A similarity-based robust clustering method. *IEEE Transactions on Pattern Analysis and Machine Intelligence, 26*(4), 434–448. doi:10.1109/TPAMI.2004.1265860

Yang, Z. G., Jiang, G. X., & Ren, L. (2004). Ellipse detection based on improved-GEVD technique. In *Proceedings of the World Congress on Intelligent Control and Automation* (pp. 4181-4185).

Yanowitz, S. D., & Bruckstein, M. A. (1988). A new method for image segmentation. In *Proceedings of the International Conference on Pattern Recognition* (pp. 270-275).

Zadeh, L. A. (1978). Fuzzy sets as a basis for a theory of possibility. *Fuzzy Sets and Systems, 1*, 3–28. doi:10.1016/0165-0114(78)90029-5

Zhang, J. S., & Leung, Y. W. (2004). Improved possibilistic c-means clustering algorithms. *IEEE transactions on Fuzzy Systems, 12*(2), 209–217. doi:10.1109/TFUZZ.2004.825079

Zhang, S. C., & Liu, Z. Q. (2005). A robust, real-time ellipse detector. *Pattern Recognition, 38*(2), 273–287. doi:10.1016/j.patcog.2004.03.014

Chapter 14
Bayesian Networks in the Health Domain

Shyamala G. Nadathur
Monash University, Australia

ABSTRACT

Large datasets are regularly collected in biomedicine and healthcare (here referred to as the 'health domain'). These datasets have some unique characteristics and problems. Therefore there is a need for methods which allow modelling in spite of the uniqueness of the datasets, capable of dealing with missing data, allow integrating data from various sources, explicitly indicate statistical dependence and independence and allow modelling with uncertainties. These requirements have given rise to an influx of new methods, especially from the fields of machine learning and probabilistic graphical models. In particular, Bayesian Networks (BNs), which are a type of graphical network model with directed links that offer a general and versatile approach to capturing and reasoning with uncertainty. In this chapter some background mathematics/statistics, description and relevant aspects of building the networks are given to better understand s and appreciate BN's potential. There are also brief discussions of their applications, the unique value and the challenges of this modelling technique for the domain. As will be seen in this chapter, with the additional advantages the BNs can offer, it is not surprising that it is becoming an increasingly popular modelling tool in the health domain.

DATA MINING IN THE HEALTH DOMAIN

As information systems are becoming more commonplace, healthcare routinely generates large clinical and administrative datasets in the process of patient care (Bates et al., 1999; Lee & Abbott, 2003; Nadathur, 2009). The collected information includes patients' history, diagnostic, therapeutic and interventions, regarding care facilities, occupancy, costs, claims and reimbursements, etc (Nadathur, 2009). Clinical

DOI: 10.4018/978-1-60566-908-3.ch014

trials, electronic patient records and computer supported disease management increasingly produce large quantities of clinical data (Becker et al., 1998; Hoey & Soehl, 1997; Matchar & Samsa, 1999; Pronovost & Kazandjian, 1999; Van der Lei, 2002).

Data generation capabilities in the Health Domain are growing faster than data analysis capabilities. Gigabyte-sized data sets are not uncommon. Two examples are the collection of functional magnetic resonance imaging (MRI) data describing brain activity (T. M. Mitchell, 1999) and the Australian Health Insurance Commission (HIC) datasets (Viveros, Nearhos, & Rothman, 1996). HIC has collected detailed claims information for the Australian population. The on-line claims file alone is said to be over 550 gigabytes containing five years of history (Viveros et al., 1996). Terabyte-sized datasets also exist. For example, a high-power microscope can rapidly obtain a 10-30 gigabytes image from a tissue sample. Thus, multiple images from a subject in a longitudinal study or a study across multiple layers of tissue can reach hundreds of gigabytes or terabytes (Kumar et al., 2008). Petabyte-sized data sets are on the way.

With the steady increase in electronic capture there has been a trend towards not only more extensive but also integrated information systems in healthcare (Bates et al., 1999; Nadathur, 2009; Staccini, Joubert, Quaranta, Fieschi, & Fieschi, 2001). There has been increasing ease of collecting data including over the networks. Linkages of clinical, administrative and external datasets are not uncommon (Stone, Ramsden, Howard, Roberts, & Halliday, 2002; Sundararajan, Henderson, Ackland, & Marshall, 2002; Williams et al., 2006). Such record linkages of routinely collected data has the potential to inform policy (Nadathur, 2009).

The trend towards increased electronic capture and data integration goes hand-in-hand with augmented efforts to standardise the capture, increasing obligation and willingness to collect quality data. This is especially seen in the recording of diagnoses; for example, the development of the International Classification of Diseases (ICD) (Hasan, Meara, & Bhowmick, 1995; Kugler, Freytag, Stillger, Bauer, & Ferbert, 2000; Stühlinger, Hogl, Stoyan, & Müller, 2000) which is the basis for refining the casemix funding found in many countries. There is also increased standardisation of nursing terminologies used to document diagnoses, interventions, outcomes, and goals in electronic systems (Lee & Abbott, 2003). Nowadays there are more stringent data collection requirements and standardisations in the form of state and national level data dictionaries (Anderson, 1986; Linnarsson & Wigertz, 1989; Moss, 1995).

With increasing availability of comprehensive data in health databases, data mining is growing in popularity. Data mining tools can go beyond mere description of data, and provide knowledge in the form of testable models and prediction of systems. Some of these analysis use techniques from machine learning.

Adopting probability theory as a basic framework *Bayesian Networks (BNs)* were introduced in the 1980s as formalism for representing and reasoning with problems involving uncertainty (Pearl, 1988). Since the beginning of the 1990s researchers are exploring its possibilities for health applications. As will be noted in this chapter, with their additional advantages the BNs can offer, it is not surprising that it is becoming an increasingly popular modelling tool in healthcare and biomedicine.

SCOPE OF THE CHAPTER

This chapter focuses on Bayesian Networks in healthcare and biomedicine. Note, when reference is made here to the 'Health Domain' it includes both healthcare (delivering care to patients, and the logistics and accounting thereof) and biomedicine (all sorts of medical, or even veterinary, research with potential bearing on healthcare).

In this chapter some background mathematics/statistics and examples are given to better understand Bayesian Networks and appreciate their potential. There are also brief discussions of the history and description of Bayesian Networks, relevant aspects of building the networks, its various applications, their unique value and the challenges of this modelling technique for the Health Domain.

The next section introduces the concepts of data analysis and places the Bayesian Network in the context of the larger data mining topic.

BACKGROUND CONCEPTS & THE CONTEXT

Why Apply Statistics to Data?

Data are usually subjected to statistical analysis for two related purposes: description and inference (Broyles, 2006; Elston & Johnson, 1995; Minichiello, Sullivan, Greenwood, & Axford, 1999). *Descriptive statistics* are used to summarise data numerically or graphically so as to be useful and yield insight about the study cohort(s). *Inferential statistics* are used to reach informed guesses or conclusions that extend beyond the immediate data alone (Greenland, 1990). In Inferential statistics, findings from a sample are generalized to pertain to the entire population. The process of drawing inferences, making predictions, and testing significance are examples of inferential statistics. Thus inferences may take the form of answers to Boolean (i.e. yes/no) questions (hypothesis testing), estimates of numerical characteristics (estimation), prediction of future observations, descriptions of association (correlation), or modelling of relationships (regression). Other common modelling techniques include Analysis of Variance (ANOVA) (for comparison of multiple groups on multiple independent variables and looking at both main and interaction effects), time series (Broyles, 2006), and data mining (Glymour, Madigan, Pregibon, & Smyth, 1996).

Data Mining, KDD, Machine Learning and Pattern Recognition

Data mining is a discipline lying at the interface of statistics, database technology, pattern recognition, machine learning, and other areas (Fayyad, Piatetsky-Shapiro, & Smyth, 1996; Han & Kamber, 2006). It is concerned with the secondary analysis of large databases in order to find previously unsuspected relationships which are of interest (Glymour, Madigan, Pregibon, & Smyth, 1997). Data mining is a process that uses a variety of data analysis tools to discover patterns and relationships in data that may be used to make valid predictions. Data mining is part and parcel of *Knowledge Discovery in Databases (KDD)* (Heckerman, 1996; Lee, Liao, & Embrechts, 2000; Mitchell, 1999).

Fayyad and co-workers describe KDD as "the nontrivial process of identifying valid, novel, potentially useful, and ultimately understandable patterns in data" (pp 40-41) (Fayyad et al., 1996). Knowledge discovery can be viewed as a multidisciplinary activity that exploits mathematics disciplines (statistics, information theory, uncertainty processing) and artificial intelligence (machine learning, pattern recognition, signal processing, expert systems, knowledge acquisition). Data mining is "a step in the KDD process that consists of applying data analysis and discovery algorithms that, under acceptable computational efficiency limitations, produce a particular enumeration of patterns (or models) over the data" (Fayyad et al., 1996) (p 41). Such models are expected to be both accurate and comprehensible to experts in the field.

Researchers from *Artificial Intelligence (AI)*, in the course of trying to understand how humans learn, attempted to develop methods for accomplishing the acquisition and application of knowledge algorithmically using computers; this they named as *machine learning*. Mitchell (T. Mitchell, 1997) described machine learning as being concerned with the question of how to construct computer program that automatically improve with experience. Developing computer programs that "learn" requires knowledge from many fields. Therefore in machine learning concepts and results from many fields can be found, including statistics, AI, philosophy, information theory, biology, cognitive science, computational complexity, and control theory (Hand, 1999). Machine learning overlaps heavily with statistics, since both fields study the analysis of data, but unlike statistics, machine learning is concerned with the algorithmic complexity of computational implementations.

Pattern recognition is a field within the area of machine learning (Bate & Edwards, 2006; Lee & Abbott, 2003). Machine learning algorithms are organized into taxonomy that is based on the desired outcome to be achieved (Draghici, 2000; Dreiseitl & Ohno-Machado, 2002; Saeys, Inza, & Larranaga, 2007). Machine learning algorithms such as decision trees, neural networks and genetic algorithms are examples of supervised learning algorithms. In the unsupervised learning approach the models are built from data without predefined classes.

There are a large number of machine learning methods available to the Health Domain (Berrar, Downes, & Dubitzky, 2003; Goldbaum, 2005; Goldbaum et al., 2005; Kim & Jung, 2003; Li & Gallin, 2005; Lucas, 2004; Maruster, Weijters, de Vries, van den Bosch, & Daelemans, 2002 ; Mitchell, 1997; Mitchell, 1999; Rupp, Wang, Rupp, & Wang, 2004; Song, Mitnitski, Cox, & Rockwood, 2004; Tigrani & John, 2005). In addition to the methods mentioned above, of particular interest to the Health Domain are methods that identify connections between input features and suggest networks of interaction, such as Bayesian Networks (Bayat et al., 2008; Blanco, Inza, Merino, Quiroga, & Larranaga, 2005; Le Duff, Muntean, Cuggia, & Mabo, 2004a, 2004b; Lee & Abbott, 2003; Lucas, 2004; Lucas, Van der Gaag, & Abu-Hanna, 2004; Rodin & Boerwinkle, 2005; Van der Gaag et al., 2008), and principled methods of dimensionality reduction such as Principal Component Analysis, Independent Component Analysis and Local Linear Embedding (Goldbaum, 2005; Goldbaum et al., 2005).

Formal construction of generalized graphic models is said (Bidyuk, Terent'ev, & Gasanov, 2005) to involve many methods of statistical simulation: examples include Component Analysis, Distribution Analysis, Hidden Markovian Models, Kalman Filters, Ising Models, etc. All of the above methods are within the framework of Bayesian graphic models and are said to be partial examples of the general formalism (Bidyuk et al., 2005; Heckerman, 1997; Heckerman & Breeze, 1995; Lee & Abbott, 2003; Lucas, 2004; Murphy, 2001; Pearl, 2000; Zipitria, Larranaga, Armananzas, Arruarte, & Elorriaga, 2008).

It should be noted that inductive inference is used as the common mechanism in knowledge discovery, data mining, machine learning, statistics, etc; namely, in disciplines that relate to learning from data. These disciplines look at raw data and then attempt to hypothesise relationships within the data, and newer learning systems are able to produce quite complex characterisations of those relationships. In other words, they attempt to discover understandable concepts. These disciplines – e.g., data mining and statistics – are not mutually exclusive, but rather represent a continuum of overlapping methods and goals all concerned with learning from data.

A BRIEF DESCRIPTION OF BAYESIAN NETWORKS

Bayes' Theorem

A BN is a directed acyclic graph that represents a probability distribution (Doan, Haddawy, Nguyen, & Seetharam, 1999; Mitchell, 1997); it encodes probabilistic relationships among variables of interest (Heckerman, 1997). Essentially, BNs use complex applications of the well-developed Bayesian probability theory, or Bayes' rule, to obtain probabilities of unknown variables from known probabilistic relationships. To understand BNs, one needs to be familiar with basic concepts such as the Bayesian probability approach, unconditional (or prior) probability, conditional (or posterior) probability, joint probability distribution, the Chain Rule, and Bayes' rule. Some of these concepts have been covered previously in this book. In the following sections the above concepts will be briefly revisited.

Thomas Bayes

At this point it is appropriate to start with the contributions of the man whose name today is so closely tied to methods in working with probability. The Reverend Thomas Bayes (1701 or 1702 to 1761) has become well known for his Theorem. Bayes did not publish any mathematical work during his lifetime under his own name. Indeed his major credited work was apparently found by a friend on his desk after his death and remained unpublished until 1763. His friend Richard Price set down Bayes' findings on probability in "Essay Towards Solving a Problem in the Doctrine of Chances" which was published posthumously in the Philosophical Transactions of the Royal Society (Bayes, 1763). That work became the basis of a statistical technique now called *Bayesian estimation*; this technique is used for calculating the probability of the probability of that event occurring on the basis of a prior estimate of its probability and any new relevant evidence.

Bayes' Rule of Conditional Probability

In short, *Bayes' rule of conditional probability* developed by Bayes concerns the prior probability of A being true without any knowledge of B. It is a widely used method of statistical inference applied to many real-world problems. The Bayesian approach is based on the concept of *posterior or conditional probability*: Pr (A/B) = x. The latter means that given an event B (and also everything that does not concern B), the probability of an event A is x. The *joint probability* of events A and B, or the probability of the two events occurring together, is denoted Pr (A, B). It is determined from the formula of total probability (Bidyuk et al., 2005): Pr (A, B) = Pr (A/B) X Pr (B) = Pr (B/A) X Pr (A). This in turn is the fundamental rule for calculating probabilities and the basis for the *Bayes' Theorem*: Pr (B/A) = (Pr (A/B) X Pr (B)) / Pr (A).

Lacave and Diez defined a finding as "a piece of information that states which certainty the value of a random variable" (Lacave & Diez, 2001)(p 2). Examples of a finding in the Heath Domain are the patient's demographic details and the facts recorded during history taking. This set of findings is called the evidence. *Probabilistic reasoning* consists of computing the posterior probability of the observed variables given the evidence; this process is called *evidence propagation*. For evidence propagation Bayes' Theorem is used directly or indirectly. The Bayes' Theorem is used when information about evidences (dependent variables) is available, and the essence of the analysis is to determine the probabilities of the original causal variables (Bidyuk et al., 2005). For example, when the conditional probability Pr (B/A) (of an event B occurring provided that an event A takes place) is available, the Bayes' Theorem allows solving the inverse problem, finding the probability of the event A if the event B has occurred.

Keith Devlin, writing for The Mathematical Association of America, expressed the opinion that Bayes' Theorem was largely ignored and unused for over two centuries before statisticians, lawyers, medical researchers, software developers, and others started to pay serious attention to it from the 1990s (Devlin, 2000).

As Devlin summarises:

"...What makes this relatively new technique of "Bayesian inference" particularly intriguing is that it uses an honest-to-goodness mathematical formula (Bayes' Theorem) in order to improve -- on the basis of evidence -- the best (human) estimate that a particular event will take place. In the words of some statisticians, it's "mathematics on top of common sense." You start with an initial estimate of the probability that the event will occur and an estimate of the reliability of the evidence. The method then tells you how to combine those two figures -- in a precise, mathematical way -- to give a new estimate of the event's probability in the light of the evidence. In some highly constrained situations, both initial estimates may be entirely accurate, and in such cases Bayes' method will give you the correct answer. In a more typical real-life situation, you don't have exact figures, but as long as the initial estimates are reasonably good, then the method will give you a better estimate of the probability that the event of interest will occur. Thus, in the hands of an expert in the domain under consideration, someone who is able to assess all the available evidence reliably, Bayes' method can be a powerful tool...." (Devlin, 2000).

In order to better understand the application of Bayes' Theorem a simple example from the Health Domain, the pathology test, is described below:

Example Illustrating Bayes' Theorem (Based on (Sutherland, 1998), with Modifications)

An inner city medical practice suspects that 10% of the patients in their practise have a disease called 'D'. The local pathology laboratory has reported that the probability of detecting this disease using their established blood test is 0.95. The false positive rate for the test is said to be 0.02. After naming the events 'patient has the D' as 'D' and the 'blood test is positive' as 'T', the above information can be summarised as follows:

Practice patients' probability of having D or Pr(D) = 0.10;
Probability of a positive blood test given that the patient has D or Pr(T/D) = 0.95; and
Probability of a positive blood test given that there is no D or Pr(T/^D) = 0.02.

Note here the notation "^" means 'no or not'. The Pr(D) denotes a *prior or unconditional probability*, i.e. the probability of an event occurring when no other information/evidence is available.

Now the four questions of interest to both the pathology unit and the clinical practice are:

Probability of patient having D, given that blood test is positive or Pr(D/T)
Probability of patient not having D, given that the blood test is negative or Pr(^D/^T)

Probability of patient not having D, given that blood test is positive or Pr(^D/T)

Probability of patient having D, given that blood test is negative or Pr(D/^T)

Naturally, the aim is to minimise or eliminate the third (false positive) and, especially, fourth (false negative) options above.

To find answer to the first question – i.e. Probability of patient having D, given that blood test is positive, or Pr(D/T) – the Bayes' Theorem can be written as follows:

Pr(D/T) = (Pr(T/D) X Pr(D)) / Pr(T)

On the right hand side of the equation the values of the numerator are already known, but not the denominator, Pr(T), or the probability of a positive blood test result. This can be calculated. There are two ways that a patient could have a positive blood test result: (a) patient has the D and the blood test is positive, i.e. D & T or; (b) patient does not have the D and blood test is positive, i.e. ^D & T. Adding together the probabilities of both these scenarios gives Pr(T):

Pr(T) = Pr (D & T) + Pr (^D & T)

Using the Second Axiom of Probability (i.e. the probability of the entire event space is 1.) one can derive:

Pr(D & T) = Pr(T/D) X Pr(D), and

Pr(^D & T) = Pr(T/^D) X Pr(^D)

This gives the answer to Pr(T):

Pr(T) = Pr(T/D) X Pr(D) + Pr(T/^D) X Pr(^D)

= 0.95 X 0.10 + 0.02 X   0.90

=   0.113

Substituting the above value into Bayes' Theorem to obtain Probability of patient having D, given that blood test is positive or Pr(D/T):

Pr(D/T) = (Pr(T/D) X Pr(D)) / Pr(T)

= 0.95 X 0.10 /   0.113

=   0.841

Probability of patient not having D, given that blood test is positive or Pr(^D/T) is

Pr(^D/T) = 1 – Pr(D/T)

= 1 -   0.841

=   0.159

To calculate probability of patient having the D given that blood test is negative, or Pr(D/^T), requires Bayes' Theorem:

Pr(D/^T) = (Pr(^T/D) X Pr(D)) / Pr(^T)

Pr(T) has been already been worked out above, so

Pr(D/^T) = (0.05 X 0.10) / (1 -   0.841)

=   0.032

Probability of patient not having D, given that blood test is negative or, Pr(D/^T), is simply:

Pr(^D/^T) = 1 -   0.032

=   0.968

The example shows how *Bayes' Theorem* can relate two events. The Theorem can also be used to relate many events by connecting them together. This we will see in an example provided later. Before giving a second example, the structure of Bayesian Networks will be explained.

BN Structure

Bayesian networks are graphic models of events and processes based on combined results from probability and graph theories (Bidyuk et al., 2005). They are said to be closely related to influence diagrams used for decision making (Bidyuk et al., 2005). Despite their name, these networks are not necessarily associated with Bayesian methods. Indeed, it is common to use frequentists methods (of likelihood function) to estimate the parameters of the conditional probability distribution. However, the name is derived from *Bayes' rule of probabilistic inference* (Murphy, 2001) which was described above.

Structurally, a BN is a *directed acyclic graph (DAG)* with a set of vertices representing stochastic variables, and a set of arcs, representing statistical dependences and independences among the variables of interest (Doan et al., 1999; Heckerman, 1997; Mitchell, 1997; Visscher, Lucas, Schurink, & Bonten, 2005). This graphical model thus specifies a complete joint probability distribution over all the variables. Therefore, the term *directed graphical model* is perhaps a more appropriate name for these networks; allowing contrast with undirected graphic models, sometimes called *Markovian random fields* (Bidyuk et al., 2005).

Now describing each of the components of this directed acyclic graph:

Nodes and Arcs

The word "*node*" is used as a synonym of the word "*variable*" or "*a dataset attribute*". Thus in a BN, each node represents a problem variable, and each *arc* between nodes represents a conditional dependency or probabilistic correlation between these variables (Bidyuk et al., 2005; Kim & Jung, 2003). A BN node is a discrete variable with a finite number of states or a continuous Gaussian random variable (Bidyuk et al., 2005). The edges between nodes represent causal relationships between them. A BN is said to be causal when all of its links are causal (Lacave & Diez, 2001). Since a BN is a DAG, no route begins and ends at the same node (Bidyuk et al., 2005).

Conditional Independence

In general, a BN describes the probability distribution over a set of variables by specifying a set of conditional independence assumptions along with a set of conditional probabilities (Kim & Jung, 2003). Each node contains a conditional probability table that contains probabilities of the node being a specific value given the values of its parents. As seen from the examples given in this chapter, the joint probability for any desired assignment of values can be computed by using Bayes' rule. A BN encodes a unique joint probability distribution, which can be easily computed using the *Chain Rule*. The Chain Rule allows the use of the knowledge of the derivatives of functions to find the derivative of the composition. Knowing the joint probability distribution, one can answer all possible inference queries by *marginalization* (summing out over irrelevant variables). *Propagation* is the process of calculating a posteriori probabilities for the non-observed node(s) based on evidences or the values of observed nodes/variables (Bidyuk et al., 2005). The term *posteriori* refers to 'from effect(s) to cause(s)'.

The types of paths (including lack thereof) between variables indicate probabilistic independence (Doan et al., 1999). If nodes (variables) are not connected by arcs, then they are considered *conditionally independent* (Bidyuk et al., 2005).

Parent Node, Causal Relationship, Absolute & Conditional Probabilities

A *causal node* is called the *parent node*. Especially in large belief networks the term *root node is used for any nodes* without parents and *leaf node* for any node without children. Child nodes are conditionally dependent upon their parent nodes. Generally a node with no parent nodes (i.e., edges directed to it) is represented by a table of *unconditional probabilities* (Bidyuk et al., 2005). Unconditional probabilities are also known as absolute probabilities. Since the root nodes have no parent nodes their tables just contain *absolute probabilities*. If a node has parents (i.e. one or several edges directed to it), then it is characterized by a table of conditional probabilities (Bidyuk et al., 2005).

Quantitative probability information is specified in the form of *conditional probability tables* (CPT) (Doan et al., 1999). For each node the table specifies the probability of each possible state of the node given each possible combination of states of its parents. That is, the table contains conditional probabilities that the node is in a specific state for definite configuration of states of its parents. The number of elements in the table of conditional probabilities of a discrete node of a BN is a product of the numbers of possible states of all of its parent nodes (Bidyuk et al., 2005). This explains why BNs are also known as *casual probabilistic networks*.

Figure 1. A three node BN

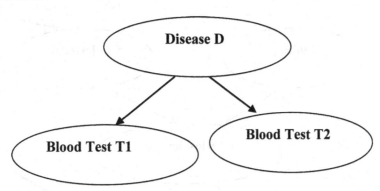

It is the probability calculation process that is behind decision-making based on BNs under uncertainty (Bidyuk et al., 2005). Uncertainties are eliminated in a BN by calculating the node state probabilities based on information about (a part of) the values of the other nodes of the network. The Bayesian approach to the analysis of uncertainties and modern methods of classical probability theory is a mathematical basis for the above (Bidyuk et al., 2005).

A Simple Example of a Bayesian Methods (modified from (Sutherland, 1998))

The example given for illustrating the Bayes' Theorem is expanded here to a three node BN (Figure 1). As mentioned in the previous example, a false negative on a blood test can be a more serious matter than a false positive. Therefore, the pathology unit has introduced a second test (T2) for detection of D disease. The two tests are independent, with an error in one not increasing the chance of error in the other. Here the disease D state of the patient drives (as represented by the arrow direction) the results in the two tests/nodes, blood test T1 and blood test T2 – in other words, the results of the two blood tests can be said to be driven or caused by the disease D.

One of question would be: If both of the blood tests are positive then what is the probability that the patient has the D, i.e. Pr(D/T1&T2). Writing out Bayes' Theorem for this case:

Pr(D/T1&T2) = (Pr(T1&T2/D) X Pr(D)) / Pr(T1&T2)

There are two values in the above equation which are not known immediately: Pr(T1&T2/D) and Pr(T1&T2). Since the two blood tests have been declared as independent, Pr(T1&T2/D) can be worked out as follows:

Pr(T1&T2/D) = Pr(T1/D) X Pr(T2/D)

The value of Pr(T1^T2) needs to be calculated. As before, Pr(T1&T2) can be calculated by breaking it down into two separate scenarios: the patient has D and both the blood tests are positive and the patient does not have D and both tests are positive. As before, applying the Second Axiom of Probability gives:

Figure 2. Part of a larger BN for stroke and heart disease

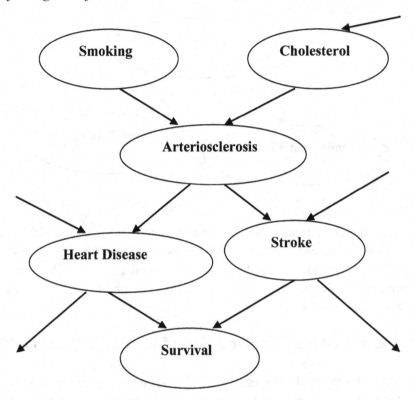

$Pr(T1 \& T2) = Pr(T1\&T2/D) \times Pr(D) + Pr(T1\&T2/^\wedge D) \times Pr(^\wedge D)$

Since the two tests are independent, the above formula can be rewritten as follows:

$Pr(T1\&T2) = Pr(T1/D) \times Pr(T2/D) \times Pr(D) + Pr(T1/^\wedge D) \times Pr(T2/^\wedge D) \times Pr(^\wedge D)$

$= 0.95 \times 0.95 \times 0.10 + 0.02`\times 0.02 \times$ 0.90

$=$ 0.09061

Using the value obtained above, Bayes' Theorem gives the following results:

$Pr(D/T1\&T2) = (Pr(T1\&T2/D) \times Pr(D)) / Pr(T1\&T2)$

Table 1. Probability distribution for stroke

Pr (stroke / Arteriosclerosis)	Pr (stroke / no Arteriosclerosis)
Pr (no stroke / Arteriosclerosis)	Pr (no stroke / no Arteriosclerosis)

$= (\Pr(T1/D) \times \Pr(T2/D) \times \Pr(D)) / \Pr(T1\&T2)$

$= (0.95 \times 0.95 \times 0.10) / \qquad\qquad\qquad\qquad 0.09061$

$= \qquad\qquad\qquad\qquad\qquad\qquad\qquad\qquad 0.99602$

Previously the probability that the patient had D, given positive result on only blood test 1 was calculated as 0.841. This has now increased to 0.996. When both the established and the new tests are positive then one is more certain that the patient does in fact have the disease.

Taking the scenario of one test being positive and the other negative, one can assume that one of the tests is giving a false negative. However, it is not known which one. The question is whether the patient has the disease D or not, i.e. $\Pr(D/T1 \& {^\wedge}T1)$. Again writing down Bayes' Theorem:

$\Pr(D/T1 \& {^\wedge}T2) = (\Pr(T1\& {^\wedge}T2/D) \times \Pr(D)) / \Pr(T1\&{^\wedge}T1)$

Knowing that the tests are independent, a similar reasoning to above can be used to calculate $\Pr(T1\&{^\wedge}T2/D)$ and $\Pr(T1\&{^\wedge}T2)$.

$\Pr(T1\&{^\wedge}T2/D) = \Pr(T1/D) \times \Pr({^\wedge}T2/D)$ and

$\Pr(T1\&{^\wedge}T2) = \Pr(T1\&{^\wedge}T2/D) \times \Pr(D) + \Pr(T1\&{^\wedge}T2/{^\wedge}D) \times \Pr({^\wedge}D)$

$= \Pr(T1/D) \times \Pr({^\wedge}T2/D) \times \Pr(D) + \Pr(T1/{^\wedge}D) \times \Pr({^\wedge}T2/{^\wedge}D) \times \Pr(D)$

$= 0.95 \times 0.05 \times 0.10 + 0.02 \times 0.99 \times \qquad\qquad\qquad 0.90$

$= \qquad\qquad\qquad\qquad\qquad\qquad\qquad\qquad 0.02257$

Substituting the above value into to the original Bayes' Theorem:

$\Pr(D/T1 \& {^\wedge}T2) = (\Pr(T1\& {^\wedge}T2/D) \times \Pr(D)) / \Pr(T1\&{^\wedge}T2)$

$= (\Pr(T1/D) \times \Pr({^\wedge}T2/D) \times \Pr(D)) / \Pr(T1\&{^\wedge}T2)$

$= (0.95 \times 0.05 \times 0.10) / \qquad\qquad\qquad\qquad 0.02257$

$= \qquad\qquad\qquad\qquad\qquad\qquad\qquad\qquad 0.2105$

A Bayesian is someone who interprets probability as degree of "belief", hence the term *Bayesian Belief Network*. In the above example the belief has increased to 0.2105 (from 0.159); thus a positive result also in the second test slightly increases our belief that the patient is indeed positive.

The interpretation given in the example above contrasts with the *frequentist interpretation* (Cloutier & Sirois, 2008; Greenland, 2000; Sheingold, 2001). There are differences between Bayesian probability and classical probability (Heckerman, 1996). Bayesian probability of an event is a person's degree of belief in that event, whereas the classical probability is the probability that an event will occur. Below, find a more sophisticated example of a BN.

A Multi Node Example of Bayesian Network

Figure 2 is a part (of a larger) BN which encodes dependence and independence information among the random variables shown, and a set of local probability distribution tables, of which one for stroke variable is shown below (Table 1).

The network and the table show that the influence of one variable on another can be assessed. This is the reason why BNs are also called *Influence Diagrams*. The digraph of the network model's stroke is depicted here as independent of heart disease with a common parent, arteriosclerosis. As seen from the previous example, when nodes (variables) are linked in the form of a network, Bayes' rule helps to predict the outcomes of events that are dependent on another event(s). Diagnostic reasoning is conducted for inferences of causes from effects. In this case, given there is heart disease the probability of causal arteriosclerosis is calculated. Causal and inter-causal inferences are conducted from causes to effects. In the example, given that there is arteriosclerosis, one can ascertain the probability of stroke or heart disease. An inter-causal inference is between causes of a common effect. Given arteriosclerosis with history of smoking, inter-causal inference is conducted to obtain the probability of high cholesterol. Mixed inferences are the combination of two or more of the other three types of inferences.

BUILDING BAYESIAN NETWORKS

Data mining using a BN consists primarily of two parts (Kim & Jung, 2003; Lee, Fung, & Fu, 2003). The first part is the construction of the BN structure or the DAG which encodes probabilistic relationships among variables. The second part is the assessment of the parameters, namely prior and posterior probabilities. This is followed by the training and testing of the network using an existing dataset.

To follow are brief discussions, with a Health Domain flavour, of the general principles underlying the construction, the methods of learning and classification.

Overview of BN Construction

Once the BN is built, it constitutes an efficient device to perform probabilistic inference. However, the building of the networks is not simple (Bidyuk et al., 2005; Lucas et al., 2004). The common steps in the construction of BNs are listed below.

Common Steps in the Construction of BNs

- Dataset selection or generation
- Selection and preparation of relevant variables
- Compilation of expert judgements and documentation of processes
- Identification of relationships among the variables and generation of network topology (nodes and edges)

- Identification of logistic constraints and assignment of probabilities for optimum network topology
- Network learning if semi or fully automatic learning is required
- If appropriate, use of the network for classification
- Sensitivity analysis and evaluation
- Presentation of the results to the user
- Feedback and refinement of the network

Since developing a BN is said to be a creative process with cyclic iteration and refinement, an ontology may be developed to support the process (Lucas et al., 2004). The following sections briefly describe the variety of ways of deriving structure and conditional probabilities from datasets.

Source of Knowledge Input

The structure and conditional probabilities necessary for characterizing the BN can be provided by domain expert knowledge or via automatic or semi-automatic learning (Bidyuk et al., 2005; A. H. Lee et al., 2003).

Domain Expert Knowledge-Based Construction

The manual building of a network structure can be solely based on a domain expert knowledge, experience and observations. Many of the BNs developed to date for real-life applications in healthcare and biomedicine have been constructed using only expert background knowledge (Lucas, 2004; Lucas et al., 2004). The common construct method is causal influence considering conditional independence (Lee et al., 2003), i.e. from cause(s) to effect(s). Potential problem with this method includes that it can be time consuming, and can be subjective and thus prone to errors and omissions.

A major part of medical knowledge concerns diseases that are uncommon or even rare. The uncommon nature of these disorders renders it impossible to collect data on a sufficiently large number of patients to develop machine-learning models that faithfully reflect the subtleties of the condition. An alternative is to develop a BN with the help of clinical experts. Lack of data is then compensated for by eliciting the structure with its associated local probability distributions from the experts (Lucas, 2001). The resulting network can be subsequently evaluated using the available dataset.

It should be mentioned here that Lucas and co-workers (2004) felt that it is still an open question as to whether or not building a BN by hand would result in a network of higher quality when compared to learning it from data,. One would expect that, in many areas of biomedicine, human knowledge of the underlying (patho) physiological processes is more robust than the knowledge embedded in a data set of limited size. However, it is believed (Lucas et al., 2004) that, to-date, there is little evidence to corroborate this expectation.

Automatic or Semi-Automatic Construction

With the increasing availability of clinical and biological data, automated learning of the networks from data is evidently the more feasible alternative (Lucas, 2004). Building of the networks can be fully or partially assisted by learning (training) algorithms. These algorithms can be applied to the process of knowledge discovery from large datasets and in determining the independence and dependence of nodes/ variables by finding direct relationships between the nodes/variables. If a comprehensive and good-quality dataset is available, a BN can be fully learnt from the data without explicit access to domain experts (Lucas et al., 2004).

Integrating background knowledge and evidence derived from data are both supported by BNs, and missing data can be handled both in the construction process and in using a BN model (Lucas, 2004). A potential consequence of the structural learning using this method is that hidden or unknown structure, frequently overlooked using conventional statistical methods, can be identified.

It should be noted here that it is easier to learn the conditional probabilities for a given structure from a complete dataset. But, it is known to be very hard to learn the optimal BN structure from even complete datasets with no hidden nodes or missing data (Kim & Jung, 2003; Murphy, 2001).

Nature of the Datasets Used for Learning

The learning datasets could be complete or incomplete, which in term has an impact on the methods of learning. Considering the above options:

Learning from Completer Data

When the dataset is complete with no missing values, the learning methods can be classified according to the space where the search is done (directed acyclic graph, space of orderings, or the space of equivalence classes), taking into account heuristics used in the search (greedy, simulated annealing, tabu search, branch and bound, floating, ant colonies, genetic algorithms, estimation of distribution algorithms, etc) (Chickering, Geiger, & Heckerman, 1994). The heuristic approach for searching for the best structure is considered superior.

Learning from Incomplete Data

When the dataset has missing values, learning is a more difficult problem. Missing data commonly exists in real world and especially in the Health Domain. The most commonly used algorithm in this case is the expectation-maximization (EM) algorithm (Lee & Abbott, 2003). The EM algorithm is an iterative algorithm that given a network structure and a database of cases, determines a local maximum estimate of the parameters by assuming that the pattern of missing data is uninformative (missing at random or missing completely at random) (Lauritzen, 1995). It consists of a step of computing the expected value of the relevant parameter and a maximisation step, which are carried out in an interleaved fashion until convergence (Dempster, Laird, & Rubin, 1997).

Methods of Learning

Generally in data mining and machine learning the distinction is made between supervised and unsupervised learning.

Supervised Learning

In supervised learning, outcome or output variables in the available Health Domain dataset are known (Lucas, 2004). The aim of model construction is to predict these outcome variables as well as other intermediate variables.

Unsupervised Learning

Unsupervised learning is used when such outcome variables are not available (Lucas, 2004). A typical application of this in healthcare is discovering diagnostic or prognostic groups in dataset.

Continuous Variables

BNs have been traditionally used to model conditional probabilities between collected variables in the medical domain (Heckerman, 1996). The example given in this chapter have nodes with categorical values and multinomial distributions. Continuous variables are often changed into more meaningful ordinal groups (e.g., 'high', 'medium' and 'low') or well accepted or published categories (e.g., age groups).

There are many continuous variables collected in healthcare: during patient examination and history taking, laboratory test results, functional status analysis and gene expressions to name a few. It is also possible to create BNs with these continuous-value nodes. The most common distribution for such variables is the Gaussian (Murphy, 2001). These variables can be related in a number of ways: directly, through mathematical formula, indirectly and through synonymy.

Algorithms for Learning

As previously mentioned, learning a BN from data involves the tasks of structure learning (identifying the graphical network structure) and parameter learning (estimating the conditional probability distributions). In many learning algorithms, the two tasks are performed simultaneously without demarcation (Lucas et al., 2004).

There are two different approaches in finding an optimal structure: search-and-score-based and conditional independence (CI) (Kim & Jung, 2003) or constraint-based algorithms (Lee & Abbott, 2003).

Using a scoring metric, a search-and-score-based algorithm searches for the best model structure in terms of the goodness-of-fit of the structure to the data (Lee & Abbott, 2003). Thus these methods search the space of all possible acyclic digraphs by generating heuristically a range of graphs and comparing these for their ability to explain the data (Lucas et al., 2004). One of the early example of this is K2 (Lee & Abbott, 2003). Other search and scoring methods use, for example, a genetic algorithm for the search and build upon the use of the minimum description length (MDL) principle (Lee & Abbott, 2003).

The other approach to learning a BN from data is to build upon the use of a dependence analysis or conditional independence (CI) or constraint-based algorithm (Lucas et al., 2004). By studying the available data set, the dependences and independences between the various variables can be extracted, for example, by means of statistical tests, and subsequently captured in a graphical structure (Lee & Abbott, 2003). The use of constraints in the learning phase enables the investigators to feed the learning algorithm with existing and well-established structural knowledge of the domain. That is, specify from available knowledge the dependence or independence among pairs of variables in the dataset, thus guiding the learning algorithm towards the best possible model (Cheng & Greiner, 2001). In practice, the CI-based learning algorithms are widely accepted to be more efficient than the scoring-based algorithms (Cheng & Greiner, 2001).

Independence tests can quickly become unreliable for larger conditioning sets and the search space of all possible digraphs can be impossibly large. In such instances learning algorithms have been proposed that take a hybrid approach (Lucas et al., 2004). These algorithms are composed of two phases. In the first phase, a graph is constructed from the data, generally using only the lower-order dependence tests. This graph is subsequently used to explicitly restrict the search space of graphical structures for the second phase in which a search algorithm is employed to find a digraph that best explains the data.

Inventing New Hidden Nodes

Usually structure learning implies finding the right connectivity between pre-existing nodes. Murphy (2001) believes that a more interesting problem is one of inventing hidden nodes, which in turn can make the model more compact.

Summary of Network Learning Methods

The case where some nodes are hidden or data are either incorrect or insufficient needs a special approach. There are four cases of network learning and these are described in Table 2 (Bidyuk et al., 2005; Murphy, 2001).

BN Classifiers

What are Classifiers?

Cheng and Greiner (2001, p 141) described classification as "the task of identifying the class labels for instances based on a set of features or attributes". Thus classification aims to identify the characteristics of the group to which each case belongs. This pattern can be used both to understand the existing data and to predict how new cases will behave. To handle classification problems a specific classes of BNs of restricted structure have become popular (Lucas, 2004; Lucas et al., 2004).

There are many problems in the Heath Domain that are classification problems, such as diagnostic alternatives, prognostic categories, survival after intervention, categories of disease burden, etc. Therefore in the Health Domain there is a great deal of experience developing classifier models based on a wide range of principles and techniques.

Table 2. Summary of network learning methods

Structure	Observability	Method
Known	Full	Maximum-likelihood estimation
Known	Partial	Expectation Maximization or gradient ascent or a "greedy" hill-climbing
Unknown	Full	Search in model space
Unknown	Partial	Expectation Maximization or Search in model space

The dataset used can be historical or one that is collected from a controlled study. Sometimes expert(s) classify a sample of cases in a dataset and this classification model is applied to the entire dataset. Learning accurate classifiers from data is an active research area.

In clinical medicine usually signs and symptoms serve to describe the characteristics of patients to be classified. For instance, one could classify cancer patients in terms of their response to a new chemotherapy agent. Data mining can be used inductively to find a predictive pattern that creates a classification model by examining pre-classified cases in the dataset.

BNs can also be used to infer the value of some target variable given the observed values of the other variables. Hence, a BN can be used as a classifier that gives the posterior probability distribution of the classification node, given the values of other attributes or features (Kim & Jung, 2003).

Fixed and Learning Classifiers

Classifiers may either be fixed classifiers or learning classifiers, and learning classifiers may in turn be divided into supervised and unsupervised learning classifiers.

One of the basic machine learning tasks is classification: that is to map examples into predefined groups or classes. This task is also referred to as supervised learning, because the classes are determined before examining. Lucas (2001) (Lucas, 2001) from his study made the observation that acquiring both structure and joint probability distributions from domain experts may result in robust classifiers, even though BNs are normally developed as declarative, reusable models, and not purely for the purpose of classification.

In the unsupervised learning approach, models are built from data without predefined classes. The goal is to organize or reduce dimensionality the unclassified data to obtain insights about internal data class structure. When the observed data can be labelled "typical" and "atypical" examples of the event of interest, supervised classifiers can be learned. Thus, the data instances are grouped together using a certain similarity metric (Friedman, Geiger, & Goldszmidt, 1997). With the help of some evaluation methods, a decision can be made about the meaning of the formed clusters (Roos, Wettig, Grunwald, Myllyma, & Tirri, 2005). The learned BN classifiers is said (Cheng & Greiner, 2001) to give very good prediction accuracy.

Classes of Classifiers

There are several different classes of BN classifiers and some of the commonly used ones are mentioned below.

A Naïve Bayesian Network (NBN) is a very simple kind of BN that naively assumes the attributes (variables) are independent and equally important (Lucas, 2004; Lucas et al., 2004).(Cloutier & Sirois, 2008). Normally not all subtleties of the interactions among the variables in the domain are reflected in such models (Lucas, 2001). Therefore, a relatively small dataset is sufficient to obtain a fairly accurate model. A NBN has the classification node as the parent node of all other nodes (Kim & Jung, 2003). No other connections are allowed in a NBN (Lucas, 2004; Lucas et al., 2004). Naïve Bayesian classifiers also have low variance (Lucas, 2001). Although the structure assumes feature independence, NBN remains robust when this criterion is not met and surprisingly outperforms many sophisticated classifiers over a large range of datasets (Cheng & Greiner, 2001).

In an effort to relax the problematic independence assumption, more general classes of BNs such as Bayesian Network Augmented Naïve-Bayes (BAN) and General Bayesian Network (GBN) have been suggested (Kim & Jung, 2003). In order to improve the NBN classifiers, there have been also some efforts for selecting feature subset in addition to relaxing independence assumption (Kim & Jung, 2003).

BAN allows attributes to form an arbitrary graph. Unlike the other Bayesian classifiers, GBN treats the classification nodes as an ordinary node. In a BN, the *Markov Blanket* of a node is the set of nodes consisting of its parents, children, and spouses. Thus the Markov Blanket of a classification node 'x' corresponds to a subset of nodes within a boundary of 'x' that shield it from being affected by any node outside its boundary. By learning the unrestricted GBN, one can get a natural feature subset by selecting nodes within the Markov Blanket of the classification node of interest (Kim & Jung, 2003).

In contrast to NBN, in a Tree Augmented Network (TAN) links are allowed between the feature variables (Lucas, 2004; Lucas et al., 2004). Research (Friedman et al., 1997; Cheng & Greiner, 2001) has shown that TAN, which incorporate extra dependences among their feature variables, often outperform NBNs. Allowing for even more complex relationships between the feature variables, as in a Forest Augmented Network (FAN), has been shown to yield still better performance.

The naïve Bayesian classifier and its variants offer the best choice when learning from a small dataset; the additional structure in the declarative models seem to be of little help in this respect (Lucas, 2001). They even outperform non-Bayesian classifiers in many circumstances.

Evaluation and Sensitivity Analysis

Evaluation of a BN is not much different from evaluation of any decision-support system. Measures such as true positive and true negative rates can be determined using test and patient data (Lucas, 2004).

There are a number of methods which give some insights into the usefulness of the constructed BN model.

As BNs are computational formalisms, it is possible to carry out cross validation (Lee & Abbott, 2003; Lucas, 2004). This is done by setting aside a fixed number of cases from a dataset and using the remaining cases to learn the underlying probability distribution, and subsequently using the set-aside cases for testing. The next step of the testing phase is to validate a trained network on new cases in a test set. For bootstrapping, where repeated random samples are taken from a dataset, evaluation of learnt models is also done on data not used in the training process (Lucas, 2004).

In Bayesian statistics assumptions are made about the prior probability distribution and the way in which prior information is updated based on observed evidence (Lucas, 2004). The resulting posteriori (or posterior probability distributions) can be examined using scoring rules, which gives insight into their quality (Lucas, 2004).

Before the network can be used in real-world, its quality and clinical value have to be established (Lucas et al., 2004). One of the techniques for assessing a network's quality is to perform a sensitivity analysis with patient data. Such an analysis serves to provide insight in the robustness of the network output to possible inaccuracies in the underlying probability distribution.

Further evaluation of a BN can be done in various different ways (Lucas et al., 2004). Examples include measuring classification performance on a given set of real patient data and measuring similarity of structure or probability distribution to a 'gold-standard' (or a paragon of excellence) network or other probabilistic model.

Evaluation of say a therapy advised by BN model is usually done by comparing this advice with that of treating clinicians or of an expert panel's opinion (Lucas, 2004).

Software for Bayesian Network

As there are many commercial and free software packages that can be used without deep knowledge about the mathematics/statistics to be applied, the emphasis of this chapter has not been on the detailed construction or calculi. Enough background has been presented to support an understanding of the basic concepts; however, it is pertinent to quickly mention the available software to provide numeric solutions to BN problems. There are reviews of software for graphical models (Lacave & Diez, 2001; Murphy, 2007). The Computer Science Department of University of British Colombia in Canada has compiled and compared a list of software (Murphy, 2008). At the end of their web page a list of other sites to explore is given. A much more detailed comparison of some of the software packages is given in Appendix B of Ann Nicholson and Kevin Korb's book, *Bayesian Artificial Intelligence* (Korb & Nicholson, 2004).

It should be noted that many software programs, such as HUGIN (http://www.hugin.comm) and Netica (http://www.norsys.com), provide parameter learning algorithms. HUGIN, BN Power Constructor (http://www.cs.ualberta.ca/~jcheng/bnpchlp/index.htm) and BN Power Predictor (http://www.cs.ualberta.ca/~jcheng/bnpp.htm), and TETRAD (http://www.phil.cmu.edu/projects/tetrad/index.htmll) are examples of CI or constraint-based algorithms. The information-theoretical algorithm of Cheng and co-worker is also an example of an algorithm taking this approach (Cheng & Greiner, 2001). An example of a system that implements search-and-score-based algorithms is Bayesian Knowledge Discoverer (http://www.bayesware.com/).

The reference list provided here is not exhaustive, but the intention was to point to a few useful websites to help with software selection.

ADVANTAGES OF BNS IN THE HEALTH DOMAIN

BNs with their associated methods have now been used in Health Domain for most of a couple decades now. In fact, most of the development in BNs has come from their use in the Health Domain. There are several significant advantages of employing BNs in health. We will now look at some of the dominant features of the Domain which makes BNs an attractive proposition.

Address Concepts beyond the Scope of Statistics

There are a number of challenges in routinely collected health datasets that might make traditional methods of statistical modelling unsuitable. They include: (a) large, noisy datasets with sometimes missing entries; (b) mixture of quantitative and qualitative data; (c) data with low time granularity, but high space granularity; (d) dynamic cycles with feedback loops, (c) large numbers of interacting agents with many multilevel and varied interactions and (d) complex (non-linear) interactions between features that are not known a priori. Granularity here refers to the level of detail of the facts stored in a dataset. Clinical datasets are multidimensional with event, space and time dependencies and therefore have: (a) different granularities in space (state, region, hospital, care location/type) organised in a hierarchy, (b) different granularities in time (year, quarter, month, day, encounter times) organised in a hierarchy, (c) different granularities in events organised in a hierarchy and (d) different diagnoses organised in a hierarchy (ICD tree, principal and other diagnosis).

The process of data analysis in healthcare is becoming increasingly complicated. Lucas (2004) attributes this to the following: (a) new techniques, such as microarrays, which has given rise to datasets with few cases described by a large number of variables; (b) the increasing need for integrated analysis of data from different sources pertaining a given topic area, including the assimilation of background knowledge in the analysis process and; (c) the employment of models to support clinical decision making. As traditional statistical methods have been unable to meet all of these requirements there has been uptake of methods such as Bayesian Network.

Generally it can be said that BN models would be easier to understand than many of the other techniques, with the nodes and arrows representing the variables of interest and the relationships of variables respectively.

BNs have also inherited some of the characteristics of mathematical statistical analysis. Since BNs are based on the assumption that the classification of patterns is expressed in probabilistic terms between predictors and outcome variables (Lee & Abbott, 2003), that is probability theory, they inherit many of the efficient methods and strong results of mathematical statistics. In addition, the output is explicitly a probability and hence can be easily interpreted. About a decade ago there were issues in calculating the probabilities, particularly in complex BNs. However, with the increasing computational power of computers nowadays such calculations are made progressively more readily.

There are a number of reasons for using causal models in artificial intelligence, especially in probabilistic expert systems (Lacave & Diez, 2001). They include: (a) as one thinks in terms of cause-effect relations, it is easier to understand; (b) the identification of invariant causal relationships permits prediction of effects of both spontaneous causes (risk factors for conditions) and actions (interventions); (c) since the necessary condition for establishing causality is statistical correlation, causality and probability are closely related; and (d) the axiomatic properties of BN (d-separations and Markov property) corresponds to probabilistic dependencies and independencies.

Bayesian statistical methods in conjunction with BNs is said (Heckerman, 1997) to offer an efficient and legitimate method for avoiding the over-fitting of data. BNs are flexible with regards to missing information and can produce relatively accurate predictions even in situations where complete data is unavailable (Lee & Abbott, 2003). Since the model encodes dependencies among all variables, it is better at handling instances where some data entries are missing (Heckerman, 1997). BNs are also less influenced by small sample size.

Lucas (2004) believes that BNs can be seen as an alternative to logistic regression. The advantage over logistic regression is that the statistical dependence and independence are explicitly represented and not hidden in approximation.

A Bayesian classifier is a probabilistic inference method based on Bayes' Theorem. When new data are introduced, this method generates a posterior probability, governed by the prior probability distribution of the dataset (Cheng & Greiner, 2001). Cloutier and Sirois (2008) recently stated that Bayesian classifiers have been shown to be superior to the logistic regression modelling technique. In the medical context it has been demonstrated (Van der Gaag et al., 2008) that Bayesian classifiers are as good or better alternatives in terms of performance, ease of construction and ease of interpretation. A major advantage of BN classifiers is their ability to produce reliable classifications even if data is incomplete in the featured nodes.

In general, based on statistical data and learning rules, BNs can improve the reliability of a model, thus being useful as an exploratory data analysis tool for studying the relationships among variables (Lee & Abbott, 2003).

Incorporate Domain Knowledge

The advantage offered by Bayesian methods is that knowledge of a background population can be taken as a starting point of a study. BNs can incorporate domain knowledge into statistical data. When used in conjunction with statistical techniques, the BN graphical model is said (Heckerman, 1997) to have several advantages for data modelling including: (a) the learning of causal relationships and therefore useful for gaining understanding about a problem domain, thus for example, predicting the consequences of a medical intervention; and (b) since the model has both a causal and probabilistic semantics it is an ideal representation for combining prior knowledge (which is often causal) with the data in hand.

Since BNs use domain knowledge in the process of knowledge discovery in a graphical format, Lee and Abbott (2003) believes that they offer a distinct advantage for nurse researchers. At the same time, the BN approach can be more robust to errors in the assignment of prior knowledge through the learning phase than other conventional statistical modelling methods (Lee & Abbott, 2003). For instance, hidden relationships among variables that might be omitted can be detected by structural learning algorithms.

The networks allows the use of domain expert knowledge in the discovery process, while other techniques rely primarily on coded data to extract knowledge (Lee & Abbott, 2003). Domain expert knowledge can be easily encoded through the use of these graphical diagrams, thus making a network structure easier to understand and the output easier to interpret. As discussed before, BN algorithms capitalise on this encoded knowledge to increase their efficiency in the modelling process and accuracy in its predictive performance (Lee & Abbott, 2003).

Adaptable and Modifiable

An important advantage of a BN is the availability of a graphical model framework of a problem, which is an appealing concept for both the Health Domain and computation. BNs can continue to improve over a period of time by adding new pieces of information. This extension of the BN requires only the addition of a small number of vertices and edges in the graph, and the related probabilities. Furthermore, BNs can be easily inspected to determine whether or not a specific piece of data provided is being taken into consideration and if necessary be forced to include that information. In this way all known features of a problem are guaranteed to be used in the calculation of the result.

Include Complex Processes & Uncertainties

BNs are said (Bidyuk et al., 2005) to be a convenient tool for the description of quite complex processes and events with both structural and statistical uncertainties. They are especially useful for the development and analysis of pattern recognition, machine learning and risk analysis algorithms (Bidyuk et al., 2005).

The main idea of constructing a graphic model is the concept of modularity or the decomposition of a complex system into simple components (Bidyuk et al., 2005). Probability theory provides consistency and a links the components into a system, thus integrating databases with graphic models (Bidyuk et al.,

2005). This approach to graphic model construction makes it possible to derive at models of processes characterized by a set of strongly interacting variables (Bidyuk et al., 2005).. In addition they help create data structures amenable for further development of efficient algorithms that can be applied in their processing and decision-making (Bidyuk et al., 2005).

These networks are also superior in capturing interactions among input variables (Lee & Abbott, 2003). This ability to capture the relationships among input variables has tremendous value in exploring data. In addition to the interest-driven data evaluation, data-driven analyses can be performed with BNs, often with interesting findings. For example, strong associations between interested variables can be discovered using Bayesian Networks.

As they can be used for simulating both static and dynamic processes, BNs are said (Bidyuk et al., 2005) to be a promising approach to simulating processes with various uncertainties. They have become increasingly popular for representing and handling uncertain knowledge in medicine, for example to assist in the diagnosis of disorders or to predict the natural course of a disorder or the most likely outcome after treatment.

In recent years BNs have emerged as a powerful data mining technique for handling uncertainty in complex domains and a fundamental technique for pattern recognition and classification (Heckerman, 1996; Heckerman, 1997; Pearl, 2000). The BN represents the joint probability distribution and domain (or expert) knowledge in a compact way. The BN with its graphical diagram provides a comprehensive method of representing relationships and influences among nodes or variables. This in turn provides a flexible representation that allows the specification of dependence and independence of variables through the network structure.

Capture Non Linear Processes

There are often non-linear relationships between factors of care and outcomes. Fixed models and linear reduction of such complex clinical environments are unlikely to be adequate methods for measuring clinical care quality and performance (Marsland & Buchan, 2005). Therefore machine learning will have a useful application here. Applications of machine learning include identifying the dominant features, or combinations of features, that affect the outcomes of a care process and performing adaptive regression and classification (Marsland & Buchan, 2005). For example, machine learning has a potential role to play in the development of clinical guidelines (Zheng, Kang, & Kim, 2008). It is often the case that there are several alternate care paths for a given condition, with slightly different outcomes. It may not be clear, however, what features of one particular path are responsible for the better results. If databases are kept of the outcomes of competing care path, then a BN can be used to identify features that are responsible for different outcomes.

Deal with Novelty Detection

Adaptive approaches should be sought for the examination of problematic patterns in clinical care, mainly because there is implicit and facilitated feedback between observed clinical outcomes, interventions and the organisation and delivery of care. BNs can be used for novelty detection and hence would be particularly useful for highlighting deviations from good clinical practice (Marsland & Buchan, 2004).

Complex Decision-Making Processes

For understanding the complex decision-making processes in health-care it is important to reason about them (Visscher et al., 2005). Since these processes often include uncertainty, BN models can be constructed to support decision-making in real-life practice as it is an excellent tool for reasoning with uncertainty (Lucas et al., 2004).

Incorporating evidence into statistical reasoning allows coherent representation of domain knowledge under uncertainty (Visscher et al., 2005). An automatically derived network in combination with human expert knowledge helps to explain better the causal relationships among the variables. This gives a better understanding and opportunities for improvement of patient specific and aspecific processes. There is also better representation of information for decision making, pattern recognition and classification functions.

Moreover, the health sector is driven to contain rising costs and improve quality of service, and thus is under pressure to utilise its data for quality improvement. In this setting, BNs are attractive as a powerful and general technique to understand complex, non-linear system dynamics. BN outputs are amenable to graphical interpretation, and provide prediction and risk estimation for specific cohorts, identifying areas for further research and quality improvement efforts.

APPLICATIONS OF BN IN HEALTH DOMAIN

The goal of data mining in the Health Domain may include discovering associations, clustering, or creating predictive (classification/regression) models. The versatility and modelling power of BNs is now employed across a variety of health fields for the purposes of analysis, prediction, diagnosis and simulation.

Applications of Bayesian Network

HEALTH CARE

Diagnostics

- Aiding diagnostic reasoning
- Computing the most likely diagnosis
- Increasing the resolution of diagnostic tests
- Medical Decision Making
- Decision Support Systems

Treatment

- Computing the highest utility
- Evaluation of new medical and surgical treatments
- Guiding optimal treatment

Prognosis

- Outcome following treatments
- Prediction of survival
- Risk estimation and Predictions of compliance
- Risk factors for disease and live style
- Prediction of patient compliance to medication
- Prediction of clinician compliance to practice guidelines

Epidemiology

- Geographical clustering
- Estimation of the best numbers
- Incidence of diseases
- Screening & Monitoring

Clinical Trials

Management

- Overall patient management tasks such as planning and scheduling
- Providing a description of the process in an adequate formalism
- Gaining a clear picture of the business process
- Improve the process of making decisions
- Better supporting policy decisions
- Predicting the future behaviour of the process's cases

Evaluation

Knowledge Acquisition

- Elements of medical reasoning
- Capturing the knowledge involved in the management of a service

BIOMEDICINE

Genomics

- Identify particular genes
- Gene expression profiling
- Interpretation of microarray gene expression data
- Analysis for shared gene functions

Proteomics

- Prediction of protein secondary structure
- Back translation of protein structure

Interactions between Genes and Protein-Protein Interactions

System Biology

- Biological image analysis
- Discovery of temporal patterns

OTHER

- Microarrays
- Text mining

CHALLENGES OF THE USE OF BNS IN THE HEALTH DOMAIN

In spite of BNs' significant advantages and power, there are some inherit limitations and weaknesses. These are highlighted below.

Assigning of Prior Distributions

Disadvantages of the Bayes' method include the different ways of assigning prior distributions of parameters and the possible sensitivity of conclusions to the choice of distributions. BNs are only as useful as quality and extent of the prior beliefs. Therefore, poor quality and inappropriate prior beliefs will distort the Network and produce invalid results.

In Building the Network

As previously mentioned, once built, a BN constitutes an efficient device to perform probabilistic inference. However, the structure and conditional probabilities necessary for characterizing the BN can be difficult to finalise and be prone to errors and omissions.

The ease of accessing huge databases in recent years has led to the development of a large number of model learning algorithms. As already pointed, out these algorithms have their own issues.

Perhaps the most significant disadvantage of an approach involving BNs is the fact that there is no universally accepted method for constructing a network from data. In addition, the computational complexities and lack of easily usable software for analyses adds to the problem.

Nature of Knowledge

Nikovski (Nikovski, 2000) believes that constructing large BNs for diagnostic applications is in many ways akin to the knowledge-engineering process employed in the creation of expert systems. However, building a BN is usually more difficult than building an expert system because a BN contains a lot of additional quantitative information which is essential to its proper performance. The statistics for filling in this numeric information are not always readily available and often the designer of the system has to make use of indirect statistics. For example, it is not always clear how combinations of diseases determine the outcome of a particular diagnostic test. Only positive and negative predictive likelihoods of that test for each individual disease are usually available and this value does not take into account other diseases that might coexist and potentially confound the outcome.

Pazzani and co-workers (Pazzani, Mani, & Shankle, 1997) argued that to be truly useful, the knowledge discovered in databases must both be accurate and comprehensible. They further ascertained that one factor that influences the comprehensibility of learned knowledge is the use of conditions as evidence for belonging to some category, when prior knowledge indicates that these conditions are evidence that an example does not belong to that category. Therefore, as with any data mining technique, the constructed BN needs to be evaluated before use for its quality and value.

In Modelling Complex Adaptive System

A healthcare system is a complex adaptive system with multiple nested interconnected parts that evolve, interact and adapt over time (Cockings, Cook, & Iqbal, 2006). The quality of care delivered by the system during an episode of care is a result of interactions between the patient and all interrelated parts of the system. The effect of a incorporating a single intervention into such a complex clinical environment may produce a result different from expected. All changes made within the system will affect all patients in different ways. Any change in such an environment will have both predictable and unpredictable effects. Isolated analyses may not be informative, as changes planned for beneficial, direct consequences may trigger indirect, adaptive effects that can be detrimental overall. BNs are quite often not practical for very complex systems with large number and combinations of variables. Complex systems are difficult to build, with the process of network discovery being either too costly to perform and/or impossible.

In Interpretation

Basic statistics texts and courses are usually dominated by classical methods of inference with only passing reference to Bayesian methods. Therefore Sheingold (2001) believes that it is not surprising that many senior analysts in healthcare that support decision making are not well acquainted or comfortable with formal Bayesian analyses.

In addition, many of the current papers and presentations of Bayesian methods do not make the method transparent or accessible, or understandable to the unskilled. Sheingold (2001) hypothesises that this could be because experts assume too much about their audience's ability to easily comprehend the material, or that Bayesian analyses are more technically difficult to apply than classical methods, or both.

SUMMARY AND FUTURE TRENDS

Data mining in the Health Domain has been motivated by the wealth of data that is now accumulating, which are becoming increasingly computerized with each passing year. Increasingly, distributed, heterogeneous, operational databases can be integrated, consolidated into a data warehouse and made widely accessible (Sheingold, 2001).

Rising costs and quality pressure on the one hand and new technologies of data processing on the other hand have created both the necessity and the opportunity for data based quality management in the healthcare (Stühlinger et al., 2000). The most important trends in managing care and developing strategies involves the collection, analysis, and dissemination of information. Larranaga and co-workers (2006) commented on how the exponential growth in the availability and amount of biomedical data has created two problems: (a) its efficient storage and management and (b) the extraction from all of these heterogeneous data of hidden biological knowledge. We are clearly at a time in which collecting data and analyses are now critical to biomedicine and healthcare decision making processes. Therefore, these datasets can be considered as strategic resources and valuable assets.

As we have seen in this chapter, the BN model can be used both for probabilistic prediction and for classification. While BNs are powerful tools for knowledge representation and inference under conditions of uncertainty, they were not considered as classifiers until the discovery of Naïve Bayes. These very simple kinds of BNs have turned out to be surprisingly effective. Consequently, the BN may compensate for many of the prior criticisms of other data mining techniques. These networks have become the most popular technique for representing and reasoning with probabilistic information. As we have seen, BNs are especially designed for causal networks or even for specific canonical problem models. Therefore it can be considered as an important emerging data mining technique in the Health Domain. In fact, BNs are gaining an increasing popularity as modelling tools for complex problems involving probabilistic reasoning under uncertainty. We have not seen the full capability of Bayesian Networks. BNs can and will be further improved in terms of learning and inference methods.

Nearly fifteen years ago Cohen envisaged that the practice of medicine is likely to be revolutionised by the convergence of two developments: information technology and evidence-based medicine (Cohen, 1995). Modelling-based healthcare management will increasingly become just as popular as evidence-based medicine. The critical technologies of health informatics, including knowledge representation, data mining, automated diagnosis, and information retrieval, can be viewed as technologies supporting the goal of knowledge discovery from datasets (Altman, 2000).

Using BN for data analysis can be viewed as the process of updating prior knowledge based on available biomedical and healthcare evidence from the collected data. The assumptions that are made in formulating this prior knowledge are obviously crucial. BNs have the virtue of being declarative models that can be reused for different tasks. They can also be employed to look at particular problems from different angles, just by varying the supplied evidence and the questions posed to the model.

The eagerness to explore the data collection in the end will, without doubt, significantly enhance the insights into various facets of the Health Domain and may result in new diagnostic, therapeutic and prognostic methods. In addition to considering global measure of efficacy, it is important that evidence-based practice incorporates evidence of benefit within the context of a particular healthcare environment of interest. The use of data mining focuses on evidence-based patterns from previous practices in the existing setting.

BNs are a promising knowledge discovery approach that clearly has several advantages over other techniques. In all likelihood, the discovery of patterns in health will unmask many questions while answering many others. The emerging questions will benefit us not only through better resource utilization but also through better patient treatment/management. As BNs are based directly on history, they represent the ultimate in evidence discovery and facilitate the updating of evidence-based practice.

ACKNOWLEDGMENT

The author is grateful to Professor Jim Warren (Chair in Health Informatics, University of Auckland, New Zealand) for the critical review of this chapter.

REFERENCES

Altman, R. B. (2000). The interactions between clinical informatics and bioinformatics: a case study. *Journal of the American Medical Informatics Association, 7*(5), 439–443.

Anderson, J. (1986). Data dictionaries - A way forward to write meaning and terminology into medical information systems. *Methods of Information in Medicine, 25*(3), 137–138.

Bate, A., & Edwards, I. R. (2006). Data mining in spontaneous reports. *Basic & Clinical Pharmacology & Toxicology, 98*(3), 324–330. doi:10.1111/j.1742-7843.2006.pto_232.x

Bates, D. W., Pappius, E., Kuperman, G. J., Sittig, D., Burstin, H., & Fairchild, D. (1999). Using information systems to measure and improve quality. *International Journal of Medical Informatics, 53*(2-3), 115–124. doi:10.1016/S1386-5056(98)00152-X

Bayat, S., Cuggia, M., Kessler, M., Briancon, S., Le Beux, P., & Frimat, L. (2008). Modelling access to renal transplantation waiting list in a French healthcare network using a Bayesian method. *Studies in Health Technology and Informatics, 136*, 605–610.

Bayes, T. (1763). Essay towards solving a problem in the doctrine of chances. *Philosophical Transactions of the Royal Society of London A Mathematical and Physical Sciences, 53*, 370-418.

Becker, R. C., Burns, M., Gore, J. M., Spencer, F. A., Ball, S. P., & French, W. (1998). Early assessment and in-hospital management of patients with acute myocardial infarction at increased risk for adverse outcomes: a nationwide perspective of current clinical practice. The National Registry of Myocardial Infarction (NRMI-2) Participants. *American Heart Journal, 135*(5 Pt 1), 786–796. doi:10.1016/S0002-8703(98)70036-5

Berrar, D. P., Downes, C. S., & Dubitzky, W. (2003). Multiclass cancer classification using gene expression profiling and probabilistic neural networks. In *Proceedings of the Pacific Symposium on Biocomputing*.

Bidyuk, P. I., Terent'ev, A. N., & Gasanov, A. S. (2005). Construction and methods of learning of Bayesian Networks. *Cybernetics and Systems Analysis, 41*(4), 587–598. doi:10.1007/s10559-005-0094-8

Blanco, R., Inza, I., Merino, M., Quiroga, J., & Larranaga, P. (2005). Feature selection in Bayesian classifiers for the prognosis of survival of cirrhotic patients treated with TIPS. *Journal of Biomedical Informatics, 38*(5), 376–388. doi:10.1016/j.jbi.2005.05.004

Broyles, R. W. (2006). *Fundamentals of Statistics in Health Administration*. Sudbury, MA: Jones and Bartlett.

Cheng, J., & Greiner, R. (2001). Learning Bayesian Belief Network Classifiers – Algorithms and System. In *Proceedings of the 4th Canadian conference on Artificial Intelligence*, Calgary, Alberta, Canada.

Chickering, D. M., Geiger, D., & Heckerman, D. (1994). *Learning Bayesian networks is NP-hard*. Redmond, WA, USA: Microsoft Research, Advanced Technology Division, Microsoft Corporation.

Cloutier, M. L., & Sirois, S. (2008). Bayesian versus Frequentist statistical modeling: A debate for hit selection from HTS campaigns. *Drug Discovery Today, 13*(11/12), 536–542. doi:10.1016/j.drudis.2008.03.022

Cockings, J. G. L., Cook, D. A., & Iqbal, R. K. (2006). Process monitoring in intensive care with the use of cumulative expected minus observed mortality and risk-adjusted p charts. *Critical Care, 10*(1), R28. Retrieved May, 17, 2006, from http://ccforum.com/content/10/1/R28

Cohen, J. J. (1995). Higher quality at lower cost - Maybe there is a way. *Academy of Medicine Journal, 73*, 414.

Dempster, A., Laird, N., & Rubin, D. (1997). Maximisation likelihood from incomplete data via the EM algorithm. *Journal of the Royal Statistical Society. Series B. Methodological, 39*, 1–38.

Devlin. (2000, February). Devlin's Angle - The legacy of the Reverend Bayes. *MAA Online*. Retrieved January, 28, 2009, from http://www.maa.org/devlin/devlin_2_00.html

Doan, T., Haddawy, P., Nguyen, T., & Seetharam, D. (1999). *A hybrid Bayesian Network modeling environment*. In *Proceeding of the 1999 National Computer Science and Engineering Conference (NCSEC)*, Bangkok, Thailand.

Draghici, S. (2000). Neural networks in analog hardware - Design and implementation issues. *International Journal of Neural Systems, 10*(1), 19–42.

Dreiseitl, S., & Ohno-Machado, L. (2002). Logistic regression and artificial neural network classification models: A methodology review. *Journal of Biomedical Informatics, 35*(5-6), 352–359. doi:10.1016/S1532-0464(03)00034-0

Elston, R. C., & Johnson, W. D. (1995). *Essentials of Biostatistics* (2nd ed.). F. A. Davis Company.

Fayyad, U. M., Piatetsky-Shapiro, G., & Smyth, P. (1996). *From data mining to knowledge discovery: An overview*. Menlo Park, CA, USA: American Association for Artificial Intelligence (AAAI) Press.

Friedman, N., Geiger, D., & Goldszmidt, M. (1997). Bayesian Network Classifiers. *Machine Learning, 29*(2/3), 131–164. doi:10.1023/A:1007465528199

Glymour, C., Madigan, D., Pregibon, D., & Smyth, P. (1996). Statistical inference and data mining. *Communications of the ACM, 39*(11), 35–41. doi:10.1145/240455.240466

Glymour, C., Madigan, D., Pregibon, D., & Smyth, P. (1997). Statistical Themes and Lessons for Data Mining. *Data Mining and Knowledge Discovery, 1*(1), 11–28. doi:10.1023/A:1009773905005

Goldbaum, M. H. (2005). Unsupervised learning with independent component analysis can identify patterns of glaucomatous visual field defects. *Transactions of the American Ophthalmological Society, 103*, 270–280.

Goldbaum, M. H., Sample, P. A., Zhang, Z., Chan, K., Hao, J., & Lee, T. W. (2005). Using unsupervised learning with independent component analysis to identify patterns of glaucomatous visual field defects. *Investigative Ophthalmology & Visual Science, 46*(10), 3676–3683. doi:10.1167/iovs.04-1167

Greenland, S. (1990). Randomization, statistics, and causal inference. *Epidemiology (Cambridge, Mass.), 1*(6), 421–429. doi:10.1097/00001648-199011000-00003

Greenland, S. (2000). Principles of multilevel modelling. *International Journal of Epidemiology, 29*(1), 158–167. doi:10.1093/ije/29.1.158

Han, J., & Kamber, M. (2006). *Data Mining: Concepts and Techniques* (2nd ed.). San Francisco, CA, USA: Morgan Kaufmann.

Hand, D. J. (1999). Statistics and Data Mining: Intersecting disciplines. *SIGKDD Explorations, 1*(1), 16–19. doi:10.1145/846170.846171

Hasan, M., Meara, R. J., & Bhowmick, B. K. (1995). The quality of diagnostic coding in cerebrovascular disease. *International Journal for Quality in Health Care, 7*(4), 407–410. doi:10.1016/1353-4505(95)00005-4

Heckerman, D. (1996). Bayesian Networks for knowledge discovery. In U. M. Fayyard, G. Piatetsky-Shapiro, P. Symth, & R. Uthurusamy (Eds.), *Advances in Knowledge Discovery and Data Mining* (pp. 273-305). Cambridge, MA, USA: The MIT Press.

Heckerman, D. (1996). A tutorial on learning with Bayesian Networks. In M. Jordan (Ed.), *In Learning in Graphical Models* (pp. 79-119). Cambridge, MA, USA: MIT Press.

Heckerman, D. (1997). Bayesian Networks for data mining. *Data Mining and Knowledge Discovery, 1*(1), 79–119. doi:10.1023/A:1009730122752

Heckerman, D., & Breeze, J. S. (1995). *Causal independence for probability assessment and inference using Bayesian Networks.* Redmond, WA, USA: Microsoft Research.

Hoey, J. P., & Soehl, S. (1997). Care maps, utilization, and outcomes: A viable solution. *The Journal of Oncology Management, 6*(6), 29–32.

Kim, I.-C., & Jung, Y.-G. (2003, July 25). *Using Bayesian Networks to analyze medical data.* In *Proceedings of the third international conference of Machine Learning and Data Mining (MLDM)*, Leipzig, Germany.

Korb, K. B., & Nicholson, A. E. (2004). *Bayesian Artificial Intelligence.* Boca Raton, FL, USA: CRC Press.

Kugler, C., Freytag, S., Stillger, R., Bauer, P., & Ferbert, A. (2000). Australian Refined Diagnosis Related Groups: Formal and inherent problems of grouping with the example of stroke care. *Deutsche Medizinische Wochenschrift, 125*(51-52), 1554–1559. doi:10.1055/s-2000-9554

Kumar, V. S., Narayanan, S., Kurc, T., Kong, J., Gurcan, M. N., & Saltz, J. H. (2008). Analysis and semantic querying in large biomedical image datasets. *Computer*, 52–59.

Lacave, C., & Diez, F. J. (2001). A review of explanation methods of Bayesian Networks. *The Knowledge Engineering Review, 17*(2).

Lauritzen, S. L. (1995). The EM algorithm for graphical association models with missing data. *Computational Statistics & Data Analysis, 19*(2), 191–201. doi:10.1016/0167-9473(93)E0056-A

Le Duff, F., Muntean, C., Cuggia, M., & Mabo, P. (2004a). Predicting survival causes after out of hospital cardiac arrest using data mining method. *Medinfo, 11*(Pt 2), 1256–1259.

Le Duff, F., Muntean, C., Cuggia, M., & Mabo, P. (2004b). Predicting survival causes after out of hospital cardiac arrest using data mining method. *Studies in Health Technology and Informatics, 107*(Pt 2), 1256–1259.

Lee, A. H., Fung, W. K., & Fu, B. (2003). Analyzing hospital length of stay: Mean or median regression? *Medical Care, 41*(5), 681–686. doi:10.1097/00005650-200305000-00015

Lee, I. N., Liao, S. C., & Embrechts, M. (2000). Data mining techniques applied to medical information. *Medical Informatics and the Internet in Medicine, 25*(2), 81–102. doi:10.1080/14639230050058275

Lee, S. M., & Abbott, P. A. (2003). Bayesian Networks for knowledge discovery in large datasets: Basics for nurse researchers. *Journal of Biomedical Informatics, 36*(4-5), 389–399. doi:10.1016/j.jbi.2003.09.022

Li, B., & Gallin, W. J. (2005). Computational identification of residues that modulate voltage sensitivity of voltage-gated potassium channels. *BMC Structural Biology, 5*, 16. doi:10.1186/1472-6807-5-16

Linnarsson, R., & Wigertz, O. (1989). The Data Dictionary - A controlled vocabulary for integrating clinical Databases and medical knowledge bases. *Methods of Information in Medicine, 28*, 78–85.

Lucas, P. (2001). Expert knowledge and its role in learning Bayesian Networks in medicine: An appraisal. In *Proceeding of the 8th Conference on Artificial Intelligence in Medicine in Europe*, Cascais, Portugal.

Lucas, P. (2004). Bayesian analysis, pattern analysis, and data mining in health care. *Current Opinion in Critical Care, 10*(5), 399–403. doi:10.1097/01.ccx.0000141546.74590.d6

Lucas, P. J. F., Van der Gaag, L. C., & Abu-Hanna, A. (2004). Editorial: Bayesian networks in biomedicine and health. *Artificial Intelligence in Medicine, 30*(3), 201–214. doi:10.1016/j.artmed.2003.11.001

Marsland, S., & Buchan, I. (2004). Clinical quality needs complex adaptive systems and machine learning. *Medinfo, 11*(Pt), 644-647.

Marsland, S., & Buchan, I. (2005). Clinical Quality Needs Complex Adaptive Systems and Machine Learning. *Studies in Health Technology and Informatics, 107*, 644–647.

Maruster, L., Weijters, T., de Vries, G., van den Bosch, A., & Daelemans, W. (2002). Logistic-based patient grouping for multi-disciplinary treatment. *Artificial Intelligence in Medicine, 26*(1-2), 87–107. doi:10.1016/S0933-3657(02)00054-4

Matchar, D. B., & Samsa, G. P. (1999). Using outcomes data to identify best medical practice: The role of policy models. *Hepatology (Baltimore, Md.), 29*(6Suppl), 36S–39S.

Minichiello, V., Sullivan, G., Greenwood, K., & Axford, R. (1999). *Handbook for research methods in health sciences* (1syt ed.). Sydney, NSW Australia: Addison Wesley Longman.

Mitchell, T. (1997). *Machine Learning.* New York, USA: McGraw-Hill.

Mitchell, T. M. (1999). Machine Learning and Data Mining. *Communications of the ACM, 42*(11), 30–36. doi:10.1145/319382.319388

Moss, E. A. (1995). Developing national health information in Australia. *Medinfo, 8*(Pt 2), 1636.

Murphy, K. (2007). Software for Graphical Models: A review. *International Society for Bayesian Analysis Bulletin, December,* 1-3.

Murphy, K. (2008, July 28). S*oftware packages for Graphical Models / Bayesian Networks.* Retrieved January 2, 2009, from http://www.cs.ubc.ca/~murphyk/Software/bnsoft.html

Murphy, K. P. (2001, October 14). *A brief introduction to Graphical Models and Bayesian Networks.* Retrieved January 5, 2009, from http://www.cs.berkeley.edu/murphyk/Bayes/bayes.html

Nadathur, S. (2009). *The value of hospital administrative datasets* [In preparation].

Nikovski, D. (2000). Constructing Bayesian Networks for medical diagnosis from incomplete and partially correct statistics. *IEEE Transactions on Knowledge and Data Engineering, 12*(4), 509–516. doi:10.1109/69.868904

Pazzani, M., Mani, S., & Shankle, W. R. (1997). Comprehensible knowledge-discovery in databases. In *Proceedings of Nineteenth annual conference of the Cognitive Science Society.* Retrieved January 4, 2009, from http://www.ics.uci.edu/~pazzani/Publications/CogSci97.pdf

Pearl, J. (1988). *Probabilistic Reasoning in Intelligent Systems.* San Mateo, CA, USA: Morgan Kaufman.

Pearl, J. (2000). *Causality.* Cambridge, UK: Cambridge University Press.

Pronovost, P. J., & Kazandjian, V. A. (1999). A new learning environment: Combining clinical research with quality improvement. *Journal of Evaluation in Clinical Practice, 5*(1), 33–40. doi:10.1046/j.1365-2753.1999.00160.x

Rodin, A. S., & Boerwinkle, E. (2005). Mining genetic epidemiology data with Bayesian Networks I: Bayesian networks and example application (plasma apoE levels). *Bioinformatics (Oxford, England), 21*(15), 3273–3278. doi:10.1093/bioinformatics/bti505

Roos, T., Wettig, H., Grunwald, P., Myllyma, P., & Tirri, H. (2005). On Discriminative Bayesian Network Classifiers and Logistic Regression. *Machine Learning, 59*(3), 267–296.

Rupp, B., Wang, J., Rupp, B., & Wang, J. (2004). Predictive models for protein crystallization. *Methods (San Diego, Calif.)*, *34*(3), 390–407. doi:10.1016/j.ymeth.2004.03.031

Saeys, Y., Inza, I., & Larranaga, P. (2007). A review of feature selection techniques in Bioinformatics. *Bioinformatics (Oxford, England)*, *23*(19), 2507–2517. doi:10.1093/bioinformatics/btm344

Sheingold, S. H. (2001). Can Bayesian methods make data and analysis more relevant to decision makers? *International Journal of Technology Assessment in Health Care*, *17*(1), 114–122. doi:10.1017/S0266462301104101

Song, X., Mitnitski, A., Cox, J., & Rockwood, K. (2004). Comparison of machine learning techniques with classical statistical models in predicting health outcomes. *Studies in Health Technology and Informatics*, *107*(1), 736–740.

Staccini, P., Joubert, M., Quaranta, J. F., Fieschi, D., & Fieschi, M. (2001). Modelling health care processes for eliciting user requirements: a way to link a quality paradigm and clinical information system design. *International Journal of Medical Informatics*, *64*(2-3), 129–142. doi:10.1016/S1386-5056(01)00203-9

Stone, C. A., Ramsden, C. A., Howard, J. A., Roberts, M., & Halliday, J. H. (2002, March 20-21). From data linkage to policy and back again: A preliminary report on the linkage of neonatal data in Victoria. In *Proceedings of the Symposium on Health Data Linkage: Its value for Australian health policy development and policy relevant research*, Tusculum House auditorium, Potts Point, Sydney, NSW, Australia. Retrieved from http://www.publichealth.gov.au/pdf/reports_papers/symposium_procdngs_2003/stone.pdf

Stühlinger, W., Hogl, O., Stoyan, H., & Müller, M. (2000). Intelligent data mining for medical quality management. In *Proceedings of 5th Workshop Intelligent Data Analysis in Medicine and Pharmacology (IDAMAP2000), Workshop Notes of the 14th European Conf. Artificial Intelligence (ECAI-2000)*.

Sundararajan, V., Henderson, T. M., Ackland, M., & Marshall, R. (2002, March 20-21). *Linkage of the Victorian Admitted Episodes Dataset*. In *Proceedings of the Symposium on Health Data Linkage: Its value for Australian health policy development and policy relevant research*, Tusculum House auditorium, Potts Point, Sydney, NSW, Australia. Retrieved from http://www.publichealth.gov.au/pdf/reports_papers/symposium_procdngs_2003/stone.pdf

Sutherland, A. (1998). *Bayesian Networks - Another example*. Retrieved January 27, 2009, from http://computing.dcu.ie/~alistair/

Tigrani, V. S., & John, G. H. (2005). Data mining and statistics in medicine - An application in prostate cancer detection. In *Proceedings of the Joint Statistical Meetings, Section on Physical and Engineering Sciences*. Retrieved January 22, 2009 from http://robotics.stanford.edu/~gjohn/ftp/papers/jsm.ps.gz

Van der Gaag, L. C., Renooij, S., Feelders, A., de Groote, A., Eijkemans, M. J. C., Broekmans, F. J., et al. (2008). *Aligning Bayesian Network classifiers with medical contexts* (No. Technical Report UU-CS-2008-015). Department of Information and Computing Sciences, Utrecht University, Utrecht, The Netherlands.

Van der Lei, J. (2002). Information and communication technology in health care: Do we need feedback? *International Journal of Medical Informatics, 66*(1-3), 75–83. doi:10.1016/S1386-5056(02)00039-4

Visscher, S., Lucas, P., Schurink, K., & Bonten, M. (2005, July 23-27). Using a Bayesian-Network model for the analysis of clinical time-series data. In *Proceeding of 2005 Artificial Intelligence in Medicine Europe (AIME) conference,* Aberdeen, UK.

Viveros, M. S., Nearhos, J. P., & Rothman, M. J. (1996). Applying data mining techniques to a health insurance information system. In *Proceedings of the 22nd Very Large Data Base (VLDB) Conference,* Mumbai, India.

Williams, T. A., Dobb, G. J., Finn, J. C., Knuiman, M., Lee, K. Y., & Geelhoed, E. (2006). Data linkage enables evaluation of long-term survival after intensive care. *Anaesthesia and Intensive Care, 34*(3), 307–315.

Zheng, H. T., Kang, B. Y., & Kim, H. G. (2008). An ontology-based bayesian network approach for representing uncertainty in Clinical Practice Guidelines. In *Proceedings of the Uncertainty Reasoning for the Semantic Web I: ISWC International Workshops, URSW 2005-2007, Revised Selected and Invited Papers* (LNAI 5327, pp. 161-173).

Zipitria, I., Larranaga, P., Armananzas, R., Arruarte, A., & Elorriaga, J. A. (2008). What is behind a summary-evaluation decision? *Behavior Research Methods, 40*(2), 597–612. doi:10.3758/BRM.40.2.597

Chapter 15
Time Series Analysis and Structural Change Detection

Kwok Pan Pang
Monash University, Australia

ABSTRACT

Most research on time series analysis and forecasting is normally based on the assumption of no structural change, which implies that the mean and the variance of the parameter in the time series model are constant over time. However, when structural change occurs in the data, the time series analysis methods based on the assumption of no structural change will no longer be appropriate; and thus there emerges another approach to solving the problem of structural change. Almost all time series analysis or forecasting methods always assume that the structure is consistent and stable over time, and all available data will be used for the time series prediction and analysis. When any structural change occurs in the middle of time series data, any analysis result and forecasting drawn from full data set will be misleading. Structural change is quite common in the real world. In the study of a very large set of macroeconomic time series that represent the 'fundamentals' of the US economy, Stock and Watson (1996) has found evidence of structural instability in the majority of the series. Besides, ignoring structural change reduces the prediction accuracy. Persaran and Timmermann (2003), Hansen (2001) and Clement and Hendry (1998, 1999) showed that structural change is pervasive in time series data, ignoring structural breaks which often occur in time series significantly reduces the accuracy of the forecast, and results in misleading or wrong conclusions. This chapter mainly focuses on introducing the most common time series methods. The author highlights the problems when applying to most real situations with structural changes, briefly introduce some existing structural change methods, and demonstrate how to apply structural change detection in time series decomposition.

DOI: 10.4018/978-1-60566-908-3.ch015

INTRODUCTION

A time series is a collection of observations of well defined data items observed through the time. An ordered sequence of values of a variable are measured at equally spaced interval. Time series analysis is a vital activity to understand and interpret the time series data in a wide range of diverse areas such as marketing, economics, commerce, industry and various science fields. Time series analysis can range from changes of demands, changes of sales, to changes of weather at different periods. Time series data and analysis serves two main goals: (a) identifying the characteristics, phenomenon or pattern represented by the sequence of the time series data, and (b) forecasting based on the identified characteristics or pattern to predict the future values. Both goals involve knowledge about the mathematical models of the time series process. Unfortunately, the patterns or characteristics of the time series data are always unclear, and time series data always involves considerable error. To interpret the time series data accurately, it requires knowledge about using and applying appropriate data analysis methods and techniques. The next section will discuss and introduce some common data analysis methods.

COMMON DATA ANALYSIS OR FORECASTING METHODS

When introducing the following methods, we assume the time series data is presented as x_t, $t = 1, 2, 3, \ldots, N$, where x_t is the observation of the variable x at time t, and N is number of observation.

ARIMA Model

ARIMA methodology proposed by Box Jenkin (1976) is one of the popular methods to uncover the hidden characteristics in the time series data, and to generate forecasts. The model is built based on the plot of the autocorrelation and partial autocorrelation functions of the dependent time series. The plot provides the information to determine which autoregressive or moving average component should be used in the model. Basically, ARIMA(p,q) model includes two independent processes. They are autoregressive process (AR(p)) and Moving average Process (MA(q)).

Autoregressive Process

Autoregressive Process can be represented as AR(p) that can be interpreted as a linear combination of prior observations, AR(p) can be summarized as:

$$x_t = \zeta + \varphi_1 x_{t-1} + \varphi_2 x_{t-2} + \ldots \varphi_k x_{t-p} + \varepsilon \tag{1}$$

where p is order of autoregressive model, ζ is the constant of the model, and $\varphi_1, \varphi_2, \ldots, \varphi_p$ are the autoregressive model parameters.

3Moving Average Process

It can be represented as MA(q). In the Moving average model, the observation can be affected by its previous error, MA(q) can be written as:

$$x_t = \mu + \varepsilon_t - \theta_1 \varepsilon_{t-1} - \theta_2 \varepsilon_{t-2} - \ldots - \theta_3 \varepsilon_{t-q} \tag{2}$$

where q is the order of the moving average model, μ is a constant and $\theta_1, \theta_2, \ldots, \theta_q$ are the moving average model parameters.

We suppose the stochastic process $\{x_t : t = 0, \pm 1, \pm 2, \ldots\}$, and its mean function is defined as $\mu_t = E(x_t)$ for $t = 0, \pm 1, \pm 2, \ldots$. In general, μ_t differs at different t. Autocorrelation is defined as:

$$Corr(x_t, x_s) = \frac{Cov(x_t, x_s)}{\left[Var(x_t) Var(x_s) \right]^{1/2}} \tag{3}$$

where $Cov(x_t, x_s)$ is autocovariance function,

$$Cov(x_t, x_s) = E[(x_t - \mu_t)(x_s - \mu_s)] = E(x_t x_s) - \mu_t \mu_s$$

The partial autocorrelation at lag k (ϕ_{kk}) is defined as:

$$\phi_{kk} = Corr(x_t, x_{t-k} \mid x_{t-1}, x_{t-2}, \ldots, x_{t-k+1})$$

that can be interpreted as the correlation between x_t and x_{t-k} after removing the effect of the intervening variables $x_{t-1}, x_{t-2}, \ldots, x_{t-k=1}$

PARAMETER IDENTIFICATION/ESTIMATION

Stationary Requirement

The data of ARIMA model has to be stationary. Stationary generally means covariance stationary. The time series $\{x_t, t = 1-k, 2-k, 3-k, \ldots, n-1, n\}$ is covariance stationary if $E(x_t) = \mu$ for all t; and $cov(x_t, x_{t-j}) = \phi_j$ for all t and any j, where ϕ_j is the lag j autocovariance of time series. It means the data should have the constant mean, variance and autocorrelation through time. When the series is not stationary, the series needs to take a "difference" transformation (i.e. $y_t - y_{t-1}$) until it is stationary, and take a log transformation to stabilize the variance.

Time Series Decomposition Model

Most time series patterns can be described in terms of three basic classes of components: Seasonal component (denoted as S_t, where t stands for the particular point in time), Trend component (T_t) and Irregular component (I_t). Trend component represents a general linear or a nonlinear component that changes over time, but it won't repeat within the time range while a recurring pattern exists within each year for the seasonal components. The irregular component represents unpredictable residual variation remaining after removing the trend and seasonal components from the original series. Trend, seasonal and irregular components are assumed to be independent, and can be assumed in different forms. Multiplicative and additive models are two decomposition models which are commonly used. In addition to these decomposition models, pseudo-additive model is used in some situations.

As we know, different months have different number of days. For example, January has 31 days. However, February has only 28 days. In order to capture good information from data, it is better to reorganize the series into equal interval. For example, it is better to have 4 weeks periods rather than monthly, or 12 weeks period rather than quarterly as different months have different lengths, or each quarter have different intervals. That means we will have 13 periods each year if we select 4-week period data.

Additive Model

Assume the original observation is represented by O_t, then the additive decomposition model can be described as:

$$O_t = S_t + T_t + I_t \tag{4}$$

The seasonal adjusted series is a series after removing the systematic calendar related influences from the original series. The seasonally adjusted data can be expressed by:

$$SA_t = O_t - S_t = T_t + I_t \tag{5}$$

The constraints for an additive model are

(1) the seasonal fluctuation averages out to zero over the year;

(2) $\sum_{j=1}^{n} S_{t+j} = 0$, $j = 1, ..., n$ with $n = 13$ for 4-weeks period series or $n = 4$ for 12-weeks period series.

Multiplicative Model

The seasonal, trend and irregular components can be written as:

$$O_t = S_t T_t I_t \tag{6}$$

The seasonally adjusted series can be expressed as:

$$SA_t = O_t / S_t = T_t / I_t \tag{7}$$

Clearly, we are not able to obtain the seasonal adjusted series if S_t contains zero values. Thus, Multiplicative is not suitable for the original observation that contains any zero value.

The multiplicative model can also be written in an additive form by taking logarithms.

$$\log O_t = \log S_t + \log T_t + \log I_t \tag{8}$$

The constraints for a multiplicative model are

$$\sum_{j=1}^{n} S_{t+j} = n \text{, for } j = 1, ..., n \text{ with } n = 13 \text{ for 4-weeks period series or } n = 4 \text{ for 12-weeks period series.}$$

Pseudo-Additive Model

When the original series contains zero value, multiplicative model will no longer be appropriate for interpreting the data. In this situation, a pseudo additive model combining the elements of both the additive and multiplicative models can be used. The pseudo-additive model can be expressed as:

$$O_t = T_t + T_t(S_t - 1) + T_t(I_t - 1) = T_t(S_t + I_t - 1) \tag{9}$$

The seasonally adjusted series is defined to be

$$SA_t = O_t - T_t(S_t - 1) \tag{10}$$

$$= T_t I_t$$

Determining Additive, Multiplicative or Pseudo-Additive Model

The pattern of time series plot provides us important information for selecting which kind of model. For additive model, we expect the seasonal pattern remains constant over time as shown in Figure 1 (a). In the Multiplicative model, the seasonal pattern increases as time increases. Besides, the series cannot dip below the zero value as shown in Figure 1 (b). However, when the seasonal pattern increases as time increase, and the series dips below zero value, we should use pseudo-additive model. In some situation, additive, multiplicative and pseudo-additive model are also applicable. As demonstrated in Figure 1 (d), the trend remains at a constant level over time and seasonal variation is small compared with the trend. Thus three models is approximately equivalent.

Figure 1.

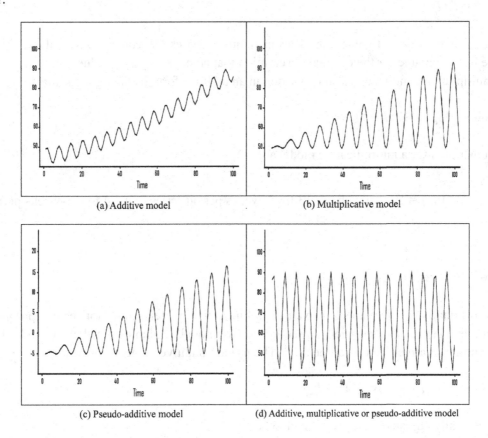

(a) Additive model   (b) Multiplicative model

(c) Pseudo-additive model   (d) Additive, multiplicative or pseudo-additive model

Example: Estimation of the Seasonal Index and Trend

When the additive, multiplicative or pseudo-additive model is determined, we can apply different techniques to estimate the trend and seasonal component. Following is the example demonstrating how we estimate the seasonal component, seasonal adjustment, and the trend of the series shown in Figure 1 (b) in the multiplicative model.

Seasonal Index

One of the common ways is to use seasonal index to represent the seasonal component. Seasonal index helps us to understand how the seasonal influence affects a particular segment of the year, and represent the seasonal component in the model. The seasonal index can be estimated using the comparison of the expected values of that period to the grand mean. Algebraically, it can be expressed as: $S_i = D_i / D$, for $i=1,2,\ldots,n$, $n=13$ when it is 4-weeks period series, and $n=4$ when it is 13-weeks period series. Where D is the grand mean, and D_i is the average value of the period i.

A seasonal index of 1.00 for a particular period indicates that the expected value of that period is 1/13 of the overall average. A seasonal index of 1.25 indicates that the expected value for that period is 25% greater than 1/13 of the overall average. A seasonal index of 0.8 indicates that the expected value for that period is 20% less than 1/13 of the overall average.

The grand mean: $D = (2245 + 2272 + 2407 + 2887) / (4*13) = 188.7$,

$D_1 = 212 / 188.7 = 1.1236$ (for January),

$D_2 = 210.8 / 187 = 1.117$, and so on.

We will obtain the seasonal index as Figure 3.

The seasonal adjustment can be obtained by: $SA_t = O_t / S_t$. Thus, the seasonal adjusted series will be shown as Figure 4.

Estimation of the Trend

One of the common methods for determining trend is to calculate a moving average of order n as following

$$\frac{x_1 + x_2 + \ldots + x_n}{n}, \frac{x_2 + x_3 + \ldots + x_{n+1}}{n}, \ldots \qquad (11)$$

Figure 2. Raw data of the sample series

	Period													
	1	**2**	**3**	**4**	**5**	**6**	**7**	**8**	**9**	**10**	**11**	**12**	**13**	**Total**
year 1	199	195	199	168	149	126	114	147	168	174	201	205	200	2245
year 2	201	191	201	172	144	124	139	145	184	175	197	196	203	2272
year 3	199	216	212	188	154	141	157	151	164	189	202	235	199	2407
year 4	249	241	204	223	208	195	182	187	208	236	250	269	235	2887
mean	212	210.75	204	187.75	163.75	146.5	148	157.5	181	193.5	212.5	226.25	209.25	2452.8

Figure 3. Seasonal index of the sample series

period	1	2	3	4	5	6	7	8	9	10	11	12	13
Seasonal Index	1.1236	1.117	1.081	0.995	0.868	0.776	0.784	0.835	0.959	1.026	1.126	1.199	1.109

Figure 4. Seasonal adjustment of the sample series

	Period												
	1	**2**	**3**	**4**	**5**	**6**	**7**	**8**	**9**	**10**	**11**	**12**	**13**
year 1	177.11	174.58	184.09	168.84	171.66	162.37	145.41	176.05	175.18	169.59	178.51	170.98	180.34
year 2	178.89	170.99	185.94	172.86	165.9	159.79	177.3	173.65	191.87	170.57	174.96	163.47	183.05
year 3	177.11	193.38	196.12	188.95	177.42	181.7	200.26	180.84	171.01	184.21	179.4	196	179.44
year 4	221.61	215.76	188.71	224.12	239.63	251.29	232.14	223.95	216.89	230.02	222.03	224.35	211.9

When the series is 4-weeks period series, we normally set $n=13$ and use a 13-period moving average to estimate the trend component.

Exponential Smoothing

Exponential smoothing was proposed by Brown and Holt. It has become one of the most popular forecasting methods. Makridakis et al (1982) and Makridakis et al, (1983) have shown that simple exponential smoothing is the best for one-period ahead forecasting among 24 other time series methods.

The simple exponential smoothing is specified as:

$$P_t = \alpha x_t + (1-\alpha)P_{t-1} \tag{12}$$

where x represents as the raw data sequence and P is regarded as the best estimate of what the next value of x will be. The weight (α) shall fall into interval between 0 and 1.

Estimation of α

The parameter α is often chosen by a grid search. Normally, we select the value of α as the best α value when that α can generate the smallest sums of square for the residual.

Causal Model

Causal model involves other variables for forecasting of our interest. The relationship between the dependent variable and independent variable will be analysed and used to build the forecasting model.

One of most popular causal techniques is multi-variable regression. Let us take a tourism demand as an example. The tourism demand model can be written as a function f():

$$D = f(Y, C, P, E)$$

where D is the tourism demand, it can be expressed in term of the number of tourist arrival, C is the cost of travel, P is the relative price level in the two countries and in an alternative destination, and E is the exchange rate.

To build and analyse the data, the simplest form is additive linear regression.

$$D = \beta_0 + \beta_1 Y + \beta_2 C + \beta_3 P + \beta_4 E + \varepsilon \tag{13}$$

where ε is the residual of the model.

However, in real practice, it is unlikely that the explanatory variables would be related to the dependent variable in such a simple way. The most common form of their relationships is multiplicative. A log transformation is thus required in the formula to reflect a more complicated relationship. (11)

$$D = \beta_0 Y^{\beta_1} C^{\beta_2} P^{\beta_3} E^{\beta_4} \varepsilon \tag{14}$$

Taking the log transformation, Equation (14) can be expressed in term of a logarithm linear form:

$$\log D = \log \beta_0 + \beta_1 \log Y + \beta_2 \log C + \beta_3 \log P$$
$$+ \beta_4 \log E + \log \varepsilon \tag{15}$$

In time series, some variables may have the seasonal variations, and others don't have. In this situation, it is better to remove the seasonal influence first. Let us take the tourism demand to explain the situation. We can easily show that more travellers visit Australia in every December than every May. However, other independent variable may not have this seasonal variations. Thus, it would be better to remove the seasonal factor (S) first. Then, the Equation (13) of the additive model will be modified as:

$$D = S + \beta_0 + \beta_1 Y + \beta_2 C + \beta_3 P + \beta_4 E + \varepsilon \tag{16}$$

When the relationship between the independent variable and dependent variable is in multiplicative form, the Equations (14) and (15) will be rewritten as:

$$D = S\beta_0 Y^{\beta_1} C^{\beta_2} P^{\beta_3} E^{\beta_4} \varepsilon \tag{17}$$

and

$$\log D = \log S + \log \beta_0 + \beta_1 \log Y + \beta_2 \log C$$
$$+ \beta_3 \log P + \beta_4 \log E + \log \varepsilon \tag{18}$$

the above coefficient can be estimated by using least square residual approach, which means we will select the value of coefficients that give the lowest possible value of $\sum \varepsilon$.

STRUCTURAL CHANGE IN TIME SERIES

In most econometric models, forecasting models or the process control, the parameters of the model or the process are usually assumed to be constant and stable over time, which means the structure or the distribution of the parameters remains the same over time. The assumption of the stable structure and the constant parameter over time poses challenges, and limits the applicability of forecasting models or econometric models. In many situations, the problem of the structural change is not addressed. When this assumption of the stable structure underlying the model is violated, incorrect inferences are drawn from the data, and forecasting performance is weakened. As a result, it leads to inappropriate decision-making in the policy. Structural change is always ignored in most conventional data mining methods. However, in reality structure change is not rare and it should be considered in many situations. For instance:

- **Economics Analysis**

Let us take an economics issue to illustrate the point. The United States labor productivity experienced a "slow down" around 1973 and "speed up" in the second half of 1990. Any economics analysis that includes the variable "labor productivity" will generate a misleading result if the researchers ignore the structural change and select a wrong time period for analysis.

- **Business Analysis**

Manufacturing companies generally plan their material purchase schedules based on the assumption that their production process is stable over time. They assume that their production rate or production yield rate is stable. The material requirements and delivery schedules are made according to the average production yield rate and production rate in the past. If the company fails to consider the change of the production process, numerous problems including production material over-stock or shortage will be generated.

The common characteristic of the above applications is that the structure of any variable may change from one stage to another, and the relationship among the variables will thus be changed.

The normal practice of forecasting and time series analysis assumes that the structure of all variables and the relationship among the variables are stable and constant over time (Hansen 2001). All available data is usually used to make the analysis. Unfortunately, when the structural changes occur in reality, the econometric models or forecasting models that are based on the assumption of the stable structure will draw an incorrect analysis result or conclusion. Some old historical data prior to the structural change becomes irrelevant and fails to reflect the new situation after the change. Empirical evidence shows that many financial and macroeconomic time series are subject to structural changes. Stock and Watson (1996) showed evidence that structural instability is found in the majority of the very large sets of fundamental time series of the US economy. When structural change is ignored, the prediction performance will be poor. Persaran and Timmermann (2003), Hansen (2001) and Clement and Hendry (1998, 1999) showed that structural change is pervasive in time series data; ignoring structural breaks which often occur in time series significantly reduces the accuracy of the forecast, and leads to misleading conclusions. Thus, the time series analysis or forecasting method mentioned in last section will no longer be valid if any structure change is found in the series. We can say that the structural change detection is one of the keys for validating our Time Series model. This section mainly discusses some of the common structural change detection methods, and demonstrates how they work.

Definition of Structural Change

The parameters of the predictive model are assumed to be consistent and constant over time. If these conditions cannot be met, it is said that structural change has occurred in the time series.

Let us take a linear regression as an example. Suppose a time series can be explained by:

$$y_t = \chi_t \beta_t + \sigma_t \varepsilon_t$$

$$y_t = \chi_t \beta_t + \sigma_t \varepsilon_t, \ t = 1,2,3,\ldots,n \text{ where } \varepsilon_t \sim N(0,1)$$

The time series is regarded to have "no structural change" if the parameters β_t and σ_t are constant and consistent over time. The change of β is defined as the change of the regression coefficients, and the change of σ can be defined as the change of variance.

The structural change can appear in many different forms. The structure may change suddenly or gradually. It may include single structural change or multiple structural changes in the time series data. The time series data may change permanently or temporarily and recover to the regular pattern after a certain period. Figure 5 is an illustration of the structural change. The seasonal effect disappeared for about two years from 1997 to 1998, and then re-appeared after 1998.

Structural Change Detection Methods

Since the classical Chow test (1960) was developed, the past decade has seen considerable empirical and theoretical research on structural break detection in time series. Chow test has been popular for many years. Chow test is expected to have F distribution, and its procedure first splits the sample into two sets of periods, then it estimates the parameters for each set of split period, and tests whether the two sets of parameters are the same.

Chow Test (F test)

The Chow Test is a particular test for detecting structural change. It tests whether the regression coefficients are the same in two separate subsamples or segments.

Suppose the time series is composed of two segments $\{Seg_1$ and $Seg_2\}$. These two segments can be interpreted by $Y=X\beta_1$ and $Y=X\beta_2$ respectively.

The regression coefficients β, β_1 and β_2 have dimension z, and there are n observations in total.

$$\text{F test} = \frac{(SSE - SSE_1 - SSE_2)/z}{SSE/(n-2k)} \tag{19}$$

Chow Test (F) has $F_{z,n-2k}$ distribution
Where

SSE = the sum of the squared residuals from the regression of the whole time series; β_1 and β_2 are assumed to be the same;

SSE_1 = the sum of squared residuals from the linear regression of the segment Seg_1;

SSE_2 = the sum of squared residuals from the linear regression of the segment Seg_2;

However, the greatest limitation of Chow test is that the break location is assumed to be known. To overcome this limitation, Quandt (1960) proposed taking the largest Chow statistic over all possible break points. His approach is to perform every possible Chow tests with all possible break locations. This approach finds the worst-case Chow statistic and the break location indicated by the largest test statistic value. Unfortunately, Quandt's approach generates another problem. He failed to consider the probability distribution of Chow test that he used in his approach. When the break location is unknown, Chow test will no longer have F distribution. Then, its critical value based on F distribution will be inappropriate. Andrews (1993) and Hansen (1992) overcome the problem of Quandt's approach and based on Chow test to develop several test statistics: SupF, AveF and ExpF with the asymptotic critical values.

Figure 5. The time plot (April 1992 – February 2000) of the monthly ILO unemployment in UK for males aged 25-49 who have been unemployed for less than 6 months

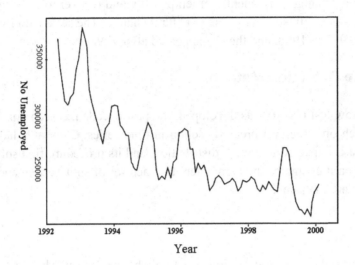

SupF, AveF and ExpF test

$$SupF = \max_{2 < t \leq T-1} F_t \tag{20}$$

$$aveF = \frac{1}{T-2} \sum_{t=2}^{T-1} F_t \tag{21}$$

$$\exp F = \log \frac{1}{T-2} \sum_{t=2}^{T-1} \exp(0.5 F_t) \tag{22}$$

where F_t is the test statistic mentioned in Equation (21) at different change point t.

Brown et al. (1975) initiated a new idea for the structural break method without relying on the assumption about the break location. They developed Cumulative Sum of Recursive Residual (CUSUM) and Cumulative Sums of Square (CUSUMS) statistics based on the recursive prediction residual.

CUSUMS and CUSUMS

Let $\{(\chi_t, y_t), t = 1, 2, 3, \ldots, n\}$ be the time series under consideration. y_t is the output observation, and $\chi_t = (x_{1t}, x_{2t}, \ldots, x_{kt})$ is the vector of the input variables.

The basic linear regression model that we use is having the output y_t with k input variables:

$$y_t = \lambda_0 + \lambda_1 x_{1t} + \lambda_2 x_{2t} + \ldots + \lambda_k x_{kt} + \varepsilon_t.$$

The following notation is used to denote the observation matrices $Y_{m,g}$ and $X_{m,g}$ which consist of $(g-m+1)$ observations in the time series starting from the mth to the gth observation.

$$Y_{m,g} = \begin{bmatrix} y_m \\ y_{m+1} \\ \dots \\ \dots \\ y_g \end{bmatrix}, \begin{bmatrix} y_m \\ y_{m+1} \\ \dots \\ \dots \\ y_g \end{bmatrix} \quad \beta_g = \begin{bmatrix} \lambda_0 \\ \lambda_1 \\ .. \\ .. \\ \lambda_k \end{bmatrix}, \beta_g = \begin{bmatrix} \lambda_0 \\ \lambda_1 \\ .. \\ .. \\ \lambda_k \end{bmatrix} \text{ and}$$

$$X_{m,g} = \begin{bmatrix} x_m \\ x_{m+1} \\ . \\ . \\ x_g \end{bmatrix} = \begin{bmatrix} x_m \\ x_{m+1} \\ . \\ . \\ x_g \end{bmatrix} \begin{bmatrix} 1 & x_{1m} & x_{2m} & . & . & x_{(k-1)m} & x_{km} \\ 1 & x_{1(m+1)} & x_{2(m+1)} & . & . & & x_{k(m+1)} \\ .. & \dots & \dots & . & . & . & \dots \\ .. & \dots & \dots & . & . & . & \dots \\ 1 & x_{1g} & x_{2g} & . & . & & x_{kg} \end{bmatrix} =$$

$$\begin{bmatrix} 1 & x_{1m} & x_{2m} & . & . & x_{(k-1)m} & x_{km} \\ 1 & x_{1(m+1)} & x_{2(m+1)} & . & . & & x_{k(m+1)} \\ .. & \dots & \dots & . & . & . & \dots \\ .. & \dots & \dots & . & . & . & \dots \\ 1 & x_{1g} & x_{2g} & . & . & & x_{kg} \end{bmatrix}$$

where $m < g$, and the $x_m, x_{m+1}, \dots, x_g$ are the row vectors.

Using the observations as the training data, the ordinary linear regression coefficients β_r can be estimated by

$$\hat{\beta}_r = (X'_{1,r} X_{1,r})^{-1} X'_{1,r} Y_{1,r}, \quad r = k+1, \dots, n-1, n$$

There are $k+1$ unknown parameters in β_r, we need to have $k+1$ row vectors to get the first estimate of β_r.

The CUSUMS statistics (Brown et al 1975) are defined as follows. The CUSUMS statistic is based on the standardized recursive prediction residual w_r. We use the estimated regression coefficients to make a one step-ahead prediction. Thus, the recursive prediction residual starts at $k+2$ after the first estimation of β is obtained.

$$w_r = (y_r - x_r \hat{\beta}_{r-1}) / d_r, \quad r = k+2, \dots, n-1, n \tag{23}$$

where

$$\hat{\beta}_r = (X'_{1,r} X_{1,r})^{-1} X'_{1,r} Y_{1,r}$$

$$d_r = 1 + x_r (X'_{1,r} X_{1,r})^{-1} x'_r$$

The CUSUM $C_0()$ and CUSUMS $C_1()$ is defined in terms of w_r:

$$C_0(r) = \frac{1}{\sqrt{n-k}} \sum_{i=k+1}^{r} w_i$$

$r=k+1,\ldots,n-1,n$ 　　　　　　　　　　　　　　　　　　　　　　　(24)

$$C_1(r) = \frac{\sum_{i=1}^{r} w_i^2}{\sum_{i=1}^{n} w_i^2}$$

$r=k+1,\ldots,n-1,n$ 　　　　　　　　　　　　　　　　　　　　　　　(25)

These statistic from Brown et al have been developed as a general method for single structural break detection. As CUSUM and CUSUMS have shown great potential and promising results in single structural break detection, a considerable amount of research has been conducted to explore its ideas and extensions. From the literature we can see the important role of CUSUM and CUSUMS in single break detection. Krämer and Schotman (1992) proposed a modified statistic from CUSUM; and the structural change is detected based on the range of the CUSUM rather than the maximum point of the absolute value of CUSUM. Bauer and Hackl (1978, 1980) proposed a MOSUMS test based on the moving sums of the recursive prediction residuals. Chu et al. (1995) proposed the recursive-MOSUM test for structural change based on the moving sums (MOSUMS) of the recursive prediction residual. Ploberger and Krämer (1992) suggested a new test developed from CUSUM, using the ordinary linear regression residual instead of the recursive prediction residual. Kuan (1994) developed the Range-CUSUM test based on the range of CUSUM. Pesaran and Timmermann (2002) suggested Reverse CUSUM for detecting the most recent break. All of the above structural break detection methods focus on testing for a single change.

Most research on structural break detection concentrates on single break detection. Very little amount of research has been conducted to deal with the multiple break detection. One of the most significant advances in multiple break detection was conducted by Inclan and Tiao (1994). They extended the main idea of CUSUMS, and proposed the centered version of CUSUMS statistic (Centered CUSUMS) and Iterated Cumulative Sums of Square algorithm (ICSS). ICSS is an algorithm which incorporates the Centered CUSUMS for multiple structural break detection. Apart from the Centered CUSUMS, some other approaches are found to deal with the multiple break detection. Bai (1997) and Bai and Perron (1998) suggested sequential estimation of multiple breaks in mean. Lavielle and Moulines (2000) proposed the Lavielle and Moulines test, and the estimation of the number of break points involves the use of Schwarz or Bayesian Information Criterion. It is also important to note that most multiple break detection methods are found to focus mainly on the change of mean. Most methods fail to deal with the change of variance. However, Bos and Hoonstrakul (2002) stated that Centered CUSUMS can detect both the change of mean and variance. He mentioned that ICSS with the Centered CUSUMS is the multiple break detection method that is able to detect both the change of mean and variance. The literature has shown that CUSUM has been widely used and extended. The Centered CUSUMS developed from CUSUMS has shown great potential in handling both single and multiple break detections for the situations with either the change of mean or variance. More research into the further exploration of Centered CUSUMS is recommended.

Centered CUSUMS

Inclan and Tiao (1994) revised the CUSUMS as described in Equation (25), and proposed the Centered CUSUMS as follows:

$$C_2(r) = \frac{\sum_{i=1}^{r} w_i^2}{\sum_{i=1}^{n} w_i^2} - \frac{r}{n}$$

$,r=k+2,\ldots,n-1,n$ (26)

Note that $C_2(r)$ has zero mean.

The test statistic for structural break detection is:

$$T = \sqrt{\frac{n}{2}} \max_r \left| C_2(r) \right|$$

(27)

Example of the Structural Change for Time Series Decomposition Model

In this example, we will demonstrate how to detect the structural change or volatility level change in the time series decomposition model. We employ the multiplicative decomposition model to analyze the series of the employed male labour force estimates in Australia from Jan 1994 to May 2008 as shown in Figure 6. The volatility level change is defined as the level change of the irregular deviation. (i.e. Irregular Deviation = abs(irregular factor-1), where abs() denotes the absolute value function. Such 'volatility' may be the impact of the new government policy. Volatility level change may be intrinsic to the data collection process, such as sampling error or non-sampling error. It may also reflect changes brought by the short-term movements of estimates which do not reflect the general underlying behaviour of the series. Changes in seasonal patterns can cause a seasonally adjusted series become more volatile, because it may take several years for seasonal adjustment process to identify and adapt to the new seasonal pattern. In this case, there may not necessarily be any increase in the volatility of the original (unadjusted) series.

As demonstrated in the previous section, we can use the multiplicative decomposition model to analyze this series, and the irregular component can be derived by the following equation:

Figure 6. Employed Male Labour force force estimate from Jan 1994 to May 2008

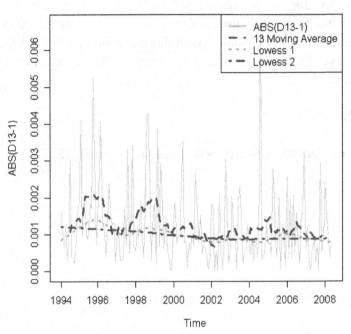

Table 1.

SupF statistic: 9.2171
SupF: P_value: 0.0387
ExpF statistic: 2.4931
ExpF: P_value: 0.02888

Irregular Factor = Seasonal adjusted series / Trend estimates.

Where seasonal adjusted series can be obtained by: Original series divided by the seasonal index, the estimation of the seasonal index is as the example in previous section. The trend can be estimated by the 13-period moving average, each period contains four weeks.

Both SupF and ExpF test statistics have indicated the volatility level change in the series as the result demonstrated in Table 1.

It seems that even Quant test (i.e. using Chow test to detect at all possible break points) is not a good test. However, the pattern of Chow test at different point provides us a rough idea when volatility level starts to change. As demonstrated in Figure 7. If the structure has been changed, it is likely that the volatility level started to change in 1999.

Figure 7. Quant test for employed male labour force estimate

Employed Male

CONCLUSION

Time series data and its analysis provide crucial information for forecasting and decision making. Accurate interpretation relies heavily on the understanding and appropriate applications of time series data analysis methods. Structural change is one of very critical factors which we should consider seriously when conducting the analysis. Detecting whether the data encompasses a stable structure and how the structural change is dealt with may also greatly determine the success of most time series analysis or forecasting methods. The structural change detection method provides a useful tool for the analysts to validate their analysis or forecasting results.

REFERENCE

Andrews, D. W. (1993). Tests for parameter Instability and Structural Change with Unknown Point. *Econometrica, 61*(4), 821–856. doi:10.2307/2951764

Bai, J. (1997). Estimating Multiple Breaks One at a Time. *Econometric Theory, 13*, 315–352. doi:10.1017/S0266466600005831

Bai, J., & Perron, P. (1998). Estimating and Testing Linear Models with Multiple Structural Changes. *Econometrica, 66*, 47–78. doi:10.2307/2998540

Bauer, P., & Hackl, P. (1978). The use of MOSUMs for quality control. *Technometrics, 20*, 431–436. doi:10.2307/1267643

Bauer, P., & Hackl, P. (1980). An extension of the MOSUM technique for quality control. *Technometrics, 22*, 1–7. doi:10.2307/1268376

Bos, T., & Hoontrakul, P. (2002). Estimation of Mean and Variance Episodes in the Price Return of the Stock Exchange of Thailand. *Research in international Business and Finance Series, 16*, 210-226. Retrieved from http://www.pongsak.hoontrakul.com/papers/ESTIMAT.pdf

Box, G. E. P., & Jenkins, G. M. (1976). *Time Series Analysis: Forecasting and Control* (rev. ed.). San Francisco: Holden Day.

Brown, R. L., Durbin, J., & Evans, J. M. (1975). Techniques for Testing the constancy of Regression Relationship over Time. *Journal of the Royal Statistical Society. Series A (General), 37*, 149–192.

Chow, G. (1960). Tests of equality between sets of coefficients in two linear regressions. *Econometrica, 28*(3), 591–605. doi:10.2307/1910133

Chu, C. S., Hornik, K., & Kuan, C. M. (1995). MOSUM Test for Parameter Constancy. *Biometrika, 82*(3), 603–617. doi:10.1093/biomet/82.3.603

Clement, M. P., & Hendry, D. F. (1999). *Forecasting Non-stationary Economic Time Series*. Cambridge, MA: MIT Press.

Hansen, B. E. (1992). Tests for parameter instability in regressions with I(1) processes. *Journal of Business & Economic Statistics, 15*, 60–67. doi:10.2307/1392074

Hansen, B. E. (2001). The New Econometrics of Structural Change: Dating Breaks in U.S. Labor Productivity. *The Journal of Economic Perspectives, 15*, 117–128.

Inclan, C., & Tiao, G. C. (1994). Use of Cumulative Sums of Squares for Retrospective Detection of Changes of Variance. *Journal of the American Statistical Association, 84*(427), 913–923. doi:10.2307/2290916

Krämer, W., & Schotman, P. (1992). Range vs Maximum in OLS-based version of CUSUM test. *Economics Letters, 40*, 379–381. doi:10.1016/0165-1765(92)90130-Q

Kuan, C. M. (1994). A Range-CUSUM test with the recursive residual. *Economics Letters, 45*, 309–313. doi:10.1016/0165-1765(94)90029-9

Lavielle, M., & Moulines, E. (2000). Least-Squares Estimation of an Unknown Number of Shifts in time Series. *Journal of Time Series Analysis, 20*, 33–60. doi:10.1111/1467-9892.00172

Makridakis, S., Anderson, A., Carbone, R., Fildes, R., Hibon, M., & Lewandowski, R. (1983). The Accuracy of Extrapolation (time series) methods: results of a forecasting competition. *Journal of Forecasting, 1*, 111–153. doi:10.1002/for.3980010202

Makridakis, S., & Winkler, R. L. (1983). Averages of Forecasts: Some Empirical Results. *Management Science, 29*(9), 987–996. doi:10.1287/mnsc.29.9.987

Pesaran, H., & Timmermann, A. (2002). Market timing and Return Prediction under Model instability. *Journal of Empirical Finance, 9*, 495–510. doi:10.1016/S0927-5398(02)00007-5

Pesaran, H., & Timmermann, A. (2003). *How Costly is it to Ignore Breaks when Forecasting the Direction of a Time Series?* (Cambridge Working Papers in Economics 0306). Department of Applied Economics, University of Cambridge.

Ploberger, W., & Krämer, W. (1992). The CUSUM test with OLS residuals. *Econometrica, 60*, 271–285. doi:10.2307/2951597

Quandt, R. (1960). Tests of the Hypothesis that a Linear Regression Obeys Two Separate Regimes. *Journal of the American Statistical Association, 55*, 324–330. doi:10.2307/2281745

Stock, J. H., & Watson, M. W. (2003). Forecasting Output and Inflation: The Role of Asset Prices. *Journal of Economic Literature, 41*, 788–829. doi:10.1257/002205103322436197

Winkler, R. L., & Makridakis, S. (1983). The Combination of Forecasts. *Journal of the Royal Statistical Society. Series A (General), 146*(2), 150–157. doi:10.2307/2982011

Chapter 16
Application of Machine Learning Techniques for Railway Health Monitoring

G. M. Shafiullah
Central Queensland University, Australia

Adam Thompson
Central Queensland University, Australia

Peter J. Wolfs
Curtin University of Technology, Australia

A B M Shawkat Ali
Central Queensland University, Australia

ABSTRACT

Emerging wireless sensor networking (WSN) and modern machine learning techniques have encouraged interest in the development of vehicle health monitoring (VHM) systems that ensure secure and reliable operation of the rail vehicle. The performance of rail vehicles running on railway tracks is governed by the dynamic behaviours of railway bogies especially in the cases of lateral instability and track irregularities. In order to ensure safety and reliability of railway in this chapter, a forecasting model has been developed to investigate vertical acceleration behaviour of railway wagons attached to a moving locomotive using modern machine learning techniques. Initially, an energy-efficient data acquisition model has been proposed for WSN applications using popular learning algorithms. Later, a prediction model has been developed to investigate both front and rear body vertical acceleration behaviour. Different types of models can be built using a uniform platform to evaluate their performances and estimate different attributes' correlation coefficient (CC), root mean square error (RMSE), mean absolute error (MAE), root relative squared error (RRSE), relative absolute error (RAE) and computation complexity for each of the algorithm. Finally, spectral analysis of front and rear body vertical condition is produced from the predicted data using Fast Fourier Transform (FFT) and used to generate precautionary signals and system status which can be used by the locomotive driver for deciding upon necessary actions.

DOI: 10.4018/978-1-60566-908-3.ch016

INTRODUCTION

Recent advances in wireless communications and machine learning techniques have jointly encouraged interest in the development of VHM systems to reduce the maintenance and inspection requirements of railway systems while maintaining safety and reliability. In this chapter, the design and possible deployment of an energy-efficient railway health condition monitoring systems has been investigated that monitor's typical dynamic behaviour of railway wagons. If a security-related incident has occurred, this system may support the operator in taking the appropriate action, communicating to the right authorities, checking the availability of rescue teams and providing all necessary information (Shafiullah, Gyasi-Agyei & Wolfs, 2007), (Smith, Russel & Looi, 2003).

Typical dynamic behaviours of railway wagons are responsible for the safe and reliable operation of freight railways. The dynamic performance is determined by the characteristics of the wagon and the irregularities in the track. Railway track irregularities need to be kept within safe operating margins by undertaking appropriate maintenance programs. Railway wagons are intended to guide the load along the track safely with minimal damage to the track and the load. Railway track is designed to interface with railway vehicles to support the load while providing a permanent path of travel. It is identified that the performance of rail vehicles running on a track is limited by 1) the lateral instability inherent to the design of the steering of a railway wagon, and 2) the response of the railway wagon to individual or combined track irregularities.

Collection of acceleration signals from the track and sending meaningful signals to the locomotive is the challenging research area. In this chapter, an energy-efficient data acquisition model has been investigated for railway applications using modern machine learning techniques. A team of Engineers from CQUniversity, Australia developed a Health Card (Bleakley, 2006), (Wolfs, Bleakley, Senini & Thomas, 2006a) system to monitor every wagon in fleet using low cost intelligent device. Bleakley (Bleakley, 2006) collected necessary field data by using dual axis accelerometers fitted to each corner of the wagon body and to the bogie side frame. Same data were collected in this study by placing three sensor nodes in each wagon body and three sensor nodes in wagon side frame. Average weighted performance measure and rule-based learning approach were used to select a suitable algorithm for this application (Garg & Dukkipati, 1984), (Wolfs, Bleakley, Senini & Thomas, 2006a), (Bleakley, 2006), (Shafiullah, Thompson, Wolfs & Ali, 2008).

To monitor lateral instability and track irregularities in this study, train wagon body acceleration signals, i.e., six degrees of freedom (DOF) or six modes of vehicle body motion: *roll, pitch, yaw, lateral, vertical and longitudinal* are investigated using machine learning techniques. Ten popular regression algorithms are used to predict vehicle vertical acceleration motion of the wagon body. The performance of different models are assessed and the most suitable algorithm for forecasting vertical displacement behaviour of railway wagons proposed based on the selected performance attributes. Finally, instead of sending or storing the collected or predicted data, only necessary events those cross the safety limits are transmitted to the driver for necessary actions in coded format using the FFT approximation technique as used in Reference (Bleakley, 2006), (Shafiullah, Simson, Thompson, Wolfs & Ali, 2008). This chapter is organized as follows: Section II discusses the existing literature. Section III presents an overview of the regression algorithms. The development of the data acquisition model is discussed in Section IV. Forecasting of vertical acceleration of railway wagons is presented in Section V. Section VI concludes the article with future directions.

LITERATURE REVIEW

Monitoring of vertical vehicle accelerations to measure track irregularities and lateral instability are current research topics. Generally, specialised track geometry measurement vehicles are used to determine track conditions. However, this alone is not a good predictor of railway vehicle response (Garg & Dukkipati, 1984), (Bleakley, 2006). Predicting vehicle response characteristics online from track measurement data has been addressed by various research organisations (Esveld, 2001), (Wolfs, Bleakley, Senini & Thomas, 2006),(McClanachan, Dhanasekar, Skerman & Davey, 2002),(Ackroyd, Angelo, Nejikovsky & Stevens, 2002),(Cole & Roach, 1996),(McClanachan, Scown, Roach, Skermen & Payne, 2001), (Palese, Bonaventura, & Zarembski, 2000). Bonaventura et al. (Bonaventura, Palese, & Zarembski, 2000) introduced the ZTLMM (ZETA-TECH Lumped Mass Model) system for predicting the response of rail vehicles to measure track geometry in real time. Car body vertical displacement (bounce), car body roll and pitch angles, vertical wheel/rail forces and vertical car body accelerations are predicted with this system. These characteristics are used to assess the safe behaviour of the vehicle (Bonaventura, Palese, & Zarembski, 2000). Freight wagon instrumentation studies have shown that severe dynamic forces occur when irregular track defect wavelengths and train speeds combine to excite a resonant mode in the vehicle (McClanachan, Dhanasekar, Skerman & Davey, 2002), (Cole & Roach, 1996). An autonomous ride monitoring system (ARMS) developed by Amtrak (Ackroyd, Angelo, Nejikovsky & Stevens, 2002) monitors peak and RMS acceleration on the 10 Hz low pass filtered signal in accordance with standard requirements outlined by the FRA (Federal Railroad Administration, 1998). This system measures wagon body and bogie motions, detects various acceleration events, and tags them with GPS time and location information. The established wireless communication techniques for the ARMS are not energy-efficient and features of its GPS system have made application difficult (Ackroyd, Angelo, Nejikovsky & Stevens, 2002). Machine learning techniques may be able to provide more efficient historical patterns than the existing system.

To improve the current track geometry inspection practices and standards, the Transportation Technology Center, Inc. (TTCI), USA (Li, Salahifar, Malone, & Kalay, 2001) developed performance based track geometry (PBTG) inspection technology. This system helps to prioritise track geometry maintenance in order to reduce the probability of derailment and is used as a new add-on to conventional track geometry inspection vehicles. This technology is developed by using a neural networks (NN) approach and many NNs have been developed (trained) from actual geometry and vehicle performance test results. Through implementation of this performance-based system in the future, railway can expect to reduce track geometry-caused train derailments and improve prioritisation of track geometry maintenance.

CQUniversity, in association with the Centre for Railway Engineering (CRE), has been investigating a health card device for railways—an autonomous device for on-line analysis of card body motion signals to detect track condition and derailment monitoring. To resolve car body motions into six degrees of freedom, the Health Card uses accelerometer and angular rate sensors with a coordinate transform. The Health Card uses FFT to efficiently convert the signal into a time-frequency spectrograph so that events can be detected according to their short-term modal content, which relates to the natural vibration modes of the vehicle system such as bounce, roll, and pitch behaviours. A detection method has been developed that provides a set of coefficients to scale the calculation according to the frequencies of interest. These are selected to match the vehicle modal responses in various degrees of freedom (Wolfs, Bleakley, Senini & Thomas, 2006a), (Wolfs, Bleakley, Senini & Thomas, 2006b). However, the absence of energy-efficient features especially for data collection, and computational load makes this system inefficient.

Hamersley Iron Pty Ltd (Trotman & Sillaots, n.d.) monitors the rail surface condition, alignment, and other track characteristics at 0.5 m intervals throughout its length using a track recording vehicle (TRV). This vehicle continuously monitors the condition of the track in order to optimally schedule track maintenance activities. These systems deal with a huge volume of data provided by the TRV which presents a difficult task as it is labour intensive as the data have to be analysed manually. To overcome these problems an intelligent track condition monitoring system has been proposed by Parkinson and Iwnicki (Parkinson & Iwnicki, 2004), to forecast track condition using NNs. This system uses statistical records of derailment and computer modelling techniques to train the NN and predicts track state for derailment risk or passenger comfort. Predicted results have been verified with the actual derailments observed. The model is developed in an iterative manner until an acceptable performance level is achieved. This system allows greater levels of confidence in the safe operation of railway vehicles at all speed.

Nefti and Oussalah (Nefti & Oussalah, 2004) used artificial NNs architecture to predict malfunctioning of railway systems due to track irregularities. Different NN structures are created to find out the best structure for predicting railway safety. Experimental analysis showed that the model performed satisfactorily and can predict the desired output with a very low error factor. In general, NN requires more computational time than other algorithms and it requires a huge amount of memory. Li et al. (Li, Stratman, & Mahadevan, 2007) investigated a machine learning approach to automate the identification process of rail wheel defects using collected data from wheel inspections. Decision tree and Support Vector Machine (SVM) based classification schemes were used to analyse the railroad wheel inspection data. The experimental results indicate that the proposed approach is very efficient, producing a classifier ensemble that has high *sensitivity, specificity* and *gMeans* values during classification.

Linear regression analysis was used to predict dynamic characteristics of worn rail pads. The curve fitting approach showed the maximum correlation of dynamic stiffness and damping of worn rail pads under preloads while achieving less than 4% error for all pads. Linear regression analysis was used to predict the deterioration rate with age of dynamic stiffness and damping coefficients (Kaewunruen & Remennikov, 2007). Duarte et al. (Duarte & Hu, 2004) have introduced a data set extracted from a real-life vehicle tracking sensor network using popular classification algorithms. This data set has been extracted based on the sensor data collected during a real world wireless distributed sensor network (WDSN) experiment carried out at Twenty-nine Palms, CA. The WDSN vehicle classification problem comprises local classification and global decision fusion. Maximum Likelihood, k-Nearest Neighbour, and SVM algorithms were used in this experiment. It has been seen that although the classification rates for the available modalities are only acceptable, methods used in multisensor networks such as data fusion will enhance the performance of these tasks.

Some problems identified in the current literature includes: absence of energy-efficient features, computation load, installation and maintenance cost and communication between wagons to the locomotive, which needs to be improved to ensure safe and secure operation of the railway industry. In this chapter, an energy-efficient condition monitoring system has been proposed that reduces computational load and overall energy consumption of the system using machine learning techniques.

REGRESSION ALGORITHMS

Regression analysis is the most significant and popular machine learning area for future decision making or forecasting of data or any incidents. Researchers already have introduced different types of regression algorithms, including popular regression analysis for time series data forecasting, tree based algorithm, rule-based learning, meta-based learning, lazy learning, neural network, and statistical learning. Currently various statistical forecasting and regression approaches are used to monitor railway wagons to ensure safety and security. This section describes the popular regression algorithms that have used to develop a forecasting model to predict front and rear body vertical acceleration of railway wagons. Rule-based learning algorithm M5Rules, PART, OneR and Decision Table, Tree-based learning M5Prime, Decision Stump, and RepTree, Meta-based learning Random Sub Space, Lazy-based learning IBK, Statistical learning based algorithm Support Vector Machine (SVM) regression, Neural Network based Multilayer Perceptron (MLP) and Simple Linear Regression (SLR) and Linear Regression (LR) have been considered in this chapter for various stages of the experiment (Witten & Frank, 2000), (Linear Regression, 2008), (Sykes, n.d.), (Regression Analysis, n.d.), (Cunninghham & Holmes, n.d.), (Aha, 1992), (Ali & Smith, 2006), (Magoulas, Plagianakos & Vrahatis, 2004), (Vapnik, 1999) (John & Kohavi, 1997). WEKA release 3.5.7 (Weka 3, 2008) learning tools have been used for experimental analysis with default parameter settings. WEKA includes a comprehensive set of data pre-processing tools, learning algorithms, and evaluation methods, graphical user interfaces and environment for comparing learning algorithms.

Linear Regression: Regression analysis (Linear Regression, 2008), (Sykes, n.d.), (Regression Analysis, n.d.) is a statistical forecasting model that addresses and evaluates the relationship between a given variable (dependent) and one or more independent variables. The major goal in regression analysis is to create a mathematical model that can be used to predict the values of a dependent variable based upon the values of independent variables. This method is called 'linear' because the relation of the dependent variable Y to the independent variables X_i is assumed to be a linear function of the parameters. The regression model is used to predict the value of Y from the known value of X and to find the line that best predicts Y from X. Linear regression does this by finding the line that minimises the sum of the squares of the vertical distances of the points from the line. The goodness of fit and the statistical significance of the estimated parameters are a matrix of regression analysis. The coefficient of determination r^2 is the proportion of variability in a data set and the value of r^2 is a fraction between 0.0 and 1.0. If r^2 equals 1.0, all points lie exactly on a straight line with no scatter; this is called best-fit situation.

RepTree: RepTree is a fast regression tree that uses information gain/variance reduction and prunes it using reduced-error pruning. It is also used as a classification tree. RepTree deals with missing values by splitting instances into pieces. Optimised for speed, it only sorts values for numeric attributes once. Pruning is used to find the best sub-tree of the initially grown tree with the minimum error for the test set (Witten & Frank, 2000).

M5Prime: The original algorithm M5 was developed by Ross J. Quinlan (1992). Later, Yong Wang's contribution improved the original model. M5Prime is useful for numeric prediction. It is a rational reconstruction of Quinlan's M5 model tree inducer. Decision trees were designed for assigning nominal categories. M5Prime extended decision trees by adding numeric prediction by modifying the leaf nodes of the tree (Witten & Frank, 2000), (Cunninghham & Holmes, n.d.).

IBK: In 1991, Aha et al. (Aha, Kibler & Albert, 1991) proposed an instance-based learning algorithm that generates classification/regression predictions using only specific instances. Instance-based learning algorithms are derived from the nearest neighbour machine learning philosophy. IBK is an implementation of the k-nearest neighbour's algorithm. The number of nearest neighbours *(k)* can be set manually, or determined automatically. Each unseen instance is always compared with existing ones using a distance metric. WEKA's default setting is $k = 1$. This algorithm performs well in application to artificial and real-world domains (Witten & Frank, 2000), (Aha, 1992).

SVM Regression: SVM is a powerful tool for classification and regression, which is based on the structural risk minimisation principle and enjoys excellent success in many real-world applications. It is a statistical based learning algorithm which has been used for binary classification in the first time. The SVM model can usually be expressed in terms of support vectors and applied to nonlinear problems using different kernel function. Based on the support vector's information, SVM regression produces the final output function. WEKA by default considers sequential minimal optimisation (SMO) for SVM and polynomial kernel with degree 1(Witten & Frank, 2000), (Ali & Smith, 2006).

Multilayer Perceptron (MLP): ANN is an information processing intelligence system that is inspired by a biological nervous system such as the brain. The most common neural network model is the MLP, known as a supervised network because it requires a desired output in order to learn. The goal of this type of network is to create a model that correctly maps the input to the output using historical data so that the model can then be used to produce the output when the desired output is unknown. WEKA uses the back propagation (BP) algorithm to train the model, though it is slower than some other learning techniques (Ali & Smith, 2006), (Magoulas, Plagianakos & Vrahatis, 2004), (Vapnik, 1999).

M5Rules: Holmes et al. (Holmes, Hall & Frank, 1999) have presented an algorithm for inducing simple accurate decision lists from model trees. Model trees are built repeatedly and the best rule is selected at each iteration. M5Rules create rule sets on continuous data and produce propositional regression rules as the IF-THEN rule format. This dictates that an attribute is considered as a class, examines the attribute and begins to construct rules that will produce the specific class value (Witten & Frank, 2000).

Decision Stump: Decision Stump is a weak learning algorithm that consists of a decision tree with only a single branch. This algorithm builds simple binary decision "stumps" (1-level decision trees) for numeric and nominal regression problems. It deals with missing values by treating "missing" as a separate attribute value. Decision stump is often used as components in ensemble learning techniques like Bagging and Boosting (Cunninghham & Holmes, n.d.).

Random Sub Space: Tin K. Ho (Ho, 1998) proposed an algorithm to construct a decision tree based classifier whose capacity can be arbitrarily expanded for increases in accuracy for both training and unseen data. The algorithm comprises of multiple trees constructed systematically by pseudo-randomly selecting subsets of components of the feature vector, that is, trees constructed in randomly chosen sub-spaces. Random subsets are selected from the training set and a classifier is trained using each subset.

PART: PART is a separate-and-conquer rule learner proposed by Frank and Witten (Witten & Frank, 2000). It is a comparatively new algorithm for producing sets of rules called "decision lists", which are ordered sets or rules. PART is developed by combining the C4.5 and RIPPER algorithms and is also called a partial decision tree algorithm. However, unlike C4.5 and RIPPER, PART does not have to perform global optimisation in order to generate rules. This algorithm works by forming pruned partial decision trees (built using C4.5's heuristics), and immediately converting them into a corresponding rule. It generates simple rules, which are easily understandable (Cunninghham & Holmes, n.d.), (Ali & Smith, 2006).

The prediction accuracy of the above mentioned algorithms, have evaluated using WEKA learning tools with classical data splitting option. In this study, a set of attributes to measure the estimation techniques performance rather than a single attribute have been considered. Prediction attributes considered in this study are given in Table 1 with their mathematical notations.

Table 1. Performance metrics attributes with their mathematical notations (Witten & Frank, 2000)

Correlation Coefficient (CC)	$CC = \dfrac{\dfrac{1}{n-1}\sum_i \left(Y_i - \overline{Y}_i\right)\left(Y^*_i - \overline{Y^*_i}\right)}{\sigma_{Y_i}\sigma_{Y^*_i}}$ where Y_i is the observation value and Y_i^* is the predicted value. σ_{Y_i} and $\sigma_{Y^*_i}$ are the standard deviation for Y_i and Y_i^*
Mean Absolute Error (MAE)	$MAE = \dfrac{1}{n}\sum_{i=1}^{n}\left(Y_i - Y_i^*\right)$
Root Mean Squared Error (RMSE)	$RMSE = \sqrt{\dfrac{1}{n}\sum_{i=1}^{n}\left(Y_i - Y_i^*\right)^2}$
Relative Absolute Error (RAE) in %	$RAE = \left|\dfrac{Y_i - Y_i^*}{Y_i^* - \overline{Y^*}}\right| x100$

ENERGY-EFFICIENT DATA ACQUISITION MODEL

Raw data collection, data pre-processing, and formatting are essential parts of developing any monitoring systems. In this section, an energy-efficient data acquisition model has been investigated for railway monitoring system using six popular regression algorithms. Initially performances of different models have been assessed based on performance attributes and relative weighted performance. Rules have been generated with the help of ranking performance and statistical analysis to select a unique classifier for the application. This newly developed model reduces the requirement to two sensor nodes in each wagon, one for the wagon body and one for the wagon side frame. This reduces energy consumption and hardware cost significantly.

Background of the Study

Health Cards (Wolfs, Bleakley, Senini & Thomas, 2006(1)), (Wolfs, Bleakley, Senin & Thomas, 2006(2)) monitor every wagon in the fleet using low cost intelligent devices. An algorithm was developed to analyse signals from accelerometers mounted on the wagon body, to identify the dynamic interaction of the track and the rail vehicle. The algorithm has been validated using collected field data including accelerations measured at strategic points on the wagon body and the bogies.

Each prototype Health Card incorporates a 27 MHz microcontroller with 256kB of onboard RAM, four dual-axis accelerometers, a GPS receiver, two low power radios, lithium ion batteries and a solar panel. Data were collected from a ballast wagon and dual axis accelerometers were fitted to each corner of the body and each side frame. The test run was a normal ballast laying operation, starting with a full load of ballast, travelling to the maintenance site, dropping the ballast on the track, and returning empty via the same route. A PC based data acquisition system was used to store data. The main purpose of the data acquisition was to provide real data that represented to the Health Card device. Data have been used to validate and demonstrate the effectiveness of signal analysis techniques and finally to develop a model to monitor typical dynamic behaviour and track irregularities (Wolfs, Bleakley, Senini & Thomas, 2006), (Wolfs, Bleakley, Senin & Thomas, 2006).

Both the vertical and lateral conditions of the railway wagon have been measured by each accelerometer. The aim of the sensing arrangement was to capture roll, pitch, yaw, vertical and lateral accelerations of the wagon body. The ADXL202/10 dual-axis acceleration sensor measured 16 channel acceleration data in *g* units, with 8 channels for the wagon body and 8 for the wagon side frame (Bleakley, 2006).

Four sensor nodes were placed in each wagon body and the locations of the sensors were front left body, front right body, rear left body and rear right body. Data collected from these four sensors are front left body vertical (FLBZ), front left body lateral (FLBY), front right body vertical (FRBZ), front right body lateral (FRBY), rear left body vertical (RLBZ), rear left body lateral (RLBY), rear right body vertical (RRBZ), rear right body lateral (RRBY).

Four sensor nodes were placed in each wagon's side fame data collected from these four sensors are front left side fame vertical (FLSZ), front left side fame lateral (FLSY), front right side frame vertical (FRSZ), front right side frame lateral (FRSY), rear left side frame vertical (RLSZ), rear left side frame lateral (RLSY), rear right side frame vertical (RRSZ), rear right side frame lateral (RRSY) (Bleakley, 2006). Sensor locations and naming convention are illustrated in Figure 1.

Data Acquisition Model

A data acquisition model has been developed for a sensor network application that reduces overall energy consumption of the existing Health Card system using six popular regression algorithms. This newly developed model can measure the same amount of data using only three sensor nodes in each wagon body.

Figure 1. Accelerometer locations and Axis naming convention (Bleakley, 2006)

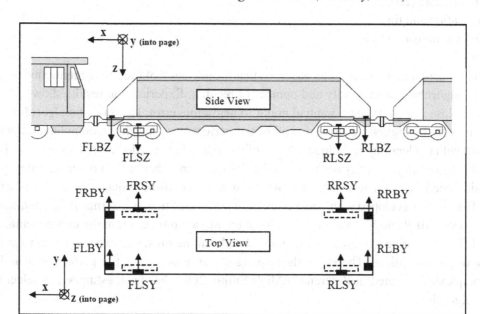

The model predicted the vertical and lateral conditions of the fourth sensor node, i.e., the sensor node located at the rear right corner of the wagon body and wagon side frame. The prediction model replaces the use of sensor nodes placed in the rear right corner of the wagon body and the wagon side fame.

Each sensor node collected both the lateral and vertical condition data. Therefore, both the rear right body vertical (RRBZ) and rear right body lateral (RRBY) conditions have been predicted using the collected data in reference (Bleakley, 2006). The rear right side frame vertical (RRSZ) and rear right side frame lateral (RRSY) have been predicted using the same data sets. After the necessary pre-processing and formatting, data have been passed into the learning algorithms. For initial data pre-processing and formatting, MATLAB (The Math Works, n.d.) and WEKA (Weka 3, 2008) learning tools have been used. Initially, six models have been developed using RepTree, IBK, M5Prime, linear regression, SVM and MLP regression algorithms to predict RRBZ condition and RRBY condition. Correlation Coefficient, RMSE, MAE, RRSE, RAE and computational complexity have been measured to evaluate the prediction accuracy. Classical data splitting options were considered to evaluate the datasets for each of the algorithms and 90 percent of the data was used for training and the remaining 10 percent for testing. The computational complexity includes both the model train period and the test set evaluation time. Later the wagon side frame condition has been predicted with the stated six learning algorithms i.e., RRSZ and the RRSY condition. With the estimated attributes' performances, the relative weighted performance has been measured for a given algorithm and suitable algorithm for the data acquisition method has been proposed. Finally, rules have been generated to select a unique classifier with the help of ranking performance and statistical descriptive analysis. WEKA release 3.5.7 with a unified platform has been used for all of the experiments. The configuration of the PC used in the experiments was Pentium IV, 3.0 GHz Processor, 1GB RAM.

For experiments, necessary data have been borrowed from the collected data of Reference (Bleakley, 2006). To cover a large experimental area, data sets were selected considering:

- train track condition
- number of data records
- train location and time
- loaded and unloaded train

From initial experiments it has been observed that the accuracy of the above mentioned metrics varies based on algorithms, data quality and number of records. Experimental results showed that all the models were close in performance and had minor to negligible error. However, no algorithm predicted the data sets with the highest accuracy for all of the performance metrics. Computational complexity also differed with the learning techniques. A few of the algorithms needed more time to classify the test set than training the model. It has been shown that IBK performs better than other algorithms in terms of correlation coefficient for few data sets. MLP and RepTree also predicted the data sets with better accuracy. The model developed with linear regression performs the best in terms of computational complexity; however, MLP and SVM required higher computational time. From the experimental results it was very difficult to come to a conclusion and to decide on the most suitable algorithm to predict rear right body wagon conditions. Therefore, the ranking performance, classifier performance and computational complexity as stated in Reference (Ali & Smith, 2006) has been estimated to select the most regression algorithm.

Table 2. Ranked algorithm performance based on correlation coefficient for the six algorithms

Algorithm	Data set 1	Data set 2	Data set 3	Data set 4	Data set 5
IBK	1.0	1.0	1.0	1.0	0.0
REPTree	0.0	0.42212	0.22889	0.75505	1.0
MLP	0.62318	0.47068	0.07833	0.09888	0.69632
SVM	0.65098	0.01653	0.00610	0.00376	0.65406
M5Prime	0.65336	0.32327	0.06815	0.64754	0.67515
Linear Reg.	0.65761	0.0	0.0	0.0	0.64293

The ranking performance for a given algorithm is estimated based on the selected attributes. The best performing algorithm on each of these measures is assigned the rank of 1 and the worst is 0. Thus, the rank of the jth algorithm on the ith dataset is calculated as stated in Reference (Ali & Smith, 2006):

$$R_{ij} = 1 - \frac{e_{ij} - \max(e_i)}{\min(e_i) - \max(e_i)} \tag{1}$$

where for example, e_{ij} is the correlation coefficient for the jth algorithm on dataset i, and e_i is a vector accuracy for dataset i. A detailed comparison of algorithm performance can be evaluated from this equation. Table 2 represents the ranked performance of correlation coefficient. The best performing algorithm on each of these measures was assigned the rank of 1 and the worst was 0.

The performances of all the classifiers have been evaluated using the total number of best and worst performances. The total number of the best and worst ranking for correlation coefficient, RMSE, MAE, RRSE, RAE and computational complexity for all the algorithms were evaluated by using the following equation (Ali & Smith, 2006):

$$C_i = \frac{1}{r}\left(\frac{s_i - f_i}{n}\right) + \frac{1}{r} \tag{2}$$

where $\rho = 2$ is the weight shifting parameter, s_i is the total number of success or best cases for the ith algorithm, f_i is the total number of failure or worst cases for the same algorithm, and n is the total number of datasets. Algorithm performances were calculated from the total number of best (1.0) and worst (0.0) rankings. Performances for all of the algorithms are given in Table 3. It has been observed that for correlation coefficients measure IBK was the best performing algorithm, while it was the worst to measure MAE. For MAE and RAE measurement, MLP was the best performing algorithm. Linear regression is the second choice to measure RAE and best performing to measure RRSE. Both IBK and MLP are the first choice to measure RMSE. Based on various accuracy measures it is observed that MLP is the best choice. Figure 2 represents the performance of different algorithms to predict rear right body wagon condition.

To select the most suitable regression algorithm, relative weighted performance have been measured for all of the algorithms with considering two different weights for ranking average accuracy and computational complexity using the following equation (Ali & Smith, 2006):

Table 3. Ranking average across test set classification problems based on different performance metrics

Algorithm	IBK	REPTree	MLP	SVM	M5P	Linear Reg.
CC	0.8	0.5	0.5	0.5	0.5	0.2
MAE	0.1	0.4	0.8	0.5	0.5	0.7
RMSE	0.6	0.5	0.6	0.5	0.3	0.5
RAE	0.2	0.4	0.8	0.5	0.5	0.6
RRSE	0.4	0.5	0.5	0.5	0.4	0.7

$$Z = \alpha a_i + \beta t_i \qquad\qquad (3)$$

here, α and β are the weight parameters for ranking average accuracy against computational complexity. The average accuracy and computational complexity are denoted by a_i and t_i respectively. The effect of the relative importance of accuracy and computational complexity was observed by changing the values of β.

Relative weighted performance was calculated by assuming $\alpha = 1$ and β is from 0.4 to 2. The average accuracy of the regression algorithms was very close to each other; however, MLP was the best and IBK was the worst. With respect to computational time SVM was the worst algorithm. Considering computational complexity and average accuracy, linear regression was the best choice and SVM performed the worst to predict the rear right body wagon condition. Figure 3 represents the relative weighted performances of the selected algorithms. However, from the above experimental analysis, it is shown that no individual algorithm performs best for all of the attributes and the performances of the

Figure 2. Regression algorithm performances

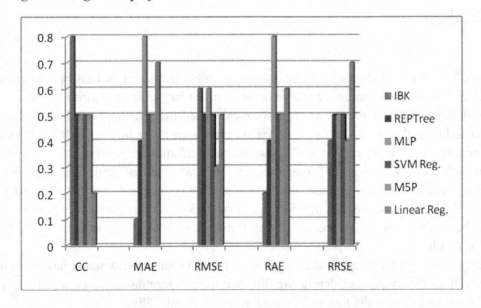

Figure 3. Overall performance of the algorithms with respect to β, assuming α =1

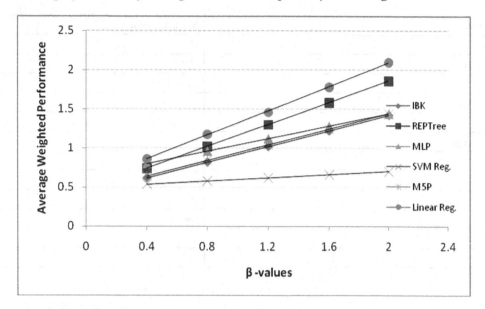

algorithms were closely related. It is also seen that computational complexity plays a significant role and greatly affects the performance of the algorithms. However, computational time is not always a vital attribute for all types of application. For this reason, both the options have been considered in this study for experimental analysis. Therefore, in the next section a rule-based learning approach using classifier approach has been introduced to select the most suitable algorithm for a particular problem.

Rule-Based Learning Approach

A rule-based learning approach using statistical analysis and ranking performance measures is proposed in this section to select a unique classifier. The selected algorithm works more efficiently and improves the overall performance of the railway monitoring systems. This study is conducted using the same regression algorithms with a large data volume. Twenty-five datasets were selected considering track condition, loaded and empty wagon condition, data record etc. This model selects a unique regression algorithm to predict sensor data of railway wagons without considering computational complexity. Twelve descriptive statistical measures were considered which are stated in Table 4. Descriptive statistics are used to summarise the relevant characteristics of any large data set and details of descriptive statistics are available in statistical books and MATLAB statistics toolbox (The Math Works, n.d.).

Rules have been generated to select the unique classifier with the help of ranking performance and statistical descriptive analysis. A data matrix has been constructed using statistical analysis and performance ranking of the algorithms. Initially, correlation coefficients have been measured for each of the twenty-five data sets with the developed six models discussed in the previous section. Data splitting test options were used to evaluate datasets in which 90 percent of the data has been used for training and 10 percent for testing. Measured correlations coefficient for the developed model with the six algorithms is stated in Table 5. The ranking performance for a given algorithm has been estimated as discussed in the previous section using equation (1) for each of the data sets. Based on the ranked performance the

Table 4. Descriptive statistics for characterization of each dataset

Statistical Name	Symbolic Name
Geometric mean	*GM*
Harmonic mean	*HM*
Trim mean	*trimmean*
Mean	*mean*
Median	*median*
Inter quartile range	*iqr*
Mad	*mad*
Range	*range*
Standard deviation	*std*
Variance	*var*
Kurtosis	*k*
Skewness	*s*

algorithms have been classified into six classes. The algorithm that achieved rank 1 for the maximum number of data sets is classified as class 1, and so on. For this experiment, IBK achieved rank 1, i.e., best performed, for a maximum 11 data sets, and so IBK is classified as class 1. RepTree has rank 1 for 4 datasets and rank 0, i.e., worst performance, for 3 data sets. On the other hand, M5 Prime has rank 1 for 5 datasets and rank 0 for 5 data sets. Therefore, RepTree and M5 Prime are classified respectively as class 2 and class 3. MLP, linear regression and SVM are classified respectively as class 4, class 5 and class 6. Classifier ranking performances for the developed models are presented in Figure 4.

Next, descriptive statistical information has been measured for each of the 25 data sets. A data matrix has been constructed with the results of statistical analysis and ranking of classifiers. Finally using the same dataset for training and testing rules has been generated to select a unique classifier for this application with the help of PART (Cunninghham & Holmes, n.d.) algorithm, which is built into WEKA learning tools.

PART has two significant parameters: confidence factor and minimum number of objects. The confidence factor is used for pruning the tree. The smaller values of confidence factor resolution more pruning and higher values require less pruning. A minimum number of objects represent the minimum number of instances per rule. The default values used in WEKA for confidence factor and minimum number of objects are 0.25 and 2 respectively. Default parameters have been tuned to select the suitable regression algorithm. Accuracy of the classifier has been evaluated based on confusion matrix. The generated rules and percentage of accuracy are summarised in Table 6. Experimental results have shown the percentage of rule accuracy for RepTree, M5 Prime and MLP has 100%; however, IBK has 91% accuracy.

Proposed model reduces power consumption of the railway monitoring systems as it requires only three sensor nodes instead of four in an existing system to collect required data from railway wagons. Data received from this newly developed model has been used to develop VHM system for monitoring vertical acceleration of railway wagons which is presented in the next section.

Table 5. Correlation coefficient for the six selected algorithms on each dataset

	IBK	RepTree	MLP	SVM	M5Prime	LR
DT1	0.92045	0.87715	0.87335	0.82435	0.79465	0.79225
DT2	0.8113	0.68905	0.7027	0.7037	0.70621	0.708
DT3	0.62715	0.711	0.73015	0.72015	0.69865	0.61025
DT4	0.56225	0.7477	0.7674	0.76235	0.789	0.6384
DT5	0.8051	0.80085	0.79055	0.71735	0.7428	0.72765
DT6	0.89425	0.74715	0.76925	0.71745	0.82055	0.74015
DT7	0.7508	0.46195	0.7342	0.7531	0.73535	0.7394
DT8	0.7626	0.6864	0.68485	0.6606	0.67875	0.6771
DT9	0.40885	0.56715	0.52575	0.4772	0.522	0.2958
DT10	0.7494	0.68515	0.686	0.66385	0.74515	0.63495
DT11	0.73235	0.71155	0.65125	0.6526	0.67005	0.6503
DT12	0.82945	0.82835	0.761	0.76695	0.7671	0.7671
DT13	0.797	0.797	0.77315	0.75475	0.80615	0.75455
DT14	0.6901	0.7307	0.72545	0.7201	0.72935	0.72045
DT15	0.67545	0.5988	0.5334	0.35015	0.36495	0.3514
DT16	0.4588	0.42515	0.35585	0.4132	0.36985	0.39845
DT17	0.01855	0.019	0.0555	0.07545	0.0774	0.0623
DT18	0.2077	0.2111	0.1464	0.08675	0.07135	0.16615
DT19	-0.0088	0.08795	0.09935	0.0081	-0.06965	0.13345
DT20	0.03605	0.0281	-0.0079	-0.03265	-0.07965	0.04675
DT21	0.124	0.1494	0.02015	0.0455	-0.01675	0.10755
DT22	0.10625	0.10375	0.05105	0.0294	0.0956	0.0251
DT23	0.15615	0.15655	0.1572	0.08425	0.1245	0.1136
DT24	0.17455	0.1154	0.1451	0.14745	0.2003	0.15045
DT25	0.4	0.4466	0.3315	0.3286	0.30415	0.3565

MONITORING VERTICAL ACCELERATION OF RAILWAY WAGONS

To monitor typical dynamic behaviour of railway wagons due to track irregularities and lateral stability, in this section vertical acceleration behaviour of railway wagons is investigated using modern machine learning techniques. To investigate vertical acceleration, initially bounce and pitch mode behaviours are identified for railway wagons. Later, models are developed with regression algorithms and predict vertical acceleration characteristics of railway wagons.

Vertical Acceleration Measurements

A three-dimensional coordinate system is normally used to describe dynamic behaviours of railway wagons having six DOF. Linear motion along the X, Y and Z axes are termed as longitudinal, lateral, and vertical translations respectively. Rotary motions about the X, Y and Z axes are termed as roll, pitch and yaw respectively as illustrated in Figure 5.

Figure 4. Classifier best performance with number of best and worst performed data sets for each algorithm

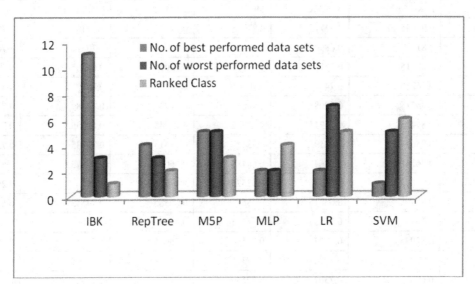

The purely vertical displacements of the wagon, i.e., deflections up and down, are called bounce mode. The rotation around the side-to-side axis of the wagon or tilting up and down is called pitch mode. The Health Card system developed by Central Queensland University (Bleakley, 2006), (Wolfs, Bleakley, Senini & Thomas, 2006a) used solid-state transducers including accelerometers and angular rate sensors with a coordinate transform were used to resolve car body motions into six degrees of freedom.

Wolfs et al. (Wolfs, Bleakley, Senini & Thomas, 2006a), (Wolfs, Bleakley, Senini & Thomas, 2006b) placed dual-axis accelerometers at each corner of the wagon body and each side frame. The aim of the sensing arrangement was to capture roll, pitch, yaw, vertical and lateral accelerations of the wagon body. ADXL202/10 dual-axis acceleration sensors measured 16 channel acceleration data in *g* units. Data was

Table 6. Generated rule-set

IBK Classifier: *IF mad > 0.0466 AND iqr > 0.1022 AND trimmean ≤ 2.4292, THEN select IBK* *IF geomean > 2.4281, THEN select IBK* *OR,* *IF mad > 0.0466 AND iqr > 0.1022 AND trimmean ≤ 2.4292, OR geomean > 2.4281, THEN select IBK* *Rule Accuracy 91%*
Rules for RepTree Classifier: *IF s > 0.1302 AND mad > 0.0466 AND range ≤ 0.1117,* *THEN select RepTree* *Rule Accuracy 100%*
M5 Prime Classifier: *mad > 0.0466 AND geomean > 2.428 AND s >0.1351,* *THEN we should select M5 Prime* *Rule Accuracy 100%* **MLP Classifier:** IF mean > 2.4282 AND range ≤ 0.1118, THEN select MLP *Rule Accuracy 100%*

Figure 5. Six degrees of freedom of wagon movement

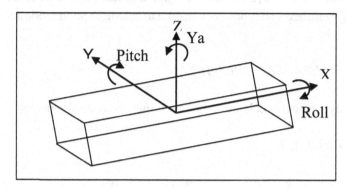

collected from a ballast wagon which had conventional three piece bogies spaced l_b = 10.97m apart. The accelerometers were spaced l = 14.4m apart. The test run was a normal ballast laying operation, starting with a full load of ballast, travelling to the maintenance site, dropping the ballast on the track, and returning empty via the same route. A PC based data acquisition system was used to store data (Bleakley, 2006), (Wolfs, Bleakley, Senini & Thomas, 2006a).

To inquire into dynamic behaviours of railway wagons, vertical or bounce and pitch mode characteristics of railway wagons are investigated, with both front and rear wagon body movements being considered for this analysis. For this experiment to calculate bounce and pitch modes of the wagon body, 3 channels of data have used out of the 16 collected, i.e., 'front left vertical, FLZ', 'rear left vertical, RLZ', and 'front right vertical, FRZ'. AFLZ, ARLZ and AFRZ are respectively the averages of FLZ, RLZ, and FRZ. Sensor locations and naming conventions are given in Figure 6.

To calculate vertical or bounce mode behaviour of railway wagons stated below equation is used:

$$VERT = [FRZ - AFRZ + RLZ - ARLZ]/2 \qquad\qquad (4)$$

Figure 6. Accelerometer locations and Axis naming convention (Bleakley, 2006)

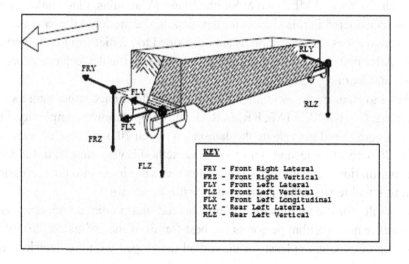

In addition to Bleakley's analysis (Bleakley, 2006), in this study l_b (the distance between bogies) and l (the distance between transducers) has been considered to calculate pitch mode acceleration. Calculated pitch mode acceleration is:

$$PITCHACC = [(FLZ - AFLZ - RLZ + ARLZ)/l] * l_b/2 \tag{5}$$

Therefore, front body vertical acceleration has been measured finally using:

$$FVertACC = VERT + PITCHACC \tag{6}$$

Rear body vertical acceleration has been measured finally using:

$$RVertACC = VERT - PITCHACC \tag{7}$$

In the next section, the experimental procedure is discussed to setup the model using selected regression algorithms to predict vertical acceleration with the help of Equations (4 - 7) stated above.

Prediction Model with Regression Algorithm

In this section, experimental procedures are discussed to develop the prediction model for monitoring of vertical accelerations of railway wagons. Models are developed both for the front and rear end of the railway wagon body using ten popular regression algorithms. A set of attributes to measure the estimation techniques' performance rather than a single attribute are considered. After necessary pre-processing and formatting, by adopting the regression method algorithms are developed to predict front and rear body vertical displacement behaviour of a railway ballast wagon with the help of WEKA learning tools. Five sets of data were used to provide a large experimental variety.

M5Rules (Witten & Frank, 2000), M5Prime (Witten & Frank, 2000), (Cunninghham & Holmes, n.d.), RepTree (Witten & Frank, 2000) and decision stump (Cunninghham & Holmes, n.d.), random sub space (Ho, 1998), IBK (Witten & Frank, 2000), (Aha, 1992), simple linear regression and linear regression (Sykes, n.d.), (Linear Regression, n.d.), (Regression Analysis, n.d.), SVM regression (Witten & Frank, 2000), (Ali & Smith, 2006), and MLP (Ali & Smith, 2006), (Magoulas, Plagianakos & Vrahatis, 2004), (Vapnik, 1999) are considered in this section for developing the model to forecast vertical acceleration behaviour of railway wagons. Initially models are developed to predict front body vertical acceleration for five data sets. After that, models for forecasting rear body vertical acceleration are developed with the same data sets and learning algorithms.

A set of attributes to measure the estimation techniques' performance rather than a single attribute are considered, including: CC, RMSE, MAE, RRSE, RAE and computational complexity. The classical data splitting option was considered to evaluate the datasets in which 70 percent of data are used for training and the remaining 30 percent for testing. This proposed method is very simple; initially it prepares input using the above formulation (Equations 4 – 7) and then feeds the input into the regression model. From the results the most suitable algorithm is proposed for this application.

Experimental results for the various algorithms showed that prediction accuracy is closely related to each other; however no algorithm performs the best for all of the estimated attributes. For the front body of railway wagons, CC is the least for the model developed with the decision stump. M5Rules,

M5 Prime, and linear regression predicted with almost similar accuracy, and the performances of these algorithms were better than for the remaining algorithms. However, they differ only in terms of computational complexity, and linear regression requires the least computational time. The model train period and the test set evaluation time also differ based on algorithms and data sets. Computational complexity of different algorithms for the front body of wagons is highlighted in Figure 7. Correlation coefficient of M5Rules, M5 Prime, and linear regression were one, i.e., actual value and predicted value were identical. Correlation coefficient of SVM regression is one, though it has higher RAE, RRSE and computational time. Considering performance attributes, it has seen that the model developed with the decision stump is the worst model to forecast front body vertical acceleration of railway wagons, though it is a good predictor in terms of computational complexity. Figure 8 describes the prediction results for the model developed with decision stump. Compare to other algorithms, MLP needs the highest computational time, though it predicted with a better correlation coefficient of 0.9975 on an average. Therefore, considering the performance metrics and execution time from this analysis, it appears the model developed with linear regression is the most suitable to forecast the front body vertical acceleration.

Models were developed with the selected regression algorithms for rear body vertical acceleration data. Model results are summarised in Table 7. It is shown that correlation coefficient is the least for decision stump. Correlation coefficients of simple linear regression, IBK, and MLP are below 1.0 but above 0.8. Results show that for M5Rules, M5 Prime and linear regression, output of all performance metrics except computational complexity is the same. However, linear regression requires the least computational time. Correlation coefficient of M5Rules, M5 Prime, linear regression and SVM is 1.0, i.e., actual value and predicted value is the same. Figure 9 represents the performance metrics of different algorithms. Therefore, considering the measured metrics from this analysis it is concluded that the model developed with linear regression is the most suitable to forecast rear body vertical acceleration data. Figure 10 describes the prediction accuracy of the model developed with linear regression.

Figure 7. Computational complexity of different algorithms for data set 1 for prediction of front body vertical acceleration

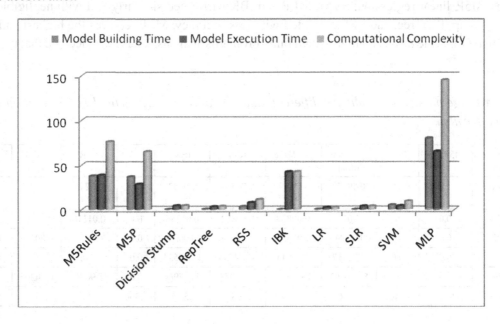

Figure 8. Prediction of front body vertical acceleration using decision stump, the worst algorithm

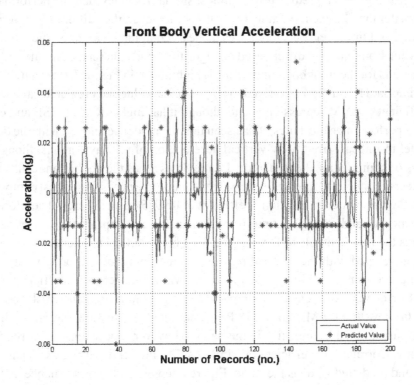

Finally, from this experiments stated above, it is observed that accuracy of the measured performance metrics varies based on algorithms, data quality and number of records. No algorithm could predict the datasets with the highest accuracy for all of the performance metrics. However, all the models performed closely and with negligible error. In terms of correlation coefficient, MAE, RMSE, RAE and RRSE, the M5Rules, M5P, linear regression, SVM, MLP and IBK performed similarly and with negligible error. Decision Stump, RepTree, and RSS predicted with less accuracy. MLP requires the highest and linear regression requires the lowest computational time. From this analysis, it has been decided that the model

Table 7. Average prediction results for different data sets of rear body vertical acceleration using regression algorithms

Performance Metrics	M5Rules	M5P	Decision Stump	REPTree	RSS	IBK	LR	SLR	SVM	MLP
Correlation Coefficient	1.0	1.0	0.49878	0.7079	0.71468	0.9453	1.0	0.8245	1.0	0.99926
MAE	0.0	0.0	0.017	0.00828	0.00882	0.00256	0.0	0.01116	0.00008	0.00016
RMSE	0.0	0.0	0.05686	0.01684	0.01744	0.0095	0.0	0.01788	0.00012	0.00012
RAE	0.0	0.0	77.5617	38.5844	41.84734	12.02534	0.0	50.34626	0.37232	0.6549
RRSE	0.0	0.0	81.89062	49.81472	53.06156	28.07964	0.0	55.90768	0.34306	3.31986
Time (s)	24.48	23.132	1.776	1.714	5.682	15.84	1.366	2.404	2.554	61.764

Figure 9. Comparisons of performance metrics with different algorithms

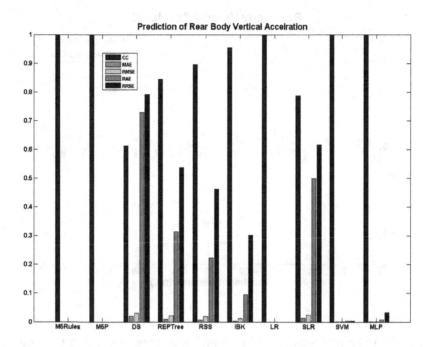

developed with linear regression is the most suitable to predict both front and rear wagon body vertical acceleration characteristics.

Spectral Analysis

Vehicle monitoring systems enable reduction of maintenance and inspection requirements of railway systems while maintaining safety and reliability. Monitoring the wagon body for instances of vertical acceleration and lateral instability has promising implications. The existing ride monitoring systems and associated standards apply peak to peak and RMS measures to detect an exception. The RMS value gives a positive valued measure of the magnitude of cyclic variation in the signal and peak to peak (PK-PK) values gives a positive valued measure of the magnitude of the extremities of the signal (Bleakley, 2006), (Wolfs, Bleakley, Senini & Thomas, 2006a).

The Federal Railroad Association (FRA) specifies safety standards for vehicle track interaction in North America. FRA specifies two levels for ride acceleration limits: level 2 (maintenance limits) and Level 1 (safety limits). For body vertical acceleration, 0.40-0.59g PK-PK is the Level 2 range and greater than 0.60g PK-PK is the Level 1 limit (Ackroyd, Angelo, Nejikovsky & Stevens, 2002). The Australian Railway Standards specify lateral and vertical accelerations for new and modified rolling stock. In this standard, measurements were to be taken from the floor level of the rail wagon, as close as possible to the bogie centre. According to the Australian ride performance standards, the peak to peak body vertical acceleration limit is 0.80g and average peak to peak body vertical acceleration is 0.50g. All acceleration signals in the Australian railway standards are to be filtered to below 10Hz (UIC leaflet 518, testing and approval..., 2003), (Queensland Rail Safety Standard..., n.d.).

Figure 10. Prediction results with linear regression model for rear body vertical acceleration

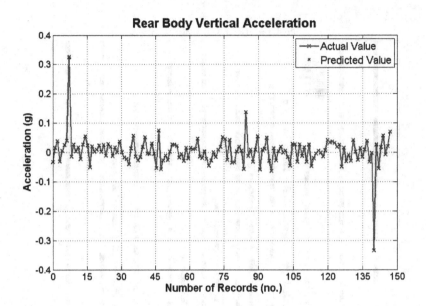

For this study the Australian Standard RMS limits according to existing ride monitoring systems have been used to monitor the signal condition. Instead of sending or storing the collected or predicted data, an FFT approximation technique with Hanning window as used in (Bleakley, 2006) generates the required signal in coded format. It extracts only necessary events of the acceleration properties of track conditions that cross the safety limits for transmission to the driver for further actions. This feature reduces data storage and communication cost, hence reduces power consumption by sending less amount of information to the driver or base station. The code has been developed in MATLAB platform (The Math Works, n.d.) to read predicted data; pre-process the data, perform the spectral analyses, and provide graphical representation to the locomotive. In this stage, data sets were used from the predicted results for the model building using linear regression, since it was selected as the most suitable algorithm during the experiment.

The filtering has been done in the frequency domain by using the FFT with Hanning window as used in (Bleakley, 2006). Wolfs et al. (Wolfs, Bleakley, Senini & Thomas, 2006a) investigated train wagon movements, and it was seen that the significant physical moments of the wagons that need to be monitored generally occur below 10 Hz. Beyond this range, extremely high accelerations can be experienced but only for very short periods to time with very little wagon movement. Therefore, the signal has been band-pass filtered to remove the low frequency content below 0.5 Hz and the high frequency content above 10 Hz. Experimental results show that typical vertical displacement has been observed some places both for front and rear wagon body. Figure 11 represents the front body vertical acceleration behaviour of railway wagons. Measured RMS values from the filtered signal for front body are represented in Figure 12. The RMS values are calculated over two second periods in steps of one sample. Typical vertical displacements observed and the RMS outputs are beyond the safety limits. Based on the measured RMS signal, a precautionary signal must be generated to send to train drivers. Signals sent to the driver through wireless communications systems for informed forward-looking decisions and initiation of suitable actions would prevent disastrous accidents from happening.

Figure 11. Front body vertical acceleration characteristics (0.5-10Hz filtered)

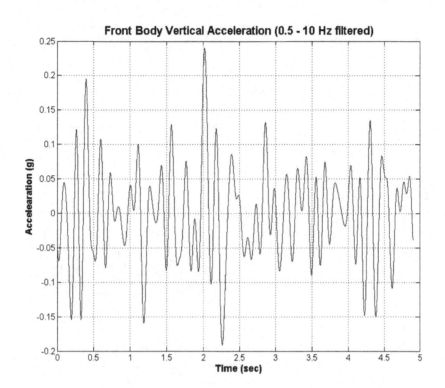

DISCUSSIONS

Machine learning techniques play a key role in developing monitoring systems for both freight and passenger railway systems to ensure safety and security, both inside the wagon and on the rail track. In this study an energy-efficient VHM system has been developed for railway that monitors typical dynamic behaviour of railway wagons due to track irregularities and lateral instability.

Initially, a data acquisition method for WSN applications was investigated using popular regression algorithms that reduce power consumption as it reduces the requirement of one sensor node in each wagon body and one sensor node for wagon side frame. Considering average ranking performance measures and computational complexity, linear regression algorithm was the algorithm best suited to predict rear right wagon body conditions; however, MLP was the most suitable considering only average accuracy of performance metrics. To select a unique classifier for the application a rule-based learning approach has been developed. All generated rules show higher accuracy except for the IBK algorithm. Rule accuracy could be increased by considering more classification problems. This research will help to reduce computational complexity, development and maintenance cost both in hardware and human inspection.

Later, a forecasting model has been developed to investigate vertical acceleration behaviour of railway wagons attached to a moving locomotive. Both front and rear body vertical acceleration phenomenon are predicted using ten popular regression algorithms. From experimental results it is shown that the approach is very effective and has predicted front and rear body vertical movement characteristics with

Figure 12. Measured RMS value for front body

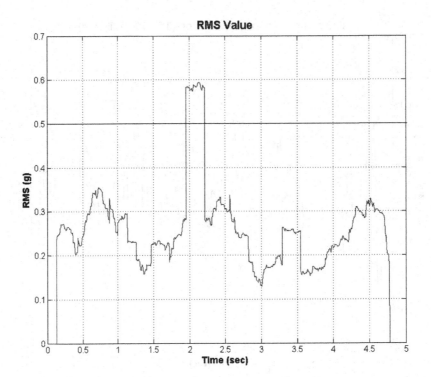

negligible errors. Metrics comprising correlation coefficient, RMSE, MAE, RRSE, RAE and computational complexity are measured from the developed model. From the performance metrics analyses it is proven that linear regression performs more efficiently than any other algorithms for this problem. Finally, with the predicted front and rear body vertical acceleration data, waveforms are developed for RMS values to monitor railway wagons using FFT.

This useful tool can be used to monitor railway systems, particularly railway track irregularities and derailment potential with integrity and reliability which reduces maintenance costs and inspection requirements of railway systems. It reduces computational cost, power consumption of the system and increases the sensor's lifetime. This is the first time that modern machine learning techniques have been used in this context which still requires verification in different areas. Therefore, it deserves further investigation that will focus on these specific areas:

- Develop data acquisition method to improve the classification and regression methods' performances
- Develop an algorithm to forecast railway health condition by integrating vertical and lateral acceleration condition.
- Investigate wireless communication system to communicate individual wagons to locomotive or driver end.
- Integrate the model with SQL database to send warning signal to driver.

REFERENCES

Ackroyd, P., Angelo, M., Nejikovsky, B., & Stevens, J. (2002). Remote ride quality monitoring and Acela train set performance. In *Proceedings of the 2002 ASME/IEEE Join Rail Conf.*, Washington DC, (pp. 171-178).

Aha, D. W. (1992). Tolerating noisy, irrelevant, and novel attributes in instance-based learning algorithms. *Int'l Journal on Man-Machine Studies, 36*, 267–287. doi:10.1016/0020-7373(92)90018-G

Aha, D. W., Kibler, D., & Albert, M. K. (1991). Instance-Based Learning Algorithms. *Journal on Machine Learning, 6*, 37–66.

Ali, S., & Smith, K. A. (2006). On Learning Algorithm Selection for Classification. *Journal on Applied Soft Computing, 6*, 119–138. doi:10.1016/j.asoc.2004.12.002

Bleakley, S. S. (2006, October). *Time Frequency analysis of railway wagon body accelerations for a low-power autonomous device.* Master's thesis, Faculty of Engineering and Physical Systems, Central Queensland University, Australia.

Cole, C., & Roach, D. (1996). Dynamic response of coal wagons during normal operation. In *1996 World Conf. on Rail Research*, Colorado, (pp. 219-231).

Duarte, M. F., & Hu, Y. H. (2004). Vehicle classification in distributed sensor networks. *Journal of Parallel and Distributed Computing, 64*, 826–838. doi:10.1016/j.jpdc.2004.03.020

Esveld, C. (2001). *Modern Railway Track*, (2nd ed.). The Netherlands: MRT Productions.

FRA 49 CFR Part 213 (1998, June 22). Track Safety Standards: Final Rule. *Federal Register, 63*(119). Federal Railroad Administration, Department of Transportation: Washington DC.

Garg, V. K., & Dukkipati, R. V. (1984). *Dynamics of railway vehicle systems.* New York: Academic Press.

Ho, T. K. (1998). The Random Subspace Method for Constructing Decision Forests. *IEEE Transactions on Pattern Analysis and Machine Intelligence, 20*(8).

Holmes, G. Hall, M. & Frank, E. (1999). Generating Rule Sets from Model Trees. In *Advanced Topics in Artificial Intelligence,* (vol.1747, pp. 1-12). Berlin: Springer.

Jo Cunningham, S. & Holmes, G. (n.d.). *Developing innovative applications in agriculture using data mining.* Tech Report, Dept. of Computer Science, University of Waikato, New Zealand.

John, G. H., & Kohavi, R. (1997). Wrappers for feature subset selection. *Artificial Intelligence, 97*(1-2).

Kaewunruen, S., & Remennikov, A. M. (2007). Response and prediction of dynamic characteristics of worn rail pads under static preloads. In *14th Int'l Congress on Sound Vibration*, Cairns, Australia.

Li, C., Stratman, B., & Mahadevan, S. (2007). Improving railroad wheel inspection planning using classification methods. In *Proc. of the 25th IASTED Int'l Multi-Conf.*, Innsbruck, Austria, Feb'07, (pp. 366-371).

Li, D., Salahifar, T., Malone, J., & Kalay, S. F. (2001). Development of performance-based track geometry inspection. In *7th Int'l Heavy Haul Conf.,* Brisbane, Australia, (pp. 461-465).

Linear Regression. (n.d.). GraphPad Software, Inc. San Diego, Tech. Rep. [Online]. Retrieved January 25th, 2008 from http://www.curvefit.com/linear_regression.htm

Magoulas, G. D., Plagianakos, V. P., & Vrahatis, M. N. (2004). Neural network-based colonoscopic diagnosis using on-line learning and differential evolution. *Applied Soft Computing, 4,* 369–379. doi:10.1016/j.asoc.2004.01.005

McClanachan, M., Dhanasekar, M., Skerman, D., & Davey, J. (2002). Monitoring the dynamics of freight wagons. In *Conf. on Railway Engineering, CORE 2002,* Wollongong, Australia, (pp. 213-221).

McClanachan, M., Scown, B., Roach, D., Skermen, D., & Payne, B. (2001). Autonomous detection of severe wagon-track interaction dynamics. In *7th Int'l Heavy Haul Conference.*

Nefti, S., & Oussalah, M. (2004). A neural network approach for railway safety prediction. In *2004 IEEE Int'l Conf. on Systems, Man and cybernetics,* October (pp. 3915-3920).

Palese, J. W. Bonaventura, C. S. & Zarembski, A. M. (2000). Intelligent system for real-time prediction of railway vehicle response to the interaction with track geometry. In *Railroad Conf. 2000. Proc. of the 2000 ASME/IEEE Joint,* (pp. 31-45).

Queensland Rail Safety Standard STD/0077/TEC Civil Engineering Track Standards Version 2. Module CETS 9 –Track Geometry. (n.d.). Queensland, Australia, Tech. Report.

Regression analysis (n.d.). Wikipedia, the free encyclopedia. Retrieved January 25th, 2008, http://en.wikipedia.org/wiki/Regression_analysis

Shafiullah, G. M., Gyasi-Agyei, A., & Wolfs, P. (2007). Survey of wireless communications applications in the railway industry. In *Conf. on Wireless Broadband and Ultra Wideband Comm.,* Sydney.

Shafiullah, G. M., Simson, S., Thompson, A., Wolfs, P., & Ali, S. (2008). Monitoring Vertical Acceleration of Railway Wagon Using Machine Learning Techniques. In *Proceedings of The 2008 International Conference on Machine Learning; Models, Technologies and Applications (MLMTA'08),* Las Vegas, NV, (pp. 770-775).

Shafiullah, G. M., & Thompson, A. Wolfs, P. and Ali, S. "Reduction of Power Consumption in Sensor Network Applications using Machine Learning Techniques", *Proceeding of the IEEE international conference TENCON2008, Hyderabad, India.*

Smith, J. Russel, S. & Looi, M. (2003). Security as a safety issue in rail communications. In *8th Aus. Workshop on Safety Critical System and Software (SCS'03),* Canberra, Australia, (pp. 79-88).

Sykes, A. O. (n.d.). An introduction to regression analysis. Chicago working paper in Law and Economics, Tech. Rep. [Online]. Available at http://www.law.uchicago.edu/Lawecon/WkngPprs_01-25/20.Sykes.Regression.pdf

The Math Works (2008). The Math Works, Inc. [Online]. Retrieved January 9th, 2008 from http://www.mathworks.com/

Trotman, M. & Sillaots, D. (n.d.). *Monitoring Rail Track Condition to Reduce Maintenance Costs*. ICN Technologies Pty Ltd, Tech Report, Australia.

UIC leaflet 518, testing and approval of railway vehicles from the point of view of their dynamic behaviour – safety track – track fatigue – ride quality. (2003, April). International Union of Railways, Paris, France, Tech. Rep.

Vapnik, V. N. (1999). An overview of statistical learning theory. *IEEE Transactions on Neural Networks, 10*, 988–999. doi:10.1109/72.788640

Weka 3. (n.d.). The University of Waikato, NewZealand, Tech. Rep. [Online]. Available March 9th, 2008 http://www.cs.waikato.ac.nz/ml/weka

Witten, I. H., & Frank, E. (2000). *Data Mining: Practical Machine Learning Tool and Technique with Java Implementation*. San Francisco: ELSEVIER, Morgan Kaufmann.

Wolfs, P., Bleakley, S., Seninin, S., & Thomas, P. (2006). A distributed low cost device for the remote observation of track and vehicle interactions. In *Conf. on Railway Engineering, RTSA*, Melbourne, Australia, (pp. 280-286).

Wolfs, P. J., Bleakley, S., Senini, S. T., & Thomas, P. (2006). An autonomous, low cost, distributed method for observing vehicle track interactions. In *Rail Conf. 2006*, Atlanta, GA.

Chapter 17
Use of Data Mining Techniques for Process Analysis on Small Databases

Matjaz Gams
Jozef Stefan Institute, Ljubljana, Slovenia

Matej Ozek
Jozef Stefan Institute, Ljubljana, Slovenia

ABSTRACT

The pharmaceutical industry was for a long time founded on rigid rules. With the new PAT initiative, control is becoming significantly more flexible. The Food and Drug Administration is even encouraging the industry to use methods like machine learning. The authors designed a new data mining method based on inducing ensemble decision trees from which rules are generated. The first improvement is specialization for process analysis with only a few examples and many attributes. The second innovation is a graphical module interface enabling process operators to test the influence of parameters on the process itself. The first task is creating accurate knowledge on small datasets. The authors start by building many decision trees on the dataset. Next, they subtract only the best subparts of the constructed trees and create rules from those parts. A best tree subpart is in general a tree branch that covers most examples, is as short as possible and has no misclassified examples. Further on, the rules are weighed, regarding the number of examples and parameters included. The class value of the new case is calculated as a weighted average of all relevant rule predictions. With this procedure the authors retain clarity of the model and the ability to efficiently explain the classification result. In this way, overfitting of decision trees and overpruning of the basic rule learners are diminished to a great extent. From the rules, an expert system is designed that helps process operators. Regarding the second task of graphical interface, the authors modified the Orange explanation module so that an operator at each step takes a look at several space planes, defined by two chosen attributes (Demšar et al., 2004). The displayed

DOI: 10.4018/978-1-60566-908-3.ch017

attributes are the ones that appeared in the classification rules triggered by the new case. The operator can interactively change the current set of process parameters in order to check the improvement of the class value. The task of seeing the influence of combining all the attributes leading to a high quality end product (called design space) is now becoming human comprehensible, it does not demand a high-dimensional space vision any more. The method was successfully implemented on data provided by a pharmaceutical company. High classification accuracy was achieved in a readable form thus introducing new comprehensions.

INTRODUCTION

Donald E. Knuth said almost twenty years ago (D. Knuth, interview, 1993): "I think the most exciting computer research now is partly in robotics, and partly in applications to biochemistry. Biology is so digital, and incredibly complicated, but incredibly useful."

In 2004, the United States Food and Drug Administration (FDA) issued a document "PAT — A Framework for Innovative Pharmaceutical Development, Manufacturing, and Quality Assurance." This document was written as guidance for a broad industry audience in different organizational units and scientific disciplines (*"Guidance for industry PAT", 2004*). To a large extent, the guidance discusses principles with the goal of developing regulatory processes of drug production that encourage innovation.

As the FDA states, the conventional pharmaceutical manufacturing is generally accomplished using batch processing with laboratory testing conducted on collected samples to evaluate quality (*"Guidance for industry PAT", 2004*). This conventional approach has been successful in providing quality pharmaceuticals to the public. However, today significant opportunities exist for improving pharmaceutical development, manufacturing, and quality assurance through innovation in product and process development, process analysis, and process control. This is where machine learning might help.

Unfortunately, the pharmaceutical industry has been generally hesitant to introduce innovative systems into the manufacturing sector for a number of reasons. One often cited reason is regulatory uncertainty, which may result from the perception that the existing regulatory system is rigid and unfavorable for the introduction of innovative systems. For example, many manufacturing procedures are treated as being frozen and many process changes are managed through regulatory submissions.

Because of the hesitancy of the pharmaceutical industry, the document encourages new production techniques with common name Process Analytical Technology (PAT). Its focus is innovation in development, manufacturing and quality assurance by removing "regulatory fear/uncertainty", utilizing science and risk-based approach to regulatory requirements and oversight. This will provide a flexible and less burdensome regulatory approach for well understood processes, creating an environment that facilitates rationale science, risk, and business decisions.

Therefore, the pharmaceutical industry needs a system for designing, analyzing and controlling manufacturing process (Schneidir, 2006). The goal of PAT is to understand and control the manufacturing process in real time. The system must be able to make the recommendation during the process to achieve higher quality of the end product. The system should follow the performance attributes, raw and in-process materials and processes. A PAT system should use multiple tools for understanding and controlling the manufacturing process: multivariate tools for design, data acquisition and analysis, process analyzers, process control tools, continuous improvement and knowledge management tools.

Figure 1. Design and control space. Control strategy is to adjust the parameters of the points in design space to get into control space.

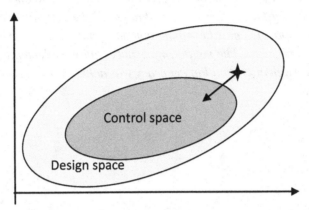

The FDA expects an inverse relationship between the level of process understanding and the risk of producing a poor quality product. The well understood process will require less restrictive regulatory approaches to manage change.

If enough data were gathered, PAT suggests constructing a design space (Desai, 2006). That is a multidimensional space that encompasses combinations of product design, manufacturing process design, critical manufacturing process parameters and component attributes that provide assurance of suitable product quality and performance. Therefore, design space is part of the space for which there is data (usually in a specific interval). Control space is defined similarly. It is the multi-dimensional space that encompasses process operating parameters and component quality measurements that assure process or product quality. It is a subset of the design space, as can be seen in Figure 1. It is considered as a "high quality area" for process parameters.

The control strategy is to mitigate risks associated with the batch failure when the critical and non-critical process parameters fall outside the control space but stay within the design space.

Machine learning methods are just becoming an appreciated technique for solving problems in pharmacy. At the same time, more research in biochemistry is done with machine learning. For example: machine learning methods such as neural networks and support vector machines have been explored for predicting compounds that interact with proteins in Li et al. (2007); machine learning based analyses on metabolic networks are presented in Plaimas et al. (2008).

In our case, the data had 100 attributes only 40 instances, because it is very expensive for the pharmaceutical company to obtain more data. However, it is also very expensive to end the production process and discover that the quality of the end product is not inside the desired specification. In this case, all of the pills have to be destroyed. On the other hand, the price of classifying the pill as good, although its quality is bad, is even greater, as the pill can do real damage to a consumer and consequently to the company. As a consequence, one needs to make a pessimistic classifier that alerts the user on all risks in the pill production. This classifier can sometimes classify a high quality product as a product of bad quality, but should never classify a product of bad quality as high quality.

The target class is the product quality. For the pharmaceutical industry there are only two possible quality classes: accepted and rejected. From the pharmaceutical point of view, every rejected product is a waste of money and resources – they would like to have flawless production. But quality can be described in more than just two terms. In reality, a product can have really good quality or really bad quality or something in between. The company experts divided product quality, in our case, into three classes: high quality, medium quality and rejected.

RELATED WORK

The data for our particular case is riddled with problems: the database is small, the data is gathered in a process, the number of negative cases is very small and there is large noise in the data. For solving this hard problem we have to combine methods that work on small databases with methods for mining data streams and methods that can produce accurate classifier despite noisy data. A special request from pharmaceutical industry is that a classifier has to offer an explanation for its prediction and be understandable even for non experts.

How much training data is enough? That is the question several researchers tried to answer (Tang et al., 2008). Algorithms learn from data and, generally, feeding them with more data improves the accuracy. This improvement, however, is asymptotical. If the training data is statistically already representative for the problem space, then a classifier will practically stop learning after a certain limit: new data will support existing patterns and will help reducing the risk of over-training, but will not add new information to the model. The actual number of required data depends on the problem, the quality of the data and the proportion between the numbers of instances against the number of attributes.

Data mining methods in general work better with large amounts of data and when used on small datasets they produce inaccurate classifiers. The main problem of these classifiers is overfitting. This means that some methods that are not very robust give very good results on training data, but when tested on real data they perform poorly. The rate of overfitting is also very dependent on input data. This mostly happens when there is not much data compared with the number of attributes, or when the data is noisy. If one has too many attributes and not much data, the state space for finding the optimal model is too wide and the algorithm often finishes in a local optimum. The problem of overfitting can be partially eliminated by suitable pre-processing and by using adequate learning methods as well as providing good input data.

Genetic researches often deal with this issues arising from the fact that there are many attributes and only a small number of samples (Ben-Dor et al., 2002). They can have more than 1000 genes and only 50 samples. They are solving the problem with attribute selection and carefully selecting data mining method that is best for their data.

Ensemble methods work well on small, noisy datasets. An ensemble of classifiers is a set of classifiers whose individual decisions are combined in some way to classify new examples (Witten & Frank, 2005). Many popular learning techniques in computer science can be conveniently described within this framework including bagging and boosting.

Hybrid intelligent systems in general achieve improvements over "single" methods. For example, in Gams and Tušar (2007), five intelligent methods were used to make prediction about the state of the person entering a building through a control point. If enough "alarms" were produced by the stand-alone modules, the overall classification was "alarm" as well.

The approach introduced within this paper is similar to bagging. Suppose the data mining task is to build a model for predictive classification, and the dataset from which to train the model (learning data set, which contains observed classifications) is relatively small. One could repeatedly sub-sample

Figure 2. Schema of the data mining process

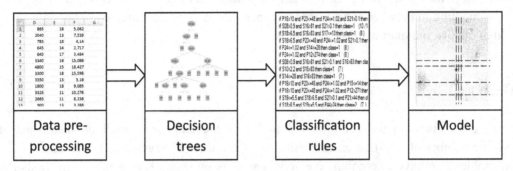

| Data pre-processing | Decision trees | Classification rules | Model |

(with replacement) from the dataset, and apply, for example, a tree classifier to the successive samples. In practice, very different trees will often be grown for the different samples, illustrating the instability of models often evident with small datasets. One method of deriving a single prediction (for new observations) is to use all trees found in the different samples, and to apply some simple voting schema. The final classification is often the one most often predicted by the constructed trees. Other weighted combinations of predictions (weighted vote, weighted average) are also commonly used.

There are several data mining algorithms for manufacturing process control (Sadoyan et al., 2006; Wang, 1999). H. Sadoyan et al. (2006) uses combination of clustering done by kNN method and rule extraction method. Cotofrei and Stoffel (2002) construct and perform data mining on events. With use of different rule induction techniques, they construct set of rules.

All of those techniques are built for very large databases. They are suitable for processes where data is gathered automatically in short time intervals. In that case, one has to deal with too many data and not with too few, like in our case.

There are several articles dealing with the use of data mining in pharmaceutical manufacturing (Wu et al., 2008; Mollan & Lodaya, 2004; Cox, 2008; Agalloco & Carleton, 2007). Mostly, however, offer overview of possible approaches and no useful applications on specific pill production process are made.

THE MINING PROCESS

Schema

We construct a classifier in four steps (Figure 2). In the first step, the data is preprocessed. Because of a small database, this is a very important step. In the second step, decision trees are built. Since decision trees on small dataset tend to overfit the data, only the best parts of trees are kept and rest of the trees are discarded. In the third step, rules are built from the best parts of decision trees. In the last step, rules are weighted and combined to a single classifier. All steps will be explained in the following sections.

There are three different uses of the model as shown in Figure 3. In phase A, the raw material is tested for quality. In phase B, the intermediate product is tested and process parameters are modified. In phase C, the quality of the end product is tested. The process will be explained in section Visualization.

Figure 3. Diagram of the application of the classification

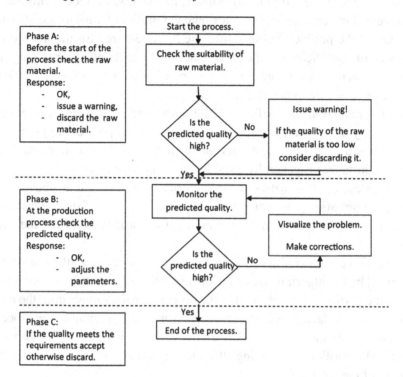

Data Preprocessing

Data preprocessing increases the accuracy of mining. On some estimates (Goharian & Grossman, 2003), 80% of mining efforts is spent on improving data quality. In case of small database, one has to pay special attention to this step. In our case, the data is preprocessed in five steps: data merging, data cleaning, data integration, data normalization and data reduction.

The first step is specific for mining data obtained in a process. A process involves sequences of actions; therefore, the attributes are also divided into several learning sets accordingly to the separate process stages. The first stage is gathering of raw materials, the second stage is the first step of production process, and so on until the last stage that consists of packaging the product and basic verification of the end product. This division reflects the sequential nature of the process. It will enable focusing on smaller subsets of data, thus achieving higher classification accuracy even during the production of new products where only part of the data needed for the classification is known.

The second step is data cleaning. Real world data is incomplete, noisy and inconsistent. In industry, the operators determine some values only to a certain degree. The values can also be wrong or misleading. Noise in the data can represent another problem. One can detect outliers and errors and correct them, but most of the noise cannot be removed. In this case one has to carefully select data mining method to compensate the error in prediction caused by noise. In our case, the expert checked all the values. Some missing values were inserted by the expert and some wrong values were removed and left unknown.

The third step involves data integration. It was established that some tests, during the process, were redundant. In this step we removed attributes that were linearly dependent.

In the fourth step, the data was normalized. Mostly, the data was divided with mass of process ingredients. This prevented the classificator to contribute variability of attributes to different sizes of pill instead to the quality of the product. For example, the force required for mixing the ingredients is in proportion to the mass of ingredients. On the other hand, the force required for mixing can be an indicator of some problems. Therefore, the force has to be first divided with the mass of the ingredients and then the normalized force is used as an attribute.

In the last step, data reduction was performed. Normally, some instances are removed, but we could not afford to remove any of the scarce instances. Since it was not possible to get more instances, the only remaining way was to select the most relevant attributes. Working with more than 100 attributes and approximately 40 instances is generally considered a very hard problem.

Attributes selection can be done with standard algorithms for ranking attributes. We compared attributes with RelieF, information gain, gain ration, and gini gain. All of the algorithms ranked the attributes in a similar order: attributes from the beginning of the process and from the end of the process had the highest rank.

If all the data would all be gathered at the same time, one could remove all the attributes except those that are highest ranked by the algorithms. But the data is gathered gradually, depending on the process stage, meaning that the attributes from the end of the process are not known until the end of the process where it might already be too late. Therefore, attributes from the beginning of the process are more important for classification than those at the end. Attribute selection in this case is a very delicate process, therefore we combined algorithms for ranking attributes, expert knowledge and took into consideration the sequential nature of the attributes.

To summarize, data preprocessing is a specialized, time consuming, important step especially for small process databases. For accurate classification, reliable data is a necessity.

Decision Tree Building

Decision trees are one of the most popular forms of knowledge representation in data mining and machine learning. For construction of decision trees, we used the C4.5 algorithm (Quinlan, 1993). Amongst other data mining methods, decision-tree based classification has several advantages: algorithms like C4.5 are well tested, reliable and robust. Even non-experts are able to understand decision-tree models after a brief explanation. On the other hand, there are some disadvantages, e.g., decision trees tend to overfit on small databases. Also, decision trees divide the attribute space linearly and therefore, it is hard to detect nonlinear rules.

We decided to build several decision trees on the data. Building many decision trees instead of only one offers several advantages. First of all, they increase reliability of the classification, as observed in bagging, boosting or ensemble techniques. Secondly, more decision trees cover more attributes. This is important for building complete design space since experts believe that every attribute is important (Banerjee et al., 2008).

Decision trees are built in several steps to reflect the sequential nature of process. First, decision trees are built with attributes from the first stage, next with attributes from the first two stages (first and second), and so on until the decision trees are constructed on all the attributes. This process of selecting attributes privileges attributes of the first stage, since they are used in all iterations of tree construction. Attributes of the last stage are used only in the last iteration, where we build decision trees with all attributes.

When constructing decision trees, one can make some choices about splitting criteria and pruning. Our decision trees were constructed with several pruning options. The default pruning options were: at least 2 examples in the leaves and post pruning with the confidence level of 0.25. The decision trees with those options on a small database lead to small, over-pruned trees. Therefore, decision trees were also built with less pruning and with no pruning. The classification trees were tested with the Weka (Witten & Frank, 2005) cross-validation for the classification accuracy. The decision trees with no pruning performed as good as trees with default pruning. This is probably due to the small database. Because of the nature of the data with many attributes and few examples, most of the trees overfit the data and are not so accurate in cross validation or later in future tests.

At each particular stage, trees were constructed on different attribute subsets. First, decision trees were built on all attributes from a specific stage. Second, the top attribute of the decision tree was removed from the attribute set and the classification tree was built again. The obtained classification trees were evaluated by cross-validation and removed if cross-validation accuracy dropped too much. The process of attribute removal was repeated until no further modification was observed. Then we repeat the process and also remove attributes that are near to the top to find out if there are other attributes that can replace them.

Building many decision trees instead of only one offered several advantages also in our case. First of all, they increased reliability of the classification, as seen in bagging, boosting or ensemble techniques. But building many decision trees also introduces some weaknesses. Because of the nature of the data with many attributes and few examples, some of the trees overfit the data and were not so accurate in cross validation or later in future tests. Specific modifications were needed.

Rule Extraction

At the end of the tree-construction phase, there is a large set of decision trees that are mostly overfit and, although one tree is easy to understand, it is difficult to go through multiple trees to decide what in the process should be changed to gain higher quality of the product. We introduced rule extraction for counterbalancing overfitting and to increase clarity of the classification result.

Furthermore, we want to maintain control over the rule construction. There are several algorithms like CN2 that could extract rules directly from the data. In contrast to decision trees, classification rules usually underfit the data. But in general it is more difficult to build large amounts of different rules than large amounts of trees. In addition, there are several algorithms and publications about e.g. random forests (Wisemann et al., 2008) which encouraged us to try first with several trees.

There are some known methods for automatic extraction of rules from trees (Witten & Frank, 2005). One method combines a divide-and-conquer strategy for decision tree learning with the separate-and-conquer one for rule learning. In essence, to make a simple rule, a pruned decision tree is built for the current set of instances, the leaf with the largest coverage is transformed into a rule, and the tree is discarded. Although commonly used, this method is not suitable for our data since it produces too few rules. One method is based on exploiting multiple viewpoints and redundancy (Gams, 2001).

To create an accurate and reliable classification model, we subtracted only the best subparts of the constructed trees and created rules from those parts. A best tree subpart is in general a tree branch that covers most examples, is as short as possible and has no misclassified examples. The redundancy in large amount of rules should compensate the decision that we use no pruning in the classification tree induction.

A rule set has to be checked, so that duplicate rules are removed. Similar rules were merged. Rules should be balanced so that all attributes are represented in a ruleset. However, the number of rules in which some attribute appears should correspond to the importance of the attribute. Therefore, some attributes occur in more rules than others. For the actual application, all the constructed rules were examined by the experts who removed the ones they did not find appropriate.

Further on, the rules were weighed regarding the number of examples and parameters. The more examples and the less parameters included, the better and more important the rule is.

The method is based on several mechanisms and expected gains. The class value of the new case is calculated as a weighted average of all relevant rule predictions. With this procedure we retain clarity of the model and ability to efficiently explain the classification result. In this way, overfitting of decision trees and overpruning of the basic rule learners are diminished to a great extend. From the rules, an expert system is designed that helps process operators.

From our testing, the best approach is based on manual selecting and merging the rules from decision trees by applying simple tools. One could argue that manual rule extraction can be the source of overfitting and inconsistencies, but it was evident that human can "see" trees and rules and can extract important rules that computer would not. Computers though, are excellent in generating statistically relevant patterns. But, experts unlike computers understand the task and the risk of overfitting.

Model Construction

After rules were refined and weighted, the final classificator was constructed. Several classifiers were considered, e. g., all rules can be considered equal and average is calculated, or different rules are treated differently and results of some rules are more important than the others.

The first classificator used a weighted average. The rules were weighted with weights equal to coverage of the rule. Since we have three classes (those are: 1, 2, 3), the classification result is a real number between 1 and 3, where 1 means the highest quality product and 3 means the lowest quality product.

By using the weighted average as a classifier, single rules are not as important as in the original list of rules. Nevertheless, a single bad ingredient can spoil the product. Therefore, we increase the importance of problematic rules by adding more rules for classes 2 and 3. In this way, in case of any doubt, rules for class 2 or 3 should prevail. As a result, the classifier is more sensitive for any "bad" attribute value; it is a "pessimistic" classifier. But it should not be too pessimistic since the pharmaceutical experts believe that a product can be of a very high quality despite some bad, but not significant parameters. On the other hand, every single rule that classifies the product as a class 3 can point to a serious problem. Therefore, each rule of this kind was carefully considered by the expert. Rules were built and selected in a way that accurate classification is possible early in the process. It is difficult to perform classical in-built cross-validation because the rules were constructed by humans. Even though, some comparison with the other methods can be done. When building decision trees, one can compare cross-validation results with methods like SVM or Naïve Bayes. Classification accuracy of the best tree is 79%, of Naïve Bayes it is 62% and of SVM 70%. This shows that decision trees are among the best methods for machine learning for this particular problem. Classification accuracy of the ensamble of constructed decision trees is lower than 79% which is due to the removal of the most informative attributes and due to overfit. The classification accuracy rose as parts of trees were converted to the rules and even more when the experts cleaned the rule set.

Figure 4. Interface of the Multi Scatterplot, the application for visualization and modeling of production process.

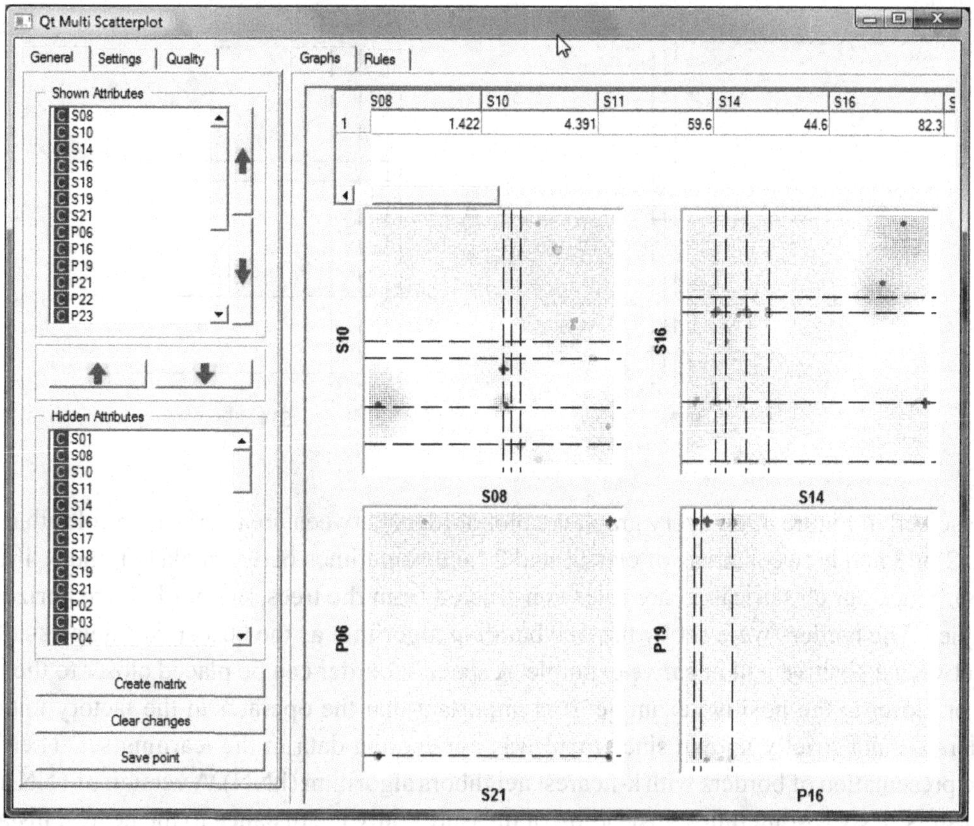

Visualization

Visualization is an important part of an application. Even the most accurate classifiers can cause confusion if no one can understand the results. In our case, there are many results a user should see at each step to successfully guide the process, but the design and control space are most relevant. Since those are in our case defined with rules; only critical rules worth consideration could be presented. In addition, the classifier should classify the product all the time between the production process, when some or most of the attributes are not known yet., thus one can choose from a limited set of rules.

The first problem is in the nature of design and control space. In principle, they can be graphically presented in a high dimensional space, where every dimension represents new attribute. But humans are not able to see in more than 3 or 4 dimensional space, and on screen only 2 dimensional (2D) figures can be presented. All higher dimensional figures can be only projections to 2D.

We decided to present a 60-dimensional design space as a set of 2D diagram, each having different attributes on the axes. There are 1770 combinations of attributes from which diagrams can be designed. An operator cannot survey them all and not all are important at the same time. The most important are attributes, whose change has an impact on improving the product quality, attributes in the rules that classify the product of class 2 or 3.

Figure 5. The design space colored with 1NN method. Red dots are of quality 3, yellow quality 2 and green quality 1.A new example is a blue cross. The user can change attribute value with a simple click on the graph.

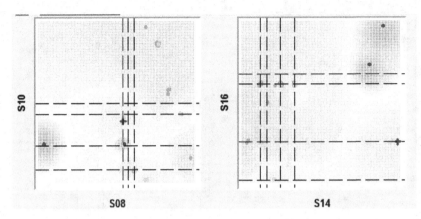

As presented in Figure 4, on every graph we plot borders between areas on which rules that classify into class 2 or 3 and between areas of class 1 and 2 (and sometimes between class 1 and 3, if that border exists). Since our classificators are rules constructed from the trees, the borders are horizontal and vertical lines. The borders were set by the tree building algorithm as the best split points usually in the middle between a positive and negative example. A specific border can be placed closer to the negative example or closer to the positive example. It is important that the operator in the factory understands that borders are not strictly known since there was not enough data in the learning set. Therefore we combined presentation of borders with k-nearest neighbors algorithm (kNN). A version of 1NN achieved the best results. 1NN is sometimes misleading; it measures only the distance to the nearest instance and does not consider combination of different attributes for classification. Therefore, the final classification is performed by the constructed classifier. However, 2D graphs with 1NN make graphical presentation very transparent.

The second problem is related to the usability of the application. The operator can interactively change the current set of process parameters in order to check the improvement of the class value. Changing parameters is done by simply clicking on the graphs. At the same time, the classifier predicts the quality of the end product. If the change causes some other attributes to become problematic, they are automatically shown in a separate window.

A further improvement is automatic finding the best combination of attributes. One would insert only the attributes that cannot be changed, for example the properties of a raw material, and the application would then set all the other attributes. We avoided this automation because of risk involved in drug production. For automatic process construction one would need more learning and testing data, which we do not have. Another important issue is that systems only help and do not make decisions. An expert should make decision for such sensitive procedures.

Application

A designer of the manufacturing process or an operator of the process is the targeted user of the designed application. The designer uses the system to test what-if situations. The operator uses the system as a

Figure 6. Example of rules and classification result

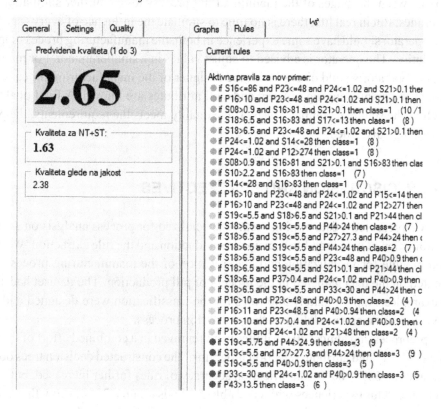

warning system that alerts on bad parameter values and as a tool for improving the product quality. The procedure of using application is in Figures 5 and 6.

When the application is started, the designer of the process inserts the data of the raw materials for the current production. The application chooses critical attributes and presents them as a set of graphs. The designer can change the values of attributes by clicking on the graphs and checking how much different attributes contribute to higher quality. After that, gradual inserting of values of attributes follow according to the expert's experience. Attributes can be interactively inserted by clicking on the graphs. The application classifies the data every time attributes are changed. Instead of graphical representation of attributes the designer can switch to a list of rules that are classifying the data. The expert can inspect all the rules to see the explanation for the predicted quality or inspects only the rules that predict problems. In this case, the expert can focus on solving the problematic attributes.

In terms of process control, the operator first enters the parameters of the raw material, which cannot be adjusted. The program then classifies the data. If it predicts a product of high quality the process continues, otherwise the program issues a warning. The operator has to decide if the raw material is of the right quality to start the process if appropriate measures are taken. In the worst case the raw material has to be discarded, which is quite uncommon.

Secondly, the raw material is processed. At the production process, quality is checked at every step. If the predicted quality is not suitable, the operator tries to find the problem with the help of the application. The operator can simulate predicted properties of the product by changing values of some attributes. Once the right combination of attributes is found, machines are set and the process is continues. The operator has some time between the stages of the manufacturing process to use further simulations and set the according machines. But in real life, there is no time to simulate the influence of every separate attribute. Therefore, the operator should have some experience in both, the manufacturing process supervision and computer simulation. The operator is advised to adjust values in a smaller manor. For major changes of the attributes, the operator should discuss with the designer of the manufacturing process.

Finally, when the manufacturing process ends, all attributes are known. A final quality prediction is made as well as the standard company tests. If the quality meets the requirements, the product is accepted, otherwise it is discarded.

CONCLUSION, DISCUSSION AND PERSPECTIVES

In this chapter we presented a data mining method specialized for process analysis on small databases. We used a combination of the ensemble decision tree induction and the rule extraction. We also provided an application module for visualization and classification of the manufacturing process. The method was implemented on the data gathered in the process of pill production. The dataset had 100 attributes and only 40 examples. Approximately 300 rules for the classification were designed and applied on a program for visualization and modeling of the production process.

During the preprocessing almost 40 attributes were removed in a combined effort of the experts from pharmaceutical industry and attribute selection programs. The constructed decision trees obtained cross-validation accuracy of 60% - 80%. Classification accuracy of rules further increased, but is not a matter of public disclosure.. Our experiences with ensemble methods (Gams, 2001) show that combination of multiple classifiers improves classification accuracy and reliability.

When one wants to extract as much useful data as possible, it is easy to end up with flooding the screen with too much data. Our method presents only the most important data. Additional information can be found on additional screens when one needs extra explanation for the classification. We believe that the chosen representation with several 2D graphs enables an important insight into the ongoing production process.

REFERENCES

Agalloco, J., & Carleton, F. (2007). *Validation of pharmaceutical Processes*. Weimar, TX: Culinary and Hospitality Industry Publications Services.

Banerjee, S., Bhatwadekar, N., Mahajan, P., Karode, P., & Mishra, A. (2008). Process analytical technology (PAT): Boon to pharmaceutical industry. *Pharmaceutical Reviews, 6(6)*.

Ben-Dor, A., Bruhn, L., Friedman, N., Nachman, I., Schummer, M., & Yakhini, Z. (2000). Tissue classification with gene expression profile. *Journal of Computational Biology*, 7.

Cotofrei, P., & Stoffel, K. (2002). Rule extraction from time series databases using classification trees. In *Proc. Applied Informatics*, Innsbruck, Austria.

Cox, S. (2008). *Pharmaceutical manufacturing handbook regulation and quality*. New York: John Wiley & Sons.

Demšar, J., Zupan, B., & Leban, G. (2004). Orange: From experimental machine learning to interactive data mining. White Paper, Faculty of Computer and Information Science, University of Ljubljana, Slovenia.

Desai, P. R. (2006). Case study: Approach for filing with PAT. In *AAPS Workshop on Real World Applications of PAT and QbD in Drug Process Development and Approval*, Arlington, VA.

Eschrich, S., Chawla, N. V., & Hall, L. O. (2002). Generalization methods in bioinformatics. In *Proceedings of the 2nd ACM SIGKDD Workshop on Data Mining in Bioinformatics*, Edmonton, Canada.

Gams, M. (2001). Weak intelligence: Through the principle and paradox of multiple knowledge. In *Advances in Computation vol. 6.* Huntington, NY: Nova Science.

Gams, M., & Tušar, T. (2007). Intelligent high-security access control. *Informatica (Ljubljana)*, *31*(4), 469–477.

Guidance for industry PAT — A framework for innovative pharmaceutical development, manufacturing, and quality assurance. (2004). U.S. Department of Health and Human Services, Food and Drug Administration.

Li, H., Yap, C. W., & Ung, C. Y. (2007). Machine learning approaches for predicting compounds that interact with therapeutic and ADMET related proteins. *Journal of Pharmaceutical Sciences*, *96*(11). doi:10.1002/jps.20985

Mollan, M., & Lodaya, M. (2004). Continuous processing in pharmaceutical manufacturing. *Processing in Pharmaceutical Manufacturing*.

Neagu, D. C., Guo, G., Trundle, P. R., & Cronin, M. T. D. (2007). A comparative study of machine learning algorithms applied to predictive toxicology data mining. *Alternatives to Laboratory Animals*, *35*, 25–32.

Plaimas, K., Mallm, J. P., Oswald, M., Svara, F., Sourjik, V., Eils, R., & König, R. (2008). Machine learning based analyses on metabolic networks supports high-throughput knockout screens. *BMC Systems Biology*, 2.

Quinlan, J. R. (1993). C4.5: Programs for machine learning. San Francisco, CA: Morgan Kaufmann.

Sadoyan, H., Zakarian, A., & Mohanty, P. (2006). Data mining algorithm for manufacturing process control. *International Journal of Advanced Manufacturing Technology*, 28.

Schneidir, R. (2006). Achieving process understanding – The foundation of strategic PAT programme. *Processing in Pharmaceutical manufacturing*.

Tang, Z., MacLennan, J., & Crivat, B. (2008). *Data mining with SQL server 2008*. New York: Wiley

Wang, X. Z. (1999). *Data mining and knowledge discovery for process monitoring and control*. Berlin, Germany: Springer.

Wisemann, S. M. (2008). Molecular phenotyping of thyroid tumors identifies a marker panel for differentiated thyroid cancer diagnosis. *Annals of Surgical Oncology*, 15.

Witten, I. H., & Frank, E. (2005). Data mining: Practical machine learning tools and techniques *(2nd Ed.)*. San Francisco, CA: Morgan Kaufmann.

Wu, H., Heilweil, E. J., Hussain, A. S., & Khan, M. (2008). Process analytical technology (PAT): quantification approaches in terahertz spectroscopy for pharmaceutical application. *Journal of Pharmaceutical Sciences, 97*(2), 970–984. doi:10.1002/jps.21004

Compilation of References

Aas, K., & Eikvil, L. (1999, June). *Text categorisation: A survey* (Tech. Rep. 941). Oslo, Norway: Norwegian Computing Center.

AccessData. Corp. (2009). *Forensic Toolkit.* Retrieved February 1, 2009, from http://accessdata.com/forensictoolkit.html.

Aciar, S., Zhang, D., Simoff, S., & Debenham, J. (2006). Recommender system based on consumer product reviews. In *Proceedings of the IEEE/WIC/ACM International Conference on Web Intelligence.*

Ackroyd, P., Angelo, M., Nejikovsky, B., & Stevens, J. (2002). Remote ride quality monitoring and Acela train set performance. In *Proceedings of the 2002 ASME/IEEE Join Rail Conf.*, Washington DC, (pp. 171-178).

Agalloco, J., & Carleton, F. (2007). *Validation of pharmaceutical Processes.* Weimar, TX: Culinary and Hospitality Industry Publications Services.

Agarwal, R., & Joshi, M. V. (2000). *PNrule: A New Framework for Learning Classifier Models in Data Mining.* Paper presented at the Technical Report.

Aggarwal, C. C., & Yu, P. S. (2000). Finding Generalized Projected Clusters in High Dimensional Spaces. *SIGMOD Record, 29*(2), 70–92. doi:10.1145/335191.335383

Agirre, E., Alfonseca, E., & de Lacalle, O. L. (2004). *Approximating hierarchy-based similarity for wordnet nominal synsets using topic signatures.*

Agrawal, R., Aggarwal, C., & Prasad, V. V. V. (2000). Depth First Generation of Long Patterns. In *Proc. Seventh Int'l Conference Knowledge Discovery and Data Mining.*

Agrawal, R., Gehrke, J., Gunopulos, D., & Raghavan, P. (1998). Automatic Subspace Clustering of High Dimensional Data for Data Mining Applications. In *Proceedings of the ACM SIGMOD Conference*, Seattle, Washington, (pp. 94-105).

Agrawal, R., Imielinski, T. T., & Swami, A. (1993). Mining associations between sets of items in large databases. In *Proc. of the ACM SIGMOD Int'l Conference on Management of Data,* Washington, DC, (pp. 207-216).

Agrawal, R., Imielinski, T., & Swami, A. (1993). Database Mining: A Performance Perspective. *IEEE Transactions on Knowledge and Data Engineering, 5*(6), 914–925. doi:10.1109/69.250074

Agrawal, R., Imielinski, T., & Swami, A. (1993). Mining association rules between sets of items in large databases. In *Proceedings of the 1993 ACM SIGMOD International Conference on Management of Data (SIGMOD'93)* (pp. 207-216). New York: ACM.

Aha, D. W. (1992). Tolerating noisy, irrelevant, and novel attributes in instance-based learning algorithms. *Int'l Journal on Man-Machine Studies, 36*, 267–287. doi:10.1016/0020-7373(92)90018-G

Aha, D. W., Kibler, D., & Albert, M. K. (1991). Instance-Based Learning Algorithms. *Journal on Machine Learning, 6*, 37–66.

Alani, H., Kim, S., Weal, D. M. M., Hall, P. L. W., & Shadbolt, N. (2003). Automatic extraction of knowledge from web documents. In *Proceedings of 2nd International Semantic Web Conference - Workshop on Human Language Technology for the Semantic Web abd Web Service.*

Alani, H., O'Hara, K., & Shadbolt, N. (2002). *Ontocopi: Methods and tools for identifying communities of practice.*

Aleman-Meza, B., Halaschek, C., Arpinar, I., & Sheth, A. (2003). Context-Aware Semantic Association Ranking. In *Proceedings of SWDB'03, Berlin, Germany*, 33-50.

Alexander, C. O. (2001). Orthogonal GARCH. In C.O. Alexander (Ed.), *Mastering Risk*, (Vol. 2). London: Financial Times-Prentice Hall.

Alexandrov, M., Gelbukh, A., & Rosso, P. (2005). An approach to clustering abstracts. In *Proc. of NLDB 2005 Conference*, (LNCS Vol. 3513, pp. 275–285). Berin: Springer Verlag.

Alharby, A., & Imai, H. (2005). IDS False Alarm Reduction Using Continuous and Discontinuous Patterns. In *Proceeding of ACNS 2005* (pp. 192-205). Heidelberg: Springer.

Ali, A. B. M. S., & Smith, K. A. (2006). On learning algorithm selection for classification. *Journal on Applied Soft Computing*, 6, 119–138. doi:10.1016/j.asoc.2004.12.002

Ali, A. B. M. S., & Wasimi, S. A. (2007). *Data Mining: Methods and Techniques*. Victoria Australia: Thomson Publishers.

Ali, S. & Smith, K. A. (2006). On Learning Algorithm Selection for Classification Applied Soft Computing, *Elsevier Science*. 6(2), 119-138.

Ali, S., & Smith, K. A. (2006). A meta-learning approach to automatic kernel selection for support vector machines. *Neurocomputing*, 70(1-3), 173–186. doi:10.1016/j.neucom.2006.03.004

Ali, S., & Smith, K. A. (2006). On Learning Algorithm Selection for Classification. *Journal on Applied Soft Computing*, 6, 119–138. doi:10.1016/j.asoc.2004.12.002

Ali, S., & Wasimi, S. (2007). *Data Mining: Methods and Techniques*. Sydney: Thomson, Australia.

Alizadeh, A. A., Eisen, M. B., Davis, R. E., Ma, C., Lossos, I. S., & Rosenwald, A. (2000). Distinct types of diffuse large B-cell lymphoma identified by gene expression profiling. *Nature*, 403, 503–511. doi:10.1038/35000501

Almonte, M., Albero, G., Molano, M., Carcamo, C., García, P. J., & Pérez, G. (2008). Risk factors for Human Papillomavirus Exposure and Co-factors for Cervical Cancer in Latin America and the Caribbean. *Vaccine*, 26, L16–L36. doi:10.1016/j.vaccine.2008.06.008

Alpaydin, E. (1993). *Multiple networks for function learning.* Paper presented at the Proceedings of the IEEE International Conference on Neural Networks.

Alpaydin, E. (2004). *Introduction To Machine Learning.* Cambridge, MA: MIT Press.

Al-Sultan, K. (1995). A Tabu Search Approach to the Clustering Problem. *Pattern Recognition*, 28(9), 1443–1451. doi:10.1016/0031-3203(95)00022-R

Altman, R. B. (2000). The interactions between clinical informatics and bioinformatics: a case study. *Journal of the American Medical Informatics Association*, 7(5), 439–443.

Ambwani, T. (2003). *Multi class support vector machine implementation to intrusion detection.* Paper presented at the Proceedings of the International Joint Conference of Neural Networks.

Ameer Ali, M., Dooley, L. S., & Karmakar, G. C. (2003). Fuzzy image segmentation using location and intensity information. In *Proceedings of the IASTED International Conference on Visualization, Imaging and Image Processing* (pp. 399-404).

Ameer Ali, M., Dooley, L. S., & Karmakar, G. C. (2005a). Automatic feature set selection for merging image segmentation results using fuzzy clustering. In *Proceedings of the International Conference on Computer and Information Technology* (pp. 337-342).

Ameer Ali, M., Dooley, L. S., & Karmakar, G. C. (2005b). Fuzzy image segmentation combining ring and elliptic shaped clustering algorithms. In *Proceedings of the International Conference on Information Technology: Coding and Computing* (pp. 118-122).

Ameer Ali, M., Dooley, L. S., & Karmakar, G. C. (2006). Object based segmentation using fuzzy clustering. In *Proceedings of the IEEE International Conference on Acoustics, Speech, and Signal Processing.*

Ameer Ali, M., Karmakar, C. G., & Dooley, L. S. (2008). Image segmentation using fuzzy clustering and integrating generic shape information. *Malaysian Journal of Computer Science.*

Ameer Ali, M., Karmakar, G. C., & Dooley, L. S. (2004a). Fuzzy image segmentation using suppressed fuzzy c-means clustering. In *Proceedings of the International Conference on Computer and Information Technology* (pp. 363-368).

Ameer Ali, M., Karmakar, G. C., & Dooley, L. S. (2004b). Image segmentation using fuzzy clustering incorporating spatial information. In *Proceedings of the IASTED International Conference on Artificial Intelligence and Applications* (pp. 878-881).

Ameer Ali, M., Karmakar, G. C., & Dooley, L. S. (2005a). Fuzzy image segmentation using shape information. In *Proceedings of the IEEE International Conference on Multimedia and Expo (ICME'05).*

Ameer Ali, M., Karmakar, G. C., & Dooley, L. S. (2005b). Fuzzy image segmentation of generic shaped clusters. In Proceedings of the IEEE International Conference on Image Processing (ICIP'05) (pp. 1202-1205).

Anderson, D., Frivold, T., Tamaru, A., & Valdes, A. (1994). Next Generation Intrusion Detection Expert System (NIDES). *Software Users Manual, Beta-Update release, Computer Science Laboratory,* (Tech. Rep. SRI-CSL-95-0). Menlo Park, CA: SRI International.

Anderson, D., Lunt, T. F., Javitz, H., Tamaru, A., & Valdes, A. (1995). *Detecting Unusual Program Behavior Using the Statistical Component of the Next-generation Intrusion Detection Expert System (NIDES)* (SRI-CSL-95-06). Menlo Park, CA: SRI International.

Anderson, J. (1983). A Spreading Activation Theory of Memory. *Journal of Verbal Learning and Verbal Behavior,* (22): 261–295. doi:10.1016/S0022-5371(83)90201-3

Anderson, J. (1986). Data dictionaries - A way forward to write meaning and terminology into medical information systems. *Methods of Information in Medicine, 25*(3), 137–138.

Andrews, D. W. (1993). Tests for parameter Instability and Structural Change with Unknown Point. *Econometrica, 61*(4), 821–856. doi:10.2307/2951764

Andrey, P., & Tarroux, P. (1998). Unsupervised segmentation of Markov random field modelled textured images using selectionist relaxation. *IEEE Transactions on Pattern Analysis and Machine Intelligence, 20,* 252–262. doi:10.1109/34.667883

Ankerst, M., Breunig, M., Kriegel, H.-P., & Sander, J. (1999). OPTICS: Ordering Points to Identify Clustering Structure. In *Proceedings of the ACM SIGMOD Conference*, Philadelphia, PA, (pp. 49-60).

Antonie, M.-L., Zaiane, O. R., & Coman, A. (2001). Application of Data Mining Techniques for Medical Image Classification. In *Proceeding of the second International Workshop on Multimedia Data and Mining,* (pp. 94-101).

Antonie, M.-L., Zaïane, O. R., & Coman, A. (2001). Application of data mining techniques for medical image classification. In O. R. Zaïane & S. J. Simoff (Eds.), *Proc. 2nd Int. Workshop on Multimedia Data Mining (MDM/KDD2001)* (pp. 94-101).

Antonio, F. S., Candenas, J. M., & Martin, F. (1999). Membership functions in the fuzzy c-means algorithm. *International Journal on Fuzzy Sets and Systems, 101,* 49–58. doi:10.1016/S0165-0114(97)00062-6

Apache jakarta lucene search engine, version 1.3. (n.d.). Retrieved from http://lucene.apache.org/

Armstrong, R., Freitag, D., Joachims, T., & Mitchel, T. (1995). Webwatcher: A learning apprentice for the world wide web. In *AAAI Spring Synopsium on Information Gathering from Heterogenous, Distributed Environments.*

Arning, A., Agrawal, R., & Raghavan, P. (1996). A Linear Method for Deviation Detection in Large Databases. In *Proceeding of 2nd International Conference on Data Mining and Knowledge Discovery* (pp. 164-169). New York: ACM Press.

Arora, S. Raghavan, P. and Rao S. (1998). Approximation Schemes for Euclidean *K-Medians* and Related Problems. In *Proceedings of the 30th Annual ACM Symposium on Theory of Computing*, Dallas, TX, (pp. 106-113).

Aroyo, L., Bellekens, P., Bjorkman, M., Broekstra, J., & Houben, G. (2006). Ontology-based personalisation in user adaptive systems. In *2nd International Workshop on Web Personalisation Recommender Systems and Intelligent User Interfaces in Conjunction with 7th International Conference in Adaptive Hypermedia.*

Asaka, M., Taguchi, A., & Goto, S. (1999). The implementation of IDA: an intrusion detection agent system. In *Proceedings of the 11th FIRST Conference.*

Athertom, T. J., & Kerbyson, D. J. (1999). Size invariant circle detection. *Image and Vision Computing, 17*, 795–803. doi:10.1016/S0262-8856(98)00160-7

Babcock, B., Datar, M., Motwani, R., & O'Callaghan, L. (2003). Maintaining Variance and *K*-Medians Over Data Stream Windows. In *Proceedings of the 22nd ACM SIGMOD-SIGACT-SIGART Symposium on Principles of Database Systems*, San Diego, CA, (pp. 234-243).

Babuska, R., Van der Veen, P. J., & Kaymak, U. (2002). Improved covariance estimation for Gustafson-Kessel clustering. In *Proceedings of the IEEE International Conference on Fuzzy Systems* (pp. 1081-1085).

Bach, M. P. (2003). Data mining applications in public organizations. In L. Budin, V. Lužar-Stiffler, Z. Bekić & V. H. Dobrić (Eds.), *Proc. of the 25th Int. Conf. on Information Technology Interfaces* (pp. 211-216). Zagreb, Croatia: SRCE University Computing Centre.

Baeza-Yates, R., & Ribeiro-Neto, B. (1999). *Modern Information Retrieval*. Reading MA: Addison Wesley.

Bai, J. (1997). Estimating Multiple Breaks One at a Time. *Econometric Theory, 13*, 315–352. doi:10.1017/S0266466600005831

Bai, J., & Perron, P. (1998). Estimating and Testing Linear Models with Multiple Structural Changes. *Econometrica, 66*, 47–78. doi:10.2307/2998540

Balabanovic, M. (1998). *Learning to Surf: Multi-agent Systems for Adaptive Web Page Recommendation.* PhD thesis, Department of Computer Science, Stanford University.

Balabanovic, M., & Shoham, Y. (1997). Fab: Content-based, collaborative recommendation. *Communications of the ACM, 40*(3), 66–72. doi:10.1145/245108.245124

Balasubramaniyan, J., Fernandez, J. O., Isacoff, D., Spafford, E., & Zamboni, D. (1998). *An architecture for intrusion detection using autonomous agents, COAST.* (Tech. Rep. 98/5). West Lafayette, IN: Purdue University.

Bandyopadhyay, S., & Coyle, E. J. (2003). An Energy Efficient Hierarchical Clustering Algorithm for Wireless Sensor Networks. In *Proceedings of the 22nd Annual Joint Conference of the IEEE Computer and Communications Societies*, San Francisco, California.

Banek, M., Min Tjoa, A., & Stolba, N. (2006). In A. Min Tjoa & J. Trujillo (Eds.), *Lecture Notes in Computer Science 4081* (pp. 185-194). Berlin: Springer.

Banerjee, A., Dolado, J. J., Hendry, D. F., & Smith, G. W. (1986). Exploring equilibrium relationships in econometrics through static models: Some Monte Carlo evidence. *Oxford Bulletin of Economics and Statistics, 48*(3), 253–277.

Banerjee, S., Bhatwadekar, N., Mahajan, P., Karode, P., & Mishra, A. (2008). Process analytical technology (PAT): Boon to pharmaceutical industry. *Pharmaceutical Reviews, 6(6).*

Barak, Y., Levy, T., Achiron, A., & Aizenberg, D. (2008). Breast cancer in women suffering from serious mental illness. *Schizophrenia Research, 102*, 249–253. doi:10.1016/j.schres.2008.03.017

Barbar'a, D., Wu, N., & Jajodia, S. (2001). Detecting novel network intrusions using bayes estimators. In *Proc. of the First SIAM Int. Conf. on Data Mining (SDM 2001).* Chicago: Society for Industrial and Applied Mathematics (SIAM).

Barnett, V., & Lewis, T. (1994). *Outliers in Statistical Data*. New York: John Wiley & Sons.

Barni, M., Cappellini, V., & Mecocci, A. (1996). Comments on 'A possibilistic approach to clustering. *IEEE transactions on Fuzzy Systems, 4*(3), 385–396. doi:10.1109/91.531780

Baronti, F. (2005). *Experimental Comparison of Machine Learning Approaches To Medical Domains: A Case Study Of Genotype Influence On Oral Cancer Development*. European conference on Emergent aspects in clinical data analaysis EACDA.

Barrus, J., & Rowe, N. C. (1998). A distributed autonomous-agent network intrusion detection and response system. In *Proceedings of the command and control research and technology symposium*, Monterey, CA.

Bastide, Y., Taouil, R. N., Pasquier, Y., Stumme, G., & Lakhal, L. (2000). Mining Frequent Patterns with Counting Inference. *SIGKDD Explorations*, (Vol. 2).

Basu, S. (1987). Image segmentation by semantic method. *Pattern Recognition, 20*, 497–511. doi:10.1016/0031-3203(87)90077-X

Bate, A., & Edwards, I. R. (2006). Data mining in spontaneous reports. *Basic & Clinical Pharmacology & Toxicology, 98*(3), 324–330. doi:10.1111/j.1742-7843.2006.pto_232.x

Bates, D. W., Pappius, E., Kuperman, G. J., Sittig, D., Burstin, H., & Fairchild, D. (1999). Using information systems to measure and improve quality. *International Journal of Medical Informatics, 53*(2-3), 115–124. doi:10.1016/S1386-5056(98)00152-X

Bauer, P., & Hackl, P. (1978). The use of MOSUMs for quality control. *Technometrics, 20*, 431–436. doi:10.2307/1267643

Bauer, P., & Hackl, P. (1980). An extension of the MOSUM technique for quality control. *Technometrics, 22*, 1–7. doi:10.2307/1268376

Baxes, G. A. (1994). *Digital image processing: Principles and applications*. Hoboken, NJ: John Wiley & Sons, Inc.

Bayardo, R. J. (1998). Efficiently mining long patterns from databases. In *Proceedings of the 1998 ACM SIGMOD International Conference on Management of Data (SIGMOD'98)* (pp. 85-93). New York: ACM.

Bayardo, R. J. (1998). Efficiently Mining Long Patterns from Databases. In *Proc. ACM SIGMOD Conference Management of Data*.

Bayardo, R. J., Jr., & Agrawal, R. (1999). International Conference on knowledge discovery and data mining. In *Proceedings of the Fifth ACMSIGKDD international conference on knowledge discovery and data mining*, San Diego, CA. (pp. 145 – 154).

Bayat, S., Cuggia, M., Kessler, M., Briancon, S., Le Beux, P., & Frimat, L. (2008). Modelling access to renal transplantation waiting list in a French healthcare network using a Bayesian method. *Studies in Health Technology and Informatics, 136*, 605–610.

Bayes, T. (1763). Essay towards solving a problem in the doctrine of chances. *Philosophical Transactions of the Royal Society of London A Mathematical and Physical Sciences, 53*, 370-418.

Becker, R. C., Burns, M., Gore, J. M., Spencer, F. A., Ball, S. P., & French, W. (1998). Early assessment and in-hospital management of patients with acute myocardial infarction at increased risk for adverse outcomes: a nationwide perspective of current clinical practice. The National Registry of Myocardial Infarction (NRMI-2) Participants. *American Heart Journal, 135*(5 Pt 1), 786–796. doi:10.1016/S0002-8703(98)70036-5

Beebe, N., & Clark, J. G. (2007). Digital forensic text string searching–improving information retrieval effectiveness by thematically clustering search results. *Digital Investigation, 4*, 49–54. doi:10.1016/j.diin.2007.06.005

Beebe, N., & Dietrich, G. (2007). A new process model for text string searching. *Advances in Digital Forensics, 3*(242), 179–191. doi:10.1007/978-0-387-73742-3_12

Belkin, N., & Croft, W. (1987). Retrieval techniques. *Annual Review of Information Science & Technology, 22*, 109–145.

Bellifemine, F., Poggi, A., & Rimassa, G. (1999). JADE - a FIPA compliant agent framework. In *Proceedings of the fourth international conference and exhibition on the practical application of intelligent agents and multi-agents*, London.

Ben-Dor, A., Bruhn, L., Friedman, N., Nachman, I., Schummer, M., & Yakhini, Z. (2000). Tissue classification with gene expression profile. *Journal of Computational Biology, 7*.

Bennett, N., Burridge, R., & Saito, N. (1999). A method to detect and characterize ellipses using the hough transform. *IEEE Transactions on Pattern Analysis and Machine Intelligence, 21*(7), 652–657. doi:10.1109/34.777377

Berkhin, P. (2002). *Survey of Clustering Data Mining Techniques.* Accrue Software, Inc.

Bernardes, M. C., & Moreira, E. S. (2000). Implementation of an intrusion detection system based on mobile agents. In *International symposium on software engineering for parallel and distributed systems*, (pp. 158-164).

Berns, A. (2000). Cancer: gene expression in diagnosis. *Nature, 403*, 491–492. doi:10.1038/35000684

Berrar, D. P., Downes, C. S., & Dubitzky, W. (2003). Multiclass cancer classification using gene expression profiling and probabilistic neural networks. In *Proceedings of the Pacific Symposium on Biocomputing.*

Berry, M. J. A., & Gordon, S. L. (2000). *Mastering Data Mining: The Art and Science of Customer Relationship Management.* New York: Wiley Computer Publishing.

Besl, P. C., & Jain, R. C. (1988). Segmentation using variable surface fitting. *IEEE Transactions on Pattern Analysis and Machine Intelligence, 10*, 167–192. doi:10.1109/34.3881

Bettini, C., Wang, X. S., & Jajodia, S. (1998). Mining Temporal Relationships with Multiple Granularities in Time Sequences. *Data Eng. Bull., 21*(1), 32–38.

Beyer, K., Goldstein, J., Ramakrishnan, R., & Shaft, U. (1999). When Is Nearest Neighbor Meaningful? In *Proceedings of the 7th ICDT Conference*, Jerusalem, Israel.

Bezdek, J. C. (1981). *Pattern Recognition with Fuzzy Objective Function Algorithm.* New York: Plenum Press.

Bezdek, J. C. (1984). FCM: The fuzzy c-means clustering algorithm. *Computers & Geosciences, 10*, 191–203. doi:10.1016/0098-3004(84)90020-7

Bhattacharyya, S. (1999). Direct marketing performance modeling using genetic algorithms. *INFORMS Journal on Computing, 11*(3), 248–257. doi:10.1287/ijoc.11.3.248

Bidyuk, P. I., Terent'ev, A. N., & Gasanov, A. S. (2005). Construction and methods of learning of Bayesian Networks. *Cybernetics and Systems Analysis, 41*(4), 587–598. doi:10.1007/s10559-005-0094-8

Bishop, C. M. (1995). *Neural Networks for Pattern Recognition.* Oxford, UK: Oxford University Press.

Bjarge, T., Engeland, A., Luostarinen, T., Mork, J., Gislefoss, R. E., & Jellum, E. (2002). Human papillomavirus infection as a risk factor for anal and perianal skin cancer in a prospective study. *British Journal of Cancer, 87*, 61–64. doi:10.1038/sj.bjc.6600350

Blake, C., & Merz, C. J. (2007). *UCI Repository of machine learning databases.* University of California. Retrieved on February 15, 2009 from http://archive.ics.uci.edu/ml/

Blanco, R., Inza, I., Merino, M., Quiroga, J., & Larranaga, P. (2005). Feature selection in Bayesian classifiers for the prognosis of survival of cirrhotic patients treated with TIPS. *Journal of Biomedical Informatics, 38*(5), 376–388. doi:10.1016/j.jbi.2005.05.004

Blanco-Fernndez, Y., & Gil-Solla, J. J. P.-A. A. Ramos-Cabrer, M., Barragns-Martnez, B., Garca-Duque, M. L.-N. J., FernndezVilas1, A., & Daz-Redondo, R. P. (2004). Avatar: An advanced multi-agent recommender system of personalized TV contents by semantic reasoning. In *Web Information Systems WISE 2004*. Berlin: Springer-Verlag.

Bleakley, S. S. (2006, October). *Time Frequency analysis of railway wagon body accelerations for a low-power autonomous device.* Master's thesis, Faculty of Engineering and Physical Systems, Central Queensland University, Australia.

Bloch, I. (1994). Fuzzy sets in image processing. In *Proceedings of the ACM Symposium on Applied Computing* (pp. 175-179).

Bloedorn, E., Christiansen, A. D., Hill, W., Skorupka, C., Talbot, L. M., & Tivel, J. (2001). *Data mining for network intrusion detection: How to get started*. Retrieved from http://citeseer.nj.nec.com/523955.html

Bollerslev, T. (1986). Generalized autoregressive conditional heteroscedasticity. *Journal of Econometrics*, *31*(3), 307–327. doi:10.1016/0304-4076(86)90063-1

Bollerslev, T., Chou, R. Y., & Kroner, K. F. (1992). ARCH modeling in finance; A review of the theory and empirical evidence. *Journal of Econometrics*, *52*, 5–59. doi:10.1016/0304-4076(92)90064-X

Bontcheva, K., Tablan, V., Maynard, D., & Cunningham, H. (2004). Evolving gate to meet new challenges in language engineering. *Natural Language Engineering*, 10.

Bos, T., & Hoontrakul, P. (2002). Estimation of Mean and Variance Episodes in the Price Return of the Stock Exchange of Thailand. *Research in international Business and Finance Series, 16*, 210-226. Retrieved from http://www.pongsak.hoontrakul.com/papers/ESTIMAT.pdf

Box, G. E. P., & Jenkins, G. M. (1976). *Time Series Analysis: Forecasting and Control* (rev. ed.). San Francisco: Holden Day.

BP. (2007). *BP America announces resolution of Texas City, Alaska, propane trading, law enforcement investigations.* Retrieved April 2008, from http://www.bp.com

Bradley, P. S., & Fayyad, U. M. (1998). Refining Initial Points for *K-Means* Clustering. *Proceedings of the 15th International Conference on Machine Learning*, Madison, Wisconsin, (pp. 91-99).

Bradley, P. S., Fayyad, U. M., & Reina, C. (1998). Scaling Clustering Algorithms to Large Databases. In *American Association for Artificial Intelligence*.

Breast Cancer Statistics (2008). Retrieved February 12th, 2008, http://www.breastcancer.org/symptoms/understand_bc/statistics.jsp

Breese, J., Heckerman, D., & Kadie, C. (1998). Empirical analysis of predictive algorithms for collaborative filtering. In *Proceedings of the Fourteenth Conference on Uncertainty in Artificial Intelligence*. San Francisco: Morgan Kaufmann Publisher.

Breiman, L. (1996). Bagging predictors. *Machine Learning, 24*, 123–140.

Breiman, L., Friedman, J. H., Olshen, R. A., & Stone, C. J. (1984). Classification Based on Gene Expressions. In *International Joint Conference on Neural Networks*, Vancouver, Canada, (pp. 1930-1934).

Breunig, M., Kriegel, H., Ng, R., & Sander, J. (2000). LOF: Identifying Density-Based Local Outliers. In *Proceeding of 2000 ACM-SIGMOD International Conference on Management of Data,* (pp. 93-104). New York: ACM Press.

Breusch, T. S. (1978). Testing for autocorrelation in dynamic linear models. *Australian Economic Papers, 17*(31), 334–355. doi:10.1111/j.1467-8454.1978.tb00635.x

Brian, H., & Dasgupta, D. (2001). Mobile security agents for network traffic analysis. In *Proceedings of the second DARPA Information Survivability Conference and Exposition II (DISCEX-II),* Anaheim, CA.

Brown, D., & Huntley, C. (1991). *A Practical Application of Simulated Annealing to Clustering*. Technical Report IPC-TR-91-003, University of Virginia.

Brown, R. L., Durbin, J., & Evans, J. M. (1975). Techniques for Testing the constancy of Regression Relationship over Time. *Journal of the Royal Statistical Society. Series A (General), 37*, 149–192.

Broyles, R. W. (2006). *Fundamentals of Statistics in Health Administration*. Sudbury, MA: Jones and Bartlett.

Buchanan, B. G. (1988). What do expert systems offer the science of Artificial Intelligence. *Proceedings of the fourth Australian conference on applications of expert systems.* (pp. 1-30). Sydney: University of Technology.

Bühlmann, P. (2006). Boosting and l¹-Penalty Methods for High-Dimensional Data with Some Applications in Genomics. In *From Data and Information Analysis to Knowledge Engineering,* (pp. 1-12). Berlin: Springer Science & Business.

Bulot, R., et al. (1996). Contour segmentation using hough transform. In *Proceedings of the International Conference on Image Processing* (pp. 583-586).

Burdick, D., Calimlim, M., & Gehrke, J. (2005). MAFIA: A Maximal Frequent Itemset Algorithm. *IEEE Transactions on Knowledge and Data Engineering, 17*(11), 1490–1504. doi:10.1109/TKDE.2005.183

Buriano, L., Marchetti, M., Carmagnola, F., Cena, F., Gena, C., & Torre, I. (2006). The role of ontologies in context-aware recommender systems. In *7ʰ International Conference on Mobile Data Management*

Burke, R. (2002). Hybrid recommender systems: Survey and experiments. *User Modeling and User-Adapted Interaction, 12*(4). doi:10.1023/A:1021240730564

Campbell, C., Li, Y., & Tipping, M. (2001). An efficient feature selection algorithm for classification of gene expression data. In *NIPS 2001 Workshop on Machine Learning Techniques for Bioinformatics,* Vancouver, Canada.

Cancer.org. (2008). Retrieved October 6ᵗʰ, 2008, http://www.cancer.org

Cannady, J. (1998). *Artificial neural networks for misuse detection.* Paper presented at the Proceedings of the National Information Systems Security Conference.

Canny, J. F. (1986). A computational approach to edge detection. *IEEE Transactions on Pattern Analysis and Machine Intelligence, 8,* 679–698. doi:10.1109/TPAMI.1986.4767851

Cantador, I., & Castells, P. (2006). A multilayered ontology-based user profiles and semantic social networks for recommender systems. In *2ⁿᵈ International Workshop on Web Personalisation Recommender Systems and Intelligent User Interfaces in Conjunction with 7th International Conference in Adaptive Hypermedia.*

Cao, H., Cheung, D. W., & Mamoulis, N. (2004). Discovering Partial Periodic Patterns in Discrete Data Sequences In *Advances in Knowledge Discovery and Data Mining* (Vol. 3056, pp. 653-658). Berlin: Springer.

Carmagnola, F., Cena, F., Gena, C., & Torre, I. (2005). A multidimensional approach for the semantic representation of taxonomies and rules in adaptive hypermedia systems. In *PerSWeb05 Workshop on Personalization on the Semantic Web in conjunction with UM05.*

Carver, C. A., Hill, J. M. D., Surdu, J. R., & Pooch, U. W. (2000). A methodology for using intelligent agents to provide automated intrusion response. In *IEEE Systems, Man, and Cybernetics Information Assurance and Security Workshop,* West Point, NY.

Casas-Garriga, G. (2003). *Discovering unbounded episodes in sequential data.* Paper presented at the Principles and Practice of Knowledge Discovery in Databases (PKDD'03), Dubrovnik Croatia.

Cassidy, A., Myles, J. P., Tongeren, M. V., Page, R. D., Liloglou, T., Duffy, S. W., & Field, J. K. (2008). The LLP risk model: an individual risk prediction model for lung cancer. *British Journal of Cancer, 98,* 270–276. doi:10.1038/sj.bjc.6604158

Cercato, M. C., Nagore, E., Ramazzotti, V., Guillén, C., Terrenato, I., & Villena, J. (2008). Self and parent-assessed skin cancer risk factors in school-age children. *Preventive Medicine, 47,* 133–135. doi:10.1016/j.ypmed.2008.03.004

Cervical cancer (2008). Retrieved February 12, 2009, from http://www.cancer.org/docroot/CRI/content/CRI_2_4_1X_What_are_the_key_statistics_for_cervical_cancer_8

Chacon, M. I., Aguilar, L., & Delgado, A. (2002). Definition and applications of a fuzzy image processing scheme. In *Proceedings of the IEEE Digital Signal Processing Workshop* (pp. 102-107).

Chan, P. K., Mahoney, M. V., & Arshad, M. H. (2003). Managing Cyber Threats: Issues, Approaches and Challenges. In *Learning Rules and Clusters for Anomaly Detection in Network Traffic*. Amsterdam: Kluwer Academic Publishers.

Charikar, M., Guha, S., Tardos, É., & Shmoys, D. B. (1999, May). A Constant-Factor Approximation Algorithm for the *K-Medians* Problem. In *Proceedings of the 31ˢᵗ Annual ACM Symposium on Theory of Computing*, Atlanta, Georgia, (pp. 1-10).

Chatzis, V., & Pitas, I. (1997). Fuzzy cell Hough transform for curve detection. *Pattern Recognition, 30*(12), 2031–2042. doi:10.1016/S0031-3203(97)00025-3

Cheeseman, P., & Stutz, J. (1996). Bayesian Classification (AutoClass): Theory and Results. In *Advances in Knowledge Discovery and Data Mining*. Cambridge, MA: AAAI Press/MIT Press.

Chen, L., & Sycara, K. (1998). Webmate: A personal agent for browsing and searching. In *2nd International Conference on Autonomous Agents*, Minneapolis, MN.

Chen, M. S., & Wang, S. W. (1999). Fuzzy clustering analysis for optimizing fuzzy membership functions. *International Journal on Fuzzy Sets and Systems, 103*, 239–254. doi:10.1016/S0165-0114(98)00224-3

Chen, T. C., & Chung, K. L. (2001). An efficient randomized algorithm for detecting circles. *Computer Vision and Image Understanding, 83*, 172–191. doi:10.1006/cviu.2001.0923

Cheng, C., Fu, A., & Zhang, Y. (1999). Entropy-Based Subspace Clustering for Mining Numerical Data. In *Proceedings of the 5ᵗʰ ACM SIGKDD Conference*, San Diego, California, (pp. 84-93).

Cheng, J., & Greiner, R. (2001). Learning Bayesian Belief Network Classifiers – Algorithms and System. In *Proceedings of the 4th Canadian conference on Artificial Intelligence*, Calgary, Alberta, Canada.

Cheung, Y.-W., & Ng, L. K. (1998). International evidence on the stock market and aggregate economic activity. *Journal of Empirical Finance, 5*(3), 281–296. doi:10.1016/S0927-5398(97)00025-X

Chickering, D. M., Geiger, D., & Heckerman, D. (1994). *Learning Bayesian networks is NP-hard*. Redmond, WA, USA: Microsoft Research, Advanced Technology Division, Microsoft Corporation.

Chinrungrueng, C., & Sequin, C. (1995, January). Optimal Adaptive *K-Means* Algorithm with Dynamic Adjustment of Learning Rate. *IEEE Transactions on Neural Networks, 6*, 157–169. doi:10.1109/72.363440

Chintalapudi, K. K., & Kam, M. (1998). The credibilistic fuzzy c-means clustering algorithm. In *Proceedings of the IEEE International Conference on Systems, Man, and Cybernetics* (pp. 2034-2039).

Chittur, A. (2001). *Model generation for an intrusion detection system using genetic algorithms*. High School Honors Thesis, Ossining High School, in cooperation with Columbia Univ.

Choenni, R. (2000). Design and implementation of a genetic-based algorithm for data mining. In A. El Abbadi, M. L. Brodie, S. Chakravarthy, U. Dayal, N. Kamel, G. Schlageter & K.-Y. Whang (Eds.), *Proc. of the 26ᵗʰ Int. Conf. on Very Large Data Bases (VLDB)* (pp. 33-42). San Francisco: Morgan Kaufmann Publishers Inc.

Chon, T.-S., & Park, Y.-S. (2008). Self-Organizing Map. *Encyclopedia of Ecology*, (pp. 3203-3210).

Chow, G. (1960). Tests of equality between sets of coefficients in two linear regressions. *Econometrica, 28*(3), 591–605. doi:10.2307/1910133

Chu, C. S., Hornik, K., & Kuan, C. M. (1995). MOSUM Test for Parameter Constancy. *Biometrika, 82*(3), 603–617. doi:10.1093/biomet/82.3.603

Chu, F., & Wang, L. (2006). *Applying RBF Neural Networks to Cancer Classification and Regression Trees*. Wadsworth: Belmont, CA.

Ciaramella, A., Cocozza, S., Iorio, F., Miele, G., Napolitano, F., & Pinelli, M. (2008). Interactive data analysis and clustering of genomic data. *Neural Networks, 21*(2-3), 368–378. doi:10.1016/j.neunet.2007.12.026

Cimiano, P., Hotho, A., & Staab, S. (2005). Learning concept hierarchies from text corpa using formal concept hierarchies. *Journal of Artificial Intelligence Research,* (24): 305339.

Cios, K. J., Chen, K., & Langenderfer, L. A. (1997). Use of Neural Networks in Detecting Cardiac Diseases from Echocardiographic Images. *IEEE Engineering in Medicine and Biology Magazine, 16*(6).

Claypool, M., Gokhale, A., Miranda, T., Murnikov, P., Netes, D., & Sartin, M. (1999). Combining content-based and collaborative filters in an online newspaper. In *SIGIR'99 Workshop on Recommender Systems: Algorithms and Evaluation,* Berkeley, CA., P. & Schafer, M. (2005). Learner modeling on the semantic web. In *PerSWeb05 Workshop on Personalization on the Semantic Web in conjunction with UM05.*

Clement, M. P., & Hendry, D. F. (1999). *Forecasting Non-stationary Economic Time Series.* Cambridge, MA: MIT Press.

Clifton, C., & Gengo, G. (2000). Developing Custom Intrusion Detection Filters Using Data Mining. In *Proceeding of 21st Century Military Communications Conference* (pp. 440-443). New York: IEEE Press.

Cloutier, M. L., & Sirois, S. (2008). Bayesian versus Frequentist statistical modeling: A debate for hit selection from HTS campaigns. *Drug Discovery Today, 13*(11/12), 536–542. doi:10.1016/j.drudis.2008.03.022

Cockings, J. G. L., Cook, D. A., & Iqbal, R. K. (2006). Process monitoring in intensive care with the use of cumulative expected minus observed mortality and risk-adjusted p charts. *Critical Care, 10*(1), R28. Retrieved May, 17, 2006, from http://ccforum.com/content/10/1/R28

Cohen, F. B. (1999). Simulating Cyber Attacks, Defenses, and Consequences. In *Strategic Security Intelligence.* Retrieved April 7, 2009 from http://all.net/journal/ntb/simulate/simulate.html

Cohen, J. J. (1995). Higher quality at lower cost - Maybe there is a way. *Academy of Medicine Journal, 73,* 414.

Cole, C., & Roach, D. (1996). Dynamic response of coal wagons during normal operation. In *1996 World Conf. on Rail Research,* Colorado, (pp. 219-231).

Cole, R. (1998). *Survey of the State of the Art in Human Language Technology (Studies in Natural Language Processing).* Cambridge, UK: Cambridge University Press.

Collins, A. M., & Loftus, E. F. (1975). A spreading-activation theory of semantic processing. *Psychological Review, 82*(6), 407–428. doi:10.1037/0033-295X.82.6.407

Comon, P. (1994). Independent component analysis: a new concept? *Signal Processing, 36,* 287–314. doi:10.1016/0165-1684(94)90029-9

Contractor, N. (2007). *From Disasters to WoW: Using a Multi-theoretical, Multilevel Network Framework to Understand and Enable Communities.* Retrieved March 8, 2009, from http://www.friemel.com/asna/keynotes.php

Contractor, N. (2008). *The Emergence of Multidimensional Networks.* Retrieved November 30, 2008, from http://www.hctd.net/newsletters/fall2007/Noshir Contractor.pdf

Cooke, C. D., Ordonez, C., Garcia, E. V., Omiecinski, E., & Krawczynska, E. G. (1999). Data mining of large myocardial perfusion SPECT (MPS) databases to improve diagnostic decision making. *Journal of Nuclear Medicine, 40*(5).

Coppini, G., Poli, R., & Valli, G. (1995). Recovery of the 3-D shape of the left ventricle from echocardiographic images. *IEEE Transactions on Medical Imaging, 14,* 301–317. doi:10.1109/42.387712

Cormen, T. H., Leiserson, C. E., & Rivest, R. L. (1990). *Introduction to Algorithms.* New York: McGraw-Hill.

Corpet, F. (1988). Multiple Sequence Alignment with Hierarchical Clustering. *Nucleic Acids Research, 16*(22), 10881–10890. doi:10.1093/nar/16.22.10881

Cortes, C., & Vapnik, V. (1995). Support-vector networks. *Machine Learning, 20,* 273–297.

Costa, M., Filippi, E., & Pasero, E. (Eds.). (1995). *Artificial neural network ensembles: a bayesian standpoint.* Singapore: World Scientic.

Cotofrei, P., & Stoffel, K. (2002). Rule extraction from time series databases using classification trees. In *Proc. Applied Informatics*, Innsbruck, Austria.

Cox, S. (2008). *Pharmaceutical manufacturing handbook regulation and quality.* New York: John Wiley & Sons.

Cpaaindia. (2008). www.cpaaindia.org, accessed 12th August, 2008.

Creighton, C., & Hanash, S. (2003). Mining gene expression databases for association rules. *Bioinformatics (Oxford, England), 19*(1), 79–86. doi:10.1093/bioinformatics/19.1.79

Crestani, F. (1997). Application of Spreading Activation Techniques in Information Retrieval. *Artificial Intelligence Review, 11*(6), 453–482. doi:10.1023/A:1006569829653

Cristofor, D., & Simovici, D. A. (2002). An Information-Theoretical Approach to Clustering Categorical Databases Using Genetic Algorithms. In *Proceedings of the 2nd SIAM ICDM Conference*, Arlington, Virginia.

Crosbie, M., & Spafford, E. (1995). Defending a computer system using autonomous agents. In *Proceedings of the 18th national information systems security conference.*

Crosbie, M., & Spafford, E. H. (1995). *Active defense of a computer system using autonomous agents,* (Technical Report CSD-TR- 95-008). West Lafayette, IN: Purdue Univ.

Cula, O. G., & Dana, K. J. (2001). Compact Representation of Bidirectional Texture Functions. In *Proceedings of the IEEE Computer Society Conference on Computer Vision and Pattern Recognition*, Hawaii, USA, December.

Cunningham, S. J., & Holmes, G. (2000). *Developing innovative applications in agriculture using data mining.* Tech. Report, Dept. of Computer Science, University of Waikato, New Zealand.

D'Avanzo, B., Vecchia, C. L., Negri, E., Decarli, A., & Benichou, J. (1995). Attributable risks for bladder cancer in Northern Italy. *Annals of Epidemiology, 5,* 427–431. doi:10.1016/1047-2797(95)00057-7

Dasgupta, D., & Gonz´alez, F. A. (2001). An intelligent decision support system for intrusion detection and response. In *Proc. of International Workshop on Mathematical Methods, Models and Architectures for Computer Networks Security (MMM-ACNS)*, St.Petersburg. Berlin: Springer-Verlag.

Dasgupta, D., & Gonzalez, F. (2002). An immunity-based technique to characterize intrusions in computer networks. *IEEE Transactions on Evolutionary Computation, 6*(3).

Dataset, (2008). Retrieved 17th August, 2008, from http://www.broad.mit.edu/cgi-bin/cancer/datasets.cgi

Dave, R. N. (1990). Fuzzy shell-clustering and applications to circle detection in digital images. *International Journal of General Systems, 16,* 343–355. doi:10.1080/03081079008935087

Dave, R. N. (1992a). Boundary detection through fuzzy clustering. In *Proceedings of the IEEE International Conference on Fuzzy Systems* (pp. 127-134).

Dave, R. N. (1992b). Generalized fuzzy c-shells clustering and detection of circular and elliptical boundaries. *Pattern Recognition, 25*(7), 713–721. doi:10.1016/0031-3203(92)90134-5

Dave, R. N., & Bhaswan, K. (1992). Adaptive fuzzy c-shells clustering and detection of ellipses. *IEEE Transactions on Neural Networks, 3*(5), 643–662. doi:10.1109/72.159055

Dave, R. N., & Patel, K. J. (1990). Fuzzy ellipsoidal-shell clustering algorithm and detection of elliptical shapes. In *. Proceedings of the SPIE Intelligent Robots Computer Vision IX, 1381,* 320–333.

Davis, B., Handschuh, S., Troussov, A., Judge, J., & Sogrin, M. (2008). Linguistically Light Lexical Extensions for Ontologies. In *Proceedings of the 6th edition of the Language Resources and Evaluation Conference (LREC) in Marrakech, Morocco 26th May - 1st June 2008.*

Deadman, D. (2003). Forecasting residential burglary. *International Journal of Forecasting, 19*(4), 567–578. doi:10.1016/S0169-2070(03)00091-8

Decker, S., & Frank, M. (2004). *The Social Semantic Desktop.* Technical Report DERI-TR-2004-05-02, Digital Enterprise Research Institute (DERI). Retrieved March 8, 2009, from http://www.deri.ie/fileadmin/documents/DERI-TR-2004-05-02.pdf

Defays, D. (1977). An Efficient Algorithm for a Complete Link Method. *The Computer Journal, 20,* 364–366. doi:10.1093/comjnl/20.4.364

Deltour, A. (2001). *Tertius extension to Weka.* Department of Computer Science, University of Bristol. Retrieved April 01, 2009, from http://www.cs.bris.ac.uk/Publications/pub_master.jsp?pubyear=2001

Dempster, A., Laird, N., & Rubin, D. (1997). Maximisation likelihood from incomplete data via the EM algorithm. *Journal of the Royal Statistical Society. Series B. Methodological, 39,* 1–38.

Demšar, J., Zupan, B., & Leban, G. (2004). Orange: From experimental machine learning to interactive data mining. White Paper, Faculty of Computer and Information Science, University of Ljubljana, Slovenia.

Denning, D. E., & Neumann, P. G. (1985). *Requirements and Model for IDES—A Real-time Intrusion Detection System,* (Tech. Rep. # 83F83-01-00). Menlo Park, CA: SRI International.

Derin, H. (1984). Byes smoothing algorithms for segmentation of binary images modelled by Markov random fields. *IEEE Transactions on Pattern Analysis and Machine Intelligence, 6,* 707–720. doi:10.1109/TPAMI.1984.4767595

Derin, H., & Elliot, H. (1987). Modelling and segmentation of noisy and textured images using Gibbs random fields. *IEEE Transactions on Pattern Analysis and Machine Intelligence, 9*(1), 39–55. doi:10.1109/TPAMI.1987.4767871

Desai, P. R. (2006). Case study: Approach for filing with PAT. In *AAPS Workshop on Real World Applications of PAT and QbD in Drug Process Development and Approval,* Arlington, VA.

Devlin. (2000, February). Devlin's Angle - The legacy of the Reverend Bayes. *MAA Online.* Retrieved January, 28, 2009, from http://www.maa.org/devlin/devlin_2_00.html

Dickerson, J. E., & Dickerson, J. A. (2000). Fuzzy network profiling for intrusion detection. In *Proc. of NAFIPS 19th International Conference of the North American Fuzzy Information Processing Society, Atlanta,* (pp. 301–306). North American Fuzzy Information Processing Society (NAFIPS).

Dickerson, J. E., Juslin, J., Koukousoula, O., & Dickerson, J. A. (2001). Fuzzy intrusion detection. *In IFSA World Congress and 20th North American Fuzzy Information Processing Society (NAFIPS) International Conf.,* Vancouver, Canada, North American Fuzzy Information Processing Society (NAFIPS). *3,* 1506–1510

Didaci, L., Giacinto, G., & Roli, F. (2002). Ensemble learning for intrusion detection in computer networks. *ACM Journal.*

Doan, T., Haddawy, P., Nguyen, T., & Seetharam, D. (1999). *A hybrid Bayesian Network modeling environment.* In *Proceeding of the 1999 National Computer Science and Engineering Conference (NCSEC),* Bangkok, Thailand.

Dodig-Crnkovic, G. (2002). Scientific Methods in Computer Science. *Proceedings Conference for the Promotion of Research in IT at New Universities and at University Colleges in Sweden.*

Dokas, P., Ertoz, L., Kumar, V., Lazarevic, A., Srivastava, J., & Tan, P. (2002). Data Mining for Network Intrusion Detection. In *Proceeding of NSF Workshop on Next Generation Data Mining* (pp. 21-30). Cambridge, MA: AAAI/MIT Press.

Doucette, P., Agouris, P., Stefanidis, A., & Musavi, M. (2001, March). Self-Organized Clustering for Road Extraction in Classified Imagery. *Journal of Photogrammetry and Remote Sensing, 55*(5-6), 347–358. doi:10.1016/S0924-2716(01)00027-2

Dourish, P., & Bellotti, V. (1992). Awareness and coordination in shared workspaces. In *Proceedings of the 1992 ACM conference on Computer-supported cooperative work*, Toronto, Ontario, Canada, (pp. 107 – 114).

Draghici, S. (2000). Neural networks in analog hardware - Design and implementation issues. *International Journal of Neural Systems, 10*(1), 19–42.

Dreiseitl, S., & Ohno-Machado, L. (2002). Logistic regression and artificial neural network classification models: A methodology review. *Journal of Biomedical Informatics, 35*(5-6), 352–359. doi:10.1016/S1532-0464(03)00034-0

DtSearch, Inc. (2009). *dtSearch*. Retrieved February 5, 2009, from http://www.dtsearch.com/

Du, Q., Faber, V., & Gunzburger, M. (1999). Centroidal Voronoi Tesselations: Applications and Algorithms. *SIAM Review, 41*, 637–676. doi:10.1137/S0036144599352836

Duarte, M. F., & Hu, Y. H. (2004). Vehicle classification in distributed sensor networks. *Journal of Parallel and Distributed Computing, 64*, 826–838. doi:10.1016/j.jpdc.2004.03.020

Dubes, R. C. (1993). Cluster Analysis and Related Issues. In *Handbook of Pattern Recognition and Computer Vision* (pp. 3-32). River Edge, NJ: World Scientific Publishing Co.

Dubes, R., & Jain, A. K. (1998). *Algorithms for clustering data*. Englewood Cliffs, NJ: Prentice-Hall.

Duda, R. O., & Hart, P. E. (1973). *Pattern Classification and Scene Analysis*. Hoboken, NJ: John Wiley & Sons, Inc.

Duin, R. P. W. (1996). A note on comparing classifiers. *Pattern Recognition Letters, 17*, 529–536. doi:10.1016/0167-8655(95)00113-1

Eberhart, R. C., Dobbins, R. W., & Webber, W. R. S. (1989). CASENET: A Neural Network Tool for EEG waveform classification. In *Proc. IEEE Symposium on Computer Based Medical System.*

Eisen, M. B., Spellman, P. T., Brown, P. O., & Botstein, D. C. (1998). Analysis and display of genome-wide expression patterns. *Proceedings of the National Academy of Sciences of the United States of America, 95*, 14863–14868. doi:10.1073/pnas.95.25.14863

El-Baz, A., Gimelfarb, G., Falk, R., & Abo El-Ghar, M. A. (2008). Automatic analysis of 3D low dose CT images for early diagnosis of lung cancer. *Pattern Recognition.*

Elston, R. C., & Johnson, W. D. (1995). *Essentials of Biostatistics* (2nd ed.). F. A. Davis Company.

Eltonsy, N. H., Elmaghraby, A. S., & Tourassi, G. D. (2007). Bilateral Breast Volume Asymmetry in Screening Mammograms as a Potential Marker of Breast Cancer: Preliminary Experience. *Image Processing, IEEE International Conference on, 5*, 5-8.

Engle, R. (1982). Autoregressive conditional heteroscedasticity with estimates of the variance of the U.K. inflation. *Econometrica, 50*(4), 987–1008. doi:10.2307/1912773

Engle, R. (2002). Dynamic conditional correlation: A simple class of multivariate generalized autoregressive conditional heteroskedasticity models. *Journal of Business & Economic Statistics, 20*(3), 339–350. doi:10.1198/073500102288618487

Engle, R. F., & Granger, C. W. J. (1987). Co-integration and error-correction: Representation, estimation and testing. *Econometrica, 55*, 251–276. doi:10.2307/1913236

Engle, R. F., Hendry, D. F., & Richard, J.-F. (1983). Exogeneity. *Econometrica, 51*(2), 277–304. doi:10.2307/1911990

Ericsson, N. R., & MacKinnon, J. G. (2002). Distributions of error correction tests for cointegration. *The Econometrics Journal, 5*(2), 285. doi:10.1111/1368-423X.00085

Ertoz, L. Steinbach, M. & Kumar, V. (2003, May). Finding Clusters of Different Sizes, Shapes, and Densities in Noisy, High Dimensional Data. In *Proceedings of the 3rd SIAM International Conference on Data Mining*, San Francisco.

Ertoz, L., Eilertson, E., Lazarevic, A., Tan, P., Dokas, P., Kumar, V., et al. (2003). Detection of Novel Network Attacks Using Data Mining. *Proceeding of ICDM Workshop on Data Mining for Computer Security* (pp. 1-10). New York: IEEE Press.

Eschrich, S., Chawla, N. V., & Hall, L. O. (2002). Generalization methods in bioinformatics. In *Proceedings of the 2nd ACM SIGKDD Workshop on Data Mining in Bioinformatics*, Edmonton, Canada.

Eskin, E. (2000). Detecting errors within a corpus using anomaly detection. In *Proc. of 2000 North American Chapter of the Association of Computational Linguistics (NAACL-2000)*, Seattle. North American Chapter of the Association of Computational Linguistics(NAACL).

Eskin, E. (2000a). Anomaly detection over noisy data using learned probability distributions. In *Proc. 17th International Conf. on Machine Learning*, (pp. 255–262). San Francisco: Morgan Kaufmann.

Eskin, E., Arnold, A., Preraua, M., Portnoy, L., & Stolfo, S. J. (2002, May). A geometric framework for unsupervised anomaly detection: Detecting intrusions in unlabeled data. In D. Barbar & S. Jajodia (Eds.), *Data Mining for Security Applications*. Boston: Kluwer Academic Publishers.

Eskin, E., Miller, M., Zhong, Z.-D., Yi, G., Lee, W.-A., & Stolfo, S. J. (2000). Adaptive model generation for intrusion detection systems. In *Workshop on Intrusion Detection and Prevention, 7th ACM Conference on Computer Security, Athens*. New York: ACM.

Eskin, E., Stolfo, S. J., & Lee, W. (2001). Modeling system calls for intrusion detection with dynamic window sizes. In *Proceedings of the DARPA Information Survivability Conference & Exposition II*, Anaheim, CA, (pp. 165–175).

Ester, M. Kriegel, H.-P., Sander, J. & Xu, X. (1996). A Density-Based Algorithm for Discovering Clusters in Large Spatial Databases with Noise. In *Proceedings of the 2nd ACM SIGKDD Conference*, Portland, Oregon, (pp. 226-231).

Esveld, C. (2001). *Modern Railway Track*, (2nd ed.). The Netherlands: MRT Productions.

Evans, D., Hersh, W., Monarch, I., Lefferts, R., & Henderson, S. (1991). Automatic indexing of abstracts via natural-language processing using a simple thesaurus. *Medical Decision Making, 11*(3), 108–115.

Everitt, B. (1993). *Cluster Analysis* (3rd edition). London: Edward Arnold.

Fagan, J. (1989). The effectiveness of a nonsyntactic approach to automatic phrase indexing for document retrieval. *Journal of the American Society for Information Science American Society for Information Science, 40*(2), 115–132. doi:10.1002/(SICI)1097-4571(198903)40:2<115::AID-ASI6>3.0.CO;2-B

Fan, J. L., Zhen, W. Z., & Xie, W. X. (2003). Suppressed fuzzy c-means clustering algorithm. *Pattern Recognition Letters, 24*, 1607–1612. doi:10.1016/S0167-8655(02)00401-4

Fan, W. (2001). *Cost-Sensitive, Scalable and Adaptive Learning Using Ensemble-based Methods*. Ph. D. thesis, Columbia Univ.

Fan, W., Lee, W., Stolfo, S. J., & Miller, M. (2000). A multiple model cost-sensitive approach for intrusion detection. In R. L. de M'antaras & E. Plaza (Eds.), *Proc. of Machine Learning: ECML 2000, 11th European Conference on Machine Learning*, Barcelona, Spain, (LNCS Vol. 1810, pp. 142–153).

Fasulo, D. (1999). *An Analysis of Recent Work on Clustering Algorithms*. Technical Report UW-CSE01-03-02, University of Washington.

Fayyad, U. M., Piatetsky-Shapiro, G., & Smyth, P. (1996). *From data mining to knowledge discovery: An overview*. Menlo Park, CA, USA: American Association for Artificial Intelligence (AAAI) Press.

Feng, Z., Zhou, B., & Shen, J. (2007). A Parallel Hierarchical Clustering Algorithm for PCs Cluster System. *Neurocomputing, 70*(4-6), 809–818.

Ferragina, P., & Gulli, A. (2007). A Personalized Search Engine Based on Web-Snippet Hierarchical Clustering. *Software, Practice & Experience, 38*(2), 189–225. doi:10.1002/spe.829

Fich, F. E. (1993). The Complexity of Computation on the Parallel Random Access Machine. In J. H. Reif, (Ed.) *Synthesis of Parallel Algorithms*, (pp. 843-899). San Francisco: Morgan Kaufmann.

Fillmore, C. (1968). *The case for case. Chapter in: Universals in Linguistic Theory.* New York: Holt, Rinehart and Winston, Inc.

Finch, S., & Chater, N. (1994). Learning syntactic categories: A statistical approach. In M. Oaksford, & G. Brown, (Eds.), *Neurodynamics and Psychology.* New York: Academic Press.

FIPA. (2005). *FIPA Specification Lifecycle, IEEE Foundation for Intelligent Physical Agents.* Retrieved December 10, 2008 from http://www.fipa.org/specifications/lifecycle.html

Flach, P. A., & Lachiche, N. (2001). *Confirmation-guided discovery of first-order rules with Tertius,* (pp. 61-95). Amsterdam: Kluwer Academic Publishers.

Flexer, A. (1996). Statistical evaluation of neural network experiments: Minimum requirements and current practice. In R. Trappl, (Ed.), *Proc. 13th Eur. Meeting Cybernetics Systems Research*, (pp. 1005–1008).

Forte, D. (2004). The importance of text searches in digital forensics. *Network Security, 4,* 13–15. doi:10.1016/S1353-4858(04)00067-4

FRA 49 CFR Part 213 (1998, June 22). Track Safety Standards: Final Rule. *Federal Register, 63*(119). Federal Railroad Administration, Department of Transportation: Washington DC.

Frakes, W. B., & Baeza-Yates, R. (1992). *Information Retrieval: Data Structures and Algorithms.* Upper Saddle River, NJ: Prentice-Hall.

Fraley, C., & Raftery, A. (1999). *MCLUST: Software for Model-Based Cluster and Discriminant Analysis.* Technical Report 342, Department of Statistics, University of Washington.

Francis, S. H. (1994). *Computer Graphics.* Upper Saddle River, NJ: Prentice Hall.

Frank, E., & Witten, I. H. (1998). Generating Accurate Rule Sets Without Global Optimization. In *The Proceedings of Fifteenth International Conference on Machine Learning*, (pp. 144-151).

Frank, J. (1994). Artificial intelligence and intrusion detection: Current and future directions. In *Proc. of the 17th National Computer Security Conference.* Baltimore: National Institute of Standards and Technology (NIST).

Freedland, S. J., Wen, J., Wuerstle, M., Shah, A., Lai, D., Moalej, B., et al. (2008). Obesity Is a Significant Risk Factor for Prostate Cancer at the Time of Biopsy. *Urology.*

Friedman, N., Geiger, D., & Goldszmidt, M. (1997). Bayesian Network Classifiers. *Machine Learning, 29,* 131–163. doi:10.1023/A:1007465528199

Frigui, H., & Krishnapuram, R. (1996). Letters: A comparison of fuzzy shell-clustering methods for the detection of ellipses. *IEEE transactions on Fuzzy Systems, 4*(2). doi:10.1109/91.493912

Fu, K. S., & Mui, J. K. (1981). A survey on image segmentation. *Pattern Recognition, 13*(1), 3–16. doi:10.1016/0031-3203(81)90028-5

Gaffney, J. E., & Ulvila, J. W. (2001). Evaluation of intrusion detectors: a decision theory approach. In *Proceedings of the 2001 IEEE Symposium on Security and Privacy*, Oakland, CA, (pp. 50–61).

Gams, M. (2001). Weak intelligence: Through the principle and paradox of multiple knowledge. In *Advances in Computation vol. 6.* Huntington, NY: Nova Science.

Gams, M., & Tušar, T. (2007). Intelligent high-security access control. *Informatica (Ljubljana), 31*(4), 469–477.

Ganti, V. Gehrke, J. & Ramakrishnan, R. (1999). CACTUS-Clustering Categorical Data Using Summaries. In *Proceedings of the 5th ACM SIGKDD Conference*, San Diego, CA, (pp.73-83).

Garg, V. K., & Dukkipati, R. V. (1984). *Dynamics of railway vehicle systems.* New York: Academic Press.

Gasch, A. P., & Eisen, M. B. (2002). Exploring the Conditional Coregulation of Yeast Gene Expression Through Fuzzy *K*-Means Clustering. *Genome Biology*, *3*(11), 1–21. doi:10.1186/gb-2002-3-11-research0059

Gath, I., & Geva, A. B. (1989). Unsupervised optimal fuzzy clustering. *IEEE Transactions on Pattern Analysis and Machine Intelligence*, *14*(7), 773–781. doi:10.1109/34.192473

Gath, I., & Hoory, D. (1995). Fuzzy clustering of elliptic ring-shaped clusters. *Pattern Recognition Letters*, *16*(7), 727–741. doi:10.1016/0167-8655(95)00030-K

Geman, S., & Geman, D. (1984). Stochastic relaxation, Gibbs distribution, and the Bayesian restoration of images. *IEEE Transactions on Pattern Analysis and Machine Intelligence*, *6*, 721–741. doi:10.1109/TPAMI.1984.4767596

Geman, S., Bienenstock, E., & Doursat, R. (1992). Neural networks and the bias/variance dilemma. *Neural Computation*, *4*, 1–58. doi:10.1162/neco.1992.4.1.1

Ghosh, A. K., Schwartzbard, A., & Schatz, M. (1999). Learning program behavior profiles for intrusion detection. In *Proc. 1st USENIX Workshop on Intrusion Detection and Network Monitoring, Santa Clara, CA*, (pp. 51–62). USENIX.

Ghosh, J. (2002). Scalable Clustering Methods for Data Mining. In *Handbook of Data Mining*. Mahwah, NJ: Lawrence Erlbaum.

Giacinto, G., & Roli, F. (2002). Intrusion detection in computer networks by multiple classifier systems. In *Proc. of the 16th International Conference on Pattern Recognition (ICPR)*, Quebec City, Canada, (Vol. 2, pp. 390–393). Washington, DC: IEEE press.

Giannella, C., Han, J., Pei, J., Yan, X., &. Yu P., S. (2003). Mining Frequent Patterns in Data Streams at Multiple Time Granularities. In *Data Mining: Next Generation Challenges and Future Directions*. Cambridge, MA: AAAI/MIT.

Gibson, D., Kleinberg, J., & Raghavan, P. (1998). Clustering Categorical Data: An Approach Based on Dynamic Systems. In *Proceedings of the 24th International Conference on Very Large Databases*, New York, (pp. 311-323).

Gildea, D., & Daniel, J. (2002). Automatic labeling of semantic roles. *Computational Linguistics Journal*, *28*(3), 245–288. doi:10.1162/089120102760275983

Giovannucci, E., Rimm, E. B., Ascherio, A., Colditz, G. A., Spiegelman, D., Stampfer, M. J., & Willett, W. C. (1999). Smoking and Risk of Total and Fatal Prostate Cancer in United States Health Professionals. *Cancer Epidemiology, Biomarkers & Prevention*, *8*, 277–282.

Glosten, L. R., Jaganathan, R., & Runkle, D. E. (1993). On the Relation between the Expected Value and the Volatility of the Nominal Excess Return on Stocks. *The Journal of Finance*, *48*(5), 1779–1801. doi:10.2307/2329067

Glymour, C., Madigan, D., Pregibon, D., & Smyth, P. (1996). Statistical inference and data mining. *Communications of the ACM*, *39*(11), 35–41. doi:10.1145/240455.240466

Glymour, C., Madigan, D., Pregibon, D., & Smyth, P. (1997). Statistical Themes and Lessons for Data Mining. *Data Mining and Knowledge Discovery*, *1*(1), 11–28. doi:10.1023/A:1009773905005

Godfrey, L. G. (1978). Testing against general autoregressive and moving average error models when the regressors include lagged dependent variables. *Econometrica*, *46*(6), 1293–1301. doi:10.2307/1913829

Godoy, D., & Amandi, A. (2006). Modeling user interests by conceptual clustering. *Information Systems*, *31*(4), 247–265. doi:10.1016/j.is.2005.02.008

Goil, S., Nagesh, H., & Choudhary, A. (1999). *MAFIA: Efficient and Scalable Subspace Clustering for Very Large Data Sets*. Technical Report CPDC-TR-9906-010, Northwestern University.

Goldbaum, M. H. (2005). Unsupervised learning with independent component analysis can identify patterns of glaucomatous visual field defects. *Transactions of the American Ophthalmological Society*, *103*, 270–280.

Goldbaum, M. H., Sample, P. A., Zhang, Z., Chan, K., Hao, J., & Lee, T. W. (2005). Using unsupervised learning with independent component analysis to identify patterns of glaucomatous visual field defects. *Investigative Ophthalmology & Visual Science*, *46*(10), 3676–3683. doi:10.1167/iovs.04-1167

Gomes, P., & Antunes, B. L. R., Santos, A., Barbeira, J., & Carvalho, R. (2006). Using ontologies for elearning personalization. In *eLearning Conference*.

Gong, Z., Cheang, C. W., & U, L. H. (2005). Web query expansion by wordnet. In *Database and Expert Systems Applications*, (pp. 166-175). Berlin: Springer Verlag.

Gonzalez, R. C., & Woods, R. E. (2002). *Digital Image Processing*. Upper Saddle River, NJ: Prentice Hall, Inc.

Gosh, A., Pal, N. R., & Pal, S. K. (1993). Self-organization for object extraction using multilayer neural networks and fuzziness measure. *IEEE transactions on Fuzzy Systems*, *1*(1), 54–68. doi:10.1109/TFUZZ.1993.390285

Gouda, K., & Zaki, M. J. (2001). Efficiently Mining Maximal Frequent Itemsets. In *Proceedings of the 2001 IEEE International Conference on Data Mining* (pp. 163-170). Washington, DC: IEEE Computer Society.

Gouda, K., & Zaki, M. J. (2001). Efficiently Mining Maximal Frequent Itemsets. In *Proc. First IEEE Int'l Conference Data Mining*.

Gowadiam, V., Farkas, C., & Valtora, M. (2005). PAID: A probabilistic agent-based intrusion detection system. *Computers & Security*, *24*(7), 529–545. doi:10.1016/j.cose.2005.06.008

Graham, D. B., & Allinson, N. M. (1998). Automatic Face Representation and Classification. In *Proceedings of British Machine Vision Conference*, Southampton, UK.

Granger, C. W. J., & Newbold, P. (1974). Spurious regression in econometrics. *Journal of Econometrics*, *2*, 111–120. doi:10.1016/0304-4076(74)90034-7

Greenberg, D. F. (2001). Time series analysis of crime rates. *Journal of Quantitative Criminology*, *17*(4), 291–327. doi:10.1023/A:1012507119569

Greenland, S. (1990). Randomization, statistics, and causal inference. *Epidemiology (Cambridge, Mass.)*, *1*(6), 421–429. doi:10.1097/00001648-199011000-00003

Greenland, S. (2000). Principles of multilevel modelling. *International Journal of Epidemiology*, *29*(1), 158–167. doi:10.1093/ije/29.1.158

Greenlaw, R., & Kantabutra, S. (2008). On the Parallel Complexity of Hierarchical Clustering and *CC*-Complete Problems. *Complexity*, *14*(2), 18–28. doi:10.1002/cplx.20238

Greenlaw, R., Hoover, H. J., & Ruzzo, W. L. (1995). *Limits to Parallel: P-Completeness Theory*. Oxford, UK: Oxford University Press

Groll, L., & Jakel, J. (2005). A new convergence proof of fuzzy c-means. *IEEE transactions on Fuzzy Systems*, *13*(5), 717–720. doi:10.1109/TFUZZ.2005.856560

Groza, T., Handschuh, S., Moeller, K., Grimnes, G., Sauermann, L., Minack, E., et al. (2007). The NEPOMUK Project - On the way to the Social Semantic Desktop. In *Proceedings of International Conferences on new Media technology (I-MEDIA-2007) and Semantic Systems (I-SEMANTICS-07), Graz, Austria, September 5-7*, (pp. 201-210).

Gu, J., Zhao, H., Dinney, C. P., Zhu, Y., Leibovici, D., & Bermejo, C. E. (2005). Nucleotide excision repair gene polymorphisms and recurrence after treatment for superficial bladder cancer. *Clinical Cancer Research*, *11*, 1408–1415. doi:10.1158/1078-0432.CCR-04-1101

Guha, S., Rastogi, R., & Shim, K. (1998). CURE: An Efficient Clustering Algorithm for Large Databases. In *Proceedings of the ACM SIGMOD Conference*, Seattle, WA, (pp. 73-84).

Guha, S., Rastogi, R., & Shim, K. (1999). ROCK: A Robust Clustering Algorithm for Categorical Attributes. In *Proceedings of the 15th ICDE Conference*, Sydney, Australia, (pp. 512-521).

Guidance for industry PAT — A framework for innovative pharmaceutical development, manufacturing, and quality assurance. (2004). U.S. Department of Health and Human Services, Food and Drug Administration.

Guidance Software, Inc. (2009). *EnCase Forensic.* Retrieved February 5, 2009, from http://www.guidancesoftware.com/products/ef_index.asp

Guil, N., & Zapata, E. L. (1997). Lower order circle and ellipse hough transform. *Pattern Recognition, 30*(10), 1729–1744. doi:10.1016/S0031-3203(96)00191-4

Gustafson, D. E., & Kessel, W. C. (1979). Fuzzy clustering with a fuzzy covariance matrix. In *Proceedings of IEEE Conference on Decision Control* (pp. 761-766).

Gutkin, A., & King, S. (2004). Structural Representation of Speech for Phonetic Classification. In *Proceedings of the 17ᵗʰ International Conference on Pattern Recognition*, Cambridge, UK.

Gwadera, R., Atallah, M. J., & Szpankowski, W. (2005). Reliable detection of episodes in event sequences. *Knowledge and Information Systems, 7*(4), 415–437. doi:10.1007/s10115-004-0174-5

Haddon, J. F. (1988). Generalized threshold selection for edge detection. *Pattern Recognition, 21*(3), 195–203. doi:10.1016/0031-3203(88)90054-4

Hale, C., & Sabbagh, D. (1991). Testing the relationship between unemployment and crime: A methodological comment and empirical analysis using time series data from England and Wales. *Journal of Research in Crime and Delinquency, 28*(4), 400. doi:10.1177/0022427891028004002

Hall, D. J., & Ball, G. B. (1965). *ISODATA: A Novel Method of Data Analysis and Pattern Classification.* Technical Report AD-699616, Stanford Research Institute, Menlo Park, California.

Hall, L. O., Ozyurt, B., & Bezdek, J. C. (1999). Clustering with a Genetically Optimized Approach. *IEEE Transactions on Evolutionary Computation, 3*(2), 103–112. doi:10.1109/4235.771164

Hamilton, J. D. (1994). *Time Series Analysis.* Princeton, NJ: Princeton University Press.

Han, J., & Kamber, M. (2001). *Data mining: concepts and techniques.* San Francisco: Morgan Kauffmann.

Han, J., Colditz, G. A., Samson, L. D., & Hunter, D. J. (2004). Polymorphisms in DNA double-strand break repair genes and skin cancer risk. *Cancer Research, 64*, 3009–3013. doi:10.1158/0008-5472.CAN-04-0246

Han, J., Dong, G., & Yin, Y. (1999). Efficient Mining of Partial Periodic Patterns in Time Series Database. In *Proceedings of the 15th International Conference on Data Engineering* (pp. 106-115). Washington, DC: IEE Computer Society.

Han, J., Kamber, M., & Tung, A. K. H. (2001). Spatial Clustering Methods in Data Mining: A Survey. In *Geographic Data Mining and Knowledge Discovery.* San Francisco: Taylor and Francis.

Han, J., Pei, J., Yin, Y., & Mao, R. (2000). *Mining Frequent Patterns without Candidate Generation (SIGMOD'00).* Paper presented at the 2000 ACM SIGMOD Intl. Conference on Management of Data, Dallas, TX.

Hand, D. J. (1999). Statistics and Data Mining: Intersecting disciplines. *SIGKDD Explorations, 1*(1), 16–19. doi:10.1145/846170.846171

Hand, D., Mannila, H., & Smyth, P. (2001). *Principles of Data Mining.* Cambridge, MA: The MIT Press.

Hansen, B. E. (1992). Tests for parameter instability in regressions with I(1) processes. *Journal of Business & Economic Statistics, 15*, 60–67. doi:10.2307/1392074

Hansen, B. E. (2001). The New Econometrics of Structural Change: Dating Breaks in U.S. Labor Productivity. *The Journal of Economic Perspectives, 15*, 117–128.

Hansen, F. R., & Elliot, H. (1982). Image segmentation using simple Markov random field models. *Computer Graphics and Image Processing, 20*, 101–132. doi:10.1016/0146-664X(82)90040-5

Hansen, L., & Salamon, P. (1990). Neural network ensembles. *IEEE Transactions on Pattern Analysis and Machine Intelligence, 12*, 993–1001. doi:10.1109/34.58871

Haralick, R. M., & Shapiro, L. G. (1985). Survey, image segmentation techniques. *Computer Vision Graphics and Image Processing, 29*, 100–132. doi:10.1016/S0734-189X(85)90153-7

Hartigan, J. (1975). *Clustering Algorithms*. New York: John Wiley & Sons.

Hasan, M., Meara, R. J., & Bhowmick, B. K. (1995). The quality of diagnostic coding in cerebrovascular disease. *International Journal for Quality in Health Care, 7*(4), 407–410. doi:10.1016/1353-4505(95)00005-4

Hastie, T., Tibshirani, R., & Friedman, J. H. (2001). *The Elements of Statistical Learning* (1st ed.). New York: Springer.

Hathaway, R. J., & Bezdek, J. C. (1986). Local convergence of the fuzzy c-means algorithm. *Pattern Recognition, 19*(6), 477–480. doi:10.1016/0031-3203(86)90047-6

Haverkos, H. W., Soon, G., Steckley, S. L., & Pickworth, W. (2003). Cigarette smoking and cervical cancer: Part I: a meta-analysis. *Biomedicine and Pharmacotherapy, 57*, 67–77. doi:10.1016/S0753-3322(03)00196-3

He, Z., Xu, X., Huang, J. Z., & Deng, S. (2005). FP-Outlier: Frequent Pattern Based Outlier Detection. *Computer Science and Information System, 2*(1), 103–118. doi:10.2298/CSIS0501103H

Hearn, D., & Baker, M. P. (1994). *Computer Graphics*. Upper Saddle River, NJ: Prentice Hall.

Heckerman, D. (1996). A tutorial on learning with Bayesian Networks. In M. Jordan (Ed.), *In Learning in Graphical Models* (pp. 79-119). Cambridge, MA, USA: MIT Press.

Heckerman, D. (1996). Bayesian Networks for knowledge discovery. In U. M. Fayyard, G. Piatetsky-Shapiro, P. Symth, & R. Uthurusamy (Eds.), *Advances in Knowledge Discovery and Data Mining* (pp. 273-305). Cambridge, MA, USA: The MIT Press.

Heckerman, D. (1997). Bayesian Networks for data mining. *Data Mining and Knowledge Discovery, 1*(1), 79–119. doi:10.1023/A:1009730122752

Heckerman, D., & Breeze, J. S. (1995). *Causal independence for probability assessment and inference using Bayesian Networks*. Redmond, WA, USA: Microsoft Research.

Helmer, G., Wong, J., Honavar, V., & Miller, L. (1999). *Automated discovery of concise predictive rules for intrusion detection*, (Technical Report 99-01). Ames, IA: Iowa State University.

Helmer, G.G., Wong, J.S.K., Honavar, V. & Miller, L. (2002). Lightweight agents for intrusion detection. *Journal of Systems and Software*.

Herlocker, J., Konstan, J., Borchers, A., & Reidl, J. (1999). An algorithmic framework for performing collaborative filtering. In *Proceedings of the Conference on Research and Development in Information Retrieval*.

Herzog, T. J. (2003). New approaches for the management of cervical cancer. *Gynecologic Oncology, 90*, 22–27. doi:10.1016/S0090-8258(03)00466-9

Hinneburg, A., & Keim, D. (1998). An Efficient Approach to Clustering Large Multimedia Databases with Noise. In *Proceedings of the 4th ACM SIGKDD Conference*, New York (pp. 58-65).

Ho, S. H., Jee, S. H., Lee, J. E., & Park, J. S. (2004). Analysis on risk factors for cervical cancer using induction technique. *Expert Systems with Applications, 27*(1), 97–105. doi:10.1016/j.eswa.2003.12.005

Ho, T. K. (1998). The Random Subspace Method for Constructing Decision Forests. *IEEE Transactions on Pattern Analysis and Machine Intelligence, 20*(8).

Hoey, J. P., & Soehl, S. (1997). Care maps, utilization, and outcomes: A viable solution. *The Journal of Oncology Management, 6*(6), 29–32.

Hofmeyr, S. A., & Forrest, S. (1999). Immunizing computer networks: Getting all the machines in your network to fight the hacker disease. In *Proc. of the 1999 IEEE Symp. on Security and Privacy*, Oakland, CA. Washington, DC: IEEE Computer Society Press.

Holmes, G. Hall, M. & Frank, E. (1999). Generating Rule Sets from Model Trees. In *Advanced Topics in Artificial Intelligence,* (vol.1747, pp. 1-12). Berlin: Springer.

Hong, J.-H., & Cho, S.-B. (2008). A probabilistic multi-class strategy of one-vs.-rest support vector machines for cancer classification. *Neurocomputing, 71*(16-18), 3275–3281. doi:10.1016/j.neucom.2008.04.033

Honig, A., Howard, A., Eskin, E., & Stolfo, S. J. (2002). Adaptive model generation: An architecture for the deployment of data miningbased intrusion detection systems. In D. Barbar & S. Jajodia (Eds.), *Data Mining for Security Applications*. Boston: Kluwer Academic Publishers.

Hoppner, F., et al. (1999). *Fuzzy Cluster Analysis: methods for classification, data analysis, and image recognition*. New York: John Wiley & Sons, Ltd.

Huang, J. J., Li, S. Y., & Ban, X. J. (2003). A fast approach to building rough data model through G-K fuzzy clustering. In *Proceedings of the Second International Conference on Machine Learning and Cybernetics* (pp. 1559-1564).

Hung, M. C., & Yang, D. L. (2001). An efficient fuzzy c-means clustering algorithm. In *Proceedings of the IEEE International Conference on Data Mining* (pp. 225-232).

Hyvärinen, A. (1999). Fast and robust fixed-point algorithms for independent component analysis. *IEEE Transactions on Neural Networks*, *10*(3), 626–634. doi:10.1109/72.761722

Hyvärinen, A. (2001). Blind source separation by nonstationarity of variance: A cumulant based approach. *IEEE Transactions on Neural Networks*, *12*(6), 1471–1474. doi:10.1109/72.963782

Hyvärinen, A., & Oja, E. (1997). A fast fixed-point algorithm for independent component analysis. *Neural Computation*, *9*, 1483–1492. doi:10.1162/neco.1997.9.7.1483

Hyvärinen, A., Karhunen, J., & Oja, E. (2001). *Independent Component Analysis*. New York: John Wiley & Sons.

Ibchelp, (2008). Retrieved August 17th, 2008 from http://www.ibchelp.org/pictures.html

Ilgun, K., Kemmerer, R., & Porras, P. (1995). State transition analysis: a rule-based intrusion detection approach. *IEEE Transactions on Software Engineering*, 181–199. doi:10.1109/32.372146

Images, (2008). Retrieved 1st of October, 2008, from http://search.live.com/images/

Inclan, C., & Tiao, G. C. (1994). Use of Cumulative Sums of Squares for Retrospective Detection of Changes of Variance. *Journal of the American Statistical Association*, *84*(427), 913–923. doi:10.2307/2290916

International Collaboration of Epidemiological Studies of Cervical Cancer. (2007). Cervical cancer and hormonal contraceptives: collaborative reanalysis of individual data for 16 573 women with cervical cancer and 35 509 women without cervical cancer from 24 epidemiological studies. *Lancet*, *370*, 1609–1621. doi:10.1016/S0140-6736(07)61684-5

Jahne, B. (1997). *Digital Image Processing*. New York: Springer-Verlag.

Jain, A. K. (1981). Advances in mathematical models for image processing. In *IEEE Proceedings* (pp. 502-528).

Jain, A. K. (1989). *Fundamentals of Digital Image Processing*. Upper Saddle River, NJ: Prentice Hall, Inc.

Jain, A. K., Murty, M. N., & Flynn, P. J. (1999). Data Clustering: A Review. *ACM Computing Surveys*, *31*(3), 264–323. doi:10.1145/331499.331504

Jain, A., & Dubes, R. C. (1988). *Algorithms for Clustering Data*. Englewood Cliffs, NJ: Prentice-Hall.

Jain, P. Mekaa, R. & Dhillon, I. S. (2008). Simultaneous Unsupervised Learning of Disparate Clusterings. In *Proceedings of the SIAM International Conference on Data Mining, Atlanta*, Georgia.

Jan, T. (2004). *Neural Network Based Threat Assessment for Automated Visual Surveillance.* Paper presented at the Proc. of International Joint Conference on Neural Networks IJCNN Budapest, Hungary.

Jansen, W., Mell, P., Karygiannis, T. & Marks, D. (1999). *Applying mobile agents to intrusion detection and response*. National Institute of Standards and Technology Computer Security Division, NIST Interim Report (IR) e 6416.

Javitz, H. S., & Valdes, A. (1991). The SRI IDES Statistical Anomaly Detector. In *Proc. 1991 IEEE Computer Society Symposium on Research in Security and Privacy,* Oakland, CA. Washington, DC: IEEE Computer Society.

Javitz, H. S., & Valdes, A. (1993). *The NIDES statistical component: Description and justification.* Technical report. Menlo Park, CA: SRI International.

Jazayeri, M., & Lugmayr, W. (2000). Gypsy: a component-based mobile agent system. In *Eighth euromicro workshop on parallel and distributed processing,* Greece.

Jee, H., Lee, J., & Hong, D. (2007). High speed bitwise search for digital forensic system. In *Proceedings of world academy of science, engineering and technology, 26,* 104-107.

Jemili, F., Zaghdoud, M. & Ahmed, M., Ben. (2007). A Framework for an Adaptive Intrusion Detection System using Bayesian Network. *IEEEXplore,* 66 – 70.

Jo Cunningham, S. & Holmes, G. (n.d.). *Developing innovative applications in agriculture using data mining.* Tech Report, Dept. of Computer Science, University of Waikato, New Zealand.

Joachims, T. (1999). Making large-scale SVM learning practical. In *Advances in Kernel Methods.*

Johansen, S. (1995). *Likelihood-Based Inference in Cointegrated Vector Autoregressive Models.* Oxford, UK: Oxford University Press.

John, G. H., & Kohavi, R. (1997). Wrappers for feature subset selection. *Artificial Intelligence, 97*(1-2).

John, G. H., & Langley, P. (1995). Estimating continuous distributions in Bayesian classifiers. In *Proceedings of the Eleventh Conference on Uncertainty in Artificial Intelligence,* San Mateo, CA, (pp. 338–345). San Francisco: Morgan Kaufmann.

Johnson, A. M., O'Connell, M. J., Messing, E. M., & Reeder, J. E. (2008). Decreased Bladder Cancer Growth in Parous Mice. *Urology, 72,* 470–473. doi:10.1016/j.urology.2008.04.028

Jong, K. (2006). *Machine learning for human cancer research,* PhD Thesis, Vrije Universiteit Amsterdam.

Julisch, K. (2001). Mining Alarm Clusters to Improve Alarm Handling Efficiency. In *Proceeding of the 17th Annual Computer Security Applications Conference* (pp. 12-21). New York: IEEE Press.

Julisch, K. (2003). Clustering Intrusion Detection Alarms to Support Root Cause Analysis. *ACM Transactions on Information and System Security, 6*(4), 443–471. doi:10.1145/950191.950192

Julisch, K., & Dacier, M. (2002). Mining Intrusion Detection Alarms for Actionable Knowledge. In *Proceeding of the 8th ACM International Conference on Knowledge Discovery and Data Mining,* (pp. 366-375). New York: ACM Press.

Jurafsky, D., & Martin, J. (2000). *Speech and Language Processing.* Upper Saddle River, NJ: Prentice Hall Inc.

Kaewunruen, S., & Remennikov, A. M. (2007). Response and prediction of dynamic characteristics of worn rail pads under static preloads. In *14th Int'l Congress on Sound Vibration,* Cairns, Australia.

Kamba, T., H. S. & Koseki, Y. (1997). Antagonomy: A personalised newspaper on the world wide web. *International Journal of Human-Computer Studies, 46*(6), 789–803. doi:10.1006/ijhc.1996.0113

Kannan, R., Vempala, S., & Vetta, A. (2000). On Clusterings: Good, Bad, and Spectral. In *Proceedings of the 41st Foundations of Computer Science,* Redondo Beach, CA.

Kantabutra, S. & Couch, A. (2000). Parallel K-Means Clustering Algorithm on NOWs. *NECTEC Technical Journal, 1*(6).

Kantabutra, S. (2001). *Efficient Representation of Cluster Structure in Large Data Sets.* Ph.D. Dissertation, Tufts University, Medford, MA.

Kaper, M., Meinicke, P., Grossekathoefer, U., Lingner, T., & Ritter, H. (2004). BCI competition 2003–data set iib: support vector machines for the p300 speller paradigm. *IEEE Transactions on Bio-Medical Engineering, 51,* 1073–1076. doi:10.1109/TBME.2004.826698

Karabatak, M., Sengur, A., & Ince, M. C & Turkoglu, I. (2006). Texture Classification By Using Association Rules. In *Proceedings of The 5th International Symposium on Intelligent Manufacturing Systems*, (pp. 96-104).

Karmakar, G. C. (2002). *An Integrated Fuzzy Rule-Based Image Segmentation Framework*. Unpublished doctoral dissertation. Monash University: Australia.

Karmakar, G. C., Dooley, S. L., & Rahman, S. M. (2001). Review on fuzzy image segmentation techniques. In *Design and Management of Multimedia Information Systems: Opportunities and Challenges* (pp. 282-313). Hershey, PA: Idea Group Publishing.

Karypis, G., Han, E. H., & Kumar, V. (1999). CHAMELEON: A Hierarchical Clustering Algorithm Using Dynamic Modeling. *Computer*, *32*, 68–75. doi:10.1109/2.781637

Kaufman, L. & Rousseeuw, P. (199). *Finding Groups in Data: An Introduction to Cluster Analysis*. New York: John Wiley & Sons.

Kautz, H., Selman, B., & Shah, M. (1997). Referral web: Combining social networks and collaborative filtering. *Communications of the ACM*, *40*(3), 63–65. doi:10.1145/245108.245123

Kazienko, P., & Dorosz, P. (2004). *Intrusion Detection Systems (IDS) Part I, WindowSecurity*. Retrieved September 23, 2008 from http://www.windowsecurity. com/articles/intrusion_detection_systems_ids_part_i__ network_intrusions_attack_symptoms_ids_tasks_and_ ids_architecture.html

Kennedy, C., Bajdik, C. D., & Willemze, R., Gruijl, Frank, R. de. & Bavinck, J. N. B. (2003). The Influence of Painful Sunburns and Lifetime Sun Exposure on the Risk of Actinic Keratoses, Seborrheic Warts, Melanocytic Nevi, Atypical Nevi, and Skin Cancer. *The Journal of Investigative Dermatology*, *120*, 1087–1093. doi:10.1046/ j.1523-1747.2003.12246.x

Kernighan, B., & Lin, S. (1970). An efficient heuristic procedure for partitioning graphs. *The Bell System Technical Journal*, *49*(2), 291–308.

Khan, J. M., Wei, J. S., Ringner, M., Saal, L. H., Ladanyi, M., & Westermann, F. (2001). Classification and diagnostic prediction of cancers using gene expression profiling and artificial neural networks. *Nature Medicine*, *7*, 673–679. doi:10.1038/89044

Kim, C. S., Riikonen, P., & Salakoski, T. (2008). Detecting biological associations between genes based on the theory of phase synchronization. *Bio Systems*, *92*(2), 99–113. doi:10.1016/j.biosystems.2007.12.006

Kim, H., & Chan, P. K. (2006). Personalized search results with user interest hierarchies learnt from bookmarks. In *Advances in Web Mining and Web Usage Analysis*, (pp. 158-176). Berlin: Springer.

Kim, H., & Chan, P. K. (2008). Learning implicit user interest hierarchy for context in personalization. *Applied Intelligence*, *28*(2), 153–166. doi:10.1007/s10489-007-0056-0

Kim, I.-C., & Jung, Y.-G. (2003, July 25). *Using Bayesian Networks to analyze medical data*. In *Proceedings of the third international conference of Machine Learning and Data Mining (MLDM)*, Leipzig, Germany.

Kim, S. Jin, X. & Han, J. (2008). SpaRClus: Spatial Relationship Pattern-Based Hierarchical Clustering. In *Proceedings of the SIAM International Conference on Data Mining, Atlanta*, Georgia.

King, R. J. B., & Robins, M. W. (2006). *Cancer biology*, (3rd ed.). London: Pearson Education Limited, UK.

Kinsella, S., Harth, A., Troussov, A., Sogrin, M., Judge, J., Hayes, C., & Breslin, J. G. (2008). Navigating and Annotating Semantically-Enabled Networks of People and Associated Objects. In T. Friemel, (ed.), *Why Context Matters: Applications of Social Network Analysis*, (pp. 79-96). Wiesbaden, Germany: VS Verlag

Kittler, J., & Roli, F. (Eds.). (2000). *First International Workshop on Multiple Classier Systems*, Cagliari, Italy, (LNCS Vol. 1857).

Klavans, J., Chodrow, M., & Wacholder, N. (1992). *Building a knowledge base from parsed definitions*. In K. Jansen, G. Heidorn, & S. Richardson, (Eds.), *Natural Language Processing: The PLNLP Approach*. Amsterdam: Kluwer Academic Publishers.

Klawonn, F., & Höppner, F. (2003). What is fuzzy about fuzzy clustering-understanding and improving the concept of the fuzzifier. In *Advances in Intelligent Data Analysis,* (pp. 254–264).

Knight, K., & Luk, S. (1994). Building a large scale knowledge base for machine translation. In *Proceedings of the Thirteenth National Conference on Artificial Intelligence,* (pp. 773-778). Menlo Park, CA: AAAI Press.

Knorr, E., & Ng, R. (1997). A unified notion of outliers: Properties and computation. In *Proceeding of 3rd Int. Conf. Knowledge Discovery and Data Mining* (pp. 219-222). New York: ACM Press.

Knostan, J., Miller, B., Maltz, D., Herlocker, J., Gordon, L., & Riedl, J. (1997). Grouplens: Applying collaborative filtering to Usenet news. *Communications of the ACM, 40*(3), 77–87. doi:10.1145/245108.245126

Kohler, R. (1981). A segmentation system based on thresholding. *Computer Graphics and Image Processing, 15*, 319–338. doi:10.1016/S0146-664X(81)80015-9

Kohonen, T. (2001). *Self-Organizing Maps,* (30, 3rd Ed.). Berlin: Springer.

Kolatch, E. (2001). *Clustering Algorithms for Spatial Databases: A Survey.* PDF is available on the Web.

Koop, K., Bakker, R. C., Eikmans, M., Baelde, H. J., de Heer, E., Paul, L. C., & Bruijn, J. A. (2004). Differentiation between chronic rejection and chronic cyclosporine toxicity by analysis of renal cortical mRNA. *Kidney International, 66*, 2038–2046. doi:10.1111/j.1523-1755.2004.00976.x

Korb, K. B., & Nicholson, A. E. (2004). *Bayesian Artificial Intelligence*. Boca Raton, FL, USA: CRC Press.

Kordic, S., Lam, P., Xiao, J., & Li, H. (2008). Analysis of Alarm Sequences in a Chemical Plant. In *Proceedings of the 4th international conference on Advanced Data Mining and Applications* (Vol. 5139, pp. 135-146). Berlin: Springer-Verlag.

Krämer, W., & Schotman, P. (1992). Range vs Maximum in OLS-based version of CUSUM test. *Economics Letters, 40*, 379–381. doi:10.1016/0165-1765(92)90130-Q

Krieger, H.-U. (2008). Where Temporal Description Logics Fail: Representing Temporally-Changing Relationships. In *Proceedings of the 31st annual German conference on Advances in Artificial Intelligence Kaiserslautern, Germany,* (LNAI Vol. 5243, pp. 249 – 257).

Krishnapuram, R. (1994). Generation of membership functions via possibilistic clustering. In *Proceedings of the IEEE World Congress on Computational Intelligence,* USA (pp. 902-908).

Krishnapuram, R. (1995a). Fuzzy and possibilistic shell clustering algorithms and their application to boundary detection and surface approximation-Part II. *IEEE transactions on Fuzzy Systems, 3*(1), 44–60. doi:10.1109/91.366570

Krishnapuram, R. (1995b). Fuzzy and possibilistic shell clustering algorithms and their application to boundary detection and surface approximation-Part I. *IEEE transactions on Fuzzy Systems, 3*(1), 29–43. doi:10.1109/91.366564

Krishnapuram, R., & Keller, J. M. (1993). A possibilistic approach to clustering. *International Journal of Fuzzy Systems, 2*(2), 98–110. doi:10.1109/91.227387

Krishnapuram, R., & Keller, J. M. (1996). The possibilistic c-means algorithm: Insights and recommendation. *IEEE transactions on Fuzzy Systems, 4*(3), 385–396. doi:10.1109/91.531779

Krishnapuram, R., & Kim, J. (1999). A note on the Gustafson-Kessel and adaptive fuzzy clustering algorithms. *IEEE transactions on Fuzzy Systems, 7*(4), 453–461. doi:10.1109/91.784208

Krogh, A., & Vedelsby, J. (1995). Neural network ensembles, cross validation, and active learning. *Advances in Neural Information Processing Systems, 7*, 231–238.

Krolzig, H.-M., & Hendry, D. F. (2001). Computer automation of general-to-specific model selection procedures. *Journal of Economic Dynamics & Control, 25*(6-7), 831–866. doi:10.1016/S0165-1889(00)00058-0

Krugel, C., & Toth, T. (2001). Sparta e a security policy reinforcement tool for large networks. *I-NetSec, 01*, 101–110.

Kruse, R., Gebhardt, J., & Klawonn, F. (1995). *Foundations of Fuzzy Syztems*. New York: John Wiley & Sons, Inc.

Kuan, C. M. (1994). A Range-CUSUM test with the recursive residual. *Economics Letters, 45*, 309–313. doi:10.1016/0165-1765(94)90029-9

Kugler, C., Freytag, S., Stillger, R., Bauer, P., & Ferbert, A. (2000). Australian Refined Diagnosis Related Groups: Formal and inherent problems of grouping with the example of stroke care. *Deutsche Medizinische Wochenschrift, 125*(51-52), 1554–1559. doi:10.1055/s-2000-9554

Kumar, S. (1995). *Classification and Detection of Computer Intrusions*. Unpublished doctoral dissertation, Purdue University, West Lafayette, IN.

Kumar, V. S., Narayanan, S., Kurc, T., Kong, J., Gurcan, M. N., & Saltz, J. H. (2008). Analysis and semantic querying in large biomedical image datasets. *Computer*, 52–59.

Kuncheva, L. I., & Whitaker, C. J. (2003). Measures of diversity in classifier ensembles and their relationship with the ensemble accuracy. *Machine Learning, 51*, 181–207. doi:10.1023/A:1022859003006

Kusiak, A., Kernstine, K. H., Kern, J. A., McLaughlin, K. A., & Tseng, T. L. (2000). Data Mining: Medical and Engineering Case Studies. In *Proceedings of the Industrial Engineering Research, Conference*, Cleveland, Ohio, (pp. 1-7).

Kusiak, A., Kernstine, K. H., Kern, J. A., McLaughlin, K. A., Land, W. H., Jr., Timothy, M., et al. (2001). Application of Evolutionary Computation and Neural Network Hybrids for Breast Cancer Classification Using Mammogram and History Data. *Evolutionary Computation, Proceedings of the 2001 Congress on, 2*, 1147 – 1154.

Lacave, C., & Diez, F. J. (2001). A review of explanation methods of Bayesian Networks. *The Knowledge Engineering Review, 17*(2).

Lane, T. D. (2000), *Machine Learning Techniques for the computer security domain of anomaly detection*. Unpublished doctoral dissertation, Purdue Univ., West Lafayette, IN.

Lang, K. (1995). Newsweeder: Learning to filter Netnews. In *12th International Conference on Machine Learning*.

Langseth, H., & Nielsen, T. D. (2003). Fusion of domain knowledge with data for structural learning in object oriented domains. *Journal of Machine Learning Research, 4*, 339–368. doi:10.1162/jmlr.2003.4.3.339

Langville, A. N., & Meyer, C. (2006). *Google's PageRank and Beyond: The Science of Search Engine Rankings*. Princeton, NJ: Princeton University Press.

Laoutaris, N., Zissimopoulos, V., & Stavrakakis, I. (2004). Joint Object Placement and Node Dimensioning for Internet Content Distribution. *Information Processing Letters, 89*(6), 273–279. doi:10.1016/j.ipl.2003.12.002

Lauritzen, S. L. (1995). The EM algorithm for graphical association models with missing data. *Computational Statistics & Data Analysis, 19*(2), 191–201. doi:10.1016/0167-9473(93)E0056-A

Lavielle, M., & Moulines, E. (2000). Least-Squares Estimation of an Unknown Number of Shifts in time Series. *Journal of Time Series Analysis, 20*, 33–60. doi:10.1111/1467-9892.00172

Lawrie, D., & Croft, W. (2000). Discovering and comparing topic hierarchies. In *Proceedings of RIAO*.

Laxman, S., Sastry, P. S., & Unnikrishnan, K. P. (2007a). A fast algorithm for finding frequent episodes in event streams. In *Proceedings of the 13th ACM SIGKDD International Conference on Knowledge Discovery and Data Mining* (pp. 410-419). New York: ACM.

Laxman, S., Sastry, P., & Umnikrishnan, K. (2007b). Discovering Frequent Generalized Episodes When Events Persist for Different Durations. *IEEE Transactions on Knowledge and Data Engineering, 19*(9), 1188–1201. doi:10.1109/TKDE.2007.1055

Le Duff, F., Muntean, C., Cuggia, M., & Mabo, P. (2004a). Predicting survival causes after out of hospital cardiac arrest using data mining method. *Medinfo, 11*(Pt 2), 1256–1259.

Lee, A. H., Fung, W. K., & Fu, B. (2003). Analyzing hospital length of stay: Mean or median regression? *Medical Care, 41*(5), 681–686. doi:10.1097/00005650-200305000-00015

Lee, I. N., Liao, S. C., & Embrechts, M. (2000). Data mining techniques applied to medical information. *Medical Informatics and the Internet in Medicine, 25*(2), 81–102. doi:10.1080/14639230050058275

Lee, S. M., & Abbott, P. A. (2003). Bayesian Networks for knowledge discovery in large datasets: Basics for nurse researchers. *Journal of Biomedical Informatics, 36*(4-5), 389–399. doi:10.1016/j.jbi.2003.09.022

Lee, W. (1999). *A Data Mining Framework for Constructing Features and Models for Intrusion Detection Systems.* Doctoral dissertation, Columbia Univ., New York.

Lee, W., & Stolfo, S. J. (1998). Data mining approaches for intrusion detection. In *Proc. of the 7th USENIX Security Symp.* San Antonio, TX: USENIX.

Lee, W., & Stolfo, S. J. (2000). A framework for constructing features and models for intrusion detection systems. *Information and System Security, 3*(4), 227–261. doi:10.1145/382912.382914

Lee, W., & Xiang, D. (2001). Information-theoretic measures for anomaly detection. *In Proc. of the 2001 IEEE Symp. on Security and Privacy,* Oakland, CA, (pp. 130–143). Washington, DC: IEEE Computer Society Press.

Lee, W., Stolfo, S. J., & Mok, K. W. (1999a). A data mining framework for building intrusion detection models. In *Proc. of the 1999 52 IEEE Symp. on Security and Privacy,* Oakland, CA, (pp. 120–132). Washington, DC: IEEE Computer Society Press.

Lee, W., Stolfo, S. J., & Mok, K. W. (1999b). Mining in a data-flow environment: Experience in network intrusion detection. In S. Chaudhuri & D. Madigan (Eds.), *Proc. of the Fifth International Conference on Knowledge Discovery and Data Mining (KDD-99),* San Diego, CA, (pp. 114–124). New York: ACM.

Lee, W., Stolfo, S. J., & Mok, K. W. (2000). Adaptive intrusion detection: A data mining approach. *Artificial Intelligence Review, 14*(6), 533–567. doi:10.1023/A:1006624031083

Lee, W., Stolfo, S. J., Chan, P. K., Eskin, E., Fan, W., Miller, M., et al. (2001). Real time data mining-based intrusion detection. In *Proc. Second DARPA Information Survivability Conference and Exposition,* Anaheim, CA, (pp. 85–100). Washington, DC: IEEE Computer Society.

Lee, Y., & Lee, C. K. (2003). Classification of multiple cancer types by mulitcategory support vector machines using gene expression data. *Bioinformatics (Oxford, England), 19,* 1132–1139. doi:10.1093/bioinformatics/btg102

Lee, Z.-J. (2008). An integrated algorithm for gene selection and classification applied to microarray data of ovarian cancer. *Artificial Intelligence in Medicine, 42*(1), 81–93. doi:10.1016/j.artmed.2007.09.004

Leuski, A. (2001). Evaluation Document Clustering of Interactive Information Retrieval. In *Proceeding of ACM CIKM'01,* (pp. 33-40). New York: ACM Press.

Levin, I. (2000). *KDD-99 Classifier Learning Contest: LLSoft's Results Overview.* Paper presented at the SIGKDD Explorations.

Levner, E., & Alcaide, D. (2006). Environmental risk ranking: Theory and applications for emergency planning. *Scientific Israel - Technological Advantages, 8*(1-2), 11–21.

Levner, E., Alcaide, D., & Sicilia, J. (2007a). Text Classification Using the Fuzzy Borda Method and Semantic Grades. In *Proc. of WILF-2007 (CLIP-2007).* (LNCS Vol. 4578, pp. 422–429). Berlin: Springer.

Levner, E., Pinto, D., Rosso, P., Alcaide, D., & Sharma, R. R. K. (2007b). Fuzzifying Clustering Algorithms: The Case Study of MajorClust. In A. Gelbukh & A.F. Kuri Morales (Eds.), *Lecture Notes on Artificial Intelligence 4827*, (pp. 821–830). Berlin: Springer.

Levner, E., Troussov, A., & Judge, J. (2009). Graph-based Mining of Digital Content. *CNGL tutorial, Dublin, Ireland, January 19-21.*

Li, B., & Gallin, W. J. (2005). Computational identification of residues that modulate voltage sensitivity of voltage-gated potassium channels. *BMC Structural Biology, 5*, 16. doi:10.1186/1472-6807-5-16

Li, C., Stratman, B., & Mahadevan, S. (2007). Improving railroad wheel inspection planning using classification methods. In *Proc. of the 25ᵗʰ IASTED Int'l Multi-Conf.*, Innsbruck, Austria, Feb'07, (pp. 366-371).

Li, D., Salahifar, T., Malone, J., & Kalay, S. F. (2001). Development of performance-based track geometry inspection. In *7ᵗʰ Int'l Heavy Haul Conf.*, Brisbane, Australia, (pp. 461-465).

Li, H. F., Lee, S., Y. & Shan, M., K. (2004). An Efficient Algorithm for Mining Frequent Itemsets over the Entire History of Data Streams. In *Int'l Workshop on Knowledge Discovery in Data Streams.*

Li, H., Yap, C. W., & Ung, C. Y. (2007). Machine learning approaches for predicting compounds that interact with therapeutic and ADMET related proteins. *Journal of Pharmaceutical Sciences, 96*(11). doi:10.1002/jps.20985

Li, J., & Liu, H. (2006). *Kent Ridge Biomedical Data Set Repository, Singapore.* Retrieved 4ᵗʰ September, 2006 from http://sdmc.i2r.a-star.edu.sg/rp/

Li, K., Huang, H. K., & Li, K. L. (2003). A modified PCM clustering algorithm. In *Proceedings of the IEEE International Conference on Machine Learning and Cybernetics (*pp. 1174-1179).

Li, L., Tang, H., Wu, Z., Gong, J., Gruidl, M., & Zou, J. (2004). Data mining techniques for cancer detection using serum proteomic profiling. *Artificial Intelligence in Medicine, 32*(2), 71–83. doi:10.1016/j.artmed.2004.03.006

Li, Y., Wu, N., Jajodia, S. & Wang, X. S. (2002). Enhancing profiles for anomaly detection using time granularities. *Journal of Computer Security.*

Liang, F. (2007). Use of SVD-based probit transformation in clustering gene expression profiles . *Computational Statistics & Data Analysis, 51*(12), 6355–6366. doi:10.1016/j.csda.2007.01.022

Liberman, H. (1995). Letzia: An agent that assists in web browsing. In *Proceedings of the 1995 International Joint Conference on Artificial Intelligence*, Montreal, Canada.

Lin, D., & Pantel, P. (2001*)*. Induction of semantic classes from natural language text. In *Knowledge Discovery and Data Mining*, (pp. 317-322).

Lin, D.-I., & Kedem, Z. M. (1998). Pincer-Search: A New Algorithm for Discovering the Maximum Frequent Set. In *Proc. Sixth Int'l Conference Extending Database Technology.*

Lincoln Labrotary. (2008). *1999 DARPA Intrusion Detection Evaluation Data Set.* Cambridge, MA: Massachusetts Institute of technology. Retrieved January 12, 2009 from http://www.ll.mit.edu/ mission/ communications/ist/ corpora/ideval/data/ 1999data. html

Lincoln, W., & Skrzypek, J. (1989). Synergy of clustering multiple back propagation networks. *Advances in Neural Information Processing Systems, 2*, 650–659.

Linear Regression. (n.d.). GraphPad Software, Inc. San Diego, Tech. Rep. [Online]. Retrieved January 25th, 2008 from http://www.curvefit.com/linear_regression.htm

Linger, R. C., Mead, N. R., & Lipson, H. F. (2004). *Requirements Definition for Survivable Network Systems.* Pittsburgh, PA: Software Engineering Institute, Carnegie Mellon University.

Lingras, P., & West, C. (2004). Interval Set Clustering of Web Users with Rough *K*-Means. *Journal of Intelligent Information Systems, 23*(1), 5–16. doi:10.1023/B:JIIS.0000029668.88665.1a

Linnarsson, R., & Wigertz, O. (1989). The Data Dictionary - A controlled vocabulary for integrating clinical Databases and medical knowledge bases. *Methods of Information in Medicine, 28*, 78–85.

Liu, J., et al. (1997). A comparative study of texture measures for human skin treatment. In *Proceedings of the International Conference on Information, Communications, and Signal Processing*, Singapore (pp. 170-174).

Lloyd, S. (1957). *Least Square Quantization in PCM's.* Bell Telephone Laboratories Paper.

Lotte, F., & Congedo, M., L'ecuyer, A., Lamarche, F. & Arnaldi, B. (2007). A review of classification algorithms for EEG-based brain–computer interfaces. *Journal of Neural Engineering, 4*, 1–13. doi:10.1088/1741-2560/4/2/R01

Lu, H., Han, J., & Feng, L. (1998). *Stock Movement Prediction and N-dimensional Inter-Transaction Association Rules.* Paper presented at the SIGMOD Workshop Research Issues on Data Mining and Knowledge Discovery (DMKD '98), Seattle, Washington.

Lu, Y., & Han, J. (2003). Cancer classification using gene expression data. *Information Systems, 28*, 243–268. doi:10.1016/S0306-4379(02)00072-8

Lucas, P. (2001). Expert knowledge and its role in learning Bayesian Networks in medicine: An appraisal. In *Proceeding of the 8th Conference on Artificial Intelligence in Medicine in Europe,* Cascais, Portugal.

Lucas, P. (2004). Bayesian analysis, pattern analysis, and data mining in health care. *Current Opinion in Critical Care, 10*(5), 399–403. doi:10.1097/01.ccx.0000141546.74590.d6

Lucas, P. J. F., Van der Gaag, L. C., & Abu-Hanna, A. (2004). Editorial: Bayesian networks in biomedicine and health. *Artificial Intelligence in Medicine, 30*(3), 201–214. doi:10.1016/j.artmed.2003.11.001

Lunt, T. F., Tamaru, A., Gilham, F., Jagannathm, R., Jalali, C., Neumann, P. G., et al. (1992). *A Real-time Intrusion Detection Expert System (IDES), Computer Science Laboratory.* Menlo Park, CA: SRI International.

Luo, J. (1999). *Integrating fuzzy logic with data mining methods for intrusion detection.* Master's thesis, Mississippi State Univ.

Ma, H., & Hellerstein, J. L. (2001). Mining Partially Periodic Event Patterns with Unknown Periods. In *Proceedings of the 17th International Conference on Data Engineering* (pp. 205-214). Washington, DC: IEEE Computer Society.

MacKay, D. J. (2003). *Information Theory, Inference and Learning Algorithms.* Cambridge, MA: Cambridge University Press.

MacKinnon, J. G. (1996). Numerical distribution functions for unit root and cointegration tests. *Journal of Applied Econometrics, 11*(6), 601–618. doi:10.1002/(SICI)1099-1255(199611)11:6<601::AID-JAE417>3.0.CO;2-T

MacQueen, J. B. (1967). Some methods for classification and analysis of multivariate observations. In *Proceedings of 5th Berkeley Symposium on Mathematical Statistics and Probability,* Berkeley, University of California Press, (pp. 281-297).

Maedche, A., & Staab, S. (2001). Ontology learning for the semantic web. *IEEE Intelligent Systems, 18*(2), 72–79. doi:10.1109/5254.920602

Magoulas, G. D., & Prentza, A. (2001). *Machine learning in medical applications* (LNAI, pp. 300 – 307). Berlin: Springer.

Magoulas, G. D., Plagianakos, V. P., & Vrahatis, M. N. (2004). Neural network-based colonoscopic diagnosis using on-line learning and differential evolution. *Applied Soft Computing, 4*, 369–379. doi:10.1016/j.asoc.2004.01.005

Mahoney, M. V., & Chan, P. K. (2001). *PHAD: Packet Header Anomaly Detection for Identifying Hostile Network Traffic Department of Computer Sciences.* Technical Report CS- 2001-4, Florida Institute of Technology, Melbourne, FL.

Mahoney, M. V., & Chan, P. K. (2002). Learning nonstationary models of normal network traffic for detecting novel attacks. In *Proc. of the 8th ACM SIGKDD International Conf. on Knowledge Discovery and Data mining,* Edmonton, Alberta, Canada, (pp. 376–385). New York: ACM Press.

Mahoney, M. V., & Chan, P. K. (2003a). Learning rules for anomaly detection of hostile network traffic. In *Proc. Third IEEE Intl. Conf. on Data Mining (ICDM)*, Melbourne, FL, (pp. 601–604). Washington, DC: IEEE Computer Society Press.

Mahoney, M. V., & Chan, P. K. (2003b). An analysis of the 1999 darpa/lincoln laboratory evaluation data for network anomaly detection. In G. Vigna, E. Jonsson, and C. Kr"ugel (Eds.), *Proc. 6th Intl. Symp. on Recent Advances in Intrusion Detection (RAID 2003)*, Pittsburgh, PA, (LNCS Vol. 53 2820, pp. 220–237). Berlin: Springer.

Makridakis, S., & Winkler, R. L. (1983). Averages of Forecasts: Some Empirical Results. *Management Science, 29*(9), 987–996. doi:10.1287/mnsc.29.9.987

Makridakis, S., Anderson, A., Carbone, R., Fildes, R., Hibon, M., & Lewandowski, R. (1983). The Accuracy of Extrapolation (time series) methods: results of a forecasting competition. *Journal of Forecasting, 1*, 111–153. doi:10.1002/for.3980010202

Malone, T. W. (1983). How do people organize their desks? Implications for designing office information systems. *ACM Transactions on Office Information Systems, 1*, 99–112. doi:10.1145/357423.357430

Man, Y., & Gath, I. (1994). Detection and separation of ring shaped clusters using fuzzy clustering. *IEEE Transactions on Pattern Analysis and Machine Intelligence, 16*(8), 855–861. doi:10.1109/34.308484

Manganaris, S., Christensen, M., & Zerkle, D. (2000). A Data Mining Analysis of RTID Alarms. *Computer Networks, 34*(4), 571–577. doi:10.1016/S1389-1286(00)00138-9

Manku, G.,S. & Motwani, R. (2002). Approximate Frequency Counts over Data Streams. *Int'l Conf. on Very Large Databases*.

Mannila, H., & Toivonen, H. (1996). Discovering generalized episodes using minimal occurrences. In *The Second International Conference on Knowledge Discovery and Data Mining (KDD-96)* (pp. 146-151). Menlo Park, CA: AAAI Press.

Mannila, H., Toivonen, H., & Verkamo, A. I. (1995). *Discovering frequent episodes in sequences.* Paper presented at the First International Conference on Knowledge Discovery and Data Mining (KDD '95), Montreal, Canada.

Mannila, H., Toivonen, H., & Verkamo, A. I. (1997). Discovery of Frequent Episodes in Event Sequences. *Data Mining and Knowledge Discovery, 1*(3), 259–289. doi:10.1023/A:1009748302351

Manso, P. M. B., Prestes, R. F., & Petraglia, M. R. (2003). Detection of ellipses using modified hough transform. In *Proceedings of the IEEE International Symposium on Industrial Electronics* (pp. 1151-1154).

Marchette, D. (1999). A statistical method for profiling network traffic. In *First USENIX Workshop on Intrusion Detection and Network Monitoring, Santa Clara, CA*, (pp. 119–128). USENIX.

Marieb, E. N., & Hoehn, K. N. (2006). *Human anatomy and physiology (7th edition)*. New York: Benjamin Cummings.

Marieb, E. N., & Mitchell, S. J. (2007). *Human anatomy and physiology lab manual, cat version* (9th edition). New York: Benjamin Cummings.

Marin, J. A., Ragsdale, D., & Surdu, J. (2001). A hybrid approach to profile creation and intrusion detection. In *Proc. of DARPA Information Survivability Conference and Exposition*, IEEE Computer Society, Anaheim, CA.

Marsland, S., & Buchan, I. (2004). Clinical quality needs complex adaptive systems and machine learning. *Medinfo, 11*(Pt), 644-647.

Marsland, S., & Buchan, I. (2005). Clinical Quality Needs Complex Adaptive Systems and Machine Learning. *Studies in Health Technology and Informatics, 107*, 644–647.

Maruster, L., Weijters, T., de Vries, G., van den Bosch, A., & Daelemans, W. (2002). Logistic-based patient grouping for multi-disciplinary treatment. *Artificial Intelligence in Medicine, 26*(1-2), 87–107. doi:10.1016/S0933-3657(02)00054-4

Maskery, S., Zhang, Y., Hu, H., Shriver, C., Hooke, J., & Liebman, M. (2006). Caffeine Intake, Race, and Risk of Invasive Breast Cancer Lessons Learned from Data Mining a Clinical Database. *Computer-Based Medical Systems*, (pp. 714 – 718).

Matalliotakis, I. A., Cakmak, H., Mahutte, N., Goumenou, A. G., Koumantakis, G., & Aydin, A. (2008). The familial risk of breast cancer in women with endometriosis from Yale series. *Surgical Oncology*, 1–5.

Matchar, D. B., & Samsa, G. P. (1999). Using outcomes data to identify best medical practice: The role of policy models. *Hepatology (Baltimore, Md.)*, *29*(6Suppl), 36S–39S.

MathWorks. T. (2009). *MATLAB - The Language of Technical Computing*. Retrieved 20 January, 2009, from http://www.mathworks.com/products/matlab/

Matlab. (2008). *Statistics Toolbox User's Guide, The MathWorksInc*, USA . Version 6.2

Matsuoka, K., Ohya, M., & Kawamoto, M. (1995). A neural net for blind separation of nonstationary signals. *Neural Networks*, *8*, 411–419. doi:10.1016/0893-6080(94)00083-X

McClanachan, M., Dhanasekar, M., Skerman, D., & Davey, J. (2002). Monitoring the dynamics of freight wagons. In *Conf. on Railway Engineering, CORE 2002*, Wollongong, Australia, (pp. 213-221).

McClanachan, M., Scown, B., Roach, D., Skermen, D., & Payne, B. (2001). Autonomous detection of severe wagon-track interaction dynamics. In *7th Int'l Heavy Haul Conference*.

McGarry, K. (2005). A survey of interestingness measures for knowledge discovery. *20*(1), 39 - 61.

McHugh, J. (2000). The 1998 Lincoln Laboratory IDS Evaluation (A Critique). In *Proceeding of RAID 2000* (pp. 145-161). Heidelberg: Springer.

McHugh, J., Christie, A., & Allen, J. (2000). Defending Yourself: The Role of Intrusion Detection Systems. *Software IEEE*, *17*(5), 42–51. doi:10.1109/52.877859

McLaughlin, R. A. (1998). Randomized Hough transform: Improved ellipse detection with comparison. *Pattern Recognition Letters*, *19*(3-4), 299–305. doi:10.1016/S0167-8655(98)00010-5

McMahon, J., & Smith, F. (1996). Improving statistical language model with performance with automatically generated word hierarchies. *Computational Linguistics*, *2*(22), 217–247.

Medasani, S., Krishnapuram, R., & Keller, J. (1999). Are fuzzy definitions of basic attributes of image objects really useful? *IEEE Transactions on Systems, Man, and Cybernetics*, *29*(4), 378–386. doi:10.1109/3468.769756

Mehmed, K. (2002). *Data Mining: Concepts, Models, Methods, and Algorithms*. Mahwah, NJ: Wiley-IEEE Press.

Michaud, D. S. (2007). Chronic inflammation and bladder cancer. *Urologic Oncology: Seminars and Original Investigations*, *25*, 260–268. doi:10.1016/j.urolonc.2006.10.002

Middleton, S., Alani, H., Shadbolt, N., & Roure, D. D. (2002). *Exploiting synergy between ontologies and recommender systems*. In Semantic Web Workshop.

Midgley, M. (2003). Biotechnology and the yuk factor. In *The Myths We Live By*. London: Routledge.

Mihalakis, A., Mygdalis, V., Anastasiou, I., Adamakis, I., Zervas, A., & Mitropoulos, D. (2008). Patient awareness of smoking as a risk factor for bladder cancer. *European Urology Supplements*, *7*, 138. doi:10.1016/S1569-9056(08)60268-7

Miheev, V., & Vopilov, A. Shabalin, I. (2000). *The MP13 Approach to the KDD'99 Classifier Learning Contest*. Paper presented at the SIGKDD Explorations.

Mika, P. (2005). Ontologies are us: A unified model of social networks and semantics. *Lecture Notes in Computer Science, 3729, Galway, Ireland*, (pp. 122-136). Berlin: Springer-Verlag.

Miller, G. A., Beckwith, R., Fellbaum, C., Gross, D., & Miller, K. J. (1990b). Introduction to wordnet: An on-line lexical database. *International Journal of Lexicography*, *3*(4), 235–244. doi:10.1093/ijl/3.4.235

Miller, G., Beckwith, R., Fellbaum, C., Gross, D., & Miller, K. (1990a). Introduction to wordnet: An online lexical database. *Journal of Lexicography, 3*(4), 235–244. doi:10.1093/ijl/3.4.235

Minichiello, V., Sullivan, G., Greenwood, K., & Axford, R. (1999). *Handbook for research methods in health sciences* (1syt ed.). Sydney, NSW Australia: Addison Wesley Longman.

Mirkin, B. (1996). *Mathematic Classification and Clustering.* Amsterdam: Kluwer Academic Publishers.

Mitchell, T. (1997). *Machine Learning.* New York, USA: McGraw-Hill.

Mitchell, T. M. (1999). Machine Learning and Data Mining. *Communications of the ACM, 42*(11), 30–36. doi:10.1145/319382.319388

Mladenic, D. (1996). *Personal WebWatcher: design and implementation.* Technical report, Department for Intelligent Systems, J. Stefan Institute [Ljubljana, Slovenia.]. *Jamova, 39,* 11000.

Mobasher, B., Jin, X., & Zhou, Y. (2004). Semantically enhanced collaborative filtering on the web. In *Web Mining: From Web to Semantic Web: First European Web Mining Forum,* (pp. 57-76).

Moehrle, M. (2008). Outdoor sports and skin cancer. *Clinics in Dermatology, 26*(1), 12–15. doi:10.1016/j.clindermatol.2007.10.001

Mollan, M., & Lodaya, M. (2004). Continuous processing in pharmaceutical manufacturing. *Processing in Pharmaceutical Manufacturing.*

Mori, J., Matsuo, Y., & Ishizuka, M. (2005). Finding user semantics on the web using word co-occurrence information. In *PerSWeb05 Workshop on Personalization on the Semantic Web in conjunction with UM05.*

Morton, K. W., & Mayers, D. F. (2005). *Numerical Solution of Partial Differential Equations, An Introduction.* Cambrdige, MA: Cambridge University Press.

Moss, E. A. (1995). Developing national health information in Australia. *Medinfo, 8*(Pt 2), 1636.

Moukas, A. (1996). Amalthaea: Information discovery and filtering using a multi-agent evolving ecosystem. In *Proc. 1st Intl. Conf. on the Practical Application of Intelligent Agents and Multi Agent Technology,* London.

Mudhireddy, R., Ercal, F., & Frank, R. (2004). Parallel Hash-Based EST Clustering Algorithm for Gene Sequencing. *DNA and Cell Biology, 23*(10), 615–623. doi:10.1089/dna.2004.23.615

Mukkamala, S., & Sung, A. H. (2003). Identifying significant features for network forensic analysis using artificial intelligent techniques. *International Journal of Digital Evidence, 1*(4), 1–17.

Murphy, K. (2007). Software for Graphical Models: A review. *International Society for Bayesian Analysis Bulletin, December,* 1-3.

Murphy, K. (2008, July 28). *Software packages for Graphical Models / Bayesian Networks.* Retrieved January 2, 2009, from http://www.cs.ubc.ca/~murphyk/Software/bnsoft.html

Murphy, K. P. (2001, October 14). *A brief introduction to Graphical Models and Bayesian Networks.* Retrieved January 5, 2009, from http://www.cs.berkeley.edu/murphyk/Bayes/bayes.html

Mutter, S., Hall, M., & Frank, E. (2004). Using Classification to Evaluate the Output of Confidence based Association Rule Mining. In *Advances in Artificial Intelligence - AI 2004,* (LNAI Vol. 3339, pp. 538-549). Berlin: Springer.

Mylonas, P., Vallet, D., Fernndez, M., Castells, P., & Avrithis, Y. (2006). Ontology-based personalization for multimedia content. In *3rd European Semantic Web Conference - Semantic Web Personalization Workshop.*

Nadaraya, E. A. (1964). On estimating regression. *Theory of Probability and Its Applications, 9,* 141–142. doi:10.1137/1109020

Nadathur, S. (2009). *The value of hospital administrative datasets* [In preparation].

Nagesh, H., Goil, S., & Choudhary, A. (2001). Adaptive Grids for Clustering Massive Data Sets. In *Proceedings of the 1ˢᵗ SIAM ICDM Conference*, Chicago, IL.

Nahar, J., & Tickle, K. S. (2008). Significant Risk Factor Extraction Using Rule Based Methods. In *IEEE International Workshop on Data Mining and Artificial Intelligence*, Khulna, Bangladesh.

Nanas, N., Uren, V., & Roeck, A. D. (2003a). Building and applying a concept hierarchy representation of a user profile. In *Proceedings of the 26th annual international ACM SIGIR conference on Research and development in information retrieval*, (pp. 198-204). New York: ACM Press.

Nanas, N., Uren, V., & Roeck, A. D. (2003b). Building and applying a concept hierarchy representation of a user profile. In *Annual ACM Conference on Research and Development in Information Retrieval archive Proceedings of the 26th annual international ACM SIGIR conference on Research and development in information retrieval.*

Nasseh, A., & Strauss, J. (2000). Stock prices and domestic and international macroeconomic activity: A cointegration approach. *The Quarterly Review of Economics and Finance, 40*(2), 229–245. doi:10.1016/S1062-9769(99)00054-X

Nattkemper, T. W., Arnrich, B., Lichte, O., Timm, W., Degenhard, A., & Pointon, L. (2005). Evaluation of radiological features for breast tumour classification in clinical screening with machine learning methods. *Artificial Intelligence in Medicine, 34*, 129–139. doi:10.1016/j.artmed.2004.09.001

Neagu, D. C., Guo, G., Trundle, P. R., & Cronin, M. T. D. (2007). A comparative study of machine learning algorithms applied to predictive toxicology data mining. *Alternatives to Laboratory Animals, 35*, 25–32.

Nefti, S., & Oussalah, M. (2004). A neural network approach for railway safety prediction. In *2004 IEEE Int'l Conf. on Systems, Man and cybernetics,* October (pp. 3915-3920).

Nelson, D. B. (1991). Conditional heteroskedasticity in asset returns: A new approach. *Econometrica, 59*, 347–370. doi:10.2307/2938260

Nepomuk Installation (n.d.). Retrieved March 8, 2009, from http://dev.nepomuk.semanticdesktop.org/wiki/UsingInstaller

Nepomuk PSEW Recommendation: Using the Recommendations View in PSEW. (n.d.). Retrieved March 7, 2009, from http://dev.nepomuk.semanticdesktop.org/wiki/UsingPsewRecommendations

Neri, F. (2000). Comparing local search with respect to genetic evolution to detect intrusion in computer networks. In *Proc. of the 2000 Congress on Evolutionary Computation CEC00, La Jolla, CA,* (pp. 238–243). Washington, DC: IEEE Press.

Nieder, A. M., John, S., Messina, C. R., Granek, I. A., & Adler, H. L. (2006). Are Patients Aware of the Association Between Smoking and Bladder Cancer? *The Journal of Urology, 176*, 2405–2408. doi:10.1016/j.juro.2006.07.147

Nikovski, D. (2000). Constructing Bayesian Networks for medical diagnosis from incomplete and partially correct statistics. *IEEE Transactions on Knowledge and Data Engineering, 12*(4), 509–516. doi:10.1109/69.868904

Ning, P., Cui, Y., Reeves, D., & Xu, D. (2004). Tools and Techniques for Analyzing Intrusion Alerts. *ACM Transactions on Information and System Security, 7*(2), 273–318. doi:10.1145/996943.996947

Oard, D. (1997). The state of the art in text filtering. *User Modeling and User-Adapted Interaction, 7.*

Oberyszyn, T. M. (2008). Non-melanoma skin cancer: Importance of gender, immunosuppressive status and vitamin D. *Cancer Letters, 261*(2), 127–136.

Olson, C. F. (1999). Constrained hough transforms for curve detection. *Computer Vision and Image Understanding, 73*(3), 329–345. doi:10.1006/cviu.1998.0728

Ordonez, C. (2006). Association rule discovery with the train and test approach for heart disease prediction. *IEEE Transactions on Information Technology in Biomedicine, 10*(2), 334–343. doi:10.1109/TITB.2006.864475

Ordonez, C., & Omiecinski, E. (1999). Discovering association rules based on image content. In *IEEE Advances in Digital Libraries Conference (ADL'99)*, (pp. 38–49).

Ordonez, C., Omiecinski, E., Braal, L., Santana, C. A., Ezquerra, N., Taboada, J. A., et al. (2001). Mining Constrained Association Rules to Predict Heart Disease. In *Proceeding of the First IEEE International Conference on Data Mining (ICDM'01)*, (pp. 433-441).

Ordonez, C., Santana, C. A., & de Braal, L. (2000). Discovering interesting association rules in medical data. In *ACM DMKD Workshop*, (pp. 78–85).

OSHA. (2005). *OSHA Fines BP Products North America More Than $21 Million Following Texas City Explosion.* Retrieved May, 2008, from http://www.osha.gov/pls/oshaweb

Otsu, N. (1980). A threshold selection method from gray-level histogram. *IEEE Transactions on Systems, Man, and Cybernetics, 9*, 62–66.

Overheim, R. D., & Wagner, D. L. (1982). *Light and Color.* New York: Wiley.

Özden, B., Ramaswamy, S., & Silberschatz, A. (1998). *Cyclic Association Rules.* Paper presented at the Fourteenth International Conference on Data Engineering (ICDE '98), Orlando, Florida.

Pacella-Norman, R., Urban, M. I., Sitas, F., Carrara, H., Sur, R., & Hale, M. (2002). Risk factors for oesophageal, lung, oral and laryngeal cancers in black South Africans. *British Journal of Cancer, 86*, 1751–1756. doi:10.1038/sj.bjc.6600338

Pal, N. R., & Pal, S. K. (1993). A review on image segmentation techniques. *Pattern Recognition, 26*(9), 1277–1294. doi:10.1016/0031-3203(93)90135-J

Palaniappan, S., & Awang, R. (2008). Intelligent Heart Disease Prediction System Using Data Mining Techniques. *IJCSNS International Journal of Computer Science and Network Security, 8*(8), 343–350.

Palese, J. W. Bonaventura, C. S. & Zarembski, A. M. (2000). Intelligent system for real-time prediction of railway vehicle response to the interaction with track geometry. In *Railroad Conf. 2000. Proc. of the 2000 ASME/IEEE Joint*, (pp. 31-45).

Park, H.-S., Kwon, O.-W., & Sung, J.-H. (2005). *Nonextraction treatment of an open bite with microscrew implant anchorage.* American Association of Orthodontists, U.S.A.

Park, J., & Sandberg, I. W. (1991). Universal approximation using radial basis function networks. *Neural Computation, 2*(3), 246. doi:10.1162/neco.1991.3.2.246

Parry, D. (2004). A fuzzy ontology for medical document retrieval. In *ACSW Frontiers '04: Proceedings of the second workshop on Australasian information security, Data Mining and Web Intelligence, and Software Internationalisation*, (pp. 121-126). Darlinghurst, Australia: Australian Computer Society, Inc.

Pasquier, N., Bastide, Y., Taouil, R., & Lakhal, L. (1999). Discovering Frequent Closed Itemsets for Association Rules. In *Proc. Seventh Int'l Conference Database Theory.*

Patcha, A., & Park, J. M. (2007). An overview of anomaly detection techniques: Existing solutions and latest technological trends. In *Computer Networks*, (pp. 3448–3470).

Paxson, V. (1999). *Bro: a system for detecting network intruders in real-time.* Paper presented at the Computer Networks.

Pazzani, M., & Billsus, D. (1997). Learning and revising user profiles: The identification of interesting web sites. *Machine Learning, 27*, 313–331. doi:10.1023/A:1007369909943

Pazzani, M., Mani, S., & Shankle, W. R. (1997). Comprehensible knowledge-discovery in databases. In *Proceedings of Nineteenth annual conference of the Cognitive Science Society.* Retrieved January 4, 2009, from http://www.ics.uci.edu/~pazzani/Publications/CogSci97.pdf

Pearl, J. (1988). *Probabilistic Reasoning in Intelligent Systems.* San Mateo, CA, USA: Morgan Kaufman.

Pearl, J. (2000). *Causality*. Cambridge, UK: Cambridge University Press.

Peeters, G., Burthe, A. L., & Rodet, X. (2002). Toward Automatic Music Audio Summary Generation from Signal Analysis. In *Proceedings of the International Conference on Music Information Retrieval*, Paris, France.

Pei, J., Han, J., & Mao, R. (2000). Closet: An Efficient Algorithm for Mining Frequent Closed Itemsets. In *Proc. SIGMOD Int'l Workshop Data Mining and Knowledge Discovery*.

Pendharkar, P. C., Rodger, J. A., Yaverbaum, G. J., Herman, N., & Benner, M. (1999). Association, statistical, mathematical and neural approaches for mining breast cancer patterns. *Expert Systems with Applications, 17*, 223–232. doi:10.1016/S0957-4174(99)00036-6

Perng, C.-S., Wang, H., Zhang, S. R., & Parker, D. S. (2000). Landmarks: a new model for similarity based pattern querying in the time series databases. In *Proceedings of the 16th Int. Conference on Data Engineering*, San Diego, CA.

Pesaran, H., & Timmermann, A. (2002). Market timing and Return Prediction under Model instability. *Journal of Empirical Finance, 9*, 495–510. doi:10.1016/S0927-5398(02)00007-5

Pesaran, H., & Timmermann, A. (2003). *How Costly is it to Ignore Breaks when Forecasting the Direction of a Time Series?* (Cambridge Working Papers in Economics 0306). Department of Applied Economics, University of Cambridge.

Pesaran, M. H., & Timmermann, A. (2000). A recursive approach to predicting UK stock returns. *The Economic Journal, 110*(460), 159–191. doi:10.1111/1468-0297.00495

Peters, G. (2006). Some refinements of rough *k*-means clustering . *Pattern Recognition, 39*, 1481–149. doi:10.1016/j.patcog.2006.02.002

Peterson, L. E., & Coleman, M. A. (2008). Machine learning-based receiver operating characteristic (ROC) curves for crisp and fuzzy classification of DNA microarrays in cancer research. *International Journal of Approximate Reasoning, 47*(1), 17–36. doi:10.1016/j.ijar.2007.03.006

Petrovic, S., & Franke, K. (2007). Improving the efficiency of digital forensic search by means of the constrained edit distance. In *Proceedings of the Third International Symposium on Information Assurance and Security*, IEEE Computer Society, (pp. 405-410).

Pfahringer, B. (2000). *Winning the KDD99 Classification Cup: Bagged Boosting*. Paper presented at the SIGKDD Explorations.

Pham, D. L., & Prince, J. L. (1999). An adaptive fuzzy c-means algorithm for image segmentation in the presence of intensity inhomogeneities. *Pattern Recognition Letters, 20*(1), 57–68. doi:10.1016/S0167-8655(98)00121-4

Pharmacy, (2008). Retrieved August 25, 2008 from http://www.pharmacy.gov.my/self_care_guide/Urogenital/Postate%20Cancer.pdf

Phillips, J., Kumar, V., & Bryden, G. (2002). Bladder Cancer. *Surgery (Oxford), 20*, 281–284. doi:10.1383/surg.20.12.281.14645

Pichard, C., & Plu-Bureau, G., Neves-e Castro, M. & Gompel, A. (2008). Insulin resistance, obesity and breast cancer risk. *Maturitas, 60*(1), 19–30. doi:10.1016/j.maturitas.2008.03.002

Pietraszek, T. (2004). Using Adaptive Alert Classification to Reduce False Positives in Intrusion Detection. In *Proceeding of RAID 2004* (pp. 102-124). Heidelberg: Springer.

Pizlo, F. & Vitek, J. (2008). Memory Management for Real-time Java: State of the Art. *IEEE Xplore*, 248-254.

Plaimas, K., Mallm, J. P., Oswald, M., Svara, F., Sourjik, V., Eils, R., & König, R. (2008). Machine learning based analyses on metabolic networks supports high-throughput knockout screens. *BMC Systems Biology, 2*.

Platt, J. (1999). Probabilistic Outputs For Support Vector Machines And Comparison To Regularized Likelihood Methods. In A. Smola, P. Bartlett, B. Schoelkopf, D. Schuurmans, (eds.), *Advances in Large Margin Classifiers*, (pp. 61–74).

Ploberger, W., & Krämer, W. (1992). The CUSUM test with OLS residuals. *Econometrica, 60,* 271–285. doi:10.2307/2951597

Pomeroy, S. L., Tamayo, P., Gaasenbeek, M., Sturla, L. M., & Angelo, M. (2002). Prediction of central nervous embryonal tumour outcome based on gene expression. *Nature, 415,* 436–442. doi:10.1038/415436a

Popanda, O., Schattenberg, T., Phong, C. T., Butkiewicz, D., Risch, A., & Edler, L. (2004). Specific combinations of DNA repair gene variants and increased risk for non-small cell lung cancer. *Carcinogenesis, 25,* 2433–2441. doi:10.1093/carcin/bgh264

Porcel, J. M., Alemán, C., Bielsa, S., Sarrapio, J., De Sevilla, T. F., & Esquerda, A. (2008). A decision tree for differentiating tuberculous from malignant pleural effusions. *Respiratory Medicine, 102*(8), 1159–1164. doi:10.1016/j.rmed.2008.03.001

Porras, P. A., & Valdes, A. (1998). Live traffic analysis of TCP/IP gateways. In *Proc. of the 1998 ISOC Symp. on Network and Distributed Systems Security (NDSS'98),* Internet Society, San Diego.

Portnoy, L., Eskin, E., & Stolfo, S. J. (2001). Intrusion detection with unlabeled data using clustering. In *Proc. of ACM CSS Workshop on Data Mining Applied to Security (DMSA-2001),* Philadelphia. New York: ACM.

Pradhan, S., Hacioglu, K., Krugler, V., Ward, W., Martin, J., & Jurafsky, D. (2005). Support vector learning for semantic argument classification. *Machine Learning Journal, 60*(1-3), 11–39. doi:10.1007/s10994-005-0912-2

Prechelt, L. (1996). A quantitative study of experimental evaluation of neural network algorithms: Current research practice. *Neural Networks, 9*(3), 457–462. doi:10.1016/0893-6080(95)00123-9

Press, W. H., Flannery, B. P., Teukolsky, S. A., & Vetterling, W. T. (1986). *Numerical Recipies. The art of Scientific Computing.* Cambridge, UK: Cambridge University Press.

Pretschner, A., & Gauch, S. (2004). Ontology based personalized search and browsing. *Web Intelligence and Agent Systems, 1*(4), 219–234.

Prewitt, J. M. (1970). *Object Enhancement and Extraction.* New York: Academics Press, Ltd.

Pronovost, P. J., & Kazandjian, V. A. (1999). A new learning environment: Combining clinical research with quality improvement. *Journal of Evaluation in Clinical Practice, 5*(1), 33–40. doi:10.1046/j.1365-2753.1999.00160.x

Pun, D., & Ali, S. (2007). Unique Distance Measure Approach for K-means (UDMA-Km) Clustering Algorithm. In *CD proceeding of The IEEE international conference,* (pp. 1-4).

Pusztai, L., Mazouni, C., Anderson, K., Wu, Y., & Symmans, W. F. (2006). Molecular Classification of Breast Cancer: Limitations and Potential. *The Oncologist, 11,* 868–877. doi:10.1634/theoncologist.11-8-868

Qin, L., Ding, L., & He, B. (2004). Motor imagery classification by means of source analysis for brain–computer interface applications. *Journal of Neural Engineering, 1,* 135–141. doi:10.1088/1741-2560/1/3/002

Quan, T. T., Hui, S. C., & Cao, T. H. (2004). Foga: A fuzzy ontology generation framework for scholarly semantic web. In *Workshop on Knowledge Discovery and Ontologies In conjunction with ECML/PKDD.*

Quandt, R. (1960). Tests of the Hypothesis that a Linear Regression Obeys Two Separate Regimes. *Journal of the American Statistical Association, 55,* 324–330. doi:10.2307/2281745

Queensland Rail Safety Standard STD/0077/TEC Civil Engineering Track Standards Version 2. Module CETS 9 – Track Geometry. (n.d.). Queensland, Australia, Tech. Report.

Quinlan, J. R. (1986). Induction of decision trees. *Machine Learning, 1*, 81–106.

Quinlan, J. R. (1993). C4.5: Programs for machine learning. San Francisco, CA: Morgan Kaufmann.

Quinlan, R. (1993). *C4.5: Programs for Machine Learning.* San Francisco, CA: Morgan Kaufman Publishers.

Rangayyan, R. M., Ayres, F. J., & Desautels, J. E. L. (2007). A review of computer-aided diagnosis of breast cancer: Toward the detection of subtle signs. *Journal of the Franklin Institute, 344*(3-4), 312–348. doi:10.1016/j.jfranklin.2006.09.003

Ratha, N. K., Jain, A. K., & Chung, M. J. (1995). Clustering Using a Coarse-Grained Parallel Genetic Algorithm. In *Proceedings of the IEEE Computer Architectures for Machine Perception*, (pp. 331-338).

Regression analysis (n.d.). Wikipedia, the free encyclopedia. Retrieved January 25th, 2008, http://en.wikipedia.org/wiki/Regression_analysis

Reissigl, C. A., Wiunig, C. H., Neyer, M., Grunser, H., Remzi, M., & Pointner, J. (2008). Chronic inflammtion of the prostate as a risk factor for prostate cancer: a 4 year follow up study. *European Urology Supplements, 7*, 226. doi:10.1016/S1569-9056(08)60618-1

Resnick, P., & Varian, H. (1997). Recommender systems. *Communications of the ACM, 40*(3), 56–58. doi:10.1145/245108.245121

Rish, J. H., & Jayram, T. (2001). *An Analysis of Data Characteristics That Affect Naive Bayes Performance.* Technical Report RC21993, IBM T.J. Watson Research Center.

Rocha, C., Schwabe, D., & Poggi de Aragao, M. (2004). A Hybrid Approach for Searching in the Semantic Web. In *Proceedings of the 13th international conference on World Wide Web, May 17-20, 2004, New York*, (pp. 374-383).

Roddick, J. F., & Spiliopoulou, M. (2002). A Survey of Temporal Knowledge Discovery Paradigms and Methods. *IEEE Transactions on Knowledge and Data Engineering, 14*(4), 750–767. doi:10.1109/TKDE.2002.1019212

Rodin, A. S., & Boerwinkle, E. (2005). Mining genetic epidemiology data with Bayesian Networks I: Bayesian networks and example application (plasma apoE levels). *Bioinformatics (Oxford, England), 21*(15), 3273–3278. doi:10.1093/bioinformatics/bti505

Rodrigues, P. S., Ruey-Feng, C., & Suri, J. S. (2006). Non-Extensive Entropy for CAD Systems of Breast Cancer Images. *Computer Graphics and Image Processing, SIBGRAPI '06, 19th Brazilian Symposium*, (pp. 121 – 128).

Roesch, M. (1999). Snort – lightweight intrusion detection for networks. In *Proceedings of the 13th USENIX Conference on System Administration Seattle, Washington*, (pp. 229–238).

Rogers, M. (2003). The role of criminal profiling in the computer forensics process. *Computers & Security, 22*(4), 292–298. doi:10.1016/S0167-4048(03)00405-X

Rogova, G. (1994). Combining the results of several neural network classifiers. *Neural Networks, 7*, 777–781. doi:10.1016/0893-6080(94)90099-X

Roli, F., & Kittler, J. (Eds.). (2002). *Third International Workshop on Multiple Classier Systems* Cagliari, Italy, (LNCS Vol. 2364).

Roos, T., Wettig, H., Grunwald, P., Myllyma, P., & Tirri, H. (2005). On Discriminative Bayesian Network Classifiers and Logistic Regression. *Machine Learning, 59*(3), 267–296.

Rosenfeld, A., & Smith, R. C. (1981). Thresholding using relaxation. *IEEE Transactions on Pattern Analysis and Machine Intelligence, 3*, 598–606. doi:10.1109/TPAMI.1981.4767152

Ross, Q. J. (1993). *C4.5: Programs for machine learning.* San Francisco: Morgan Kaufmann Publishers.

Rübenkönig, O. (2006). *The Finite Difference Method (FDM) - An introduction.* Albert Ludwigs University of Freiburg.

RuleQuest. (2008). *RuleQuest Data mining tools, RuleQuest Research Pty Ltd.* Retrieved November 12, 2008 from http://www.rulequest.com/download.html

Rumelhart, D. E., & McClelland, J. L. (1986). *Parallel Distributed Processing: Explorations in the Microstructure of Cognition* (Vol. 2). Cambrdige, MA: The MIT Press.

Rumelhart, D. E., Hinton, G. E., & Williams, R. J. (1986). *Learning internal representations by error propagation in parallel distributed processing, 1,* 318–362. Cambridge, MA: MIT Press.

Rupp, B., Wang, J., Rupp, B., & Wang, J. (2004). Predictive models for protein crystallization. *Methods (San Diego, Calif.), 34*(3), 390–407. doi:10.1016/j.ymeth.2004.03.031

Ruspini, E. H. (1969). A new approach to clustering. In *Proceedings of the IEEE Conference on Information and Control* (pp. 22-32).

Ryan, J., Lin, M.-J., & Miikkulainen, R. (1998). Intrusion detection with neural networks. In M. I. Jordan, M. J. Kearns, & S. A. Solla (Eds.), *Advances in Neural Information Processing Systems*, (Vol. 10). Cambridge, MA: The MIT Press

Sadoyan, H., Zakarian, A., & Mohanty, P. (2006). Data mining algorithm for manufacturing process control. *International Journal of Advanced Manufacturing Technology*, 28.

Saeys, Y., Inza, I., & Larranaga, P. (2007). A review of feature selection techniques in Bioinformatics. *Bioinformatics (Oxford, England), 23*(19), 2507–2517. doi:10.1093/bioinformatics/btm344

Said, S. E., & Dickey, D. A. (1984). Testing for unit roots in autoregressive-moving average models of unknown order. *Biometrika, 71*(3), 599–607. doi:10.1093/biomet/71.3.599

Sakr, R., Rouzier, R., Salem, C., Antoine, M., Chopier, J., Daraï, E., & Uzan, S. (2008). Risk of breast cancer associated with papilloma. [EJSO]. *European Journal of Surgical Oncology*, 1–5.

Salton, G., & McGill, M. (1983). *Introduction to Modern Information Retrieval*. New York: McGraw-Hill.

Salton, G., Wong, A., & Yang, C. (1975). A vector space model for automatic indexing. *Communications of the ACM, 18*(11), 112–117. doi:10.1145/361219.361220

Salzberg, S. L. (1997). On comparing classifiers: Pitfalls to avoid and a recommended approach. *Data Mining and Knowledge Discovery, 1,* 317–328. doi:10.1023/A:1009752403260

Sanchez, D., & Moreno, A. (2005). A multi-agent system for distributed ontology learning. In *EUMAS,* (pp. 504-505).

Sander, J., Ester, M., Kriegel, H.-P., & Xu, X. (1998). Density-Based Clustering in Spatial Databases: The Algorithm GDBSCAN and Its Applications. *Data Mining and Knowledge Discovery, 2*(2), 169–194. doi:10.1023/A:1009745219419

Sanderson, M., & Croft, W. B. (1999). Deriving concept hierarchies from text. In *Research and Development in Information Retrieval*, (pp. 206-213).

Sandor, O., Bogdan, C., & Bowers, J. (1997). Aether: An Awareness Engine for CSCW. In H. Hughes, W. Prinz, T. Rodden, & K. Schmidt (eds.), *ECSCW'97: Fifth European Conference on Computer Supported Cooperative Work, Lancaster, UK* (pp. 221-236). Amsterdam: Kluwer Academic Publishers.

Sauermann, L. (2005). The semantic desktop - a basis for personal knowledge management. In Maurer, H., Calude, C., Salomaa, A., and Tochtermann, K., (Eds.), *Proceedings of the I-KNOW 05. 5th International Conference on Knowledge Management*, (pp. 294–301).

Sauermann, L., Bernardi, A., & Dengel, A. (2005). Overview and outlook on the semantic desktop. In Decker, S., Park, J., Quan, D., & Sauermann, L., (Eds.), *Proceedings of the First Semantic Desktop Workshop at the ISWC Conference 2005*, (pp. 1–18).

Sauermann, L., Kiesel, M., Schumacher, K., & Bernardi, A. (2009). Semantic Desktop. *Social Semantic Web, 2009,* 337–362. doi:10.1007/978-3-540-72216-8_17

Sauermann, L., van Elst, L., & Dengel, A. (2007). Pimo – a framework for representing personal information models. In *Proc. of the I-SEMANTICS 2007*, (pp. 270–277).

Schaner, M. E., Ross, D. T., Ciaravino, G., Sorlie, T., Troyanskaya, O., & Diehn, M. (2003). Gene expression patterns in ovarian carcinomas. *Molecular Biology of the Cell, 14*, 4376–4386. doi:10.1091/mbc.E03-05-0279

Schapire, R. E., Freund, Y., Bartlett, P., & Lee, W. S. (1998). Boosting the margin: A new explanation for the effectiveness of voting methods. *Annals of Statistics, 26*(5), 1651–1686. doi:10.1214/aos/1024691352

Scheffer, T. (2001). Finding Association Rules that Trade Support Optimally Against Confidence. In *Proceedings of the 5th European Conference on Principles and Practice of Knowlege Discovery in Databases(PKDD'01)*, Freiburg, Germany, (pp. 424-435). Berlin: Springer-Verlag.

Scheffer, T. (2001). Finding Association Rules that Trade Support Optimally Against Confidence. In *Proceedings of the 5th European Conference on Principles and Practice of Knowlege Discovery in Databases(PKDD'01)*, (pp. 424-435). Freiburg, Germany: Springer-Verlag.

Schiffman, M., Castle, P. E., Jeronimo, J., Rodriguez, A. C., & Wacholder, S. (2007). Human papillomavirus and cervical cancer. *Lancet, 370*, 890–907. doi:10.1016/S0140-6736(07)61416-0

Schlogl, A., Lee, F., Bischof, H., & Pfurtscheller, G. (2005). Characterization of four-class motor imagery EEG data for the BCI-competition. *Journal of Neural Engineering, 2*, L14–L22. doi:10.1088/1741-2560/2/4/L02

Schneider, A. (2000). Weighted possibilistic c-means clustering algorithm. In *Proceedings of the IEEE International Conference on Fuzzy Systems* (pp. 176-180).

Schneidir, R. (2006). Achieving process understanding – The foundation of strategic PAT programme. *Processing in Pharmaceutical manufacturing*.

Scholkopf, B., Sung, K.-K., Burges, C. J. C., Girosi, F., Niyogi, P., Poggio, T., & Vapnik, V. (1997). Comparing support vector machines with Gaussian kernels to radial basis function classifiers. *IEEE Transactions on Signal Processing, 11*(45), 2758–2765. doi:10.1109/78.650102

Schumacher, K., Sintek, M., & Sauermann, L. (2008). Combining Fact and Document Retrieval with Spreading Activation for Semantic Desktop Search. In *The Semantic Web: Research and Applications, 5th European Semantic Web Conference, ESWC 2008, Tenerife, Canary Islands, Spain, June 1-5, 2008 Proceedings* (LNCS Vol. 5021, pp. 569-583). Berlin: Springer.

Schwarz, G. (1978). Estimating the dimension of a model. *Annals of Statistics, 6*(2), 461–464. doi:10.1214/aos/1176344136

Sequeira, K., & Zaki, M. (2002). Admit: A nomaly-based data mining for intrusions. In *Proc. of the 8th ACM SIGKDD International conf. on Knowledge Discovery and Data mining*, Edmonton, Alberta, Canada, (pp. 386–395). New York: ACM Press.

Shafiullah, G. M., & Thompson, A. Wolfs, P. and Ali, S. "Reduction of Power Consumption in Sensor Network Applications using Machine Learning Techniques", *Proceeding of the IEEE international conference TENCON2008, Hyderabad, India*.

Shafiullah, G. M., Gyasi-Agyei, A., & Wolfs, P. (2007). Survey of wireless communications applications in the railway industry. In *Conf. on Wireless Broadband and Ultra Wideband Comm.*, Sydney.

Shafiullah, G. M., Simson, S., Thompson, A., Wolfs, P., & Ali, S. (2008). Monitoring Vertical Acceleration of Railway Wagon Using Machine Learning Techniques. In *Proceedings of The 2008 International Conference on Machine Learning; Models, Technologies and Applications (MLMTA'08)*, Las Vegas, NV, (pp. 770-775).

Sharkey, A. J. C., & Sharkey, N. E. (1997). Combining diverse neural nets. *The Knowledge Engineering Review, 12*(3), 231–247. doi:10.1017/S0269888997003123

Sharma, A., & Paliwal, K. K. (2008). Cancer classification by gradient LDA technique using microarray gene expression data. *Data & Knowledge Engineering, 66*(2), 338–347. doi:10.1016/j.datak.2008.04.004

Shehata, S., Karray, F., & Kamel, M. (2006). Enhancing text clustering using concept-based mining model, In *Proceedings of the IEEE International Conference on Data Mining (ICDM)*, (pp. 1043-1048).

Shehata, S., Karray, F., & Kamel, M. (2007). A concept-based model for enhancing text categorization, In *Proceedings of the 13th ACM SIGKDD International Conference on Knowledge Discovery and Data Mining (KDD)*, (pp. 629-637).

Shehata, S., Karray, F., & Kamel, M. (2007). Enhancing search engine quality using concept-based text retrieval, In *Proceedings of the 13th IEEE/WIC/ACM International Conference on Web Intelligence (WI)*, USA.

Sheingold, S. H. (2001). Can Bayesian methods make data and analysis more relevant to decision makers? *International Journal of Technology Assessment in Health Care, 17*(1), 114–122. doi:10.1017/S0266462301104101

Shen, M., Chapman, R. S., He, X., Liu, L. Z., Lai, H., Chen, W., & Lan, Q. (2008). Dietary factors, food contamination and lung cancer risk in Xuanwei, China. *Lung Cancer (Amsterdam, Netherlands), 61*, 275–282. doi:10.1016/j.lungcan.2007.12.024

Shen, Y., Shi, H., & Zhang, J. Q. (2001). Improvement and optimization of a fuzzy c-means clustering algorithm. In *Proceedings of the IEEE Instrumentation and Measurement Technology Conference* (pp. 1430-1433).

Sheshadri, H. S., & Kandaswamy, A. (2007). Experimental investigation on breast tissue classification based on statistical feature extraction of mammograms. *Computerized Medical Imaging and Graphics, 31*, 46–48. doi:10.1016/j.compmedimag.2006.09.015

Shook, D. (2004). *Alarm management* [white paper]. Retrieved July 7, 2004, from http://www.matrikon.com/download/products/lit/Matrikon_Alarm_Management_Whitepaper.pdf

Shyu, M.-L., Chen, S.-C., Sarinnapakorn, K., & Chang, L. (2003). A novel anomaly detection scheme based on principal component classifier. In *Proceedings of the IEEE Foundations and New Directions of Data Mining Workshop*, Melbourne, FL (pp. 172–179).

Sibson, R. (1973). SLINK: An Optimally Efficient Algorithm for the Single Link Cluster Method. *The Computer Journal, 16*, 30–34. doi:10.1093/comjnl/16.1.30

Sieg, A., Mobasher, B., Burke, R., Prabu, G., & Lytinen, S. (2005). Representing user information context with ontologies. In *Proceedings of the 3rd International Conference on Universal Access in Human-Computer Interaction*.

Sigurbjörnsson, B., & van Zwol, R. (2008). Flickr tag recommendation based on collective knowledge. In *Proceeding of the 17th international conference on World Wide Web, Beijing, China*, (pp. 327-336).

Sinclair, C., Pierce, L., & Matzner, S. (1999). An application of machine learning to network intrusion detection. In *Proc. 15th Annual Computer Security Applications Conference (ACSAC '99)*, Phoenix, (pp. 371–377). Washington, DC: IEEE Computer Society.

Singh, S., & Kandula, S. (2001). *Argus - a distributed network-intrusion detection system*. Undergraduate Thesis, Indian Institute of Technology.

Sinha, A. P., & Zhao, H. (2008). *Incorporating domain knowledge into data mining classifiers: An application in indirect lending*. Paper presented at the Decision Support Systems.

Slagell, M. (2001). *The Design and Implementation of MAIDS (Mobile Agents for Intrusion Detection System)*. Master's thesis, Iowa State University, USA.

Smaha, S. E. (1988). Haystack: An intrusion detection system. In *Proceedings of the IEEE Fourth Aerospace Computer Security Applications Conference*, Orlando, FL, (pp. 37–44).

Smith, J. Russel, S. & Looi, M. (2003). Security as a safety issue in rail communications. In *8ᵗʰ Aus. Workshop on Safety Critical System and Software (SCS'03)*, Canberra, Australia, (pp. 79-88).

Smith, J. S., Green, J., Gonzalez, A. B. D., Appleby, P., Peto, J., & Plummer, M. (2003). Cervical cancer and use of hormonal contraceptives: a systematic review. *Lancet, 361*, 1159–1167. doi:10.1016/S0140-6736(03)12949-2

So, M. K. P., & Yu, P. L. H. (2006). Empirical analysis of GARCH models in value at risk estimation. *Journal of International Financial Markets, Institutions and Money, 16*(2), 180–197. doi:10.1016/j.intfin.2005.02.001

Sobti, R. C., Gupta, L., Singh, S. K., Seth, A., Kaur, P., & Thakur, H. (2008). Role of hormonal genes and risk of prostate cancer: gene-gene interactions in a North Indian population. *Cancer Genetics and Cytogenetics, 185*, 78–85. doi:10.1016/j.cancergencyto.2008.04.022

Song, X., Mitnitski, A., Cox, J., & Rockwood, K. (2004). Comparison of machine learning techniques with classical statistical models in predicting health outcomes. *Studies in Health Technology and Informatics, 107*(1), 736–740.

Spafford, E. H., & Zamboni, D. (2000). Intrusion detection using autonomous agents. *Computer Networks, 34*(4), 547–570. doi:10.1016/S1389-1286(00)00136-5

Spath, H. (1980). *Cluster Analysis Algorithms.* Chichester, UK: Ellis Horwood.

Specht, D. F. (1990). Probabilistic neural networks. *Neural Networks, 3*, 109–118. doi:10.1016/0893-6080(90)90049-Q

Spetch, D. F. (1991). A general regression neural network. *IEEE Transactions on Neural Networks, 2*(6), 568–576. doi:10.1109/72.97934

Spirkovska, L. (1993). *A summary of image segmentation techniques* (NASA Technical Memorandum).

Srikant, R., & Agrawal, R. (1996). *Mining Sequential Patterns: Generalizations and Performance Improvements.* Paper presented at the 5th Int. Conf. Extending Database Technology (EDBT), Avignon, France.

Staccini, P., Joubert, M., Quaranta, J. F., Fieschi, D., & Fieschi, M. (2001). Modelling health care processes for eliciting user requirements: a way to link a quality paradigm and clinical information system design. *International Journal of Medical Informatics, 64*(2-3), 129–142. doi:10.1016/S1386-5056(01)00203-9

Staniford, S., Hoagland, J. A., & McAlerney, J. M. (2002). Practical automated detection of stealthy portscans. *Journal of Computer Security, 10*(1-2), 105–136.

Staniford-Chen, S., Cheung, S., Crawford, R., Dilger, M., Frank, J., Hoagland, J., et al. (1996). GrIDS – A graphbased intrusion detection system for large networks. In *Proc. of the 19ᵗʰ National Information Systems Security Conference*, Baltimore, MD. National Institute of Standards and Technology (NIST).

Statnikov, A., Aliferis, C. F., Tsamardinos, L., Hardin, D., & Levy, S. (2005). A comprehensive evaluation of multicategory classification methods for microarray gene expression cancer diagnosis. *Bioinformatics (Oxford, England), 21*(5), 631–643. doi:10.1093/bioinformatics/bti033

Steckley, S. L., Pickworth, W. B., & Haverkos, H. W. (2002). Cigarette smoking and cervical cancer: Part II: a geographic variability study. *Biomedicine and Pharmacotherapy, 57*, 78–83.

Stefani, E. D., Boffetta, P., Ronco, A. L., Deneo-Pellegrini, H., Acosta, G., Gutiérrez, L. P., & Mendilaharsu, M. (2008). Nutrient patterns and risk of lung cancer: A factor analysis in Uruguayan men. *Lung Cancer (Amsterdam, Netherlands), 61*, 283–291. doi:10.1016/j.lungcan.2008.01.004

Stein, B., & Busch, M. (2005). Density-based cluster algorithms in low-dimensional and high-dimensional applications. In *Proc. of Second International Workshop on Text-Based Information Retrieval, TIR05*, (pp. 45–56).

Stein, B., & Nigemman, O. (1999). On the nature of structure and its identification. [Berlin: Springer.]. *Lecture Notes in Computer Science, 1665*, 122–134. doi:10.1007/3-540-46784-X_13

Steinbach, M., Karypis, G., & Kumar, V. (2000). A Comparison of Document Clustering Techniques. In *Proceedings of the 6ᵗʰ ACM SIGKDD International Conference on Knowledge Discovery and Data Mining*, Boston, MA.

Steinhaus, H. (1956). Sur La Division Des Corp Materiels En Parties. *Bull. Acad. Polon. Sci.*, Cl. *III, IV*, 801–804.

Stephen, O., Freedland, J., Wen, J., Wuerstle, M., Shah, A., Lai, D., et al. (2008). Obesity Is a Significant Risk Factor for Prostate Cancer at the Time of Biopsy. *Urology*.

Stock, J. H., & Watson, M. W. (2003). Forecasting Output and Inflation: The Role of Asset Prices. *Journal of Economic Literature, 41*, 788–829. doi:10.1257/002205103322436197

Stone, C. A., Ramsden, C. A., Howard, J. A., Roberts, M., & Halliday, J. H. (2002, March 20-21). From data linkage to policy and back again: A preliminary report on the linkage of neonatal data in Victoria. In *Proceedings of the Symposium on Health Data Linkage: Its value for Australian health policy development and policy relevant research*, Tusculum House auditorium, Potts Point, Sydney, NSW, Australia. Retrieved from http://www.publichealth.gov.au/pdf/reports_papers/symposium_procdngs_2003/stone.pdf

Stühlinger, W., Hogl, O., Stoyan, H., & Müller, M. (2000). Intelligent data mining for medical quality management. In *Proceedings of 5th Workshop Intelligent Data Analysis in Medicine and Pharmacology (IDAMAP2000), Workshop Notes of the 14th European Conf. Artificial Intelligence (ECAI-2000)*.

Sundararajan, V., Henderson, T. M., Ackland, M., & Marshall, R. (2002, March 20-21). *Linkage of the Victorian Admitted Episodes Dataset*. In *Proceedings of the Symposium on Health Data Linkage: Its value for Australian health policy development and policy relevant research*, Tusculum House auditorium, Potts Point, Sydney, NSW, Australia. Retrieved from http://www.publichealth.gov.au/pdf/reports_papers/symposium_procdngs_2003/stone.pdf

Sutherland, A. (1998). *Bayesian Networks - Another example*. Retrieved January 27, 2009, from http://computing.dcu.ie/~alistair/

Sykes, A. O. (n.d.). An introduction to regression analysis. Chicago working paper in Law and Economics, Tech. Rep. [Online]. Available at http://www.law.uchicago.edu/Lawecon/WkngPprs_01-25/20.Sykes.Regression.pdf

T˝olle, J., & Niggermann, O. (2000). Supporting intrusion detection by graph clustering and graph drawing. In *Proc. of Third International Workshop on Recent Advances in Intrusion Detection (RAID 2000)*, Toulouse, France, (LNCS Vol. 1907). Berlin: Springer.

Takahashi, I., Matsuzaka, M., Umeda, T., Yamai, K., Nishimura, M., & Danjo, K. (2008). Differences in the influence of tobacco smoking on lung cancer between Japan and the USA: possible explanations for the 'smoking paradox' in Japan. *Public Health, 122*, 891–896. doi:10.1016/j.puhe.2007.10.004

Tan, P.-N., Steinbach, M., & Kumar, V. (2005). Association Analysis: Basic Concepts and Algorithms. In *Introduction to Data Mining*, (pp. 327-414). Reading, MA: Addison-Wesley

Tang, Z., MacLennan, J., & Crivat, B. (2008). *Data mining with SQL server 2008*. New York: Wiley

Taxt, T., Flynn, P. J., & Jain, A. K. (1989). Segmentation of document images. *IEEE Transactions on Pattern Analysis and Machine Intelligence, 11*(12), 1322–1329. doi:10.1109/34.41371

Tchienehom, P. L. (2005). Profiles semantics for personalized information access. In *PerSWeb05 Workshop on Personalization on the Semantic Web in conjunction with UM05*.

Teevan, J., Dumais, S. T., & Horvitz, E. (2005). Personalizing search via automated analysis of interests and activities. In *Proceedings of the 28th annual international ACM SIGIR conference on Research and development in information retrieval*, (pp. 449-456). New York: ACM.

Terveen, L., Hill, W., Amento, B., McDonald, D., & Creter, J. (1997). Phoaks: A system for sharing recommendations. *Communications of the ACM, 40*(3), 59–62. doi:10.1145/245108.245122

The Math Works (2008). The Math Works, Inc. [Online]. Retrieved January 9th, 2008 from http://www.mathworks.com/

Tho, Q. T., Hui, S. C., Fong, A., & Cao, T. H. (2006). Automatic fuzzy ontology generation for semantic web. *IEEE Transactions on Knowledge and Data Engineering, 18*(6), 842–856. doi:10.1109/TKDE.2006.87

Tigrani, V. S., & John, G. H. (2005). Data mining and statistics in medicine - An application in prostate cancer detection. In *Proceedings of the Joint Statistical Meetings, Section on Physical and Engineering Sciences*. Retrieved January 22, 2009 from http://robotics.stanford.edu/~gjohn/ftp/papers/jsm.ps.gz

Tizhoosh, H. R. (1997). *Fuzzy image processing*. Berlin, Germany: Springer. Retrieved from http://watfast.uwaterloo.ca/tizhoosh/fip.htm

Tolias, Y. A., & Panas, S. M. (1998). Image segmentation by a fuzzy clustering algorithm using adaptive spatially constrained membership functions. *IEEE Transactions on Systems, Man, and Cybernetics, 28*(3), 359–369. doi:10.1109/3468.668967

Trotman, M. & Sillaots, D. (n.d.). *Monitoring Rail Track Condition to Reduce Maintenance Costs*. ICN Technologies Pty Ltd, Tech Report, Australia.

Troussov, A., Judge, J., & Sogrin, M. (1997, December 13). *IBM LanguageWare Miner for Multidimensional Socio-Semantic Networks*. Retrieved March 8, 2009, from http://www.alphaworks.ibm.com/tech/galaxy

Troussov, A., Judge, J., Sogrin, M., Akrout, A., Davis, B., & Handschuh, S. (2008c). A Linguistic Light Approach to Multilingualism in Lexical Layers for Ontologies. In *Proceedings of the International Multiconference on Computer Science and Information Technology*, (pp. 375–379).

Troussov, A., Judge, J., Sogrin, M., Bogdan, C., Edlund, H., & Sundblad, Y. (2008b). Navigating Networked Data using Polycentric Fuzzy Queries and the Pile UI Metaphor Navigation. *Proceedings of the International SoNet Workshop*, (pp. 5-12).

Troussov, A., Sogrin, A., Judge, J., & Botvich, D. (2008a). Mining Socio-Semantic Networks Using Spreading Activation Technique. In *Proceedings of I-KNOW '08 and I-MEDIA '08, Graz, Austria, September 3-5, 2008*, (pp. 405-412).

Tsai, H., Horng, S., Tsai, S., Lee, S., Kao, T., & Chen, C. (1997). Parallel Clustering Algorithms on a Reconfigurable Array of Processors With Wider Bus Networks. In *Proceedings of the IEEE International Conference on Parallel and Distributed Systems*.

Twellmann, T., Meyer-Baese, A., Lange, O., Foo, S., & Nattkemper, T. W. (2008). Model-free visualization of suspicious lesions in breast MRI based on supervised and unsupervised learning . *Engineering Applications of Artificial Intelligence, 21*(2), 129–140. doi:10.1016/j.engappai.2007.04.005

UIC leaflet 518, testing and approval of railway vehicles from the point of view of their dynamic behaviour – safety track – track fatigue – ride quality. (2003, April). International Union of Railways, Paris, France, Tech. Rep.

Valdes, A., & Skinner, K. (2000). Adaptive model-based monitoring for cyber attack detection. In *Recent Advances in Intrusion Detection Toulouse*, France, (pp. 80–92).

Van der Gaag, L. C., Renooij, S., Feelders, A., de Groote, A., Eijkemans, M. J. C., Broekmans, F. J., et al. (2008). *Aligning Bayesian Network classifiers with medical contexts* (No. Technical Report UU-CS-2008-015). Department of Information and Computing Sciences, Utrecht University, Utrecht, The Netherlands.

Van der Lei, J. (2002). Information and communication technology in health care: Do we need feedback? *International Journal of Medical Informatics, 66*(1-3), 75–83. doi:10.1016/S1386-5056(02)00039-4

Vapnik, V. (1998). *Statistical Learning Theory*. Mahwah, NJ: John Wiley and Sons.

Vapnik, V. N. (1999). An overview of statistical learning theory. *IEEE Transactions on Neural Networks, 10*, 988–999. doi:10.1109/72.788640

Veer, L. J. V., Dai, H., Vijver, M. J. V. D., He, Y. D., Hart, A. A. M., & Mao, M. (2002). Gene expression profiling predicts clinical outcome of breast cancer. *Nature, 415*, 530–536. doi:10.1038/415530a

Verwoerd, T., & Hunt, R. (2002). Intrusion detection techniques and approaches. *Computer Communications*, 1356–1365. doi:10.1016/S0140-3664(02)00037-3

Viinikka, J., Debar, H., Mé, L., & Séguier, R. (2006). Time Series Modeling for IDS Alert Management. In *Proceeding of 2006 ACM Symposium on Information, computer and communications security,* (pp. 102-113). New York: ACM Press.

Vilalta, R., Carrier, G., C., Brazdil. P. & Soares, C. (2004). Using Meta-Learning to Support Data Mining. *International Journal of Computer Science & Applications, 1,* 1, 31 – 45.

Vinnakota, S., & Lam, N. S. N. (2006). Socioeconomic inequality of cancer mortality in the United States: a spatial data mining approach. *International Journal of Health Geographics,* 5–9.

Visscher, S., Lucas, P., Schurink, K., & Bonten, M. (2005, July 23-27). Using a Bayesian-Network model for the analysis of clinical time-series data. In *Proceeding of 2005 Artificial Intelligence in Medicine Europe (AIME) conference,* Aberdeen, UK.

Vittayakorn, S., Kantabutra, S., & Tanprasert, C. (2008). The Parallel Complexities of the *K-Medians* Related Problems. In *Proceedings of the 5th International Conference on Electrical Engineering/Electronics, Computer, Telecommunications and Information Technology,* Krabi, Thailand, (pp. 9-12).

Viveros, M. S., Nearhos, J. P., & Rothman, M. J. (1996). Applying data mining techniques to a health insurance information system. In *Proceedings of the 22nd Very Large Data Base (VLDB) Conference,* Mumbai, India.

Voorhees, E. M. (1986). Implementing Agglomerative Hierarchical Clustering Algorithms for Use in Document Retrieval. *Information Processing & Management, 22*(6), 465–476. doi:10.1016/0306-4573(86)90097-X

Wallace, C., & Dowe, D. (1994). Intrinsic Classification by MML – The Snob Program. In *Proceedings of the 7th Australian Joint Conference on Artificial Intelligence,* Armidale, Australia, (pp. 37-44).

Wan, S. J., Wong, S. K. M., & Prusinkiewicz, P. (1998). An Algorithm for Multidimensional Data Clustering. *ACM Transactions on Mathematical Software, 14,* 153–162. doi:10.1145/45054.45056

Wang, F., & Zhang, Q. J. (1995). An Improved *K*-Means Clustering Algorithm and Application to Combined Multicodebook/MLP Neural Network Speech Recognition. In . *Proceedings of the IEEE Canadian Conference on Electrical and Computer Engineering, 2,* 999–1002.

Wang, J., Han, J., & Pei, J. (2003). Closet+: Searching for the Best Strategies for Mining Frequent Closed Itemsets. In *Proc. ACM SIGKDD Int'l Conference Knowledge Discovery and Data Mining.*

Wang, K., He, Y., & Han, J. (2000). Mining frequent itemsets using support constraints. In A. El Abbadi, M. L. Brodie, S. Chakravarthy, U. Dayal, N. Kamel, G. Schlageter & K.-Y. Whang (Eds.), *Proc. of the 26th Int. Conf. on Very Large Data Bases (VLDB)* (pp. 43-52). San Francisco CA: Morgan Kaufmann Publishers Inc.

Wang, S., Zhou, M., & Geng, G. (2005). Application of Fuzzy Cluster Analysis for Medical Image Data Mining. In *Proceedings of the IEEE International Conference on Mechatronics & Automation,* (pp. 631-636).

Wang, W. Yang, J. & Muntz, R. (1997). STING: A Statistical Information Grid Approach to Spatial Data Mining. In *Proceedings of the 23rd Conference on VLDB,* Athens, Greece, (pp. 186-195).

Wang, X. Z. (1999). *Data mining and knowledge discovery for process monitoring and control.* Berlin, Germany: Springer.

Waring, J. F., Jolly, R. A., Ciurlionis, R., Lum, P. Y., Praestgaard, J. T., & Morfitt, D. C. (2001). Clustering of Hepatotoxins Based on Mechanism of Toxicity Using Gene Expression Profiles. *Toxicology and Applied Pharmacology, 175*(1), 28–42. doi:10.1006/taap.2001.9243

Warrender, C., Forrest, S., & Pearlmutter, B. A. (1999). Detecting intrusions using system calls: Alternative data models. In *Proc. of the 1999 IEEE Symp. on Security and Privacy,* Oakland, CA, (pp. 133–145). Washington, DC: IEEE Computer Society Press.

Watanabe, H., Yakowenko, W., Kim, Y., Anbe, J., & Tobi, T. (1996). Application of a Fuzzy Discrimination Analysis for Diagnosis of Valvular Heart Disease. *IEEE Trans. On Fuzzy Systems.*

Watson, G. S. (1964). Smooth regression analysis. *Sankhya Series, 26,* 359–372.

Wei, L. M., & Xie, W. X. (2000). Rival checked fuzzy c-means algorithm. In *Proceedings of the Acta Electronica Sinica* [Chinese] (pp. 63-66).

Wei, W., & Mendel, J. M. (1994). Optimality test for the fuzzy c-means algorithm. *Pattern Recognition, 27*(11), 1567–1573. doi:10.1016/0031-3203(94)90134-1

Wciss, G. (1999). *Multi-Agent System: A modern approach to distributed artificial intelligence.* Cambridge, MA: The MIT Press.

Weka 3. (n.d.). The University of Waikato, NewZealand, Tech. Rep. [Online]. Available March 9th, 2008 http://www.cs.waikato.ac.nz/ml/weka

White, S. D. M., & Frenk, C. S. (1991). Galaxy Formation Through Hierarchical Clustering. *The Astrophysical Journal, 379,* 52–79. doi:10.1086/170483

Widyantoro, D. H., & Yen, J. (2002). Using fuzzy ontology for query refinement in a personalized abstract search engine. In *10th IEEE International Conference on Fuzzy Systems,* (pp. 705-708).

Wikimedia, (2008). Retrieved October 2, 2008, from http://upload.wikimedia.org.

Wikipedia, (2008). Retrieved August 20, 2008 from http://en.wikipedia.org/wiki/Bladder_cancer

Wilkinson, B., & Allen, M. (1998). *Parallel Programming, Techniques and Applications Using Networked Workstations and Parallel Computers.* Englewood Cliffs, NJ: Prentice Hall.

Williams, T. A., Dobb, G. J., Finn, J. C., Knuiman, M., Lee, K. Y., & Geelhoed, E. (2006). Data linkage enables evaluation of long-term survival after intensive care. *Anaesthesia and Intensive Care, 34*(3), 307–315.

Windeatt, T., & Roli, F. (Eds.). (2003). *Multiple Classier Systems, 4th International Workshop, MCS 2003.* Guilford, UK: Springer.

Winkler, R. L., & Makridakis, S. (1983). The Combination of Forecasts. *Journal of the Royal Statistical Society. Series A (General), 146*(2), 150–157.

doi:10.2307/2982011

Wisemann, S. M. (2008). Molecular phenotyping of thyroid tumors identifies a marker panel for differentiated thyroid cancer diagnosis. *Annals of Surgical Oncology,* 15.

Witten, I. H., & Frank, E. (2000). *Data Mining: Practical Machine Learning Tools with Java Implementations.* San Francisco: Morgan Kaufmann.

Witten, I. H., & Frank, E. (2000). *Data Mining: Practical Machine Learning Tool and Technique with Java Implementation.* San Francisco: Morgan Kaufmann.

Witten, I. H., & Frank, E. (2005). *Data Mining: Practical machine learning tools and techniques,* (2nd Ed.). San Francisco: Morgan Kaufmann.

Wolfs, P. J., Bleakley, S., Senini, S. T., & Thomas, P. (2006). An autonomous, low cost, distributed method for observing vehicle track interactions. In *Rail Conf. 2006,* Atlanta, GA.

Wolfs, P., Bleakley, S., Seninin, S., & Thomas, P. (2006). A distributed low cost device for the remote observation of track and vehicle interactions. In *Conf. on Railway Engineering, RTSA,* Melbourne, Australia, (pp. 280-286).

Wong, H.-S., & Wang, H.-Q. (2008). Constructing the gene regulation-level representation of microarray data for cancer classification. *Journal of Biomedical Informatics, 41*(1), 95–100. doi:10.1016/j.jbi.2007.04.002

Wu, E. H. C., Yu, P. L. H., & Li, W. K. (2006). Value at Risk estimation using independent component analysis-generalized autoregressive conditional heteroscedasticity (ICA-GARCH) models. *International Journal of Neural Systems, 16*(5), 371–382. doi:10.1142/S0129065706000779

Wu, H., Heilweil, E. J., Hussain, A. S., & Khan, M. (2008). Process analytical technology (PAT): quantification approaches in terahertz spectroscopy for pharmaceutical application. *Journal of Pharmaceutical Sciences, 97*(2), 970–984. doi:10.1002/jps.21004

Wu, P. S., & Li, M. (1996). A novel hough transform for curve detection. *IEEE Transactions on Systems, Man, and Cybernetics, 4,* 2722–2727.

Xu, X., Ester, M., Kriegel, H.-P., & Sander, J. (1998). A Distribution-Based Clustering Algorithm for Mining in Large Spatial Databases. In *Proceedings of the 14th ICDE Conference*, Orlando, Florida, (pp. 324-331).

Yang, F. Q., Sun, T. L., & Sun, J. G. (2006). Learning hierarchical user interest models from web pages. *Wuhan University Journal of Natural Sciences*, *11*(1), 6–10. doi:10.1007/BF02831694

Yang, L., Peterson, P. J., Williams, W. P., Wang, W., Hou, S., & Tan, J. (2002). The Relationship Between Exposure to Arsenic Concentrations in Drinking Water and the Development of Skin Lesions in Farmers from Inner Mongolia, China. *Environmental Geochemistry and Health*, *24*(2).

Yang, M. S. (1993). A survey of fuzzy clustering. *Mathematical and Computer Modelling*, *18*(11), 1–16. doi:10.1016/0895-7177(93)90202-A

Yang, M. S., & Wu, K. L. (2004). A similarity-based robust clustering method. *IEEE Transactions on Pattern Analysis and Machine Intelligence*, *26*(4), 434–448. doi:10.1109/TPAMI.2004.1265860

Yang, Z. G., Jiang, G. X., & Ren, L. (2004). Ellipse detection based on improved-GEVD technique. In *Proceedings of the World Congress on Intelligent Control and Automation* (pp. 4181-4185).

Yanowitz, S. D., & Bruckstein, M. A. (1988). A new method for image segmentation. In *Proceedings of the International Conference on Pattern Recognition* (pp. 270-275).

Ye, N., Emran, S. M., Chen, Q., & Vilbert, S. (2002). Multivariate statistical analysis of audit trails for host-based intrusion detection. *IEEE Transactions on Computers*, 810–820. doi:10.1109/TC.2002.1017701

Yeh, J.-Y., Wu, T.-S., Wu, M.-C., & Chang, D.-M. (2007). Applying Data Mining Techniques for Cancer Classification from Gene Expression Data. *International Conference on Convergence Information Technology*, (pp. 703-708).

Yeung, D.-Y., & Chow, C. (2002). Parzen-window network intrusion detectors. In *Proc. of the Sixteenth International Conference on Pattern Recognition*, (Vol. 4, pp. 385–388), Quebec City, Canada. Washington, DC: IEEE Computer Society.

Yeung, D.-Y., & Ding, Y. (2003). Host-based intrusion detection using dynamic and static behavioral models. In *Pattern Recognition*, (pp. 229–243).

Young, N. E. (2000). Greedy Approximation Algorithm for *K-Medians* by Randomized Rounding. In *Proceedings of the ACM-SIAM Symposium on Discrete Algorithms*, San Francisco, CA.

Zadeh, L. A. (1978). Fuzzy sets as a basis for a theory of possibility. *Fuzzy Sets and Systems*, *1*, 3–28. doi:10.1016/0165-0114(78)90029-5

Zaki M., J. & Hsiao, C-J. (2005). Efficient Algorithms for Mining Closed Itemsets and Their Lattice Structure. *IEEE Computer Society, 17*.

Zaki, M. J. (2000). Generating Non-Redundant Association Rules. In *Proc. Sixth ACM SIGKDD Int'l Conference Knowledge Discovery and Data Mining*.

Zaki, M. J. (2000). Scalable algorithms for association mining. *IEEE Transactions on Knowledge and Data Engineering*, 12.

Zaki, M. J. (2000). Sequence Mining in Categorical Domains: Incorporating Constraints. In *Proceedings of the Ninth International Conference on Information and Knowledge Management* (pp. 422-429). New York: ACM.

Zaki, M. J., & Hsiao, C. J. (1999). *CHARM: An efficient algorithm for closed association rule mining*. New York: Rensselaer Polytechnic Institute.

Zaknich, A. (1998). Introduction to the modified probabilistic neural network for general signal processing applications. *IEEE Transactions on Signal Processing*, *46*(7), 1980–1990. doi:10.1109/78.700969

Zaknich, A., & Attikiouzel, Y. (1988). *An unsupervised clustering algorithm for the modified probabilistic neural network*. Paper presented at the IEEE International Workshop on Intelligent Signal Processing and Communications Systems, Melbourne, Australia.

Zaknich, A., & Attikiouzel, Y. (1993). *Automatic optimization of the modified probabilistic neural network for pattern recognition and time series analysis.* Paper presented at the Proc. First Australia and New Zealand Conference Intelligence Information System, Perth, Australia.

Zalane, O. R. (2008). Principles of knowledge discovery in databases. *Bioinformatics (Oxford, England), 19*, 1132–1139.

Zhang, B., Pham, T. D., & Zhang, Y. (2007). *Bagging Support Vector Machine for Classification of SELDI-ToF Mass Spectra of Ovarian Cancer Serum Samples* (LNCS Vol. 4830). Berlin: Springer.

Zhang, G. P. (2000). Neural Networks for Classification: A Survey. *IEEE Transactions on Systems, Man and Cybernetics. Part C, Applications and Reviews, 30*(4), 451–462. doi:10.1109/5326.897072

Zhang, J. S., & Leung, Y. W. (2004). Improved possibilistic c-means clustering algorithms. *IEEE transactions on Fuzzy Systems, 12*(2), 209–217. doi:10.1109/TFUZZ.2004.825079

Zhang, S. C., & Liu, Z. Q. (2005). A robust, real-time ellipse detector. *Pattern Recognition, 38*(2), 273–287. doi:10.1016/j.patcog.2004.03.014

Zhang, T., Ramakrishnan, R., & Livny, M. (1997). BIRCH: A New Data Clustering Algorithm and Its Applications. *Journal of Data Mining and Knowledge Discovery, 1*(2), 141–182. doi:10.1023/A:1009783824328

Zheng, H. T., Kang, B. Y., & Kim, H. G. (2008). An ontology-based bayesian network approach for representing uncertainty in Clinical Practice Guidelines. In *Proceedings of the Uncertainty Reasoning for the Semantic Web I: ISWC International Workshops, URSW 2005-2007, Revised Selected and Invited Papers* (LNAI 5327, pp. 161-173).

Zhu, A.-L., Li, J., & Leong, T.-Y. (2003). Automated Knowledge Extraction for Decision Model Construction: A Data Mining Approach. In *Proc. of AMIA Annu Symp.* (pp. 758–762).

Zhu, J., Rosset, S., Zhou, H., & Hastie, T. (2005). Multiclass adaboost. *Technical Report #430.*

Zhu, Y. M., Webster, S. J., Flower, D., & Woll, P. J. (2004). Interleukin-8/CXCL8 is a growth factor for human lung cancer cells. *British Journal of Cancer, 91*, 1970–1976. doi:10.1038/sj.bjc.6602227

Zhu, Y., & Yan, H. (1997). Computerized tumor boundary detection using a Hopfield neural network. *IEEE Transactions on Medical Imaging, 16*, 55–67. doi:10.1109/42.563666

Zhu, Y., Williams, S., & Zwiggelaar, R. (2004). A survey on histological image analysis-based assessment of three major biological factors influencing radiotherapy: proliferation, hypoxia and vasculature. *Computer Methods and Programs in Biomedicine, 74*(3), 183–199. doi:10.1016/S0169-2607(03)00095-6

Zhu, Y., Williams, S., & Zwiggelaar, R. (2006). Computer technology in detection and staging of prostate carcinoma: A review. *Medical Image Analysis, 10*(2), 178–199. doi:10.1016/j.media.2005.06.003

Zipitria, I., Larranaga, P., Armananzas, R., Arruarte, A., & Elorriaga, J. A. (2008). What is behind a summary-evaluation decision? *Behavior Research Methods, 40*(2), 597–612. doi:10.3758/BRM.40.2.597

About the Contributors

Dr. A B M Shawkat Ali has been involved over the past 12 years with research and teaching in Australia and overseas universities at undergraduate and postgraduate levels. He holds a PhD in Information Technology from Monash University, Australia on Statistical Learning Theory: Support Vector Machine. He is a author of a Data Mining text book published by Thomson and have published over 55 book chapters, journals and conferences paper in the area of Data Mining, Bioinformatics, Telecommunications and Sensor Networking.

Dr. Yang Xiang is currently with School of Management and Information Systems, Central Queensland University, Australia. His research interests include network security and distributed systems. In particular, he is currently working in a research group developing active defense systems against large-scale network attacks and new Internet security countermeasures. He has published 80 journal and conference papers in network security, such as IEEE Transactions on Parallel and Distributed Systems. He has served as Program/General Chair for the 11th IEEE International Conference on High Performance Computing and Communications (HPCC 2009), the 3rd International Conference on Network and System Security (NSS 2009), the 6th IFIP International Conference on Network and Parallel Computing (NPC 2009) and the 14th IEEE International Conference on Parallel and Distributed Systems (ICPADS 2008). He has been PC member for many international conferences such as IEEE ICC, IEEE GLOBECOM and IEEE ICPADS. He has served as guest editor for ACM Transactions on Autonomous and Adaptive Systems, Computer Communications, Journal of Network and Computer Applications, and Future Generation Computer Systems. He is on the editorial board of Journal of Network and Computer Applications.

* * *

Dr. Ameer Ali has born in Dhaka, Bangladesh in 1977. He completed his B. Sc. in Computer Science and Engineering in 2001 from Bangladesh University of Engineering and Technology, Dhaka and PhD in IT in 2006 from Monash University, Australia. Currently, he is working as an Assistant Professor in the Department of Electronics and Communication Engineering, East West University, Dhaka, Bangladesh. He has more than 20 published articles in both reputed international journals and conferences. His research interests are image processing, segmentation, fuzzy clustering, telemedicine, vendor selection using fuzzy techniques, and networking.

Cristian Bogdan is a researcher at the Royal Institute of Technology, Stockholm, Sweden. He approached the topic of Spread of Activiation from the field of Computer Supported Collaborative Work, where he became interested in large semantic networks of interrelated objects. Cristian is also interested in a number of related fields such as end-user programming and interface modeling, and also drives two open source software projects developing applications in these fields. He is a computer engineer by training and vocation, and received his PhD in 2003 with a thesis on IT Design for Amateur Communities, written in a multidisciplinary, socio-technical tradition.

Dr. Dmitri Botvich is a principal investigator at Telecommunications Software & Systems Group of Waterford Institute of Technology, Ireland. His research interests include mathematical modeling, mathematical and computational algorithms, bio-inspired methods, network resource management, queuing theory, system modeling, optimization methods.

Sunil Choenni (1964) holds a PhD in database technology from the University of Twente and a MSc in theoretical computer science from Delft University of Technology. Currently, he is heading the department of Statistical Information Management and Policy Analysis of the Research and Documentation Centre (WODC) of the Dutch Ministry of Justice. His research interests include data mining, databases, information retrieval, and human centered design. He published several papers in these fields.

Prof. Dr. Matjaz Gams (http://dis.ijs.si/Mezi/) is professor of computer science and informatics at the Ljubljana University and senior researcher at the Jozef Stefan Institute, Ljubljana, Slovenia. He teaches several courses in computer sciences at graduate and postgraduate level at Faculties of Computer science and informatics, Economics, etc. His research interests include artificial intelligence, intelligent systems, intelligent agents, machine learning, cognitive sciences, and information society. His publication list includes 500 items, 70 of them in scientific journals. He is an executive contact editor of the Informatica journal and editor of several international journals. He is heading the Department of intelligent systems, was member of the governmental board of the JS Institute, president of several societies, cofounder of the Engineering Academy of Slovenia and the Artificial Intelligence Society and Cognitive sciences in Slovenia; currently president of ACM Slovenia. He headed several major applications in Slovenia including the major national employment agent on the Internet, the expert system controlling quality of practically all national steel production, and the Slovenian text-to-speech system donated to several thousand users.

Raymond Greenlaw received a BA in Mathematics from Pomona College in 1983, and an MS and a PhD in Computer Science from the University of Washington in 1986 and 1988, respectively. Ray is a professor of Computer Science at Armstrong Atlantic State University; he is the Distinguished Professor of Computer Science at Chiang Mai University in Thailand. Ray holds a visiting professorship at the University of Management and Science in Kuala Lumpur, Malaysia. He has won three Senior Fulbright Fellowships (Spain, Iceland, and Thailand), a Humboldt Fellowship (Germany), a Sasakawa Fellowship, and fellowships from Italy, Japan, and Spain. He has published fifteen books in the areas of complexity theory, graph theory, the Internet, parallel computation, networking, operating systems, theoretical Computer Science, the Web, and wireless. He is one of the world's leading experts on P-completeness theory. His books have been used in over 120 Computer Science and Information Technology programs in the US, as well as internationally, and have been translated into several languages. Ray has lectured throughout the world presenting over 185 invited talks. He serves as a Computing Accreditation Commissioner (CAC) for ABET and was elected to the CAC Executive Committee in 2008. His research papers have appeared in over 60 journals and conference proceedings. His research has been supported by the governments of Germany, Hong Kong, Iceland, Italy, Japan, Malaysia, Spain, Taiwan, Thailand, and the US.

Dr. Xiangjian He is the director of Computer Vision & Recognition Laboratory at the University of Technology, Sydney. He holds PhD degree in Computer Science. His main research interests include computer vision and networking.

Dr. Tony Jan is a Senior Lecturer of Computer Systems and Networks at the University of Technology, Sydney, Australia. He holds PhD degree in Computer Science, Masters Degree in Electrical and Information Engineering and Bachelor (Honours) in Electrical and Communications Engineering from the University of Sydney and the State University of Western Australia respectively. Prior to lectureship, he was a research fellow at the University of Sydney. His main research interests are in statistical signal processing and machine learning. He has authored more than 50 articles in premiere international journals and conference proceedings in machine learning and neural networks.

John Judge is a researcher in the IBM Dublin Software Lab working as part of the LanguageWare team. He previously worked in the National Centre for Language Technology in Dublin City University, where he received his Ph.D. in 2006 for a thesis entitled "Adapting and Developing Linguistic Resources for Question Answering Systems." He joined IBM in 2006 as part of the LanguageWare Team. He carried out research and development work for IBM's participation in a 3 year integrated EU project called NEPOMUK, where the IBM team is developed tools for semantic analysis of text. These tools allow for semi-automatic production of semantic meta-information needed for content management. He is currently working to productise natural language processing and semantic web technologies and as a consultant in developing bespoke text analytics solutions.

Sanpawat Kantabutra received a BA in Accounting from Chiang Mai University in Thailand in 1991, an MS in Computer Engineering from Syracuse University in the US in 1996, and a PhD in Computer Science from Tufts University in the US in 2001. He is currently an assistant professor of Computer Science in the Theory of Computation Group in Chiang Mai University and a Royal Golden Jubilee scholar of the Thailand Research Fund. His areas of research are design and analysis of algorithms, algorithm complexity and intractability, parallel algorithms and architectures, graph theory and algorithms, and combinatorics. He has published his research regularly in leading international conferences and journals and has served as a program committee member for several international conferences. He has also regularly refereed papers for leading journals such as IEEE Transactions on Pattern Analysis and Machine Intelligence, IEEE Signal Processing Letters, and IEEE Transactions on Systems, Man, and Cybernetics. In addition, he has also been invited to teach and give research talks nationally and internationally.

Savo Kordic was born in 1962. He is a Ph.D. candidate and a sessional lecturer at Edith Cowan University (ECU), Western Australia. His research interests include data mining and programming.

Chiou Peng LAM is the Postgraduate Coordinator for the School of Computer and Information Science (SCIS) at Edith Cowan University. Her main research interests include machine learning, pattern recognition, data mining and software engineering.

Eugene Levner is Professor of Computer Science at Holon Institute of Technology and Bar-Ilan University, Israel. His main scientific interests are design of computer algorithms, optimization theory, and clustering and classification of digital content. He is author/co-author of seven books and more than 100 articles in refereed journals. His Citation Index is 410, and h-index is 15. He is the full member of the International Academy of Information Sciences, a member of editorial boards of four international journals.

Huaizhong Li was born in 1964. He received the PhD degree in Electrical and Computer Engineering from The University of Newcastle, Australia in 1996. He is a chair professor at Wenzhou University, Wenzhou, Zhejiang, China. His research interests include data mining, software engineering, artificial intelligence, automatic control, and computer applications.

Xie Li, born in 1942, professor and Ph. D. Supervisor of Computer Science and Technology, Nanjing University, Nanjing, China. His current research interests include distributed computing and advanced operation system. E-mail: xieli@nju.edu.cn. Postal mail address: Department of Computer Science and Technology, Nanjing University, Hankou Road, Nanjing, P. R. China, 210093.

W.K. Li is a Chair Professor, Department of Statistics and Actuarial Science, The University of Hong Kong. His research interests include time series analysis, stochastic analysis, financial and insurance risk management and environmental statistics. He is an Elected Fellow of the American Statistical Association and the Institute of Mathematical Statistics. He has papers published in top journals including *Biometrika, Journal of the Royal Statistical Society Series B, Journal of the American Statistical Association, Annals of Statistics*, etc. He served as the Board of Directors of International Chinese Statistical Association from 2006 to 2007 and the President of the Hong Kong Statistical Society from 2000 to 2003.

Shyamala G. Nadathur. The career commenced in with post-graduate qualifications Biomedical Sciences and experiences encompassing hospital and research laboratories, pharmaceutical industry and public health projects. Additionally have completed a master's in health management and worked for over a decade in project and program management roles in the health sector. Through the various roles having experienced the importance of good and timely information for planning, operations and quality has developed a keen interest in health informatics (HI). There have been opportunities to undertake a number of IT courses including post-graduate qualification in IS. The HI doctorate project sets out to obtain value out of administrative datasets and see if they are able to inform about the current clinical presentation, process and outcome of care. Over the years there has also been some involvement in tertiary level teaching including IT/IS. Professional affiliations include membership of the Public Health Association of Australia and Associate Fellow of the Australian College of Health Service Executives. There is also continued involvement in the Health Informatics Society of Australia, including in the capacity of Executive Member of the Victorian branch.

Kwok Pan Pang obtained the PhD from Information Technology faculty of Monash University in Australia, Master degree in Information Technology from Queensland University of Technology in Australia, and Honor degree in Statistics from Dalhousie University in Canada. He has more than 15 years of practical experience in applying statistical and time series analysis/prediction in manufacturing industry. He is now working in the research area of the tourism time series including forecasting and analysis. His research interest includes data mining, machine learning, econometrics and time series analysis.

GM Shafiullah currently is a PhD student at CQUniversity working on wireless sensor networking and machine learning technology. He is graduated in Electrical and Electronics Engineering from Chittagong University of Engineering & Technology (CUET). He obtained Masters of Engineering from CQUniversity, Australia on "Application of Wireless Sensor Networking for Train Health Monitoring". He has published 10 book chapters, journals and conferences paper in the area of Data Mining, Railway Technology, Telecommunications and Sensor Networking. Mr. Shafiullah has more than eight years of professional experience in the field of Information and Communication Technology (ICT).

Dr. Thompson Graduated from Latrobe University in Melbourne Australia with first class honors degrees in both Electronics Engineering and Physical Science in 2000 and the Andrew Downing award for the highest grade point average in physics. Adam also gained a scholarship to complete his honors in physics at LaTrobe University. After graduation he worked for a Clyrcom Communications in Australia where he was a design engineer then in 2001 Adam commenced a PhD candidature at RMIT University in Melbourne Australia, with a focus on Digital Signal Processing. In 2004 Adam graduated with several international journals and many more conference publications. From 2004 – 2006 Adam was the senior hardware engineer at MTData in Melbourne Australia. Dr Thompson is currently an academic at Central Queensland University in Australia where he conducts research into communications, automated flight and rural farm management all with a focus on Digital Signal Processing. Currently he is a regular reviewer for Elsevier Digital Signal Processing Journal.

Dr. Tich Phuoc Tran received his Bachelor of Software Engineering (2005) and Bachelor of Information Technology with a First class honours (2006) from the University of Technology, Sydney (UTS). He was awarded with a University Medal for his excellent academic achievement. He also holds a PhD degree in computing sciences. His research interests include data mining, theoretical development of ANN models and network security.

Dr. Alexander Troussov is chief scientist in IBM Ireland Centre for Advanced Studies (CAS) and chief scientist of IBM LanguageWare group. He has published more than 30 peer reviewed journal and conference papers and has 5 patents. In 2000 he joined IBM as the Architect of IBM Dictionary and Linguistic tools group, known now as IBM LanguageWare group. As CAS Chief Scientist, Dr. Alexander Troussov leads IBM Ireland's participation in the 3 year integrated 6th framework EU project NEPOMUK, and is one of the creators of IBM LanguageWare Miner for Multidimensional Socio-Semantic Networks, which is a unified API that helps in creating solutions for social computing, semantic processing, and activity-centered computing for networks of people, documents, tasks, etc.

Dr. Pohsiang Tsai received his Bachelor of Science degree with first class honours and a PhD degree in information technology (2005) from the University of Technology, Sydney (UTS). His research interests include biometrics, computer vision, data mining, and machine learning.

Gulden Uchyigit has a PhD in Artificial intelligence and data mining from Department of Computing, Imperial College, University of London. She is senior lecturer at the department of Computer Science and Mathematics, University of Brighton. She has authored over 30 papers in refereed books, journals and conferences. She serves on the programme committees of several international conferences and has organised and chaired several workshops in the area of data mining and personalization systems.

Joris L. van Velsen (1977) holds a PhD in theoretical physics from Leiden University and a MSc in applied physics from the University of Twente. He authored several papers on quantum physics and solid state physics. Currently, he is a researcher at the department of Statistical Information Management and Policy Analysis of the Research and Documentation Centre (WODC) of the Dutch Ministry of Justice. His research interests include model selection and time series analysis.

Professor Peter Wolfs is the Western Power Chair in Electrical engineering at the Curtin University of Technology, in Perth, Australia. His special fields of interest include electrical power quality; intelligent power grids; railway traction systems; electric, solar and hybrid electric vehicles; rural and renewable energy supply. Professor Wolfs is a Senior Member of IEEE, a Fellow of Engineers Australia, a Registered Professional Engineer in the State of Queensland. He is the author of more than 150 technical journal and conference publications in electrical engineering.

Edmond H.C. Wu received a B.Sc. degree in applied mathematics and computer science from South China University of Technology, China in 2002 and an MPhil. degree in mathematics in 2004 and a Ph.D. degree in Statistics in 2007 from The University of Hong Kong. He is now a postdoctoral fellow at School of Hotel and Tourism Management, The Hong Kong Polytechnic University. His research interests include data mining, time series modeling and financial risk management.

Fu Xiao, born in 1979, Ph. D. Candidate of Department of Computer Science and Technology, Nanjing University, Nanjing, P. R. China. Her main research interests include network security and machine learning. E-mail: fuxiao1225@hotmail.com. Postal mail address: Department of Computer Science and Technology, Nanjing University, Hankou Road, Nanjing, P. R. China, 210093.

Jitian Xiao was born in 1958. He received the Ph.D degree in Computer Science from The University of Southern Queensland, Australia in 2001. He is a lecturer and doctoral supervisor at Edith Cowan University, Western Australia. His research interests include databases and applications, data mining, software engineering and artificial intelligence, etc

Ming Xu is an associate Professor in the Institute of Computer Application Technology, Hangzhou Dianzi University, P. R. China. He received the doctor degree in computer science and technology from the Zhejiang University in 2004. His research interests include computer and network forensics, file caving, intrusion detection, p2p, computer and network security. He has published more than 15 articles in journals and conference proceedings.

Hong-Rong Yang received the B.S. degree in computer science from the Hangzhou Dianzi University, in 2006. He is currently a master candidate the Hangzhou Dianzi University, P. R. China. His research interests include data Classification, computer and network security. Currently, he is a member of IET.

Philip L.H. Yu is an associate professor, department of statistics and actuarial science, the University of Hong Kong. He has published more than 50 research papers in statistical modeling, financial data mining and financial risk management. Currently, he serves as an associate editor of *Computational Statistics and Data Analysis*. He is the developer of portimizer, a software for portfolio optimization and asset allocation, which won the best web services applications for smart client in 2005. He has more than 10 years of consulting experience for financial institutions in areas such as investor risk profiling, optimal asset allocation and capital adequacy in risk management.

Ning Zheng is a Professor in the Institute of Computer Application Technology, Hangzhou Dianzi University, P. R. China. His research interests include computer and network forensics, file caving, computer and network security, CAD, and CAM. He has published more than 60 articles in journals and conference proceedings.

Index